FUNNY WA

TO BE

A HERO

by

John Fisher

Sid Fie

FUNNY WAY TO BE A HERO

by
John Fisher

Designed by Andy Spence

preface

Published by Preface 2013

10 9 8 7 6 5 4 3 2 1

Copyright © John Fisher 2013

John Fisher has asserted his right to be identified as the author
of this work under the Copyright, Designs and Patents Act 1988

First published in Great Britain in 1973 by Frederick Muller Limited
This revised and expanded edition first published in 2013 by Preface Publishing
20 Vauxhall Bridge Road
London, SW1V 2SA

An imprint of The Random House Group Limited

www.randomhouse.co.uk
www.prefacepublishing.co.uk

Addresses for companies within The Random House Group Limited
can be found at www.randomhouse.co.uk

The Random House Group Limited Reg. No. 954009

A CIP catalogue record for this book is available from the British Library

ISBN 978 1 84809 313 3

Dust jacket illustration and design by Arthur Rambo

Designed by Andy Spence
www.andyspence.co.uk

Printed and bound in China by C&C Offset Printing Co., Ltd

for my mother and father then…

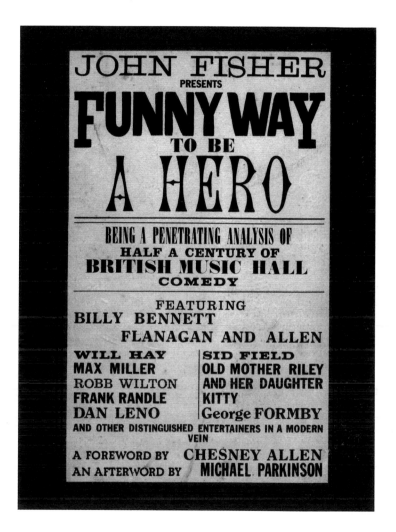

…and for my sister, Ann, now

Contents

Endpaper: *Arthur Askey rehearsing for the 1952 Royal Variety Performance at the London Palladium*
Author's Note: *Max Miller at the 1950 Royal Variety Performance at the London Palladium*

Preface to the New Edition

Let me know where you're working tomorrow night – and I'll come and see YOU!
[Chosen by John Osborne for his epitaph, 1975]

Little did I realise as I put the finishing touches to the manuscript of *Funny Way to be a Hero* almost forty years ago that any publisher would be interested in taking it on, let alone that it would act as a calling card throughout a career spent in television production, for much of that time working with many of the names featured in these pages in addition to so many more who enjoyed prominence on the world's comedy stage. Nor did I anticipate that in due course the book, eventually published by Frederick Muller in 1973, would inspire a television series – *Heroes of Comedy* – which would run for a decade on Channel Four, often expanding the original focus on variety-based talent into the domain of comedy acting and revue. No attempt has been made to reflect that wider canvas in this new edition – maybe a subsequent volume could remedy that – but I have taken the opportunity to treat in greater detail six subjects who were, for whatever reason, marginalised or ignored first time around.

It seems inconceivable that at the original time of writing the career of Tommy Cooper was only just maturing into full star status. Les Dawson, too, had still to become a national institution. The same applied to the Two Ronnies. It could be argued that Barker and Corbett were never a full-blown variety attraction, but the way they effortlessly recreated its ambience on television through a period of fifteen years identifies them squarely within the tradition. The same must be said of Benny Hill, who shied away from live performance to concentrate on television only to become in the process the most internationally famous of the performers in this book. Arthur Askey maintained until the end of his days that he was not really a variety turn, but his constant presence on the variety stage, together with his influence on British radio and television comedy, demands a fuller appraisal at this later stage. And in her day no name made a bigger impression on the halls than Gracie Fields, mistakenly dismissed in the first edition on the grounds that she was principally a singer, when in fact her comedic talents were more than a match for her ability to hit the high notes.

Inevitably much has happened in the realm of comedy since first publication, much of it reflected in the afterthoughts I have appended to each chapter. Not least, more than a few of the performers discussed in detail have departed this world, and I have transferred the general thrust of their chapters from the present to the past tense, while reserving any new observations for the afterthoughts themselves. It is here that from time to time I have taken the liberty of recounting where relevant personal experiences of knowing and working with a subject. Any modifications made in the main body of the text have been to correct errors, shed anachronisms, plug a few gaps and clarify. Hypothetical performers or performers in general have for the most part been referred to in the masculine case, not least because comedy of this kind remains a male-dominated profession. This is not meant to reflect on the comedic skills of those women who have held their own against their male counterparts and continue to do so.

The Foreword and Afterword so graciously provided by Chesney Allen and Sir Michael Parkinson respectively have been left intact, happy reminders of when the world was young and one's future hopefully spelled fulfilment in the career path one had chosen. I little knew then how much a book undertaken to drive home a personal crusade that popular comedy should be treated with prestige and respect would help me along the way.

Foreword by Chesney Allen

This memory man's fantastic book should bring laughter and pleasure to a great many people. To the real followers of the great music hall days, the fans – one might almost say addicts – this is a 'must'. To the youngsters of today, who have it I think all too easy, but with starlight in their eyes and a foot on the ladder of fame, it is an education.

Having spent more than sixty years actively engaged in show business and in the music halls, I was amazed that the author, who is I believe quite young, could have acquired all this knowledge of the events in the lives of his characters, incidents the general public never knew.

Knowing most of the characters, some intimately, conjures up so many happy memories for me. The author must have spent many, many months researching and retelling the funny stories and routines between these covers. And he has done his homework really well, going back over those wonderful years when the only gimmicks that kept those household names at the top of their profession for decade after decade were sheer talent and arduous basic training.

This is a book that will be eagerly sought for, not only by the elderly and middle-aged but as a tremendous help and guidance to the embryonic star of the future: the magnetism to hold an audience that could only be acquired after years and years of 'apprenticeship in the long grass', the number twos and number threes in the small towns of the provinces; the painstaking perfection of acts and timing, getting to know each audience and its particular likes and dislikes – in fact, becoming a part of the audience, without barriers between watcher and watched; and then, with luck (this is important too), a 'potential' could become a lasting star – not just a sudden overnight success that could vanish as swiftly as it appeared.

I can well remember the first week I had to stay away from my London home. It was in 1912, West Hartlepool, where I was joining the Lodge Percy Stock Company at the Grand Theatre (we stayed a week in each town with a different play every night – nowadays Stock is called Repertory). My mother cried and my landlady in West Hartlepool took me through my lines in a 'combined' (now called a 'bedsitter'), repeatedly telling me that I was too young to be away from home.

It saddens me that so much has been lost to the realms of the past, because I firmly believe there is a permanent place in life for real variety, something to capture the harmless and healthy vulgarity of that atmosphere of the old music hall. Still, I wonder how many millions watch *The Good Old Days* on TV, which, like the old stars, goes on for year after year, proving that there is a demand even in the 70s for this type of entertainment.

Flanagan and Allen: 'Underneath the Arches'

My sincere congratulations go out to this young author. He's given me so many laughs and brought so many memories back. I only wish, for me, it could all begin again – every moment of it.

1973

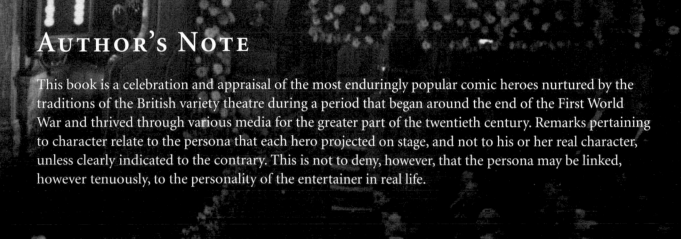

Author's Note

This book is a celebration and appraisal of the most enduringly popular comic heroes nurtured by the traditions of the British variety theatre during a period that began around the end of the First World War and thrived through various media for the greater part of the twentieth century. Remarks pertaining to character relate to the persona that each hero projected on stage, and not to his or her real character, unless clearly indicated to the contrary. This is not to deny, however, that the persona may be linked, however tenuously, to the personality of the entertainer in real life.

Dan Leno: 'The Monarch
of All Comedians'

THE LITTLE DOG LAUGHED...

Only mediocrity can be trusted to be always at its best. Genius must always have lapses proportionate to its triumphs.
[Max Beerbohm on Dan Leno, 1904]

It has always been the same. In 1887 a mournful page in the *Dictionary of National Biography* proclaimed that 'genuine pantomime drollery expired with Grimaldi'. And yet the following year the now legendary Dan Leno made his Drury Lane pantomime debut as the wicked baroness in charge of an unruly pair of 'babes in the wood'. The year Leno's own fragility proved fatal, Sid Field, one of the most revered of subsequent comedians, was born. And then forty-six years later at the Royal Variety Performance in November 1950, while nothing could compensate for the death nine months earlier of the creator of 'Slasher Green', two contrasting young performers, Max Bygraves and Frankie Howerd, both made a special impact on the Palladium stage. The previous year, their colleague Tony Hancock had made his radio debut as a guest on *Variety Bandbox* on the very day the great broadcasting comedian Tommy Handley died. The comic tradition of the music hall, despite its depressing habit of being declared at its last gasp whenever one of its prominent exponents meets his, would appear to have had a remarkable ability for rebirth and regeneration.

No one can regret the passing of the social conditions that gave birth to the original entertainment. Music hall flourished from about 1850 and had run its course by the time of the Armistice in 1918, to be replaced by the more streamlined genre of variety. The social climate of the earlier time had encouraged a cruel, abrupt division between the upper and lower classes, and the genre more than thrived on the selfish influence of a privileged few in imposing upon the less fortunate a spurious satisfaction with their sparse lot alongside a guilt-ridden fear of ever being able to enjoy the milk-and-honey existence from which they were excluded. When seen at a remove of several decades, the commercially focused 'On Mother Kelly's doorstep' view of those days through the rosy perspective of music hall gaiety makes the predicament of that majority appear all the more sad.

With competition advancing from the mechanised media in so many forms – cinema, radio, the gramophone – the need for a snappier, more streamlined entertainment became inevitable. With variety, the acts became more diverse, the duration of the performance more compact, and the accompanying distractions of food and drink, always at hand during an authentic music hall evening, were kept at bay. The curious mix of discipline and enforced conviviality created by the gavel-wielding chairman also disappeared. Fortunately one commodity survived – the talent. It would have been regrettable had the skills and techniques fostered in the original halls proved incapable of permeating other show business forms. All important were that first vital, electric moment of contact between audience and performer, the calculated progression in gauging audience reaction and meeting audience demand within the framework of an act, the sheer human energy that sustained the whole. The social climate and the media may have changed, but the high-powered concentration of all the verve and vigour, comic brio and diablerie that a performer could muster at any one moment in his act remained a potent entertainment force. Since the first platform for performance was erected in this country, the British public has grasped with open arms the opportunities for release afforded by its jesters and clowns, and variety allowed that practice to continue.

Of course, in any generation the dejected cry goes up among self-indulgent nostalgists that the performers of today pale into insignificance beside those of yesteryear. It is obviously impossible to ascertain levels of superiority when those contrasted are generations apart, and it is unfair to dismiss on this basis the acknowledged greats of later years, performers who themselves have attained such a high degree of individuality that any change, any 'improvement' in their persona could only destroy it. Whatever the varying talents of successive generations, later performers might well be expected to be better than those of earlier times. In 1919 T. S. Eliot, discussing 'Tradition and the Individual Talent' from the poetic viewpoint in his essay of that name, wrote: 'Someone said: "The dead writers are remote from us because we know so much more than they did." Precisely, and they are that which we know.' In the same way the performers of today have a far richer, because longer, tradition to draw upon. However crucial for success the individuality of any performer may be, that individuality will have been partly influenced by his predecessors, particularly those he himself has most admired. This process, demanding as it will be until the true essence of individuality is distilled, must not be confused with what Eliot calls 'blind or timid adherence' to the successes of others. Moreover, please do not think that the analogy between poet and music hall performer is obscure. In *The Use of Poetry and the Use of Criticism* Eliot himself wrote, 'Every poet would like to convey the pleasures of poetry to a larger audience... All the better, then, if he could have at least the satisfaction of having a part to play in society as worthy as that of the music hall comedian.'

Although the variety stage eventually became a platform for the talents of the most motley assortment of entertainers, embracing magic and menagerie, big band and ballerina, and a zany zigzag of countless novelty acts, the emphasis of this book is upon the clowns, comics and buffoons, who always boasted the highest degree of sheer personal popularity, not merely for the laughter they raised, but because of the basic social identity they shared with the bulk of their audience, an identity firmly fixed in this world and not the superhuman universe conjured up by a Houdini, Pavlova or Walford Bodie, the ace hypnotist of his time. The predecessors of the funny men and women to be met in these pages were the original lifeblood of the music hall before it became more diversified and hence variety: those countless singers of comic songs so often performed in eccentric character, in particular Dan Leno, the archetype of the modern stand-up comedian in that he was the first to break away from song and address his audience in the style of conversational speech. His biographer J. Hickory Wood wrote,

From the time he virtually abandoned clog-dancing and began to grow in favour as a London comedian Dan Leno steadily developed his entertainment in one special direction. One calls his performances on the halls 'songs' for want of a pithy word that is better; but they were not really songs at all. They were diverting monologues in a style of which he was as undoubtedly the originator as he was its finest exponent. With him the character was the first consideration; the amusing wealth of monologue or 'patter' was the means whereby he gave his audience an insight into that character, while the verses struck one as being, in most cases, a somewhat unnecessary interlude.

To list Leno's many notable contemporaries would at this stage be futile. Later we shall see the achievements of many of them reflected in the jesters who took their places at the top of a unique profession, one of noble descent from the popular semi-improvised *mimus* or comic spectacle of classical antiquity, through the buffoons of medieval drama, the court jester, the Zanni and Arlecchini of the Italian *commedia dell'arte*, and the harlequinade of the later English pantomime, which saw its peak in the genius of Grimaldi. By 'descent' is not suggested a direct handing-down from one fashion to the other. Rather there is some quintessential element peculiar to all the above and suggesting that one could look back even further than classical antiquity to find something vaguely representing music hall as we know it.

There is, however, one quality which the comedian unquestionably shares with his more exotic colleagues. It accounts for the fundamental difference between performers on the so-called legitimate and illegitimate stages. The straight actor becomes complete only when supported by the sturdy prop that is the amalgam of director's guidance, playwright's text, designer's brush and the physical presence of the rest of the cast. Conversely, the music hall or variety stage became the Mecca of the individualist. Not for the solo artist the well trodden clearly signposted path of the legitimate actor. To quote from a significant article, 'Evening Shadows in the Music Hall', published in *The Times* during July 1961, 'His is the lonely road of self-education, copying from this one here and that one there, until he finds his own strength and the particular medium fitting the gift which nature bestowed upon him. How difficult those groping years are, only the seeker would know and only the honest would tell.' The vein of melancholy that runs through the article brings home all the more vividly the isolated world of our jesters, jugglers and clowns. Relying almost entirely on their own resources, they are essentially their own producers. This is not to say that they never cross over into the realms of the legitimate stage, collective revue and musical comedy. But never have they been completely absorbed. When Robey played in *Henry IV Part I*, Secombe in *Pickwick*, Howerd in *The Dream*, always there were those outrageous eyebrows, that gurgling giggle, that uneasy fidget playing respectively their own independent and yet somehow integral parts.

All members of the variety profession have their sights set on the same immediate target, the demands imposed upon them by the live flesh-and-blood audience with which they are always at their greatest ease, an audience they will coax and coddle to be cooed and caressed in return. The essential nature of the technique required to meet these demands is difficult to pin down in words, since a precise notation does not really exist, the performer being a law to himself, with no automatic complementary pole of reference for written analysis. In 1946 Ernest Short wrote in his *Fifty Years of Vaudeville* that he had found,

> no principles governing the craft of vaudeville, apart from the value of hard work. If there is one, it lies in the importance of rhythm which pervades all the dramatic arts. The outstanding vaudeville stars have known how to punctuate song and patter so that song and patter meant something fundamentally different to what they did when a man or woman with a lesser sense of rhythm sought to give them life.

George Robey in characteristic make-up, swishing a pre-Chaplin cane, and in his sketch as the Prehistoric Man

Although one would not wish to disregard 'the value of hard work', one does see in the 'rhythm' mentioned by Short the key to the controlled mood that distinguishes the acts of the great comics, progressing from all-important initial impact, through subtly placed minor climaxes of guffaw, gusto, frenzy, or pathos, right up to the culmination, which must still leave the audience clamouring for more, the whole pervaded by an almost extra-sensory awareness of the need for either acceleration or relaxation, effusiveness or economy, contrast or sameness. Nothing may be left to chance, and yet always the basis of the act must remain flexible; today's audience may be in Glasgow, tomorrow's in Bournemouth; today's may be randy, tomorrow's respectable. The backbone of the comedian's art must be one of adaptability and improvisation. Never must he be inwardly baffled, never at a loss. The overall performance may give the impression of life at great speed, and yet speed for speed's sake is not essential. In all the great performers there is a carefully controlled economy of movement and gesture. At any definite moment there would appear to be a carefully plotted position for each limb, each physical feature. The vigour of variety technique is to intensify, to accentuate the existing material, not to speed through it in half the time. One recalls the title of one of Marie Lloyd's songs, 'Every little movement has a meaning of its own'. One recalls Jimmy James and a cigarette, Sandy Powell and a false moustache, a million and one minute gestures that telegraphed their way to the back of the gods.

The unremitting sense of alertness and control at any one moment in a performance serves to emphasise a further basic difference between the variety artist and his 'legitimate' counterpart. While no one would dispute that it is the aim of every clown to ensure that his audience is happier, more excited, more invigorated, even more enlightened at the end of his act than at the beginning, his is essentially the impact of something here and now, the happy, thrilling or pathetic moment, as distinct from the happy, thrilling or pathetic ending towards which the actor will find himself working. Moreover, that moment of experience stands a mere cipher without an audience to complement it. The so-called illegitimate stage represents a far more reciprocal medium between audience and performer than straight theatre. As the actor is the interpreter with regard to his role within the play, so the variety artist stands revealed as the collaborator. We must now take a more detailed look at the audience, his partner in this collaboration and the pivot on which the performance turns.

Henri Bergson went straight to the heart of the matter in his terse essay *Laughter*: 'You would hardly appreciate the comic if you felt yourself isolated from others. Laughter appears to stand in need of an echo.' It is a matter of mass psychology. Few things are more personal, more restricted than a sense of humour, and yet one is more prone to laugh at something one would not have found individually funny, if you have the laughter of a neighbour to urge you on. In vacuo, the sound of laughter itself is often enough to arouse more. The communal bond inherent in an audience raises one's risk of infection from laughter. Those who were private and restrained individuals upon entering the theatre, have now in the hazy hypnotic comfort of a dark once-smoky security become merged into an anonymous throng, their solidarity to be established in laughter and song, their inhibitions ready for the shedding, the process far less difficult because shared. And so, following the course of echo, crash, and thunder detailed by Bergson, the mere titter will in turn gain the increased prestige of chuckle, guffaw, even happy hysteria.

One can see in the process a throwback to the ancient Roman festival of Saturnalia, when social chaos, topsy-turvydom and unashamed licentiousness were the rule of the day. The music hall, like the Saturnalia, represents the spring, the release catch to that frivolous, irresponsible, jack-in-the-box element within us all. Any attempt to restrain it is merely to harm its more steadfast counterpart, a sober reliability that can only be refreshed by this intermittent intoxication. One criterion for comic success, however, would appear to be never to allow the members of an audience to be conscious of their loss of individual identity. And so in the largest auditoriums the greatest stars will appear to address themselves to you alone, whether cosseted in the front stalls or remote in the back row of the balcony. You go away from the theatre feeling that the performance could have been staged for you personally. Significantly the medium is the one dramatic form where the performer's line of vision continually extends beyond the footlights.

The fact that no joke is complete until it gains the response of laughter stipulates that the audience itself fulfils by far the greatest need of the comedian on stage. This is further underlined by the characters of many of the great comics themselves. However brash and extrovert they may appear in performance, they are predominantly shy and reserved when first met offstage. This is not to dispute their basic desire for applause and recognition, but to emphasise the psychological block that stands in its way. Their chosen profession is a defence mechanism against this fundamental insecurity. Onstage they no longer have to worry that their own personality may be superseded by that of a mere face in the crowd. They have the licence to shed their inhibitions without embarrassment, because this is the place where such abandon is expected of them. And so a conspiracy is formed between the members of the audience and the artist, the former energising the latter and providing by way of applause and laughter a springboard for the comedy. Thus the shape of the act, the show, is determined by a combination of their reactions and that rhythm already described. The audience itself is part of the act.

To realise the full value of direct communication with an audience, one has only to consider the predicament of performers working in the mechanised media. The cinema comedian, for example, does not have this immediate audience reaction – laughter or the lack of it – to which he can adjust the timing of his own performance. In the disjointed process that constitutes film-making it is all too easy to lose sight of the audience altogether. The solution of many of the great screen comedians to this problem helps to emphasise the advantage of the live theatre as the medium more essentially conducive to laughter-raising. At the height of their anarchic powers the Marx Brothers would take a stage version of their forthcoming film on tour to test it before a live audience, adjusting their material appropriately before shooting began. During the heyday of Laurel and Hardy, Stan would view their new films secretly in the company of a preview audience, and then adjust the length of their various camera-looks to coincide with the audience's laughter. Sometimes they would even shoot new material, if there seemed to be audience demand for it at a specific point in the action. Only after these adjustments had been made would the film be released.

On this page and over: a gallery of undisputed music hall greats, all of whom had an influence on subsequent British comedy. Clockwise from top left: T. E. Dunville, Lily Morris, Marie Lloyd, Gus Elen, Will Fyffe and Billy Merson

*Clockwise from top left: Harry Champion,
Mark Sheridan, Sam Mayo, Alfred Lester,
R. G. Knowles and Arthur Roberts*

Clockwise from top left: Harry Lauder, Jack Pleasants,
Albert Chevalier, Harry Tate and Charles Coborn

Far more damaging for the comedian working in film is the rigid straitjacket so often imposed upon these boisterous instinctive beings by the medium's obsession with a conventional dramatic storyline with a beginning, middle and an end. This is, of course, directly contrary to the true nature of music hall and variety, where the assertion of pure self holds sway, where the performer *is* rather than *acts*. When Twentieth Century Fox and MGM took away from Laurel and Hardy the licence and spontaneity they had been allowed with director Hal Roach, their films swiftly deteriorated. The same sad course occurred with Buster Keaton. All this emphasises what was said earlier about the variety artist as his own producer. He will only shine on the silver screen, if he can retain an uncontrived spontaneity and a basic artistic control over his work, and at the same time overcome the rigid machinery of film, a world of definitive positions, changing lenses and the editor's scissors. The clown's essential timing must thrive alongside that of editor and director, and not be swamped by them. This is to be Chaplin or Jacques Tati, and not, sadly, Sid Field, Morecambe and Wise, or the latter-day Danny Kaye.

It is ironic that the cinema should have been unable to capture the true magic of so many of the great British variety comedians, because it was the British music hall, quite as much as American vaudeville, that so markedly informed the early days of film comedy, the cinema arriving just as the comic tradition of the early halls was in full flight. The British Film Institute possesses a fleeting yet remarkable fragment of film entitled *Little Tich et ses Big Boots*, shot in Paris in 1900, in which Tati discerned the whole origin of the comedy that cinema has made its own. The acrobatic skill, the stylised – almost ritualistic – movement and pantomime that were later to hallmark Chaplin, Keaton and their colleagues are all tellingly present. Equally revealing with the added advantage of sound are sequences of a later date featuring such notable performers as Charles Coborn in full strut as 'The man who broke the bank at Monte Carlo'; George Robey, the self-styled 'Prime Minister of Mirth', declaiming, 'I stopped, I looked, I listened;' Percy Honri with his 'Concert-in-a-Turn'; Lily Morris bemoaning, 'Why am I always the bridesmaid?'; and Gus Elen complaining, 'It's a great big shame.' Forgotten now is the British series of one- or two-reelers made by Homeland Films, a company formed in 1915 by a group of music hall artists that included Charlie Austin ('Parker PC') and Billy Merson. In the same period Will Evans transferred some of his famous sketches to the screen, the most notable from a cinematic point of view being 'Harnessing a Horse', while his nephew Fred Evans achieved even more consistent success with his *Pimple* series, in which he played an absurd knockabout of a dandy.

The list of British music hall comedians who in the early days of cinema emigrated to America to make good in the new medium is impressive: Charlie Chaplin and Stan Laurel, both at one time members of Fred Karno's *Mumming Birds* company, Lupino Lane, James Finlayson, and Jimmy Aubrey and Billie Reeves, two further Karno graduates. Much of

Little Tich and his Big Boots: forerunners of screen comedy

W. C. Fields' formative period was spent in the British music halls, billed as 'The Distinguished Comedian and Greatest Juggler on Earth, Eccentric Tramp'. Although it is has been claimed that Chaplin was most influenced by the seedy swell created by the French comedian Max Linder, Bob Monkhouse in *Films and Filming*, October 1965 quotes Linder himself as saying that he learned 'as much from Chaplin as he ever learned from me', and that from 1905 to 1914, while Linder was working for Pathé, he 'drew much from my tutors in London'. These included Dan Leno and Billy Ritchie, another Karno alumnus, described as 'the best masters of finesse to visit the Varieties'. Almost certainly the Anglo-French favourite Harry Fragson had his own influence on Linder. Ironically, however, it was the American and French cinemas that were to benefit, even though the ideas and techniques were so often traditionally British. Not until the 1930s was our own cinema genuinely enriched from the variety tradition. But even with the Crazy Gang, Will Hay, George Formby and later Norman Wisdom the medium would so often prove a barrier to the freedom and spontaneity that hallmarked their key work on stage. In spite of the flair of directors like Marcel Varnel and Walter Forde for expanding and developing the talent of these personalities, there was still nothing quite like coming face to face with their true idiom in the flesh.

Above: Fred Karno's 'Mumming Birds' company in 'A Night in an English Music Hall'; right: Lupino Lane

Television might at first appear even more restrictive than the cinema, and yet it is a far more honest medium. The straitjacket imposed by the insistence on storyline no longer exists, television being recognised as an all-perceiving retina of events, shows, discussions and spectacles of all kinds. Though the performance, as in film, will be seen through a variety of camera angles, it need not be a disjointed procedure for the artist, the act being taped continuously and not with cinema's ever-recurring need for adjustment between shots. The performer can therefore retain the sense of cumulative thrust that gives that extra impact to a performance. A live transmission even heightens the impact. Unlike its film

Bruce Forsyth: a latter-day Lord of the Revels

equivalent, the television studio can provide the basic reaction of an audience to guide the performer, and once in a while an excuse comes along to shoot the performance in the theatrical setting it was made for. The success of the old-time music hall show *The Good Old Days*, and the many variants of the original *Sunday Night at the London Palladium*, in which a young Bruce Forsyth first demonstrated to a wider public his spontaneous control of an audience, was in large part due to their ability to make the secluded family circle feel as if it was rubbing shoulders with the theatre crowd. Whether, however, television's private nature can ever allow the domestic group to become an actual extension, uninhibited, unshockable and anonymous, of the true theatrical Saturnalia that is music hall is perhaps doubtful. This is not, moreover, to condone canned laughter, that spineless substitute for an actual audience. Nor is it to suppose that the successful televising of the variety artist is an automatic procedure. One despairs at the number of comedy punchlines, magical secrets and speciality act climaxes that have been destroyed by some frenzied director in the fear that he is not visualising enough. Equally dangerous is the determined resolve to make television an essentially close-up medium. The great variety comedians could be as funny and as meaningful with their feet and hands as with their faces, including ironically Hancock, perhaps the most close-up-worthy of all the television clowns. Comic success in the medium has always presupposed a combination of appreciation and flexibility in the director. Morecambe and Wise, who appeared to translate the basic traditions of variety comedy so effortlessly to the small screen, had in their key producer/directors Colin Clews and John Ammonds what amounted to equal partners in their act. Only on the live stage or cabaret floor, however, will the performer ever be the undisputed master of the situation. It is predominantly in these surroundings that the subjects of this book have won their greatest acclaim, true to their music hall heritage.

The genuinely funny men and women celebrated in this volume can be seen to represent a special elite who became successful because they could be simultaneously identified as ordinary people and as stars in spite of themselves. With their attitudes often firmly rooted in the working class, there is no mistaking the well defined depth of personality, the supreme confidence, the intrinsic funniness of the great comedian. There comes a time in such a career when the personal style becomes so refined as to render, should the performer wish, script and patter subsidiary. The celebrated dramatic critic James Agate wrote, 'That every artist should abound in his own sense was never truer than in the music hall. Nobody knew this better than Little Tich exploiting dwarfishness, and the elder Formby revelling in melancholy.' With George Robey the wink of an eyebrow could bring the house down. Later came Max Miller exploiting a winsome lechery, Sid Field a camp innocence, Tommy Cooper a dysfunctional dexterity and Ken Dodd a manic gift for the absurd. All the performers discussed in these pages developed over the years a distinct idiom – a coat hanger for their personality – that set them and their attitude to audience, material and the outside world apart from all others. Here are not merely funny men, but popular heroes in their own right. Moreover, it should be stressed that at a time when celebrity culture runs rampant regardless of any need for talent to substantiate it and nonentities can be elevated to pseudo-hero status overnight with the right public relations machinery, it is reassuring to find heroes who have illuminated the way we live and are such for what they have done, for what they were and are. A triumph, in fact, for real merit.

The anticipation that has always greeted the appearance of the great comedian on stage is as intense as any that precedes the entry of the bullfighter into the arena or the cup-final teams onto the Wembley pitch. The Saturnalian function of their task when they do eventually step forth can only add to their prestige. Appearances no longer have to be kept up, but exist to be shattered to smithereens. Authority and the dull rules of everyday life may now be vigorously resisted. The prodigal, the bohemian holds sway, to the benefit of both spectator and society, whose fantasy lives the funny man embodies. Perhaps the energy, spirit, excitement generated by the great entertainers *is* as highly charged as that of the more conventional hero, whether superhuman athlete or Olympian god, an energy symbolic of the kind of power that ruthlessly and irresistibly demands to be set upon a pedestal. Even more persuasive may be our subconscious realisation, as we laugh at the great funny men, that theirs is the most pressurised task in entertainment. People will forgive mediocrity in sport, drama, music, but they will not forgive the comedian who fails to raise a laugh. No other entertainer has to face the uncertainty presented at each performance by that immediate and automatic indicator of his or her success or failure, namely the laughter of the audience, or the gnawing silence that is its only alternative. The clapping of hands may be anything from enthusiastic response to a polite, yet reluctant gesture, but laughter will always be true to itself. People will never be fooled by what is not funny. And it is reassuring that, however cheated one may feel by the person who deliberately sets out and yet fails to amuse, one's admiration for the jester whose performance gives disappointment a wide berth will endure far longer than the laughter with which one first greets his antics. None of us should kid ourselves that the task is easy. All of us hold Max Beerbohm's sentiment on Dan Leno quoted at the head of this chapter to our hearts.

This admiration is further underlined by a feeling of sympathetic concern for our comic heroes, many of whom, partly to stress their unique quality, make themselves out to be in some way inferior to the audience. The defect may be physical, mental, social, moral, but always it stands revealed as a virtual licence to amuse. It would be wrong, however, to presume that such shortcomings are always merely put on for the performance. While Wisdom's idiocy and Hay's deviousness were entirely theatrical, George Formby Senior's convulsive cough, with its attendant line 'Coughin' well tonight,' was the result of a tubercular condition that eventually killed him. While Jimmy James, the music hall's greatest drunk impersonator, was a strict teetotaller, the anxiety and rankling dissatisfaction that hallmarked Tony Hancock's comic persona were in real life aggravated to the point of self-destruction. One is led to think of the subtle interchangeability that exists between the comic and tragic masks, which, to quote Colin MacInnes in *Sweet Saturday Night* – a work to which this author is extremely indebted for its disciplined yet devout study of the authentic music hall period from 1840 until 1920 – 'the grin of comedy seems to be groaning, and the groan of tragedy to be grinning'. Certainly one is reminded that the lives of so many comic heroes have been riddled with tragedy and hardship, made to appear even more lamentable when set against the happiness these same persons spend their working hours giving to others.

It may be argued that the struggles and sufferings of comedians' early lives, both childhood and those difficult years spent trying to gain a foothold in the most precarious of professions, are an essential part of their training, imparting the ability to laugh off disappointment or distress when it cannot be denied or averted. To say in retrospect, however, that the suffering was beneficial is not to say that it was alleviated in any way when it occurred. It is not to relieve the pressures of the job they undertake. It is not to alter the fact that so many have died violently or prematurely, bankrupt or forgotten by their public. Later we shall meet specific cases of later years; in earlier times, Mark Sheridan, buoyant and 'one of the b'hoys', the exhilarating performer of 'I do like to be beside the seaside', shot himself after a hostile reception in Glasgow; Harry Fragson was shot by a father jealous of his success; T. E. Dunville, the grotesque specialist in nonsense songs – 'A little boy; a pair of skates; broken ice; heaven's gates!' – drowned himself in the Thames when his red-nosed brand of humour appeared to go out of fashion; Marie Lloyd collapsed on stage when only fifty-two, fatally exhausted by failing health, the insistent demands of performance and her disastrous marriage to jockey Bernard Dillon; Dan Leno died even younger, aged forty-four, worn out by the pressures of his craft and the curses that accompanied it. Max Linder was only forty-two when he entered into a suicide pact with his young wife. And the list could – and will – continue.

Like all forms of mass entertainment, the music hall has often been dismissed by the culturally arrogant as tawdry, naive, meaningless escapism. Such criticism is as pretentious and galling as the assumption upon which it is based, namely that all serious theatre is indisputably good and all light entertainment degradingly bad. One has to see the good and the bad in both worlds, to realise that the comedian is as dedicated to his task as the straight actor, that his public makes as valuable a contribution to keeping the British theatre alive as the restricted numbers of Shakespearean connoisseurs or the habitués of the newest and weirdest of experimental theaters. A newspaper headline once famously proclaimed, No one gives Ken Dodd a grant, do they? – or words to that effect. It is a measure of his success that the question has never arisen. We tend to forget that Shakespeare was the popular entertainer of his own day, the boisterous, vulgar element in his work long delaying his acceptance as a serious poet. No one would deny, however, that the great funny men, without ever losing their place in the popular affection, have lifted the whole robust art of music hall onto a higher, more distinguished plane, to be praised by both critics and theatrical snobs alike who would otherwise have no time for the tradition. But it was only because the general public, with its acute instinct for picking winners from among hundreds of lesser artists, got its priorities right in the first place that such eulogies have been forthcoming.

This book, then, is an attempt to define the appeal of the greatest comedians nurtured and sustained by the British variety tradition, to pin down the talent that so often transcended the material at their disposal, and to give some idea to successive generations of, quite simply, what they *did*. It is a notorious fact that a comedian's material does not thrive on the printed page. It is possible, however, to re-create mentally the movements and body language, the delivery and characterisation, the stage geography of the comedian as one reads the dialogue or an account of his actions, and it is hoped that, where possible, readers will use their imagination in this way. And where these facets are strange territory, there will be hints and descriptions to help in this respect.

There has evolved a tendency in studies of great comedians to place the emphasis upon 'hidden' meanings in their work and qualities that go beyond the true province of the funny man, a case of slapstick with a message. Intellectually impressive as this may be, it is to be doubted whether the performers themselves were or are conscious of such profundity in their work. Donald McCaffrey, in his study of *Four Great Comedians*, namely Chaplin, Keaton, Harry Langdon and Harold Lloyd, put the matter in a healthier perspective when he wrote of the clown, 'Primarily, this little fellow who is dancing in the wind, thumbing his nose, or embracing the good things of life, is concerned with the pleasure of laughter which he promotes. He is, in short, an entertainer; a bearer of happiness. It is not necessary to excuse him, to apologise for him, to elevate him. As if making us laugh were of little significance!' Such is the view taken by this book. As such it is an affirmation of a priceless hilarity. It is also an unashamed act of hero worship. What redeems it is that the heroes are real.

AFTERTHOUGHTS

Readdressing this opening chapter forty years on has been encouraging on two counts. While mediocrity in modern comedy abounds, the individuality of the greats dealt with in this volume has been handed down to a new generation of entertainers quite as distinctive and as representative of their time as the giants that loom within the pages that follow. Just as this book found itself charting an impromptu family tree of British comedy from the time of the music hall to the end of the variety era, it could be a worthwhile enterprise to continue that theme from the 60s heyday of Howerd, Cooper and Dodd

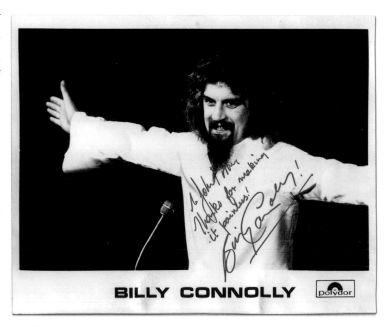

BILLY CONNOLLY

through the folk-club-inspired chapter of Billy Connolly, Max Boyce, Jasper Carrott and Mike Harding to the 'alternative' success of Ben Elton, Rik Mayall and the school of *The Young Ones*.

The word alternative is misleading, of course, because all comedy to be meaningful has to provide an alternative to what has gone before. Indeed in recent years the pendulum might be said to have swung back to a certain traditionalism, a form of 'reverse alternative'. The links between Lee Evans and Norman Wisdom, say, or Eddie Izzard and Frankie Howerd, do not require an inner grasp of the workings of comedy to spot or to understand. The links between Izzard and Robb Wilton, each with his cultivated brand of indecisiveness, may be less obvious. Indeed a comedy version of Kim's Game begins to suggest itself with the idea of matching spiritual pairs across the generations. Dare one suggest Eric Morecambe and Vic Reeves; Elsie and Doris Waters and French and Saunders; Billy Bennett and Harry Hill – surrealists both; Les Dawson and Jack Dee – downbeats ditto; Tommy Cooper and Joe Pasquale – magicians at a tangent; Joyce Grenfell and Victoria Wood; Tony Hancock and Ricky Gervais; Bernard Manning and Peter Kay; Al Read and Peter Kay again; Dick Emery and Harry Enfield; the Goons and the

Mighty Boosh? At the risk of frightening the more devout followers of these modern names, they all embody something of the spirit of the old-timers, irrespective of changing social attitudes, the elusive canard of political correctness, the more adult nature of much of their material and the need to be seen to be creating that material for themselves as the norm rather than the exception.

On the second count, it is unquestionable that more serious attention is given to comedy today, albeit not always in the popular mainstream, but in the critical columns of the more serious newspapers and their broadcasting equivalent. It has cast off its cultural-Cinderella status, even if at a price. The halcyon days when Handley, Hancock and Morecambe and Wise could through one or other of the broadcast media have half the British population laughing at them at any one time have been sacrificed to a multi-channel Internet culture that may nevertheless bear a greater similarity to the original business structure of the variety theatre and music hall than one might suppose. Not *everyone* went to the music hall to sing along with Marie, to the local Empire to cheer on the Cheeky Chappie; but today courtesy of YouTube everyone *can* sit at their laptop and summon up an extraordinary variety bill of yesterday's greats, provided they have the right names to enter into their search engine.

That said, comedy will always need the live arena both as its nursery and as the scene of potentially its greatest triumphs. When *Funny Way to be a Hero* was first published the variety clubs that briefly took over from the last few remaining variety theatres were well advanced in bringing live comedy to the masses in an environment actually more in keeping with the spirit of the original music halls, where food and drink were always attractions alongside what happened on stage. The boom was short-lived because the economics were faulty, the clubs unable to sustain the huge salaries paid to the top stars in a giddy display of one-upmanship between one establishment and another. Performers will always find stages to play, however, and in recent years the circuit of smaller comedy clubs that have appeared with their focus on a younger clientele has helped to keep a vibrant tradition alive. The newer clubs have a restricted economic viability insofar as their seating capacity is limited and the big names come expensive. But while it became a cliché at one stage to describe stand-up comedy as the new rock and roll, the willingness and ability of today's biggest names to play the largest arenas in the manner of rock bands has injected the kind of excitement into comedy aficionados that used to be generated by Max Miller or Ken Dodd at the London Palladium.

My doubt is whether the new generation of funny people is or will be loved in the way that the subjects of this book were and still are. This may be because their vulnerability is less, their susceptibility to tragedy and self-doubt not so obvious. Certainly the abiding stature and unconditional respect that the old guard continues to attract seem a world apart from the more cynical, shallower age in which we live. To surmount that, their comic heirs will have to prove themselves true heroes.

LONDON
PALLADIUM
OXFORD CIRCUS, W.1.
5.40 TWICE NIGHTLY 8.15
GEORGE BLACK'S SHOW SHOP of 1940
... THE LITTLE DOG LAUGHED
A TERRIFIC CAST OF 80 INCLUDING
GEORGE BLACK'S CRAZY GANG
NERVO & KNOX
FLANAGAN & ALLEN
NAUGHTON & GOLD
AMERICA'S FUNNIEST ACT
WILLIE. WEST & McGINTY
A BILLION BUILDING BLUNDERS
MATINEES: WED., THURS. & SAT. AT 2·15
CONDOS BROS.
WORLD'S GREATEST TAP DANCERS
DAN DONOVAN
MARION WILSON
PATRICIA LEONARD
SHERMAN-FISHER'S PALLADIUM GIRLS
SYD RAILTON
SIX HANDSPRING ACROBATS FREDIANIS
JIMMY HADREAS
A LESSON IN DANCING
EDNA SQUIRE-BROWN
OXFORD CIRCUS TUBE STATION NOW OPEN Only One Minute's Walk
General Theatre Corporation, Ltd.
Managing Director: MARK OSTRER
POPULAR PRICES OF ADMISSION
TELEPHONE: GERRARD 7373
DIRECTION: GEORGE BLACK
Resident Manager: C. T. HUTCHISON

Yours militarily
Billy Bennett.

BILLY BENNETT: ALMOST A GENTLEMAN

It was Christmas Day in the cookhouse and the place was clean and tidy,
The soldiers were eating their pancakes – I'm a liar, that was Good Friday.
In the oven a turkey was sizzling and to make it look posh, I suppose,
They fetched the battalion barber, to shingle its parson's nose!

Billy Bennett was the apotheosis of the 'low' comedian. His billing, 'Almost a Gentleman', with the stress on the first word, was the most apt in variety history. Bennett was a trier and, however much he fell short of the demands of polite society, seemed pleased with the front he presented to the world. His comic idea was vividly expressed by shrunken dress suit, chunky hob nailed army boots, flapping shirt dicky, red silk handkerchief tucked into waistcoat top, thickset face counterbalanced by unclipped walrus moustache, curlered quiff of jet-black hair and lady's garter for a watch fob. His head bulged from his ever-tight wing collar like a lollipop about to explode. The eccentric appearance, exaggerative of a poverty with which one can't quite sympathise, evoked instant laughter. In one hand he sometimes carried a flattened opera hat, in the other a pre-Satchmo crumpled handkerchief to dab away the ever-recurring beads of sweat on his fringed brow. As one critic put it, clothes made not only the man, but the 'Almost'. Here at a glance was Chaplin – with the gristle.

He was born William Robertson Russell Bennett in 1887, the son of John 'Jock' Bennett, one half of a slapstick team, Bennett and Martell, billed on the music halls as 'Those Murderous Knockabouts'. The son graduated through playing the hind legs of an elephant and a whirl as an acrobat before becoming a comedian himself. The First World War, in which he served as a farrier sergeant with the 16th Lancers and won the Distinguished Conduct Medal and the Belgian Croix de Guerre, provided the opportunity. As a 'canteen comic' during the hostilities he was able to develop the forceful style of comic attack that underpinned an immense popularity terminated only by his death on 30 June 1942. On leaving the army he went briefly on the stage as a soldier act, retaining the khaki in front of the footlights as 'The Trench Comedian'. His second date, however, was scheduled for the Theatre Royal, Dublin. When the manager discovered that his music consisted of 'Tipperary' and other martial airs, not a particularly wise choice for an Irish audience at that time, Bennett, with no other material at his disposal, had no alternative but to improvise a quick disguise for his own safety. The false moustache, the hair, all literally fell into place, investing the soldier act with an air of conscious burlesque. Before long the army uniform would be discarded in favour of the ill-fitting evening dress in the city of his upbringing, Liverpool. The army boots, however, stayed. The facade had evolved and the branding was registered.

He was chiefly famous for his parody monologues, surrealist travesties of the hybrid style of George R. Sims and Bret Harte. Their very nature tend to make versified monologues boring and predictable, but

Bennett threw common sense overboard and added a sparkling surprise quality whereby no one knew what would ever come next. He delivered this inspired material with a cumulative gusto that imparted a rhythmic logicality to what was otherwise nonsense. His manner was the matter-of-fact approach of the urgent elocutionist, declaiming his material in a raucous non-stop foghorn of a voice.

> Friends, Romans, countrymen, lend me your ears, because I have a story to tell.
> Lend me your ears; if you've not got them with you, your noses will do just as well.

Having announced that his next poem had been written by the greatest of living authors, he would continue, 'And when I finished writing it…' Indeed, most of his material came from his own pen, but his air of seriousness stressed the apparent humour of all such claims. He never let the mask of gravity slip.

Once in a while he would discard his usual slipshod attire in favour of more relevant, but equally ludicrous, clothes: he may have been dressed as 'almost a sailor' saying 'farewell to his horse'. No one ever discovered what did become of that poor animal, but with couplets as appealing as

> The little sardines had gone into their tins
> And pulled down the lid for the night

and

> I saw lots of water on top of the waves
> And I found a lot more underneath

no one really cared. As 'almost Napoleon' he gave a burlesque of the tragedy at Waterloo, his main concern being the suffering of the Highland regiments in the high wind.

> On came the gallant Scotch Brigade,
> Their kilts in the wind were blowing.
> None of them knew where the wind came from,
> But they all knew where it was going.
> Bullets flew by with a sizzle,
> Bagpipes and gas pipes roared.
> I stood the shots well, but Napoleon fell
> When they told me that *(here he would interpolate the name of the local football team)* had scored.

Bennett as himself

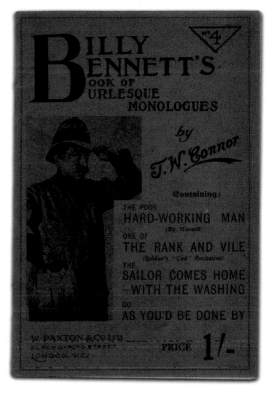

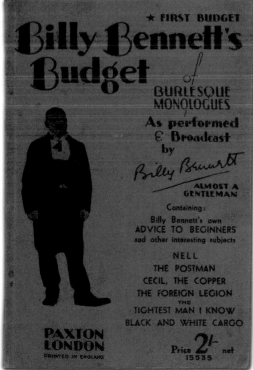

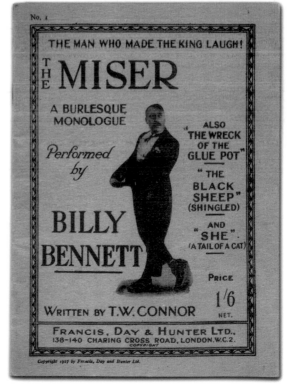

Most notable was his return to khaki as a Kiplingesque explorer complete with short, baggy pants and tent for sun hat, as he trudged along the never-ending road to Mandalay, swigging for survival from a hot-water bottle in the agonising heat. Whatever the bottle contained, it prompted lines like

> There's a farm on the horizon,
> Looking eastward to Siam;
> We could have some ham and eggs there,
> If they had some eggs and ham!
> But they've only got one hen –
> They call her Mandy, by the way –
> But they've found out she's a cock;
> That's why they can't make Mandy-lay!

> There were no maps for soldiers
> In this land of Gunga-Din,
> So they picked the toughest warrior out
> And tattooed on his skin.
> On his back he's got Calcutta,
> Lower down he's got Bombay,
> And you'll find him sitting peacefully
> On the road to Mandalay.

In more conventional costume he would describe unconventional meetings of the League of Nations held to discuss such matters as whether red cabbage is greengrocery, on which side of the road kippers ought to swim, the possibility of a 'bandy-legged gherkin' being a 'straight cucumber's child', and where a duck keeps its quack when its tonsils have been removed. At the most unlikely of meeting places, namely Berwick Market, he paraded a formidable array of geographical freaks, including kilt-wearing Hebrews, Yorkshire-speaking Scandinavians, shorthand-speaking Scots and Greeks with beards of bubble and squeak.

In 'The bookmaker's daughter' one met Nell, the elder of twin sisters, 'first past the post' by 'two minutes at most', who, when older, gave completely new meaning to a phrase like 'laying on the field' and saved the day for her father by riding the slippery steed Black Pudding in a pair of 'red-flannel non-skids'. Another formidable Bennett female was featured in 'She was happiest when she was poor'. For this hapless soul, wealth had meant an increase in weight from 'seven stone four' to 'eighteen stone six', six double chins that reached the floor, and the need to sleep with one leg in bed and the other up the chimney! Slightly more palatable, if equally outrageous, was the tale of 'The green tie of the little yellow dog'. Mad Carew donates his tie to his mistress for her pet. This is affixed to the animal's tail by means of the madman's misplaced tiepin. The dog gains a subtle and just revenge on Carew by planting his mistress's false teeth in his bed. By way of conclusion:

There's a cock-eyed yellow poodle to the north of Gongapooch,
There's a little hot cross bun that's turning green,
There's a double-jointed wop-wop doing tricks in who-flung-dung,
And you're a better man than I am Gunga-Din.

One does not need to know that 'Gongapooch' is an actual Hindustani colloquialism for 'arseholes' (first included in this parody of Kipling's 'Gunga-Din' during a performance before King George V; with his knowledge of the language the monarch was the only one to appreciate the full joke) to realise that Bennett had no time for delicacy. There ran through his entire work a vein of coarse physicality, a red-nosed obsession with anatomy, whereby an innocent phrase like 'gathering of the clans' immediately conjured up a grotesque festering image only a hair's breadth from mental vomiting. Bennett's was a world where one grew corns on one's chest and milked cows with a spanner. Catharsis in comedy can take many forms. The monologues aside, the typical Bennett gag fell comfortably into the same category.

My wife's father has a long beard. He looks as though he has eaten a horse and left the tail hanging out!

This brother had a single hair on the end of his nose. It was so long that every time he sneezed it cracked like a whip. One night he took a pinch of snuff and flogged himself to death!

There was the man who had to be taken to hospital after breaking his fingers while cracking jokes to a deaf mute, as well as the Scot who broke his neck trying to lick off the 'medicinal' whisky rubbed on his back. Bennett's preoccupation with false teeth, tattoos and obesity was as abiding as Ken Dodd's with tickling and Spike Milligan's with knees in later years. But he always fell short of evoking actual nausea through a tactical surrealism, a quality that identifies him even further with Milligan, and with Dodd especially – the Liverpool upbringing and the whole low comedy ethos being mutual.

The combination of bizarre fantasy and the down to earth is a technique that had been popular with Leno, whose patter was similarly rich with instances of time out of joint, impossible anatomical situations and inanimate objects endowed with a life of their own. Bennett carried on this freewheeling tradition, one that made it possible to look as far as one can see and then a little further, to anticipate the present by having done things in the future, to travel in vehicles that remain empty. Bennett's postman was strikingly reminiscent of Leno's shopwalker, tramping the streets so much that he had to resort to turning his legs up at the ends when his feet had been worn away. In his act – to no one's surprise – hot dogs wore pullovers, gooseberries shaved, tears had a habit of running up the spine and black puddings were regarded as white slaves. In his *In Praise of Comedy* the philosopher James Feibleman has pointed out the close parallel between comedy and surrealism, and it is easy to see in this the secret of Bennett's humour: 'The classic method of comedy is evident in the technique of the surrealists. The juxtaposition of objects and hence of relations which do not seem to have any good reason for belonging together lies at the bottom of all surrealists' work.' With its madcap word associations and inverted logical reasoning, there was certainly much in Bennett's style that foreshadowed the work of absurdist dramatists like Ionesco, Pinter and Beckett. More significant in literary terms is the clear line of descent from Bennett back through Leno to the century of Lear and Carroll. Indeed, the sense of incongruity shared by all four was a quality intrinsic to the spirit of music hall, as discernible in Little Tich's elongated boots, Chirgwin's white diamond eye make-up or Cinquevalli's attire as a human billiard table as in its verbal absurdities. On the variety stage of the 1920s and 30s Bennett stood as the continuing personification of this quality.

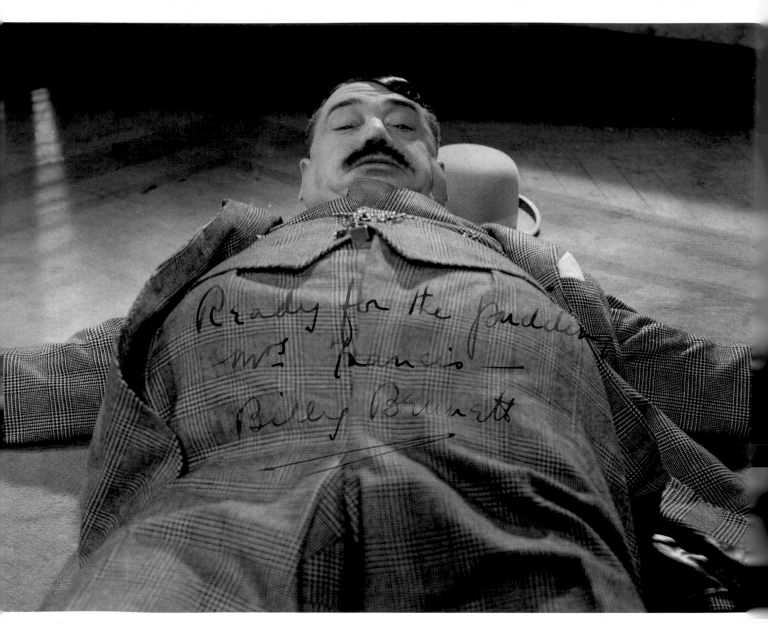

His boisterous juicy delivery as a monologist made up for his shortcomings as 'almost a ballet dancer' – he thought nothing of interlacing his verses with a pot-bellied attempt at perfectly valid ballet steps – and as a singer. To hear his turbulent baritone reproduced today is to hear one of the least engaging of the voices on those scratchy 78s bequeathed by the last years of the halls. And yet there are two songs with which he will always be associated. Both made comedy of the tragedy of social injustice and one listens to them now uneasily. The pathos needs a far more featherweight touch than Bennett can provide, while the irony appears unnecessarily contrived. 'Don't send my boy to prison' is the plea to a relentless judge from a poverty-stricken mother whose son has been imprisoned for a minor crime committed to save the family from starvation. The problem is knowing whether Bennett's treatment is meant to be comic or not. The human emotions within the lyric are not the stuff of comedy and yet it seems impossible that Bennett gave them the serious treatment they appear to demand. The other number is somewhat less disquieting and gave Bennett his signature tune, namely 'She was poor, but she was honest', with its recurring lines:

> It's the same the whole world over,
> It's the poor what gets the blame.
> It's the rich what gets the pleasure.
> Isn't it a blooming shame?

The lyric tells of a humble provincial girl who travels innocently to the big city to become the prey of a wealthy Lothario.

> Then the rich man took her riding,
> Wrecker of poor women's souls.
> But the devil was the chauffeur
> As she rode in his Royce Rolls.

Eventually forsaken, she jumps into the Thames. Taken for drowned, she is dragged onto the bank, only to get up and sing the inevitable refrain.

An intriguing facet of Bennett's career is that at the height of his popularity as 'Almost a Gentleman', he mysteriously smothered this known persona with a completely different style of presentation. Donning black face, thick white rubber-ring lips and a grey bowler, he assumed the identity of Moses Washington Lincoln in the cross-talk act Alexander and Mose, formed in November 1930 in the early days of radio broadcasting at Savoy Hill. The identity of the two wisecracking blackface minstrels was at first kept a secret, but the act's popularity soon made a leak inevitable and by May 1931 they were appearing together on the halls. Alexander was first played by James Carew, who was essentially an actor rather than a variety performer. The act seems not to have taken full flight until Carew left to pursue a cinematic career in the latter part of 1931 and was replaced by Albert Whelan, an already established Australian variety performer, famous for his debonair delivery of songs and stories like 'The three trees' and 'The poacher and the bear', and as the first entertainer to boast a signature tune. Standing centre stage, he would commence his own act by casually removing his top hat, coat and gloves as he whistled 'Der Lustige Brüder' ('The Jolly Brothers') waltz. His own 'Gentleman' compensated for all the shortcomings implied by Bennett's 'Almost'. They were a popular combination, and a profitable one, as it was possible for them, with just a few minor supporting acts, to dominate a whole variety bill. They would each perform their solo act in the first half and then emerge again at the end of the show in make-up as Alexander and Mose, an act with an appeal totally distinct from that of their alter egos.

They managed to impart to the basic cross-talk act an authentic 'bones and tambourine' atmosphere and all the traditional wheezes of the minstrel show corner men. Bennett as Mose affected a continual air of laziness to the disgust of his would-be corrector, Alexander, who had greater difficulties with the language than most immigrants. Their dialogue, delivered in a languid nasal drawl as dark as molasses, would go something like this:

Alexander: Is you residing in a peaceful residential neighbourhood?

Mose: No. The people upstairs was jumping about and shouting at two o'clock this morning.

Alexander: Did they disturb your sleep?

Mose: No. I wasn't sleeping.

Alexander: What was you doing?

Mose: Playing the saxophone.

Alexander: Why be an athletic disciple of Orpheus?

Mose: Sez which?

Alexander: Why are you learning the saxophone?

Mose: I'se going to a party.

Alexander: When is the party?

Mose: At Christmas.

Alexander: Last Christmas you promised to send me a turkey and that turkey never arrived.

Mose: I didn't know it was going to get well again!

Alexander: Use your ligaments, boy, and don't percolate.

Such an act is inconceivable today. That it was possible not so long ago must be based on the understanding that during the early vaudeville period the American negro regarded his white-as-black counterpart in the minstrel show line-up less as a suggestion of his own inferiority, more as a token comic type, formalised long beforehand like the stingy Scot, the foppish dandy or the innocent rustic as another static emotionless comic mask. It is interesting to note that on the early London music hall stage the negro, whether made up white or not, far from being a figure who was looked down upon with ridicule, was elevated to such a romantic level that subsequent stars like Little Tich and Harry Champion began their careers as 'coon' performers in attempts to curry early popularity. G. H. Elliott affectionately carried this tradition over into the 1950s with his 'Chocolate Coloured Coon' characterisation. Renowned for his dignity and a hauntingly elegiac vocal quality, he died, like Whelan, twenty years later than Bennett in 1962, the year the record-breaking *Black and White Minstrel Show* followed the Crazy Gang into London's Victoria Palace. The world has now moved on.

Happily Bennett never allowed his 'Mose' character to take over completely from 'Almost a Gentleman', even though in May 1931 he did feature the blackface routine in one of his four appearances in a Royal Variety Performance. In those of 1926, 1933 and 1934 his aspirant to gentility held sway. He was forthrightness itself: suggestion was a technique unknown to him. With the rugged pride of a refuse collector by royal appointment, he stood in the direct line of Rabelais, Sterne and Swift. He also enjoyed a priceless direct access to his audience, an audience he took by the scruff of its neck and told what it could do if it did not like his approach. The understanding, however, was never on anything other than an old pals' basis. They might wonder how he got away with what he did, but they were laughing at the same time.

AFTERTHOUGHTS

Playwright John Osborne, a staunch advocate of the halls in their dying days – vide his creation of the fading music hall comic Archie Rice in *The Entertainer* – paid Bennett the ultimate compliment by naming the second volume of his autobiography *Almost a Gentleman*. The first had been entitled *A Better Class of Person*. Osborne, whose relish for the practitioners of robust comedy is preserved on videotape in a memorable sequence where he and Sir John Betjeman are observed guffawing at a live recording of Max Miller, would almost certainly have put Bennett in this category as well. It is tempting to imagine the ex-cavalryman cast as Archie's father, although I guess the dustman Alfred Doolittle in *Pygmalion* may have been closer to the spirit of Bennett's act.

Stanley Holloway, who made the part of Doolittle his own in the musical version, *My Fair Lady*, worked with Bennett on many occasions and provided a fascinating insight into the real character of his friend, whom he saw as 'frank, forthright and a man who led his life in a most orderly fashion. If he arranged to play golf with someone it was like an army manoeuvre. If the time fixed was for, say, 10 a.m., Bill would be waiting there on the first tee, and if the other man didn't turn up punctually Bennett would never wait for him. He'd start playing on his own and his opponent would jolly well have to catch up with him!' Bennett never married and referred to himself as 'God's gift to lonely women'. He had no shortage of lady friends, and if they stayed the night at his apartment they were given strict instructions to be off the premises before his 'daily' arrived at eleven. An uncomplicated man, he was appreciated for the bluntness that never deserted him. He once shared a bill with the bandleader Jack Payne, not the most popular man in the profession. 'Can anybody lend me twopence?' asked Payne. 'I want to phone a friend.' Bennett obliged: 'Here's sixpence. Phone the lot!'

One story from Bennett's war career embraces the public and the private man. After the Armistice he and a colleague were detailed to clear out the NAAFI store at a small French town. They sold everything they could, only to be left with a couple of large sacks of Epsom salts of the equine variety. Not knowing what to do with them, in the dead of night they tipped the lot down a well. Billy's eyes lit up as he described the aftermath: 'Do you know, after that the place became famous as a health spa!'

'Well, it rhymes!'

WILL HAY: THE FOURTH FORM AT ST MICHAEL'S

Hay: You distinctly asked me how high was a Chinaman!
Young boy: I didn't ask you. I told you.
Hay: Eh?
Young boy: I simply said, 'How High is a Chinaman.' How High is his name and he's a Chinaman and he keeps a laundry.
Hay: Who does?
Young boy: How High!

The self-styled head of St Michael's embodied more comprehensively than any of his contemporaries on the British variety stage the combination of stealth, greed and meanness of spirit that the critic Eric Bentley discerned as the major force in the comic universe, 'the itch to own the material world' that is the basis of so much comedy: 'In how many comic plots there is theft or the intention of theft! If men did not wish to break the tenth commandment, comic plotting, as we know it, could never have come into being.' Will Hay was the epitome of disrepute, an imposing upstart in an outwardly respectable arena, that of privileged preparatory education. His seedy pedagogue had nothing to teach, would have been incapable of passing on knowledge if this had been otherwise and just about managed to scrape along by opportune cribbing from his own pupils.

Destined to become the most popular light sketch performer of his day, he was born, the son of an engineer, William Thomson Hay in Stockton-on-Tees on 6 December 1888 and, like Robey and Wilton ahead of him, gave up a career in engineering to enter show business. His stage apprenticeship was spent as a member of a Derbyshire concert party and subsequently a minstrel troupe on the Isle of Man. A spell with Fred Karno's company likewise provided experience. It was as the ersatz academic that he first achieved and later sustained fame, originally in a musical sketch entitled 'Bend Down', inspired by the experiences of his schoolmistress sister, Elspeth. Each verse chronicled the misbehaviour of a pupil in an unruly classroom, culminating in a whack of the cane.

Today while taking object lessons I said, 'Now, boys, look here.
What does the little busy bee give us? Now be quite clear.'
One boy shouted, 'Please, sir, stings!' Another shouted, 'Beer!'
But when one shouted, 'Beetroot!' I said, 'Do they?
Come here, bend down.' *Swish*!

He toyed with the idea of dragging up as a grotesque school ma'am before deciding to concentrate upon her shifty male equivalent. As 'The Schoolmaster Comedian' he prospered, like Bennett, to the extent that his career embraced four Royal Variety Performances, though over a more impressive span of twenty years: at the Alhambra in 1925, the Coliseum in 1928 and 1945, and the Palladium in 1930.

It is significant that Hay did not look like a comedian: his offstage expression was typically earnest and scholarly. And yet the addition of mortarboard tilted at rakish angle, tattered gown and the famous pince-nez perched precariously halfway down a disdainful nose soon set him aside as an eccentric at an almost red-nosed level, though in a interview in the *Era,* January 1928, he would admit to only 'caricature'.

> Modern audiences require a more intellectual type of comedy. In my sketch I portray school life in caricature. It is not burlesque, but an exaggerated portrayal of English character – a particular living type of schoolmaster; I have no doubt there are schoolmasters of my type living today. I pick out the peculiarities in a schoolmaster and exaggerate them in the same way as an artist when making a caricature of a man will exaggerate his prominent nose or his big chin or other outstanding features. These exaggerations not only make the picture amusing, but serious also, because it is a likeness to the man portrayed. The old-fashioned type of red-nose comedian did not portray any living character at all.

If the character looked grotesque, it was certainly played with the utmost seriousness. However ludicrous the argument, lesson or debate, there was not so much as a hint of a smile to suggest that it was to be regarded as anything other than the strenuous intellectual exercise it set out to be. No schoolmaster ever put such grim meaning behind the simple introduction 'Good morning, boys,' uttered in the sharp, sarcastic, snapdragon tone that was its owner's most immediate defence against the confusion into which he would inevitably find his lesson plunged. Back would come the wearily-chanted echo 'Good morning, sir,' the most consistent cue for the telltale sniff or deprecating cough with which Hay could express indifference, contempt or disbelief. His hand would brush against his chin in equivocation. He would peer at the 'boys' through his pince-nez with eyes as shifty as pebbles in a kaleidoscope. Around the whole proceedings hung an aura of the shabbiest gentility.

The boys, of course, were as important to the act as Hay. Films he subsequently made without the regular members of his team show that he was happiest when he had their zany support. One must not imagine, however, that the sketch comedian or member of a double act has an easier task than the solo performer. Whereas the latter is able to concentrate immediately upon establishing direct contact with his audience, the members of a double act or sketch team have the twofold task of maintaining the necessary dramatic contact with each other, as well as connecting beyond the footlights. Hay himself was well aware of the responsibility this placed upon the other members of his team.

> When I begin to prepare a sketch, I study seriously the situations which are likely to raise a laugh. I look upon these situations as a series of mines which have to be exploded at certain intervals, because to raise a laugh you have, metaphorically speaking, to make an assault on the minds of the audience.

These mines have to be exploded at definite times, and when I am on the stage, my duty is not necessarily to be funny, but to see that all the mines are sprung at the psychological moment, and also have the correct amount of explosives in them to obtain the greatest effect on the audience.

A comedian working solo, of course, can regulate the explosions as he wishes, but it is far more difficult to do so when one is working with assistants, because he has to see that his assistants do not discharge the mines, as I have said, too soon or too late. When I get a new assistant I always impress upon him the importance of timing the gags correctly. As an illustration, I refer to a heavy wheel which has to be set in motion. It requires a certain amount of energy to rotate it, but once it has been rotated, it requires very little impulse to keep it going.

With Will Hay Junior and H. Gordon Saunders

The membership of the act changed over the years, but a basic combination of two pupils remained the nucleus for most of the time, one a sly stupid bewhiskered octogenarian, who collected his pension on the way to school, the other a fat precocious youth who knew far too much to be tolerated elsewhere. Both prospered under the dictatorial wing of their dysfunctional headmaster, helping Hay to prove what in our own schooldays we had all hopefully surmised, that mortarboard and dunce's cap were interchangeable. At first Hay found a single character adequate, but the addition of the old man added a new dimension to his work. The boy was always brighter than he was, but the two of them could always outwit the dotard. In this way Hay was able to steer a middle course, still the butt of most of the jokes, but able to gain the upper hand for comic flexibility from time to time. In the early years the young know-it-all and the dim-witted senior were played by Hay's nephews, Bert and Cyril Platt, then more prominently by Will Hay Junior and H. Gordon Saunders respectively, but a more notable duo was provided by Moore Marriott's senile 'Harbottle' and Graham Moffatt's squealing, Billy Bunter-style 'Albert'. The latter pair were Hay's staunch henchmen in many of his films, where the three-sided ritual was often transferred to wider fields of authority and administration.

'The Fourth Form at St Michael's' underwent many adventures as its history was chronicled in stage sketches throughout the 1920s and 30s. 'The Beginning of St Michael's' satisfied the curiosity of all those who ever wondered how such an incongruous trio ever came together in one classroom. Opening with a chance encounter between 'plain-clothes' headmaster and new boy in a quiet country lane, the latter has no sooner asked the way to the school than he is announcing his plans to get the head to 'clear out'.

Hay: I don't understand slang.
Young boy: I'll make him vamoose.
Hay: Oh, you mean bunk!

The boy boasts of his notoriety for killing schoolmasters and that the new school is to be the stage for his next murder. The scene changes to the famous classroom, where we meet an ancient railwayman who has just returned to school to find out why he should have spent his last sixty-five years tapping wheels. Meanwhile Hay has donned cap and gown and revealed his identity to the young scoundrel. His earlier sly reticence now takes its revenge upon his opponent's loud-mouthed cockiness and flagellation runs riot.

This sketch was not the only time Hay's act opened against a rural backdrop. In 'Gambling' he comes across the new boy and the old man playing an alfresco game of banker. He reproachfully interrupts the game, but is soon lured into playing himself. Hay is fleeced, a policeman approaches, the boys run, and the headmaster successfully saves himself by pretending to the law that he is an innocent schoolboy himself. Back at school, Hay gets back the money the others filched from him. The law again arrives on the scene, but if the headmaster has had the foresight to change places with the new boy in good time, he has not taken into account the flogging he will receive from his pupil, at last presented with a perfect opportunity to masquerade as the figure of authority. The exchange of roles between boy and master was a recurrent theme in Hay's sketches. In 'Inkstain's Theory' he arrives on stage with trousers torn, having caught them on a nail as he was sliding down the banisters. The lesson that follows is interrupted by a solicitor who announces that a pupil has inherited the school, though luckily the will, in its small print, does save the head from being fired. The routine enabled Hay to indulge his genuine fascination with scientific subjects, albeit from a comic perspective.

Young boy: I don't think you know anything about it yourself.
Hay: About what?
Young boy: About the construction of matter.
Hay: Oh, is that what it is?
Young boy: Yes.
Hay: In that case I do know something about it.
Young boy: Right, well how do they split the atom?
Hay: How do they what?

Young boy: Split the atom.

Hay: Well, that all depends on how they want it splitting – whether with the grain or across the grain.

'Entomology' saw a journey made in reverse direction from school to countryside. Every course of study that can be pursued successfully within four walls having failed, the trio, equipped in the cause of natural history with mallet, Stilton cheese, mantrap and penny whistle, track down a beetle to its lair. The hideous scarlet creature refuses to be caught. Frolicking about the stage on its secret wire with a squirrel's elusiveness, it completely ridicules the human determination that plagues it. Eventually mallet and mantrap bring Hay himself to the ground, where he stays, even after the boys take off the stretcher which is supposed to carry him.

The academic level at St Michael's was obviously set at the most abysmal low, and if the level of humour used to emphasise this was often that of the schoolboy howler, the public was prepared to tolerate its naivety for the skilful characterisations of Hay and his team. Moreover, the whole set-up could not fail to evoke a distinctive nostalgic quality for those not too far removed from their own schooldays. In Hay's academy the most significant fact about the Magna Carta was that it was signed above the dotted line, while no one was quite sure whether 'Hastings 1066' was a telephone number or the time of a train. By way of definition, radishes were 'vegetables with knobs on', Joan of Arc was Noah's wife, and a martyr 'a pile of wood with a man on top'. In a pre-metric age his attempt to explain the difference between troy weight and avoirdupois came out something like this:

Hay: Troy weight was invented by – er – Helen of Troy, and avoirdupois comes from three French words. *Avoir* – to have, *du* – of the, and *pois* – er – pois? Er – (*at last with sudden enlightenment*) peas!

Young boy: Peas?

Hay: Yeh.

Young boy: Why peas?

Hay: Well – because – er – in the reign of Louis XIV, they used peas as weights. See? So many peas to the magnum.

Old boy: Please, sir.

Hay: Yes, what is it?

Old boy: Please, sir, what did they do in the winter?

Hay: What did who do in the winter?

Old boy: The shopkeepers, sir.

Hay: Well, what do you mean – 'What did they do?' They didn't shut up if that's what you mean.

Old boy: No, sir. I mean what did the shopkeepers do, sir? They be out of season in the winter.

Hay: What are you talking about? Shopkeepers don't go out of season at all.

Old boy: No, sir. I mean the peas, sir.

Hay: Oh – the peas – oh – well – they used tinned peas then.

Old boy: Yes. But please, sir, wouldn't tins of peas weigh much heavier, sir?

Hay: Oh, God! Well look – they took 'em out of the tins and – er – will you shut up? Keep quiet!

The stubborn octogenarian and the pert fat boy made sure Hay was hounded and caught at every turn, his lessons turning into a mental obstacle race that exercised his powers of verbal evasion to the utmost, until his indignation burst, quiet was demanded with the vulgar roar of a rabble rouser and recourse had to a stack of canes.

In view of the splendidly hopeless verbal tangles in which headmaster and pupils found themselves, it is not surprising that when the question 'What's your name?' featured in the script, the boys found themselves with surnames such as Watt or Weighley (pronounced 'Why'). Moreover, the confusion experienced by Hay as he struggled to enter the appropriate name in his register was only increased when it came to recording that Reginald Clarence D'Arcy, for example, lived at Ware. Illogical argument and cross-purpose were the very fibre of Hay's humour. The tag lines to individual jokes may not be inspiring, but the aggravated confusion which led to them was built up with an earnestness that only enhanced the fun along the way.

Young boy: Can you tell me who it is who dies the most awful death?

Hay: Er – no. Who does?

Young boy: A sculptor.

Hay: A sculptor?

Young boy: Yes.

Hay: Oh, does he?

Young boy: Yes

Hay: I never knew that before.

Young boy: Well, say 'Why?'

Hay: Hmmm?

Young boy: Well, say 'Why?'

Hay: Why?

Young boy: Because I want you to.

Hay: You want me to what?

Young boy: Say 'Why?'

Hay: Why?

Young boy: Because you have to.

Hay: I have to what?

Young boy: Say 'Why?'

Hay: Eh? What do you want me to say?

Young boy: 'Why?'

Hay: I don't know what you want me to say; how can I say it?

Young boy: I told you. I want you to say 'Why?'

Hay: You know, I don't think we speak the same language. Listen, ask Harbottle. Let him have a go at it.

Young boy: Here, Harbottle. Say 'Why?'

Old boy: Yes.

Young boy: What?

Old boy: Yes.

Young boy: Yes what?

Old boy: I don't know.

Hay: That's all right. Leave him out. He's hopeless. Now listen, what do you want me to say?

Young boy: 'Why?'

Hay: Well, I've said it half a dozen times already.

Young boy: Oh yes. Well, a sculptor dies a most awful death because he makes faces and busts.

Hay: Any more questions like that, my boy, and I'll bust you!

Hay stood for everything that could be construed as dodgy in a figure of authority. He knew it, and his boys knew it, and never was he more essentially himself, hedging and ingratiating, than when his own ignorance was about to be exposed. And yet the corruption and deception on display in a Hay sketch were completely harmless, offset by a blundering inefficiency at any task undertaken. When challenged by a sceptical pupil that he was not a qualified teacher, all he could bring forth as proof of his BA was a certificate signifying election to the Royal and Ancient Order of Buffaloes.

Young boy: Buffaloes? What do you think we want to be? Cowboys?

Hay: Well, that's... that's Oxon, isn't it?

The only way he could get to know the answers to the questions he set was by 'marking' the book of the bright boy first. In 'Rebellion', the boys succumbed to militant action, threatening withdrawal of fees by their parents if they did not pass their exams. The same bright pupil was puzzled why six questions he had answered correctly were marked wrong.

Hay: You had those questions last year, didn't you?

Young boy: Yes, I had the same questions last year and put the same answers and you marked them right then.

Hay: Well, what about it?

Young boy: Well, what do you want to mark them wrong now for?

Hay: Well, things have changed since last year, haven't they?

The one certainty in life was that at St Michael's facts, dates, formulae, conjugations were all as variable as clouds in the sky.

FUNNY WAY TO BE A HERO

Hay was in his mid-forties when in 1933 he made his first film, a Pathé short entitled *Know Your Apples,* which led to a distinguished if belated cinematic career embracing nineteen full features over a ten-year period. He wisely divided his time on celluloid between his favourite schoolmaster role and variations that signified some other shady, pompous authoritarian, whether magistrate in a loose adaptation of Pinero's farce *The Magistrate* (*Those Were the Days*), policeman (*Ask a Policeman*), fireman (*Where's That Fire?*), or prison governor (*Convict 99*). *Old Bones of the River* took the trio as far as Africa, where we find Hay attempting in vain to impart his special knowledge to the children of the jungle, who have already learned everything from qualified missionaries, while *The Goose Steps Out* saw the blustery rascal masquerading as a German officer teaching Nazi recruits – most notably a young Peter Ustinov – how to salute the Führer with a not very subtly disguised V-sign. The saga of Narkover by J. B. Morton, Beachcomber of the *Daily Express*, provided an excellent vehicle for his schoolmaster characterisation in several films, commencing with *Boys Will Be Boys* in 1935. Only Will Hay could have played Dr Smart Allick. If only because of his presence, therefore, it is ironic that the producers should have diluted the name in the final scenario to Dr Alexander Smart!

Oh, Mr Porter!, reminiscent of Keaton's *The General* with its climactic locomotive chase, has a justifiable claim to be considered the most notable British comedy of the 1930s. Superbly crafted by writers Marriott Edgar and Val Guest and Hay's most effective director, Marcel Varnel, it features the comedian as stationmaster William Porter, dispatched out of sight by his superiors to the decrepit Irish halt of Buggleskelly, manned by the equally decrepit Moffatt and Marriott, who spend their time bartering tickets for food and cultivating tomatoes in the signal box. Hay brings all his reserves of self-importance to the new post, while revealing his total inadequacy for the task. He once said that he 'gloried in the idea of an inefficient man doggedly trying to do a job of which he is utterly incapable'. That was never shown to better effect than here. Anxious to implement a new regime, he flounders in a mire of zero respect, enmeshed in a plot that involves espionage and gunrunning. Only a set of comic circumstances lead the incompetent trio to emerge triumphant. Set against a lovingly observed, if caricatured, rural Irish background, *Oh, Mr Porter!* demonstrated clearly how much the sheer illogic of Hay's comic idiom gained when set in a realistic but incongruous framework. This is the key to the enduring success of all his best work and explains why, of all the top British variety comedians who took advantage of the cinematic medium in the 30s, artistically Hay was by far the most successful. Today the humour of his films remains crisp and invigorating, and his brash assurance has lost none of its attack. It is not difficult to see why his style was so adaptable to the camera. As long as the cinema demanded a scenario synonymous with plot, narrative and storyline, rather than allowing comedians the licence to perform freely according to their own ethos – in other words to pursue that spontaneity enjoyed by Chaplin and Keaton in the early days of film-making – the finished product could not help but appear false and contrived. The plots of Hay's films are no less contrived than those of Lucan or Formby, but whereas in their case one would have been happier watching simply a never-ending quarrel with Kitty or a carefree ukulele tour of all those lamp posts against which a naive lover ever wistfully leaned, Hay's own world was one of scheming, contrivance and petty intrigue. The twists and turns of his plots were more than the right thing for a character that

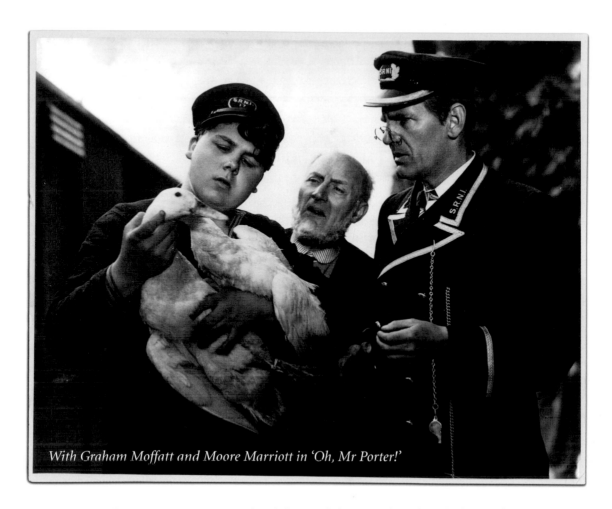

With Graham Moffatt and Moore Marriott in 'Oh, Mr Porter!'

lived by twists and turns. To repeat Bentley: 'If men did not wish to break the tenth commandment, comic plotting, as we know it, could never have come into being.'

It is significant that Hay, both as a solo entity and together with his team, had parallels in contemporary Hollywood. He would have been the perfect match for W. C. Fields, and it is interesting to note that Hay, like Fields, started on the halls as a juggler. It has been reported that he was inspired to learn the skill as a result of seeing Fields on tour in Manchester in 1908. Selfish arrogance and pig-headed stubbornness, deviousness and dishonesty were traits common to the two performers. Within the confines of the cinematic storyline, Fields was the more successful. In *The Art of W. C. Fields* William K. Everson writes, 'Like Fields, Hay was frequently trapped by his own schemings. But while Fields could bluff his way out of any situation by convincingly assuming the pose of an expert, Hay's attempts at bluff merely got him into more trouble.' To go on to say, however, that Hay was a far less likeable character than his American counterpart, 'with fewer redeeming traits', would appear to be a paradoxical and, as far as Fields himself is concerned, unfair judgement, in view of the determination with which both openly shunned sympathy and pathos.

In the 1930s the team of Hay, Marriott and Moffatt was also the nearest British approximation to the Marx Brothers. The incompetent blunders of the Hay team were much closer to the anarchistic activity of the Marxes than the essentially seaside-postcard humour of the Crazy Gang, more often quoted as the British equivalent. Hay and Groucho shared the same sly suspicious outlook, outrageously typified by ill-fitting pince-nez in one case and painted moustache in the other; Albert and Chico had in common a saving impudence, a resilient independence; the aged Harbottle and the mute Harpo had their prolonged periods of silence punctuated by flashes of sudden inspiration. As with the Marxes, no one member of the team ever became exclusively prop or foil to another. Each existed in his own right, part of a well-balanced comic whole. It is apt that the first comedy routine the Marxes played in their early vaudeville days was a sketch entitled 'Fun in Hi Skule' or 'School Days', which greatly influenced the biology class scene in their epic attack on the established education system, *Horse Feathers*. Thus Hay, Fields, and the Marxes are inseparably linked, although it would be impossible to say that one side of the Atlantic influenced the other. Suffice to say that Hay would have been far more aware of Fields' work than vice versa (Hay's films meant little in the United States, although he had made a successful stage tour there in 1927) and that any British combination that looked as if it might rival the Marxes in popularity was bound to be fondly welcomed by UK film distributors.

Parallel to the grimly serious determination with which Hay tried to overcome the havoc that held sway in his classroom was a happily serious disposition offstage, which found expression in frequent appearances on the BBC's *The Brains Trust* and an absorbing interest in astronomy, his studies in which were officially recognised by his election as a Fellow of the Royal Astronomical Society. He built his own observatory at his home in Hendon and in August 1933 made the notable discovery of a large white spot on Saturn. Two years later he published a book on his avocation. *Through My Telescope* was later reprinted for the use of the Home Guard in the Second World War. In 1942 he temporarily gave up his theatrical work to help the war effort, joining the navy as a sub-lieutenant in the Special Branch of the RNVR to instruct the Sea Cadet Corps in astronomy and navigation.

His final years were dogged by ill health. He died from a stroke on 18 April 1949, having been inactive professionally from an earlier stroke for two and a half years. During that time it was said he had lost seven eighths of the personality that had made him a star. His inability to adjust his astronomical instruments and the home-made clocks he had set to one fifth of a second made him even more morose. It was ironic that his death should occur at what was then the scholastic retiring age, but 'The Schoolmaster Comedian' had been far luckier than most professional funny men in that offstage he had been openly encouraged to be serious and, therefore, himself.

AFTERTHOUGHTS

Alongside the Billy Bunter novels of Frank Richards, and perhaps to an extent because of them, Hay's popularity thrived in spite of the ignorance among the general public of the world of private preparatory education. Even today his name and image are shorthand for the vagaries and inefficiency within the wider teaching profession, appearing in the educational pages of the more serious newspapers on a regular basis. In any game of word association his would be the first comedian's name to come to mind at the mention of 'curriculum'. Perhaps it is not surprising that few names in comedy appear to have inspired so much apparent trivia.

Almost entirely self-educated, Hay was fluent in French, German, Italian, Norwegian, Afrikaans and Latin. He also possessed the strange ability to write what appeared to be nonsense on a blackboard, only to turn it upside down to reveal a coherent statement of some kind. He would repeat the process with whatever people cared to dictate to him, although it is not clear whether he ever displayed the skill on stage. Apart from his comedy appearances on traditional radio programmes, he was probably the first variety comedian to assume the role of quizmaster over the airwaves, taking the job seriously and not using it as a medium for comedy as more than a few stand-up practitioners have done on television in recent years. As such he presented the 'Double-or-Quits' cash quiz section of the wartime entertainment show *Merry-Go-Round* on twenty-five occasions from May 1944. So another link is established with Groucho Marx, who on *You Bet Your Life* made the question master role his own on American television in the 50s, although using the vehicle as a springboard for ad-libbing, a skill that Hay never openly displayed.

In my biography of the later comedian I reasoned that without Tony Hancock there would have been no Steptoe, no Alf Garnett, no Captain Mainwaring, no Alan Partridge, no David Brent. Ergo, without Will Hay… His influence on subsequent British comedy may be seen as considerable, if only for the impact he made, by their own admission, on Hancock himself and his most enduring writers, Ray Galton and Alan Simpson. The spirit of Will Hay, his seedy grandeur and the lowly social realism of his milieu, were alive and well in East Cheam during those halcyon days of radio comedy in the decade or so after he died. Together Hancock and his co-star Sidney James were spiritual heirs to the schoolmaster comedian, Sid majoring on the duplicity and the lad himself on the pretension and indignation that Hay used as a smokescreen to hide his ignorance. In a radio episode from 1955 entitled 'The Red Planet' Galton and Simpson turned their attention to astronomy, when Hancock discovers a new planet, which he thinks is on a collision course with the earth. In fact Sid has decided to play a trick on his crony by painting on the lens of his telescope a red spot that he makes bigger every day. It is difficult not to see the show as subconscious homage to the older performer, who – serious man that he was – would surely have applauded the programme, endorsing as it did his two great loves of laughter and learning. Although Hay's material was always wedded to the joke, an element rigorously shunned by Hancock and his writers, the emphasis he placed on character within the sketch format signified a step forward from his colleagues and rivals on the halls, and together with his elaborate use of wordplay and sense of the inadequacy of language as a means of communication pointed the way forward to the more sophisticated sketch comedy of the 1960s and beyond, most notably in the work of the Two Ronnies.

Hay also foreshadowed Hancock in another way. At the peak of his fame, with the triumphs of *Oh, Mr Porter!*, *Convict 99* and *Ask a Policeman* still only recent memories, Hay decided to end his screen partnership with Moffatt and Marriott and to shift his film operation from Gainsborough to Ealing Studios. Just as twenty years later Hancock exercised an inner need to expand his horizons by distancing himself from Sid James and leaving the BBC for ITV, so the risk of stagnation and repetition set in to plague Hay, who dug in his heels in spite of protests from many who had his interests at heart. As he insisted to his agent, 'I've no intention of being one of a three-legged act.' He brought in 'silly ass' Claude Hulbert as his sidekick in *The Ghost of St Michael's* at the new studio towards the end of 1940. There would be five more films in his lifetime. The standard remained high, but for many some elusive chemistry was missing. As one critic said, it was rather like *Hamlet* without the ghost.

It is doubtful whether the future impact of Hay's career resonated with the young Hancock as he devoured Hay's movies on first release in his local picture house. According to a devoted friend, many years later Hancock ushered in his last new year rewatching *Oh, Mr Porter!* on a juddering television screen which had to be thumped into stability. Hancock could always be bounced out of depression by certain lines from the film. The friend would play Harbottle to Hancock's Mr Porter:

Every night when the moon gives light,
The miller's ghost is seen.
As he walks the track
With a sack on his back...

'And his earhole painted green!' chimed in Tony. Harbottle's explanation for Albert's eccentricity – 'He plays with the pixies' – was guaranteed to bring Tony out in hysterics. Hancock is not the only one of a later generation of comedians who rated Hay highly. Ronnie Barker, with Hay's mastery of comic reaction in mind, described him as 'the best straight man there ever was', while Ken Dodd, no mean wordsmith himself, openly cherishes the importance Hay gave to words and the need to use the right one at the right time to convey the maximum meaning. Eric Morecambe drew parallels with the great Jack Benny – perhaps there can be no higher praise. Morecambe and Wise never made it in America – they had no need to – but had the film industry been organised differently Will Hay just might have done. Even when he was snivelling behind the most devious plan, he was a class act.

UP THE OLD NARKOVIANS

WORDS & MUSIC BY....
LESLIE SARONY
&
LESLIE HOLMES

FROM THE FILM
"BOYS WILL BE BOYS"

A Gainsborough Picture

DIRECTED BY
WILLIAM BEAUDINE
Starring
WILL HAY
with
GORDON HARKER

THE CINEPHONIC MUSIC Co.Ltd.
DEAN HOUSE,
2,3 & 4, DEAN STREET,
LONDON, W.I.

6D

Flanagan and Allen: The 'Oi!' Comedians

(Bud crosses the stage with a suitcase)
Allen: Where are you going?
Flanagan: Taking my case to court.
(Bud returns with a larger suitcase)
Allen: Where are you going now?
Flanagan: Taking my case to a higher court.
(Bud returns carrying a coat hanger and before Ches has a chance to speak...)
Flanagan: I lost my suit! Oi!
(He scarpers to the wings)

The traditional double act, featuring crosstalk between low comedian and straight man, is a direct derivation from the earliest comic drama with its ironist and impostor, knave and fool, Belch and Aguecheek combination. And yet, while there may be nothing new in the interrelationship between two such figures, thriving as it does on a constant diet of insult, ridicule and repartee, an ambiguous blend of antagonism and good fellowship, many great acts achieved a startlingly individual identity within the tested formula. One could be forgiven for supposing that Murray and Mooney, whose bill matter was 'Even Their Relations Think They're Funny', created the form. Whether they did or merely popularised it on an unprecedented scale is debatable, but certainly the now legendary 'I say, I say, I say,' 'I don't wish to know that' and 'Kindly leave the stage' were first used with lasting effect by them during the 1930s. Harry Mooney (1889 – 1972) the clown delivered the first, while the other Harry, the dignified Murray (1891 – 1968), always had the other two up his sleeve by way of retaliation.

Charlie Clapham (1884 – 1959) and Billy Dwyer (1890 – 1943) were another combination. Clapham and Dwyer were so popular with radio audiences from 1926 until Dwyer's death that they would make their entrance from what the *Era* mistook 'for a cross between the "Time, gentlemen, please" gates of a public house and the lift of a Park Lane hotel', in other words an outsize wireless cabinet. Their act was billed as 'In a Spot of Bother', the latter usually caused by mythical cow 'Cissie', who had a habit of creeping into the conversation on the weakest of pretexts. The combination of the gullible gormless grotesque and the shrewd pompous know-all reached its zany apotheosis in the late 1940s and early 50s with the 'Up the Pole' act of cousins Jimmy Jewel and Ben Warriss, of whom more later and of whom Mike and Bernie Winters and Cannon and Ball became later approximations. Something more subtle after years floundering for their best style was achieved by Eric Morecambe and Ernie Wise, an audience with whom also awaits towards the end of this volume.

Of all the double acts of the earlier variety period, none is remembered more lovingly than that of Flanagan and Allen. It differed curiously from the others, namely in the absence on stage of any deep antagonism between the two partners. Any disagreements they shared were fleeting, superficial, a pretext for single gags and nothing deeper. Whereas in other acts rivalry informs the whole atmosphere, the essential ethos of Bud and Ches was one of pure and simple comradeship. That they had first met in the First World War and were to reach the peak of their career together just before the Second would appear to have had some influence on this aspect of their style. That they saw themselves as buddies in a troubled world where both had experienced the difficulties of succeeding single-handed is clear from Ches's background. The traditional double act of the halls was a crystallisation of the double plot, high life and low life, expounded by literary critic William Empson in his pastoral theory. On the top level there is the well dressed socially secure straight man, on the lower the layabout, the labourer as funny man, guaranteed to put his superior in some ludicrous situation before the night is out. And yet while Ches and Bud fitted visibly into these two roles, there was never any question that they were now anything but socially equal. However debonair Ches may have appeared, however much his early social background differed from Bud's, you knew that he had since been tempered by the same straits and misfortunes as Bud himself.

> You see we're two very ordinary people,
> Jogging along and glad to be.
> For the simple folk we are
> We thank our lucky star,
> My pal and me.

Bud was born Chaim Reuben Weintrop of Polish–Jewish parents in Spitalfields on 14 November 1896. By the age of ten he was a call boy at the Cambridge Music Hall in Shoreditch. His performing career began when he appeared at the nearby London Music Hall as 'Fargo, the Boy Conjurer'. At fourteen he ran away from home, in effect walking to Southampton and working his passage on a liner to New York. There he jumped ship and stayed in America until 1914, years that saw him amid other adventures playing the modest role of pageboy in a Broadway production. He first met Chesney Allen, two years his senior and a legitimate actor until war commenced, in 1917, in an *estaminet* in the French village of Poperinghe. Born William Ernest Allen in Brighton on or around 5 April 1894, the son of a master builder, he did not renew his acquaintance with Bud until a chance meeting in Piccadilly Circus after the war, when he was appearing in the Criterion farce *You Never Know, You Know*. Many permutations would occur before Bud and Ches came together as an act. For Bud there would be a spell as Chick Harlem, blackface comedian, one with army pal Roy Henderson as Flanagan and Roy, another with Jack Buckland as Flanagan and Poy, lean periods spent as a taxi driver and as a boxer. Chesney would leave the straight theatre and form another double act, Stanford and Allen. While Bud was appearing with Buckland at Kilmarnock, he was summoned by Florrie Forde, the music hall queen of the chorus singers, to join her touring show, *Flo and Co.*, specifically to replace Stan Stanford in Allen's act. To Bud's surprise he found Chesney had since become Forde's manager – this in addition to his performing activities.

Bud had originally changed his name to Flanagan in revenge upon an Irish sergeant major whose anti-Semitism he had been forced to endure during the war; he kept the promise he made then that the CSM would be laughed at for evermore. By sheer serendipity Flanagan was also Florrie Forde's maiden name and the title of one of her most famous songs. Flanagan and Allen made their first appearance together, as 'singing comedians', in Forde's company at the Keighley Hippodrome in 1926. Things did not fall into place immediately, but by a form of osmosis Chesney's relaxed style enabled the initially forceful Bud to adopt a more casual approach on stage. Even so, when Forde ceased revue production at the turn of the decade, the act went through a low period during which, in 1931, Bud and Ches contemplated turning to bookmaking for a living, but a successful week at the Argyle in Birkenhead, a theatre where Harry Lauder, Ella Shields of 'Burlington Bertie' fame and George Formby Senior had all enjoyed early successes, led to a booking for Val Parnell at the Holborn Empire and in turn to their debut at the London Palladium for the week commencing 5 October in the company of the magician Frakson and, topping the bill, Peter Dawson, the Australian bass baritone who climaxed his act with a spectacular First World War scena, with the trenches in silhouette and troops marching up the line.

Bud and Ches during the early years

The act they now developed was a simple combination of songs and crosstalk, with Bud and Ches portraying two strolling troubadours, the latter elegantly dressed in traditional contrast to Bud's shabby bulging evening suit beneath mangy ankle-length raccoon coat. Bud would hustle on stage, the upturned brim of his battered boater accentuating his jug-handle ears and expansive leer. And yet the face was a sensitive one, capable of a smile that beamed to the very back of the gods. From a distance they might have resembled a melancholy dancing bear with its patient cultured keeper. The backdrop most probably depicted the Thames Embankment, not too far removed from the setting of their theme song, 'Underneath the arches'.

In their heyday their humour could claim the most distinctive verbal style on the halls, one rooted in Flanagan's constant pleasure in making ridiculous periphrastic mistakes. In the world of surrealist fantasy they created, Lord Beaverbrook became Lord Otterpond, Golders Green Silverer's Black, Ramsgate Sheep's Door. When at last with Ches's help Bud did correct himself, he would shout 'Oi!' to which straight man, orchestra and eventually audience would echo 'Oi!' in return. So frequent were Bud's verbal stumblings, his scripts came to resemble the notes of a psychologist in a word association test. Although in print such humour seems forced and mechanical, it is easy to understand its relevance at a time when the immigrant community in London's East End would have still struggled to make a foreign tongue its natural idiom. It was also stylistically distinctive, yet easy for the general public to imitate in casual conversation, enjoying the additional bonus of a shameless running gag to help it on its way. In the following only Bud's soft fruity intermittently Jewish accent and Ches's clarifying genteel tones have to be imagined. Ironically the rapid-fire delivery of the sequence is directly contradictory to any difficulty one may have expected Bud to have had through his own immigrant origins.

Ches: They tell me you left college.
Bud: I couldn't get on with the chemeesestry.
Ches: Chemeesestry?
Bud: Chemeesestry – cutipharmical work.
Ches: Cutipharmical work?
Bud: Cartiphumical work.
Ches: Cartiphumical work?
Bud: Yes. You've got to have a stiff ticket.
Ches: A stiff ticket?
Bud: A stiff ticket.
Ches: A certificate!
Bud: A certificate. Oi!
All: Oi!
Bud: You see you're making up crispictions.
Ches: Crispictions?
Bud: Yes – for people that are snowing.
Ches: Snowing?
Bud: Ailing! They go to a sisiskian.
Ches: They go to a physician.
Bud: Or a sturgeon.
Ches: A sturgeon? A surgeon.
Bud: And he gives them a crispiction.
Ches: He gives them a prescription.
Bud: Well, they take it to Slippers.
Ches: Take it to Slippers?

Bud: Shoes.
Ches: Shoes? They take it to Boots!
Bud: Boots! Oi!
All: Oi!

Their style may be best summed up by a riddle, 'When is a riddle not a riddle?' The lines above are not exactly riddles, but they have the same feel, the same concise tautness as those early exercises of one's imagination. Imagine an Egyptian scene, the conversation on slaves.

Bud: The fellow's in bandages?
Ches: You mean bondage!
Bud: No I don't. That's whisky!

While their humour possessed a surrealistic tone, their songs always stayed much closer to reality. Both in the numbers Bud wrote himself and those they performed by others, Florrie Forde's influence was easily discernible. While her strident vocal style was far removed from the gentle harmony of her protégés, all their songs were, like hers, poignantly evocative of the past, of friends and faces, scenes and sensations no longer accessible and at once painful and reassuring when recalled to mind. Their own style was in fact far more appropriate to this kind of material, Ches's precise plaintive enunciation echoing Bud's endearing huskiness, modelled upon the singing voice of his boyhood idol Alec Hurley, 'The Coster Comedian' (who was, incidentally, Marie Lloyd's second husband). Bud once described the effect Hurley made: 'His voice was like silk, he never shouted – but you could hear him at the back of the hall. Instead of going out to them, he made them come to him.' Certainly Bud's singing voice was far easier on the ear than the rasping tones of Albert Chevalier and Gus Elen, both contemporaries of Hurley and the two great names of the coster comedian tradition, within which Bud himself, with his cheeky independence and utter self-confidence, fitted so effortlessly.

Today many of their numbers may appear excessively sentimental, but if one first considers critic F. R. Leavis's apt definition of sentimentality as 'emotion in excess of the facts' and then considers the period that gave birth to the majority of their songs, an age that saw the Great Depression, the rise of nationalistic militarism on the Continent, a world war, the insecurity bred by nervous anticipation of that war, a pervading atmosphere of uncertainty and disillusionment, then the wistfulness and yearning to which they gave voice seem quite in place. That they should reflect the period in which they were written is a characteristic shared by all the great songs in the music hall canon. Bud's own songwriting instinct was shrewdly, if simply, in touch with this need to connect. Moreover, as Colin MacInnes explains, one must distinguish between two types of sentiment: the synthetic, 'moon in June' variety, and the kind occasioned by genuine emotions and events and as such inextricably rooted in people's actual experience. 'Can't we meet again and let's be sweethearts?', 'Do you recall the day you went away?', 'Nice people, with nice manners, but got no money at all', 'Home town' with its tumbledown shanty-style streets and old schoolhouse door tumbled through at four, all represent authentic popular feeling and were interpreted by Bud and Ches with an honesty and respect totally devoid of patronage.

Seldom absent from their songs was a concern for the underdog of society and for the gutter-spun philosophy that sentimentalised poverty as riches. One knew instinctively as they sang that the attitude to life embodied in their lyrics had itself been conditioned by their own experiences in leaner times, that there had been occasions when the rain had entered their shoes, when their dreams and schemes had fallen on stony ground. But one also knew that the spirit which could induce two lonely destitute vagabonds to sing

> Free – no one could be luckier than we,
> Nature never had a lock or key,
> Isn't that the way it ought to be?

was also largely responsible for their eventual success.

> We're always on the outside, on the outside always looking in.
> We never know how fortunes are made,
> For the sun when it shines finds us both in the shade.
> We're always on the ebb-tide,
> But we'll keep on trying till we win,
> For we know someday we're gonna be on the inside,
> Instead of the outside, always looking in.

Moreover, it informed their comic philosophy. Bud had no doubts about his position as a funny man: 'The clown is a clown because he deliberately puts himself in a position where he's looked down upon.'

The most successful, the most famous song Bud and Ches ever sang was 'Underneath the arches'. More than any other, it caught the mood of the Depression, with its lilting melody and poignant account of nights spent exposed to all weathers on cobblestone beds and of subsequent joy at approaching daybreak.

> Pavement is my pillow, no matter where I stray;
> Underneath the arches, I dream my dreams away.

It was Bud's own composition, and he once explained to broadcaster Benny Green how the melody came to him during a depressed moment in his dressing room at the Derby Hippodrome in 1926. In Green's words, 'He had merely started to whistle and soon found himself with a complete tune. Being untrained as a musician, Flanagan was obliged to sing it over and over to himself to make sure the tune did not evaporate.' The following week it received its first public performance at the Pier Pavilion, Southport. Later in their career they would re-create that performance on stage, evoking memories of that year by reading the nostalgic headlines from a newspaper of the time: GERTRUDE EDERLE – 18-YEAR-OLD AMERICAN – FIRST WOMAN TO SWIM THE CHANNEL, CHARLIE CHAPLIN NOT TO RETIRE, CHURCHILL'S UNPOPULAR BUDGET – 5 PER CENT TAX ON ALL LEGAL BETS, BBC ASKS FOR NINE SHILLINGS INSTEAD OF SEVEN AND SIX FOR A WIRELESS LICENCE. For those who remembered, this frequent presentation ensured that the song lost none of its original impact in later more prosperous times.

The war inevitably influenced much of their material, providing them with some of their most memorable songs. 'Run, rabbit, run' is said to have been inspired by an early Luftwaffe raid on the Shetlands during the Phoney War, a raid that numbered a single rabbit as its sole casualty. The carcass was stuffed and sent to Bud, who during the run of the show *The Little Dog Laughed* would nightly carry the poor specimen onto the Palladium stage and sing a variation of Noel Gay's original lyric.

> You didn't run, rabbit, run, rabbit, run, run, run,
> When the German planes dropped their bombs, bombs, bombs.
> Bang, bang, bang went the anti-aircraft guns,
> But, unlike the Nastis, you didn't run, run, run.

The same show featured 'We're gonna hang out the washing on the Siegfried Line' in a scene with an actual clothes line of underwear, the seat of each garment bearing a name: Hitler, Himmler, Goebbels, Ribbentrop and, the largest pair of all, Goering. There was also 'The umbrella man' from *These Foolish Things*, a patently innocent number with Ches portraying a street umbrella repairer and odd-job man who will mend anything from an apple cart to a broken heart. The latter song, with its *toodle-looma-looma* chant and tune suggestive of pattering rain on a blustery day, survives well. At that tense time its comforting carefree lilt was coloured by the identification of Prime Minister Neville Chamberlain as the man with the umbrella both before and after the Munich crisis. All three numbers reveal a vivid sense of living for the present, determination to grin and bear, to regard as a joke the unpleasant effects the war was having. Even if their impact on both forces and civilians was not as great as that of Vera Lynn's 'We'll meet again', or the favourite song of the war, 'Lili Marlene', ironically appropriated from the enemy, it seems wrong to regard them, as MacInnes does, as 'imbecilities'. Seen as carefree antidotes to misery, they do at least profess a certain innocence, and are far removed from the defiant flag-waving and mock-glamorous notion of duty and bravery that one meets in the music hall songs of the Crimean, Boer and First World Wars.

The cosy singing style of Bud and Ches represents a welcome change from the aggressive confidence of earlier patriotic singers, from The Great MacDermott to Harry Lauder, with their easy appeal to jingoistic emotion totally divorced from any humane consideration of the actual facts of war, any realisation that their very patriotism was itself fanning rather than extinguishing the flames of hostility. Not that Flanagan and Allen did not cross this line. The sheet music of 'If a grey-haired lady says "How's your father?"' or 'Mademoiselle from Armentières' bore the dubious caption 'A message from an oldun of 1914 to a youngun of 1939 – the most human song of the war', while their recording of 'The Smiths and the Jones', in which along with 'the Kellies and Cohens' and all those united in the war effort, they are seen as 'democracy's sons' with 'right on their side', doing a 'job that must be done', is so full of clichés, let alone blatantly exaggerated optimism, that it is wholly contrary to the gentle whimsicality of the novelty numbers just discussed and the wistfulness of their other songs at this time, songs not referring directly to specific aspects of the war, but nevertheless greatly influenced by what was happening. In the austerity of those years many must have believed that good times were a thing of the past. The very titles of 'Don't ever walk in the shadows', 'Yesterday's dreams' and 'Don't believe everything you dream' admit an honest pessimism that is confirmed by their lyrics. Moreover, what optimism is suggested by the reprise number 'Round the back of the arches', a wartime return to old haunts, and by the title song of their film *We'll Smile Again*, is nothing if not tear-stained.

Today Flanagan and Allen are more likely to be recalled for their unique style of close-harmony singing than their crosstalk comedy. One reason may be that Bud's comic bravura would be displayed to even better effect in later years as a member of the Crazy Gang. The initial step towards this dual career was taken on his behalf by producer Val Parnell on 30 November 1931, when under the auspices of George Black he presented the first *Crazy Week* at the London Palladium. Not that this bill featured Flanagan and Allen. The nucleus of the cast on that occasion consisted of Nervo and Knox, Naughton and Gold, Caryll and Mundy, and Eddie Gray. The format of the show was based on a new style of revue that Nervo and Knox, beginning with *Young Bloods of Variety* in 1925, had been presenting for several years around the provinces, allowing them to get hilariously involved in the other acts on the bill, a seemingly spontaneous style no doubt influenced by Fred Karno's Krazy Komics, the original of all the comedy groups, both here and in America, whose speciality was well ordered chaos. As we have already seen, Karno's company, famed for its *Jail Birds* and *Mumming Birds* presentations, had proved in the early years of the century a prolific nursery of subsequently great comedians. In addition to Chaplin and Laurel there were Fred Kitchen (1872 – 1950), famed for his mock-serious and hilariously complicated lecture 'How to Cook a Sausage', and Harry Weldon (1881 – 1930), noted for his portrayal of the incompetent 'Stiffy the Goalkeeper', the whistle in his voice and the catchphrase ''S no use.' Joe Boganny's Lunatic Bakers, the Six Brothers Luck, Charlie Baldwin's Bank Clerks and Will Casey's Court were the intriguing names of other prominent groups of knockabout comedians contemporary with Karno, a school to which music hall star Harry Tate, forever surrounded by stooges, also belonged.

There would be a second *Crazy Week* before Black would decide to hold a *Crazy Month* in June 1932 and bring in Bud and Ches, by now regulars at the theatre, to swell the already large cast of clowns. Bud explained in his autobiography, *My Crazy Life*, how the other comics were not anxious to welcome two newcomers to their fold. The show's immediate success, however, dispelled any doubts Bud, Ches or anyone else may have had. To conjure up the ambience of that production one need only mention that

CLAPHAM & DWYER

Clockwise from top left: Clapham and Dwyer, Murray and Mooney, Nervo and Knox, Caryll and Mundy, Naughton and Gold

at different times during the show Bud could be seen chasing a screaming chorus girl all over the auditorium with an axe, while during the interval he was to be found serving hot dogs to the audience from the stage. Another *Crazy Month* soon followed, then a third, *March Hares*, the first Crazy show with a distinct title. The Crazy Gang were in full flight and would dominate the Palladium scene until the war years with a succession of lavish revues, each running about eight months, beginning with *Round About Regent Street* in 1935, *O-Kay for Sound* (1936), *London Rhapsody* (1937), *These Foolish Things* (1938) and the already mentioned *The Little Dog Laughed* (1939). Bud and Ches, minus the rest of the gang, were also featured at the same theatre in the shows *Life Begins at Oxford Circus* (1935), in company with Jack Hylton and his Band, Florence Desmonde and Stanley Holloway; *All Alight at Oxford Circus* (1936) with Harry Roy and his Band; and in *Swing is in the Air* (1937) with Vic Oliver and Hylton again. Whether officially Crazy productions or not, the presence of Flanagan and Allen guaranteed that they shared the same ramshackle improvisation and rollicking audience involvement that now more than ever underlined the art of music hall as deriving from the *commedia dell'arte* of four hundred years previously and the Atellane farces of Roman times. If that seems obscure, for '*commedia dell'arte*' read 'comedy by pros', for 'Atellane farces', 'gags from the East End'.

'O-Kay for Sound' from left to right: Naughton, Flanagan, Knox, Allen, Gold, Nervo

Of the other members of the original pool of Crazy Gang talent Jimmy Nervo (1897 – 1975) and Teddy Knox (1896 – 1974) were the most influential. They joined forces in 1919, and soon became famous for their slow-motion wrestling and a burlesque of a Greek dance called 'The Fall of the Nymph' with Jimmy as Diana and Teddy as her pursuer. There was also a supreme parody of two Russian ballet dancers. In the latter the disciplined poise of one was at cross purposes with the elephantine clumsiness of the other until – in a later version – a sensual balloon with a will of its own came between them with even funnier effect. As well as being stop-at-nothing comics, they were also extremely capable acrobats. In the *Era* of January 1927 Nervo provided an insight into why their ballet routine would come to be regarded as a classic and be performed in a simplified form by later notables such as Billy Dainty, Danny La Rue and Ronnie Corbett.

There must be a sequence of meaning; and you must interpolate a story all the time. That is where a lot of people who do our kind of stuff make a mistake. They have no rhyme or reasons for falling. There is a great amount of technique in burlesque. It is this technique that makes the show. Like the ordinary ballet dancers we have always reasons for doing our different poses and situations. It would be no use my jumping into Knox's arms if there were no reason for doing so.

Glaswegians Charlie Naughton (1887 – 1976) and Jimmy Gold (1886 – 1967) started their career together even earlier in 1908. They first met on a Glasgow building site and decided to use their work experience as the basis of a slapstick act, sometimes billed as the 'Napoleons of Fun'. Within a short time they had become the acknowledged experts in the art of splashing whitewash over a pantomime stage or plastering themselves with paste as they proceeded to wallpaper a kitchen. In their world water existed quite simply for splashing around, eggs for smashing, soggy dough for catapulting into the gallery. Trying to make a plank fit across two trestles in their decorating sketch – 'Turn it round the other way' – also became a classic. Membership of the Crazy Gang gave them round-the-year slapstick scope. Billy Caryll (died 1939) and Hilda Mundy (died 1969), who left to pursue a career in radio and in the process provide more room for Bud and Ches, were best known for their interpretation of the traditional drunk act within a domestic scenario, their bill matter 'The Good Companions – but not for long' hinting at the discord to come. Finally 'Monsewer' Eddie Gray (1898 – 1969), regarded by many as the supreme droll, deserves more space than can be given here and will be treated in the following chapter.

If you combine so many distinctive comic elements, it is impossible not to produce an erratic chemical reaction. The atmosphere of the Crazy Gang shows was one of hoax and mayhem on both sides of the footlights, the whole theatre a vacuum for lunatic exuberance. The comedians would invade the auditorium, scattering rice in their wake, taking turns as usherettes, sending ticket holders to the wrong seats. Even the printed programme carried a notice that said 'the Palladium clocks aren't right'. Halfway through a wirewalker's act the Gang would come on in turns and have furious arguments with the orchestra as the performer remained poised precariously in mid-air. A juggler could never guarantee that his clubs would not be lubricated overnight, or a leaden ball be substituted for one with the requisite bounce. There was the notorious occasion the Gang had the theatre fireman inform a famous theatrical animal supplier that the dogs she was providing for one of the production numbers had to be fireproofed before they would be allowed on stage. She took him at his word and within minutes was chasing all over London trying to find a canine fireproofer. At a later period impresario Jack Hylton used to come straight from his office to the Victoria Palace, keeping a dress suit in Bud's dressing room ready for a quick change. Over the course of a few weeks the trousers were dispatched daily to an obliging tailor to be shortened just ever so slightly each time. Hylton's ultimate reaction when he finally twigged is not recorded. Then there was the time a Madame Tussaud's Chamber of Horrors sequence was included in a Crazy show and a rigid Jimmy Gold was substituted beneath the dust sheet supposed to cover Dr Crippen. When a stagehand went to lift the 'dummy' onto the stage, Gold wriggled and the stagehand fainted. The publicity attracted by such behaviour meant that no one could take any member of the Gang seriously. There were times when what might have started as harmless fun collided with something approaching sadism. One night, as understudy Peter Glaze carried a showgirl in his arms up a narrow flight of steps onto the stage from the auditorium, Bud whipped the glasses off Peter's nose with the line 'I told you you could see without them.' Glaze was virtually blind without and only just managed to avert a calamity.

The Little Dog Laughed would be the last full-scale Crazy Gang show to be featured at the Palladium. Several years of indecision were ahead for Bud and Ches. Flanagan and Allen went into *Black Vanities* at the Victoria Palace with Frances Day and Naunton Wayne, and then into *Hi-De-Hi* for Jack Hylton at the Palace, renewing their acquaintance with Florence Desmond and Gang stalwart Eddie Gray. At the end of the war, however, the performing partnership came to a close, ill health – described by Bud as 'rheumatism and nerves' – forcing Ches to retire from active performing, although he would subsequently become the Gang's agent and manager.

That the Gang should come together again after the war, albeit without Ches, does not appear to have been as obvious then as it might in retrospect. Emile Littler presented Bud in the revue *The Night and the Laughter* at the Coliseum in September 1946, but as one critic said, it was 'like asking Bud to bat at both ends in a Test Match'. Littler's own terse comment summed up the situation: 'Not enough laughter!' Val Parnell, the Palladium boss, was not convinced that the public would accept the Crazy Gang recipe as before, and it was Jack Hylton, now turned impresario, who in a momentous leap of faith instigated the revival with the aptly titled *Together Again* at the Victoria Palace on 17 April 1947. The Crazy Gang, now comprising Nervo and Knox, Naughton and Gold, and Flanagan (Eddie Gray would not rejoin the fold until 1956), would assume almost continual residence at this theatre until they finally disbanded in 1962, six years before Bud's death. *Together Again* would run for no fewer than 1,566 performances. *Knights of Madness* (1950), *Ring out the Bells* (1952), *Jokers Wild* (1954), *These Foolish Kings* (1956), *Clown Jewels* (1959), *Young in Heart* (1960), the titles of their successive shows, all had the ring of perpetual youth and their self-identification with court jesters, two prime reasons for their continued success and their becoming a national institution. Even without Ches, Bud would continue to record memorable songs, most notably 'Hey, neighbour' from *Knights of Madness*, 'Maybe it's because I'm a Londoner', written by Hubert Gregg for *Together Again*, and 'Strollin'', written by Ralph Reader of *Gang Show* fame and used in *Clown Jewels*.

Cleaning up in 'These Foolish Things'

On the basis of their electric verve and anarchic irreverence for order and authority, there has always been a tendency to consider the Crazy Gang a native approximation of the Marx Brothers. But whereas the Marxes maintained an overriding subtlety, the keystone of the Gang's humour was vulgarity in the broadest, rowdiest sense of the word. Although the Gang made several movies, celluloid failed to capture their true spirit, which is better evoked by comparison with the hurly-burly style of Olsen and Johnson's *Hellzapoppin* revue and at a later date by the Carry On ensemble put together by film producer Peter Rogers, arguably the true spiritual heirs to George Black's ragamuffin crew. The knockabout assault of the Gang was aimed at both public and private life. No one within the Establishment was safe from attack, bearing out Mack Sennett's definition of the essence of comedy: 'contrast and catastrophe involving the unseating of dignity'. When questioned about the offensive qualities of his humour, Bud would reply, 'You mean my dressing up as a clergyman and running a gaming party in the vestry? That's not being offensive. That's cheek!' The explicit sexual nature of much of their material also invaded the private world of the individual. 'Sexual' may be too tenuous a word; 'scatological' or 'anatomical' more apt. Whichever is used, the comic potential of breasts, bottoms and urinals, chamber pots, bedpans and hernias appears to have been inexhaustible. The whole panoply of the seaside postcard was theirs for the taking.

Knox: My wife and I have been married for ten years and we've got nine children, but I haven't seen her since the day we were married.
Flanagan: You have nine children and you've never lived with your wife?
Knox: Mark you, I write to her every day.
(*There follows an interruption from a stage box*)
Gray: I'll be back in a minute.
Gold: Hey, where are you going?
Gray: I'm going to borrow his pencil!

At a time when stage material was constantly vetted by the Lord Chamberlain's office, their routines obviously attracted close scrutiny, but were inherently innocent. Their approach to sexual themes was infantile, at most adolescent, the erotic often blurred with the excretory. This gathered comic momentum after 1947 as the five jesters advanced in age, unashamed of vaunting their sexual energy, and revealed a banality far removed from the uninhibited eroticism of the *Oh! Calcutta!* era that hovered on the horizon. Scarcely a Crazy Gang show went by without them losing their trousers or donning skirts and brassieres. The transvestite moments of their shows are among the most memorable. *These Foolish Kings* saw them dressed as bedraggled charwomen, incited by a game of one-upmanship to outdo the more affluent blasé sunbathers on the roof of the block of luxury flats next door. There followed a dragbag of a fashion show as they paraded the oddest assortment of voluminous bloomers, rainbow vests and Union-Jack-adorned chemises. At one point Bud took a steel rod from his bosom and clanked it down on stage: 'Curse these corsets!' The climax of his own *déshabillé* saw him padlocked to his chemise. One critic captured the event admirably: 'For one wild moment I wondered what brave man could ever espouse such a wild, black-haired, leering wanton, and how he ever imagined a mere padlock would chain her to respectability!' In *London Rhapsody*, and again in *Clown Jewels* they were featured 'In the shadow of Eros', this time as formidable flower sellers or, to quote the song they sang, 'Six little broken blossoms, six faded flowers'. In their final show there was an outrageous burlesque of the 'Ascot Gavotte' scene from *My Fair Lady*. Dowagers had never been more overpowering. On another occasion their well upholstered incarnations as 'Principal boys from panto' played visual havoc with sexual identity.

Trousered highlights from Crazy Gang shows included 'Prehistoric Regent Street' from *Round About* with Bud and Ches as two ancient bookmakers dealing in stone money. It was said that for several years afterwards George Black attributed his favourite gag to this sketch, when Bud said to Ches, 'Be careful not to take any bad money. There's a lot of cement knocking about.' The christening scene from *These Foolish Kings* featured Charlie Naughton as baby with Bud as the most unlikely of parsons. The cherubic lisping Naughton was a natural for the part: journalist René Cutforth described him as having the look of 'a hamster who's swallowed a tennis ball'. The gags were vintage: 'Let's give 'im a nice biblical name. Like Isaiah. One eye's 'igher than the other;' the action violent: a cake exploding, crockery smashing, a baby being flung from the window with Punch and Judy nonchalance. The Pyramus and Thisbe sequence from *A Midsummer Night's Dream* was featured in the same show. For the record, and to enhance any subsequent reading of that passage, Bud took the lead, a wistful Naughton played Thisbe, Knox was Quince, Nervo Lion, a bored Gold was Moon, and the impregnable Gray a sturdy Wall. 'The Fathers' Sketch' had the 'down and out' fathers of the Gang interrupting from the stalls and invading the stage. Bud would then ask Jack Hylton where *his* father was. It transpired he had left home many years ago and had since disappeared. As he explained, a dazzling blonde would stride down the aisle, step on stage, fling her arms around the dazed Hylton and exclaim she was his new stepmother. This was the cue for Bud to look at his own 'father' in disgust, smack him in the face and roar, 'Why don't you go out and get married?' Curtain! This sketch originated in *Life Begins*, one of the non-Crazy shows, though in later years it would be played by various members of the Gang proper. Its rowdy, almost callous knockabout was typical. Then there was Bud's original presentation of 'Strollin'': as he sang the chorus, the others would walk on, each with a dog on a lead. Sometimes the dogs would behave, sometimes not.

The Crazy Gang were the heroes of everyone who had been plagued by the pomposity and pretension of others. Their technique had an hypnotic effect: on fellow performers who, realising they could not fight the lunatic atmosphere that pervaded the theatre when the Gang was on hand, would relax into the party spirit, imparting to their own performances a piquant edge that made all the difference to box-office returns; on audiences who, in a theatre where performers spilled over into the auditorium, were literally engulfed in the happy-go-lucky atmosphere. Also admirable was the skill with which the members of the Gang, whether double acts or solo, managed to keep their separate identities while merging at the same time into the larger whole. But if over the years Bud came to be seen as the cornerstone of the act, its accepted leader, he always seemed to maintain a certain aloofness without in any way detracting from the essential teamwork. There was something about his at once guilty yet innocent grin and those glistening yet melancholy eyes that suggested an awareness of life that the others could not project. Only he could switch instantaneously from the brusque knockabout to the convincing delivery of sentimental songs. Always in later years the big scene at the Victoria Palace would be shared by Bud, a motheaten fur and a crushed straw hat, even though Ches was no longer by his side. He became the court jester of his day and featured, usually with the Gang, in no less than fifteen royal performances between 1932 and 1965, Ches often coming out of retirement for these special shows in which the laugh was always on the Royal Box. In 1958 he was awarded the OBE. The morning he went to Buckingham Palace for the investiture, he took one look at the courtiers assembled and then doubled back to Prince Philip: 'That's a smashing house you've got for a matinee!' If that doesn't work for you, try this one. During the presentation of performers to the royal family after one Royal Variety Performance, Philip asked Flanagan what he was doing next. Bud replied, 'Well. I've got a crate of brown ale in the dressing room. I thought we might all go back to your place!'

AFTERTHOUGHTS

The final performance by the Crazy Gang was given at the Victoria Palace on 19 May 1962. It was an emotional occasion with a eulogy penned by Sir John Betjeman and recorded messages from Jack Benny, Bob Hope, Danny Kaye and Sophie Tucker. A sprightly Chesney Allen bounced on stage to perform with his old partner and Jack Hylton wielded the baton in the orchestra pit. In a radio report of the event René Cutforth declaimed, 'We were all agreed in my part of the house, some of us with tears, that something English, human and admirable had departed from this mortal scene.' Bud continued to stay in the spotlight, here and there in pantomime, on television and on the one-night circuit. He popped up on *Sunday Night at the London Palladium,* where both he and Bruce Forsyth were seen to be sporting the initials B. F. on their blazers. This was considered risqué for its day. Just about the last thing he did was to record the song 'Who do you think you are kidding, Mr Hitler?' for use as the signature theme for the sitcom *Dad's Army.* A clever pastiche by Jimmy Perry and Derek Taverner of a typical Flanagan and Allen number, it is what he'll be remembered for by a younger generation today.

It is ironic that of the members of the Crazy Gang Chesney Allen, the first to retire from performing, should outlive them all. Bud died from a heart attack on 20 October 1968. He had been predeceased in 1967 by Jimmy Gold, whose real name was McGonigal and who through illness had missed most of the last two productions at the Victoria Palace, although with assistance from his colleagues he managed to appear on the moving final night. Bud in turn was outlived in order of survival by Eddie Gray; Teddy Knox, at one stage known as the boy juggler Chinko; Jimmy Nervo, originally a member of the acrobatic team The Four Holloways; and Charlie Naughton. It should be remembered that for all the popularity of Flanagan and Allen, the key catalysts for the formation of the Gang had been Nervo and Knox. While Bud was seen by the public as master of the revels, Jimmy and Teddy, with an assist from Eddie Gray, had been the first to forge the style, while behind the scenes Jimmy Nervo remained the true architect of anarchy from the first Palladium week to the last gala evening. Nervo and Knox always secured top billing and were allegedly the highest paid.

This book owes much to Bud Flanagan and Chesney Allen. When I submitted the original manuscript to publishers Frederick Muller, I did so in the knowledge that they had produced a string of show business autobiographies, but had not connected them with the publication of Bud's autobiography, *My Crazy Life*. The managing editor had got to know and respect Bud's representative in the process and his first reaction back in the early 1970s was to send my manuscript to him for assessment. That, of course, was Chesney, and his endorsement became more concrete with the contribution of the Foreword, which retains its position in this volume. Later it was my good fortune to work in television with this special gentleman. He was involved in a short Indian summer of a comeback when Patrick Garland and the Chichester Festival Theatre mounted their spectacular stage tribute to the Crazy Gang in 1981. In *Underneath the Arches* Christopher Timothy portrayed Ches to Roy Hudd's Flanagan, but that did not prevent Ches making a surprise appearance on stage with Roy every night, recreating the scene of years gone by, when they would sway in song together at the microphone, Allen always behind, one hand on Flanagan's shoulder, a reassuring presence for Bud and for all of us during the darkest of times as his clear recitative complemented the husky tones of his partner.

My memory of him backstage at Chichester on the opening night holds great poignancy. He had not formally appeared before a paying public for many years, yet the contents of the battered make-up box that had travelled with him from his first beginnings as an actor were set out meticulously on his dressing table as if nothing had changed, while his enthusiasm remained that of a twenty-year-old. This most self-effacing of men epitomised professionalism from another era, and one felt at once privileged and sad to be in his presence. In 1982 the show went on to triumph in the West End at the Prince of Wales Theatre, and I treasure the photo of the theatre marquee that Roy Hudd signed to me in thanks for the help I had given the production. It is annotated, 'Thanks for putting a shilling in the meter.' Chesney joined the West End company on stage for the opening night, but his health was fading and he died during the year-long run on 13 November 1982. Allen's contribution to the Gang on stage before the war has been overlooked through his absence after the conflict, but there can be no question that the team was the better for the class and dash of decency he added to the rorty mix, not to mention the sheer diplomacy he must have exercised on behalf of his renegade partner on more than a few occasions.

An unexpected corollary of the Flanagan and Allen story came about in 1969 when the artists Gilbert Proesch and George Passmore, now universally known as Gilbert and George, paid homage to the double act with their living sculpture in which immaculately suited and wearing gold make-up they mimed their way – sometimes for eight hours at a stretch – through a continuous recording of Bud and Ches singing 'Underneath the arches'. Their slow rotatory movements echoed perfectly the lazy swaying of the original and imparted an air of the music hall to their work that has never been completely absent since. Their most recent pictures based on London newspaper billboards provide a vivid commentary on the social life of the capital today as the song lyrics of the halls did all those years ago. One is reminded of the less familiar Flanagan and Allen song, 'We're always on the outside, on the outside always looking in,' a position routinely shared by great artists and comedians alike.

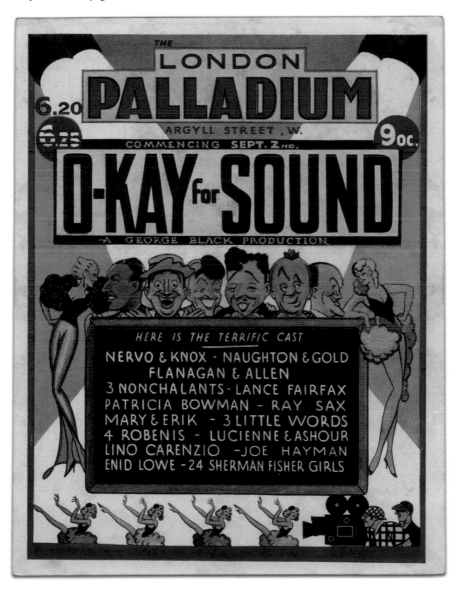

'MONSEWER' EDDIE GRAY: JUST A WOLF IN SHEEP'S CLOTHING

Allen: Who let *him* on? *(observing the renegade, Monsewer Eddie Gray)*
Flanagan: Who let him *live*?

Although Eddie Gray was for long periods an integral part of the Crazy Gang, it would be wrong to regard this chapter as a mere afterthought to the preceding one. Humorist Paul Jennings wrote in *The Times* that he regarded the Monsewer, the cause of countless pilgrimages to Chiswick or New Cross Empire, as 'the funniest man in the world'. Sir John Betjeman, when invited by a London newspaper to lunch with the person he would most like to meet, chose Eddie Gray. He was a black swan of comedy, a comedian's comedian who commanded the respect of all other successful comedians. The proof is in his immense influence, in the way the catchphrases of the master later became the clichés of lesser clowns. He was personally responsible for what became far more than the two theme gags of the early Crazy shows: 'They're working well tonight' and 'I saw it last week at the Holborn.' His comic persona suggested a run-down seediness that surely conveyed to his fellow performers a distinct truth about the less glamorous side of their profession.

Offstage Gray might have passed for a bank clerk from that area where the metropolis overspills into the Surrey fringe. Onstage he was the archetype of the red-nosed comedian, wearing his telltale props – battered topper, steel-rim spectacles and false moustache reminiscent of some grotesque eel – with the bravura of a scarecrow ready for all comers. Beneath was a deadpan expression that refused not to be taken seriously, but the threadbare evening dress with its incongruous scarlet waistcoat belied his whole flamboyant approach to dignity. The most blatant giveaway was his speech, an appalling display of 'fractured' French interspersed with a brusque cockney idiom, with which he insisted, like so many inferior exponents of magic and juggling, on giving a running commentary on his obviously visual act.

> *Monsewer*: Now, ce soir – that's foreign for this afternoon – moi's gonna travailler la packet of cards – *une* packet of cards, not deux, *une*. Now I have 'ere an ordinaire packet of playing cards – cinquante-deux in numero – fifty-two in number – ein, swine, twine, and every card parla la même chose. I cutee in deux with vingt-six ici and vingt-six there-ci…
> *Heckler*: I object.
> *Monsewer*: You object? What to, sir?
> *Heckler*: Making fun of my language.
> *Monsewer*: But who are you, sir?
> *Heckler*: I am the Bulgarian consul.
> *Monsewer*: But I'm talking French.
> *Heckler*: Oh, sorry!
> *Monsewer*: Voulez-vous obliger moi and turn it up?

However much his French was peculiar to the Stratford-at-Bow of Chaucer's Madame Eglantine, this linguistic trick, reminiscent of the play Anglo-French entertainer Harry Fragson had made of his own bilingualism at the turn of the century, did originate in Paris, from Gray's arduous attempts to make himself understood to continental stagehands: 'Moi's gonna get la hoop an' throw it to one side and vous goin' to catch it.' Later, back in England, he recalled his experiences as an anecdote offstage and the resultant laughter gradually edged the joke into his act. The tag Monsewer was Val Parnell's inspiration, a legacy from early Crazy Gang shows.

"WELL, IT'S THE CURSE OF THE GRAYS!"

Born Edward Earl Gray on 10 June 1898, the son of a Pimlico fruiterer and not, as he would insist, descended from 'a long line of bachelors', he was at the age of nine apprenticed by his father to a troupe of boy jugglers. His habit of playing about with the fruit on the family stall had first suggested a juggling future. Five years later, in 1912, he met Jimmy Nervo, then a wire-walking member of the Four Holloways, at the Tower Circus, Blackpool, and the first seeds of the Crazy Gang were sown. By 1919 he was working with Nervo and Knox in prototypes of the Crazy productions that were to revolutionise variety in the 1930s. Not unnaturally he was featured, as we have seen, in the first Palladium *Crazy Week*. From the beginning his impish personality was indelibly marked upon all that the Crazy Gang was subsequently to achieve. No one in the profession would gain greater notoriety, and at the same time respect, for perpetrating jokes on- or offstage. On one occasion when appearing in a show with Tommy Trinder they had rehearsed a new gag at Gray's insistence. It should have gone something like:

Trinder: What did you have for breakfast?
Monsewer: Haddock.
Trinder: Finnan?
Monsewer: No. Thick 'un!

When it came to the performance, no sooner had Trinder delivered the first line than the poker-faced Gray replied, 'Cornflakes', and carried on juggling. For once Trinder was at a loss for words. On another occasion, about to leave a prison after entertaining the inmates, he drew the attention of the duty guard to the concert party's paper tearer and whispered, 'Who's this bloke? He wasn't with us when we came in.' The unsuspecting victim was immediately led away. Gray is said to have originated the gag in which posing as a borough surveyor he would ask a passer-by to hold the end of a tape measure very still against a wall while he went round the corner to measure the distance between one part of the building and another. Once round the corner he would approach another unsuspecting stranger with the same request and then, under the pretext of having to fetch his 'sextant for the hydrographics', take refuge in a nearby cafe to see how long the two victims would stick to their posts. Eddie claimed that the duration of the world tape-measure-holding record exceeded three hours. Tricks like these as much as his own stage act helped Gray to earn his reputation among his fellow pros. He was the ace joker because he had no intention of giving anything away. He was the complete deadpan, exuding a fervent seriousness that never belied his most cunning schemes.

Not that he was never on the receiving end of such behaviour himself. The story goes that his own comedy juggling routine only gathered momentum when Nervo and Knox plastered his clubs with grease. In later years the act would settle down into a happy medium between erratic slapstick and brilliant skill, but it was nothing for Nervo or Knox to start tickling his neck through the backcloth as he approached the climax of a difficult trick or release a cascade of cabbages from the flies as he balanced the proverbial billiard cue on the tip of his chin. As a juggler, though, he was a superb technician, allegedly the first to feature the stunt with three apples in which one gradually disappears as it is munched in flight. In the 20s he used to conclude his act in semi-darkness, dancing as he swung the clubs about with reckless abandon. It was when he decided to reverse the order of these two routines and found himself forced to gulp down an apple breathless from dancing, that he gained his first ever laugh on stage and the urge to pursue comedy further, long before the fractured French and Crazy identification of later years.

However great his skill with the hoops and the clubs, once he *had* decided to play for laughs, there was no question of his act being taken seriously. 'I'm an absolutely sensational juggler. I'm a better juggler than I am a burglar and I might tell you I can see just as well in the dark as I can without a light.' His performances subsequently teemed with gags and gambits that have passed into comedy lore. Having put 'la glasses in la skyrocket', he'd be unable to find his clubs on the floor and eventually start juggling with only two clubs and a coin. There was the now classic trick in which he caught a bouncing ball in his ample sweater only for it to emerge at the neck and continue on its upward rebound. As he juggled six balls, they would get higher and higher until out of sight of the audience and then in an instant come crashing down, no longer six but hundreds. On other occasions he would nonchalantly bring disaster upon himself. No sooner had he got his clubs twirling in their usual rotation than he would walk away for no apparent reason, leaving the gaudy objects to plummet to the boards: 'Beautiful clubs! You can't buy them. There were only about eight million made, you know!' He would break off from juggling china plates to aim a couple into the wings, 'perhaps hoping,' as Kenneth Tynan observed, 'to maim some stagehand'. Certainly stagehands did nothing to stop the constant interruptions to the act, whether vagrant members of the cast falling in his path as they strolled across the stage or stray cyclists weaving their way through the intricate tracks of his dancing hoops. However persecuted he may have been, he never lost his temper. He knew, and we knew, that his own box of tricks and wiles was far superior to any hanky-panky others might attempt to carry out on him. This inward self-satisfaction was his revenge. As Agate described him, his air was that of 'an income-tax inspector taking a busman's holiday'.

Like all great practitioners of his art he always had one eye fixed on achieving the hitherto impossible, on pushing his talent that one daring step beyond his established limit. 'Now before I attempt my trick, I must ask the attendant to clear the back row of the hupper-circle, as that's where I usually finish on my flaming bicycle. Voulez-vous kindly tell the audience to scarper? Otherwise, to take a ball of chalk.' Again, shuffling across the stage on his knees, juggling and balancing some object on his head at the same time, he would confide lugubriously to the audience, 'This is the trick I usually broadcast.' Such remarks brought one face to face with the inner spirit of the man, the full complexity of his character. One never quite knew who was supposed to be kidding whom, the uncertainty informing the comic tension of his performance. When he asked a stooge 'to donner au moi a favour. Bring me a café-au-lait without malc,' was he making a genuine, if ignorant, request or just testing the individual's own intelligence? He would stand there helpless on stage as other members of the Gang proceeded to strip the clothes from his back. When told it was all in fun, he exclaimed, 'Oh! As long as you don't really mean it.' Jennings recalls the typical greeting to an old friend visiting his dressing room between houses: 'Wonderful to see you, but look, I've only got twelve minutes, got to change from finale costume to opening, get a bite to eat, write a couple of letters,' and then as the visitor apologetically made for the door, 'Tell you what, why don't you come and see me between shows?'

His comedy was not confined to juggling and offstage hoaxing. There were the hilariously hackneyed card tricks during which one was reminded of the Somerset Maugham exchange: '"Do you like card tricks?" he asked. I said, "No." He did five.' There was the glorious sight of him coaxing a troupe of performing dogs, not one of which would do anything he said. There were the mock-Shakespearean recitations, the blurred story of Romeo and Juliet as delivered in his rugged cockney being the special favourite. *Clown Jewels* saw juggler turned psychoanalyst in a sketch with Teddy Knox as the patient. The Monsewer drew a square, a circle and a triangle on a blackboard. Knox had to say what they reminded him of and suggested 'a woman getting into bed, a woman already in bed, and a woman getting out of bed'. 'You must be woman-mad,' said Gray, to be capped by a triumphant Knox, 'But who's drawing the

dirty pictures?' The final show, *Young in Heart*, at one stage saw the battered topper exchanged for artist's beret. 'Is it cheaper in the nude?' asks the lady sitter. 'Not really, but I'll oblige just the same,' answers Gray as he slithers out of his smock. The same show saw him 'On the Square' dressed like Lord Nelson, pointing to a suitcase and explaining proudly, 'I've got about four gross of pigeons in there who will make themselves dizzy at my slightest word.'

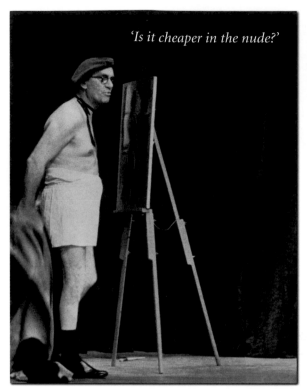

'Is it cheaper in the nude?'

'On the Square'

The one solo performer who belonged to the original Crazy Gang concept, he was able, like Flanagan in the later years, to remain aloof, bringing a spicy edge to the comic traditionalism symbolised by the others, more than once stealing the show, and yet because of his unique style proving an invaluable member of the team when they were lucky enough to have him in their midst. The year after the last Crazy Gang performance he consolidated the many successes of a lengthy career with a featured role as Senex in *A Funny Thing Happened on the Way to the Forum*, the American musical staring Frankie Howerd at the Strand Theatre. In retrospect Howerd's bedraggled quality placed him firmly in Gray's tradition. Less well known, but preserving Gray's own sense of comic indifference within a juggling framework, was Rob Murray, a laconic Australian who gave a jaundiced commentary on life as he staggered around the stage with cane, ball, and hat brilliantly manipulated in controlled slow motion. 'Don't clap for God's sake, or we'll drop the bloody lot.' Not that he ever did. He became a unique fixture of British variety in the 1950s and 60s, his billing 'Juggling under Protest' being as spot-on as his dazzling technical prowess. However, Gray's most obvious successor was Tommy Cooper. They were different from most other comedians in that they were as funny, if not funnier, offstage than on-, inhabiting a world where, as Roy Hudd has pointed out, only they made sense. They were larger than life eccentrics, and it is hard to think of any who fit into that category today. Gray last worked in variety in Brighton in 1969. The next day he went to see his friends Elsie and Doris Waters down the road in Eastbourne. They called him up on stage, whereupon he received a standing ovation. As he made his way back to his seat, he doubled up in pain. 'Bloody indigestion again,' he told his wife. The following morning he died.

A few months before his death Gray appeared on a radio show with, again, Tommy Trinder, who paid him the sincere and spontaneous tribute that nobody had ever worked with the Monsewer without being able to say at the end of the week that the funniest gag they had ever heard had been cracked by Eddie Gray. His own response was predictable: 'I'd like to second that.' Those who knew him have continued to voice such remarks about this latter-day merry-andrew not un time, not deux times, but all times until the end of their days.

AFTERTHOUGHTS

It was only after the first edition of this book went to press that I was told what might qualify as the definitive Eddie Gray practical joke. If there were enough people passing by, he would walk up to a pillar box and shout down the slot, 'Well, how did you get in there in the first place?' This was only the prelude to a feigned conversation that ended with the reassuring, 'It's all right. Don't panic. Look, I'll nip around to the post office and get a key. Just hang on.' By this time a crowd had gathered in anxious suspense to see the rescue that was not to be. Roy Hudd was once in Gray's company when he pulled the gag and adds flesh to the bare bones: '"I don't believe this," Eddie said to the crowd. "There's a postman in there. He fell inside the box as he was collecting the letters and the door closed behind him. Look, you keep him talking while I sort this out." As Eddie went on his errand, these poor souls attempted to continue the dialogue: "Oh God, I think he's fainted. He's not answering!"'

Gray must have had a thing about pillar boxes. On his way to the Victoria Palace one afternoon with Charlie Naughton in tow he noticed some workmen about to cement one into position on Westminster Bridge Road. He whisked out his membership card for the Variety Artistes' Federation and, unrecognisable and totally credible in his street clothes, assumed the identity of 'Mr Shankers, Post Office Pillar Box Siting Officer'. Having asked to see their plans he assumed command: 'Yes, this is right, but it has to be the other way round. You see, it's very difficult for the scrimpsen scrayville to undulate the cordwinder unless it is. Do you see?' 'Yes.' 'Right then, we'll check once we've instigated the traffic-fill at the junction box.' And that is why in those days anyone wishing to post a letter in the vicinity of the Victoria Palace took their life into their hands. Had the workmen looked Gray in the eye they might have discerned the demonic glare of a mad trickster. Otherwise there was nothing to give him away. Stunts such as these were perpetrated anonymously and gave no publicity to the Crazy Gang whatsoever. Only a psychoanalyst would have had access to any deeper meaning.

Hopefully his individual stature in these pages will make up for the fact that within the business structure of the Gang he was always considered the humblest of the seven. His lack of 'remooneration' itself became a subject for humour. When he rejoined the team in 1956 he was rumoured to be on only thirty-five pounds a week. When a journalist enquired if this was so, the maestro added that in order to make ends meet he had been forced to undertake a daily milk round. He acquired a reputation as the only variety star who would never sign a contract, and his unwillingness to cooperate with certain managements may have contributed to him being paid less than his talents were worth. Much as he was loved by his closest colleagues, his aloof independent air was not entirely stage pretence. When the master manipulator Cardini appeared on one of the Palladium Crazy shows, the programme credits included the line: 'The cigarettes used by Cardini – collected by Eddie Gray.' Merely the hint of this cut-price Machiavellian recycling the tobacco to sell at Oxford Circus a short step away would have been worth the price of admission.

Fleet Street did grant Sir John Betjeman his wish to lunch with his hero. Afterwards, as they strolled down the Strand, Eddie stopped a tall young man apparently lost in thought and asked him where he was going. Before he could answer, Gray had launched into a one-sided conversation along the lines of 'How's the boss? Is he well?' The man was nonplussed and eventually Eddie had the good grace to let him go on his way: 'Well, give him my regards. Give him my good wishes. Tell him you've seen me and I'll be calling him soon.' As they strolled on, the poet laureate asked how long he had known the lad. 'Never seen him before,' replied the Monsewer. In Betjeman's words, 'That's the secret of humour. The unexpected.'

From left to right: Dave O'Gorman, Charlie Chester, Eddie, Arthur Askey, Joe O'Gorman and Charlie Naughton with a fly on his nose

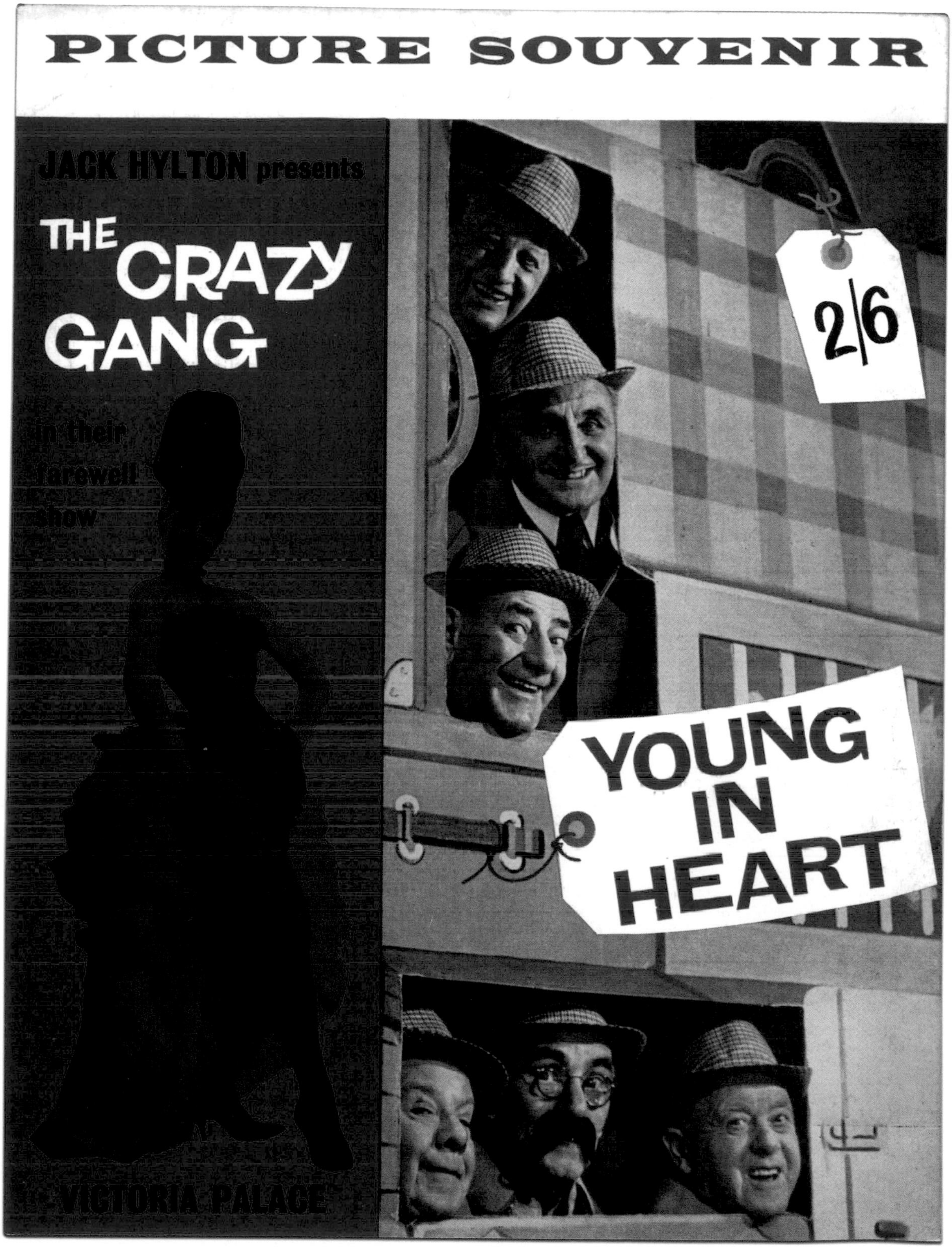

PICTURE SOUVENIR

JACK HYLTON presents

THE CRAZY GANG

in their farewell show

VICTORIA PALACE

2|6

YOUNG IN HEART

LUCAN AND McSHANE: OLD MOTHER RILEY AND HER DAUGHTER KITTY

> *McShane*: Why do you object to me speaking to my boyfriends?
>
> *Lucan*: I don't object to you speaking to your boyfriends. It's what you're speaking about to them that worries me.
>
> *McShane*: Don't let that worry you. I only speak about the same things that you spoke about when you were courting.
>
> *Lucan*: Oh, you ought to be ashamed of yourself! How did you know? I mean, who told you? I deny it!

The sophisticated image of sexual satire and caricatured glamour that – notably through the success of Barry Humphries as Dame Edna Everage – has defined the art of female impersonation in later years has tended to obscure the fact that arguably the most consistently popular drag artist of the last century was a performer who, far from embodying an attitude of extravagant coiffure and cosmetic illusion, represented the spirit of earthy domesticity to be found in every backstreet granny who ever put on bonnet and shawl. The main point of similarity between Arthur Lucan as Old Mother Riley and the more sophisticated Australian is that they both injected into their characterisation a far greater depth than is suggested by the mere visual gag of a man dressed in woman's clothes. It is hard to imagine though that in his day Lucan would have met with the popular acclaim Old Mother Riley brought him, had he veered away from the idea of the old Irish washerwoman in favour of a more urbane character.

Arthur Lucan had not always played the dame. He was born Arthur Towle, the son of a groom, in Boston, Lincolnshire on 16 September 1885. An early interest in theatricals led at the age of nine to him playing the part of a native when measles decimated the cast of a local production of *Robinson Crusoe*. Eventually he ran away from home and found himself busking on the sands at Skegness and Blackpool, before signing a seven-year apprenticeship with a Pierrot company known as the Musical Cliftons, appearing at Colwyn Bay and Llandudno. Arthur toured with the troupe to Ireland, where he fitted into the role of a rough-hewn Irish character comedian, complete with red nose, baggy trousers and diminutive hat. In 1910 he grasped the opportunity of writing a pantomime for the Queens Theatre, Dublin. Arthur was allowed to produce and to play the part of grandmother to *Little Red Riding Hood* himself. To play the title role he discovered a thirteen-year-old, whose mother was a midwife and father a fireman, singing in a local music arcade. Born on 19 May 1897, Catherine McShane was prevented from playing the star role by the local authorities as she was underage. But Towle enjoyed his first success as a dame and found a wife in the process. He married Kitty on 25 November 1913, when she was only sixteen. Considering 'Towle' lacked an authentic Irish ring, he remedied the matter in Dublin, where the Lucan Dairy inspired his subsequent stage name. He would continue to play the dame intermittently in pantomime and kept up his trek around the provincial halls until a major breakthrough occurred when in August 1925 the archetypal sketch featuring the old Irish mother and her lively colleen was brought to the Alhambra, London in a bill topped by Harry Tate and Little Tich. It first bore the title 'Come Over'.

Lucan: So you have a sweetheart?

Kitty: Yes, mother.

Lucan: Was that the boy I saw you with on the corner?

Kitty: Yes, mother.

Lucan: Well, tell me everything that passed between the two of you.

Kitty: Oh, mother – not *everything*!

Lucan: Well as much as you can without making me blush.

Kitty: We were talking about getting married.

Lucan: Come over…

(*Comic business ensues as Lucan walks across stage dragging Kitty with her*)

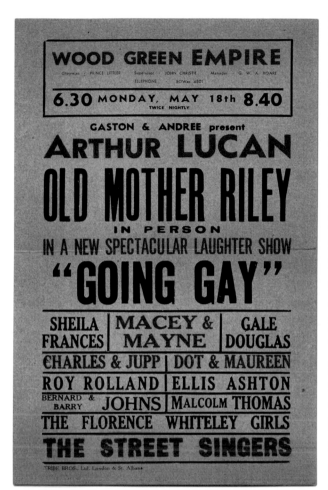

Lucan, however, had not yet decided to concentrate entirely upon female impersonation. In March 1927 he was playing principal comedian in the revue *Irish Follies* at the Wood Green Empire, his dame characterisation being only a part, even if the most notable, of his total offering. On that occasion he presented 'The Old Match-seller and her Balloons', the sketch he later featured in his first appearance at the London Palladium in August 1932. Onto a stage representing the Thames Embankment staggered a dishevelled white-haired, old lady clothed in rusty black. 'Matches, penny a box... matches, penny a box...' The match-seller and the later Old Mother Riley had much in common. To her increasing indignation she had been moved on once already 'and by a Special!' Then to her new pitch comes a damsel in distress, played by Kitty, whose future husband has failed to arrive at the altar. The old lady has her own view on such matters: 'Every man before wedlock should be padlocked!' Even then the main humour derived from the old lady's interruptions, interjections and caustic remarks – 'His teeth are like stars... they come out at night' – but there was pathos too as first the two women try to console each other on the park bench and then the girl wanders off to leave the old lady alone. 'There's laughter and tears, smiles and regrets, sunshine and flowers, but we must all carry on to the end,' says Lucan. Shrugging her shoulders with more than a touch of Chaplin about her, she shuffles offstage, repeating her opening cry, which fades away into the distance: 'Matches, penny a box... matches, penny a box...' There couldn't have been a dry eye in the house. As she said in another context, 'I like a good cry. Saves me washing me face!'

When they presented this act at the Liverpool Empire in August 1935, the critic of the *Liverpool Echo* wrote, 'His acting was something quite outside the range of the ordinary "dame" comedian. Mr Lucan does not of course play the part "straight", but he never gets completely out of character. It is no small achievement thus successfully to combine what is in method and in effect realistic acting with excursions into slapstick comedy.' This technique would lift the Irish washerwoman above the usual run of dames and enabled her to exist as a specific personality in her own right, with her own identity, until his death. G. S. Melvin with his Girl Guide characterisation, Douglas Byng, Norman Evans, Danny La Rue and Dick Emery as blonde bombshell Mandy with her recurring catchphrase 'Ooh, you are awful, but I like you!' all created individual female types, but not the specialised characterisation sustained by Lucan to the blanket exclusion of his own personality. Only Rex Jameson's Mrs Shufflewick and Dame Edna Everage have been her equal in this regard.

The Giddy Hiker—You'll Like "Her"

Above: G. S. Melvin; right: Dick Emery as Mandy with an unknown suitor: 'Ooh, you are awful, but I like you!'

The sketch that set the seal on Old Mother Riley and her daughter Kitty was 'Bridget's Night Out', in which the anonymous Irish mother and Bridget were soon to achieve and change identity respectively. This was included in the Royal Variety Performance of 1934. Its basic theme is that of a mother waiting up into the early hours for her wayward daughter to return home. When Kitty does arrive, she refuses to do the washing-up her mother has been saving for her. In disgust Old Mother Riley hurls a rolling pin across the stage, and gradually plate after plate, crock after crock, all precariously poised on the miles of shelving fitted around the stage set, shatter to smithereens. The subtlety of the knockabout is only revealed in the final moments when amid the mountains of broken china Lucan just cannot get that last plate to shatter. That it eventually does so only emphasises that not a single piece of china has been left unbroken. The sketch gave Lucan full scope for his enormous range of facial and bodily contortions and his delightful sense of the absurd. The sheer ludicrousness of the line 'She's left me all alone and she knows I can only read the clock when it strikes' is only brought home when the clock does eventually strike three: 'Oh dear! It's one o'clock three times!' The name Old Mother Riley itself did not pass into common currency until 1937, when Lucan made the film of the same name, but he must have long recognised the widespread potential in the character he had created.

To cast eyes on the old matriarch was to observe the height of the grotesque, a quality that the formidable old harridan always took pains to emphasise herself.

> *Kitty*: Do you know where I went, mother? I went to a museum.
> *Lucan*: Went into a museum?
> *Kitty*: Yes, went into a museum.
> *Lucan*: What did you go into a museum for? Was it raining?
> *Kitty*: No, darling, it wasn't raining. I went to see an ancient curiosity.
> *Lucan*: An ancient curiosity?
> *Kitty*: An ancient curiosity.
> *Lucan*: You had to go out to a museum to see an ancient curiosity?
> *Kitty*: Well I. . .
> *Lucan*: Why didn't you come home to see your mother?

She goes on to explain that she found Kitty's father in a museum: 'He looked at some monkey skulls, looked at me, and said, "Darwin was right!"' Her claim to be reminiscent of a museum exhibit did not end, however, with the eager emaciated face, with its lean hungry look symbolic of a harsher, less affluent age, framed by its bedraggled black bonnet with the incisive cord-elastic. Her spindly, scrawny body appeared as brittle as parched seaweed: one could almost see the bones sticking out of the voluminous black dress that reached to the ground. Her limbs gave the impression of being not double but treble-jointed, leading to inevitable entanglements with tables and chairs. One recalls the bare spiky elbows bent sharply downwards with the hands clasped at eye level to express deepest aggravation or ecstatic joy. And over her shoulders were the tattered remains of a shawl that could not possibly shrink any further. Lucan was an acknowledged master of make-up, and once the appeal of Old Mother Riley was established, he never appeared onstage in men's clothes. Countless people would throng around the stage door to see what he looked like in real life, but they would seldom recognise him.

Onstage, however, there was no mistaking the rasping 'Irish' tones that heralded her boisterous entry: 'Good evening blackguards, bodyguards, coal yards and fireguards. It's me, Mother Riley, just blown in for a breath of fresh air.' Such an introduction set the scene for the steady stream of incoherent chattering that punctuated the act at regular intervals. To say that she relied upon mispronunciation as a comic gambit is an understatement. Never did anyone's tongue and teeth get into such confusion. No sooner would the word she intended spring from her lips than it would bring a whole chain of unnecessary, often inconsequential words in attendance. In short, her mind, her sense of meaning and of mathematics could not keep up with her tongue. It was common for her to rebuke Kitty: 'Oh, it's disgusterating, disgraceful, delicious, delightful. I mean…!' By way of autobiography: 'I spent my childhood, my womanhood, my motherhood, my… eh?… my falsehood in a museum!' To Kitty, by way of curiosity: 'Is it a staff dance, a barn dance, a rumba dance, or a fan dance?' By way of self-sympathy: 'I've got one foot in the grave, one foot in a bed sock, and I'm kicking the bucket with the other!'

The chaos in her life was just as sweeping. Who else outside the nonsense world of pantomime would have worn twenty underskirts, warmed their corsets in the oven overnight and kept her vest and sundry other articles in the bread bin? And yet for all her absurdity, Old Mother Riley possessed a definite credibility, a strict, even if zany fidelity to working-class life. Her meaningless gossip, her reliance upon the lesser creature comforts, namely her chair, her fire and her gin, her determination and strength in straitened circumstances, all combined to suggest that whatever her vulgarity, her brashness, here was a touching portrayal of someone who was only too true a figure, indeed still is, within British society.

The central pivot around which her life revolved was of course her daughter Kitty, in whom she cherished an intense protective pride. Kitty's shortcomings would make her mother at once fierce, fretful and fidgety. Her unpunctuality, her aspirations to a sophistication that betrayed her humble origins, her presumption that her poverty-stricken mother, her 'darling mummy, jewel of the whole wide world', would be able to provide the financial means to turn such hopes into reality, her skittish gallivanting, all had to reckon with Old Mother Riley's cantankerous conservatism.

Lucan: If you think for one split second that you're going to bring a man into my family with a name like Adolphus, you've got another think coming. If he comes near my establishment, I'll scuttle him, I will.

Kitty: But mother, darling, I love Adolphus.

Lucan: Love him? How can you talk of love?

Kitty: Why shouldn't I talk of love? You fell in love once when you married my father.

Lucan: Yes, I married your father, but you want to marry a stranger. And your father had a good, healthy name. No Adolphus about him.

Kitty: What was my father's name?

Lucan: John Patrick Murphy Spud Riley!

Moreover, even if the old lady was uneducated in the conventional sense, Kitty proved the whetstone for the sharpest of wits.

Lucan: Is he (*the latest boyfriend*) fond of kissing?
Kitty: Don't be silly, mother. Of course he is.
Lucan: (*with a contemptuous squawk*). How do you know?

Then came the catchphrase rebuke: 'The shame on you!'

Theirs was essentially a love–hate relationship, but the pathos often present in such a situation was never allowed to become irksome, simply because sympathy was either blatantly asked for or cunningly contrived. Her hard-done-by armoury of unwantedness, old age, ill health and loneliness rivalled Albert Steptoe's, and it is surprising how many points of reference are shared between the geriatric rag-and-bone man and his son, Harold, on the one hand, and washerwoman and Kitty on the other. Both maintain the same basic equilibrium between offspring trying to be better than they really are and parent obstinately determined to see they stay at first base. When Kitty decided to stay at home to comfort her mother although more enticing attractions beckoned from outside, Old Mother Riley's gratitude knew no bounds: 'I'll give you a party. I'll open a tin of sardines – and make you a *strong* cup of tea.' Kitty's restlessness arose naturally from her inability to reconcile such luxuries with her own idea of the good life. And yet, if the Rileys, like the characters created by Ray Galton and Alan Simpson, could not live together in peace, they could not live apart at all. Both situations highlight the horror of the blood tie, interminable and indissoluble, between two people who, while knowing more than they ever want to know about each other, are at the same time mutually indispensable. As the 'darlin' darter', Kitty McShane embodied a gushing glamour, artificial, theatrical and with a dash of the fairground. By itself the personality would have been cloying, the speech too affected, but in performance both were admirably counterbalanced by the brisk down-to-earth belligerence of her partner. That Kitty succeeded in sustaining the spirit of a lovely young Irish colleen through into her mid-fifties invited criticism from some quarters, but in fact this only emphasised the blood tie with the much older female.

The dizzying heights of popularity they achieved are best evidenced by their phenomenally successful cinematic career. After a cursory appearance in *Stars on Parade*, one of those variety compilations on celluloid of which the 1930s were fond, they were launched into films properly by John Argyle, who gave them two cameo roles in *Kathleen Mavourneen*. That was in 1937. Within the year the eponymous *Old Mother Riley* was geared by the same producer to their own specific talents, the first of a series of fifteen films, which subsequently saw the naive old washerwoman in Paris, as an MP, in the army, in high society, in business, haunted by ghosts (this film is of special interest as it is the only one in which Lucan is seen as a man – he played not only Riley, but a crook who disguised himself as her), in circus ownership, as a private eye, overseas, back home again, undertaking a 'New Venture', as a headmistress, in the jungle, and finally in 1952, this time without Kitty, meeting the Vampire (namely Bela Lugosi)! The films cleaned up at the provincial box office, and yet not until 1949, twelve on in the series, did one receive a West End showing prior to general release. Children especially enjoyed the predominant knockabout element, and for many years afterwards the films were shown at juvenile Saturday morning matinees throughout the country.

The neglect of Old Mother Riley by a West End audience that before long would devour the latest Carry On epic was characteristic of an attitude that existed towards the supposedly unsophisticated provinces in the days before television, an attitude that made, for example, Frank Randle, the brilliant drunk and senile impersonator, a superstar in Blackpool and a relative unknown south of Nottingham. Lucan's films had a decided bias towards the North Country market, but Old Mother Riley, helped by frequent radio exposure, was able to extend her reputation far beyond the regional limitations the industry might have foreseen for her popularity. The character represented a unique hotchpotch of provincial traits which helped to broaden the comic appreciation of the country as a whole. Lucan was born in Lincolnshire; his readiest audience was spread throughout Lancashire and Yorkshire; the content of his act with its endearing blarney and quaint illogicality was unmistakably Irish; and yet in essence this was the Irish of the Liverpool dockside and neighbouring industrial towns. At the London Palladium in December 1943 the revue *Look Who's Here* was built around their talents. The entire second half was given over to 'The Tearing of the Green', a loosely connected series of songs, sketches and dances set in an Irish village and featuring revue star Richard Haydn, just returned triumphant from Hollywood, as guest artist. In spite of production by Robert Nesbitt and choreography by Wendy Toye, the raucous humour of Old Mother Riley was unable to sustain anything more than a short run, but happily Lucan had no need to rely on the West End stage. His hybrid regional pedigree provided its own security.

Lucan sustained his characterisation right until his death in 1954, appearing at all the leading provincial variety houses, usually as the focal point of a full-scale revue, a series that culminated in *Old Mother Riley in Paris*. He was last seen onstage at the Theatre Royal, Barnsley on 14 May 1954. The following Monday the show was about to open at the Tivoli, Hull. Onstage Ellis Ashton played the comedy mayor who had to introduce the old lady to cast and audience. Unbeknown to Ashton as he made the announcement, Lucan had collapsed in the wings with a heart attack and died shortly afterwards in his dressing room. His death was kept from the audience, and an understudy, Frank Seton, took his part for both houses that evening.

It was a tragic end, made even more so by the disappointments and setbacks suffered in his final years. The partnership with his wife had broken up in 1951, when Kitty, having opened a beauty salon in London's Mayfair, decided to concentrate on her business interests. Towards the end, moreover, it had not been the happiest of relationships. Often when rowing on stage as mother and daughter, they were vicariously acting out their private life as husband and wife. During their last film together they never met on set. They would come into the studio on separate days for their individual shots to be taken. The scenes would be intricately pieced together during the editing process. Lucan naturally persisted in his attempts to keep alive the legend of Old Mother Riley, but without Kitty the spirit had gone. Financial worries made matters worse. Kitty had invested their money in business ventures, one of which, the beauty salon, lost between £30,000 and £40,000. Lucan himself admitted a surtax debt of about £15,000 to the Inland Revenue, even if at the London bankruptcy court two months before his death they had only claimed £10,051. Although they were living apart, since 1951 he had paid about three quarters of his income to Kitty. It is ironic that his own comment on this tangled situation had a typical Riley ring: 'All I owe is income tax. I have never owed a man a penny in my life.' After Lucan's death, Kitty attempted a comeback with Roy Rolland, a brilliant impersonator of Lucan's style and once a regular understudy. The public knew, however, that 'Old Mother Kelly' was nothing more than an impostor, however remarkable the resemblance may have been. Kitty herself died ten years after her husband on 24 March 1964.

By his complete absorption in the role of his chosen character, Lucan set himself head and shoulders above all others in a tradition that went back to the medieval mystery plays. The garrulous shrew who was Noah's wife in the Chester cycle could have been written with Lucan in mind. It was originally a drag role and there was never any question of a woman herself playing such a knockabout character. According to theatre critic Clement Scott, Dan Leno's drag speciality was women of 'the lodging house and slavey type', a perfect description of the old Irish washerwoman. Leno's Mrs Kelly and Lucan's Mrs Riley would have got on splendidly together. In July 1941 the *News Review* described the latter as 'the champion of the underdog, a hater of shams, a Valkyrie of the backstreets'. However absurd her eccentricities, it was easy to peer beyond these and see that she possessed an intense awareness of life's tragedies. It was a subtle, humane, as well as outrageous characterisation and it became legendary. Many have been the actors and drolls who have kept alive the tradition of Ugly Sister, Widow Twankey and Charley's Aunt on the boards, but there was only one man who could do full justice to the part of the hearty, yet sad, Irish harridan.

AFTERTHOUGHTS

Rereading my appraisal of Arthur Lucan, I realise that I gave scant emphasis to two roles that played a key part in his life, namely the acrobat and the alcoholic. That he became prey to alcohol is understandable if only to counteract the pressures of his domestic life, let alone the well established burden of the comedian's role. 'I'd make meself a cup o' tea, if I could find me corkscrew' was a harmless enough line onstage, but indicative of the Dutch courage perhaps inevitable in the presence of the megalomaniac monster that McShane had become.

Just as he never appeared for his last performance, an understudy taking his place as the undertakers were called, so it has since come to light that understudies saved the day on many more occasions when alcohol prevented him going onstage. Audiences were unaware of the change. Full marks then not only to Frank Seton, but also to Roy Rolland and George Beck, his most frequent double, for making their efforts so convincing, not least because of the extreme physicality that accounted for so much of Arthur's appeal. Few who saw him will forget his remarkable acrobatic prowess, as he whirled his arms and legs around like a windmill going in several directions at once. There was an incredible moment when he seemed to leap a foot into the air, applying a scissor-like movement to his legs to get them properly crossed before he sat down.

In more recent years the suggestion of a harsher version of Old Mother Riley has manifested itself for a more brittle age in Paul O'Grady's startling if severe creation Lily Savage. Today the phrase 'single parent' has a different connotation and for 'washerwoman' one has to read 'scrubber' of another kind: Lily has to resort to more carnal means to earn an 'honest' bob or two. It is a shame that apart from the odd pantomime appearance the nature of show business today has distanced her creator from his alter ego to pursue a successful career as a talk-show host. This is miles away from the authentic atmosphere of the halls, where Savage would have been in her true element. Grady, like Lucan, is a kind and sensitive man and one senses that he knows that only too well.

Jack Le White was a magnificent old-timer from a long-established circus family whose musical speciality act with his own wife often toured with the Lucan and McShane show. In his autobiography *Rings and Curtains*, he recalled the time Kitty decided to focus upon her beauty parlour: 'Arthur did his best to carry on with the show, but Kitty took to following after him and creating scenes until it became necessary to ban her from going backstage. So many times we had heard her telling Arthur to drop dead in her reverberating stage whisper. In the end, that is what he did.' It is a chilling epitaph.

Traditional festive fun with, from left to right and from top downwards, Kitty and Arthur, Frank Randle, Bud Abbott and Lou Costello, Joe E. Brown, and Stan Laurel and Oliver Hardy

MAX MILLER: THE CHEEKY CHAPPIE

**There'll never be another, lady. No, there'll never be another.
When I'm dead and gone, the game's finished!**

No comedian was more immediately identifiable from his bill matter than Max Miller. And yet, as a description, 'The Cheeky Chappie' was lacking because Max was so much more. He was flamboyant, outrageous, sensational. Every facet of his personality was so vividly accentuated that the words 'larger than life' would have achieved their cliché status through their application to him alone. He would charm thousands with the accurate boast 'There'll never be another!' There never was and never will be. He was the undisputed master of his trade, who took the art of communication with a live audience to a zenith never repeated with greater panache and personal assurance.

His sense of stagecraft was unerring, his entrance the most anticipated in variety. As the applause for the preceding act died away, whatever music had been playing would cut out and the stage plunged into darkness for ten seconds. As quiet fell over the auditorium, people would wonder why the show had stopped – ten seconds is a long time in such a context – but then of a sudden the band would launch into his signature tune, 'Mary from the dairy', the lights would come up, the spotlight would hit the prompt corner and then, at the precise moment for maximum applause, Max grinning from ear to ear would swagger on in all his technicolour glory. The band would keep playing as he took off his ankle-length coat to reveal one of his dazzling suits of floral chintz. Let's imagine it depicted buttercups or daffodils. He directed his gaze at a woman in the front row, 'D'you like it, lady? I've just had a mustard bath!' Only on the end of the gag did the music stop, at which point the audience suddenly heard the volume of its own laughter. The impact must have been electrifying.

His skill enabled him to reduce the most cavernous auditorium to the intimate surroundings of your own front room. He used to say, 'You need to be close enough to them so that you can nick a shilling from an old girl's handbag without her knowing.' As he leaned across the footlights his expressive eyes scanned the audience like searchlights, making direct contact with everyone in sight. 'There's a lady over there got opera glasses on me. She thinks I'm a racehorse!' He understood that laughter was contagious and developed the technique of addressing the one lady in the house with an irrepressible cackle, wherever she might be. Miller knew how to maximise her presence to his best advantage, working on the single outlet until the whole house echoed in the same way. On *Max at the Met*, the live recording of his act made at the Metropolitan Music Hall, Edgware Road on 30 November 1957 – *the* classic recording of comedy in performance – one can hear the process. Miller had as shrewd an insight into his profession as anyone, as he showed when he described it to a young Bob Monkhouse: 'Comedy, son, comedy is the one job you can do badly and people *won't* laugh at you, but it's the one job you can do well and they will.' In Bob's own words, 'He had the magic of a magnet and that informed all his comedy. He drew you to him, made you laugh and wouldn't let you go until he had.'

The son of a builder's labourer, Max Miller was born Thomas Henry Sargent in Brighton on 21 November 1894 and maintained throughout his performing life an identification with that resort's brash glittering grandeur. If the Royal Pavilion and the West and Palace Piers were magnificent, so were Max's clothes: the immaculate white trilby with its brim accentuated snappily to one side, the stunning silk suits with their flowery patterns and enormous plus fours, the two-tone co-respondent shoes, the extravagant kipper tie. 'I know exactly what you're saying. You're saying to yourselves, "Why is he dressed like that?" I tell you why I'm dressed like this: I'm a commercial traveller and I'm ready for bed!" One famous costume featured a mass of white daisies against a blue background, while his suit of red, white and blue for the 1937 Royal Variety Performance prompted the remark 'I know how to dress for these occasions – nice and quiet.' At such events he would stand out like a red admiral against a swarm of cabbage whites. Maybe this gaudy splendour was a secret link to his early love of the circus, although the nearest he got to working with one was cleaning the animal cages for a week for a travelling show visiting the seaside resort. Life was hard, and when the rent could not be paid the family was often forced to perform a moonlight flit to another part of town. Other early jobs included a milk round, serving in a fish and chip shop, and spells as a golf caddie and a motor mechanic. As a youth he loved showing off and earned the nickname Swanky Sargent after putting on a pair of spats rescued from some nob's dustbin over the rags that passed for his trousers.

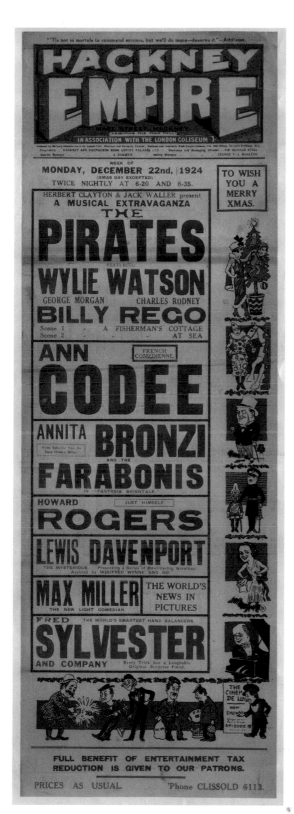

When war was declared in 1914, he volunteered for the Royal Sussex Regiment, which led to an exchange that could have come out of a music hall sketch.

> *Recruiting officer*: Your name?
> *Max*: Sargent, Sergeant.
> *Recruiting officer*: Are you trying to be funny? I asked you your name.
> *Max*: Harry – Sargent.
> *Recruiting officer*: What's your surname, you idiot?
> *Max*: Sargent, Sergeant.

In time he would be posted to India, where he helped to found a concert party called The Lightners. In later life he recalled, 'I took all the women's parts, so I was always going to the captain and saying, "How are the horses?" You see, when one of the horses died, I used to get their tails and make them into wigs.' The following year he saw service on the front line in Mesopotamia, an experience that saw him blinded by shellfire for three days and led to a commitment to helping the sightless that lasted to the end of his life. After demobilisation he returned to Brighton and joined Jack Sheppard's concert party, performing alfresco on Brighton beach. Here he met Kathleen Marsh, a contralto and child impersonator. They were married in 1921. The year before, at her suggestion, he had dropped the name Harry Sargent in favour of Max Miller. For a while they attempted a double act, but it was soon obvious from his rapport with an audience that he should concentrate on being a solo turn. Once established as a performer in variety, however, it could be said that he never entirely cut himself off from the traditions of the Pierrot tradition, his colourful stage clothes echoing its billowing costumes and its links to the harlequinade. By May 1929 he had worked his way up to his first booking at the London Palladium, where he returned twice in the same year and would be featured on his first Royal Variety Performance in 1931.

Even before he became a dancer and light comedian with Sheppard he had worshipped the brilliant blackface minstrel and music hall star G. H. Elliott (1884 – 1962), then innocuously billed as 'The Chocolate Coloured Coon'. This admiration continued throughout Miller's career, and if Max placed the emphasis on comedy at the expense of singing and the soft-shoe shuffle, he still maintained the neatness of presentation and care for detail that hallmarked the lilting performer of 'I used to sigh for the silvery moon'. Even when he was secure in his position as a major star, he would take time out from his own touring schedule to catch up with his hero, still registering on the boards as part of the *Thanks for the Memory* company of old-timers. The ease with which Elliott danced met its match in the fluency of Miller's tongue. The tone of his voice was crisp and snappy, and one could be forgiven for thinking that donkeys evolved for the sole purpose of enabling him to talk the hind legs off them.

Above: Max's hero, G. H. Elliott
Right: an early publicity postcard of Max with monocle and moustache

MAX MILLER.

Armed with a disarming smile and a roving eye, he would chatter ad infinitum with a sense of rhythm that marked him out as unmistakably the greatest, if only because the easiest to listen to, stand-up comedian of his generation. But while he was garrulous, Max was in no way verbose, adroitly using emphasis and repetition within a line to communicate with maximum effect. Not a word was wasted, not a phrase longer than it needed to be. More than that of any other British comedian of the time, his speech took wing. He would crouch forward, one foot planted firmly upon the footlights, to relate his lecherous escapades. However eccentric his appearance, his face was friendly and 'straight', and belied his habit of dodging imaginary missiles as he went striding up and down the apron. He never needed the practice this piece of business gave him; his own attack on those out front was flawless and 100 per cent effective. Linked to this was his mastery of the offstage look to the imaginary adversary in the wings, the theatre manager who was gunning for him on some matter of time or taste, a technique developed with equal brilliance in later years by Frankie Howerd. 'It's people like you who give me a bad name,' Max would chide the crowd, turning to the wings to check whether some sinister authority figure was coming to apprehend him.

However, it was far more than his stagecraft and verbal fluency that made him pre-eminent among his kind, more even than the air of impudent authority that invested all the jokes he told – whether original or of the more predictable, parochial type – with the stamp of his own copyright. More than any other performer he embodied that quasi-Saturnalian function discussed in the first chapter, whereby in the warm security of the theatre an audience of essentially respectable citizens can sit guiltless, conscience-free as their most secret desires are acted out by the amoral anarchic jester on stage.

I had a shocking dream the other night – a shocking dream. I dreamt three of my pals and myself – we went to hell – yes! And when we got down there the devil said to the first one, 'What are you doing here?' He said, 'I don't know. I haven't done anything wrong. I've never neglected the wife. I never go with women. And I don't smoke. I don't know why I'm here.' He said to the other one, 'What about you?' He said, 'Well, I'm the same as him. I've never neglected the wife. I don't go with women. I don't smoke. I don't drink. I dunno why I'm here.' And the third one exactly the same. Then he turned to me and said 'What about you, Miller?' I said, 'I'm entitled to be here.' I said, 'I've done everything wrong. I've neglected the wife. I've gone with women.' He said, 'You're the boy I'm looking for. Do you know what I'm gonna do?' I said, 'No.' He said, 'I'm going to burn the other three and you and I are going to have a night out!'

The release provided by laughter forestalls any hint of guilt or shame. The dramatist John Osborne, who tapped into aspects of Max in creating the character of the variety comedian Archie Rice for his play *The Entertainer*, put his finger as near as possible on the secret of this facet of his stage presence: 'When he was on the stage he generated a sense of danger. You thought this is somebody who is dicing, gambling, and is going to get away with it.' Without question, Max was all out for mischief, tempting authority all the time, a characteristic trait since childhood when, caught red-handed scrumping in an orchard, he successfully bribed the farmer to 'take it out on my hide and don't bother about sending for a policeman'. No one could restrain him and on stage Max went along his own unrepentant slippery path. 'I don't care what I say, do I? I don't! I don't! Honest I don't!' He emphasised the fact many times, grinning at his audience in his own saucily wicked way. He was repaid not only with laughter, but with breathless gasps of delighted surprise from every figure of so-called respectability out front. Only by listening to a recording of a live Max Miller performance can one now realise how frequently such gasps punctuated the patter.

If that sense of danger may be said to represent a precipice, his blatant – but endearing – exoticism brought him that much closer to its brink. His vanity was that of a peacock crossed with a parrot. The one bird would plume itself, but only the other could shout out about it. 'Miller's the name, lady. There'll never be another, will there? They don't make 'em today, duck!' Haven't I got a nice figure, lady?' And always he assured you, 'You can't help liking him, can you?' He conducted this offensive in so amiable a manner that any doubts the public may have had that it was mere exhibitionism were soon dispelled. No performer could stay top of the bill for thirty years without a genuine sincerity towards his audience and the ability to convey this quality to them personally. Hence the confidential manner with which he attempted to prove the truth of his outrageous statements, or declare, 'The songs I sing I do write myself, and you can only hear them when I sing them – nobody else dare sing them!' He was the paragon of garishness, whose world revolved around saloon bar, breezy promenade, greyhound track and an endless succession of boarding houses. Whatever jobs he had done before the stage claimed him, one guesses that the Cheeky Chappie the public knew would not have wished to have been associated with such a background of mundane, honest toil. There is a recording of him singing 'If I were not upon the stage, someone else I'd like to be', but after we have been introduced to his prospective taxi driver, window cleaner, barrow boy, 'clippie' and butcher – 'Five Max Millers at the price of one!' – he lets out a raucous laugh of self-satisfaction. Secure in his own insecurity, he thrived on his raffish existence to the total exclusion of any alternative.

And then there were the occasions when it appeared that he had gone too far, that he had actually tottered over the edge. His gags were catalogued in two now-legendary books, one white and one blue, graded according to strength, which he proudly displayed on stage. Somewhere in the latter volume came the story of the black washerwoman's surprise encounter with the elephant's trunk, the one about what didn't happen when an unmarried couple shared the same bed with a pillow down the centre to make it all 'religious', and the one about the unsuccessful attempts by a judge to gain a precise definition of what

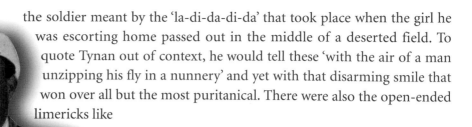

the soldier meant by the 'la-di-da-di-da' that took place when the girl he was escorting home passed out in the middle of a deserted field. To quote Tynan out of context, he would tell these 'with the air of a man unzipping his fly in a nunnery' and yet with that disarming smile that won over all but the most puritanical. There were also the open-ended limericks like

> Jack and Jill went up the hill
> Just like two cock linnets.
> Jill came down with half a crown.
> She wasn't up there two…' Ere, there's a funny thing!

And even more notorious:

> When roses are red,
> They're ready for plucking.
> When a girl is sixteen,
> She's ready for…' Ere!

Max never had any need to finish. He just let the audience do it for him, as his own silence (often innocent, as when it forestalled a word like 'minutes') fed their imaginations.

The more popular the Blue Book became, so the White Book assumed its own bluish tinge. It is a peculiar facet of the English language that the most unlikely word can be forced into a completely new, albeit risqué, meaning simply through its context, however strained the parallel may appear on close reflection. In this way the White Book assumed its own vivid sexual connotation. Add to this Max's skilfully timed pauses, his sidelong glances, the occasional insinuating wink, and it is not surprising that he became the master of the double entendre.

I met a pal of mine the other day. I said, 'Charlie, they tell me that you're married now.' He said, 'That's right.' I said, 'Well, now you know what's what.' He said, 'What?' I said, 'Now you know what's what.' He said, 'What d'you mean?' I said, 'Well, if you're married, you must know what's what.' He said, 'I think you're crazy.' And he started walking home, and as he was walking home he kept saying to himself, 'Now you're married, now you know what's what.' Well, when he got home that night, he got into the bedroom. The wife was in bed. So he took all his clothes off and he switched the light out. He didn't want to get out again, see! And he was in the dark and he was feeling around in the dark, see. And all of a sudden he said, 'What's that?' And the wife said, 'What's what?'

A great roar of laughter would engulf the theatre. As it subsided, Max would jump in with 'And there it was, on the mantelpiece all the time!'

There was scarcely a word or phrase in the English language that he could not make suggestive: 'I rang the doorbell and this woman answered it. She said, "Yes?" I said, "Wait a minute! I haven't asked you yet!".' He had only to say, 'I went to the chemist's yesterday.' He hadn't said anything remotely funny, but the audience knew that there was only one thing Max would go to the chemist for, and it certainly wasn't a toothbrush.

Like his own comic hero George Robey before him, he played throughout the self-alleged innocent, delighting his audience even further as he blamed them for mentally racing ahead of what he had actually said. 'I know exactly what you're saying to yourselves. You're wrong! I know what you're saying. Oh, you wicked lot! You're the kind of people who get me a bad name.' And Max was usually right: so much of his material was completely inoffensive per se. However, whether the true agenda was ambiguously inferred, subtly implied or vividly explicit, there is no escaping the fact that the point of his humour was more spirited, shameless and healthily lascivious than the equivalent of Robey's 'honest vulgarity' a generation earlier. In the early 1930s Robey himself wrote somewhat high-handedly,

> It is scarcely possible to move a yard without seeing some new entertainment advertised as having so-called sex-appeal, but I would prefer to give it the plain John Blunt name of filth-appeal. It is undermining the character of the younger generation. It is putting into their heads such thoughts as no decent minds would carry. The music hall, much maligned though it is, does not do this. It shows father bathing the twins, not seducing the typist. We artists of the variety world would try to teach people to laugh at things. We don't encourage them to break the canons of decent society.

In the light of what the Cheeky Chappie went on to typify, these remarks and the picture of Robey's humour they conjure up today appear nothing if not stunted and stodgy, a product of narrow mindedness and a job only half done. The layers of unconscious irony in Robey's declaration that (his idea of) 'honest vulgarity is the finest antidote I know to present-day hypocrisy' contain their own just rebuke.

Max was great because he did go so far as to seduce the typist, to break those 'canons of decent society', whereas Robey was no more daring than a naughty boy exchanging smutty stories in secret on a

Sunday-school outing. Robey's attitude persisted in the so-called champions of music hall, who obstinately played down the momentous breakthrough achieved by Marie Lloyd and more than a few others in establishing the music hall as the original 'permissive society'. What Orwell said of comic postcards may also be applied to risqué comedians.

It will not do to condemn them on the ground that they are vulgar. *That is exactly what they are meant to be*. Their whole meaning and virtue is in their unredeemed lowness. They are a harmless rebellion against virtue. They express only one tendency in the human mind, but a tendency which is always there and will find its own outlet, like water. On the whole, humans want to be good, but not too good, and not quite all the time.

Hence the subversive quality of all jokes, not merely those that give obscenity and adultery a hearing, but also laziness, avarice, stealth, every aspect of behaviour hostile to the smooth working of society and the demands of convention. Far from presenting a serious threat to morality, they represent a respite in the uphill struggle to uphold such a code. Once relieved, one can return happily to the task of meeting one's responsibilities. Without relief, those very responsibilities are that much more likely to go by the board. As long as the public laughed at Max, one could be sure that the codes that the anti-Miller brigade – composed almost exclusively of chiding magistrates, BBC officials and 'wives-who-won't' – feared most in danger were absolutely safe. Only if the laughter had stopped, if there had been nothing outrageous left in Max's patter because his own sexual code had become the accepted norm, would they perhaps have had cause for concern. As it happened, the protests only enhanced the cheek of the Cheeky Chappie. But one must always remember that underpinning this cheek was a brilliantly skilful technique that Osborne himself equated with genius. It would be wrong to suppose, in the light of the above, that any joke with heavy sexual implications can be acceptable from the lips of any comedian. Max had the master touch when it came to handling such material; no music hall comedian ever had a more sweeping licence to rebel against the accepted morality, not least because no comedian provided a more telling sounding board for the sensibilities of the audiences who revelled in his every indiscretion. They were as oxygen to each other.

There was this little girl. She keeps biting her nails and her mother says, 'Stop biting your nails, because you know what'll happen to you?' She says, 'What'll happen to me?' Her mother says, 'You won't half get fat if you bite your nails.' She says, 'Well, I won't bite them any more.' Well, her mother took her shopping, got on the bus and there's a fellow in the corner of the bus weighing about twenty stone. And she said, 'Mum, I'll get like that, wont I.' She said, 'You'll get worse than that, if you bite your nails.' She said, 'Well, I won't bite 'em any more.' And after shopping they got on another bus, and there's a blonde sitting in the corner, she's carrying a bit of weight as well... *that's what I like about you, you're so quick – you're quick!*... and the kiddie kept looking at the little girl and the blonde kept looking at the kiddie. And the blonde, she couldn't stand it any longer, so she said to the kiddie, 'Do you know me?' And the kiddie said, 'No, but I know what you've been doing!'

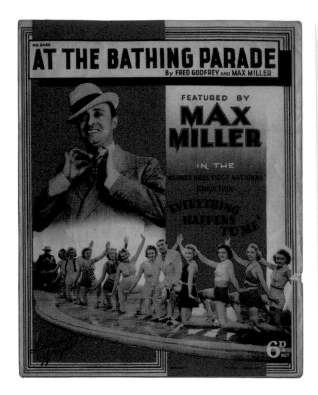

No one, of course, knew what Max had that the others hadn't more than the girls who were the main preoccupation of his scandalous persona.

> I'm known as the Cheeky Chappie,
> The things I say are snappy,
> That's why the pretty girls all fall for me.

His comic songs were about little else. There were girls on bikes and girls at bus stops; Spanish girls who knew their onions and Swiss girls who smiled and said, 'Hello'; girls who were 'a little bit and some more, not quite so much and then perhaps'; landladies charging 'thirty shillings all in and I don't want any children'; fan dancers who fell and damaged their fans; girls 'wearing slacks that bring out all the facts, and bring out the police force as well!' Nor must we forget the unwilling girls, the girls who hadn't found out, the girls who were different from other girls and those the stork had already put the wind up! Max himself made his preference very clear.

> I like the girls who do,
> I like the girls who don't.
> I hate the girl who says she will,
> And then she says she won't.
> But the girl I like the best of all,
> And I think you'll say I'm right,
> Is the girl who says she never does,
> But she looks as though she m…' Ere, listen!

And then, more specifically, alongside Lulu, Josephine and Annie and Fanny, there was 'Mary from the Dairy', whose love for Max may not have been spontaneous but who did reward him with an everlasting signature tune for the role she was forced to play after falling among the buttercups and daisies the time the buttercups were suspiciously full of margarine! One feels the only member of the opposite sex he would never have won over, however hard he schemed, was Marie Stopes. It would have meant being far too careful, not being himself at all. Incidentally, by origin Mary was not a farm girl, rather a direct reference to a waitress at the Express Dairy in London's Charing Cross Road, the cafe where the variety profession congregated for gossip and self-support, and where Max bought the number from songwriter Sam Kern.

Perhaps Max saw his prodigious sexual energy as a hereditary trait. Certainly he would proudly refer to his own beginnings.

> I said to my father, I said, 'Dad, I want to get married.' He said, 'All right, son, who do you want to marry?' I said, 'I'd like to marry Miss Green.' He said, 'You can't.' I said, 'Why not?' He said, 'She's

your half-sister. When I was a lad I had a bike and I got around a bit.' I said, 'All right, I'll marry Miss White.' He said, 'You can't. She's your half-sister. Forget about it.' Well, I was a bit despondent and I walked around. My mum said to me, 'What's wrong with you?' I said, 'Well, I said to dad I wanted to marry Miss Green, and he said I couldn't because she was my half-sister. I said, "All right, I'll marry Miss White." He said, "You can't. She's your half-sister."' She said, 'Look, you go and marry which one you like. He's not your father anyway!'

As he got older his philosophy became easily defined: 'Whether you're rich or whether you're poor, it's nice to be rich, and whether you're married or whether you're single, it's nice anyway.' Once married, the Cheeky Chappie developed a subtle variation on the traditional marriage joke in which the husband is perpetually henpecked and plotting seduction, while the wife triumphantly and suspiciously holds sway at home. One never gained the impression that Max was henpecked in the defeatist sense of the word; one knew for certain that in the world he created for himself on stage his wife, perhaps realising his rampant promiscuity was too much for her even to attempt to check, could boast her own sexual independence. This Max seemed to accept quite happily as consistent with his own personal view of morality.

> I went home the other night. There's a fellow standing there, not a stitch on! Can you imagine that, lady? How's your memory, girl? He hasn't got a stitch on. I called the wife in. I said, 'Who's this?' She said, 'Don't lose your temper, Miller. Don't go raving mad.' I said, 'I'm only asking a fair question. Who is it?' She said, 'He's a nudist and he's come in to use the phone!' There's a clever one from the wife, aye?

Stories like this, however, and remarks like 'I wouldn't say my wife was pretty. I wouldn't say she was ugly. Sort of pretty ugly!' belied the fact that in real life his marriage to Kathleen endured for forty-two years until his death.

This sexual athlete among comedians could even get a sensual thrill out of the guitar with which he accompanied his catchy little songs. Strumming gently to get into tune, he'd sigh with great satisfaction, 'That's nice, Maxie. That is nice. I like that, Maxie.' And then, striking a flat note, he'd enquire of the conductor, 'That's down, isn't it, Ivor? That one's down. Must be the cold weather!' But neither his way with a guitar nor an account of his wife's sex life would ever thrill the audience so much as his racy accounts of his own activities with the 'girls who do'.

> She said, 'Will you come up to the flat and have coffee and games?' I said, 'I'll come up, but don't bother with the coffee. Not straight away!' So I went up. She had a marvellous flat. Two beautiful armchairs – but we didn't bother with those – and she had a lovely bearskin in front of the fire. I was glad the fire was on! So was she, I think! Well, it was raining outside, and there are only two things to do when it's raining, and I don't play cards…

John Osborne described Max as 'a beautiful, cheeky god of flashiness. A saloon-bar Priapus'; to James Agate he was 'brilliant and suave and subtle'; while Ivor Brown, distinguishing between the tough and the tender among comedians, saw in him 'an ace among the bully boys'. This last description is somewhat misleading. While the Cheeky Chappie was unmistakably masculine, indelibly heterosexual, his whole stage personality professed an aura of sexual ambiguity, focused upon the pale feminine make-up, the soft fresh complexion, the dazzling clothes, the neat almost delicate appearance, and not least the thin layer of doubt in lines like 'He's a boy, isn't he? I hope so!' or, as he removed his coat to reveal one of those florid suits, 'What if I am?' In short, while the anonymous male element in his audience was ready to identify with him in his sexual adventures, the female element, which may otherwise have been afraid of an out-and-out bully boy, was itself free to fall for him. He posed no macho threat, the hint of ambiguity a cunning device for making a possible audience of 'girls who won't' into 'girls who are willing'. 'Haven't I got a nice figure, lady? No, I have. Haven't I, ducky? No honest… I'm not drawn in, honest I'm not. I'm all muscle!' And he won them over even further when, breaking away from his patter, he would sing his occasionally sentimental songs. Refreshingly these were not always about unrequited love – 'You broke your promise' – but also about sincerity as in 'Be sincere', a parent's love for its child in 'Something money can't buy', and a strong maternal affection in 'My old mum' and 'Don't forget your first sweetheart'.

Top of the bill by the early 1930s, Max had reached his impertinent peak by the outbreak of war, a time when the public was more anxious than ever to indulge in the relaxation of standards his act could provide. For a while he made his professional home between the Holborn Empire and the London Palladium, with occasional forays into the wilds of Hackney, Finsbury Park, Wood Green, Shepherd's Bush and the other suburban outposts with their Empire theatres intact, always returning to his beloved Brighton on the last train home, which on more than a few occasions a tolerant guard would keep waiting for him at Victoria. In December 1939 he starred in the revue *Haw-Haw!* at the Holborn Empire. It ran until the end of July 1940. The following month he opened in *Applesauce*, the last revue at the Holborn Empire before it succumbed to the Blitz. This show, the title of which delightfully suggested the special piquancy of his style, transferred to the Palladium in March the following year, where it played for a further 462 performances. Second billing, incidentally, went to Vera Lynn, billed then not as 'The Forces' Sweetheart', but as 'Radio's Sweet Singer of Sweet Songs'. Here, at the height of hostilities, Miller would walk onstage holding a carrier bag, reach inside and bring out a cabbage – 'Hitler's head' – followed by a turnip – 'Hitler's nose' – and then two potatoes. This in itself was enough to raise a laugh. Then came the coup de grace: 'No, you're all wrong – King Edward's!' He returned to the Palladium for two lengthy variety seasons during the hostilities, the second run of twenty weeks in 1944 being the longest for a single turn in a straightforward variety show – as distinct from production show – in the history of the theatre. Another morale-boosting gambit during this period involved wearing around his neck the sort of box used by civilians to carry their gas masks. As he jiggled the container up and down his eyes made contact with every woman in the crowd. 'Do you know what I've got in here? Do you know what I've got? It's not me gas mask – it's not me gas mask. Hitler's secret weapon, I've got in here!' To prove his point, he reached inside and produced a long pink phallic object. 'Look! A German sausage!'

In keeping with his maverick status, he found himself in trouble with the authorities on more than one occasion. But he always seemed to have the audience on his side. Generally, the more attempts were made to restrain him, the more audacious he became. More than once he was chided by the BBC, but each time Max, intent anyhow on rationing his broadcasting appearances for fear of overexposure, revelled in the resultant publicity that could only raise his phenomenal theatre fees. More than once he (or the theatre management) was fined £5 for a joke considered too blue by some priggish magistrate; it was a cheap price to pay for its passage into folklore. *The joke* for which he was supposedly banned by the BBC has followed a similar route, although I have never met anyone who heard it when it was supposedly broadcast or been able to trace any formal documentation of the incident. 'I was walking along this narrow mountain pass – so narrow that nobody else could pass you – when I saw a beautiful blonde walking towards me. A beautiful blonde, with not a stitch on. Yes, not a stitch on, lady. I didn't know whether to block her passage or toss myself off!'

Roy Hudd thinks he was too clever to have used a joke as bald and as obvious. Max knew perfectly how to ride the line between filth and subtle innuendo. Part of his skill was never to go too far, but to leave the audience thinking that one day he just might. He was totally outrageous, but never blue in a mucky sense. If the colour applied at all, it was more in keeping with the defining sparkle of his laser-beam eyes.

Whatever ban did or did not apply, by the 1950s Max was broadcasting regularly again on BBC radio, on *Variety Fanfare, Henry Hall's Guest Night, Workers' Playtime* and *Mid-Day Music Hall*. And it seemed a foregone conclusion that, when in 1951 the BBC mounted a special *Festival of Variety* gala to coincide with the Festival of Britain, he should take his rightful place alongside Gracie Fields, Danny Kaye, George Robey, Ted Ray and Robb Wilton. The biggest laugh of the evening came when Max avowed he had performed 'without the slightest sign of vulgarity'. And besides there was always Radio Luxembourg, the pioneer commercial station, from which during the Second World War the Germans had relayed the outrageous Nazi propaganda pronouncements of the broadcaster William Joyce, the original Lord Haw-Haw, from whom George Black had taken the title of Max's Holborn Empire vehicle.

Then there was the controversy over the Royal Variety Performance at the Palladium in 1950, during which Max overstayed his allotted time of six or seven minutes by at least ten more. When Charles Henry, the producer, tried to call him off from the wings, Max's direct reply was 'I'm not coming off. If the Americans can go on (a reference to Jack Benny, who had committed the same sin earlier in the show and got off scot-free), I'm gonna have a go.' He certainly deserved those extra minutes. From his entrance brandishing a jewelled walking stick and his opening line – 'Hello, lady. Look. Do you see that? I've been to the tower today. The crown jewels will look funny without that!' – he had the most difficult of all audiences in the palm of his hand. Backstage things were not so happy, nervous performers thrown even further off course in a show in which timing is supposed to run with split-second precision, if only to meet the demands of the royal schedule. Afterwards Val Parnell vowed Miller would never play one of his theatres again. Max was unrepentant: 'I'm sorry, Val, but you're £100,000 too late!' Needless to say, the renegade was back topping the bill at the Palladium within a couple of years. As he remarked, 'If you make money for people, they have a wonderful way of forgetting.' Around that time Miller was one of only a handful of British performers – Gracie Fields, Norman Wisdom and vocalist Donald Peers were others – who could fill a theatre of the stature of the Palladium on the strength of their name alone. He would eventually command a weekly salary of £1,500, plus a percentage, which at the time made him the highest-paid British variety comedian.

His status bought him a Rolls-Royce (plus a Lanchester for going around town and a De Soto to carry the golf clubs), a cabin cruiser moored at Henley and the unofficial fiefdom of half Brighton. Contributing to this status was his cinematic career. His first film appearance was a cameo lasting three minutes in J. B. Priestley's *The Good Companions* in 1933. In this he appeared with John Gielgud, seemingly ad-libbing his way through his role as a song plugger and stealing all the notices, confirming for those who suspected that much of his vocal style was founded on his observation of the 'Roll up, roll up, come a little closer' technique of the sideshow barkers and cheapjacks who paraded their wares along the Brighton seafront in his youth. After further cameos he went on to star between 1935 and 1940 in a series of eight comedies for Warner Brothers, all of which featured his tremendously fast patter. His best film role was as the bookmaker Educated Evans in the eponymous film of the Edgar Wallace novel and its successor, *Thank Evans*. Had he lived into the 80s he would have provided the stiffest competition for

George Cole as the shady used-car dealer Arthur Daley in the television series *Minder*, his Evans characterisation as synonymous with suspect capitalism in the 30s as Daley was in the Thatcher era. He was, however, essentially a live performer, his film career being in no way essential to his stage success, as it was in the case of Formby or Lucan. Indeed his fame was assured before entering either film, radio or recording studio. Never was he happier than when he had a flesh-and-blood audience to play with. That is why his most valuable film is the 1940 feature *Hoots Mon!* in which he plays an alter ego, Harry Hawkins, billed as 'England's Funniest Comedian'. This provides a valuable visual record of parts of his stage act, right down to his whistling, his soft-shoe shuffle, the cartwheel across the stage, for which he didn't use a double, not to mention his spectacular attempt at the splits. Halfway down he would say, 'First half first house, second half second house,' or 'Tomorrow,' if it *was* the second house.

Above: Max as Educated Evans
Right: Max with Beryl and George Formby aboard Max's cabin cruiser in 1950
Far right: a page from Max's scrapbook

When he topped the bill at the London Casino in October 1947, Lionel Hale, theatre critic of the *Daily Mail*, dubbed him 'The Pure Gold of the Music Hall', a label which with the peacock vanity of his stage character he proudly used until the end of his career. He died in semi-retirement from complications following influenza after a long period of ill health beset by cardiac problems in his beloved Brighton on 7 May 1963. One of the last people to enjoy his company was his friend John M. East, who recalled acting as companion on what proved to be Max's last visit to London. Having met at Victoria, they then at Max's insistence walked in companionable silence to Piccadilly, through Green Park, past Buckingham Palace and back to the station. It was time for the old stager to catch his train. As John expressed his affection to the older man in what he rightly sensed was a last farewell, the master replied, 'Good of you to say so, but I haven't got a very high opinion of myself.' Then a twinkle flashed in his eyes as he added, 'But the Cheeky Chappie – he was a great bloke, wasn't he?'

You like me lady don't you ?

Here's a little song beautifully
written and beautifully sung

Well you've got to look smart, haven't you?

What if I am?

Dance

Splits? No it hurts me, lady

Afterthoughts

Since his death nothing in British comedy has compromised the supremacy of Max Miller as the foremost theatre comedian of his generation and beyond, although Ken Dodd has come very close. In Miller's favour was his ability to streamline his effectiveness into a tight twenty- to thirty-minute routine: nobody missed the last bus home because he overran. His standing as a folk hero was truly cemented when alongside Tommy Handley, W. C. Fields and Laurel and Hardy he made up the comedy contingent in Sir Peter Blake's iconic 1967 cover design for the Beatles' album *Sgt Pepper's Lonely Hearts Club Band*. His identity with his beloved Brighton has similarly been perpetuated with the recently installed statue in the Royal Pavilion Gardens, perhaps somewhat redressing the balance for the loss to fire and assorted planning hazards of the resort's treasured West Pier.

In his lifetime one of his proudest boasts was that theatre managements never lost money with Miller, and later in life when he discovered one venue had not done as well as expected at the box office that week, he instructed his agent to find out the extent of the loss. He then sent a cheque to cover the shortfall of £100 to the impresario who had booked him. The theatre was the Theatre Royal, Kings Lynn, the recipient of the cheque Joe Collins, the father of actress Joan. There may well have been similar incidents. Max famously never bought a drink for anyone, but such stories go some way towards proving the lie of his meanness. He never traded upon parsimony as an integral part of his stage persona in the manner of the great American comedian Jack Benny, but the reputation persisted regardless and towards the end of his life Max took delight in telling the joke against himself.

So I went into this pub to have a drink, and six teddy boys walked in and one of them said, 'Give us six whiskies and what are you having?' I said, 'I'll have a whisky.' They said, 'Give him a large one, give him a large one.' I had a large whisky and this fellow called for six more and said, 'Give him one.' So I had another large whisky. I had six large whiskies with these teddy boys and I looked at the clock... half past ten. I said, 'Sorry, I've got to be going now.' So one of them said, 'Just a minute, aren't you Max Miller?' I said, 'Yes.' He said, 'You've got a lot of property in Brighton, haven't you?' I said, 'Yes, I've got one or two hotels and about half a dozen houses.' He said, 'Well, you want to sell one of them and buy a round of drinks!'

In real life he was a quiet-living man who, as John East's recollection shows, had the wisdom to distance himself from his creation. In fact, he was a great humanitarian, his closet philanthropy extending from lending his spacious mansion at Ovingdean, just outside Brighton, to St Dunstan's for the use of blind servicemen for the duration of the war to countless unrecorded acts of kindness to people who had fallen on hard times, often visiting Brighton magistrates' court incognito to pay the fines of drunks and vagrants. On one occasion for several days he placed his Rolls and chauffeur at the disposal of a sad old-timer whose wife had been hospitalised many miles away.

As for those drinks, Roy Hudd and Eddy Kay, Roy's erstwhile stage partner, were once invited by Max for a drink in the bar to discuss their act during the interval. At first the last question he seemed interested in was 'What'll you have?' However, when the doors swung open and the audience surged in, the star was immediately bombarded with offers of liquid refreshment: 'Oh, Max, what'll you have?' 'Oh, I'll have a Scotch and my two friends here will each have a beer,' said Miller. He then turned to Roy and whispered, 'Let them buy it. It gives them a thrill.' An exceedingly young Barry Cryer once spent a morning with him before a radio broadcast from London's Playhouse Theatre. In the course of the morning Cryer was treated to two cups of tea, half a packet of cigarettes and two beers. He felt honoured. Max later told Cryer that 'he was not disposed to buy drinks for seventeen strangers, only for friends'. As John Osborne remarked, at a time when the top rate of income tax was 19/6 in the pound, he was entitled to hold on to what he'd earned.

It is difficult given the shock value of so much that passes for comedy today to assess Miller against the contemporary scene. He prided himself that he never swore on stage, and if he could be let out of his particular purgatory to be reconstituted in all his exotic glory for one last night, it is hard to imagine he would have to swear today. Social values have inevitably changed over the last fifty years, but when listened to on the lustrous recordings he has left behind he remains truly fresh and spectacularly funny in a manner achieved by few of his contemporaries. It all comes back to that rhythm, carrying audiences along on a wondrous wave of enjoyment that recognises neither time nor place. In his day he was the ultimate alternative. But while I cringe at the antics of relatively feeble performers who might pretend to his crown – on radio phone-ins, hosting ubiquitous award shows or crudely strutting their stand-up stuff in today's clubs and arenas – I have to admit that I don't know whether he is turning in his grave or cheering them on, critical of their lack of technique maybe, but living through them the glorious thrill of cocking a snook at the Establishment. No one did it better than Max. His special skill was to do so with style and without displaying an iota of malice towards a single member of his potential public.

One searches for the most fitting accolade with which to end this assessment. Perhaps it derives from the occasion the ill-disciplined high jinks of the Crazy Gang were getting out of hand and backstage discontent at the Palladium was threatening the future of the show. Impresario George Black called an early-morning rehearsal and gave the team a dressing-down which ended with the pertinent observation 'You're all bloody lucky to be here. As acts outside the Crazy Gang, you'd be hard pressed to make a living. Take Max Miller. He's got more talent in his little finger than any of you have got in your whole body – remember that!'

Perhaps it comes from a later time. There wasn't a single comic of the post-war generation who wasn't energised by Miller's example, and Tony Hancock, who first trod the boards at sixteen years old in homage to his idol as 'The Confidential Comic', was no exception. In what was the last major interview he gave – to the Australian magazine *Chance* – just before he took his own life, he nominated Max as the outstanding British comedian of his lifetime: 'This was a very kind man. He was very much underwritten.

He did charity privately, which was never known. And so he died. And everybody said he was very mean. He wasn't though. He was terribly funny… the greatest front-cloth comic we've ever had.'

Perhaps one should let the performer and his performance speak for themselves, like that night at the Brixton Empress when the audience reaction was slower than usual and Max exhibited a mastery of stage control shared by none. Halfway through his act he sauntered offstage, walked behind the backcloth, had a few words with the stagehands, then re-entered from the other side. The stage was empty for a good sixty seconds. To the audience it seemed like an eternity, but Max retained complete command. 'I'm back – just to make you appreciate me all the more. Haven't I got lovely blue eyes, lady? Do you fancy me, girl? You do? Well, you've got good taste.' At the risk of repetition, 'There'll never be another, lady. No, there'll never be another!' There was scant conceit to the remark, because it was true.

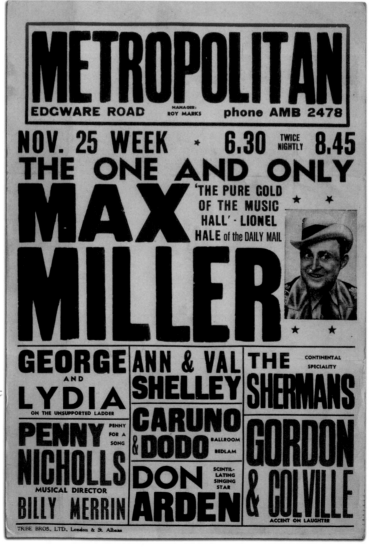

*Max Miller on his way to the
London Palladium in 1953*

Robb Wilton: 'The day war broke out...'

This customer goes into a pub and he says to the feller behind the bar, 'Excuse me, pal, but could you let me have a Scotch and soda without flavour?' The feller behind the bar said, 'Certainly, sir, with pleasure. What flavour would you like it without?' So the customer says, 'Blimey, I hadn't thought about that! What flavour have you got it without?' So the barman looks up at some bottles on the shelf and he says, 'Wait a minute. I've got it without vanilla. I've got it without lime juice. I've got it without lemon. But,' he said, 'I've got it *with* peppermint.' The customer says, 'Oh 'ell, that's the one flavour I wanted it without!'

Small-town politics, petty officialdom and magistrates' courts were far from Lewis Carroll's mind when he visualised the perplexing rabbit hole that led so weirdly to Alice's frenetic adventures. And yet the man whose flustering comic charm was to find its cosiest outlet amid the former would have been surprisingly at home in that curious tunnel. In his article 'Alice on the Stage', in the *Theatre*, April 1887, Carroll wrote

And the White Rabbit, what of *him*? Was *he* framed on the 'Alice' lines, or meant as a contrast? As a contrast distinctly. For *her* youth, audacity, vigour, and swift alertness of purpose, read elderly, timid, feeble, and nervously shilly-shallying, and you will get *something* of what I meant him to be. I am sure his voice should quaver, and his knees quiver, and his whole air suggest a total inability to say 'Bo' to a goose!

It is not hard to see Robb Wilton's Mr Muddlecombe in those lines, right down to the stipulation 'elderly', emphasising that however successful Wilton had been on the variety stage during his early years, it was not until late in life that radio brought him his own peak in popularity.

If the success of the Muddlecombe saga led people to forget his earlier prominence, it must have completely obscured from memory an even earlier period of theatrical activity. Born Robert Wilton Smith on 28 August 1881 in Everton, Liverpool, at the age of eighteen Robb, like George Robey before him, abandoned a tentative career in engineering and in 1899 entered the straight theatre as a member of the stock company at a Liverpool venue known by locals as the Old Blood Tub. Such was the popular demand for melodrama in those days. If Wilton was usually cast as the villain, there was seasonal compensation at pantomime time when he would switch to playing dame. Two rewarding incidents did occur, however, during the months given over to blood and thunder. It is alleged that once when playing a prison warder he unwittingly donned a cap several sizes too small for him. Now with the task of evoking sobs, he found that only chuckles were forthcoming. As the appeal of melodrama declined, he determined to become a comedian, the minuscule hat he so often wore on stage in later years becoming his first trademark. His first engagement outside the warm security of the stock company was at the Liverpool Lyric, from which it was a short step to the Liverpool Pavilion. There he was seen by Sir Walter de Frece, who gave him a three-year contract which led in turn to his first London appearance, at the Royal Holborn in 1909 billed as 'The Confidential Comedian'. The second incident was again a contradiction of the laws of melodrama. While playing in *Greed of Gold* at the Alexandra Theatre, Hull in 1903, the villain, admittedly offstage, wooed the heroine, played by Florence Palmer, and won. Robb gained more than a wife. If Wilton was to emerge as one of the finest of all sketch comedians, her active participation in his act was to prove invaluable.

Whether in his sketches or in his solo act, the predominant mood of a Wilton performance was one of quiet puzzled thoughtfulness. When the situation became more perplexing, the increased anxiety seldom resulted in the raising of his phlegmatic Lancastrian drone, but rather in the controlled interplay of hand and mouth in one of a number of carefully studied gestures – playing a tune upon his teeth, rubbing his chin, chewing his little finger or passing an anxious hand over an equally anxious brow. Always more profound meditation would leave him even more bewildered, while his physical build, thickset and stocky, only emphasised the slow, effortless yet deliberate approach.

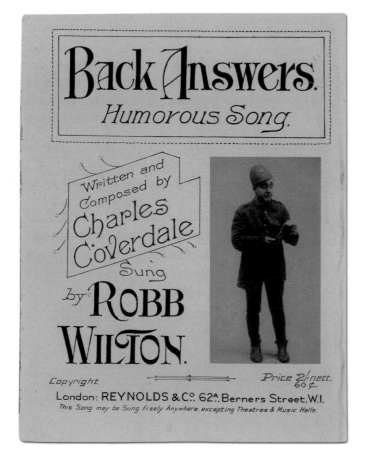

An air of bored nonchalance and harassed ineptitude characterised those solemn officials who were the pivotal figures of his stage sketches. 'Sherlock Bill' presented him in sole charge of a modest police station trying to come to terms with a woman who has voluntarily confessed to poisoning her husband. Casually the admission is entered in the ledger. However, only when the constable has blatantly asked her what she wants the police to do about it, does one find oneself on true Wilton territory. Her reply that she is offering herself up befuddles him still further. Petty trivialities take precedence over critical emergencies. 'That's made a mess of the books, that has,' he complains, sinking gradually into an abyss of upended logic, until finally engulfed by his refusal to have anything to do with her and his own preoccupation with his evening meal.

In 'The Fire Chief' the calm, to be expected in a station with no telephone, is shattered by another agitated female whose house is on fire. His attempts to engage her in conversation about the weather fail. He hands her a form to fill in, only to be advised by the woman that this should wait until the fire is extinguished. Concerned for her husband's plight, she dashes back to the scene as Wilton calls after her, 'Could you try to keep it going till we get there?' Eventually he unhooks a speaking tube and makes contact with Arnold, his assistant, who is busy doing the football sweep. 'You mustn't let things like that interfere with duty,' he sternly remonstrates, and then, after the requisite pause, 'What have I drawn?' He continues:

Arnold, how are we fixed for petrol? I know it's no good for putting fires out, you blithering... Have you got enough to get you there? What? Enough to get there and not get back? Oh well, it's no good going if you can't get back. Oh, I see, Arnold, you think you can manage it? Well, it's a pretty big fire... (aside)... should be by now! Well, I'll leave that to you and Harry then, Arnold. Oh, I say, Arnold... take the dog with you... It'll be a run for it!

By now the woman has returned to watch the conflagration from a distance. She sees the fire engine arrive and Arnold climb the ladder. He is about to enter the blazing building when Robb protests, 'He mustn't do that – he's got the football sweep money on him!'

In another sketch the daily duties of his 'Prison Guv'nor' entail interviewing a murderess who has refused to leave even though her sentence is up. For once he is firm, but at her pronouncement that she will merely search for another victim he declares, 'Very well, but we can't promise you the same cell. With race week coming in, we're bound to be full up!' Later a Magwitch type pays him a social call, the friendliness of which is only marred by the convict's remark that whenever he has imbibed a couple of whiskies he feels a compulsive urge to kill a prison governor. Eventually he finds himself at the ruffian's mercy, fingers around his throat. The full absurdity of the situation is not brought home, however, until the telephone rings, the governor answers and, finding it to be a wrong number, mutters impatiently, 'Always interrupting when I'm busy.' Casually he replaces the receiver and succumbs again to the intoxicated assault of his guest.

'Dope' was an extension and elaboration of 'Sherlock Bill'. The setting was transferred from more congenial Britain to gangster-infested America, but the desire to poke fun at his own background in melodrama was again prominent, as was his recurring inability to see the difference between normal and abnormal, logical and illogical. Anne, the vampire, has just committed murder when Wilton, as the detective, bursts in upon her. After the traditional confession she adds, 'Now go and call the police.' Wilton is outraged at this suggestion, which he naturally construes as a direct aspersion on his efficiency. As he explains, his leaving would provide her with the opportunity to escape. He has a better idea: 'I'll stay here; you go for the police.' If his attempt at an American accent won less favour with his admirers than his cautious northern drawl, the logic of the situation was happily poised upon as shaky a foundation as ever.

While his mock officials hadn't the foggiest idea what was expected of them, their awareness of the surrounding world was possibly more acute than that of his soldier in the sketch entitled, with apologies to playwright R. C. Sherriff, 'His Journey's End'. Twelve years after the armistice of 1918, he is still hibernating in his dugout 'just to be on the safe side' when he finds a Frenchman planting cabbages at the threshold. Nobody has told him the war is over. In his anxiety to take his wife a present on his return to Blighty, a spare bomb has to suffice. Unfortunately it far too closely resembles her Christmas pudding, one of those domestic terrors that, along with pestering relatives, would appear to make home life no more attractive than his recent environment. The bomb inevitably finds its way into the oven, only to blow up Wilton in his flurried attempt to save the rest of the family from disaster. Not, however, until the laughter of anticipation has been milked to its greatest extent.

Perhaps for Wilton his most influential sketch was 'The Magistrate'. Included in the Royal Variety Performance of 1926, it foreshadowed his subsequent success as radio's Mr Muddlecombe JP. Sadly it fell prey to cuts and timing complications in the royal show, but this was perhaps significant. The fear of such a fate befalling the biggest star on such an occasion would eventually pass into the catalogue of theatrical superstition. Ironically, the humour of the sketch was itself predicated on the notion that the entire human race is the constant prey of superstitious terror of a more general kind. One moment sees Wilton courageously bracing himself to face the burglar now breaking into his house, the next wilting pitiably as the picture destined to drop fifteen minutes before its owner is due to die falls with an ominous thud. This dialogue between courage and cowardice persisted in Wilton's work, a reminder of his early days at the Blood Tub and now seen through the comic perspective provided by his flustered, blethering stage persona, appropriately garnering delighted laughter rather than muffled screams.

It was not until the late 30s that Wilton introduced Mr Muddlecombe JP to radio and found himself undisputed top of the bill as a variety attraction. If the germ of the idea had been in 'The Magistrate' and the other confused officials soldiering on as they attempted to combine dignity and inaction, the vast possibilities it presented were not realised until Wilton began to visit local police courts as a means of relaxation on provincial variety tours. The amusing cases he heard and the eccentricities of the magistrates themselves soon led to the institution on the airwaves of the 'Court of Not-so Common Pleas' with Mr Muddlecombe in the chair. One broadcast in which Muddlecombe, presiding while under the influence of drink, invites a glamorous lady complainant to meet him in the local when the court rose provoked a protest from the Magistrates' Association. The official reply of Lord (then Sir John) Reith, the director general of the BBC, reflected the feelings of countless Wilton fans whose letters poured into the offices of the national press. All stressed that the broadcast was so farcical – the charges had included racing tortoises within the thirty-mile limit – that in no way could it be regarded as any reflection on the judicial system. Perhaps Wilton knew otherwise, even if he did express surprise at the protest.

Wilton proved an expert broadcaster. B. C. Hilliam, Flotsam of the comic song duo Flotsam and Jetsam, and himself a master of the medium, wrote in the *Stage* in 1937, 'One can almost see the mobile hand passing over the puzzled countenance at pointed intervals. Some artists sound as if they drop their mannerisms at the mike; Robb's sort sound as if they are all there.' It was a natural development, therefore, when the activities of Mr Muddlecombe expanded beyond the courtroom, his career of ineptitude spreading over a wider field. Returning, for instance, to his native village of Nether Backwash, he became chairman of the district council, an account of his activities being presented to the public under the series title *Public Futilities*. One meeting of the council was to discuss the building of a bypass, a project welcomed by Mr Muddlecombe but opposed by the village shopkeepers.

Mr Muddlecombe: But we must keep up with the times, be up to date. Bless my life, every decent town these days has its bypass!
Shopkeeper: My argument is that we don't have enough passers-by to want a bypass.
Mr Muddlecombe: No. But the passers-by who do pass by, if they had a bypass to pass by, would be able to pass by the bypass.

Even if it means pulling down private property, Mr Muddlecombe is convinced.

Mr Muddlecombe: Private individuals cannot be specially considered in a matter of so great importance to the welfare of the city, the – er – town, the – er – Nether Backwash. It is all perfectly clear to me that sacrifices must be made by one and all if our noble aims are to succeed.

He is convinced, that is, until his own house is included in the demolition schedule.

Mr Muddlecombe: I'd no idea that this bypass would mean the pulling down of so much property.
Surveyor: A bypass is not possible without.
Mr Muddlecombe: Then you mean that the whole of the High Street must be removed?
Surveyor: Decidedly!
Mr Muddlecombe: And that property belonging to Major Todd?
Surveyor: Absolutely!
Mr Muddlecombe: And all Meredith's farm buildings, and my house and grounds?
Surveyor: Most essential!
Mr Muddlecombe: But that's all there is of Nether Backwash!
Major Todd: Then it simply means that for Nether Backwash to have a bypass, Nether Backwash has got to be entirely removed?
Surveyor: Quite!
Mr Muddlecombe: But if there's no Nether Backwash, there's no need for a bypass?
Surveyor: None whatever.
Mr Muddlecombe: Then we will not be having a bypass!

The decision is final, the seal set on insignificance.

On radio intermittently between 1937 and 1948, Mr Muddlecombe was equally confusing in series called *Office Hours* ('the place looks more like a pub than a solicitor's office'), *At Home*, and, most surprisingly, towards the end of the Second World War as the fairground manager in the variety series *Hoop-La!* The hostilities themselves, however, provided Wilton with the most famous of his extra-legal activities. To quote the immortal monologue:

> The day war broke out, my missus said to me, 'What good are you?' I said, 'How d'you mean, what good am I?' 'Well,' she said, 'you're too old for the army, you couldn't get into the navy, and they wouldn't have you in the air force, so what good are you?'... I said, 'There'll be munitions.' She said, 'How can you go on muni –' I said, 'I never said anything about going on munitions. I said there'll *be* some.' 'Well,' she said, 'all the young fellers'll be getting called up and you'll have to go back to work.' (*After a perfectly judged pause*) Oooh, she's got a cruel tongue!

Robb Wilton as Mr Muddlecombe JP

As things stand, he doesn't have to go back to work: 'I'm a lamp lighter.' Instead he joins the Home Guard, 'for the duration, unless it finishes before then'. Not that Wilton, Harry Bates, Charlie Evans and all his other mates ever strayed far in their duties from their HQ, a little hut situated conveniently behind their local, the Dog and Pullet. As for the enemy, he has to admit he's never met Hitler. 'Well, how're you going to know which is him, if they do land?' asks the wife. 'I've got a tongue in my head, haven't I?' responds Robb.

While Jack Warner's 'Garrison Theatre' radio character with his famous line 'Mind my bike' addressed itself directly to the troops, Wilton secured his success by turning to comic advantage the realisation that this was essentially a civilian war. Not only were civilians as involved as those in uniform, but they far outnumbered the troops. He could hardly now escape becoming a national figure. Henpecked and war-harassed, he became firmly rooted in a world of waste paper for the war effort and twenty-six coupons for a suit. It was also a world of so called middle-class respectability: aspidistras in the front room, pianos being tuned which no one can play, and jumble sales of things people buy but have no use for. The great significance of Wilton's Home Guard was that, whereas in his earlier sketches he had portrayed an amateur masquerading as a professional, now *everyone* was an amateur. He was the hero of all those who ever fumbled their way through pike drill in preparation for the invasion that never was, all those who managed to escape into civil defence for an evening at the local away from the trials of domestic life. He was the hero of many.

Jack Warner, the star of radio's 'Garrison Theatre', later to become famous as television's Dixon of Dock Green

The name of Muddlecombe was appropriate. It suggested the confusion he so often brought in his wake as well as evoking the spirit of muddling through that characterised the British civilian during the conflict, a bewildered tenacity that helped the man in the street to emerge triumphant from the troubles of the time. This myth, together with all that Wilton's humour stood for during the war, was lovingly re-created in later years by television's *Dad's Army*, fronted by the brilliantly assessed performance of Arthur Lowe (1915 – 1982) as the self-appointed Captain Mainwaring, po-faced and implacable, whose self-esteem remained as impervious to attack as the shores of seaside suburbia that his men defended against the amorphous enemy in their own ramshackle way. Almost a decade before *Dad's Army* took to the air in 1968, another sitcom regular, Harry Worth (1917 – 1989), staked his own claim to following in Wilton's footsteps as the bumbling defensive blunderer, bewildered innocent and man upsetting the machine. Like Wilton he revelled in his own determined insistence that, whatever the shambles, his way remained

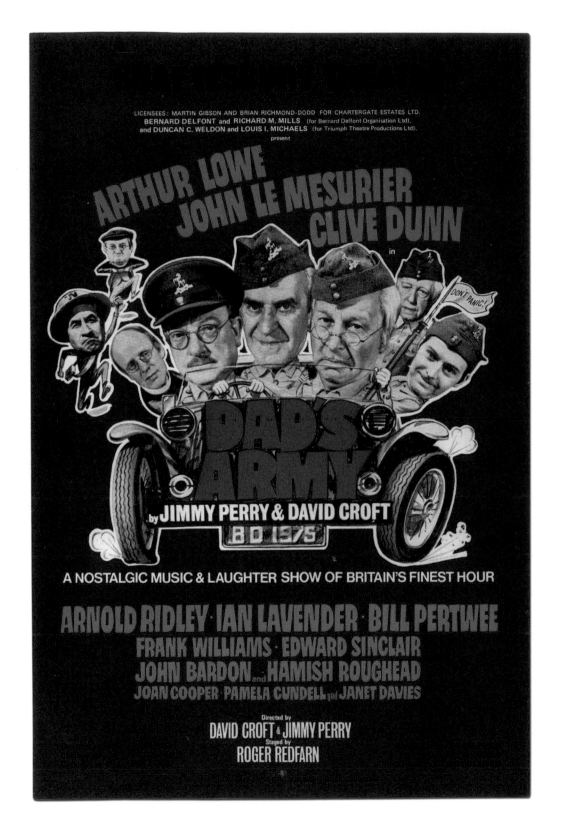

the correct one. Wilton too had doubtless been influenced by precedent. Minor officialdom had been parodied ahead of him by cockney comedian Charles Austin (1877 – 1942) as Parker PC, a character inspired by Austin seeing the notice To Let displayed in a vacant police station; by the lugubrious Alfred Lester (1872 – 1925) in his sketch 'The Village Fire Brigade' – the brigade was not of much use, but, as he explained, looked good in a procession between the Ancient Order of Foresters and the scavengers; by Wilkie Bard (1877 – 1944) as another police constable, whose patrol duties were discharged from the luxury of his shady hammock – 'I'm here if you want me;' by George Robey, both as a barrister and as the mayor of Mudcumdyke.

Wilton was perhaps more qualified as an actor than his predecessors. Indeed, on the day war broke out in 1939, he was on tour playing the part of the photographer in J. B. Priestley's *When We Are Married*, and fourteen years later as a witness in the Chancery Court in a case whereby Eastbourne Corporation unsuccessfully claimed exemption from entertainment tax for a series of summer concerts, he described himself as a 'character comedy actor'. And yet throughout his variety career he confined himself to basically the same characterisation. However much the costume changed – from fireman to soldier to Muddlecombe himself – the persona beneath remained constant, a character perhaps best summed up by his line: 'We have many grave responsibilities, but at the moment I cannot think of any.' This gives a hint of the determination with which he maintained an almost quixotic stand against the urgencies and tedium of everyday life. In doing so he performed a valuable, albeit escapist, function, his success at which was emphasised by the welcome local magistrates extended to him and by his own admission that the best audience he ever had for his policeman sketch was one composed entirely of policemen.

Even when he was telling disconnected jokes in a stand-up act, as during his last radio broadcast in *Blackpool Night* in August 1956, nine months before his death on 1 May 1957, the special aura of his most famous sketches and monologues was still present. As a teller of jokes, Wilton now became essentially a third party, no longer portraying his own adventures, but relating those of others. It is very hard, however, to disassociate the usual protagonist of the sketches from the subjects of his stories, highlighting as they do the same dialogue between mechanical common sense and Wilton's own imaginative absurdity. We know instinctively that the latter will not hold water, but this does not deny it a persuasive hopeful logic all its own, all the more acceptable because of our usual heedless acceptance of the alternative. Significantly, the opening cue for laughter had by this time become almost telegraphic. Having switched immediately after the war to 'The day peace broke out', he soon discovered that only the first two words were essential.

> *The day* Charlie Evans and me spent a night in Blackpool, a pal of Charlie's promised to give us a run around the town. So we got into the car and we were off and all of a sudden a policeman pulled us up and he said to the fellow who was driving, 'Hey, do you know you've got no lights on this car?' This fellow said, 'I don't need lights; I know every inch of the town.'

Two fellows going over the – er – going over to New York. They know each other, but they don't meet until they get into mid-ocean. One fellow sees the other. He says, 'Hello, Harry. Are you going over?' He said, 'Aye! Are you?'

Charlie Evans and me, we didn't half have a night out the other night. We didn't get home till about three in the morning. And Charlie – he's dead scared of his missus, Charlie is. And he was in a state! But he thought of an idea. He got all the fire irons together, strung 'em together, and tied 'em round his neck. As he was going upstairs, of course, the devil of a clang and bang and a noise all the way up and Charlie – he said to himself – he said, 'She'll never hear me with all this noise!'

Until the end of his career Wilton's greatest asset was his style of delivery, so suited to radio with its halting pauses, its frequent repetitions, its tuts and its ers, all carefully scripted and delivered at a quiet emphatic pace as if he really were making the words up as he went along. No philosophy ever had a more winning mouthpiece. This was a voice, one feels, specifically created to express muddle, and in the unhurried fashion that muddle would itself demand. It could also express irritation, exasperation, but never full-blooded anger, however great the provocation. Nor did its effect derive merely from the way words were pronounced, but from the semantic tangle in which they found themselves enmeshed in conversation. This snatch from a discussion between the Muddlecombes should give some idea:

Mrs Muddlecombe: Oh dear, that clock's wrong again. It's ten minutes fast.
Mr Muddlecombe: Well, I have to keep it ten minutes fast or it won't go.
Mrs M: And I don't know what's happened to the sundial in the garden. I usually put the clock right by that, but that's two hours slow, and I don't know how you alter sundials.
Mr M: Well, you can't alter sundials, dear. Don't be so stupid. You can't alter sundials.
Mrs M: Well, what's the good of them when they go wrong if you can't alter them and put them right. I looked at it at one o'clock today and it was only eleven by it.
Mr M: Well, we're two hours ahead of the sun now the clocks have been put on two hours. But you can't put a sundial back, dear. You can't if the sundial is really right. But it's – er – two hours wrong. That's all that's the matter with it.
Mrs M: How can it be right, if it's two hours wrong?
Mr M: Well, because if it was right, we'd be wrong.
Mrs M: Who would?
Mr M: Hmm – everybody.
Mrs M: Well, how do you mean?
Mr M: Now wait. Loo-loo-look! The clocks – everybody's clocks – not only ours – everybody's. They've been put forward two hours for summertime, haven't they?
Mrs M: I'm not talking about the clocks! I'm talking about the sundial.
Mr M: Yes, yes, yes, well. That's two hours behind the clocks.
Mrs M: That's what I'm saying. It's two hours slow.

Mr M: No, no, it isn't. It's right.

Mrs M: But if it's two hours slow, how can it be right?

Mr M: Because the clocks are two hours fast.

Mrs M: Oh! Then the clocks are wrong?

Mr M: No, no, no! The clocks are right?

Mrs M: Yes, but you've just said the clocks are two hours fast.

Mr M: But so they are.

Mrs M: Well, how can they be right?

Mr M: Because, they'd be wrong if they were right.

Mrs M: Oh dear, what are you talking about?

Mr M: Wait a minute, Agnes. Wait a minute. Look, the clocks are two hours fast.

Mrs M: Yes, well that makes the sundial two hours slow.

Mr M: No, no! The sundial can't be slow.

Mrs M: But, if it's two hours behind the clocks, it must be slow.

Mr M: Now, wait a minute – look – what time is it now?

Mrs M: Oh! Ten to nine.

Mr M: Yes, that's right, but it's ten to seven, and at ten to eleven it will be ten to nine, so that it'll be a quarter to seven at a quarter to nine in the morning. You don't seem to have grasped things, Agnes. You don't understand.

Few would try to follow such a conversation, but many derived pleasure from the comic nightmare of communication it represented. Moreover, however exaggerated it may be, such humour cannot but underline how tortuous a means of communication language is, how cautiously one should tread the verbal path. The style was typical of Wilton and he even embodied it – in simplified form – in a song. It was called 'Back answers'.

I'm subject to colds and they make me quite deaf,
And then I can't hear what you say.
A fellow once asked me if I'd have a drink
And I heard that *with* a cold by the way.
As we drank we got chatting of girls we had met.
I described a sweet bird dressed in red.
My description was good and my pal went half mad.
'Twas the girl he was going to wed.
He said, 'I'll punch your head;' I said, 'Whose?' he said, 'Yours.'
I said, 'Mine?' he said, 'Yes;' I said, 'Oh!'
He said, 'Want to fight?' I said, 'Who?' he said, 'You!'
I said, 'Me?' he said, 'Yes;' I said, 'No!'
So we then got to words, and he said, 'You're a cad.'

I said, 'Cad?' he said, 'Yes;' I said, 'Who?'
He said, 'Who?' I said, 'Yes;' He said, 'You.'
I said, 'Me?' he said, 'Yes.'
So, of course, then I knew!

Fellow performer Ted Ray said of Wilton that he 'had warmth in greater measure than any living comedian'. Certainly for someone who set himself the task of commenting upon the ridiculous world around him his manner was reassuringly gentle. One is tempted to use the word satire, but the barbed bitterness that acts as the adrenaline of the latter is totally absent from his work. What one finds instead is a true love for humanity. Meanwhile Mr Muddlecombe himself was never happier than when supposedly sorting out a pile of papers.

We can't hurl it all out higgledy-piggledy. We must have method of some kind. Now look, you'd better grab a couple of handfuls of it, and I'll grab hold of a bunch and – er – now – Mrs Golightly – give her a handful as well. Then throw them all onto the floor and start sorting them out between us. That's the only thing! Here you are. Now Adolphus (*his office boy*) – there you are. And I'll get hold of these. Empty them on to the floor, Mrs Golightly. That's right. That's the idea. Now, you put yours on top, Adolphus. I'll put these on the top of yours, you see. That's all we want. *System!* That's all!

It all remained, of course, as higgledy-piggledy as ever. For Robb Wilton there was no other way.

AFTERTHOUGHTS

Within the sketch format Wilton proved himself a master comedy character actor, and were he around today there is no doubt he would be in constant demand for situation comedy. This should not detract, however, from his spontaneous sense of humour offstage, of which there are many examples. Towards the end of his career he found himself playing a footballers' social club. Things were not easy for him as driving rain beat a tattoo on the corrugated-iron roof, and the strains of band practice by the Boys' Brigade next door conspired to make things worse. When on top of all this a waiter dropped a tray of drinks, Robb remarked with his resigned sigh, 'I think they're trying to train me to be a police horse.' On another occasion the following exchange was reported to have been overheard between Wilton and a lone individual he had never met before. The fellow was literally crying into his beer.

Robb: Whatever's the matter?
Man: Oh, it's being here by myself.
Robb: Well, I'm here now.
Man: I mean being by myself in life. I'm so terribly lonely.
Robb: Oh, cheer up. What'll you have to drink?
Man: A large brandy.
Robb: A large brandy? No wonder you're bloody lonely.

Perhaps the best example of his mordant wit – previously attributed wrongly to Jimmy James – centred upon the time he shared lodgings on tour with Arthur Askey. The star-conscious landlady had converted her stairwell into a signed portrait gallery of the names of the day. As they climbed the stairs, she wasted no time in assuring them they would be staying in the best digs in the land: 'You see, we've had Gracie here, and Bud and Ches, and George and Beryl!' As they reached the top of the landing they were confronted by a reproduction of Leonardo's *The Last Supper*. 'Oh,' commented, Robb, 'and I see you've had Dr Crock and his Crackpots here as well!' Arthur later related, 'She slung us out there and then!' Dr Crock and his ensemble were a comedy orchestra whose onstage zaniness and musical unpredictability were matched by their overall appearance of clownish disreputability.

Wilton wrote most of his own material, sometimes with his wife and stage partner, Florence, although in later years under pressure from the demands of radio the Muddlecombe oeuvre was considerably enhanced by the writer and producer Max Kester. Wilton's star billing on stage and radio did not transfer to films, although he brightened up at least a dozen movies with his cameo performances, aside from innumerable shorts of his sketches made for Pathé. Among the most memorable of these excursions are guest appearances as a magistrate in Gracie Fields' *Love, Life and Laughter* in 1934 and Arthur Askey's *The Love Match* nineteen years later. Stars as secure as these two had no fear of being upstaged in their own movies, which of course they were.

George Formby: 'It's turned out nice again!'

Well, this man went into a talent agent's office and said he did parrot impersonations. The agent said, 'I'm sorry. I can't use you. Bird impersonators are ten a penny.' The man said, 'That's a pity,' turned, and flew out of the window!

The essence of George Formby's professionalism amounted to more than the appeal of his irresistible grin, flawless ukulele technique and cracked Lancashire tones. At no point in his performing career did he appear anything more than an enthusiastically talented amateur doing something for the sheer fun of it. He himself once admitted, 'I wasn't very good, but I had something the public seemed to want.' This only emphasises the amateur's touch. His stage act varied little from the day in 1925 when he first incorporated the strum machine into his performance until his premature death in March 1961, a cosy medley of those broad catchy songs that he made his own and the haggard out-of-date jokes to which he would cling with loyalty when other top-liners had long forsaken them, with a special fondness for parrot gags – like 'knock, knock' jokes, a comedy craze of an earlier time. But while the basic material of the act may not have been very good, and was certainly in the beginning stereotyped and conducive to anonymity, the technique with which it was delivered came to reach a perfection as spectacular as the performer himself was endearing, his modesty genuine. It is hard to believe that George, the perpetual innocent, ever became aware of any improvement in that technique over the years.

George Formby held the notable distinction in the variety profession of becoming the even more famous son of an already famous father. George Formby Senior (1875 – 1921), known in the north of England as the Wigan Nightingale, was perhaps the most tragic figure of the authentic music hall period. He created the character 'John Willie', the archetypal gormless Lancashire lad, the epitome of northern humour born of misery and deprivation, pathetic for his diffidence, poverty-stricken clothing and persistent bronchial cough. The latter prompted many asides to the musical director: 'Coughin' better tonight; coughin' summat champion.' 'Come on – I'll cough you for a shilling,' he would challenge the orchestra. Ironically, the more he coughed, the more the audience laughed. But while no audience ever did die laughing, for George the cough proved not merely painful but eventually fatal. He had long been aware of his tubercular condition, but the pull of the boards and the natural desire to make as much future provision for his family as he could in the years left to him destroyed any possibility of recuperation. To discover the peculiar essence of his stage character one has only to scan the titles of his songs: 'I'm such a hit with the girls', 'One of the boys', 'Looking for mugs in the strand', 'Since I parted my hair in the middle'. But however much his persona tried to justify itself among what he considered superior company, there was always the cough above all else to let George down and evoke gales of laughter from the auditorium. His most memorable number had him 'Playing the game in the west', a self-styled daredevil or young dog adrift in the daring city, flirting with the girls, throwing his money about and determined not to return home till a quarter to ten on his one night out. The most telling indication of his talent and professional status is that Marie Lloyd herself would deign to watch only two of her contemporaries: one was Dan Leno, the other George Formby Senior.

Above and below:
George Formby Senior

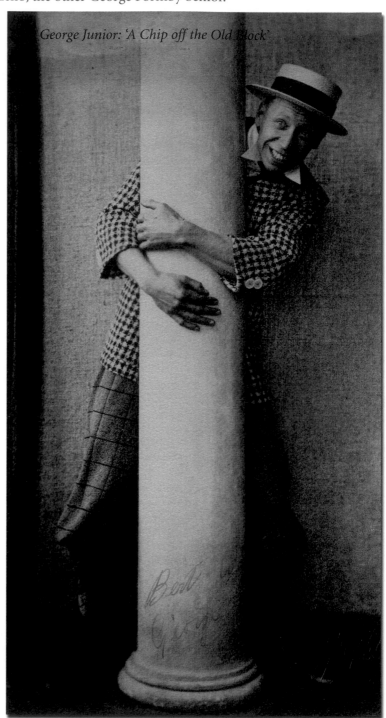

George Junior: 'A Chip off the Old Block'

The son was born on 26 May 1904 in Wigan, where his father's fertile imagination coined the phrase Wigan Pier to describe the small landing stage on the branch of the recently opened (1894) Manchester Ship Canal, which connected Wigan with Warrington. The family surname was Booth, and young George was not originally destined for the theatre. Later in his career he remarked, 'I never saw dad on the stage. He wouldn't let me. He used to say, "One fool in the family's enough."' He was born blind and was not able to see until some weeks later when a coughing fit removed the obstructive caul while he was crossing the River Mersey as a babe in his mother's arms. His boyhood was spent at a riding stables, where he trained as an apprentice jockey. He did in fact become the youngest ever jockey to compete professionally when he entered a race in Lord Derby's colours at the age of ten weighing an incredible three stone thirteen pounds. His own eventual overweight, his father's death and the subsequent plagiarism of George Senior's material by lesser performers led him to break his previous resolution never to tread the boards, and in April 1921 he made his first professional appearance at the Hippodrome, Earlestown. Anxious not to trade on his father's reputation, he adopted his mother's maiden name and was first billed as George Hoy. By August 1924, however, he had achieved the heights of a West End booking at the Alhambra Music Hall in Leicester Square and assumed the Formby name. Initially his mannerisms and style were similar to those of his father and the ukulele had yet to be added to the act. That month he treated the London audience to a burlesque of a shabby depressed man, in the idiom of his father, singing appropriately 'I'm a jockey', together with, as if to stress that he did have definite ideas of his own, a skit on an anarchist complete with plum-pudding bomb, sweeping cloak and slouch hat. From around this time dates another sketch set in an auctioneer's, in which George discovers he has bought six picture postcards for sixpence: 'Eee, I've been done – they've got no stamps!' Then there was his burlesque of another of nature's losers, a man with one leg in plaster attempting to balance as he fends off with two sticks the dog pestering the cast.

It was not long before he developed his own individual style. Both father and son paraded an air of good-natured gormless naivety, but while the father was mournful, lugubrious, subdued, the son had a lighter, fresher, more attractive approach, typified by the resilience with which he would meet the blows fate dealt him, the smile of perpetual wonder as he met them, and always the unspoken suggestion that lurking behind the ingenuousness was a subtle cunning which knew that the solution to life's problems at any level mentally more demanding than that of simple high spirits was doomed to failure. Certainly George Formby knew no other way and yet always emerged triumphant. It is ironic that while his father's trademark had been a hacking cough, his own should be a warm throaty chuckle, the perfect vocal complement to the batter-pudding face, glistening eyes and horse-toothed grin.

The cornerstone of any Formby performance was provided by the usually predictable ditties that he described with characteristic simplicity as 'me daft little songs'. In his lifetime he recorded no fewer than 189 of them, and when his recording contract expired in 1946 it was supposed that the supply had become exhausted. And yet after his death over two hundred unrecorded songs were discovered. He sang them in a cracked voice, jaunty and enthusiastic, unmistakably Lancashire, and once likened with vivid accuracy to a 'fire bellows masquerading in the top register of a mouth organ'. What he lacked in vocal quality, he made up for in his faultless pointing of the lyrics, the instinctive jogging of his swivel neck to right or left and the suggestive wink emphasising those crucial moments of double entendre with the casual precision of a metronome. But for his engaging ukulele technique the songs were not musically inspiring, all falling into a similar pattern, permutations of a handful of basic tunes. However, that essential 'this'll make you whistle' quality was always present, underpinned by the calm confidence of the performer as he sang them that everybody else would soon be doing the same.

Formby's vocal repertoire thrived on a world of appalling mothers-in-law, henpecked husbands and nudists either brazen or bashful but never in between, of satin bloomers, faulty plumbing and charabanc rides. It was a world where births were always multiple, the birds above did everything but sing, laxatives were inevitably too powerful and gout was the greatest calamity that could befall man. It was the world of the seaside comic postcard, and the similarity was not merely one of subjects, but also of treatment. One can discern an eerie parallel between the garish, monotonous yet happy expanses of colour that characterise the popular art form and the persistent rhythms that form the basis of the Formby numbers, between the crude forceful quality of the line drawing in the former and the blatant poetic licence that frequently distinguishes the rhyming and word order in the latter. And yet both, because rather than in spite of these faults, remain unmistakably alive and warm, true to that niggling, humiliating side of life which we do not necessarily welcome but have to accept, and which, if we are to accept, we might as well do so with laughter.

The world of Donald McGill and his fellow artists, however, became stereotyped for the simple reason that in its escapism it was commenting upon a society already stereotyped, dreary and monotonous. It was hidebound by an attitude that said that the greatest adventure for the working class was its annual visit to the seaside (an attitude that in the 1930s had a distinct truth, and persists still if you equate Majorca with Blackpool), by the fact that the more tedious a man's working day, the less varied will be his leisure hours. It was the same depressing world as that of the people who bought the postcards, only seen from an outrageously comic perspective. By way of contrast, Formby's songs were often refreshingly adventurous in the new horizons they encompassed. As Orwell pointed out, in the seaside postcard foreigners seldom if ever appeared, unless one includes the inevitable Scotsman with his short kilt and scrawny knees. The characters of some of Formby's most famous numbers, however, ranged from 'Madame Moscovitch, the Moscow witch', a Gypsy palmist who unfortunately continued to talk in Russian when she read your palm, and yet

> If you pay a quid then she
> Will unfold her mystery,
> And you'll see much more
> Than you did before
> Of the Russian Gypsy Queen!

to the Indian 'Hindoo-Howdoo-Hoodoo-Yoodoo-Man', ninety-nine years old and smoking opium and bits of rope all day.

A princess gave him pearls and said, 'For all your love I yearn,'
But jewels could not compare with what he went and gave her in return!

There was 'Don Pedro, the great bullfighting hero, the Lancashire Toreador', who turned out to be none other than George himself.

They cheer me,
And when the bull gets near me,
To show how far a brave man can go,
With the bull I dance the tango.

He was altogether more enterprising than his two-dimensional cardboard counterparts, restricted by way of relaxation to sex, alcohol, seaside and the great outdoors. Nothing made George happier than when he was 'Riding in the TT races'.

In a fifty-mile race I am the best.
I ride five miles and skid the rest!
So come along and see me
Riding in the TT races;
Easier than hopscotch,
Beating all the topnotch aces.

In 'The best of schemes' we find him 'a rascal for sport', full of overzealous self-confidence, accepting a hundred-pound bet that he can swim the Channel. After swimming for fourteen hours in the freezing water:

I reached the other side and said, 'The money I'll take,'
And then I found I'd swum the Serpentine by mistake.

Another good scheme had gone wrong.

Even the conservative rhythms of the most typical Formby numbers went out of their way on at least two occasions to celebrate, even if by parody (while still remaining distinct Formby material) what were then more sophisticated imported musical trends. On the other hand, it was impossible for the robust overpowering art of McGill ever to acknowledge the equally stylised and subsequently more influential graphic styles that in 1930s America immortalised the adventures of Tarzan, Superman, Dick Tracy and Li'l Abner in newspaper strip format, and would come to revolutionise popular art in this country, rescuing it from the rut typified by the earlier *Comic Cuts* tradition. 'John Willie's Jazz Band' was at once a nominal tribute to Formby's father's famous character and a burlesque of an American rhythm expert, the personnel of the band having been largely recruited among the 'coal-black pit shafts down in Wigan land'. Far removed from Tennessee, their combined musical talents were strangely capable of turning black puddings white with fear, and when they came inevitably to play on Wigan Pier itself, the first reaction of passers-by was to fill their ears with sand. Then there was the craze for popular vocalists to attach the meaningless phrase 'do-de-o-do' to everything they sang. Formby, unlike the majority, refused to dismiss this as nonsense. Characteristically his song 'Do-de-o-do' was literally restricted to thoughts of money, home cooking and female rabbits, never the sheer joy of carefree musical improvisation.

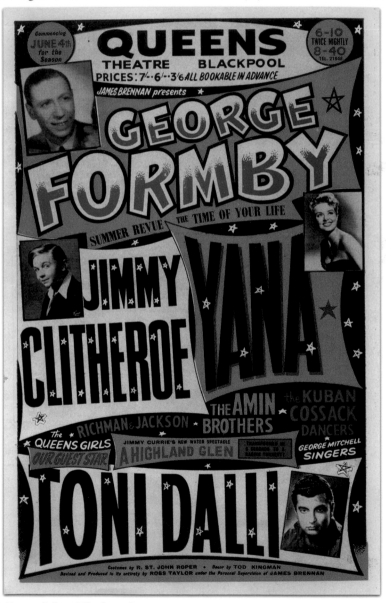

George's last Blackpool season, 1960

However, whatever scope the songs offered for the variety, adventure and innovation denied to the graphic tradition, it was against the background of the seaside comic postcard that Formby was most at home.

> With me little stick of Blackpool rock
> Along the promenade I stroll.
> It may be sticky, but I never complain,
> It's nice to have a nibble at it now and again.
> Everyday, wherever I stray, the kids all round me flock.
> One afternoon the band conductor up on the stand
> Somehow lost his baton; it flew out of his hand.
> So I jumped in his place and then conducted the band
> With me little stick of Blackpool rock.

In the 1930s and 40s the theatres of Blackpool were a spiritual home to Formby, and it was at the Queen's Theatre in 1960 that he appeared in his last summer show. It is hard now to imagine his rollicking jaunty little tunes being composed without the people who stroll along that most flaunting of promenades in mind. His round face with its famous cheeky grin could have been specially moulded for inserting in those life-size cutouts, so favoured by beach photographers for giving the frowziest of old maids a Miss World figure and the most tormented of husbands even knobblier knees and hairier legs. There was one song, however, that took Formby back even closer to his roots than numbers like 'Swimmin' with the women' and 'Sitting on the top of Blackpool Tower'. 'In a little Wigan garden', essentially comic-realist in its treatment of the more depressing side of industrial Lancashire life, he sang with a vivid poignancy that rendered the lyric dignified, touching and humane. George, forsaking grand park, hills and dales, clung loyally to a postage-stamp plot of gravel and fought a losing battle against the encroaching smoke and grime in a garden where crocuses croaked with gasworks smog, whatever did grow grew upside down, and the scented breezes that wafted down from the chimneys were not the most conducive to the success of a courting career.

> In a little Wigan garden,
> With me little Wigan knees,
> Getting stung with bumblebees,
> Between the cabbage and the peas;
> 'Neath the Wigan water lilies,
> Where the drainpipe overflows,
> There's my girl and me,
> She'll sit on me knee,
> And watch how the rhubarb grows.

There was an affinity with Lowry as much as with McGill. The analogy with the great artist is not strained. Images of Formby's father with his spindly body suggest he could have walked out of a Lowry landscape.

There were, of course, three songs which became more quintessentially Formby than any other numbers he recorded, and without singing which he was never allowed to leave the stage: 'Chinese laundry blues', 'When I'm cleaning windows' and 'Leaning on a lamp post'. The first tells of a Lancastrian oriental, Mr Wu (another foreigner), whose business has been on the decline ever since he became distracted by his love for a Chinese girl. The result is a calamitous chain of scorched underwear, shrunken vests and Sunday shirts that somehow end up with 'perforated rudders'.

> Oh Mr Wu,
> What shall I do?
> I'm feeling kind of Limehouse Chinese laundry blues.
> This funny feeling
> Keeps round me stealing.
> Oh, won't you throw your sweetheart over do?

Eventually he marries her instead, 'The wedding of Mr Wu' providing a logical sequel, the church decorated with the washing from the backyard line and the ukulelified ting-a-ling-ling oriental tones of the laundry blues substituted for the wedding march. To many the oriental motif may appear surprising in the context of Formby's sturdy Lancashire roots, but as J. B. Priestley pointed out in his socially aware travelogue *English Journey* in 1934, 'a boy could look pure Liverpool and prove to be three parts Chinese', so prolific was the Chinese population in the county in the 30s.

'When I'm cleaning windows' brought Formby even greater fame. George himself is now the worker rather than the onlooker, even though the work in hand gives both mind and eye the greatest of opportunities for wandering from the prescribed task. The song was virtually the private spectacle of 'What the butler saw' transformed into mass entertainment, the whole point being the peeping Tom's view George obtained of other people's lives.

> At eight o'clock a girl she wakes,
> At five past eight a bath she takes,
> At ten past eight my ladder breaks,
> When I'm cleaning windows.

Dipsomaniacs who drink their bath water, frustrated old maids on the lookout for action, talkie queens divested of all make-up, honeymoon couples for whom the phrase parlour tricks takes on a completely new meaning, all fell under his prurient gaze. No wonder he couldn't keep his mind on his work. The window motif proved so successful that it eventually worked its way into other songs, and in 1940, eight years after the first recording of 'Chinese laundry blues', the film *Let George Do It* featured the song 'Mr Wu's a window cleaner now', the laundry having obviously failed to survive the Depression years.

> He had his eyesight tested, a most important matter,
> Through a bathroom window a lady he peeps at her.
> His eyesight's getting better,
> But his nose is getting flatter,
> 'Cause Mr Wu's a window cleaner now.

Most of George's numbers came deliciously near the knuckle, but their performer had a unique charm that combined naughtiness with niceness in the quaintest, old-fashioned way. As such they could never offend. However risqué they became, they always just steered clear of explicit sex, redeemed by a shiningly innocent display of double entendre. Everyone, prompted by the Formby wink and the blatantly contrived context so essential for squeezing new outrageous meanings out of otherwise withered words, would have their own audacious idea of what George really had in mind when he sang of his magical wand, his gas mask, Auntie Maggie's remedy, Mr Wu's chopstick, and of course his little stick of Blackpool rock, not to mention the ukulele itself.

The final song of the famous trio, however, 'Leaning on a lamp post', was devoid of all innuendo and comic intention and represents the most perfect expression of his charm. Unashamedly sentimental in his infatuation for the girl who may or may not present herself, Formby sang it throughout his career, never outgrowing it, perhaps because in his later years it conjured up for the majority of his audience the image of the younger George Formby of the 30s.

> There's no other girl I would wait for,
> But this one I'd break any date for.
> I won't have to ask what she's late for;
> She wouldn't leave me flat, she's not a girl like that.
> Oh, she's absolutely wonderful, and marvellous, and beautiful,
> And anyone can understand why.
> I'm leaning on a lamp post at the corner of the street
> In case a certain little lady passes by.

It is the most individual of his songs, the theme inherited from his father, and yet it maintains a significant relationship with the others. Doubtless when the lyric's hopeful lover does leave his lamp post to marry some 'little lady', they will be destined for many years of domesticity, either cosy or calamitous. However painful those years may prove, however soon that couple lose their good looks and sex-appeal, the marriage state will remain inviolate, the bond inviolable. The tone of the lyric, the poignant yearning of the tune, the kind of people one may easily infer as involved suggest no alternative. As such it represents the moral background outlined by Orwell as essential to the success of society, the moral code that provides the springboard for all the jokes that are the basis of the comic postcard. This one serious song informs the comedy of all the others. While Max Miller bravely went all the way in shunning sexual respectability, Formby, in not taking the whole journey, curiously went part of the way towards promoting it, towards setting up the Aunt Sally to be knocked down.

Unlike the more representative Formby numbers, 'Leaning on a lamp post' was a product of the prolific songwriting talent of Noel Gay, who gave the 30s such numbers as 'Run, rabbit, run', Lupino Lane's 'The Lambeth walk' and Tommy Trinder's 'All over the place'. The others were by and large a result of various collaborations between Formby himself, Harry Gifford, Fred E. Cliffe (all three responsible for 'Windows'), Ernie Latta and Jack Cottrell (solely responsible for 'Mr Wu'). It is difficult to arrive at an accurate estimate of Formby's own musical ability. Certainly his ukulele accompaniment to the songs was as intrinsic a part of their appeal as the lyrics or his own personality, although to be accurate it was not a ukulele he played, but a banjulele or ukulele banjo. He paraded his high-speed technique as insistently as if it were some symbol of authority or virility, complementary to his basically innocent, gormless, put-upon personality. He has been acclaimed by experts as the finest rhythm banjulele player this country has produced, the creator of the style that made him famous, which he so often featured minus lyric as his numbers came to a close, a sequence technically labelled 'sequence of seven followed by stop, roll, bounce and flicker'. However, in his final television broadcast for the BBC in December 1960 he stated quite openly that he had never been able to tune the instrument. As a result banjuleles in different keys were often made available for different numbers, on stage a whole array of them set up on a settee. Nevertheless, it is impossible to imagine his act without its shuffling background rhythms. He usually included one memorable piece of byplay. At some stage during a song he would absent-mindedly turn his instrument the wrong way round, strings towards his chest, and carry on strumming regardless. It is encouraging to think that even if his musical ability did deserve the praise it receives from the experts, he was still able to poke fun at it.

Of the many leading variety stars of the 1930s and 40s who lent their talent to the cinema Formby was arguably by far the greatest commercial success in the medium. In 1932, determined to break into films and yet with no offer forthcoming from the production companies, he set to and made a crude short entitled *Boots, Boots*, which featured the songs 'Why don't women like me?' and 'Sitting on the ice in the ice rink', for a modest £3,000 in an equally modest fourteen days over a garage in London's Albany Street. This and a similar effort, *Off the Dole*, proved so popular in the smaller cinemas, particularly in the north, that before long he found himself under contract to Basil Dean's Ealing Studios and Associated Talking Pictures Limited at an astronomical £100,000 a year. Between 1938 and 1943 he was, on the evidence of the Motion Picture Herald Poll, Britain's top cinema box-office attraction, beating even his Lancashire compatriot Gracie Fields and all American competition. In 1941 he moved from Ealing to Columbia, and by the end of his film career in 1946 had completed a total of twenty-one feature films. They were an enormous success in every country of the world, including the USSR – where he was allegedly awarded the Order of Lenin in 1943 and for a while enjoyed a popularity rating second only to Stalin – but excluding the USA. There, as Norman Wisdom would find out twenty years later, people were unable to come to terms with the grass-roots traditions of British comedy.

The films themselves, which included *Feather Your Nest, Keep Your Seats Please, Spare a Copper* and *It's in the Air*, were all a simple undemanding concoction of sincere naivety, open-eyed innocence, stunning vitality and, of course, his songs. Nor must one forget the traditional hair-raising chase with madcap speed – 'Ooh, mother!' – rather than Keatonian subtlety as its keynote. The eager simpleton, George always comes out on top, whatever the pitfalls and chaos the scenario subjects him to: 'Aha, never touched me!' In the end he always gets the girl in spite of his difficulty in dating her in the first place. But luckily he is never at a loss for a song with which to cover up his embarrassment. The songs themselves often suggest that the process is so much easier.

> She started to undress and timidly she looked round;
> Said, 'Thank God I am rid of him, for he's homeward bound.'
> But when she pulled the bedclothes down, now guess what she found?
> Why, the Lancashire toreador!

Apart from a glittering film career and sporadic variety appearances at the London Palladium Formby remained essentially a provincial attraction until October 1951, when impresario Emile Littler presented him in his first West End production show, *Zip Goes a Million*, at the Palace Theatre, Shaftesbury Avenue. The show, yet another lease of life for *Brewster's Millions*, featured George as Lancashire lad Percy Piggott, committed to spending, or rather squandering, a million dollars in four months if he wishes to inherit a further eight million. The theme was one of 'take seven letters – no make it telegrams – they're more expensive!' The action took place predominantly in Texas and New York, but a cruise to a certain Raratonga Island was involved where George was crowned king with, yes, ukulele for orb and sceptre! Any doubts he may have had that the south of England would not tolerate his particular brand of humour in other than short spells were soon dispelled. Both his performance and the production – described by one critic as having the elegance of a Bond Street box with an Eccles cake inside – met with both critical and popular acclaim. Moreover, apart from the zestful title number, the show at last gave George, by way of 'Ordinary people', a song to rival 'Leaning on a lamp post' in its honesty and unfrivolous charm.

He was not to play in the musical for long. Early the following year he suffered a severe heart attack that threatened to end his career, but within eighteen months he was back at the Palladium in the production show *Fun and the Fair*, joined by a distinguished cast that included Billy Cotton and his Band, Terry-Thomas, and the Deep River Boys. Here he revived with Audrey Jeans the honeymoon sketch he had so long ago performed with his wife, Beryl Ingham, a former champion clog dancer, before concentrating upon ukulele and songs. The sketch had been a tour de force of the road shows with which they had toured the provincial circuits in the 1920s and 30s prior to Formby's film fame. If ever there was corn as high as an elephant's eye, it was here, deriving from the nervous attempts made by the groom – George in a cloth cap to offset his violently spotted pyjamas – to join his bride between the covers. Everything is done to stall for time: measuring the bed for size, checking under the bed, nervously taking a run at it to get in, falling short, shivering on the edge, checking the bounce of the mattress only to hit hard against a plank, the pretext for the creaking line 'Well, we won't get much sleep in there tonight – real seaside board!' The teasing innocence of the bride towards her own role in the scenario adds its own layer of suspense to what they both know lies ahead. When it appears that nothing further could possibly delay consummation of the act, a telegram arrives from George's mother, conveying instructions concerning his investments in a building society, which in the heat of the moment are misconstrued by our hero: 'Do nothing till you hear from me!'

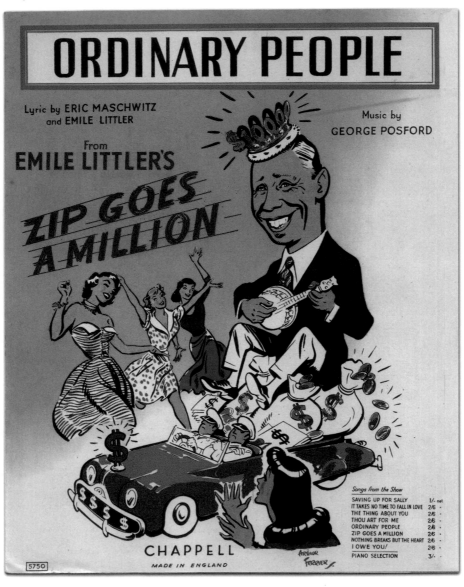

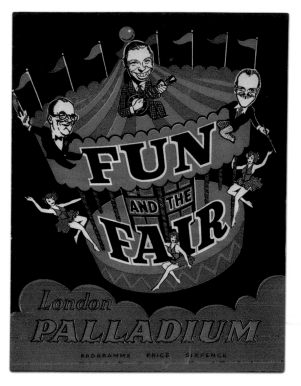

His coronary condition was to dog his career until the end. In 1956 he returned to the Palace to play Idle Jack in the pantomime *Dick Whittington*. There then followed a lull until summer seasons in Great Yarmouth in 1959 and Blackpool in 1960. However, at Christmas that last year his wife died, his heart gave way again under the strain, and he had to leave the cast of his Bristol pantomime. Unlike his films his real-life story had no happy ending. Less than two months later he announced plans to marry a thirty-six-year-old schoolteacher, Pat Howson, whom he had known since she was nine. The excitement proved too much, and the condition he had laughingly called Mr CT for so long, with the same tragicomic disrespect for life with which his father had scorned his own ill health, finally ended his days on 6 March 1961. Mr CT was not to be laughed at.

The last years of his married life had been far from happy, his Roman Catholicism clashing both with Beryl's atheism and with the thought of divorce to facilitate marriage to his future fiancée, whom he had allegedly loved since 1954. Instead he endured the strain of maintaining the public illusion of a happy marriage, a task not made easier by Beryl's excessive drinking. After the war he certainly had no financial need to work, and the fact that he did was probably to occupy a mind otherwise worried by domestic matters.

It is hard though to believe that he would ever have succeeded without Beryl, the real-life counterpart to all those leading ladies who in his films had spurred him on to greater, more daring things. In the BBC broadcast of 1960 he admitted the difficulty he experienced in reading. Beryl always had to read the small print, get to grips with contracts, negotiate with hard-headed impresarios. 'I'll always be grateful to Beryl for that,' were the words of a man who on stage presented what was probably a conscious caricature of his real self, an awestruck provincial lost in the world of big business. There can be no doubt that to set George on the road to stardom and ensure that he stayed at the top once he got there, Beryl exerted a brutal hold over him. Although the love interest in his films was never aimed at anything other than apple-for-the-teacher level, she always made sure it was provided by a different girl. Moreover, with the exception of Googie Withers at the end of *Trouble Brewing*, when both capsized into a brewery fermenting tank, he kissed only one leading lady on the lips, and that was Beryl herself, in *Boots, Boots*. She hit the roof when she discovered that the director of *Trouble Brewing*, Anthony Kimmins, had given the secret instruction to Withers: 'Make it a whopper!'

From the date of their marriage in 1924 she almost literally never let him out of her sight, later handing him daily an allowance of five shillings as she took scrupulous care of the hard-won thousands – thousands which after the war enabled George to buy Beryl a new Rolls-Royce every year and marked him out as one of the richest British entertainers of the time. Her first impression of him back in 1923 had been straight to the point: 'If I'd had a bag of rotten tomatoes with me I'd have thrown them at him.' However, from the moment she took him in hand she smartened him up and smoothed him down. Even today a cloth-cap image of him as a north country comedian persists; but after Beryl's treatment George was nothing if not immaculately turned out, from his dark Brylcreem-slick hair with its disciplined parting and the sheen of one of his own gramophone records, to the tailored dinner jacket worn at all times on stage during his standard act. The lighter fresher approach was essential if he was to stand out against his father.

George with Beryl

Today his songs remain instantly recognisable, so easily can one pin the performer to the tune. There are still Formby imitators who earn a modest living on the club circuit and crop up from time to time on television reality shows. It may appear surprising that lines like the following – based on the assumption that if someone shouts 'knickers' the world will fall about its ears – can still make an audience laugh.

Now Mr Wu – he's got a naughty eye that flickers!
You ought to see it wobble when he's ironing ladies' (*prim pause*) blouses!

That said, it would be several decades before a spiritual heir, Benny Hill, would prove that the success that eluded George in the USA was not entirely unachievable. In spite of the increased frankness and permissiveness of our age, perhaps the old taboos are still as rigid as before. Perhaps the laughter depends on context and anticipation, the plan of the lyric and the memory of the original performer. More probably it hinges on a distinction between our public and private selves. Certainly the average man may be more permissive now than he was a generation or two ago, but he has not yet reached the stage where he is prepared to admit to strangers, even close friends, exactly how much further he is prepared to go, whether in speech, behaviour or in judging others.

Formby's original success was a distinct product of another age, those bleak years of the 1930s and early 40s, years of doubt, depression and Hitler, when his remarkable gift of being able to inspire happiness all around him, even when things went wrong, was most readily acceptable to all the ordinary people he later celebrated in song, but whom he never regarded with anything approaching condescension. In the words of another song he was

> …not stuck-up or proud,
> I'm just one of the crowd;
> A good turn I'll do when I can.

That his appeal was primarily to the underdog, the humble, the masses, is emphasised by the observation by Colin MacInnes that, unlike other great music hall performers, throughout his peak period he went almost completely ignored by highbrows and the sophisticated. As MacInnes explains, the latter had at least known of the existence of Marie Lloyd and Harry Lauder, if only by way of disapproval. The critical accolades that came the way of Max Miller, Sid Field, even the Crazy Gang were not directed at him. Perhaps matters were remedied somewhat when he was awarded the OBE in 1946 – largely in recognition of his morale-boosting efforts during the war when it is estimated he played to something approaching three million service personnel in combat zones. It is surprising to learn that although he did appear privately at Windsor Castle, his entire career encompassed only two Royal Variety Performances, at the Palladium in 1937 and the Blackpool Opera House in 1955. And yet to the countless ordinary people who saw his films, bought his gramophone records, responded to his magnetic stage personality, whistled his tunes throughout those tragic times, his sheer simplicity was utterly irresistible.

AFTERTHOUGHTS

More than fifty years after his death people still tend to grin when Formby's records are played, while the frequency with which his legacy reverberates through popular culture in the most unlikely of places is testament to his durability as a folk icon. A garland of trivia embraces the ward in *Coronation Street's* Weatherfield General Hospital named after him, the part played by 'When I'm cleaning windows' in the unofficial curriculum of Alan Bennett's *The History Boys*, the sinister use of his films to depress morale in the sci-fi sitcom *Red Dwarf* and his existence as a make-believe boxing partner to Muhammad Ali in the stand-up fantasising of Eddie Izzard. Of course, the greatest compliment paid to him came from the Beatles. Lennon and McCartney's 'When I'm sixty-four' could, were its lyric not so knowing, have been composed for him, a tribute to the cosy domesticity that informed his act from a later age when marriage had already started to count for less. George could well have imparted a second layer of meaning to references to mending a fuse when the lights have failed. Listen carefully to the *Sergeant Pepper* recording and you can almost hear Paul essay a muted 'he-he' at more than one point. George Harrison was a fully paid-up member of the George Formby Society, an accomplished ukulele player and a true fan who was genuinely attached to songs that in his words 'you just can't sing without smiling'. In the version of John Lennon's 'Free as a bird' remastered for *The Beatles Anthology* in 1995, the track ends with Harrison performing a burst of ukulele in Formby style, over which is dubbed Lennon voicing George's catchphrase 'Turned out nice again' played in reverse. Formby – as portrayed by an actor on a traditional music hall stage – is depicted in the closing scenes of the accompanying video. As for Beryl, her habit of emerging with all the splendour of the Queen Mother at the end of George's act to commandeer the applause and confirm the image of married bliss, was commemorated by Morecambe and Wise, no less, when the buxom Janet Webb made her regular impudent entrance at the end of their show.

It is now generally considered that the one-man show performed by Formby on BBC Television on 16 December 1960 under the banner of *The Friday Show* was the perfect swansong, if not in fact his greatest performance. Broadcast live only nine days before Beryl's death, the programme revealed him as plumper and greyer than many would have remembered him, but over forty minutes he showed that his rapport with an audience was still as taut as a hawser, as he sang his famous songs and in what amounted to a self-conducted confessional chatted his way through a lifetime of secrets. 'No girls, no dancers, no acrobats, no conjurors, not even a guest star – only me and the uke. But I'm going to tell you a few home truths I've never told in public before.' Without a trace of self-pity he not only opened up about his semi-illiteracy and musical limitations, but the part Beryl had played in the business side of his success. He went on to express his regret at not having a family, a regret underlined by the advice given to a pet goldfish going out into the big watery world in his performance of the song 'Swim little fish'. At another moment tears welled in his eyes as he listened to a recording of the father he hardly knew. His poise in talking to the camera – never the easiest skill to master for performers used to projecting to the back of vast theatres – is remarkable, his control of his narrative totally relaxed and conversational, in spite of moments when the old gaucheness seemed never too far away. His sincerity lit up the screen as he turned to the matter of the audience itself: 'People say to me, "How did you become a star?" Huh, that's a daft question! I mean, what do we do? We don't do anything. We don't *become* stars. You people *make* us stars. We wouldn't be any good without you. And our present stars today – if they believe anything different, they're crazy! I shall always be grateful to the public for what they've done for me.' If he was faking sincerity then he deserves to be remembered as our greatest actor, but true humility has a way of asserting itself. It never did so with greater dignity than on this occasion.

EALING STUDIOS presents

GEORGE FORMBY

GRADE A

Turned out nice again

ANOTHER SMASH HIT FROM EALING STUDIOS

Produced by
MICHAEL BALCON

Directed by
MARCEL VARNEL

DISTRIBUTED UNITED ARTISTS

TOMMY HANDLEY: 'IT'S THAT MAN AGAIN!'

Hello! Is that Turner, Turner and Turtle? It is? Then good morning, good morning, good morning. It's that man again. That's right, Tommy Handley.
[The opening words of the first *ITMA*]

At the beginning of the Second World War, when *ITMA* at last brought Tommy Handley undisputed national fame, a stage version of the compulsive radio show featuring members of the regular cast toured the provinces. It was greeted everywhere by full houses, but proved a pitiable failure. No cost had been spared in the production, but even a lavish budget and the expert staging of Robert Nesbitt could not disguise the fact that it simply was not funny, that the carefree, happy-go-lucky Handley, the biggest hero so far created by the new medium of radio, projected a totally different personality on stage. Only when shielded by the security of the microphone did the essential Handley truly sparkle. The new medium and the gentle friendly comedian with the crackerjack voice could have been made for each other. Ted Ray, a spiritual successor with similar roots, described him as the greatest comic script reader of all time; Ted Kavanagh, who wrote the *ITMA* scripts, referred to his 'uncanny instinct for a line; an ear that detected the slight misplacing of a word, the most minute variation in timing'. His powers of inflection could make the most inert line sound funny; his rapid-fire speed in delivering a string of wisecracks dazzled Bob Hope; and yet only the radio, when listened to in the privacy of one's own home, was capable of doing full justice to this verbal subtlety. Millions caught the habit of listening intently.

Tommy was born in Toxteth Park, Liverpool on 17 January 1892, the son of a cow keeper, who died while Tommy was still a babe in arms. His theatrical preoccupation at an early age was primarily visual – a schoolboy's obsession with facial disguise, a spell like Bud Flanagan as a boy conjuror with a flair for practical jokes, activities perhaps foreshadowing the lyric of his eventual signature tune:

> Mother's pride and joy,
> Mrs Handley's boy,
> Oh, it's useless to complain.
> When trouble's brewing, it's his doing,
> That man – that man again!

On the strength of a passable baritone, he would become increasingly involved in amateur concert party work, much in demand during the First World War, and by 1917 had landed a small part in a northern touring company production of *The Maid of the Mountains*. It was not until he joined an army concert party later that same year, however, that the comedian lurking inside him finally exploded any idea of remaining a serious singer. The years immediately after the war saw him working for a short time in partnership with Jack Hylton at the piano (Hylton became a lifelong friend and Handley would tour under his banner later in his career); in December 1919 opening at the Metropolitan, Edgware Road with Bobby Howes in a touring burlesque entitled *Seasoned to Taste*; and the following year appearing in a concert party in Wales with Tom Walls and Leslie Henson – generally leading the usual life of a variety performer touring the provinces.

So far there had been nothing outstanding in Tommy's career: he had been lucky, but remained unknown and undistinguished. The association with Walls and Henson was the first step in a more favourable direction. They had decided, at first with Handley's disapproval, to revive a wartime skit on an army court martial written for improvised performance to the troops by Eric Blore, later to become famous as the unctuous butler in many Hollywood films. Entitled 'The Disorderly Room', it began a seemingly never-ending tour of the halls at the Shepherd's Bush Empire in 1921, and became Handley's first claim to national acceptance, if not to full star status. By December 1923 the sketch had achieved the recognition of a Royal Variety Performance at the London Coliseum, with Tom Walls and Ralph Lynn receiving billing above Handley. Although in 1942 he would go to Windsor Castle to record a special edition of *ITMA* before George VI, it is a possible indication of his shortcomings as a stage performer that in the twenty-six years following the Coliseum accolade

Tommy in 'The Disorderly Room'

he would grace only one more Royal Variety show, in 1938, in no more than a gratuitous walk-on appearance at the same theatre in a 'Lambeth Walk' finale with 249 other names of varying distinction. Still, the demands placed on a solo star performer were vastly different from those imposed by a vehicle for six relatively anonymous ones, a sketch uncannily anticipating the crazy exploitation of verbal humour to characterise *ITMA* in later years. Not that Handley in the early 1920s saw himself reaching the topmost rung of the ladder. In his biography of the comedian, Kavanagh gives as his own opinion that if Tommy had believed he would one day do so he would not have played in that same sketch so often. He clung to it as the mainstay of his repertoire continually from 1921 until the early 40s. Towards the end it became a crutch to fall back on for what might have proved difficult personal appearances. When the stage version of *ITMA* floundered, the routine found its way into a hastily revised version of the show. By that stage it could not appear but outmoded, a lifebelt turned millstone.

In the early 20s, however, even if it looked as if Handley might become known for nothing else, there was something fresh about the way the words of an army courtroom were fitted to the music of popular songs. Handley played the officer in charge who, in his initial speech to the prisoner accused of stealing the personal effects of a fellow soldier, parodied the George Robey hit 'In other words'.

> It appears you waxed excessively convivial,
> With fine fermented produce you had strife.
> You gazed upon the vintage when 'twas crimson,
> When bacchanalian revelry was rife.
> You've partaken of thoracic lubrication,
> With ambrosial nectar you were somewhat lined.
> It clearly states you were non compos mentis,
> In other words. . . you was blind!

But however incomprehensible this may appear, Tommy would often change gear halfway through and come out with something like

> You've partaken of the tittifolol bazooka,
> With the Skimsons and the Skamsons on your mind.
> When the Cleethorpes are magoozlum in the zimzam,
> In other words. . .

He was already establishing himself as a master of sheer gibberish, the one man who could talk double-double-Dutch and make himself understood. In its debunking of military red tape the sketch also reflected the humanitarian side that would reveal itself more and more in Handley's persona as the years progressed. By the time the prisoner has given his own evidence, the sergeant is reduced to tears and the culprit himself sentenced to 'Blighty'!

It is a mark of the early popularity of 'The Disorderly Room' that during the latter half of 1922 Tommy should have been tempted to try a variation on the theme, a comic-musical version of a civil court action for divorce. It was entitled 'Wrangle v. Wrangle' and featured a verbal duel between Tommy as Mr Wrangle and his mother-in-law to the tune of 'Colonel Bogey'. The formula was basically the same and Tommy secured bookings at the Coliseum, the Alhambra and the leading provincial halls, but this meant little. As always the public wanted the original and not a substitute.

In 1924 Handley was featured in the Palladium revue *The Whirl of the World*, which starred Nellie Wallace, Billy Merson, and Nervo and Knox. Of even greater significance that year, however, was his successful audition for the BBC at Savoy Hill, the turning point of his entire career. It was fortuitous that a man born to be a radio comedian should have been present at the embryo stage of the medium. The fact that he had not yet achieved full star status meant that while known names had ahead of them the frustrating task of adapting their already established techniques and personalities to an alien medium, Handley was quietly allowing the medium to influence him according to its own needs. There followed a succession of radio revues (wireless concert parties) with names like *Radio Radiance, Inaninn, Handley's Manoeuvres, Tommy's Tours* and *Hot Pot*. These earliest years of wireless activity were the busiest in his career, since radio fame increased his variety bookings. Then in December 1934 came a new departure, the formation of a double act with Ronald Frankau as 'Mr Murgatroyd and Mr Winterbottom'. The former, an old Etonian renowned for his sophisticated songs in concert party and cabaret, had, like Handley, developed a remarkable flair for the modern form of quick-fire topical patter. That they should combine forces was not at all surprising in spite of their differing social backgrounds. They had appeared together in 1930 as 'North and South', with Tommy as a down-to-earth Lancastrian and Frankau all an old Etonian was supposed to be. One of Frankau's songs included the lines

> The preparatory school, the public school and the varsity
> Produce a kind of fellow who is a scarcity.

The new act bypassed such attitudes with an original twist. Now they were nothing if not social equals. Neither Murgatroyd nor Winterbottom professed to be the straight man, each using the last thing said by the other as the lead into the next wisecrack. They enjoyed their greatest success with burlesque commentaries on such national sporting events as the Grand National and the Boat Race, often broadcast on the evening of the event. The dialogue was always delivered at a pace worthy of the race itself. The sheer outrageousness of the puns, a presage again of *ITMA*, was presumably the reason for them to be delivered as hastily as possible.

These styles of presentation, however, were still far removed from a series of storyline shows, a trend pioneered in the USA by performers like Amos 'n' Andy, Jack Benny, and George Burns and Gracie Allen, and as we shall see in the next chapter foreshadowed loosely in this country by Arthur Askey and *Band Waggon*, first broadcast in January 1938. Although they were satisfied with the immense popularity of the first native example of what John Watt, then the BBC's top variety entrepreneur, later wittily described as the 'Great God Series', it appears that the programme planners were not convinced that the Askey success could be replicated easily. And so the initial brief for Britain's second comedy series was for an anglicisation of the Burns and Allen format with Tommy as the George Burns figure. He certainly possessed the speed required to put across the streamlined American style, and was the obvious choice for the series, but the project proved abortive and hardly got beyond the script-conference stage. It was futile to approximate Handley with Burns in any way. He far more obviously fitted the description the distinguished gruff-voiced American gave of Gracie, his wife and stage partner, namely that she had been 'vaccinated with a gramophone needle'. However, on 12 July 1939, the first of a projected series of six fortnightly programmes entitled *It's That Man Again* went on the air. All obvious American colouring had been sidestepped by the star, his pioneering producer Francis Worsley and scriptwriter Ted Kavanagh.

The title, not yet abbreviated, was a catchphrase of the period, used by the popular press as a headline every time Hitler called for *Lebensraum* and already adopted by the British with that smiling yet uneasy air of defiance that masquerades for fear.

Not until war was declared and programme schedules were disrupted as a result did the programme begin to assume the character by which it would become known. The initial series, with Tommy as the owner of a radio broadcasting ship able to transmit whatever he liked, was abandoned after four episodes. By the third week of September the show had regrouped with a new supporting cast as a weekly transmission. Tommy himself emerged as Minister of Aggravation and Mysteries, provided with accommodation by courtesy of the Office of Twerps – a comment on the sudden mushrooming of vast new ministries at that time of greatest national emergency, ministries never short of advice to give every national news bulletin.

> *Handley*: Take a memo. 'To all concerned in the Office of Twerps: Take notice that from today, September the twenty-tooth, I, the Minister of Aggravation, have power to confiscate, complicate and commandeer –'
>
> *Dotty, the Secretary (played by Vera Lennox)*: How do you spell 'commandeer', Mr Hanwell?
>
> *Handley*: Commandeer – let me see. (*Sings*) Comm-on-and-eer, comm-on-and-eer, Tommy Handley's wag-time band, comm-on-and-eer, etc... Er, where were we? 'I have the power to seize anything on sight.'
>
> *Dotty*: Oh, Mr Handpump – and me sitting so close to you!
>
> *Handley*: Keep your mind on your memo. 'From today onwards Jack Hylton's Band is placed entirely at the service of this ministry, for work of the utmost national annoyance, and all sufferers from syncopation must report immediately to me, when they will receive a first fiddle copy of the "Warden's farewell to his whistle". Signed TH, on behalf of *ITMA*.'

The abbreviation of the title to *ITMA* was a comment on the proliferation of initials flaunted on vehicles to obtain right of way not only by important organisations, but also self-important individuals – ARP, RNVR, WVS, VET, and so on. What is remembered as the traditional *ITMA* format would not arrive until the beginning of the third series in 1941. Here Tommy found himself evacuated (with a pension from the OOT as long as he stayed away) to become mayor of Foaming-at-the-Mouth, the archetype of the small inefficient seaside resort where annual holidays corresponded to mechanical habit. The programme had been renamed *It's That Sand Again!* ('ITSA – ITSA – ITSA date!') but would revert to its right and proper title for the fourth series. It was, though, *ITSA* that first saw the total fusion of the basic *ITMA* ingredients, the first brilliant exploitation of the comic potential of radio to conjure up the absolutely fantastical. Here were the zany procession of almost Carrollian figures through the famous *ITMA* door, the command of surrealism, the distinctive musical arrangements, the intricate verbal texture of lightning puns and catchphrases reminiscent of no less than Joyce's *Finnegan's Wake*, the delirious speed and sharp staccato style of delivery not only reflecting the faster quicker-witted world that had seen the birth of electronic entertainment, but imparting a new energy to gags of a greater age. This would remain the framework of the programme until Handley's sudden death at the beginning of 1949. Throughout, new characters were continually introduced into the framework. At the end of the war Tommy would be appointed governor of his own never-never island, Tomtopia, while the programme underwent an almost complete change of supporting characters; and yet still the mixture remained at once fresh and comfortably as before, largely due to the ingenuity sustained by Kavanagh in the invention of those weird eccentrics who seemed to be attracted to Handley like bees to a honey pot. Certainly any profile of Tommy cannot be complete without a brief glance at the main members of that screwball cavalcade.

One actor who was at Tommy's side in the first programme and remained there until the last was Jack Train, a later stalwart of the radio panel game *Twenty Questions*. His first notable creation was the haystack-moustached Fusspot, assistant controller at the OOT, an appointment that could well have prompted from others his own constant complaint that everything was 'most irregular, most irregular'. Then came Funf, the ubiquitous German spy with a ghost-like talent for materialisation, whose signature line 'This is Funf speaking,' delivered in a threatening Teutonic accent at the distant end of a telephone, continued on the lips of an admiring public long after the character's presence in the show had diminished and there remained any comic point in having an insidious enemy agent lurking at every corner. One of Train's characters would survive the war years, the bibulous Colonel Chinstrap, with his habit of twisting Tommy's remarks into an offer of liquid refreshment.

Handley: I'd better look round this stall. It needs a complete clear-out.
Train: Bring the beer out – a good idea, Handley. I say, I'd wish you'd stand still when you're talking to me.
Handley: I am standing still.
Train: That's what you think. There, you turned a somersault! And there's a lizard going into your breast pocket!
Handley: Colonel, where have you come from?
Train: Trafalgar Square, sir. I danced round all the Xmas trees.
Handley: Trees? I only saw one.

Train: That's the worst of being sober – you only see things by halves. What about a drink, sir?
Handley: Listen, Colonel, with a head like yours, why don't you try a swim in the Serpentine?
Train: Try a gin and turpentine? I don't mind if I do!

Together with Horace Percival as 'Claude', Train played the 'Cecil' half of the pair of broker's men given to wallowing in hideously ultra-polite conversation and an over-the-top concern for each other's well-being, as signified by their traditional opening and closing lines: 'After *you*, Claude.' '*No*! After *you*, Cecil.'

Percival also played the lugubrious diver who figured in what was arguably the most successful of all the *ITMA* catchphrases: 'Don't forget the diver, sir; don't forget the diver.' This was one of the few *ITMA* characters inspired by a real person, a pathetic one-legged diver from Handley's boyhood who, butterfly net in hand, helmet at his feet, would cry out to the hordes of day trippers at the New Brighton pier head, 'Don't forget the diver, sir; don't forget the diver. Every penny makes the water warmer.' There was Sam Scram, played by bespectacled Sydney Keith, the nearest Tommy ever got to a right-hand man, who was prone to making breathless announcements like 'Gee, boss, sumpin' terrible's happened. I had the whole set-up working sumpin' wonderful. It was a honey. You was in hook, line and sinker. It was a lalla. Gee! I'd done a marvellous job for you, boss, and then…'

In post-war years Deryck Guyler made his initial mark in the company of his fellow Liverpudlian, first as Sir Short Supply of the Ministry of Food, constantly carping at Tommy and strangling the success of his projects with red tape, and then as Frisby Dyke, an unashamed comic exploitation of the Merseyside accent, with his signature line 'They don't never tell no one nothing these days, do they?' and sequences like

Guyler: Hey, whacker! What sort of a job's this you've got?
Handley: A tough one – to make success here is going to be a stiff tăsk.
Guyler: 'Tăsk', Tom? The word is tarsk – don't you understand? Tarsk.
Handley: Oh, is it? Well, since you're so clever, how about găs măsk?
Guyler: It's not găs măsk, Tom – it's gars măsk…

And so on, fifteen years before the Beatles. Guyler went on to become one of our most distinguished comedy character actors, his magnificent comic policemen and brassy peak-capped authoritarians enlivening every film or television series in which they appeared.

And then there were the female members of Handley's staff led by the blousy Mrs Mopp immortalised by Dorothy Summers, the 'corporation cleanser' with her introductory query 'Can I do you now, sir?' her request to 'dust the dado', her weekly gift for Tommy (part out of generosity, part a test of his imagination in what became a weekly guessing game) and her famous abbreviated farewell still used to this day: 'TTFN – Ta-ta for now.' The record length Tommy achieved with his own shortened goodbye was 'NKABTYSIRWU' or 'Never kiss a baby till you're sure it's right way up.'

Diana Morrison played the bullying Miss Hotchkiss, the secretary who swept into Tommy's life with the ultimatum, 'Hotchkiss is the name. Have you anything to dictate? I'll give you a week's trial; if I find you steady, sober, and reliable, I'll stay!' She *did* stay and came to idolise him in the end. Mona Lott, played by Joan Harben, was the grousing hypochondriac washerwoman with the haunting cockney voice and the now legendary reply to Tommy's continual advice that she should keep her 'pecker up': 'I always do, sir – it's being so cheerful as keeps me going.' She provided possibly the most poignant of all the *ITMA* characters of either sex, though none the less hilarious for that. And then there was Sophie Tuckshop, the overweight schoolgirl played by a young Hattie Jacques, prone to bouts of giggling amid her gastronomic excesses and their attendant suffering, but always finally assuring one with a contrite squeal 'but I'm all right now'.

To understand Tommy's relationship with each character is to realise that at any one point in the programme the masks of straight man and clown were interchangeable between the supporting character of the moment and the star himself. Tommy represented the one ordinary person in a society of eccentrics. And yet the very presence of his kindly squire in this world called his own sanity into question and left him appearing the most moonstruck of them all. Kavanagh explained just how indispensable this air of ambiguity was to the programme.

On the face of it, it would have appeared that these characters, let loose before the microphone, would give all the laughs needed. But they would have failed utterly without the pivot round which they all whirled. Tommy rarely left the microphone for the entire half-hour show, bluffing his way out of awkward situations, suave, seriously light-hearted, allowing others to score off him, distributing the laughs equally between himself and his opposing number.

The same could have been written twenty years later of the equally assured though more leisurely Kenneth Horne, when, courtesy of the writers Marty Feldman and Barry Took, he found himself at the helm of *Round the Horne* in the assorted company of Julian and Sandy, Seamus Android, Daphne Whitethigh, Rambling Sid Rumpo, J. Peasmould Gruntfuttock and Dame Celia Molestrangler among others.

Each *ITMA* character had its own instantly recognisable catchphrase, most of which survived with something approaching an almost tattoo-like permanence. The phenomenal influence of the programme on a people at war can best be gauged from the way these lines found themselves in common currency at moments of the severest hardship, far removed from the overt frivolity in which they were first delivered. Bomber pilots became Claude and Cecil to one another over the intercom as they queued up over targets. 'Don't forget the diver' were sometimes the last words spoken by fighter pilots as they plunged into enemy airspace. 'TTFN' would likewise bring home the mad futility of war with horrific incongruity on the failing lips of bomb victims and butchered soldiers. There was a report of a small boy trapped by debris after a bombing raid, crying out to the head of the demolition squad, 'Can you do me now, sir?' One should never forget that a war was raging for about 170 of the total of 310 *ITMA* shows.

Less easy to repeat in times of crisis were the tricks with sentence structure – 'catch-syntax', perhaps. One thinks of the inverted sentences of Basil Backwards, played by Hugh Morton, with his greeting 'Sir, morning good! Coffee of cup? Strong too not. Milk have rather I'd.' As infuriating was Horace Percival's Mr Whats'isname, living as he did in a vague world of 'what-you-may-call-its', 'you-knows', and incomplete sentences. The word-juggling would reach its zenith with the spelling routine shared by Tommy and Signor So-So, the falsetto-voiced 'foreign secretary' portrayed by Dino Galvani, originally conceived as an Italian equivalent to Funf.

Galvani: Ah, Mr Hangnail, you sent for me? Again you have an attack of the anno domini – yes?

Handley: No. Only a touch of the tittifolols – a kind of concert party on the chest. I want a thorough overhaul, Dr So-So.

Galvani: First I test your blood. You're anaemic.

Handley: No. You're thinking of Jack Train. He's a mimic.

Galvani: I think you glup your food.

Handley: Glup my food? You mean gulp my food?

Galvani: Yes. Glup your food.

Handley: Listen. G – U – L – P. Glup.

Galvani: You mean gulp. Now I feel your plus.

While much of the humour may appear mechanical, the success of *ITMA* was personal to its listeners, accurately expressing what they were thinking and were anxious to communicate at the time, and yet still remaining far enough removed from the war and its aftermath to lighten the gloom of sticky tape on windows, 'London can take it', ration books, gas masks at the ready, and carrots in every conceivable edible form. Mildly satirical, but never vicious, it united the whole community, embracing intellectuals, workers and servicemen in the same sense of fun. By necessity radio had now become the principal entertainment medium for all classes. For a decade Handley did as much for national solidarity as any politician and with remarkably little flag-waving, albeit the victory edition '*Victma!*' indulged itself quite uncharacteristically in two compliments to Churchill. 'Hip Hip,' exclaimed Handley. A horse was heard. 'What's that?' 'Three cheers for Winny,' Tommy replied. The second was an openly patriotic song, 'We're glad we walked behind the man who smoked the big cigar!' sung by the whole cast as they supposedly paraded through the streets. But for all this, not only did the same programme feature Handley on the make, the brains behind a fiddle involving the sale of Union Jacks, but eventually separated from the parade, left to sing to himself in a deserted alley. In *ITMA* patriotism was far from sacred.

Not so obvious was the influence *ITMA* would have on later comedy shows, with its speed of delivery, its quick-fire succession of short scenes and verbal non-sequiturs, its surrealist overtones, all breaking away from the traditional music hall sketch orientation of *Band Waggon*, and anticipating *Take It From Here*, and even more so *The Goon Show* and *Round the Horne*. In Kavanagh's own assessment of his intentions as scriptwriter when first entrusted with the *ITMA* project, one can see the seeds of what would later flower into the Goons. 'My own idea of radio writing was an obvious one – it was to use sound for all it was worth, the sound of different voices and accents, the use of catchphrases, the impact of funny sounds in words, of grotesque effects to give atmosphere – every device to create the illusion of rather crazy or inverted reality.'

The normal ratio of chaos to convention became reversed in the most inspired *Hellzapoppin* tradition. But even without what proved to be a revolutionary format, Handley would have remained *the* great radio comedian. His voice, with its cheery cadences and warm introductory line 'Hello, folks,' had an infectious vitality that immediately won a place in the heart of a distressed nation more than ever in need of friendship, not to mention the zest and zing he brought to the lives of its people. When he died suddenly at the height of his career on 9 January 1949, the consequence of a cerebral haemorrhage, possibly in turn the result of years of constant anxiety and worry – Kavanagh explains how he was as nervous at the end of his career as he had been at the beginning – the appalling sense of loss felt by an adoring public alone testified how a funny man can not only be elevated to hero status, but absorbed into the very pattern of our lives.

AFTERTHOUGHTS

In his eulogy at Handley's memorial service at St Paul's Cathedral the Bishop of London declared that the comedian 'was one whose genius transmuted the copper of our common experience into the gold of exquisite foolery. His raillery was without cynicism, and his satire without malice.' At the time it hardly needed saying, but there had been moments when some had disagreed. In my possession is a letter dated September 1939, in which Handley found himself defending the tenor his humour would take for the duration of the war. In the wake of the first wartime *ITMA* transmission he thanks his correspondent, one Oliver Rees of Swansea,

> for your candid criticism, but I cannot agree with your protest. My ridicule is not against the German people. I too know many who are personal friends. It is only the language that I burlesque. By the same rule I should have had protests from the Office of Works, which I call Office of 'Twerps', but no one has written as yet… If by chance you listened to Germany the other evening at nine o'clock you would have heard an announcer – speaking in perfect English – suddenly break into a newsreel item and say that 'the English were swine'. After that I don't think it matters what I say, and anyhow all material is passed by the Ministry of Information before it is broadcast. I'm afraid that a sense of humour is the only thing that will help to win the war.

ITMA catchphrases were further celebrated on postcards

By the end of hostilities there could be no questioning Handley's last statement. That he should have to defend himself so punctiliously at the beginning is indicative both of the extreme impact of *ITMA* at the time and the conscientiousness of the man.

In his introduction to a published edition of *ITMA* scripts in 1974 the novelist and poet P. J. Kavanagh, who happens to be the son of Ted, wrote of the man he observed from a privileged closeness as a child.

> Tommy was handsome, almost in a leading-mannish sort of way, but there was a telltale crinkle at the corners of the eyes that mocked the effect of his electric presence even while he included you inside it… Like all great performers he shone in the radiance of his effect on others. No one who had ever met him would call him 'only' a radio comedian, as though that is a minor form of art. Perhaps it is, but there was nothing minor about his presence.

Maybe my assessment of Handley as a stage performer does him an injustice; maybe he could have shone as brightly on stage with material more worthy of him. But there is no doubt that he knew his own strengths. When the possibility of putting *ITMA* onto television was explored in the immediate post-war years, Handley was totally resistant, insisting that the programme was 'produced *for* and broadcast *in sound, and should remain so*'. He was fittingly included on Sir Peter Blake's cover design for the Beatles' *Sergeant Pepper* album. Even today the *ITMA* catchphrases resurface in headlines and cartoon captions. More than anyone he helped to deflate the pomposity that was endemic in sound broadcasting during his heyday. On his death the BBC news bulletins reported 'the death of Mr Thomas Handley', refusing to use the familiar version of his name that registered him as the friend of millions. Most importantly, that friendship was cherished at a time when many needed it most.

To John —
I thank you!
Arthur Askey

ARTHUR ASKEY: 'BEFORE YOUR VERY EYES!'

Big: Don't you realise you're supposed to make people laugh?
Stinker: Why, don't I make you laugh?
Big: Well, you make me scream, but that doesn't help the listeners. They can't see you!

Onstage no comedian displayed a more irrepressible sense of fun than Arthur Askey, although strictly speaking he was not at heart a music hall or variety performer. He lacked the shrewd attack of a Miller, the steel verve of a Trinder and, once established as a star, concentrated for the greater part of his theatrical career on farce and musical comedy, in the tradition of West End stalwarts like Leslie Henson, Stanley Lupino and Bobby Howes. His persona was that of a boy rascal in an adult body. The phrase 'hop skip and jump' could have been coined for him; it seemed there was scarcely a moment when he remained still on stage, all the while entertaining with his silly little songs accompanied by their equally silly little dances, the exaggerated mime of his excited hands and his expansive pixie grin. Instantly recognisable from the small frame of his body and the large frames of his spectacles, he had only to issue his rallying call, 'Hello, playmates,' in a voice that embodied the infectious throaty chuckle he made his own to bring us all to the frolicsome level of the playground where intuitively his performances took place. That he was able to maintain this persona without strain or embarrassment into his early eighties was as remarkable as his boast that one so tiny never in all his days needed a microphone to reach the back of the gallery.

He always appeared to be enjoying the proceedings on stage quite as much as his audience and once commented, 'And even if very occasionally I am *not*, then it is my business to make it appear that I *am*.' With Arthur it all came down to attitude. There is no reason to doubt the sincerity of his claim that he never suffered stage fright in his life. One would doubt the claim if made by almost any other performer, but everything about Askey points to the jester as optimist. 'I've never died,' he used to say, adding after a pause, 'I've been critically ill.' When things weren't going too well early in the run of one pantomime, he was heard to comment, 'This *will* be funny when we've worked it up!' For a non-attacking comic, he had the instinctive ability to lift a show – any show – when it was flagging. Such longueurs occur frequently in Royal Variety Performances and never more so in 1972, when compère Dickie Henderson found himself playing the fall guy in an especially tedious juggling act halfway through a particularly lethargic bill. Then on walked Arthur, unbilled and unannounced, ostensibly to take Dickie's place as the butt of the act. The theatre erupted on seeing him, and Askey responded as only he could, 'Hello, playmates… ay-thang-yew… This is where the show picks up.' And it did. You could see this little man lifting the whole production by the bootstraps. Single-handedly he saved the evening.

Like Tommy Handley he was born in Liverpool – on 6 June 1900, in the small dockland area known as The Holy Land comprising the streets named after David, Jacob, Isaac and Moses. The nickname he acquired at school – where years later an observant fellow pupil, Paul McCartney, would spot his name carved on a desk – clung to him through life and in time provided the inspiration for his signature tune.

> Big-Hearted Arthur, they call me,
> Big-Hearted Arthur, that's me.
> Clean if I'm not very clever,
> But only 'cause I've got to be.

As a schoolboy his musical activities were dominated by being a chorister. In 1910 he made what may have been his first solo appearance, as the boy soprano who sang 'Oh for the wings of a dove' at the consecration of the Lady Chapel of Liverpool Cathedral, standing on a hassock to see over the top of the stalls. After school he worked for eight years as a clerk in what he always referred to as the Tonsils and Adenoids Department of the Liverpool Education Office, broken only by six months in the Welch Regiment towards the end of the First World War.

Much of his spare time in Liverpool was spent performing in amateur concert party. Inspired by childhood holiday memories of watching a Pierrot troupe called The Jovial Jesters in Rhyl, for a short time he even ran his own group entitled The Filberts. Wounded soldiers often provided a captive audience. By 1924, however, he could resist the lure of the professional stage no longer and against the wishes of his parents joined the Song Salad concert party at the Electric Theatre, Colchester. The engagement marked the formal beginning of a comic apprenticeship that would last for fourteen hard yet halcyon summers spent chiefly on the Isle of Wight and at Margate, with time in between for pantomime, masonic concerts and the emerging medium of radio. It became hard not to picture his trim square-shouldered physique in pompoms and ruffle, the large head with its bewildered horn-rims and beaming watermelon smile beneath the conical white cap of the true Pierrot. 'Did you ever see such a funny little bloke as me?' he used to sing. No one *looked* quite as funny as Arthur Askey.

Concert party expected a softer, more relaxed approach from its comedians than music hall. As Ted Ray once explained, 'I'm a typical music hall comedian. Arthur is a gentle comedian who played to a gentle audience at the seaside while I was fighting for my life on the halls in Sunderland.' In other words, Arthur's audience was on holiday, but whoever went to Sunderland for sand and sunshine? Ted used to stride on announcing he didn't want any applause, but would they please give him a ten-yard start. Arthur skipped on, chirped, 'Hello, playmates,' and had everyone captivated in seconds. If the weather was fine, the performance would be alfresco, on an open stage on sand or pier with deckchairs for the stalls; when it rained the show would be moved indoors to the makeshift surroundings of the town hall. Indoors or out, Arthur was able to develop an infallible sense of audience control. However, when he eventually found himself playing the variety circuits on the back of his radio success, he did express concern to

managements that the bigger auditoriums and the stricter time restraints of the variety bill might work against him. He need not have worried. His audiences were comprised mainly of *Band Waggon* fans, many of whom had never been in a music hall in their lives. To the end of his days, however, Askey always favoured the more intimate, subtler conditions of his earliest successes. In this light it is not difficult to see why he took so fluently to the new media of radio and television. Nothing could be more relaxed or intimate than entering the audience's homes.

Askey made his first radio broadcast in 1933, although his big break did not occur until May 1937. *The Coronation Revue* was scheduled in celebration of the coronation of King George VI, and George Robey and Max Miller were invited to share the duties of compère. Max was unhappy having to read from a script, so he dropped out and Arthur was invited to step in. At first things did not augur well. At rehearsal Robey kept taking the young pretender's lines. On air, however, Askey, encouraged by his wife May, ad-libbed and completely lost the grand old man of music hall, stealing the show. He was officially reprimanded by the powers at Broadcasting House – the offending words were 'hell' and 'lousy' – but then showered with glory. The BBC was looking for its first resident star comedian in response to recent trends in American radio in a show that would go out on the same station on the same night at more or less the same time each week, although Arthur had to wait until after his final Shanklin summer season for the idea to turn into reality. The *Daily Mail* reported, 'It's a step nearer the regularising of programmes which makes for easier and more discriminate listening.' Until then only the news and the magazine programme *Monday Night at Seven* had enjoyed a fixed slot in the schedule.

Band Waggon, described as 'a brand new, scintillating, epoch-breaking show', would today be classified as broken comedy with musical interludes. It debuted at 7.55 p.m. on Wednesday 5 January 1938. In its lifetime its duration wavered between 45 minutes and an hour. The first few episodes were uninspired, and the series seemed doomed until Askey grasped the creative reins and with help from his willowy new straight man, Richard 'Stinker' Murdoch (1907 – 90), began to contribute to the scripts. He argued whimsically that if the BBC was going to describe him as its resident comedian, he should literally live on the premises. And so in a pioneering dig at the Establishment Askey and Murdoch became residents of their famous fictitious flat on top of Broadcasting House. The comic invention of the show never aspired to anything above a conventional comic-strip level, but its predictability and triviality made it at once charming and comforting. 'Big' and 'Stinker' acted out their own private fantasy life in this new-style treetop-house of the technological era. Sharing the abode was a whole menagerie of unpaying guests, which included Hector the camel, Basil and Lucy the pigeons, and Lewis the goat.

    Stinker: A goat in the flat? What about the smell?
    Big: Oh, he'll get used to it

Arthur with Richard Murdoch on the roof of the BBC

Lewis was present in a milk-yielding capacity to obviate the necessity for a daily climb up forty-nine stairs (to be biologically accurate it should have been Louise). Sanitary arrangements were provided by the announcers' bathroom on the floor below. As for culinary matters, they found the best way to boil eggs was to put them in a kettle which they let down on a string into the fireplace of Lord Reith, the director general. One chorus of 'Hands, knees and boomps-a-daisy' signified soft-boiled, two choruses hard. Their main contact with the outside world was Mrs Bagwash, their charwoman and mother of the notorious Nausea, intended to provide love interest for Arthur. The mother's work was always in slipshod evidence, but neither woman actually spoke over the air. Other readily identifiable motifs were their fanatical admiration for Reginald Foort, the BBC organist, the daily chore of polishing the six pips for the time signal and the gag about cutting a pattern from a rug for Arthur's 'combs'.

One resident feature was 'Chestnut Corner', described as 'an interesting collection of old jokes you might never have heard again'.

> *Stinker*: That's a nice little dog you've got. What's his name?
> *Big*: I call him Corset.
> *Stinker*: Corset?
> *Big*: Cos he's tied up all day and let loose at night!

> *Stinker*: I haven't seen your girl for a long time. Has she kept her figure?
> *Big*: Kept it? She's doubled it!

Without the comedy sound effects that punctuated the punchlines, 'Chestnut Corner' would have seemed a throwback to the age they were leaving behind. Until then comedians on radio had simply stood at a microphone and replicated their stage act. *Band Waggon* was driven more by dialogue, vocal characterisation and sound effects than by jokes per se. A mountain of tin cans and assorted paraphernalia was kept in the studio to be demolished on cue, while Nausea's presence was registered by a thud as she fainted at the mike. The key to success was to engage the visual imagination of the audience in the sound medium. Everything was paving the way for *ITMA*, *The Goon Show* and the golden age of radio comedy that was to follow.

In this regard, more important than the jokes were the catchphrases, which served Arthur in good stead until the end of his life. First to register in the national psyche was 'Ay-thang-yew,' subconsciously modelled on the mechanical reply of the bus conductor of the 1930s as he collected his fares. It was the preface to a complete phrasebook that would go on to include 'Ah, happy days,' 'It isn't the people who make the most noise that do the most work,' 'Don't be filthy,' 'That's tantamount to a rebuff,' 'Doesn't it make you want to spit?' and 'Light the blue touchpaper and retire immediately!' Murdoch consistently referred to Arthur as 'You silly little man', while Arthur naturally greeted the listeners with 'Hello, playmates.' Askey also claimed that it was on *Band Waggon* that he first coined the epithet Auntie for the BBC, long before Ben Elton, a bespectacled comedian from a different planet, featured in the television series *The Man from Auntie* in the early 1990s.

For a while Arthur may well have been the most famous man in the country after Neville Chamberlain and the royal family, his success reflected in Askey merchandise which included dolls, puppets, badges, his own children's annual and pole position in the comic *Radio Fun*. Between December 1938 and March

1939, a crucial time in British political history, listening figures reveal that the show attracted a larger percentage of the potential audience than the six o'clock news. When the show was about to return, a month after the outbreak of war, the chancellor of the exchequer, Sir John Simon, addressed the Commons with the kind of optimism that hallmarked Askey's style: 'We are getting back to normality. *Band Waggon* will be back on the air next week.' Arthur boasted of the show's mention in *Hansard* until his death. The little man's humour and resilience perfectly complemented the mood of the country on the threshold of its darkest hour.

The last programme of the series was transmitted on 2 December 1939. There had been fifty-one regular editions in total over three seasons, by which time *Band Waggon* had become the victim of Askey's own personal success with the plethora of opportunities it opened up for him. The impresario and band leader Jack Hylton had wasted no time in acquiring the stage rights from the BBC. He *couldn't* put it on without Arthur, resulting in a West End season starring the little man at the Princes Theatre (now the Shaftesbury), a provincial tour and a final season in town at the Palladium during the summer of 1939. Commercially Hylton now had the upper hand over Auntie, but Askey was secretly relieved when the radio run came to a close, fearing that the show's high standard would drop under the strain of having to find new material each week. There was talk of resuming *Band Waggon* after the war once Murdoch had emerged from the RAF (another complication), but there he had teamed up with another sparring partner, Kenneth Horne, the outcome of which was the long-running series *Much-Binding-in-the-Marsh*. Askey subsequently went on to star in a long string of other radio shows, including *Big's Broadcast*, *Forever Arthur*, *Arthur's Inn*, *Hello Playmates* and *Askey Galore*. Arthur never did less than shine, but none of them had quite the same impact as *Band Waggon*.

As he capered onto the stages of the biggest theatres in the land, Arthur – a Little Tich for a modern age – quickly discovered that one of his trump cards was his size. People came to see what he looked like, and there was always a gasp – conditioned by all those radio references to him as 'Big' – when all 5 feet 3½ inches of him made its first entrance. 'Hello, playmates. It's all right – you're not being diddled. This is all there is!' His sheer physicality as he rolled his shoulders up and down, projected his elbows like jug handles, protruded his posterior and did his funny little shuffle like a speeded-up figure on a Swiss clock only emphasised the lack of inches. Askey's success on radio was concurrent with that of Walt Disney's *Snow White and the Seven Dwarfs* in the cinema. He was later likened by one critic to a 'bespectacled Donald Duck not giving two quacks for anyone' as he waddled irrepressibly through a show and it is satisfying to imagine him as the eighth member of Snow White's gang, or even as the inspiration for an animated Pied Piper rallying all the curious creatures that inhabited the world of his songs, concert party gems now finding a setting on bigger stages. At some point during the war with a recording contract to deliver on average a new record every two months, he interrupted the run of nonsense songs and morale-boosters like 'The washing on the Siegfried Line' and 'The thing-ummy-bob (that's going to win the war)' to make a hit recording of 'Give a little whistle', the Jiminy Cricket number from Disney's *Pinocchio*. It could have been written for him.

Of his musical menagerie, the first and most famous number was the bee, the subject of a lyric written by fellow concert party veteran, Kenneth Blain. In Askey's hands the lyric became transformed as he buzzed around the stage, his hands in overdrive as they simulated the flight of the humble bumble.

> Oh what a glorious thing to be
> A healthy grown-up busy busy bee,
> Whiling away the passing hours
> Pinching all the pollen off the cauliflowers.

The song never left his repertoire, to be joined in quick succession by a whole parade of wriggling worms, sonorous death-watch beetles, 'chirrup chirrup' little birds, impudent pixies, non-stop-nibbling moths, blissfully degenerate seagulls and more, created by Blain or others, sometimes by Askey himself.

> Flying very high, flying very low,
> You can never catch me, oh dear no.
> Flying round a liner, racing neck and neck,
> Then our favourite pastime, playing hit the deck.
> Just a silly seagull, that's all –
> Fly away Peter, fly away Paul.

It was all performed with effortless ease. Audiences may well have assumed he was making it up as he went along.

Jack Hylton did more than introduce Askey to the mainstream variety circuit; he also secured for him a contract for the film version of *Band Waggon*, which launched Arthur upon a respectable cinematic career embracing nine features for Gainsborough Pictures during the hostilities, and resuscitated for four more during the 1950s. Arthur took to the new medium without trouble, and first time around his performances, not least their musical interludes, captured the mood of the moment. *I Thank You* in 1941 opened with him starting a new day, tending to his ablutions and getting dressed on a crowded underground platform among the still-slumbering bodies of people who have taken refuge from the Blitz of the night before. As he prances among them singing the Noel Gay success 'Hello to the sun', it is impossible not to be warmed by the optimism he projects, as if he already knows he'll emerge from the makeshift air-raid shelter to discover a cloudless blue sky.

> I'm up with the lark,
> As soon as it's day.
> I tear off the bedclothes
> And throw them away.
> Before the day has really begun,
> I'm ready to say 'Hello to the sun.'

He had always wanted to star in musical comedies, and the films led to notable success in four major West End musicals. Between 1943 and 1952 *The Love Racket*, *Follow the Girls*, *The Kid from Stratford* and *Bet Your Life* were all tailored to his talents. He may well have done more had this style of show not been overtaken by the more naturalistic success of productions like *Oklahoma!* and *South Pacific*. Similarly his work in two films based on dramatic successes, *The Ghost Train* and *Charley's Big-Hearted Aunt*, convinced Jack Hylton that he had the acting ability to carry a non-musical show, as proved by his impact in the north-country farce *The Love Match* both in Blackpool and at London's Palace and Victoria Palace Theatres during 1953 and 1954. It was his success in the film version of Glenn Melvyn's play that brought Arthur back to favour in the film studios.

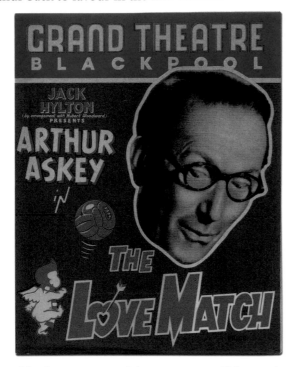 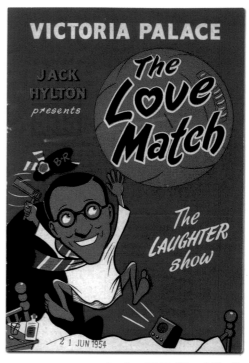

Arguably the most surprising moment of his movie career was a sequence in the 1943 film *Miss London Limited*, where *sans* spectacles he assumed the character of Harpo Marx, with less assured assistance from Evelyn Dall as Groucho and Jack Train as Chico. It was remarkably convincing, and underlined his facility as a physical clown. One of his big scenes in *The Love Racket* saw him impersonating George Bernard Shaw, for which permission was reluctantly granted by GBS himself and only at the last minute: 'There's no reason why you shouldn't do it because I won't be coming to see it.' Arthur wore Norfolk jacket, knickerbockers and a full chin of whiskers, while the dialogue went:

Actor: May I bid you a good morrow, gentle sire?
Askey: Not bloody likely!
Actor: Are you Shaw?
Askey: I'm certain!

Because it allowed him free rein to ad-lib, theatre would always prove a happier medium for Askey than film. In the same show he had to walk offstage at one point with a plaster bust under his arm. As he swung round he accidentally caught the head on the scenery. It rolled into the middle of the stage and he had to return to pick it up. 'Never lose your head on a first night,' he joked and brought the house down.

For all his success, come the early 1950s Arthur could have been forgiven for feeling swamped by the new generation of comedians blossoming after the Second World War. Askey held his nerve and very soon was bringing to the new medium of television the same acumen and inventiveness he had brought to radio fifteen years earlier. In April 1952 the BBC launched *Before Your Very Eyes*, the title taken from the phrase with which he had always introduced his nonsensical piano playing in his concert party act. He soon showed that he knew instinctively what to do with the camera, treating it like a member of the audience sitting in a deckchair at Margate or Shanklin. Like quicksilver he would switch from interacting with those around him in the studio to confiding behind the back of his hand to the home audience, never failing to make comic capital out of prop failures or forgotten lines. Directors were kept on their toes as with characteristic intrepidity he targeted a camera to share a backstage secret with those at home – 'Isn't it funny where this room ends' or, in a foreign legion sketch, 'Fancy the desert finishing here' – or pushed his face into the lens to invite them to study his complexion: 'Can you see my freckles, viewers?' Sometimes he'd even address himself to the director: 'We're flogging a dead horse, here. They've all gone to bed.' No one understood better how to exploit the limitations as well as the advantages of the new medium. It helped his style that the show was live and scarcely used more than two cameras. As veteran radio producer Mike Craig observed, 'He never rushed; he just took his time and we hung on to every word, every nuance, every flicker of an eyelid.' At the end of a show he would sign off and then holding his nose drop out of frame as if submerging himself underwater. The device suggested itself to Askey when he noticed directors not fading out performers after their final 'Good night', leaving them high and dry with fixed grins on their faces.

Before Your Very Eyes was not the first live comedy sketch show on television – Terry-Thomas had paved the way with the imaginative *How Do You View?* as early as 1949 – but there was still a sense that history was repeating itself. Askey provided the first truly big hit of the television era, as he had done on radio many years before, bringing an impish spirit and *joie de vivre* to the electronic vacuum of the television studio that has never been properly acknowledged. The show ran for three series, in the last of which as a gimmick he introduced a dumb blonde, the big-breasted model Sabrina, who seemed to do nothing but breathe deeply. She proved to be the most eye-catching of foils, eliciting from the big-hearted little man the nickname the Hunchfront of Lime Grove. It was a strange move for the cleanest of all comedians, but to the relief of the BBC hierarchy Askey never behaved offensively towards her. In 1956 he decamped with the show and Sabrina to the new commercial television channel for a further three series. Although he would quip, 'Twice the money for half the rehearsal!' the move was equally a show of loyalty on Askey's part to Jack Hylton, a major shareholder in the new enterprise.

Askey was ever-present on one channel or another virtually to the end of his life, never more at home than on shows like the *The Good Old Days* or *Sunday Night at the London Palladium*, where audiences were given a glimpse of the material that had stood him in good stead in concert party or on his early variety tours. His act as such showcased material from long-forgotten pantomimes, cajoling the crowd into monosyllabic responses.

> What, no milk?
> *Dear, dear, dear, dear, dear!*
> This is getting quite a habit,
> I shall have to milk the rabbit.
> *Dear, dear, dear, dear, dear!*

He also had a soft spot for another routine, in which, with a nod to Billy Bennett, he recalled his return from service in the foreign legion.

> I landed in England last Tuesday,
> It wasn't so hard to detect it.
> For I'd sand in my whiskers and sand in my hair,
> And sand where you'd never expect it.
> Now here I am back entertaining,
> Singing songs ancient and new,
> Striving and straining to get a good laugh
> Out of boss-eyed palookas like you.

Since the time of his radio success the centrepiece of his stage act had invariably been his attempt to coax Rachmaninov's Prelude in C sharp minor out of a concert grand. The concept had been a mainstay of the repertoire of his gravelly voiced idol Leslie Henson, and in more eccentric guise would later boost the popularity of Max Wall. Askey brought a lighter touch to the idea. 'I come before you as a walking miracle of modern musical achievement. Six weeks ago I couldn't tell the black notes from the white notes, but today we washed the piano and I can pick out the white notes quite easily.' At the Palladium as late as 1974, the *Guardian* theatre critic Michael Billington took special delight as Askey approached the piano 'circuitously with a series of leaps, jumps and pirouettes that make you think he is going to dance with it rather than play it'. But play it he could, among, that is, the comic mileage to be gained from flexing his fingers, flipping his tails the right side of the piano stool, and generally reconciling his size to the bulk of the instrument. Then, when well advanced with the Prelude, he would unexpectedly be sidetracked down the route of a more popular dance-band number of the day – like 'Memories' or 'Destiny' – and have to struggle to get back on course with the comment, 'Well, it went very well at the Brownies' concert!'

Jokes were never an important element of an Askey stage show, as they were with the likes of Miller, Trinder and Ray. Far more important was his attitude towards them, enabling him to score with the weakest of material. By taking the mickey out of a joke – 'I must tell that badly – I don't know – but anyway…' – he was able to mock himself ahead of the audience. This produced as big a laugh as any joke and in the process the gag was bad no more. His asides in this context were priceless. 'Every one a little gem – it will go better next time!' he used to quip. He once owned up to possibly the worst joke he ever told: 'You have all heard of Nelson Riddle. Well, I'm his twin brother, Jimmy Riddle. We're alike as two peas.' As he said, 'It didn't exactly die; it gave a death rattle in the form of a ripple of laughter!' On the night Arthur sighed, 'Sometimes yes… sometimes no.' His timing was perfect and he got the laugh he wanted. It all came down to his concert party training. 'How does he think them up? And the next one, please!' In his own words, 'It's not really enough for me to crack a joke verbally; my entire body has to rock in sympathy with it.' Nor did the age of the material worry him. 'I've been working this material for fifty years. Which all goes to prove Abraham Lincoln wrong: you *can* fool all of the people all of the time!' Bob Monkhouse once said of him, 'By constantly undermining what he did, he made it all the funnier.'

As he grew older, he defied his age more cheekily than any comic before or since. On the occasion of that Palladium appearance in 1974, he greeted the audience, 'Last week Josephine Baker, this week me, next week Grimaldi.' In the Royal Variety Performance of that year he sang a parody of 'Ol' Man River' from *Show Boat*.

> Ol' man Askey, that ol' man Askey,
> Though somewhat dated, he feels elated,
> Rejuvenated, he still keeps rolling along.

He sold the number with a youthful assurance linked to an air of self-deprecation that once again dominated the show.

> Tell that joke, get no laugh,
> Not a blinking soul wants an autograph!

The last line was never true, of course, even from a generation that had not been born when he made his first impact on the wireless. In his final years no performer became a greater national institution in pantomime: he could claim that between 1957 and 1968 he had played mother to no less than David Whitfield, Cliff Richard, Frank Ifield, Engelbert Humperdinck and Jimmy Tarbuck at the London Palladium alone. Typically he played down his prowess: 'I'm not a great dame. I don't even put false boobies on. It's just Arthur Askey in a frock.'

Offstage Askey was an unpretentious man of great dignity, who for all his love of the stage mistrusted the limelight and disdained the fripperies and false camaraderie of so much of show business. After a performance he would often leave the theatre by the quickest means possible: taking off his spectacles he would put on his hat, pull up the collar of his coat and mingle with the crowds leaving the auditorium. With magical panache one of the most recognisable men in the land became invisible. The ruse only worked, however, when he had a friend beside him to guide the way. Without his glasses he could hardly see where he was going. But he never short-changed his public; as he once said, 'I begin my performance when I leave my house in the morning.' His final years were marked by great sadness as his beloved wife May, 'my darling little missus', suffered from early-onset dementia; she died in 1974. Supported by the love of his daughter Anthea, a staunch trouper in her own right, her family and his sister Rene, he kept on working. He received the OBE in 1969, and then the CBE in 1981. That he did not progress to a knighthood was a shameful albeit typical anomaly of the honours system. In the business of comedy few have been a star for at least four generations, let alone a success in every single medium they have tackled.

A heart attack in 1978 signalled the beginning of the end, although he recovered sufficiently from it to play the Royal Variety Performance that year. No one would have expected otherwise. As he said, 'Performing is like breathing in and breathing out with me. It's no effort at all.' However, in the summer of 1982 doctors diagnosed gangrene in one of his legs, the result of circulation problems following the coronary. He entered hospital and died on 16 November having had both legs amputated. Anthea recalled how the desire to raise a laugh never deserted him. When the man came to measure him for his artificial legs, Arthur said, 'Well, you can put the tape measure away. I'm a six and seven eighths?' Without a touch of self-pity, he joked that even without them he'd still be able to play the front end of a pantomime horse. At a tribute lunch held in his honour in 1974, Ernie Wise had announced, 'I am half of a double act; Arthur is half of a single act.' Ernie could have had no inkling then of the unconscious irony his comment would one day acquire. That the most agile, most mobile of all comedians should have suffered such an end was a fate which he of all men least deserved.

The spark of anarchy that Askey ignited over the airwaves was kept ablaze in the years to come by names as disparate as Spike Milligan, Kenny Everett, Michael Barrymore and even Chris Evans. For all their combined brilliance, none of them came near to matching the little man for sheer *good* humour. Occasionally cynical but never cruel, he maintained his dignity both on- and offstage in a way that would have qualified him for legendary status with or without the laughs. After his death it was left to Anthea to take care of the more than 8,000 cards and messages of goodwill that had arrived for her father during his hospitalisation. His friend Jimmy Jewel paid him the finest tribute: 'He showed great courage. I don't know a greater man.'

Arthur made something like twelve appearances in the annual Royal Variety Performance. Ken Dodd was present on one occasion, when at the end of the dress rehearsal producer Robert Nesbitt addressed the whole cast onstage, thanking everyone for their efforts and wishing them good luck for the ordeal ahead. At this point a lone voice had the audacity to make itself heard: 'Mr Nesbitt?' 'Yehss,' queried the great man. 'In your opinion,' dared Arthur, 'which one of us stood out?' In an instant the cold formality of the moment dissolved and everyone relaxed into laughter. Not for nothing had Arthur Askey in his early days once been billed as 'The Ultra-Violet Ray of Sunshine'.

TED RAY: FIDDLING AND FOOLING

It's a wisecrack that knows its own father!

I've got a fiddle, home, dog, motor-car, wireless set, cinematograph – and a wife. So I should worry!

Merry 'Cripps-mas' and an 'Attlee' New Year from Ted Ray and may 1948 bring us prosperity and plenty, even if comics have to change their routines!
[Seasonal greeting placed in the *Performer* Christmas edition, 1947]

The art of the radio comedian as exemplified by the skills of Askey and Handley was maintained at the top level by their honorary fellow Liverpudlian Ted Ray. In addition to the adroitness with which he handled the mechanised medium of the wireless, Ray was also a brilliant stage performer and at the peak of his career ensured that the one skill adroitly complemented the other. That career did not officially begin until Charles Olden, born the son of popular northern comic Charlie Alden in Wigan on 21 November 1905, fulfilled his first professional engagement as a small-time dance-band violinist in Liverpool, where his family moved a short time after his birth. With a flair for comic vocal extemporisation he developed a solo act under the name of Hugh Neek, which must qualify as one of the most off-putting stage names ever devised. This then evolved into the act of Nedlo (Olden backwards), the Gypsy Violinist, in which Ted was at first forbidden by contract to utter a single word. It was not long, however, before the quips crept back in between the tunes, and after a successful debut in the capital at the London Music Hall, Shoreditch in May 1930 the pseudo-Romany name was changed to Ted Ray in honour of the British golfer who had won the United States Open Championship in 1920. The Gypsy costume had already been abandoned two years earlier in favour of white evening dress and stiff collar. But formal dress was not considered particularly conducive to comedy and, through a flash of inspiration, Ted found himself not only changing his style overnight, but also helping to set a trend. To quote from his autobiography, *Raising the Laughs*:

I did not realise it, but I had experienced the birth pang of an idea which was to alter not only my whole approach to comedy but my career as well… As clearly as though a voice had spoken the words aloud I found myself thinking: You've been wrong all along. Why keep yourself aloof from the audience? Why not be *one* of them? Forget all about comic make-up, the white bowler hat, those fantastic, ridiculous props. Why, there's no need even to bother about a dinner jacket. Just be human. Stroll on to that stage in an ordinary suit, just as if you'd walked in from the street.

By March 1932 the casual, intimate, modern Ted Ray set the seal on his break with the tradition of the grotesque when he made his debut at the London Palladium. He was billed unobtrusively as 'Ted Ray: A Newcomer', but the immediate impact of his success may be measured by the fact that at the first house on Monday night he was second act after the opening chorus line; at the second house he was second act after the interval! Moreover, by the end of the week, the top of the bill, Harry Green, a Jewish comedian of passing repute, had him doing a spot in his own act as well. Ted soon became a big name on the variety stage, playing the Palladium many times in subsequent years, though ironically, since his peak period coincided with the invasion of Hollywood stars in the late 1940s, he never had one of that theatre's big production shows built around his talents in the way that vehicles were provided for Miller, Trinder and the Crazy Gang. However, Ted often found himself introducing the American stars to a bewildered British public, including the much publicised Danny Kaye on his first triumphant visit in 1948. Although their comic styles were miles apart, the ballyhoo surrounding Kaye's visit was so intense that it was to Ray's credit that the press should spare copy to praise him as the artist who carried the banner of British talent fluttering defiantly in the face of the best of Hollywood. One newspaper carried the headline WHICH IS BETTER – KAYE OR RAY?, and in the Royal Variety Performance at the Palladium that year Ted was a tremendous hit, Kaye a resounding failure. The following year he again participated, filling the final spot that Kaye had held the year before.

On the variety stage Ray's two most recognisable trademarks were his fiddle, played with a passable musical ability inherited from his father and grandfather, who had both been skilled violinists, and a direct voice with a built-in twang that was all its own. The structure of the act changed very little after that first London engagement at Shoreditch, although, as the general standard of stage choreography improved, the sequence he once described as 'gags, violin, song, dance' was curtailed. Fiddle and voice were interdependent, the former a prop for and a pointer to the gags, the latter the means of keeping the audience itself at a pitch of anticipation until he did eventually play. 'I started very young. When I was three, I used to play on my parents' nerves. And when I was four, the neighbours clubbed together and bought me a violin. I practised for a whole year and when I was five they clubbed together again and bought me a chopper. When I was nine, I appeared at the Albert Hall and played Rachmaninov. I nearly beat him too!' An idea of the closely knit texture of his 'fiddling and fooling' can be gained from Ray's own analysis of his act in the theatrical newspaper the *Stage* during September 1951. Likening it to a chain of quips, stories, gags and asides, he went on, 'the big laughs I aim for every seven seconds; then there are the ripples of good feeling in the audience – the smaller links; all being woven into a pattern that ends with the song that takes me offstage'.

However scientific Ray's approach, he was not the only performer on the British variety stage to combine comedy with violin playing, following in a tradition established in the USA by Jack Benny and Henny Youngman. Vic Oliver (1898 – 1964) was quite as adept as Ted at storytelling and the art

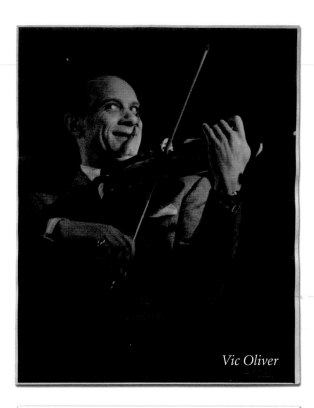

Vic Oliver

Jimmy Wheeler

of the throwaway line – 'What has Paganini got that I haven't got? Except hair!' – and was an even better musician, having been a professional concert soloist on the staff of Graz Opera House. During his later years he did in fact divide his time between comedy and serious concert work. However, his social contacts – between 1936 and 1945 he was married to Sir Winston Churchill's actress daughter, Sarah – would appear to have cramped both his appeal and his style, which did, however, enjoy the considerable advantage of an attractive natural Austrian accent. Jimmy Wheeler (1910 – 1973), who reached his peak with considerable television exposure in the 50s, was as gruff as Oliver was sophisticated, the archetypal beer-stained bash comic. Wearing battered trilby and shaggy moustache (fashioned out of rabbit fur), he scorned the smoother approach of the other two, and became famous for his rough and ready departure line 'Aye, aye, that's yer lot!' What set Ted Ray apart from Vic and Jimmy was his ability to maintain a common touch contrary to the slickness of his presentation. His act had at once the class of one and the unpretentiousness of the other. In this double quality one can see the influence not only of those slightly older performers whom Ted came to emulate if only for the kindness and warmth he detected in their humour – namely Robb Wilton and the Scottish character comedian Will Fyffe, not to mention the Liverpool auctioneer whose superb timing and easy-going line of patter had in the early years taught the aspiring young comedian much about the technique of handling an audience – but also of the many American performers he introduced to the British public and who made up for what they lacked in warmth before an alien audience with the sheer slickness of their delivery. Hence the unmistakable transatlantic tone in Ray's voice;

but, as Bud Flanagan remarked in *My Crazy Life*, British variety artists were becoming highly susceptible to American influence, 'especially their way of talking', as early as the 1900s, so this was not as revolutionary as it may have appeared.

It is as a radio wit that Ted Ray will be most vividly remembered, and it is perhaps surprising that until 1949 his connection with broadcasting was only slight. In 1939 the BBC decided to profit from the current success of the Crazy Gang with a radio equivalent entitled *Just Fooling*, featuring Ted, Dave and Joe O'Gorman, and Binnie Hale. The outbreak of war, however, prevented the show from continuing the success of its first and only broadcast, and Ted had to wait another ten years before getting a comparable opportunity with the first six tentative editions of *Ray's a Laugh*, possibly the most apposite title ever boasted by a radio comedy series. The show began on 4 April 1949 and eventually ran for twelve years, not least thanks to the combined writing skills of Ronnie Hanbury, Eddie Maguire, George Wadmore and Ted himself among others.

Although a more realistic programme than *ITMA*, which it could be construed as replacing, over the years it developed its own zany circus of catchphrases and characters. The most notable members of this select group included gangster Al K. Traz, who was in love with a girl named Penny Tentiary, and Serge Suit, an amiable Russian whose tongue always fell short of getting to grips with the English language: 'I lerewike to hear Tchaikerowovsky's Serewugar Plerewum Ferewairy.' Both were portrayed by an unknown Peter Sellers, at his most chameleonesque early best. Sellers also played an eccentric female who could hardly speak for the giggles, before going on to announce, 'My name's Crystal Jollibottom, you sauce box!' Graham Stark was transformed into Tommy Trafford, who would declare in weather-beaten proud Lancastrian tones, 'If you haven't been to Manchester, you haven't lived.' Bob, of the popular songs-at-the-piano duo Bob and Alf Pearson ('We bring you melody from out of the sky, my brother and I') would in cute ingratiating tones supply the legendary reply to Ted's familiar question 'What's your name, little girl?' – 'Jenn-eee-ferr,' the stress distributed equally over all three syllables. In the case of Mrs Hoskin and Ivy, forerunners of Les Dawson's 'Cissie and Ada', Bob as the former had Ted to partner him in verbal drag. The victim of incessant hypochondria, Mrs Hoskin would recount, 'It was agony, Ivy,' and Ivy would chirpily enquire, 'What happened, Mrs Hoskin?' This was the cue for the mythical Dr Hardcastle to creep into the conversation, the mention of his name providing the cue in turn for Ivy's excited gasp and the words, 'Young Dr Hardcastle! He's loo-vely, Mrs Hoskin… He's loo… ooo… vely!'

However essential the above eccentrics were to the show's success, they were fringe benefits. The sketch format in time became dominated by the domestic situation between Ted and his radio wife, played for the most part by the Australian Kitty Bluett. This portrayed a world of odd jobs that never get done, of the breakfast newspaper as an Iron Curtain barring communication, of concealed pay rises and marital ultimatums, of burnt toast and burst pipes. Although clichés of domestic existence and married life are not funny per se, once an audience has identified with the domestic detail in this type of comedy, the laughter of recognition takes over. Not the first in this country to exploit this style of humour via dramatic situation, Ted must have long realised its obvious appeal. The couple he and Kitty portrayed shrewdly represented neither the world of kitchen sink nor smart Chelsea, but rather the happy medium of anonymous suburbia. Moreover, however much their adventures were based on fact – many of the incidents that subsequently amused the radio audience had happened in the homes of various members of the production team – they could all claim an element of improbability. If the show did break the bounds of realism severely, though, it was in representing Ted and Kitty as living far beyond the means of a junior clerk. As such the programme may be likened to Barry Appleby's original 'Gambols' cartoon strip, which was at once wish-fulfilment fantasy and a vicarious means of expression for the ordinary person who observes things in everyday life which amuse, impress or intrigue him but which he is unable to express consciously for himself, however acute the observation. Ted himself admitted in a 1957 *Radio Times* interview, 'I like to feel when Kitty and I are doing one of our sketches that all over the country married couples are looking at each other and saying, "But darling, that's exactly what happened to us the other day."' He was also honest enough to admit that at the core of the series was a 'rationale of tediousness'. But tedium never set in, not least because of the unpredictability of the eccentric parade of supporting characters. Perhaps the most famous of these was one that never had a chance to put its case to the microphone. After Will Hay's schoolboys, Robb Wilton's office boy and Funf, it provided a most original scapegoat.

> *Ted*: Before you go to sleep, Kitty, listen to this advert. 'For Sale, set of ornamental rabbits – suitable for garden – owner going abroad.'
> *Kitty*: Ted, they would be nice in the garden – why don't you buy them?
> *Ted*: Not likely. I wouldn't be able to tell the difference between *them* and *him*!
> *Kitty*: Who's *him*?
> *Ted*: *That ginger tom from next door*!

Apart from Kitty Bluett, the supporting actor who became most identifiable with the programme was Carry On stalwart Kenneth Connor, remembered as the sheepish little man – brother-in-law, lodger or boss's nephew – with the quivering tremble lodged in his throat, upon whom Ted could only just refrain from committing physical violence; or, once Connor had changed this accent into the most nasally contorted of all, as the surly individual with the stock introduction 'My name is Sidney Mincing, and I happen to be the proprietor of this [whatever it may have been that week] emporium.'

'It's that ginger tom from next door again!'

Throughout his career Ray's most valuable asset was his quick-fire talent for repartee, which marked him out as one of the nimblest wits in show business, as proved by his presence on panel shows like *My Wildest Dream*, *Jokers Wild* and *Does the Team Think?* One gained the impression, perhaps unfairly, that this wit was based on the most copious of memories, to which were committed thousands of well tried quips and gambits, all filed away mentally, waiting to be summoned with hair-trigger certainty as the situation demanded, rather than being essentially creative in the manner of his American counterparts like the dour Fred Allen or the zanily intelligent Groucho Marx. It is easy to call to mind many witticisms of the latter pair, but it is hard to recall readily anything that originated distinctly from Ted Ray. And yet his reputation is its own answer to such doubts. The *commedia dell'arte*, the root of the music hall as we know it, was improvisational only in so far as it did draw upon such a stock of tested material. Ray used to boast, 'Give me any keyword and I'll give you four jokes.' There is no reason to doubt his claim.

Reporting on his appearance in the Royal Variety Performance of 1952, the *Stage* wrote that Ted had 'not only advanced with the times, but often been in advance of them in style and technique. More than any other contemporary comedian he has been able successfully to combine radio and stage.' Spry and youthful-looking into advanced age, he was seen in his own series on television for only four years between 1955 and 1959. He may simply have been ahead of his time. Fred Allen, who was comparatively ignored by the medium himself, once said that the really big star name of television comedy would eventually be the performer who could simply sit and talk to people before the cameras in that intimate confidential manner so obviously demanded by the living room. As a sit-down as distinct from stand-up comedian, Ted Ray's own contributions to shows hosted by serious, if friendly, interviewers, suggest that, had he been born thirty years later, or had television been invented thirty years earlier, he could well have fulfilled Allen's prediction in this country. As it is, Allen may have been paving the way for his young Irish namesake, Dave Allen (1936 – 2005), real name David Tynan O'Mahoney, who as a skilled raconteur proved a spiritual descendant of Ray, a fact obscured by his anarchic but thoughtful irreverence for our most sacred taboos. And yet while the world of Allen's humour admitted to a harsher reality, a more caustic appraisal of human nature than the cosy domesticity promoted by Ted, Allen's hold on the popular audience was no less compulsive, his grip on the new medium, as predicted by the American, intimate and sure.

Dave Allen: 'TV is immediate – this show is recorded!'

Afterthoughts

I have a special fondness for Ted Ray for two reasons. The first radio comedy series I ever registered as a child was *Ray's a Laugh*, the first joke I can recall – perhaps because I had to ask my parents to explain it – being one cracked by Ted on the occasion he took Kitty to Paris for the weekend. She told him that she was just popping out of the hotel to see the *magasins* and Ted countered with a line to the effect that she had no need to do that; they had lots of magazines in their room already. I was not much more than five years old at the time, with no knowledge at all of the French language, let alone its word for shops. Secondly, no other comedian ever defined more succinctly, more practically the word that has become the cornerstone of comedy technique. Asked to define timing, he replied, 'Timing? You don't talk while the audience is laughing. It's as simple as that!'

In its twelve-year run over eleven series *Ray's a Laugh* eventually notched up 358 episodes, not including the occasional one-off seasonal special. As such it overtook *ITMA*. In retrospect what makes the statistic more staggering is the fact that for a large part of this time Ted was also appearing in a whole range of other radio variety and comedy shows, not least *Calling All Forces*, *Spice of Life* and *Ted Ray Time*, helping to make him the most recognisable voice in comedy during the 1950s.

Sadly the final years of this most genial of jesters were marked by a fall from grace when in 1975 he was convicted of dangerous driving while under the influence of alcohol, having smashed into three other vehicles and then rammed a lamp post. He appeared to recover, but after returning to hospital for further treatment died suddenly on 8 November 1977, cause of death being registered as heart failure. In fact the accident left him in severe pain, and when he made what may have been his last television appearance, as a guest of the magician David Nixon a short while before he died, he was ironically reduced to performing his stand-up routine sitting on a stool. Meanwhile Dave Allen would make the piece of furniture his own as he became the first stand-up comedian to risk doing his act sitting down alone with a glass of whisky and a cigarette, taking shots at religion – 'I'm an atheist... thank God!' – and his native Irish culture, and blazing a path not only for *Father Ted* and Graham Norton, but also as inspiration at a wider level for the Jack Dee and Ben Elton generation.

Of Ted's fellow fiddlers, Jimmy Wheeler was the least accomplished. Apparently he could play only one tune, 'Mistakes'. On one occasion he was asked by a theatre manager to vary his repertoire: 'Can't you play anything else?' 'Of course I can. What do you want,' replied the maestro, '"Fascination" or "Kiss Me Again"?' The manager said, 'Yes, play "Fascination".' Jimmy, somewhat disgruntled, replied, 'All right then. I'll play "Fascination", but don't blame me if it sounds like "Mistakes"!' While Wheeler's image remained as subtle as a toilet brush, Vic Oliver moved in different circles entirely. It is said that Vic was once present when Churchill was asked whom he most admired. The great man replied, 'Mussolini.' When asked why, he answered, 'Because he had the good sense to shoot *his* son-in-law!' But Oliver could take a joke against himself. No line summed up his approach better than the one he asked compères to deliver by way of an introduction when appearing on a variety bill: 'Ladies and gentlemen, whenever we are privileged to present a truly great artist, we always refer to them solely by their surname – Gigli, Menuhin, Callas, Heifetz – so we are now proud to present Mr Vic Oliver!' Ted once explained why so many comics played the violin: 'If they couldn't sing a song, they had to have some means of getting offstage… You can't just finish and stand there with your face hanging out, especially with a hard audience, so the fiddle enabled you to get off with dignity.' Ted never signed off without it.

Ted as Nedlo, the Gypsy Violinist

Sid Field: 'What a performance!'

Heckler (from the circle of the theatre): Well, what are you?

Field (as Slasher Green): I am a discovery.

Heckler: Discovery? What's that?

Field: Like I have been found.

Heckler: Why?

Field: No, no, you don't seem to understand. I am not lost – I have been sorted out.

Heckler: Yes – sorted out of what?

Field: Sorted out of people what want to go on, see. The theatre magnates, they go round finding them and they take them away from a good home where they are happy and comfortable and put them on the stage and make money out of them.

The early life of Sid Field grimly underlines the heartaches and frustrations of a precarious profession. There has always been irony in any suggestion of overnight success after strenuous years of graft and grind; in Field's case those years amounted to thirty, a period in which provincial respect chafed against professional obscurity. It was not until 1943 that *Strike a New Note*, a purposely anonymous revue at the Prince of Wales Theatre, brought him at last to the notice of a discriminating public. Anonymous is accurate. It contained initially no stars as such. All the artists were billed alphabetically, in a programme that bore a prophetic footnote headed, 'Here is youth,' even though Sid himself, at thirty-nine, was far from a youthful age for the start of a meteoric West End career: 'These boys and girls have been gathered from every part of the country. All are players of experience, needing but the opportunity to make themselves known. They have worked, they have learned; this, then, is their chance to show what they are worth.'

Sid did show his worth. Within three weeks the posters were amended to feature as star-billing 'Sid Field – The New Funny-man'. Amid the clamour and cheers of that first night, 18 March 1943, the critics paused to ask where such a genius had been hiding. Grateful yet cynical, Sid could reply that only six weeks before he had been playing London's Finsbury Park Empire, territory out of bounds to the sensitive metropolitan theatre critics of the day. Luckily their praise for the new production, which also featured Derek Roy, Zoë Gail, Jill Manners, and in support a very young and for that occasion unpartnered Eric Morecambe and Ernie Wise, helped to notch up a total of 661 performances. Sid followed this with *Strike it Again*, which ran for 438 performances from 28 November 1944, with Wendy Toye and Billy Dainty as auxiliary members of the cast. Then, on 11 October 1946, the curtain went up on the first of 778 performances of *Piccadilly Hayride*.

Playing second comic lead to Field in this show was Terry-Thomas (1911 – 1990), who with gap-toothed grin and a grandiose line in waistcoats and cigarette holders would later become the first comedian to make more than a flickering impression in British television and subsequently became Hollywood's favourite idea of the Englishman-about-town as silly ass. His principal contribution here was the routine 'Technical Hitch', in which he played a pioneer radio disc jockey whose fortuitous talent as an impressionist saves the day when just before going on air he trips and all the records he is about to play are smashed to smithereens, a routine featured many times in later years and one of the most original frameworks conceived by a stage impressionist for his skills.

Field's three revue successes were all staged at the Prince of Wales Theatre, by the end of the decade almost a permanent showplace for his talent, in comfortable contrast to the hectic days of provincial touring, a travelling see-saw of a routine in which he had been trapped since childhood. He was born

Sidney Arthur Field on April Fools' Day 1904, and began his theatrical career when a small boy, dressing up in his father's outsize trousers, boots and wing collar to perform back-garden impersonations of Chaplin in the Sparkbrook district of his native Birmingham. Once when he ventured into the street, he caused chaos and was pulled home by the ear by a policeman with a philosophy that Field himself would later disprove: ''Ere, we've got one Charlie Chaplin – we don't need any more.' Apart, however, from an ability as an amateur impressionist and his admiration for his father's whimsical personality – 'Apart from Chaplin, my old man [a cane and whip maker by trade] was the funniest chap I ever knew. He used to have tea under the table. Then he'd say, "What are you laughing at?"' – there was nothing about Field's background to suggest a theatrical career. Certainly the young boy had no professional ambition in this direction. His mother, though, was persistent, determined that her son should tread the boards.

At the age of eleven he found himself, along with three precocious boys and ten spiteful girls, unhappily billed as 'The Kino Royal Juveniles'. This first professional engagement lasted no more than a day and the horrid junior troupe was reduced to the unlucky number Sid thought it deserved. A year later the sensitive young Chaplin impersonator rejoined them and, by now inured to their ribbing, stayed. At fourteen he would find himself understudying Wee Georgie Wood and eventually outgrowing the job. Then would come the long, tedious provincial haul, punctuated only by a tour of Australia in the early 1930s. For several years he himself took the part of straight man and comedian's labourer, first for the mercurial touring-revue comic Jack Herbert, and then for another, Duggie Ascot, names which mean little today. The accent in his own act at this stage of his career was on the singing and dancing of a light juvenile lead, in the tradition of his idols Jack Buchanan and Fred Barnes – the Novello of the music halls. Although funny offstage, Sid was apparently scared of the thought of actually *having* to make people laugh.

The West End was still a distant Utopia, but August 1929 did see Field at the Hammersmith Palace of Varieties supporting Ascot in a revue futuristically entitled *Hot Ice*. The following year he acted as straight man to what remains another obscure name, George Norton. One night Norton's excessive – and, as far as Field was concerned, portentously ironic – drinking occasioned his dismissal from the cast. In the emergency Sid had no alternative but to take over the lead in the golfing sketch they performed. He had edged his way to top billing, and by April 1933 was tentatively encroaching upon the elusive West End, top of the bill at Finsbury Park Empire in *The Revue of the Moment*, billed as 'The Destroyer of Gloom'. However, an additional barrier to top-flight recognition was now thrown across his path by an exclusive contract to William Henshall, incorporating an annual option on his services by the provincial impresario. Field was as secure as any unrecognised variety artist could be, but would find himself forced to work for Henshall with diminishing goodwill for ten years, during which the clown whose constant ambition was to be a top West End star had no option but to reject the tempting offers that kept coming his way. Field had to wait until 1942 for this legal straitjacket to be loosened. Impresario Val Parnell then saw him with Jerry Desmonde in a Nottingham pantomime. It was a short step to *Strike a New Note*, and the circuit-prisoner of the 30s swiftly became the comic talking-point of the 40s.

It is futile to attempt to describe Sid Field's comic persona in a few words. He represented a whole gallery of dubious, yet adorable, always extraordinarily detailed caricatures, whether bumptious spiv or apprentice golfer, moonstruck musician or exasperating photographer, yet always remaining himself, the distinctive Field ethos never failing to assert itself through the surface of the characterisation. J. B. Priestley compared this spirit to that of Dickens's 'genial monsters', in that both seemed to belong to some distant happier planet. The key to this analogy lay in his extraordinarily plastic face, at once as innocent as a baby and as astute as the most prosperous of barrow boys, a face which in 1944 put Agate, not knowing where the eyes ended and the nose began, in mind of 'those mystery ships which do not reveal their secret until they go into action'. Through the slightest glint of an eye, the merest flicker of a smile, Sid could melt the most frigid of audiences. As one critic accurately remarked, he had only to wink with the side of his mouth to be funny. And yet if his shrewd, apparently exhaustive character ability and unlimited range of facial expression were poised at genius level, he also brought to everything he did the special permanent quality that qualified him as one of the greatest individual clowns. His great secret was that whatever level of sophistication his characters aspired to, beneath the surface he remained the naive schoolboy to whom mischief meant unlimited joy. His stolid lumbering frame resisted the facile pathos of the little man, but the wide winsome blue eyes, the air of battered innocence made it inevitable that a measure of pathos should obtrude. Of course, the moment it did so, Field himself, as if brandishing an invisible catapult, was the first to jeer it offstage. The logic of many of his sketches was poised at nursery level. He was an overgrown baby, forgetful and squabbling, yet bringing to his audience the same pleasure and comfort that a normal child can contribute to family life. Waving a triumphant rattle in the face of his audience, he generated the warmth of a child's tea party where he could have spilt tea, smeared cream, thrown cake on an indulgent audience and got away with it. And yet, however dominant Field's own personality, like Harry Tate with his check cap and cranked-up propeller of a moustache before him, he belonged firmly to the tradition of music hall comedy that demanded a step back from the footlights into a designer's set, forsaking intimate patter for the comic situation. The simpler that situation, the greater its appeal and comic potential, although the basic requirements remained the same, namely the need to strike off at a tangent from the accepted norm, transmute order into chaos, render the easiest task an insurmountable obstacle.

While Field's versatility makes generalisations of character difficult, there was an essential difference between the two sketch performers. Tate – in his own words 'master of the situation' and a 'stickler for system' – was always the central cause of the disintegration and chaos. His self-confidence matched his self-delusion; as far as he was concerned, he was never beaten, was always cock-a-hoop, even though the audience had taken the hint long before that at the root of things it was Tate who was being scored off by his team of oddly assorted 'boys', Tate who didn't really have a clue. Field, whether as golfer, billiards player or 1940s wide boy, brought a basic humility and honesty to the Tate prototype. Ramshackle inefficiency may still have been the order of the day, and yet one knew that if this was Field's fault, he was still doing his best. He could never grasp why so much fuss should be made as a result of his actions and, appalled and amazed, would complain in sullen flattened tones, 'What a performance!' He could admit to the chaos, because he never visualised himself as its cause. For Tate, fully conscious of his own failings, to make such an admission would have been social suicide, and this he knew well to avoid.

Whereas the older performer employed a whole team to back him onstage, Field's main prop at the peak of his career was Jerry Desmonde (1908 – 1967), who joined him in 1942. Desmonde's real name was James Robert Sadler, and in later years he would provide an admirable foil for Norman Wisdom, but it was as the urbane complement to Field's rampant inadequacy that he first gained recognition. Here was the traditional double act of unctuous intolerant straight man and daft distraught clown at its most brilliant. Once Sid had coaxed an audience into laughing at a certain point in a routine he would hold the script in abeyance and milk that one situation for maximum laughter, going outside the sketch framework and reaching out to the audience on more direct terms. In such a situation few straight men have matched Desmonde's flexibility. Sid and Jerry had an instinctive feel for one another which meant that at any moment the former could telegraph to the latter to continue as arranged. The threads would be gathered unerringly and the audience would be completely unaware of any significant deviation having taken place. Desmonde became not only the pivot around which Field revolved, but his alter ego. In this way every performance, however different, became the definitive one. The sketches in which they appeared remain among the most prized memories of those who saw them. They all required on Field's part an individual costume and – although, as we have seen, only at surface level – a different personality. In these respects he again differed from Harry Tate.

The most famous occasion when Desmonde's dignity fell prey to Field's gushing idiocy was in 'Following Through', the golfing routine inherited from Norton and featured in *Strike a New Note, Strike it Again* and the Royal Variety Performance of 1945. The sketch represented a gradual descent into an ever-deepening abyss of Aguecheek misapprehension on the part of Sid. One was led to expect the worst from his first entrance in plus fours carrying a lilac flower and explaining wistfully, 'Isn't that a be-oo-tiful colour? He-li-o-trope! What a be-oo-tiful word!' Bullied by Desmonde and caddy Alfie Dean into playing a game, Sid is told to prepare the tee. For this he will need some sand: 'Tea with sand? I'm not drinking that sturf [*sic*] – more like cocoa!' This difficulty smoothed over, Jerry is ready to begin: 'Let's go.' Sid starts to return to the clubhouse. Summoned back he changes physical gear into a sulking frenzy, his gawky, skew-eyed look the link between Harpo Marx's 'Gooky' expression and Norman Wisdom's 'Gump', his large floppy cap swivelled round with peak upturned. As Jerry explains, 'When I say "Let's go", I don't mean "Let's go"; I mean "Let's go"'. Sid is not convinced. With a matronly despair he exclaims 'What a per-*form*-ance! I can't understand what's come over you, Humphrey. You're not like this when we're painting together.' His inability to understand the simplest logic places him firmly in line with the character from comic antiquity who, wanting to sell his house, carries a single brick about as a sample. Even a curt rejoinder from Desmonde leaves Field nonplussed.

> *Desmonde*: Skip it! What are you jumping over the ball for?
> *Field*: Well, you said 'Skip it!'

Desmonde: No, no! Get behind the ball.

Field: But it's behind the ball all round. What a performance!

Desmonde: Come on! Square up to that ball. (*Sid starts to box*) No. Not like that, silly. Keep your eye on the ball (*Sid kneels down and does so*) Ah! Get up. Address the ball.

Field: Dear ball.

Desmonde: Get up.

Field: No. You've smacked me!

At each exchange Field becomes more sheepish and appears all the more innocent. His interpretation of Desmonde's instructions assumes its own metaphysical aspect. There *is* a justification somewhere. Not that this impresses Jerry, his eyes fixed in a blood-curdling stare. The whole routine is punctuated by retaliation of the purest knockabout kind. The bullying Desmonde continually enquires 'What are you doing that for?' and Sid instinctively buffets him across the chest with his forearm, a peculiar defence mechanism which Eric Morecambe kept alive in his own exasperated assaults on a similarly pestering Wise during their early television days. Sulking like a child and pronouncing his words with a slow, rounded, tongue-tip precision, he regrets not having attended his music lesson with Miss Fanthorpe.

Sid with Jerry Desmonde: 'Following Through'

Field: Miss Fanthorpe's kind.
Desmonde: Miss Fanthorpe might be kind, but she can't play golf.
Field: No, but she can play the piano and the flute.
Desmonde: But who wants to play the piano and the flute?
Field: Miss Fanthorpe!

By now Sid is laughing, and we could be forgiven for supposing that the tantrums are over. However, Desmonde's bullying persists. Told to address the ball 'with the face of the club', Sid holds the handle at the point nearest the iron head to talk to it; told to swing the club 'back, back, slowly back', he *walks* back and away from the ball until it suddenly dawns that he can't now hit the ball in that position. The professional is at his wit's end.

Desmonde: When I say 'slowly back', I don't mean 'slowly back'; I mean 'slowly back'.
Field: Well, let's pick flowers.

Gradually, though, Sid's speech takes on a glow of enlightenment.

Field: Look, when you say 'slowly back', you don't mean 'slowly back'; you mean 'slowly back'. Sthilly! [*sic*] You should have said.

For one brief moment they are 'all friends again', emphasising the sense of companionship and shared values inherent in sport, which in turn underlines the failure of communication at all other moments between Sid and Jerry, and perhaps explains why sport was so often a focal point of the music hall sketch. Two girls now approach. Told to shout 'Fore!' Sid thinks that 'daft' and bellows, 'Get out of it.' They take no notice and walking nonchalantly in front of Sid pocket the ball, the 'fourth' they've found today. Thwarted again he lapses into another Wisdom-style frenzy, jerking along mechanically and justifying all his own favourite adjectives – 'daft', 'silly', 'Oh, you *naughty* boy,' 'Don't be so *foolhardy*.' As if this *reductio ad absurdum* has not gone far enough, Jerry now takes out another ball. On the cue 'Belt it,' Sid's hands go instinctively to his waist; 'Get down to it,' and he starts to descend; 'No, I mean stand up and get down to it!' Eventually Sid does hit the ball, but the true climax of the routine is not in the sound of shattering glass caused by his success, but in the look of hurt pride in his eyes, a look which says far more effectively than any words that he *has* done *his* best. There was now only one thing which Jerry could say: 'I didn't really mean it, Sidney.'

The same agonies of bewilderment and frustration, the same look of wounded dignity, hallmarked the billiards routine featured in *Piccadilly Hayride* and the Royal Variety Performance of 1946, in which Sid, 'the novice', was taught to play by Jerry, 'the old hand', with the services of Alfie Dean as 'the marker'. Once more he is humiliated by surface technicalities. 'Strike,' roars Desmonde, at which Sid puts down his cue and lolls against the wall. 'Pocket the ball,' yells the expert. And so, coyly shifting his gaze between audience and the red, Sid casually hides the ball in his trouser pocket at the very moment Jerry's eyes are averted. The latter, surprised to hear that he has carried out his instruction, is anxious to know which pocket it is in. Taking a deep breath Sid sighs, 'Ahhh – guess!' The appealing eyes glisten with mischievous glee – billiards has been reduced to a nursery game. Jerry now has to quiz his way around the table: 'This one?' – 'No.' – 'That one?' – 'No.' – 'That one?' – 'No. You're getting warm.' – 'That one?' – 'No.' – 'Well, which one?' And then with a triumphant meticulousness Sid exclaims '*This* one!' One moment jubilant, the next he drives his cue through cloth and table, pretext again for the huffish gibber, the sullen tantrum.

'*Portrait Study*'

While the world of golf course and billiards room was one of male gamesmanship, the salon of Field's fashionable blonde-wigged velvet-coated photographer (as featured in *Strike it Again*) was nothing if not a repository for feminine gossip, a place where tea and biscuits were of more importance than the process of taking photographs. From the first entrance of Sid's friend, Whittaker, slightly late through having fallen off his bicycle – 'You see, I told you not to buy one with a crossbar' – we could be in the company of two mutually-adoring gossiping old matrons, the host all but licking the guest with pleasure and affection. There is the feminine preoccupation with headwear, in this instance Desmonde's 'tricky' mayoral hat, which Sid simply must try on, not that it suits him because his hair 'hasn't been done'. 'So that's a mayor's hat, eh? Looks like one of those flappers we used to get from the Maypole when we were kids!' As he swishes it through the air like the folded paper toy the childish aspect of the Field persona once again flashes to the surface. Then comes the serious business of getting tea, each falling backwards in his attempt to help the other.

Desmonde: I know, let me cut the bread and butter.
Field: No, it's already cut and the butter's wiped on and everything.

Refusing to make light of the task in hand, Sid keeps dashing off into the side room, falling over the camera legs as he does so. Field made a habit of tripping over invisible obstacles when the real thing failed to present itself. Eventually he emerges with the tea trolley and they sit together, Sid poised precariously on the edge of his seat in his anxiety to hear all the latest gossip. With ecstatic effeminacy he exclaims 'Oh, I'm *sooo* happy,' a line which you knew he not only meant, but which for all its simplicity became on his lips one of the funniest in the whole of music hall crosstalk. Of course, all they do have to talk about is the weather: 'Oh dear! Hasn't it been cold? Really, I haven't known how to move!'; the business of pouring tea: 'Forgive me pouring that way, but I used to drown my tie' (after pouring each cup Sid awkwardly brings the teapot down to within six inches from the floor to let the drips fall on the carpet); the plate of cakes, which they juggle between themselves with exaggerated finesse: 'Did you make them yourself?'; and their own well-being. Sid's photographer is not without self-pity: 'I'm terribly busy – a big house to clean – can't get up the stairs like I used to – never been the same since my last operation – fourteen weeks on my back with my leg up, I was.' Then they begin to prepare for the actual photographic session. At first the mayor is told he has his hat on 'side-saddle' (that is from ear to ear), whereas the photographer wants it at right angles to this position. 'That's right – more in keeping with the nose!' The difficulties Sid now experiences in getting his subject, 'bobbing about like the squirt from a siphon', into just the right position are interminable, both parties wavering between spiteful recrimination and lavish adoration. Behind the sitter's chair is a screen, one side of which is blank, while the other depicts a wood scena. Sid asks Jerry to turn the screen round – 'I can't see the mayor for the trees' – but when he does so, he is completely hidden by it and a spontaneous game of hide and seek ensues. 'This mayor's so utterly stupid, I could scream,' despairs Field. Pacing out the correct number of steps between sitter and tripod, he suddenly loses mental track and breaks into a run as if to bowl at cricket; then, his mistake suddenly dawning, he apologises fawningly. Eventually Jerry is seated correctly and Sid squats beneath the black camera cloth. 'Show me your teeth. No, don't take them out.' 'Marvellous, absolutely wonderful. Come and have a look. Oh, silly!' 'Let's put some books on the table. That gives the impression you can read!' The light dims and the photographer has to borrow a shilling from his client. The sitter sneezes and Sid remonstrates, 'I've never seen such a baby mayor! Even I'm not afraid of this.' There is hardly any need to add that when Sid does come to press the bulb, not only his equipment but any confidence he may have had disintegrates in a flash of smoke.

Of all Field's characterisations, the photographer was the most ground-breaking. The height of grotesque effeminacy, it set a trend in gossipy camp humour that the more jagged personality of Frankie Howerd would fully exploit in the years after Field's death. The partnership between photographer and client also predated the Julian and Sandy combination of Hugh Paddick and Kenneth Williams in *Round the Horne*, even though the sexual ambiguity of the later duo was far less subtle. Certainly all these performances blatantly underline the theory proffered by Tynan on seeing 'Portrait Study', that comedy is in part rooted in 'the exposure of all that is womanish in man, the unveiling of feminine traits beneath the masculine exterior'. Interestingly an early draft of the sketch – written by the celebrated *Punch* humorist Basil Boothroyd – reveals that before the photography motif was added it was entitled 'Tea Party' and began with a spoken introduction that left no doubt about the sexual ambivalence it contained: 'In this topsy-turvy world, where most women are doing men's jobs, we would like to give you our conception of "if men had a tea party like the women do".'

'The Blizzard of the Bells'

As a professor of music in 'The Blizzard of the Bells' from *Strike a New Note* Field donned a hideous tail-suit which had seen far better days with a gaudy red waistcoat beneath. The stage setting offered a conglomeration of tubular hanging bells, while his accent veered towards a combination of stilted camp and robust German. His conversation with the orchestra leader starts relevantly enough: 'My speed is absolutely colossal – sometimes I finish before the audience!' but degenerates into personal trivia uttered with the photographer's finicky politeness: 'Yooo keep r-r-reasonably well? That's r-right. The boys?

That's r-right.' When he first attempts to play, one bell falls to the ground. Then the head falls off the hammer. He comes to the front of the stage again, commences a long sentence, and just manages to get to the end, writhing to the ground as he does so. 'Oh, I am a foool – I *must* remember to breathe when I speak . . .' But once more he forgets and again ends up breathless and gasping, sagging at the knees into a forlorn pile. This sketch certainly saw the birth of Frankie Howerd's trademark wheeze. The conductor's suggestion that they play 'Sleigh Bells across the Sahara' brings the reply 'There's no such thing; you're having me on! Aren't you?' As he speaks Sid gets his lips stuck in a pursed position and makes much play with his fingers before adjusting them back to normal. He eventually gets to play the bells, but then suddenly the whole instrument collapses. This is the cue for Desmonde to intervene in his part of heckler in a stage box. He questions whether Sid ('I beg your very, very pardon') really knows anything about music. He queries the musician's bicycle clips, which Sid removes, and the table of clocks and cheap trinkets to the left of the stage, which Sid, standing to attention, proclaims are 'Prizes!' It was normal for the whole act to end in bedlam with even a pack of hounds dashing across the stage!

There was another musician in Field's repertoire, the seedy cinema organist from *Piccadilly Hayride* who offered 'Fragrant Moments' as he tried desperately to live up to his glittering facade of chromium plate and white tuxedo. Swinging round the organ as if it were a dodgem car, cringingly leading the audience in an over-the-shoulder chorus of 'Lily of Laguna', playing 'We'll gather lilacs' as waltz or foxtrot, ballad or gallop, he yet maintained the basic dignity common to all Field's characters, smiling, winking and waving like an early electronic Liberace. In addition there was his drunken, myopic man-about-town, billed as one half of 'four other fellows' in 'I'm going to get lit up when the lights go up in London', a scene built around the evocative wartime song by Hubert Gregg in *Strike a New Note*; the mock-Shakespearean episode in *Piccadilly Hayride* presented by the 'Old Nick Theatre Company' with Sid as King John tripping over his royal mantle and phoning the executioner at the Tower. 'Is that you, Archie? Can you take off an 'ead? You can get it done before tea? And I say, Archie, save us a couple of nag sides;' Sid as amateur landscape artist in *Strike it Again*, disturbed by the precocious criticism of a frightful St Trinian's-type schoolgirl and, assuming his most engaging smile (calculated by Agate to woo an elephant at a hundred yards), retorting, 'Why don't you go and play a nice game on the railway lines… with your back to the oncoming engines?' and then calming her with a bottle of lemonade. 'Get the bottle well down your throat.'

Possibly his most famous characterisation, however, remains Slasher Green, pride of the Elephant and Castle, he of the overlong check overcoat ('You don't want them any longer than this – it looks silly!'), ludicrously padded shoulders, rakish trilby and two-tone shoes. Here was the coster type at a stage of subtle development from the tradition of music hall stars like Gus Elen and Albert Chevalier, the flashy, immaculate spiv, the cockney tempered with basic Americanism. His walk, a shambling jaunty occasionally leg-shaking affair, made for a magnificent entrance. At first dazed – the continual shadow-boxing and the murmured 'Don't worry – I'll get him in the next round' giving him away before he begins – he is asked by Desmonde what he is going to perform. It is talent night and a song is by far the easiest way out, but first the perky Slasher must have ample room to move. 'I should keep well back, son, cos I keep gettin' round.' With two stamps on the floor he launches himself into the chorus: 'You ought to see me on Saturday night; oh what a wonderful sight!' Halfway through the orchestra stops. 'Wot yer turned it up for – broke down, 'ave yer?' Desmonde, disconcerted, taps him on the shoulder, and quick as a flash Slasher comes back with 'Turn it up – you'll have me out of shape!' After all he is 'a discovery – that's someone who's sorted out of people – all the people what want to go on the stage so that they can stop in bed in the morning! Huh! He doesn't understand, does he? Keep well back, son. There's a good boy.' Weaving back and forth across the stage, he then attempts a 'bit of dancing – makes a change' but is unable to give any precise information to the drummer about his routine. 'A somersault, double somersault, don't know what I'll do yet – might change me mind in mid-air.' Then one of his shoulder pads works its way round to the back of his coat, giving him a hunchback appearance. Thrown off course by the shock of its loss, he tells the drummer not to play: 'It works me up too much.' The whole point of the act within an act is that by the end nothing worthwhile will have been accomplished. Slasher Green is 100 per cent bluff, his whole facade spelling out the insecurity of pretence. Even the aggressiveness is only put on. Beneath the shadow-boxing is a coward, and because of this he was in total contact with his audience. If they laughed, Slasher would stop and laugh back, and then they would laugh back again and louder. He was nothing if not one of the crowd. After all, it was only for the crowd that he 'put it on'.

The remarkable depth and detail of his character range was Field's greatest technical achievement, entailing a fantastic repertoire of accents, wavering between the rounded manicured vowels of the photographer, the pouting exasperation of the golfer and the hoarse back-throated cockney of the wide boy. But, the basic characterisation aside, there was about him a quaint unexpectedness – you never knew exactly which voice, pose, attitude he would next break into in any one sketch. In an edition of the *Tatler* dated February 1948 he admitted, 'It's not so much what I say that's funny, it's the way I say it – and I say it different every time.' Later in the same article when discussing 'Slasher Green': 'Spivs? They're a type, the same all over the place in their own particular way, whether you find them in Balham or Birmingham. In London I play Slasher as a cockney, in Brum as if he was a local boy.' Proof of his motley genius came with the emergence of many prominent comedy performers of subsequent years. In addition to Howerd's wheeze and surrender to amazement, there was the give and take between Morecambe and Wise, Max Bygraves' warm directness, Tony Hancock's despair, Terry-Thomas's genteelness, the spiv-like quality of Arthur English on 50s radio and George Cole in the St Trinian's films, Jimmy Edwards' musical mayhem, Norman Wisdom's frenetic incoherence, Dick Emery's coy campness, Harry Secombe's genial daftness, Benny Hill's moon-faced innocence, even Olivier's archness as Archie Rice. All reveal more than a trace of Field's influence. Not that Sid himself had not been influenced by the less well-known names with which he spent the early part of his career.

To confirm Field's influence one has only to sit through a showing of *London Town*, the abysmal million-dollar failure of a British attempt to duplicate the traditional-style Hollywood film musical. Made in 1946 to exploit Field's arrival as the great new comedy star, it fell like the first films to headline Max

Bygraves (*Charley Moon*) and Harry Secombe (*Davy*) into all the traps, not least an unimaginative plot, hackneyed show business setting and the lack of any attempt to adapt the comic talent of the star to the new medium. Luckily, however, albeit unimaginatively, it does contain intact a permanent record of five of his sketches (Slasher, musician, golfer, drunk and photographer), even though it conveys no idea of the laughter generated by the same routines in an authentic theatre setting. As a musical it deserved instant oblivion; as a comedy, on the strength of those sketches alone, no English film has a greater right to be seen again. As one watches Field, it is impossible to dissociate his performance from a ghostly one-man parade of these later comedians. Field's own comment would probably be no different to his analysis of his own quality at the time of his success: 'I suppose I'm just peculiar altogether.'

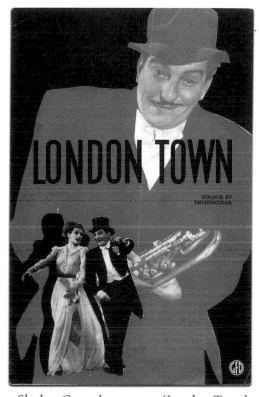

Slasher Green looms over 'London Town'

Sid as the Cardboard Cavalier

The synthetic *London Town* was not Field's first film. In 1939 he had been featured in an inauspicious comedy entitled *That's the Ticket*. It was made in three weeks and remained unnoticed. Two years after *London Town* came *Cardboard Cavalier*, an historical romp with Sid as a Cromwellian barrow boy, Sidcup Buttermeadow, helping to restore Charles II to the throne. Like its predecessor it only succeeded in capturing Field's true magic intermittently, most notably in his bickering scenes with Desmonde as Colonel Lovelace, the king's aide; a sequence in which he posed as a Russian dancing master with Margaret Lockwood – Nell Gwynne in the film – as his assistant Madame Nowigotcha; and another sequence as a buxom matron under the unfamiliar influence of barley wine, flickering her eyelashes with bravado and flirting outrageously with the Protector himself: 'You great, big, beautiful Cromwell.'

Sid relaxes with 'Cardboard Cavalier' co-star, Margaret Lockwood, at the 1948 London Olympics

While his film career proved disappointing, his stage stock rose. At the beginning of 1949 he returned to the Prince of Wales Theatre, ready to realise his full acting potential for the first time as Elwood P. Dowd, the wistful dipsomaniac with the invisible six-foot-one-and-a-half-inch rabbit 'Harvey' as a mascot, in the Pulitzer prize-winning play of the same name. This was at the insistence of its author, Mary Chase. However, in spite of his phenomenal success in the role – all the more remarkable since it entailed keeping in careful check all the mannerisms and catchphrases that had rocketed him to his earlier success on the very same stage – there was a bitter irony inherent in his portrayal of Dowd, stemming from his own offstage alcoholism. In the very early years this weakness had led to many weeks out of work, fostering as it did an inevitable reputation for unreliability; at the peak of his career it still remained the Dutch courage, first suggested by a domineering mother, needed to face an audience. It is alleged that Field was dependent on alcohol by the age of thirteen. At heart he was a worrier and a romantic, living from day to day, favouring the sentimental ballad to the actual material he performed, songs like 'You can't keep a good dreamer down', which he featured in *London Town*. Dreaming, however, could not disguise the fact that in 1949 he was a sick man. After seven months in *Harvey* he suffered a breakdown that took him out of the show for four and a half months. He returned on Boxing Day and died following a succession of heart attacks on 3 February 1950 at the sadly premature age of forty-five, with, as Tynan has observed, alcohol and self-criticism his pallbearers. His fellow performers lost the most respected exponent of their art, a position he would continue to hold for many years. Somehow the words of Leigh Hunt quoted by Agate on the death of Harry Tate are even more poignant in Field's case.

> The death of a comic artist is felt more than that of a tragedian. He has sympathised more with us in our everyday feelings, and has given us more amusement… it seems a hard thing upon the comic actor to quench his airiness and vivacity – to stop him in his happy career – to make us think of him, on the sudden, with solemnity – and to miss him for ever… it is something like losing a merry child.

The Sid Field tragedy was that the 'happy career' of arguably the greatest comic talent of his generation should be stopped barely seven years after its first major success. The analogy to a merry child had become astonishingly relevant.

AFTERTHOUGHTS

I shall never forget the afternoon in the late 60s when I sat transfixed in a small BFI viewing room in a dingy alley off Charing Cross Road, cocooned from the outside world all the better to appreciate what flickering evidence remained on celluloid of the comic genius that was Sid Field. Twenty-five years later I sat equally transfixed in the stalls of the Queen's Theatre on Shaftesbury Avenue when one of our greatest actors brought the clown to life in a manner one might only have been granted had Aladdin's lamp been within reach. With immaculate timing and grace, David Suchet uncannily added flesh to many of the images I had seen on distressed celluloid, conveying above all the deep intoxication with the desire to make people laugh that was Field's ultimate gift, and communicating to a modern audience his golden glow in a way that old movie clips could not. Suchet's triumph was compensation for what might have been had the comedian lived into the television age or conquered the medium of the cinema. All great comedians are actors, of course, but quintessentially Field had the potential to be a star character actor in the mode of Guinness, Gambon and Suchet himself.

That Sid could have succeeded on television in the type of format that served Benny Hill, Dick Emery and Stanley Baxter is obvious. Indeed his influence extends through them into the later work of Harry Enfield, Paul Whitehouse and *The Fast Show*, Matt Lucas, David Walliams and *Little Britain*. However, his greatest influence was arguably not in the area of sketch comedy at all, but on Tony Hancock, who went as far as to name his first two cars Sid and Harvey in honour of his hero. When I was writing my biography of the later comedian, Graham Stark shared with me the moment in the immediate aftermath of World War Two when as two struggling hopefuls he and Hancock first set eyes upon Field at the Prince of Wales. 'We were kicking the seats in front of us – it was so funny – he was magic – we'd never laughed so much.' Stark recalled the moment in the Shakespearean burlesque in which Sid played King John. Taking one look at the man-at-arms standing nearby in full armour, Field commented, 'You wanna get a fourteen-pound hammer and put a crease in them.' At that moment a convulsed Hancock turned to his friend and whispered, 'He's the one. He's the one for me.' The ability to give an inconsequential line comic depth was only one attribute that would in due course find an echo in Hancock's work. The qualities of 'Stone me!' moroseness, of 'How dare you!' indignation were others. It helped that Sid, like Tony, had been born in Birmingham.

In his appearance on *The Frost Programme* in January 1967 Hancock brilliantly conjured up the magic of his hero for a whole new audience.

> And Jerry Desmonde would come on and say, 'Now ladies and gentlemen, with great pleasure I would like to introduce England's leading exponent of the tubular bells, Mr Eustace Bollinger.' And Sid would come on with two mallets, and a terrible wasp waistcoat and bicycle clips – which have always seemed to me to be funny anyway. He used to say to the musical director, 'What do you think I should play?' and he'd say, 'Why don't you play Beethoven's 15th Movement of the 7th Symphony in E flat minor with the modulated key change to G flat major?' and Sid had a good long look at him, and then he got hold of one of these mallets and said, 'Yes, I thought you'd suggest something like that,' and tried to belt him with this stick. Then the orchestra all rose up and tried to clout him with their violins, so nobody was in any doubt as to what the relationship was for a start! Then a voice from the box said, 'Maestro,' but Sid knows it's not true. That was the beauty of it. Anybody calling him 'Maestro,' he knew the man was a fool. And on a table by the side he'd got a Ludo set, a toy fire engine, a toy poodle – by the side of these tubular bells – and this bloke in the box says, 'Maestro, what's all the junk on the table?' 'Junk?' 'Yes, what is all that junk on the table?' 'That's not junk,' says Sid. 'That's prizes!' That paralysed me. You could just imagine him sort of cycling up from Sidcup or somewhere, with his clips on and all this gear on his bike. Most of it is in your imagination. Like any great comic, Sid relied a great deal on the imagination and warmth of his audience.

Field was not a wisecracking wit in the manner of contemporaries like Flanagan, Trinder and Ray, but there is no doubt that he was capable of turning an economical word or two to comic advantage at the appropriate moment. His frequent understudy, Jack Tripp, himself later a revue comic and pantomime dame of repute, took delight in telling of the occasion a statuesque chorus girl brushed past him in the wings at the Prince of Wales. In Jack's words she was wearing 'just about one feather, two milk bottle tops and a five-foot-high jewelled headdress'. She had the courtesy to address the star: 'Good evening, Mr Field.' 'Hello,' replied Sid. 'Working?' In such moments a lifetime of comedy is distilled.

FRANK RANDLE: 'BAAA... I'VE SUPPED SOME ALE TONEEET!'

(*As the Old Hiker*) **I was talking to an old woman down the road... Eeeh, she were cheeky. I said, 'I think you look like a blue-nosed monkey.' She said, 'Well, we all come from monkeys, and it wouldn't worry me if my grandfather was a great big hairy ape with a tail that long.' (***He indicates length of tail***) So I said, 'No, but it would worry your grandmother.'**

Frank Randle's appearance on stage provided the clue both to his boundless energy and the persistence with which he refused to be controlled by those who crossed his path off it. His whole body overflowed: inquisitive pop-eyes which appeared to be attached to invisible springs; a dominant drooping nose which recalled the peering Mr Chad of wartime graffiti fame; dangling arms which in their aimless semaphoric wanderings appeared longer than they actually were; legs which, in voluminous trousers two sizes too short and cocoon-style shoes two sizes too large, stood splayed, often swaying, as insecure as Dan Leno's shopwalker with 'the bottoms of my legs bent up to make feet'. When he walked, his loose-limbed body had the floppy dignity of a seal, and this was the only equipment he needed to split an audience's sides, but he added a wide range of facial contortions and the verbal resources of a quirky Lancastrian mutter, both made more distinctive by his much-vaunted toothlessness, even in pantomime.

Cinderella: Of course you can't kiss me, Buttons. You've got no teeth.
Randle: No, but I could gi' yee a nasty suck!

More likely than not he had taken his dentures out at the beginning of his act and thrown them at the stalls.

He would have made the perfect scarecrow in an anglicised version of *The Wizard of Oz*, but there are deeper if more obscure roots in popular American mythology. More than any British comedian of his era he resembled the trickster archetype of Native American culture, a body comprising an assortment of independent self-functioning units. Right hand, for example, fights with left; limbs are detachable; sexual organs carried in a box. This inability to control and come to terms with one's complete physical self recalls the effect of all the great acrobatic clowns. Randle, however, always managed to succeed in giving the impression that his acrobatics were wholly improvised, not rehearsed with mathematical leg-kicking precision, but an honest attempt to experience rough and tumble at first hand. He allowed his knobbly limbs to wander all over his act, like a doodler yielding to a pencil on a scribble pad. But if trickster Randle looked as if his body could disintegrate at any moment, the personality he pegged onto the visual characterisation also bore a striking relevance to the myth. According to critic Joan Westcott, quoted in an early 1970s *TLS* article on screen comedy, the totem was, like Randle, 'a creature of instinct and great energy', functioning as 'rule-breaker... a spanner in the social works'. In the words of anthropologist Paul Radin, among its most notable traits was a 'wandering and unbridled sexuality'. Randle had a slap-happy disregard for the brushes he experienced with both authoritarians and flirts. The incoherent anger aroused in him by the former: 'I'll poke me eye in your finger!' and the only-so-slightly-hurt suspicion he felt when rebuffed by the latter:

> *Girl*: You're not polished enough.
> *Randle*: What yer take me for? A coffin?

never dampened his shameless good spirits for long, never brought home to him the truth that he was other than the sophisticate by birth he imagined.

He radiated a total disregard for sympathy and had more than a touch of the barrack room in his make-up. The army was, in fact, a target of ridicule in many of his sketches. In 'Twerp of the Jungle' he would appear as Private Sans Grey Matter, a name shared by lieutenant, sergeant, three other privates, in fact all the other participants. Something like the Randle atmosphere was re-created in the years immediately following his death by Granada Television's *The Army Game*, in which Bernard Bresslaw as the dimwitted Private 'Popeye' Popplewell, Alfie Bass as Private 'Excused Boots' Bisley and Michael Medwin as Corporal Springer fell in as a company of misfit grotesques under the beady eye of Bill Fraser's Sergeant Major Claude Snudge. Sadly none of them had quite the full measure of Randle's exuberance to enable the series to take full comic flight, although that did not prevent it becoming the most successful sitcom of ITV's early years. Other Randle routines included his 'Vulgar Boatman' in 'Any More for A-Sailing', in which, clay pipe in hand, he evoked memories of characters he had seen on Blackpool front, trying to earn a crust by coaxing day trippers afloat for a few minutes on the Irish Sea: 'Any more for a sailin'... Room for two more... Yer know there must be a whist drive on somewhere ...Yer know it gets that quiet at times round 'ere, I can 'ear me 'air grow.'

Frank as the Old Hiker

His speciality, however, was the spiky geriatric of eighty-two, with overemphasised potbelly, wispy woolly wig, wire-rims perched at the tip of his nose and a libido beyond containing. Maybe it was in 'Wanted a Housewife' with the sex-crazed Randle married four times – 'If the Lord keeps providing 'em, I'll keep buryin 'em' – and bluntly assessing the favours of a possible fifth spouse (a member of his company in drag) as his hand wandered up inside 'her' ample petticoats: 'I want to get to the point at once!' Maybe it was in 'Grandpa's Birthday', with further comic mileage guaranteed not only by the appearance of his old flame but also by 'Grandpa's father'. Here snuff became a very special comic tool, and a nightshirted Randle could milk five minutes of laughter from the swaying pompom at the tip of his floppy woolen bed cap. Most famous of his senile characters was the gnarled, drunken hiker, based on a veteran athlete who used to take part in the Manchester to Blackpool Whit Walk in the 1920s. This was usually played as a solo routine – 'Baaa... I've supped some ale toneeet!' – and was all the more effective for that. Here his preoccupations are legs (his own, with reference to his walking), girls and ale, in reverse order of importance.

Eeee, well I've walked through Europe, Arope, Irope, Syrup, Wallop, Jollop! Aye, I'm the daddy of all hikers. Me eighty-two and just look at these for a pair o' legs. I tossed a sparrer for these and lost... By gum, I don't like these new boots of mine. They're givin' me corns a bit o' gyp today. I was troubled with a corn. I went to one of those chiropuddle fellers – Dr Scollops. He had a look. I said, 'How about this corn?' He said, 'There's no corn there!' It was a collar stud in me sock. Yes, three weeks I'd been plagued with that.

I just passed a couple o' tarts up road yonder. Eeeee, they were a couple o' hot 'uns. Aye. One went like this 'ere comin'. I took no notice… much!!! I said to her, I said, 'Not today, love… I'd rather 'ave a Kensitas.' I took one of 'em for a bit of a walk. We went five miles and neether of us spoke a word. At the finish I said to her, 'A penny for thy thoughts.' Ooh! She gave me such a clout across lug. I said, 'What's to do with yer? I only said, "A penny for yer thoughts."' 'Eeee,' she said, 'I thought yer said, "A penny for me shorts."'

Funny, you know, I said to the landlord of the pub where I got this – I said, 'It's a bit thin, mistah.' 'Aye,' 'e said, 'you'd be thin if you'd come up same pipes as this ale 'as.' Aye. 'E said, 'I bet you've never tasted our bitter?' I said, 'No, but I've paddled about in it!' Eeee, that just reminds me. I once sent a bottle o' beer away like this to be analysed. They must've got mixed up at other end. They sent me a postcard saying, 'Dear sir, your horse is in perfect condition!' Eeeeee, aye.

Even if he matches his own description of a 'monkey up a stick', he also 'fairly sizzles', ecstatic at still being alive, anticipating the amazing vitality of Ken Dodd's fictional old folk of later years. 'I'm as full of vim as a butcher's dog – I'm as lively as a cricket. Why, I'll take anybody on of me age and weight, dead or alive, and I'll run 'em, walk 'em, jump 'em, fight 'em… aye… and I'll play 'em dominoes!'

Or challenge them to a drinking bout perhaps? To Randle, self-styled 'All-slops', ale was measured at 'thirty-six burps to a bottle', and these punctuate this part of his act with reverberating effect. 'I'll sup it if it keeps me up all night,' he exclaims between his distinctive belching and gargling, as recognisable as catchphrases, however succinct and crude. He was brash and grotesque, but without sinking into pathos he managed to maintain that mellow comic melancholy that the Crazy Gang also possessed in their latter years. 'It's only t' other day I went to a funeral. I was comin' away from graveside – a chap looked at me – he said, "How old are yer?" I said, "I'm eighty-two." "Aye," he said, "I don't think it's much use thee goin' 'ome at all."'

Randle was baptised Arthur Hughes in Wigan, where he was born on 30 January 1901, the illegitimate son of a domestic servant, Rhoda Hughes. He later took the name of McEvoy when his mother married a former soldier of that name, although the man was not his natural father. After a varied career as waiter, butcher's boy, bottle washer and tram conductor, he commenced his show business career in 1918 as one of the Three Ernestos, a trampoline and tumbling act, at Blackpool Tower Circus. Within a few years he had renamed himself Arthur Twist, combining his acrobatic skills in a comedy act along Chaplinesque lines. Not until he joined another trampoline act, the Bouncing Randles, did he settle on the name he would use until the end of his life. By 1929, with the help of Jack Taylor, the northern impresario who specialised in 'Long Tours of the Number Twos', Frank Randle was launched on a solo career as a character comedian. He eventually achieved phenomenal success in two spheres, film and road shows, the latter touring package deals, usually mounted by the star himself, which enjoyed an ironic vogue as variety proper waned.

Albert Modley

Contemporary with Randle in the road show stakes were two magnificent Yorkshire drolls whose presence continued to add warmth to the British entertainment scene long after the touring device had played itself out. Albert Modley, 'Lancashire's favourite Yorkshireman', toured for many years with *On with the Modley*. He first achieved distinction in the early 1930s as the original 'Enoch' to Harry Korris's 'Mr Lovejoy', the nucleus of the radio show *Happidrome*, and himself achieved radio fame as a resident comedian in *Variety Bandbox* during the late 1940s. Born in Liverpool in 1901, he moved to Barnsley at an early age. Few comedians have ever projected more successfully their sheer enjoyment at the task in hand. His act with its chirpy improvised patter – 'My eyes are bad – I keep running' into pubs' – developed into a musical speciality encompassing a Chico Marx line in Joanna-bashing and a session at the drums which transformed into a mock tram front. His philosophy was spelled out by his catchphrase, 'Eeeh, isn't it grand when you're daft!' He died in 1979.

Equally notable was Sandy Powell, the bespectacled Rotherham-born (1900) droll who boasted a smile as benevolent as the man in the moon in the old Creamola advertisement. He reached his peak in the 30s when his asthmatic plea 'Can you hear me, mother?' became the first radio catchphrase to cling to the lips of a new eager public. At the same time recordings of his sketches, particularly 'The Lost Policeman', often with a sporting theme, sold in excess of a record seven million. He died in 1982, but not before enjoying a deserved, if freak, comeback with his burlesque of a harassed military ventriloquist battling on against all odds with a disintegrating dummy with a life of its own, his false walrus moustache inadequate at concealing the lip movements it is meant to obscure, and an unwieldy sword: 'The finest blade in the world, the Wilkinson... Oooh!' The moment when he plunged the blade via clenched fist back into its scabbard represented literally the most painfully comic in variety. 'Ventriloquism, that is the thing of the day,' he would wheeze blandly. His pride in his supposed talent was matched only by the level of his later despair. 'Everybody'll know how it's done!' He had been evolving this routine throughout his career, from the moment he conceived the idea of a mere two-minute gag to follow the substandard ventriloquist booked by a careless agent into his show. Gradually one gag snowballed into a classic fifteen-minute sketch. Ironically its Indian summer brilliance only served to underline the childish inanity of the material he recorded when he was indisputably top of the bill in the 1930s.

Sandy Powell: 'And now the female voice'

The road show meant that a more coherent production with glossier production values could play the lesser halls, the smaller towns. Randle's contribution to the genre had the initially appropriate title *Randle's Scandals*. More exotic elements in the company included The Mandalay Singers, showing as the *Stage* once reported, 'considerable power in operatic snippets and solo items'; Ali Ben Hassan's Whirlwind Moroccans; and in chief comedy support Gus Aubrey and Ernie Dale. The show played to full houses for years, invariably earning Randle £1,000 a week even in locations remote from the main entertainment centres. In fact it was when he attempted to conquer the West End that Randle met with least success. He had played London's Alhambra in 1935 and flopped. It took seventeen years for him to return to London's theatreland. In February 1952 Jack Hylton presented Randle and company in a venture so eccentric that the mind now boggles. Those who imagined that the magpie tendencies of one entertainment medium towards another had reached a nadir with the 1950 film *The Twenty Questions Murder Mystery* now witnessed the even more depressing spectacle of *TeleVariety*. Randle enjoyed top billing despite having no relevance to the world of television. The only appeal for viewers was provided by a stage presentation of the *What's My Line?* panel game chaired by Gilbert Harding with a panel that included Elizabeth Allan and hypnotist Peter Casson. No reception was ever more harsh, no press more prejudiced against a comedian than on that first night. The charge of tastelessness and crudity was almost unanimous. Only the *Guardian* saw Randle in his true 'highly professional' colours. Financially the show was a disaster and closed after two weeks. If Randle made an error, it was only in uncharacteristically apologising for his material at the end of his act on the opening night. The following week, however, found him cherishing the last laugh, conveniently booked at short notice into the Metropolitan, Edgware Road with his *New 1952 Scandals* playing to enthusiastic packed houses. It is a misconception that, his two West End dates excepted, he never played south of Birmingham. Meanwhile the *Stage*, in defence of an entertainer they valued for his honest presentation of many taboo aspects of everyday life, wrote, 'Down at the Met, up in Manchester, almost anywhere else you like to mention, ordinary decent people who in their unsophisticated way keep the music hall alive, seem to have the advantage of recognising a good thing when they see it, and of not being afraid to let themselves go.'

Meanwhile 'up in Manchester' his most ardent followers had to be content with the latest Randle film offering. Had he been born twenty, even ten years previously, Randle might well have achieved the Hollywood eminence of Laurel or Chaplin. He was a natural for the Keystone knockabout tradition but had to be content with the same bottom-drawer productions one associates with Formby and Lucan. The Randle films went without West End release or national press coverage, and yet, as John Montgomery explains in his survey of film comedy, in most northern towns he was a bigger box-office attraction than Flynn, Dietrich or Robert Taylor. All the Randle films were produced by the Manchester-based Mancunian Film Corporation operating from a converted chapel in Dickenson Road, Rusholme – later a BBC television studio – under John Blakeley, who had produced the first Formby efforts *Boots, Boots* and *Off the Dole*. The best remembered today are the Somewhere series produced between 1940 and 1948 and comprising *Somewhere in England*, *Somewhere in Camp*, *Somewhere on Leave*, *Somewhere in Civvies*, and *Somewhere in Politics*. In the first three, all army farces, Randle was joined by Harry Korris from *Happidrome*, now with the diminutive Robby Vincent as Enoch ('L-e-t m-e t-e-l-l y-o-u...'). On other occasions he was supported by animated rubber-necked genius Nat Jackley and ebullient 'Two-Ton' Tessie O'Shea.

Nat Jackley

In total Randle made ten feature films, the last in 1953, *It's a Grand Life*, in which he co-starred with Diana Dors, but by 1947 he had already found it necessary to finance his cinematic activities in partnership with Blakeley. Maybe Randle's capricious temperament offstage demanded this financial guarantee. On his death the *Daily Express* described him as 'the bad boy of show business'. He quarrelled with everyone from the stage-doorkeeper to the Lord Chamberlain. The latter quarrels were especially frequent, the cause general – the use of supposedly offensive material – or specific – once for burlesquing Handel's *Messiah* in touring revue. His counsel on one of these occasions aptly described him as 'the type

Above: Tessie O'Shea provides larger than life support for Randle on the big screen
Left: Randle joins forces with Korris, Vincent and regular sidekick Dan Young

of man who would be quick on the draw, but would shoot at the wrong man'. Not surprisingly tales out of school abound. In a radio tribute comedienne Renée Houston described the occasion the Randle show was playing to poor business in Brighton. She and her husband and stage partner Donald Stuart were requested to help out. On the Saturday night Randle strutted into their dressing room with an apology: 'I've got news for you – I can't pay you anything, but I've bought a doll for the little girl.' Renée was forty-two at the time! The same programme demonstrated how Randle's stage persona blurred into his private life. On trial in Blackpool, his adopted town, for dangerous driving along the front, which was divided into promenade, tramline and road, he explained unashamedly to the judge that, yes, he had had 'a gill or two'. He was going along in his Rolls, had seen a driver approaching, had waved him aside several times with no success, and since he had taken no notice, 'Oh well, 'ell! And I hit 'im!' 'And you realise, Mr Randle,' the judge replied, 'you hit a tram?'

In 1954 he left the cast of an Oldham pantomime on Christmas Eve, after giving only two performances as Widow Twankey. He then announced his break from the stage and intention of writing a book exposing the 'mental pygmies of show business'. The book never materialised and he made a triumphant comeback in touring revue. By now, however, his health was worsening and the tax authorities did not make life easier when a demand for £56,000 left him virtually bankrupt. Variety's greatest exponent of the comic potentiality of old age was never to know it himself. His final years were dogged by tuberculosis and cirrhosis of the liver. He died technically of gastroenteritis in Blackpool on 7 July 1957, at the age of fifty-five. If one may use Gracie Fields as a barometer of professional opinion, she described Frank Randle as 'the greatest character comedian that ever lived'. But how much of his near-infamous character was clever disguise by a master rascal who thought nothing on one occasion of setting fire to the hotel where he had received bad service, only he could tell.

AFTERTHOUGHTS

Not too long into the so-called alternative comedy era I recall a headline proclaiming comedy 'the new rock and roll'. The phrase meant little, other than possibly to highlight that comedy had been the old rock and roll as well. No comedian had a greater reputation for being subversive than Frank Randle, not merely onstage but in the lifestyle he subscribed to when alcohol and paranoia took control of his actions. Since this chapter was written, the roll call of his misdemeanours has extended itself to include further incidents poised on the borderline of slapstick and irresponsibility. There was the occasion he agreed to give a charity performance at a town hall and was so disgusted with the food provided for his company that he paid five pounds for the lot and used it to hurl at the sedate oil portraits of the ex-mayors staring down at them from the walls of the reception room. There was the time when in a mad act of vengeance he threatened to bombard Accrington from an aeroplane with toilet rolls, only to be forestalled by a pilot whose course was set for York; it never happened, but it might have done. There was the occasion at the Hulme Hippodrome in 1956 when a disagreement over an unpaid bar bill led to the systematic trashing of his dressing room. The poet Jeff Nuttall, who wrote an impressionistic portrait of the comedian in 1978, caught the fury of the moment: 'He takes the whisky from his glass and hurls the glass into the dressing-room mirror… he takes the axe from the firepoint in the corridor. He cracks it down on the sink. A swing at the row of wardrobe hooks brings the whole fitting hanging adrift into the room, splattering plaster. It sticks outward like a fractured limb. The carpet torn loose from the lino, tacks like dragons' teeth along the edges, is calico in his hands. The velvet curtains likewise.'

Jimmy Casey, radio producer son of Jimmy James, Randle's friend and rival, provided as sane an assessment of such behaviour as there may ever have been: 'You don't know how much of this sort of thing comes through frustration – of what happened to you when you were down and, when you get there, my God, you're going to make them pay for it and they're going to do what you want… I think probably he had a monstrous chip on his shoulder from what happened in the early days.' However much his early life affected his psychology, there is no question that at a physical level the acrobatic skills he acquired at a young age were ingrained in him as permanently as an extension of his DNA. His films are a revelation in this regard, revealing him to have no equal as a physical comedian among his contemporaries in this country, as if the bounce of continual trampolining had been contained within him like a perpetually wound-up spring, leaving him with limbs of elastic and a boneless body impervious to harm. In one sequence he precariously attempts to climb upstairs while drunk, defying gravity as he teeters on the edge of each step with a precision that disguises itself as recklessness; in another he takes a bath with his clothes on, his soggy long johns filling with air to make him an instant Michelin man who might be expected to bounce his way into the final credits. At the end, when his body was racked by booze and tuberculosis, he was still capable of turning a double cartwheel down the glittering staircase of the finale scene of his last pantomime.

Randle was dubbed by writer Tom Moreland 'the stormy petrel of show business', but he was also a religious man and died in the Roman Catholic faith. During one of his final engagements in variety the sick Randle locked himself in his dressing room to say his prayers. The call boy knocked on the door: 'Two minutes, Mr Randle.' Amid the coughing and the spluttering he answered, 'Fuck off, I'm praying.' His unique combination of physical skills and subversive behaviour make it hard to point to a natural successor.

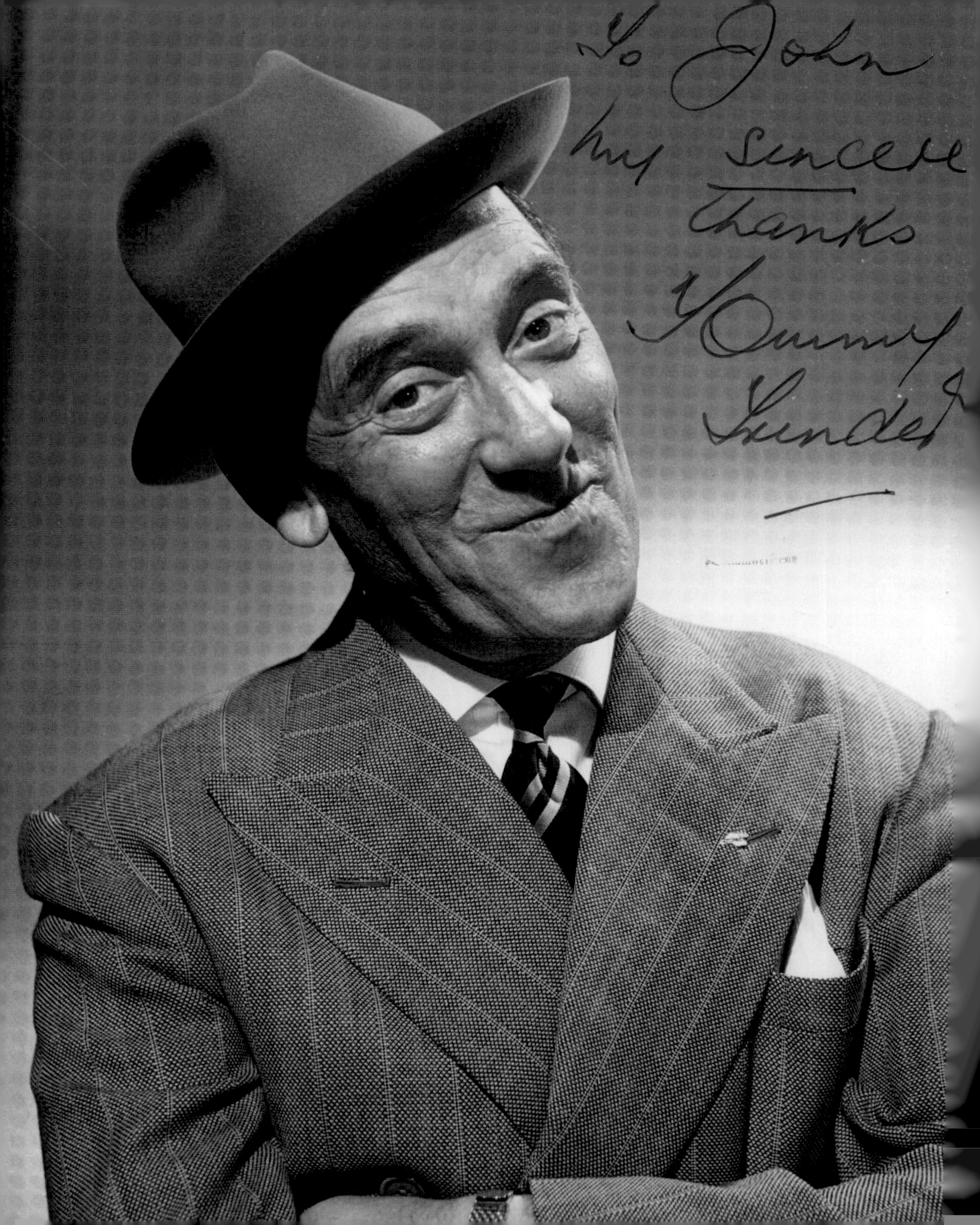
To John
my sincere
thanks
Tommy
Trinder

TOMMY TRINDER: 'YOU LUCKY PEOPLE!'

A man was walking down Whitehall and asked a passer-by, 'Which side is the War Office on?' He answered, 'Ours, I hope!'

Few comedians have succeeded without a sense of driving egotism. Tommy Trinder converted his into a joke itself. At the peak of his career in the early 1940s he paid as much as £265 a week to advertise his jutting chin on twenty-five massive eight-foot-high hoardings, strategically placed on the most prominent sites in London. All but one of them read, IF IT'S LAUGHTER YOU'RE AFTER, TRINDER'S THE NAME. YOU LUCKY PEOPLE! The odd one out, opposite Aldgate underground station, was printed in Hebrew. The slogan made him famous, while his unabashed flair for publicity permeated every aspect of his life and performance. Not only did he persuade the theatre's musical director to wear a jacket with TRINDER blazoned across his shoulders, but his initials are even said to have been a major influence in his becoming teetotal. As he used to joke of his car registration number TT1, 'That's because I was the first to sign the pledge!' Every word, every gesture contributed to a publicist's field day. He wasted no time in assuring audiences they had been swindled into buying theatre programmes when the only item of interest in them was to announce that he was appearing: 'Trinder's the name. That's T-R-I-N-D-E-R. And for the benefit of any Americans in the audience,' he would swagger, 'I am the English Bob Hope!' At the peak of his career, not least through his association with a leading football club, it was hard to keep him out of the headlines. He skilfully juggled an infallible instinct for self-advertisement with the dedication and loyalty of a tolerant public, not least through his ability to ensure the laughter lived up to the hype.

One pitfall of the P. T. Barnum approach to publicity is that it tends to obscure the hard work and dedication invested in success in the first place. Tommy was born Thomas Edward Trinder, the son of a tram driver on the Hammersmith – White City route, in Streatham on 24 March 1909. Subsequently his career encompassed a week's engagement as boy vocalist at Collins Music Hall – later in life he used to joke, 'I had a voice like Julie Andrews, only more feminine'; a spell in Will Murray's Casey's Court company – a survival of the Karno style and forerunner of the Crazy Gang; a period when he worked under the inverted name Red Nirt; and years of hard slog around the lesser provincial halls as second act in the first half or first in the second, when for most of the time he was forced to work in front of a distracting backcloth of advertisements. 'You had to walk about to give every advertisement a chance. If you blocked out the ad for somebody's fish and chip shop there would be complaints.'

Firmly established by the late 30s as a contemporary comedian, he would subject his audience to a barrage of topicality delivered with machine-gun gusto in his brash cockney – 'I only speak the way I do to come down to your level' – his lean angular frame towering over the footlights with vulture-like superiority. Veering between innuendo and cynicism, insult and repartee, he relied on his up-to-dateness, the ability to twist not only every headline, but what was happening every minute, every second in the world around him to his own advantage. With his wide mischievous grin fixed securely above an extravagantly aggressive jaw, he was in control of the whole situation, his insolent disdain of individuals and institutions characterised by his most usual attire, mismatched evening dress and irremovable well worn trilby. Otherwise there was not obviously much of the clown about him, certainly no floral suit or tattered fur. His tearaway presence matched the sense of urgency that pervaded his delivery.

His success was particularly remarkable when one considers the bold brittle nature of his style. He was never happier than when audience-baiting, practically daring those in the stalls to take a poke back at him. The nearest his performance ever came to pathos was in the possibility of his own disappointment at not being heckled, or at not being able to interpret the slightest hint from the house as a heckle. But such barren moments were never allowed. He was never without a cutting remark to keep everyone on their toes, as caustic as scouring powder with a tongue to match.

No individual laughter, sir. The others have all paid as much as you!

What's the matter, madam? Lost your bike?

Thank your husband for sending you, madam. You must be unbearable at home!

Well now, before I declare the meeting closed, are there any questions?

(*To a late arrival*) Get yourself mechanised, sir.

During wartime he particularly relished targeting senior service personnel. On one occasion a rear admiral arrived late at the Palladium, to be greeted with 'Good evening, sir. Of course, you had to wait for the tide to come in.' On another occasion he remarked, 'We can't have officers walking in late. It makes this look like an ENSA concert.' Then, after the briefest of pauses, 'No, you can't tell me off. I'm a civvy!' The beaming eyes scanned the auditorium with a look that tolerated no nonsense. There was something about his hectoring style that made it too easy to dismiss him as a barrack-room lawyer of a comedian, but his was never a case of ignorance masquerading as know-how. So sure was his control of an audience, you couldn't knock Trinder down. The act was the incarnation of cockney bravado, and whatever insecurities may have lurked beneath the surface, the audience was never allowed a glimpse. Besides, the posters had already conditioned the crowd for what to expect, made them succumb to his impudent attack before he ever darted on stage to the thrusting rhythms of his signature tune, 'Tiger rag'. Incidentally it was Trinder who gave the service entertainment ENSA its humorous tag, 'Every Night Something Awful!'

His verbal abrasiveness and brilliance at deflation were certainly in tune with the stringent, propaganda-and-censorship-ridden times that coincided with his greatest success, namely the 1940s, when after seventeen years hard apprenticeship on the variety halls he took as naturally to the Palladium stage as the Crazy Gang had done the previous decade, the stage where on Sunday nights he would be reinstated for three and a half years in the mid-50s as spearhead of Independent Television's flagship show, *Val Parnell's Sunday Night at the London Palladium*, his cocksure personality setting the tone for the programme and indeed for much of commercial television in the UK in those pioneering days. Brought in by impresario George Black in 1939 to bolster the appeal of the stage version of the Askey–Murdoch *Band Waggon* revue on its transfer to the Palladium, he landed a part with Flanagan and Allen in that theatre's *Top of the World*, a show forced to close after only four performances through bombing. He then gained another chance in *Gangway* with Bebe Daniels and Ben Lyon, the show that made his Palladium reputation. George Black was now ready to build his next show, *Best Bib and Tucker*, around Trinder himself. In April 1947 came a similar revue, *Here, There and Everywhere*. Sandwiched between the two was *Happy and Glorious*, the longest-running of all such Palladium shows, which ran for 938 performances from October 1944 into 1946.

For their time these shows were gaudy, expensive, boisterous, arrogant – profuse, pretentious packages of cosmetics and plastic, chiffon and nylon, microphones and high kicks. As metropolitan escapism they were the perfect vehicle for the Trinder personality, one characterised not only by an aggressive ego, but by a strong vein of smoking-room masculinity that appealed to the countless servicemen who kept the shows running for such long periods. His comedy was always rooted firmly in a man's world, the jokes as often dealing with sport as with sex, the two often inescapably blurred; there was a moment in his act when he offered to gag about any sport the audience cared to mention. One recalls the account of his first Rotary luncheon speech: not knowing what to talk about he spoke on sex, and with great success. However, when he got home he felt embarrassed and told his wife he had spoken on yachting. The following morning she met someone who had been there the night before. Told of his triumph she replied, 'I don't see what he can know about it. He's only done it twice. The first time he was sick; the second time his hat flew off!' And there was his genuine interest in football and close if controversial association – as director and chairman – with Fulham Football Club. At times the team became a somewhat tedious part of his stock in trade as a professional comedian, a straight man eleven times over.

> We've got two Chinamen playing for us now: one called We Won Once and the other How Long Since!

> One of our players was just going to put his head in his hands and missed!

> We have now introduced cliff-hanging into our training!

But as Tommy explained in his defence, 'I had to crack gags about Fulham because you can run down your own club in the way a man can run down his own wife, but nobody else can.' The players were reputedly not impressed, but the association with the club went back a long way. The flat where he grew up as a boy was only a hundred yards from the club ground at Craven Cottage. The young Tommy used to sneak in along the riverbank without paying. 'I studied the tide tables, not the fixture list, and I only saw Fulham play when the tide was out!'

However much Trinder clung to the bootlaces of professional football to consolidate his masculine camaraderie and even to emphasise his own working-class roots, there were two hilarious routines in which he stepped completely out of character into the dubious, and for him surprising, area of camp. Infringing on Crazy Gang territory, there was the puzzling ambiguity of his impersonation of a leggy principal 'boy' singing 'Strolling down the Strand'. It would have been hard to decide what was more distracting: the monstrous eyelashes capable of sweeping the path ahead of him or the rib-tickling confusion of the idea of a man impersonating a girl impersonating a man. He was offered even more spectacular scope in his unforgettable impression of Carmen Miranda, the always extravagantly dressed Brazilian Bombshell with her towering fruit-salad hat.

> *Trinder* (*as Miranda*): I'll go and get my torso ready.
> *Bystander*: You mean trousseau.
> *Trinder*: Don't be silly, that's always ready!

Tommy as Carmen Miranda

228

The routine, when featured in a full-scale South American production sequence in *Best Bib and Tucker*, had none other than Edmundo Ros and his Band to beat out the rhythms as Tommy sang, 'No! No! No! … I told Columbus… You've discovered enough tonight.' Eyelashes, in competition with the chin, were again the centrepiece of the impersonation.

With his brusque cockney patter Trinder can be seen to have carried on the tradition of two renowned figures of the earlier London music hall stage: Harry Champion (1866 – 1942), who used to punch out his immortal numbers like 'Any old iron' and 'I'm Henery the eighth, I am!' with the same authority with which a nerveless Trinder punched home his jokes, and Arthur Roberts (1852 – 1933), an early master of the quick-witted improvised humour delivered staccato-style that Trinder used to vigorous effect. Champion's sometime bill matter, 'The Express Train Comic', was especially apt. There was, however, another music hall old-timer, not a cockney, in whom the Trinder personality was also vividly reflected. R. G. Knowles (1858 – 1919), a native of Ontario but a British subject, used to bill himself as 'The Very Peculiar American Comedian'. As successful in this country as across the Atlantic, he pioneered the knife-edge audience-alienation technique that came to be most readily associated with Trinder. His patter, which was based largely on comedy advice to young people in love, and his eccentric appearance – seedy frock coat, battered topper, clean but ragged white trousers – do not readily suggest Trinder, but there was more than a hint of the later performer in his husky voice and habit of shuffling up and down the stage as he delivered his material.

After a few low-budget excursions into films, in 1939, on the back of his Palladium success, Tommy was signed by Ealing Studios. His film career now entered its most successful phase, bucking the trend of the personality vehicles associated with the likes of Formby, Miller and Hay and placing the emphasis on his ability as a fine natural actor. As such he provided a link with the socio-realist comedies with which the studio became increasingly identified after the war. *The Foreman Went to France* was based on the real-life Melbourne Johns, a factory worker who goes to occupied France to retrieve valuable machines supplied by his armaments factory lest they fall into enemy hands: Tommy is one of the two soldiers who help the foreman, played by Clifford Evans, along his way. *Champagne Charlie* gave him the chance to portray the Victorian music hall star George Leybourne, while *The Bells Go Down* was a tribute to the work done by the auxiliary fire brigade during the Blitz. In this, Tommy, wisecracking till the end, lays down his life on screen. Racing up a ladder to rescue a colleague trapped in a blazing building, he finds himself stuck on a ledge when the floor gives way. Trinder is not discouraged: 'I reckon that puts us off duty!' Then with a thunderous crash the whole building collapses. We see Tommy cross his arms in front of his face before the screen is engulfed in smoke. When the film opened in the West End in 1943, Trinder was starring at the Palladium. One night a couple came into the theatre late. The comedian immediately singled them out. 'This isn't the cinema, you know. You can't see me do the act again. If you want that you'll have to go to the Empire, Leicester Square.' For once Tommy had met his match. The man replied, 'No, I've come to see you die here!'

In any anthology of music hall wit, few would figure more impressively than Trinder. In Britain he helped to set a fashion for the spontaneous unrehearsed often unsympathetic ad-lib that symbolises the authority equal to any emergency of the variety performer. Not that the most notable of Trinder's one-liners were delivered in the theatre. There was the exchange with a morose Orson Welles when Trinder opened in cabaret at the Embassy Club on the day Rita Hayworth divorced the movie genius:

> *Trinder*: Trinder's the name!
> *Welles*: Well, why don't you change it?
> *Trinder*: Is that a proposal of marriage?

Not long after the abdication of Edward VIII, Tommy found himself at Windsor Castle in conversation with King George VI.

> *King*: Well, Trinder, you've done well since I saw you last.
> *Trinder*: You haven't done so badly yourself, sir!

Tommy always took pride in the cufflinks presented to him by the monarch when they next met. Then there was the banquet with the Duke of Edinburgh as guest of honour and Trinder proposing the toast. 'Mr Chairman, may it please your Royal Highness, your Excellencies, your Eminence, ladies and gentlemen… (*and then as the toastmaster – resplendent in his scarlet coat – caught Trinder's eye*)… and, you'll pardon me, but the fox went that way!'

As memorable, even if more premeditated, was the line he used in *Gangway*: 'Here I am at last at the London Palladium, where I've always wanted my name in lights, and blimey they've got a blackout.' He would always follow through with his delighted boastful chortle, the insistent puffing of the cock-sparrow chest, both signifying his satisfaction that there was no occasion to which he couldn't rise. Not the least of these were the Royal Variety Performances – he appeared in five between 1945 and 1980 – where he was sometimes entrusted with the pre-show television-style warm-up of what can be a notoriously frigid audience, one before whom some of the biggest stars have floundered. Most notable was the occasion when he read aloud what the critics had written damning the poor reaction of the intimidated and/or blasé audience at the previous year's show, remarks like 'They frightened the artists by their aloofness' and 'They kept their eyes on the Royal Box rather than the stage.' Trinder aimed his rebuke like an arrow, its disdainful *twang* deafened by the laughter it evoked: 'If I'd had such lousy write-ups, I'd never show my face in a theatre again, yet you lot are here again, bold as brass!'

The epitome of the compulsive talker-cum-jester to be found in many a saloon bar, given half the chance he would have stayed up half the night poking fun at every available target. On one occasion he had to improvise for an hour and a quarter when a power failure held up transmission of *Sunday Night at the London Palladium*. Then, when the show at last made the air, he still had the strength to enter with 'And welcome to *Monday Morning at the London Palladium*!' Trinder knew no such thing as bored embarrassment and had the answer to every predicament that set out to ensnare him. Shrewd and wholly self-satisfied, he took the art of self-promotion to comic extremes, never asking for sympathy because he never needed it. Sadly he never got around to writing his autobiography, but used to joke that he had the title standing by. *Ham and Ego* summed him up at one level, but there was more to Trinder than self-belief. The professionalism, the swiftness of his delivery, the finger on the pulse of his times, all contributed to an entertainer who deserves to be remembered far more than he is.

AFTERTHOUGHTS

This great attacking comedian died on 10 July 1989. He had been appointed CBE in 1975, but, that moment of glory aside, his latter years saw a shift into a twilight zone of fame, defined by nostalgia programmes and the after-dinner circuit, without the full elevation to national-treasure status that longevity brought, say, to Askey and Wisdom. 'They tell us things are bad. Do you realise that in thirty years these will be the good old days?' His television career never fully recovered after he allegedly slighted ATV boss Lew Grade and discovered he was being replaced on the Palladium show in the press. As late as 1983 it was sad to see him working at less than full power on a pantomime bill as a Chinese policeman in a lacklustre production of *Aladdin* at London's Shaftesbury Theatre. He was billed beneath a cast whose combined achievements stood not a chance of matching what he had accomplished in his heyday. Around that time I asked him why he carried on. He replied, 'I don't have to do it for the money. I do it for the importance.' The words explain more clearly than most the vocational pull of being a professional funny man. Trinder's tenacity and professional force of purpose never deserted him, even if his sense of timing did. He died within the same twenty-four hours as Laurence Olivier. One can only guess at the barbs fired in the actor's direction at the Pearly Gates. To be upstaged in the obituary columns, as Trinder unsurprisingly was, seems like a cruel joke to one who was never consciously upstaged in his life.

Today the world of professional football maintains its links with comedy, not least through the ongoing enthusiasm of Frank Skinner and David Baddiel. In their organisation and media reach, both worlds have changed immeasurably since Trinder's day. The comedian was the first club chairman to pay a player one hundred pounds a week, namely Johnny Haynes in 1961, when the maximum wage was abolished. At the time Trinder said, 'Johnny Haynes is a top entertainer and will be paid as one from now on.' Now the earnings of top soccer players tend to outstrip those of comedians. The support of both, however, remains subjective: among colleagues the choice of one's favourite funny men can be as emotive a matter as one's favourite team. Trinder can take satisfaction from the fact that he brought to comedy the touch of excitement, the edge of hostility that will inform a great football match. In any team of his comedy contemporaries he would have been automatic choice as centre forward, his headlong charge on goal corresponding exactly to his relentless pounding of the Palladium audience.

Regarding that autobiography, Tommy was not of a literary disposition. He once told me he cherished three books in his library. They were the *AA Guide*, *Rothman's Guide to Football* and *Funny Way to be a Hero*. It made my day!

A no-holds-barred publicity brochure at the height of Tommy's career

Tommy in 'Beat the Clock' on 'Sunday Night at the London Palladium'

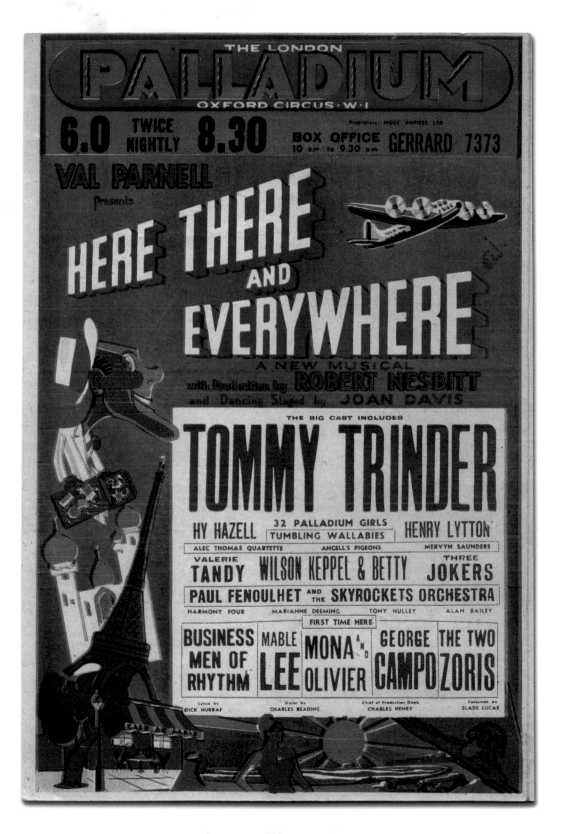

Jimmy James: The Staggering Comedian with the Stuttering Feet

There's a knack in this chipping business. The knack is you get hold of the potato between the forefinger and thumb like that and you get hold of the handle (*of the knife*) like that, and it's 'On, pull, chop – on, pull, chop.' There's four movements. I bet you thought there was only three. I could tell by your face. You didn't see me take the potato out of the bucket! I'll show you again. It's 'On, pull, chop – on, pull, chop.' Only get your fingers out quick. Get your fingers out, otherwise you'll think you've got more chips than you've chopped. Bad chipsters, you can see them all over the country walking about like this. (*Holds up hand with two digits missing*). You can always tell a bad chipster. He'll come into a pub and say, 'Four pints.' (*Holds up index and little finger only*) He forgets, you see.

The leading practitioners of music hall comedy have always shown exquisite attention to detail in carrying out the most basic of tasks. One recalls Little Tich putting on his shoes, Robb Wilton wiping a brow, Sid Field pouring a cup of tea, Max Miller tuning up a guitar, even Stan and Ollie twiddling fingers and a tie respectively. Nowhere was it more explicit than in the act of Jimmy James. One calls to mind his way with a cigarette. Every draw became a breathtaking battle with equilibrium as he weaved precariously between his two stooges. Aiming in a wide arc at an anxious mouth, he would miss all of three times before at last catching it for the briefest of moments between the suction pads that passed for his lips. Then, his neck swivelling as he puffed jaggedly to right and to left, the smouldering butt would take off once again on its swooping flight at the end of his arm. James could have built an entire act around that cigarette alone.

Certainly few were ever more diverting at smoking, however hard many tried. At other times while talking he would stamp out a cigarette, raise his foot, and with a minimum of bending convey butt from shoe to pocket. Countless comics attempted to squeeze a laugh from this gambit, but only James ever came near to obtaining full mileage from the gag. He succeeded because he gave the impression he was doing it without knowing that he was. With James it always happened on the offbeat, in the middle of a sentence; others would feature it during a break in patter, as an item in its own right, thus investing it with an importance it did not warrant that could only prove fatal to the laugh.

This same attention to detail was apparent in the way be could express the subtlest change of feeling through the mere shrug of a shoulder, the glint in an eye, the casual tilt of the headpiece of the moment, whether top hat or bowler. His skill achieved a perfect outlet in his toper routine. The music hall's role as a champion of alcoholic excess was as longstanding as its support of bawdiness and illicit sex. Alongside James, however, all other comedy drunks, while they may have been exempt from the charge of plagiarism, still appeared nothing but watered-down imitations – even those of Sid Field, who openly acknowledged his debt to Jimmy, and Frank Randle, who merely used the device as a further means of projecting his own high-voltage knavery. The bulbous nose, searching bloodhound eyes, straggling black brows and fissured complexion, all contributed to James's cautious 'Shhh…' characterisation. As he lurched sluggishly across the stage to the significant strains of 'Three o'clock in the morning', the top hat was raffishly askew, the shirt front drooped, index finger and thumb of outstretched hand clutched that wilting cigarette, the other hand anchored in his trouser pocket. When he spoke he did so with that extra emphasis all topers assume when trying to prove they're stone cold sober. This was James's secret – all his imitators were trying to prove they were drunk. Ironically, offstage James was a staunch teetotaller, unlike Field or Randle who both allowed the characterisation to gain too much of a grip on their private lives.

'Shhh…'

This portrayal – first developed for a study of a bridegroom who gets drunk at the reception and finds himself locked out on his wedding night – was one of three routines James came to rely upon as his career matured, and yet in the other two, the 'Chipster' and 'Shoebox' routines, the effects of alcoholic excess, if not the predominant comic motif, were never allowed to recede entirely into the background. Thus he would turn to one of his stooges and with a pecking movement find himself looking over his shoulder into a mysterious void, the heads prevented from colliding by a hair's breadth because at that split second the hoped-for object of his attention had similarly misjudged a turn to him. This appeared to happen with the inevitability of Newton's pendulum whenever James turned his head; the sheer precision of it was the result of timing practised to the nth degree. As such, equal credit must go to his two henchmen: 'You wouldn't think they were the two fellers who cut the cables at Bath races, would you?' One wore an ample below-knee-length overcoat and mop wig, and was called Hutton Conyers after a village on the Ouse near Ripon, a name chosen by James on sudden impulse while driving through Yorkshire between shows; the other affected a shrunken suit, deerstalker and the equally improbable name Bretton Woods after the New England venue of the international monetary conference of 1944.

Jimmy with son Jim Casey (left) and nephew Eli Woods

'Hey, are you putting it around that I'm barmy?'

The personnel changed many times during James's career. The slightly aggressive Conyers – 'Hey, are you putting it around that I'm barmy?' – was notably played in turn by James's brother-in-law Jack Darby, his son Jim Casey (then billed as Cass James and later a BBC radio producer responsible for the long-running *Clitheroe Kid* series) and Roy Castle, that brilliant little-boy-lost among musical comedians, who between 1956 and 1959 abandoned his own stage act to serve what he considered was a vital comic apprenticeship with Jimmy. The even simpler Woods, often referred to as Eli, was played by Jack Casey, James's nephew, often featured on Les Dawson's television show in later years as Eli Woods and hauntingly reminiscent with his tall warped appearance of photographs of George Formby Senior, persistent stutter replacing tragic cough. Both Woods and Conyers were incapable of fully adjusting to the world, and James excused their presence as his 'discoveries', at once tolerant and, because embarrassed, disdainful: 'It must be gonna rain if they come this far up the river.'

With Roy Castle, Eli and a shoe box

James's own persona was nothing if not ambivalent. There was something granitic in the presence he generated on stage. His gruffness, his gambler's attire suggested a native provincial version of Edward G. Robinson. But there was also a gentleness and melancholy. Roy Castle got something of this across when he said that James's 'humour walked the stage in suede clogs'. Upbraid his stooges as he did, he managed to maintain an undercurrent of sadness in sympathy with them.

The act had its own distinctive conversational formula, dominated by what the *Guardian* described on James's death as his 'voice of Durham clay'. Whether drunk or sober, he had a fastidious way of shaping a sentence, the lilting cadences of which were admirably offset by the boisterous heckle and the tentative stutter of his two partners. James despised jokes per se, anticipating Tony Hancock by many years, his own definition of a comedian being 'a man who says things funnily, not a man who says funny things.' Like the great American droll Jack Benny, he was unafraid of silence after a remark, never afraid to wait for the laugh. His verbal technique found perfect expression in his lecture on the art of potato chipping, featured in his one Royal Variety Performance in 1953, in which he exposed the secrets of a champion chipster who had managed to steer clear of the occupational 'batter's elbow' and 'permanent wink', both demonstrated with imaginary fillet and invisible splutter and shown to be devoid of any effete sexual ambivalence once explained.

It was, however, in his routine with the shoebox that the individual components of James's world were seen to work with the most perfect cohesion, the vague otherworldliness of Woods and Conyers seen at its most effective. Conyers' bumptious 'Hey, are you putting it around that I'm barmy?' sparked off a chain of misunderstanding focused on the box he nursed protectively under his arm. He had just returned from the unlikely post of colonial secretary in Egypt, where he had been presented with two man-eating lions.

Jimmy: Where do you keep them?
Conyers: In this box.
Jimmy: I thought I heard a rustling!

As James tried to persuade the even more retarded Woods to get two coffees – 'This is gonna be a long job' – Conyers went on to describe the giraffe he received in Nyasaland.

Jimmy: Where do you keep it?
Conyers: In the box.
Jimmy (*to Eli*): Get on the phone. I'll keep him talking till they come.
Conyers: Are you telling him about the giraffe?
Jimmy: No, I'll tell him. (*To Eli*) He's got a giraffe in that box.
Eli: Is it black or white?
Jimmy: I'll ask him. (*To Conyers*) He wants to know if the giraffe is black or white.
Eli: No, the coffee I mean.

Finally a visit to India had yielded an elephant. James is about to ask the obvious.

Jimmy: No, he couldn't! Is it male or female?
Conyers: No, an elephant.
Jimmy: I don't suppose it makes any difference to you whether it's male or female.

Eli: It wouldn't make any difference to anyone but another elephant.
Jimmy: I shall have to stop you going to these youth clubs. (*To Conyers*) Where do you keep the elephant? In the box?
Conyers: Don't be silly. You couldn't get an elephant in there.
Jimmy (*knowingly*): Of course not. You couldn't get an elephant in there. There's no room.
Eli: He could ask the giraffe to move over a bit.
Jimmy: Why don't you go to a museum and get stuffed?
Conyers: I keep the elephant in a cage.
Jimmy: Of course. And where do you keep the cage?
Conyers (*echoed by Jimmy*): In the box!

They would invariably end by expressing their new found solidarity in song. After the agonies of coaxing out the correct key – 'Fah – FAH – fah – FAH' – James would lead the trio close-harmony style in the cosy melody of 'I want to hear my dear old Granny's song at twilight', Johnnie Ray's 'Such a night', or at a later date 'Kisses sweeter than wine'.

James possibly saw the sentimentality of the final song as a safety valve in the face of those who detected the slight undercurrent of menace that existed in his work, the same quality that stood exposed at the end of the first act of David Storey's *Home* when both couples are finally revealed as inmates of some kind of mental institution. When James volunteers, 'Well, there'll be room in the van for the three of us,' he confirms he no longer stands apart from the derangement of the other two, a point for which we have already been prepared more subtly. His sometime introduction of the gangling Eli as a daredevil parachutist is a case in point. The plan was for Eli to jump out of an aeroplane 20,000 feet above the theatre, plummet through the roof and not pull the ripcord until he was only ten feet above the stalls.

Eli: But what if the parachute doesn't open?
Jimmy: You can jump ten feet, can't you?

His dialogue – manic, imaginative and concise – brings to mind names like Beckett and Pinter, ahead of its time on a popular level and maybe the reason why in a long career James, for all his brilliance, never fully made it as a top-of-the-bill attraction. However, his long career as staunch supporting act or workmanlike top of lesser-than-Palladium bills, secured him the indelible respect of all those connected with his profession, not least his fellow funny men, who alone understood those painful devoted years spent working towards the topmost rung of popular acclaim. In the eyes of Robb Wilton, he was 'the greatest timer who ever walked on a stage'.

His specialised recognition as a comedian's comedian stemmed also from his reputation as an ad-libber, his ability to spin laughs out of a chance remark. He had no qualms about overrunning his time, improvising on the spur of the moment. Once when asked by a BBC producer exactly what he did on the stage, he replied, 'I'm glad you brought that up; it's been worrying me for years!' This was the cue for a madcap description of how 'Jimmy James and Co.' opened in Chinese costumes harmonising to 'Sleepy lagoon' as they swung upside down from a wire, the climax coming 'when we spin the bowls of goldfish from strings held in our teeth'. During the Blitz he was playing Eccles Crown Theatre when a mine blew in every door in the auditorium. Pointing to the back of the stalls he bawled, 'Get 'em out! It's that wedding party at the back that's causing all the trouble. Tell 'em to come in or stay out!' He had already been ad-libbing over the noise of bombs and anti-aircraft guns for forty-five minutes. His confidence in the ad-lib, however, is best underlined by the fact that he was possibly the only comedian who ever gave a complete broadcast off the cuff on what was without question a scripted show. When a guest on *Star Bill* during the early 1950s, he somehow lost his script crossing the stage and forced a white-faced Tony Hancock, acting as host, to ad-lib a double act for nine minutes. From that moment Tony was confirmed as James's greatest fan. On a similar occasion he appeared with Eli and son Jim on the summer radio show *Blackpool Night*. As he walked on, again his script fell to pieces and he refused to look at another. While his son alternated between anger and hysterical laughter, the father ad-libbed for ten minutes around his disdain that the BBC couldn't afford three paper clips. 'If anyone should go without, it should be one of you two. I'm the star.' The last laugh, however, went to Eli. He had been silent for five minutes – not surprisingly since the others hadn't spoken to him – when James put the question:

Jimmy: You haven't spoken, but I'll bet you've been thinking?
Eli: Oh yes.
Jimmy: What have you been thinking about?
Eli: I was thinking… this is a hell of a place to rehearse!

James's real name was Casey, which he changed when an agent booking him work in Wales suggested it would receive no welcome in the valleys. He was born in Stockton-on-Tees on 20 May 1892, his father a steelworker by day and music hall clog dancer by night. Jimmy himself began in show business as a twelve-year-old juvenile featuring 'Terry, the blue-eyed Irish boy', a repertoire of five dances, a whistling routine and a standing jump over a five-bar gate! He persisted with his singing, joining a group called Will Netta's Singing Jockeys, and only became a comedian by accident in 1925, standing in when the lead comic in the company at Longton in Staffordshire quit. Four years later he was already playing second top to Jack Hylton's Band for George Black Senior at the London Palladium. In January 1948, when Mickey Rooney led the Hollywood invasion of the theatre that persisted into the 50s, James was again in support. When after the first night the American entertainer consulted Jimmy as to what had gone wrong with his act, he gave a straight answer: 'You haven't got one!' James graciously worked on the American's 'act', even appearing in an impromptu sketch with Rooney. He saved the face of the star, but to the national press there was little doubt who was the real success of the season.

Sadly James's latter years were dogged by financial difficulties. Excessive generosity to friends and an addiction to gambling – where possible theatre bookings were always arranged to coincide with race meetings – led to bankruptcy proceedings on three occasions, in 1936, 1955 and 1963, the third time with a deficiency of no less than £15,542. The final lap of his career comprised a tired variety tour with pop star Adam Faith, a co-starring role as the manager to a gormless boxer played by Bernard Bresslaw in a disastrous BBC television series, *Meet the Champ*, and a token spot in a mock revival of *Old Time Music Hall* at the Comedy Theatre during early 1964. But the old gruffness had not entirely lost its bite. Around that time he made an appearance on television's *Sunday Night at the London Palladium* which proved little short of sensational, so much so that Hancock, just back from another 'rest cure', rang him in his dressing room to say it was the funniest ten minutes he had enjoyed in years – 'I pissed myself!' A heart attack forced James's retirement from the stage in September of that year. He died from pulmonary complications eleven months later on 4 August 1965, but not before his fellow comedians had staged their own tribute at the Prince of Wales Theatre. They called it a tribute, but it also doubled as a benefit, unique in show business for someone still very much alive, even if bedridden. Tribute or testimonial, as a gesture it made its own comment on the regard in which he was held by a grateful profession, as well as paying a few bookmakers' bills. In 1963 he had declared in the bankruptcy court, 'I have now won the official receiver outright!' As his son Jim Casey said, humour like that could never know defeat.

AFTERTHOUGHTS

According to Roy Castle in his autobiography *Now and Then*, the shoebox routine evolved from a two-minute gag told backstage to Jimmy by the 50s singing star Dickie Valentine, suggesting that the classic sketch was a much later addition to the comedian's repertoire than one might have supposed. The full routine eventually played for about twelve minutes, a fact discovered in the early 1980s when Roy's appearance on the *Parkinson* show triggered thoughts of a revival. Word had filtered through that James Casey was by now a dead ringer for his dad and that Eli was alive and well and managing to scrape some sort of living on the northern club circuit. All parties agreed and the decision was taken to allow Roy to finish his interview with a reconstruction of the famous sketch. I shall never forget sitting with Michael Parkinson watching the trio during rehearsals. It was variety heaven as everyone in the studio responded to the classic lines. But there was a snag: the performance ran far longer than the five minutes we had estimated. As producer, I looked at my watch apprehensively, knowing that it would be impossible – and unethical – to shorten the sequence with cuts. Parky had read my mind and leaned over with a word of reassurance: 'You leave it as it is – we owe ourselves this one.' The success of the item led to a new career for Casey that incorporated a Royal Variety Performance and other major television appearances. Some time later it was reported back to me that Eli Woods had declared how grateful he was that bills could now land on his doormat without him needing to worry how they would be paid. That warmed my heart.

A moment offstage for the comedians' comedian

Onstage there was a certain gravitas in the way James stood there between the two zanies on either side of him. Offstage there was something equally down to earth and practical in his approach to comedy, however things were going that night. As he once confided to the young Castle, 'I know it's funny, you know it's funny, last week it was funny, last night it was funny, so if they don't laugh tonight, *they're* wrong!' They seldom were. Roy told me that within the profession James was attributed with the longest laugh ever recorded at the London Palladium. It occurred when he played there on a variety bill, at the time when the Second World War was at its most threatening with the sound of air-raid sirens and doodlebugs a constant reminder of a world where laughter might have seemed to have no place. In those days he would introduce Eli as a whistling contortionist: 'He whistles "Bird songs at eventide" and does the splits – two things at one and the same time.' Jimmy then took a quick pull on his cigarette before adding, 'And if the sirens go, he'll probably do *three*!'

And it was true about Eli – whose stutter was genuine – playing the clubs as a stand-up comedian. One night the audience became a little more vociferous than any comic would have welcomed. He held up his hand and announced, 'I've g-g-g-got s-s-s-some gr-gr-gr-great hec-hec-hec-heckler stoppers – i-i-i-if y-y-y-you'll… wait!'

Nellie Wallace:
'The Essence of Eccentricity'

ARE WOMEN FUNNY?: FROM NELLIE WALLACE TO DAME EDNA

A man may kiss a maid goodbye,
The sun may kiss a butterfly,
The morning dew may kiss the grass,
And you my friends… farewell!
[Curtain speech of Nellie Wallace]

The variety stage knew few women with the attack and ruthlessness essential to the comedian to break down the inhibitions of an audience into uncontrollable laughter. Whereas acidic wit was championed by the fair sex – witness the success of revue stars like Hermione Gingold, Beatrice Lillie and Joyce Grenfell – jokes as such seemed to drop uneasily from feminine lips, while knockabout was considered even less becoming. Gracie Fields, the performer with greatest claim to be styled the Joan of Arc of variety, was like Marie Lloyd, her predecessor, an exception, helped by her perception by much of the public as a singer who happened to lapse into comedy. Great comedians have exploited what they have perceived as the funniness of women, but it does not seem likely that George Burns's scatterbrain Gracie Allen, Howerd's put-upon pianist or the girl Eric Morecambe experimentally called Sid, would have been funny if themselves left in charge of a stage, unable as they were to comprehend the laughter they evoked in the presence of their male colleagues.

The reason for the dearth of funny women can only be guessed at. One mainstay of the great funny man is his subtle exploitation of his own foibles and inadequacies. Is it reasonable to expect women, supposedly often anxious to preserve their mystery and allure, to wish to lay bare their shortcomings? Moreover, the laughter produced by the deliberate flaunting of failings can be seen as a necessary defence mechanism against them. Women may simply have no need of this kind of laughter. Certainly, unlike men, they appear to have no need of jokes as an instinctive feature of social contact. Moreover, those funny ladies who came near to achieving anything like the notoriety of a Formby or a Miller on the variety stage tended to reveal a masculine attitude to their work, sidestepping any element of femininity, of sexual attractiveness that might obtrude into their stage characterisations and placing the emphasis on their ugliness, their ungainliness. It was no easy task, but the air of independence this gained stripped away pretensions in howls of laughter and provided inoffensive scope for the most suggestive material, otherwise taboo when spoken by a glamorous woman and likely to cause uneasiness among both sexes. Just as the Americans, however, appear to have had fewer scruples about glamorous women as jesters – we came to accept the impish sophisticated Lucille Ball as a clown of distinction, while neither Mae West nor Marilyn Monroe had qualms about flaunting their sexuality in the cause of laughter – so it would be wrong to assume that this country has always regarded knockabout and bawdiness as a male prerogative. We should not forget that in Chaucer's time even nuns had licence to be as earthily hilarious as the men. The funny women of the halls, in fact, were not so much pioneers as revivalists reduced to non-feminine methods in a feminine cause.

Prominent within that tradition on the music hall and variety stage was Nellie Wallace, often billed as 'The Essence of Eccentricity'. Born in Glasgow on 18 March 1870, she made her first appearance at the age of six as one of The Three Sisters Wallace, an act that combined singing and clog dancing. She made her first London solo appearance in 1903, and in 1910, by which time she had entered the glorious middle age that would inform her brilliant characterisation, was featured in the opening programme at the London Palladium. Cyril Fletcher once described her as a hybrid of 'the Duke of Wellington and Ken Dodd', a telling description of her nose and teeth in turn. To this could be added a nonexistent chin, a mangy scrap of hair and an even mangier wisp of fur – 'me bit of vermin' – around a scrawny neck. Other well emphasised props included restrictive high-button boots, a gaudy tartan skirt, an ample grey jacket and a small battered Glengarry hat from which stood erect the long tail feather of a pheasant. Her characterisation was grotesque, but to many a yearning spinster poignantly natural. This exchange from her sketch 'Queen of Clubs' by Bob Weston and Bert Lee, as performed at the Holborn Empire in 1932, more than sums up her constant humiliation at the hands of the opposite sex.

> *Man*: I wonder why a woman as intelligent as you troubles to run a club like this.
> *Nellie*: I'm doing this to forget a man.
> *Man*: Crossed in love?
> *Nellie*: No, worse. I've been run over.

Halfway through the song 'The blasted oak', a favourite meeting place, she became more explicit.

> This is the third time that I've been jilted – me first was a sailor, me second a soldier and me last a baker. Oh what a nippy little bit of goods my sailor was! I can see him now. He used to pull me to him, sit me on his knee and say, 'Any old port in a storm.' He hadn't had a storm lately. Ah, but he was the one – my soldier, my buxom blue-eyed soldier. He never took me out in the light. He said I was best in the gloaming.

Her wandering expressive hands and high-pitched adenoidal voice also found scope in songs like 'I lost Georgie at Trafalgar Square', 'Geranium' – a mock-sentimental ballad about a maiden whose tears watered the plant until her true love's return, and 'My mother said, always look under the bed', which continued

> Before you blow the candle out,
> To see if there's a man about.
> I always do, but you can make a bet,
> It's never been my luck to find a man there yet!

Her sketch 'Finesse' presented Nellie as a debutante in skin-tight evening gown. Exuding hope and joy, she would bound staccato-style onto the stage. 'It's excitement – all excitement! If you're fond of anything *tasty*, what price me?' Performing an entrechat in each corner, she drops her fan and unable to bend has to lie outstretched on the boards to retrieve it. By now there is no need for her to look at the clock and exclaim in surprise 'Strange! He promised to be here at 9.30. It's now 12 o'clock' for her audience to realise that feminine allure is not her special preserve.

Her ugliness was all the more striking in the light of her persona's self-delusion: 'I was so ugly when I was a child. That's why I've grown up so pretty.' The refrain of that number ran, 'I wish I was young again,' suggesting she was content anyhow to be distant from the stereotyped glamour and beauty associated with her sex. This combination of attitude and appearance, together with her rorty confidential delivery, rendered material that would have invited shock and suspicion on the lips of a lady completely inoffensive. Nor must one forget the lascivious wink, which could alone compensate in laughter for the sorrow one may have felt for Nellie at the mercy of the ruthless Romeos who haunted her ever-hopeful imagination. She died on 24 November 1948, having continued working through the heyday of variety as a member, alongside Randolph Sutton, G. H. Elliott, Gertie Gitana, Talbot O'Farrell, Billy Danvers and Ella Shields, of Don Ross's *Thanks for the Memory* company. It was in this grouping three weeks before her death that she appeared in the Royal Variety Performance at the Palladium, surprisingly the only time she was accorded that honour and fittingly at the theatre which she had not only opened, but where in 1924 as the lead in the revue *Whirl of the World* she scored her greatest triumph, caricaturing Yasmin in a burlesque of Basil Dean's elaborate production of *Hassan*, Juliet to Billy Merson's Romeo in a burlesque of the balcony scene, and as a boarding-house harridan adept at packing twenty-four visitors to the current Empire Exhibition at Wembley into one bed. A contemporary of Marie Lloyd, she succeeded her as the queen of low comedy, able to convey a whole world of meaning by the mere lift of an eyebrow, a despairing sniff, the slightest rearrangement of that withered tippet of fur. Her reputation as one of the greatest pantomime dames of her era, Widow Twankey her speciality, is a lonely beacon of her own sex in a field dominated by drag.

The tradition of the woebegone eccentric as the driving force in British female comedy was successfully continued in the 1940s and 50s by the sisters Elsie and Doris Waters (1893 – 1990 and 1899 – 1978), their 'Gert and Daisy' partnership providing a rallying call for housewives and servicemen alike during the worst days of the Second World War, during which they maintained a comforting presence on radio. On stage Daisy's torn raincoat, Gert's tattered yellow jumper, the dangling string bag, became to a vast public symbols of people they really knew, whose overheard conversation cut across the tedium of bus queues, shop queues, sluggish suburbia in general. The personal confidences of the two charwomen, revolving around Daisy's husband Bert, Gert's longstanding fiancé Wally, neighbour Old Mother Butler, the insurance man, a husband's eating habits, what's on at the pictures, were all delivered in a languid cockney that expressed self-righteous scorn for anything other than the working-class way of life. Their style had a racy closeness to reality and would find an echo in the parade of old biddies from Ena Sharples onwards who down the years allowed a nation to while away the time with them in the bar of *Coronation Street*'s Rover's Return. True to its origins, the act was developed from the actual comments of two cockney girls at a fashionable wedding at which the Waters sisters, originally in concert party as a musical duo featuring humorous songs from Doris to Elsie's violin accompaniment, were also bystanders. 'Gert and Daisy' were the last of the amusing doubles that persisted among the funny women of the music hall, a tradition that also embraced the irrepressible Houston sisters Billie and Renée, Beattie and Babs, Lorna and Toots Pounds, and Ethel Revnell and Gracie West, who, billed as 'The Long and the Short of It', became famous through their act as two cockney kids.

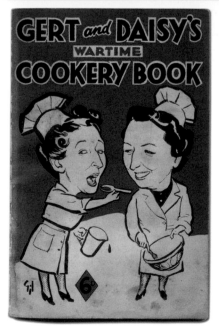

Above left: Elsie and Doris Waters as Gert and Daisy
Above right: Ethel Revnell and Gracie West

Hylda Baker (1905 – 1986) shared the distinction with Wallace of beating the men at their own game as a pantomime dame of impact. No better placed socially than her predecessor, she brought to the variety stage an air of cocky defiance in her portrayal of the archetypal ever-so-slightly-snobbish gossip, always hopeful of moving to a better class of neighbourhood but whose accent, clothes and demeanour only caricature her aim. Her string of well-rounded malapropisms also help to give her away: 'No one has dallied with my afflictions, and I say that without fear of contraception!' Born in Farnworth, near Bolton, the daughter of touring comedian Harold Baker, she began her career on the boards when ten years old. The act for which she would become famous, however, did not develop until the Second World War when she conceived the idea for a sketch based on her observation

Hylda Baker

that when a tall girl and a short girl, both friends, were together, the latter would invariably act as spokesman for the two. In this way the monolithic Cynthia evolved, a spindly spinster the better side of middle age, 'blonde with sort of aquamarine features and her hair in a nutcracker suite'. In reality a man in skirts, 'she' stood at the back of the stage silent and motionless with a transparent stare, 'not all she should be', while Hylda – under five feet in height and bedecked with straggling boa and capacious handbag – bustled bossily through her routine with the fearsome energy that would dispose of a week's washing in five minutes. 'Where have ya been? We've stood standing here waiting for you. I told you to be soon, didn't I? "Be sooon," I said. "Be soooon." (*And then confiding to the audience*) She just looks through ya! No, I wouldn't care, but she knows, y' know! She just won't let on, that's what!'

It is arguable that the true spirit of Nellie Wallace was best kept alive in the 1950s and 60s by a man, namely Rex Jameson (1924 – 1983), who in the persona of Mrs Shufflewick preserved the sharp tragi-comic edge of the original. Terribly refined and yet, in her own words, 'broadminded to the point of obscenity', she resided in Wimbledon, 'all cut glass and tennis balls'. Clutching her handbag and wearing drop-pearl earrings, red gloves, damson velvet coat, a hat fashioned from wax fruit and feathers and the obligatory skimpy fur ('known in the trade as untouched pussy, which is unobtainable in London at the moment'), her slightly baffled appearance distilled that shabbily genteel world where cut flowers were always kept the other side of the curtains for the benefit of the neighbours and pavements were principally meant for dogs to be walked along. Once well known on the variety stage as 'Bubbles Latrine with her educated sheepdogs', she admitted – with careful enunciation – to having been married in the distant past to a pheasant-plucker. While the gawky Wallace placed the emphasis on comedy songs, the tiny drab Mrs Shufflewick presented an intriguing monologue about an evening begun innocently in the local and concluded naked, all but her hairnet, on top of the number 29 double-decker bus, the sozzled centre of attention for countless sober eyes. 'As if they'd never seen a woman naked on the top of a bus before!' Her mind befogged by continual gin and tonics, she would yap on quietly about booze and sex, admittedly mincing over the more embarrassing words, but still in a manner that would be hard to take from an actual female, however talented. Her life's philosophy was based on lewdness. Given a choice of 'death or dishonour' pinioned against a brick wall in a blind alley by a sailor, she is quite convinced that she is 'not dying yet'. With 'I'll tell you one thing – if I'm not in bed by half past eleven, I shall be going home,' we are obviously closer to inverted Max Miller than Nellie Wallace, but even if Mrs Shufflewick,

Below: Rex Jameson as Mrs Shufflewick

250

'weak-willed and easily led', was clearly one jump ahead of Nellie both socially and sexually, they share many points of reference, not least their red-nosed enthusiasm for the task in hand, their naive optimism, the sheer delicacy with which both elicit from their audience an element of genuine pity and concern alongside the gross and the grotesque.

The complexity of the Shufflewick characterisation far outweighed the superficial effect obtained by the countless contributors to the drag phenomenon of the 1960s, where pancake make-up, a synthetic wig and elaborate costumes and accessories were all that were required to convert minimal talent into an apparently acceptable, if suspect, product. As epitomised by the success of the brilliant Danny La Rue (1927 – 2009), the glamorous woman became the aim of most female impersonators. Rex Jameson himself belonged to the older tradition graced by the pantomime dames of Leno, Robey, Malcolm Scott, Wilkie Bard, Tommy Lorne and George Jackley, and brought to perfection, as we have seen, by Arthur Lucan. It is significant that Jameson's favoured term for what he did was dame comedian and not female impersonator or drag performer. When he first appeared on the scene he was often billed simply as 'Mrs Shufflewick' and many in the audience had no idea he was not a woman. Sadly the alcohol-induced aspect of his characterisation crossed over into reality, and during the last ten years of his life it was difficult for him to perform without sitting down.

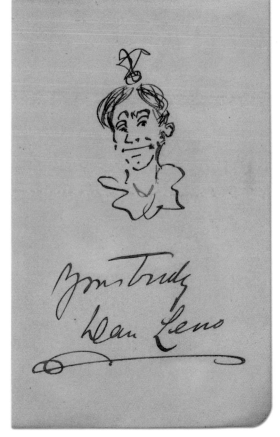

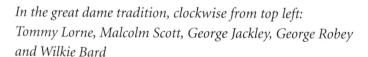

In the great dame tradition, clockwise from top left:
Tommy Lorne, Malcolm Scott, George Jackley, George Robey
and Wilkie Bard

La Rue himself, an Irish-born graduate from the chorus of post-war all-male revues with uneasy titles like *Forces in Petticoats* and *Men Only* achieved national fame via massive success in West End cabaret, where his eponymous nightclub off Hanover Square became a shrine to the so-called Swinging Sixties. His comedy was based for the most part on the portrayal of one particular type, the assertive, high-powered, brassy career woman. To know the prototype was to acknowledge that the lacquered pagoda wigs, the extravagant baroque gowns, the emphatic décolletage, all cornerstones of his impersonation, were nothing if not realistic. These represented the social antithesis of the hard-done-by type conveyed by Wallace and Baker, Lucan and Jameson and their colleagues. La Rue acknowledged a personal debt to Sabrina, Diana Dors, Elizabeth Taylor, the socialite Lady Docker, all personalities who, as Roger Baker pointed out in his exhaustive study *Drag*, flaunted their feminine exuberance in a pioneering attempt to break the tedium of the previous decade, a period when the star of the observant La Rue was still in the ascendant. His acute observation, however, mirrored not only the finer details of the opposite sex – how women walk, hold a handbag, glance at their nails, flicker their eyelashes, size up a man – but the panache required by the woman if such details are not to caricature themselves. Because he had this special flair, La Rue's characterisations remained feminine without ever appearing effeminate. And yet the key to his originality was that at times his inner self barely pretended to be a woman at all. Sweeping on stage in silk and sequins, he would surprise the crowd by bawling 'Wotcher, mates' in a voice fixed far more firmly in the bass clef than his customary husky squeal.

In *Grace, Beauty and Banjos*, an illuminating trawl through the billing matter of a century of music hall and variety performers, the actor Michael Kilgarriff, noting the scarcity of funny women on the halls, ventures to suggest that while the public have 'no objection to female comics, it has never cared for women who put their femininity at risk'. The huge success of La Rue in the 1960s and 70s would serve to underline the observation, the drag performer providing a vicarious means for both men and women to laugh at the opposite sex without embarrassment. It is difficult to think of a corresponding female performer from within variety – as distinct from a straight actress adept at comedy – who could have challenged his success.

AFTERTHOUGHTS

Since 1973 the comedy scene has witnessed the regular arrival of women to rival their legendary counterparts of the variety period, headed by Victoria Wood, Dawn French and Jennifer Saunders, Caroline Aherne (better known as Mrs Merton), Catherine Tate and Miranda Hart. All were given their major opportunity by television; all have to an extent taken advantage of more relaxed attitudes to what would once have been regarded as taboo on female lips. Only Wood and Saunders have steered (at times) away from the obvious caricature that would at one stage have been obligatory; some would have adapted to the live medium of 'twice nightly' more easily than others. The fact remains that irrespective of the greater licence allowed by changes in social attitudes and the greater acceptance of women in all the professions, professional funny women still constitute a minority, as men themselves do within the nursing profession or, for that matter, women inside the boxing ring. Perhaps the successful stand-up performer Jenny Eclair came close to the heart of the matter: 'Men start practising being funny early on. It's the way parents treat them. With girls, it's "Doesn't she look pretty?" Boys take more teasing. Also, men don't communicate or talk to each other. Their way of making friends is to make them laugh. A woman, however, tells her friends serious truths, showing "I trust you with secrets".'

Meanwhile there are two omissions from the earlier edition that have to be repaired. Somewhere in the territory between Wallace and the Waters sisters resided the now largely forgotten but hugely successful Suzette Tarri (1881–1955). I recall her distinctly as one of the first voices I was able to identify on the midday variety shows that were such a feature of the wireless during my childhood. Tarri did not become a star until her late fifties, having entered the entertainment profession as a child violinist and contralto, but concert party and in turn variety eventually claimed her for comedy, where she portrayed 'Our Ada', another cockney cleaning lady, who used to refer to herself as 'the only living woman still awaiting the answer to a maiden's prayer'. Her billing was apt and would have done Wallace proud: 'Still on the Shelf'. She invariably began her act by walking on to the strains of 'Red sails in the sunset', before launching into a plaintive dissertation on love and would-be married bliss.

> You know, I did think that romance had come to me one day last week. There was a knock at me door and when I opened it, a gentleman said, 'Good heavens, Carole Lombard!' Oh, he was ever so nice to me. He said that in the excitement of meeting a glamorous film star double – that was me, see – he'd almost forgotten what he'd called about. I didn't have the pluck to tell him I'd spent all me savings on a vacuum cleaner. That's five I've got now!

Hearing her recordings today one notes that her throaty chuckle had a sexy edge to it that would only have been lost on a boy of six or seven. Ken Dodd once acknowledged the help and advice she gave him when he first contemplated a show business career. Study the photograph of Tarri in performance. I cannot believe it is a coincidence, but she seems to be holding a feather duster in her hand. That was long before Dodd appropriated the device for his tickling stick. The trouble with props is that they seldom register their presence on radio.

A different approach to the female grotesque, neither old maid nor scrubber of floors, was taken by Beryl Reid (1919 – 1996), who on the back of her radio success through five seasons in *Educating Archie* shot to the top of the bill in variety in the 1950s, even though her gangling schoolgirl character 'Monica' – 'Aren't I the absolute terminus?' – had been a mainstay of her work as a live performer for some time. A perfect foil to the cheeky ventriloquial puppet, in her gymslip and straggling pigtails she suggested a reject from St Trinian's, her posh lisp helping to extract every last ounce of laughter from lines like 'I've got thum thticky boiled thweeth in the pocket of my knickerth, but they're all covered in penithillin.' Her catchphrase 'Jolly hockey sticks!' passed into the language to suggest a certain kind of female whose enthusiasm derives from a public school games-orientated background. When the radio show wanted another character she went into creative overdrive and devised 'Marlene – from the Midlands'. With huge dangling earrings like frisbees and a groovy line in contemporary dance-hall lingo, she would extol the praises of her boyfriend Perce, stretching the acceptability of the Brummie accent to its limits, 'Ooh, he's lovely, is moy Pierce. Oi think he's terrifick… He *sends* me,' before signing off with her trademark 'Goodnight, each!' In one of her favourite routines she would knock her girlfriend Deidre: 'She's not loike me, you know. She's common. Deidre says her complexion is sallow. Oi call it yellow. With her yellow face and her little black eyes, she looks like a small portion of prunes and custard!' Few would have guessed that in the years to come Reid would become one of Britain's most respected straight actresses, winning her colours on stage and screen as the controversial lesbian soap star in Frank Marcus's *The Killing of Sister George* and progressing to important work at the National Theatre and the RSC and much else besides. But then Hylda Baker had surprised the world with her contributions to the films *Saturday Night and Sunday Morning, Up the Junction* and *Oliver!*

Beryl Reid as Monica

It is fitting to return to Wallace, who, it should be noted, became like Tarri a happily married wife and mother. After her death Nellie had no greater champion than Sir Alec Guinness, who in his autobiography recalled the impression she made on him as a child of seven on a school-holiday visit to the London Coliseum. It was not love at first sight. In the beginning her parrot-beak nose and a walk that gave her the appearance of being always bent forward from the waist – 'as if looking for someone to punch' – conveyed a witch-like appearance. Later in the show, however, she made the transition from eccentric and vulgar to giddily surreal when she appeared in a sketch in nurse's uniform, on hand to assist in an operation. The patient was wheeled on covered with a sheet and Nellie stood to prim attention as the surgeon went to work with a giant carving knife. At regular intervals she dived under the sheet and with triumphant glee extracted a succession of impossible items: a flat iron, a hot-water bottle, a live chicken. Finally with a look that said everything, she got to insert a long rubber tube in the body. When she blew down this, the body inflated rapidly and covered by the sheet took to the air. Nellie jumped and capered all around the stage in an attempt to catch it, but to no avail. Guinness is less precise about the exact end. By now he had fallen off his seat with laughter. He particularly recalled her high-buttoned boots and expressed the wish that they would end their days cared for 'in some eccentric museum', where when darkness falls they would 'shed their primness, take up idiotic positions and tap out some old, raucous, ribald music hall song'. How I would love to find them and give them that home!

Nellie Wallace

Towering above all the funny ladies, of course, is the all-glamorous all-comforting figure of that global megastar Dame Edna Everage. Since Maurice Chevalier and Marlene Dietrich few performers have implanted themselves on the international consciousness with such vivid clarity, such devastating panache. Her achievement may well be the most towering in recent comic history, but with her Australian roots and origins in satirical cabaret she falls outside the remit of this volume. In any case, it is hard to imagine her venturing to play a week at the New Cross Empire or the Attercliffe Palace, even though in recent years pantomime at Wimbledon has been within her orbit. However, I have it on the authority of her mentor and manager Barry Humphries that in the late 1940s and early 50s when the horizons of his protégée might have been expected to be focused on not-too-distant parenthood and running a home in the halcyon community of the Melbourne suburb of Moonee Ponds, her attention was often distracted by the humorous interludes on the radio provided by records of top British variety names of the day like George Formby, Sid Field, Cyril Fletcher and his 'Odd Odes', and Kenneth and George, the Western Brothers, extolling the virtues of the old school tie in their faux la-di-da accents. The wireless provided the great lady with a first enticing glimpse of music hall, and I am sure that Gracie and Nellie, not to mention Elsie and Doris, were well to the fore in this company. Also influential must have been Douglas

Douglas Byng, DLE: Dame of the Liverpool Empire!

Byng (1893 – 1987), the nightclub 'queen', whose shrill voice and sharp technique came to the fore in the presentation of a whole harem of strong-willed female grotesques from 'Doris, the Goddess of Wind' to Boadicea and Nell Gwynne. Everage's comedic education was further advanced when top names like Tommy Trinder and Arthur Askey came from the home country to play Australia's stages in person: it was a revelation for an insecure young woman to see these lone figures stand on a vast stage and address an audience of thousands in casual conversation, as intimately as if she had been chatting across her own garden fence. One can hear her now: 'Call them old-fashioned, darlings, but Tommy and Arthur both have a lot to answer for!'

Right: Dame Edna Everage appears by arrangement with Barry Humphries Enterprises

'I hate all men except Max Miller,
Aunty Grace, 1930'
(From Max's photograph album)

GRACIE FIELDS: THE LASS FROM LANCASHIRE

If we can't spin, we can still sing!
[To the mill-workers in the film *Sing As We Go***]**

Now, I'm going to sing a few choruses and if you'd like to join in, you can do,
and if you don't, it doesn't matter – I'll speak to you just the same!
[To the forces in France]

Although she was unquestionably the most successful female variety performer of her day, some might question the inclusion of Gracie Fields in this volume. For all her success she could divide audiences between those who were devoted to the sublime effects she achieved as a serious singer to the exclusion of her comedy, and those who voted for her incomparable handling of a comedy song and would prefer to have skipped the less frivolous parts of her repertoire. And yet she had no need to play off one side against the other. She also possessed an all-conquering sense of audience control that united both camps as deftly as she was able on occasion to combine her skills within a single song.

There exists a live recording made at the Holborn Empire in 1933 of her singing an early country standard, 'There's a cabin in the pines'. She alternates effortlessly between pathos and send-up, switching from coloratura clear to corncrake rasp as if Joan Sutherland were in duet with a feminine version of James Durante: 'Sorry that I went away... *Cor blimey!*' Ultimately the comedy has to win through, as it did over Tommy Cooper's magic and Victor Borge's prowess at the keys. It first did so early in her career as she experimented with burlesque vocal gymnastics when audiences grew restive during her rendition of sentimental ballads that may have seen better days, a process acted out effectively within the rags-to-stardom plot of her film *The Show Goes On*. One is reminded of one of those comedy gymnasts sacrificing potential Olympic gold in the cause of laughter. 'Our Gracie' has a total right to be put on a comic pedestal within these pages, however many recordings of 'Ave Maria' she may have sold. When she played New York's Palace Theatre in 1930, she was billed as the 'funniest woman in the world'. Her voice had the splendour of a stained-glass window and the inbuilt power to shatter itself to smithereens for slapstick effect.

Fields was able to fuse her two appeals through an unerring ability to identify with her audience, at first at a northern provincial level, then gradually expanding to national and international acceptance, transcending class and accent en route, but always astute enough to reject the airs, graces and false values often thrust upon a star – a movie star especially – by success. She knew implicitly when to rein in the tears evoked by a hymn or a sentimental song and surrender all to the hilarity of a comedy number or shaggy dog story. Few summed her up better than the author J. B. Priestley, who wrote several of her screenplays and knew her well: 'She was independent, saucy, sharply humorous, bossy, maternal, blunt in manner but deeply feminine… she was the people in all the little backstreets, now with a full audience and the lid off.' He could have added, 'humble, shrewd, ironic, unaffected and the scourge of pretension'. For all her artifice, there was nothing artificial about her. And she knew full well what she was doing. She once likened it to weaving a silver thread between herself and the theatre audience. During the Second World War she was regularly accompanied by Ivor Newton, sometime pianist to Chaliapin and Piatigorsky. His anxiety summed up her intuitive feel for the mood of the crowd: 'There was never a rehearsal; I lived the whole time on my nerves, sure that she herself would never go wrong.' That she never went wrong for the best part of six decades regardless of her superficially opulent lifestyle and the ups and downs of her personal life is itself testimony to her talent.

Not that there was any doubt that once she was on stage everyone was under strict instructions to have a good time. Trilling the high notes as she entered, she would cut across the applause with the strident errand boy's whistle that she made her own. A couple of numbers later she would take off her fur stole and throw it across the piano. 'Only wore it for swank,' she would admit, before adding, 'Hope someone dusted the piano,' or, 'You've all seen it now, so I needn't bother!' It was soon time to spell out her agenda: 'Right, we'll forget we're at the Holborn Empire. Imagine we're in our front room and we're having a bit of a do. We've had a nice tea – some boiled ham and lettuce, and a tin of salmon and we're all right now.'

The Palladium impresario George Black recalled the occasion she appeared to break the first rule of stage technique, never to turn your back on an audience and walk upstage before the laughter and applause have subsided. Gracie did so, paused and then with her back still turned began to sing. The audience was expecting to be launched into a second wave of laughter when they were suddenly brought to silence by the pure liquid notes of a semi-religious melody, 'Three green bonnets'.

> At exactly the right moment, known to her by instinct, she turned her head, then her body, and began to walk slowly down the stage singing. The house was hushed, breathless. As the last notes died away I heard a gasp. And I, who had been a hardboiled showman since boyhood, and thought I knew all the tricks of the trade, felt what the audience felt. For here was no trick. This was blazing sincerity – a heart speaking to the hearts of the world.

As so often, the clue was in the detail. She could achieve a similar bond with the briefest of comic moments, as in her first film, *Sally in Our Alley*, when she is about to sing the theme song that came to symbolise her appeal. She has her back momentarily to those gathered to hear her sing. She is wearing what was for her an uncharacteristically glamorous bare-shouldered evening gown. In a mid-shot she first turns her head over her left shoulder and then repeats the move over her right, before the tips of her right fingers creep into the bottom of frame to sneak a scratch on her bare back. As she turns around to face the camera to sing, she acknowledges her indiscretion (nice girls don't relieve an itch in public) by biting her lower lip like a child caught with a hand in the cookie jar. The sequence is over in seconds. It is funny, but more importantly assures her audience she would never rise above her true station in life.

With accompanist and songwriter Harry Parr-Davies

She was a total paradox, the core ordinariness she projected able to coexist with the quite extraordinary quality of her multifaceted talent. A lesser performer would have been set up for life if blessed with merely her vitality or versatility, her comic spontaneity or amazing vocal range. She also knew, or sensed she knew, her limits. The grand diva Tetrazzini once offered to coach her, but she declined, with the result that within the classical canon she seldom progressed further than an aria from *La Traviata* or the Bach – Gounod setting of 'Ave Maria'. Whatever their good intentions, people who demanded for this great star a supposedly more exalted platform missed the main point about her. She needed fingertip contact with her roots, and any medium other than the brash variety stage or the low-budget films concocted for her would have let her down.

With the mechanised media of radio, cinema and the gramophone to help her, Gracie was almost certainly the first northern English artist completely to captivate the southern public without – *vide* George Formby Senior – having to compromise her identity or mocking her origins in any way. She was famously born Grace Stansfield over her grandmother's fish and chip shop in Rochdale on 9 January 1898. Jenny, her stage-struck mother, strove to eke out the modest family income by taking in theatricals' washing and contrived to time her pick-ups and deliveries to coincide with the show, taking young Gracie along with her to watch from the wings. The daughter never forgot her mother's instructions at that time: 'Keep your eyes about you, young Grace. Watch everything you can. That's the only way you'll learn.' Jenny soon spotted the girl's singing potential as Gracie trilled her way though the songs she had heard on those Hippodrome visits. Anxious to secure her daughter an escape from the industrial landscape, Jenny entered her for a talent contest when she was seven. She tied for first place, and soon became part of a succession of juvenile troupes with names like Haley's Garden of Girls and the Nine Dainty Dots.

However, her father Fred, who worked at an engineering works, was less convinced that this was the future he desired for his daughter. He insisted that from the age of twelve she follow the accepted routine of someone of her class and work in the cotton mills from six to noon, then attend school in the afternoon. The arrangement was short-lived. A chance to deputise for an act at the Hippodrome renewed her confidence. Gracie was fourteen when she took the train to Blackpool to appear as one of Charburn's Young Stars. It was around this time that she shortened her surname to stand out on a variety bill. There was no question now of her professional status, although nothing of note occurred in her career until 1915, when she joined the company of a touring revue, *Yes, I Think So*, for over a year. The principal comedian was Archie Pitt. Few outside his own circles would have recognised the name, but he would go on to exert probably the greatest influence of anyone on her future career. Pitt produced a similar show, *It's a Bargain*, the following year. It continued for two and a half years. In effect they were biding their time for the big break. It arrived in 1918 with Pitt's production *Mr Tower of London*. The show claimed Gracie's attention for the next seven years, taking her from run-down halls in small coal-mining communities to every venue of note in the provinces, as well as a prestigious run in 1923 at London's Alhambra music hall. By the time she left the show after more than 4,000 performances in 1925 she was a national figure and married to Archie. In later years Gracie's forthrightness kept from no one the fact that the marriage was one of convenience and not romance. As she conceded in her autobiography, 'He was not my Svengali, but he was a passable imitation.' The marriage was dissolved after six years of what she once described as 'star-spangled humiliation'.

In fairness, Pitt had long sensed that the gauche young redhead who came under his wing embodied an indefinable combination of talents, and he was as determined as her mother had ever been that she should reach the top. He also provided the perfect nursery environment for her emerging comedy skills. One sketch involved Gracie being locked in the Chamber of Horrors at Madame Tussaud's. Another had her playing a dizzy maid to a nouveau riche family in a short frilly skirt that showed off her long thin legs encased in twisted black stockings full of holes. As she proceeded to lay the table she went into a cod-acrobatic routine, twisting them into semaphoric patterns and kicks of which Max Wall would have been proud. 'Did I ever tell you that my grandmother was Baroness Farquharson and that my father of course was Baron –' boomed someone, to which Gracie interrupted, 'Pity your mother wasn't!' Along the way she inevitably got to spill soup over the guests. There was her bow-legged washerwoman, a character that would have brought back memories of the days when the theatricals' laundry steamed up the back room at home, and the operatic diva delivering a pitch-perfect aria from *Carmen* or *Rigoletto*, who is unexpectedly obliged to substitute gobbledegook for the foreign phrases she cannot remember. Nothing was absolutely set in stone, and Gracie's improvisational gifts were encouraged.

Her success inevitably led to a film career, which commenced with *Sally in our Alley* in 1931. By now she was no longer living with Pitt, although he continued to play a role in her career, contributing to the screenplay of this and the next movie, *Looking on the Bright Side*. There was nothing about these films to suggest that the cinema had found its female Chaplin equivalent, but their pick-me-up quality made

them the perfect vehicles for the Depression era and Gracie pre-empted the screen success of George Formby by four years. They also made her the highest-paid British star of the decade. Excluding cameo appearances there were fourteen bona fide starring vehicles up until 1946, the last six of which were technically American productions, although only the final three – *Holy Matrimony, Molly and Me* and *Madame Pimpernel* – were actually made in America. Her British pictures were almost all masterminded by Basil Dean at Associated Talking Pictures out of Ealing Studios. The three American films shot in England for Twentieth Century Fox between 1938 and 1939 (*We're Going to be Rich, Keep Smiling* and *Shipyard Sally*) were directed by the ebullient Italian film director Monty Banks, who had already directed *Queen of Hearts* for Dean at Ealing.

In her films Gracie for the most part epitomised the working girl battling against the system amid a conventional farrago of clichéd misunderstandings and rags-to-riches aspiration. Motifs from her real-life story flit across the screen as if to test the knowledge of the most zealous fan, and she is never allowed to lose the common touch, even to the extent of forfeiting her romantic ideal if the climactic love match strikes the wrong note. When she fails to win the man, it is enough that she has kept the mill open (*Sing As We Go*), upheld the throne of a Ruritanian kingdom while saving the finances of a children's hospital (*Love, Life and Laughter*) or even saved the show through her own triumphant success (*The Show Goes On*). Altruism is always to the fore, provided she still has scope for an average of four or five songs a picture. She was fortunate to come across 'Sally' so early. A live performance in which she omitted to sing it, her trademark headscarf looped around her hair, was as inconceivable as Christmas without Crosby. It has been estimated that she must have performed it every other day for almost half a century. That it was a song written for a man to sing never seemed to matter.

> When skies are blue, you're beguiling,
> And when they're grey, you're still smiling!
> Sally! Sally! Pride of our alley!
> You're more than the whole world to me!

As early as 1933 she was prefacing it in the theatre with the prophetic line, 'I bet I'm singing it when I'm seventy!' She had sung it at the second of her ten appearances in a Royal Variety Performance in 1931 – the first had been in 1928 – and it was her sole contribution during her surprise appearance on the occasion of her last, in special tribute to the Queen Mother in 1978.

A prophecy that might have been made as readily by any of her admirers is that with the outbreak of hostilities in 1939 Gracie with two decades of success behind her would have gone on to symbolise the British wartime spirit as our undisputed national heroine. A famous painting from these years by Dame Laura Knight depicts with dazzling technical accuracy a skilled munitions worker at her bench 'screwing a breech-ring'. Her concentration sets off her plain beauty, one devoid of glamour. Her name is Ruby Loftus and in another context she could have been Gracie herself, working in the mill as depicted with documentary precision in the opening titles of *Sing As We Go*, the Fields film that alongside *Shipyard Sally* best celebrates productivity and solidarity in the workplace. The hearts of the nation went out to Loftus as the painting, unlike anything Knight had atempted before, achieved widespread publicity and Ruby became a national wartime heroine. That was the level Fields might have achieved, opposite sides of the same coin, the mechanic and the entertainer, but both no-nonsense hard-working public servants. The subsequent sentimentalisation of less versatile talents as forces' sweethearts and similar sobriquets, however agreeably they sang, disguises the fact that no female entertainer was potentially more important to the country's morale than Gracie. Besides, for all her radiance and personality there was not a wife or girlfriend in the land who would have seen her as a threat.

Things did not work out quite that way. At first she poured all her efforts into war work and the rigours of troop entertainment, in spite of the fact that she was still recovering from cancer surgery from which she nearly died a few weeks before war was declared. Things were complicated, however, when in March 1940 she married Monty Banks (real name Mario Bianchi) following her divorce from Pitt shortly before. The threat of Banks' internment as an enemy alien when Italy entered the war, even though he had lived in America since the age of ten, led to a discussion of her dilemma at the highest political level. Churchill advised her to repair with Banks to Canada, adding, 'If you want to work for Britain, it's no good earning English pounds, but if you can earn American dollars for Britain, you will be doing her the greatest service you can.' It was not the first time he had supported in herculean circumstances one half of a union emotionally committed for help and support to the man or woman they loved. It was argued by some that at such a time there were far worse fates than internment, but any accusation of naivety levelled at Gracie has to be tempered by the part played by the man with the big cigar in the course she took.

At considerable financial sacrifice, Gracie toured throughout North America, raising vast sums for British war charities. 'I know you were expecting Betty Grable in a bathing suit, and all you got is an old gal in a frock, but I'll do my best.' Meanwhile she was denounced in the British press for deserting her homeland with her wealth and jewellery, intent on sitting out the war in America. She later admitted, 'Every British newspaper screamed I had deserted my own country… I was a traitor… I had run away… I'd smuggled heaven knows what fortunes out. I was stunned.' But one can understand the feelings of the man in the street, as if the figurehead of Britannia on our mightiest warship had been spirited away to safe storage for the duration of hostilities. It could not have helped that she did not have one instantly recognisable song that identified her to the exclusion of all other singers with the conflict, in the way that 'Sing as we go (and let the world go by)' had served for the Depression. Indeed, after 1940 her recording career fell away gradually, not to resume again until 1947. 'Wish me luck as you wave me goodbye' from *Shipyard Sally*, released only weeks before the war began, should have fitted the bill and certainly became a standard of her repertoire. Maybe the jaunty optimism of the number was better suited to a Flanagan or a Formby than a performer who for all her comic brio could have effortlessly epitomised the sadness of the times. Even the unbearably poignant 'I'm sending a letter to Santa Claus (to bring daddy safely home to me)'

did not fulfil the requirement, centred as it was on the nursery and not conventional romance. Meanwhile Vera Lynn scored her biggest success with 'We'll meet again'.

Torn between love, duty and compromise, and in spite of contractual obligations in the United States, Gracie did in fact return many times to her homeland during the troubles, performing in shipyards and munitions factories, as well as travelling to troop bases as far afield as the Far East, the South Pacific, India and North Africa. In time she received an official apology from Parliament over the matter of the money and possessions she had allegedly taken overseas, and when the war was over the love and affection felt towards her by the British public regained its former strength, but those closest to her knew that wartime events had cast a shadow over her life that – however clear her conscience – never completely faded from her view. After the war she began to take life at a slower pace, alert to the need for reflection as she pulled together the loose ends of a career that apart from a couple of movies had been sacrificed financially to the war effort. By now she had acquired the home on the Italian island of Capri, *La Canzone del Mare* – The Song of the Sea, where she would seek refuge during the rest of her days. A BBC radio series, *Gracie's Working Party* helped to ease her back into popularity in 1947. But the big challenge came when she accepted an offer to top the bill at the London Palladium in 1948. It was here she showed she had lost none of her ability to win over an audience. Her agents, Bert and Lillian Aza, had been concerned when she appeared to offer a cover version of the Edith Piaf hit 'La vie en rose' as her opening number for the big occasion. They were decidedly nervous when on the opening night the first bars played by the orchestra revealed that their protests had been in vain – until she sang. Gracie had provided the melody with a new set of English lyrics. They had nothing to do with the meaning of Piaf's original, but no words could have better suited the moment of reconciliation and return.

> Take me to your heart again,
> Let's make a start again,
> Forgiving and forgetting…

If only wars had been fought in theatres! It was as if she had never been away. And, as she showed that triumphant night, she could still execute a high kick and turn a cartwheel with the best of them.

No performer in the entire music hall canon left a greater legacy of comedy songs, the titles of which have entered the language. Many held a mirror up to the everyday experience of her working-class public, while the words often invited her to interpret them as character studies, like the one about the girl who took her harp to a party, 'but nobody asked me to play… so I took the darn thing away'. She managed to invest that last line with a weariness that made you feel the burden of the wretched instrument. In a similar category lived the sad but determined spinster hoarding the tokens of an idealised domestic bliss in her 'little bottom drawer'.

> One Persian rug – one china jug
> And some beautiful silverware from Woolworth's store,
> With a book by Doctor Fife on *How to Be a Perfect Wife*,
> All packed up in my little bottom drawer.

'I never cried so much in all my life' recounted a visit to the cinema by a highly strung movie fan, the title providing the refrain to the various episodes in this melodrama to end all melodramas.

> As she faced the blinding snowstorm and came trudging through the town,
> Oooh… I never cried so much in all my life!
> And when I saw her carrying her baby upside down,
> Oooh… I never cried so much in all my life!

Gracie's continual use of song title as refrain guaranteed increasing laughter and converted many of them to the status of catchphrases in their own right. In 'Turn 'Erbert's face to the wall' she bemoaned a miscreant who has brought disgrace on her family, but not before turning the rest of the household to evil ways, providing another excuse for mounting anxiety and mock tears. With 'What can you give a nudist on his birthday?' she entered the world of Donald McGill cartoons – 'a watch chain would look silly, draped across the front of Willie' – while 'Keep it in the family circle' revolved around a very large and putrid Stilton cheese to which all at home had become attached in spite of its alarming potential as a source of poison gas and proven ability to scare the daylights out of the waxen effigies in the Chamber of Horrors.

Especially ironic seem those songs that in retrospect appear to reflect details of her personal life. 'The wickedness of men' is a subject on which she might be expected to have become an expert, embracing a learning curve that took in both the landlady's son who allegedly sexually abused her at the age of ten and the faithless Archie Pitt. Admonishing her audience that there's so much an honest working girl has got to lose, she adds

> Instead of saying, 'No,' at first,
> Say, 'Yes,' and then refuse.

'She fought like a tiger for 'er 'onour,' with its painful line, 'He said "Gertcha, I won't hurt yer,"' mirrored the same theme. 'Out in the cold, cold snow' made reference to a husband who gambled away his fortune and cast its subject into the frozen wastes of wherever (Monty Banks died a relatively wealthy man, but his extravagant gambling habits were of great concern to his wife and her family). 'Fonso, my hot Spanish knight' extolled the romantic virtues of mainland Europeans, a category to which both her second and third husbands belonged. Interestingly she herself proposed to the latter, a gesture in keeping with one of her biggest hits, 'Walter, Walter, lead me to the altar!' in which she pleads she has no wish to die an old maid and doesn't 'cost too much to keep in food'.

> Walter, Walter, mother thinks you oughter,
> So take me while she's in the mood!

Rivalling this number as her most requested comedy success was 'The biggest aspidistra in the world', with its clever build of audience expectation through the pregnant pause before the delivery of the title line, as in 'Oooh… I never cried so much in all my life!'

> When father's 'ad a skinful at his pub, the Bunch of Grapes,
> He doesn't go all fighting mad and getting into scrapes.
> You'll find 'im in 'is bearskin playing Tarzan of the Apes
> Up the… *biggest* aspidistra in the world!

In 1938 'Aspidistra' became her biggest-selling comedy recording, with worldwide sales of over a million, more even than 'Sally'. On the outbreak of war she adapted the lyrics to signal her intent to 'hang old Hitler from the very highest bough of the… *etcetera*!' The new recording came to the attention of the German high command. In May 1940, two days after she was secretly recalled from the hotel in northern France where she had been based for ENSA, an enemy bomb fell on the property, reducing her room to ruins and killing seven people. Around this time a German magazine declared, 'Gracie Fields has earned for England the equivalent of a hundred new Spitfires. She is adjudged a war industry and should be therefore treated accordingly.' Churchill may have been justified for wanting her to get far away.

In live performance none of her comedy numbers was more effective than 'Rochdale hounds'. Presaging the success of Joyce Grenfell with a similar technique in later years, Gracie was able to people the stage with the imaginary characters of the hunt as vividly as the revue artist conjured up the members of her recalcitrant nursery class – even to the extent of Gracie's George being an unexpected forebear of Grenfell's 'George, don't do that!' At a gentle gallop, the band provided appropriate 'tantivy' accompaniment while she briefly left the stage to put on her hunting clothes, before emerging in comical hunting garb.

> Come on, lads. Come on, come on, dogs. Go on, dogs. (*Gracie emerges*) Go on, little uns and big uns. Go on, go on in front. Go on, start picking up scent. George, come on. Come out of that pub. You've been in all morning. You won't know whether you're hunting for horses or hunting for dogs. I don't know. Come on. (*She switches briefly to an affected accent*) Good morning, Lord Alphonse, 'ow are you? 'Ow's your 'orse? I'm very glad. (*She switches back*) Come on, George. Give us a leg up. Keep still, mare, keep still. Steady, steady, now, right, go! Hey, hey, you pie can, I want to get onto it, not over it. Come on now, keep steady. That's right, up! Eee, I don't think I better sit side-stroke. I'm sure to slip off. No, I'll sit like Tom Mix does. That's better. The only thing is I'll sit like it for six weeks after. Eee, I say, this horse is bony. Oi, come on, stick 'em in a bit, love. Go on, gee up. Go on, follow, dogs. That's the way. A nice steady pace. That's beautiful. Hey, hey, never mind this 'ere fence. Go round it! Heh, I think we're winning. Heh, there's nobody with us. We've won! You're doing all right. Eee, there's something funny here. Here, pie can, you're following wrong dogs, come on. There's road to greyhound track. Can't you read? Go on, gee up. You better catch others up, go on. Go on, I'll stand for it. I'll never be able to sit for it. Go on, go on. It's all right, go on. You keep going. I am! Go on, go on, we're doing all right. I know one thing. I'll stick to knitting after this! Go on, dogs, go on, dogs, keep on in front. Go on, you're all right. Go on, look out, my horse is bucking. Look out, hey, stop it. There's a dog down there. Kick it off, get it off! Hee, hee, the cheeky thing! Did you see that? It was taking my horse for a gas lamp!

As she cantered around the stage, the physical tour de force would have reminded those with a privileged knowledge of Parisian music halls of Jacques Tati's breathtaking pantomime of a horse and its rider at the same time. It was almost an anticlimax when she left the supreme spontaneity of this for the song proper, in which we discover that the Rochdale hunt relied on a Battersea blend of whippets and Alsatians, bulldogs and Dalmatians. A cat has to make do for a fox and her uncle's steed has a coal wagon attached.

As the above reveals, she could mock the accent and mores of the upper classes with relish, but by the mid-1930s they too had taken her to their hearts and had either missed the joke or didn't care, even though many of them probably fell into the category that preferred her more serious vocalising. On the occasion of her first Royal Variety Performance, Queen Mary is reported to have said to her afterwards, 'I prefer you singing songs like "Come into the garden, Maud" (*sic*) to the common ones.' Critic James Agate, who championed her for the role of St Joan, went halfway to make amends when he declared of her lighter fare, 'No other artist could invest this howling, defiant drivel with such exquisite and unerring pathos and sincerity.' She attempted to please everybody, of course, and over the years her pure legato made magic of titles as diverse and potentially mundane as 'Danny Boy', 'Scarlet ribbons', 'Christopher Robin', 'Now is the hour', 'Little old lady' and 'Around the world'. She never messed around with the numbers her core public might hold sacrosanct in any way.

In even greater contrast with the more serious songs were the jokes she told with energy and gusto. She kept a special selection already typed in a folder for perusal by the Lord Chamberlain at any time and dipped into them as and when she saw fit. She boasted of their cleanness and had no trouble then with what might be frowned upon as stereotypical or politically incorrect today.

It happened on the train to Glasgow. Every time the train stopped, a little old Scotchman clambered over his neighbours, hurried down the station platform and scampered back aboard just as the whistle blew. Finally one of the passengers said, 'Look here. What's the idea, jumping off and on again every time we stop? What's going on?' The little Scotchman was worn out. He said, 'I've been to London to see a heart specialist. He told me my heart's liable to stop at any minute, so I'm taking no chances. I'm just paying my fare from station to station!'

The Home Guard was practising manoeuvres and this big six-foot farm lad with a shotgun was posted as sentry. He heard someone walking towards him in the darkness and called out, 'Halt! Who g-g-g-goes th-th-there?' The footsteps stopped. He could see a little fellow standing there, but there was no answer. 'Who g-g-g-goes there?' he repeated. Still no answer. 'Why d-d-d-don't you say something?' he demanded. At that point a sad little voice spoke up. 'And h-h-have you th-th-think I'm making f-f-fun of you! N-n-not me!'

An Irishman was standing on the corner of a very busy street. He was dying to get over to the other side, but the lights had gone wrong and they sent a policeman down who knew nothing about traffic, and he's standing there terrified, going 'Traffic, pedestrians, traffic, pedestrians, traffic, pedestrians.' Suddenly Pat called across, 'Oi, when are you going to let some of the Catholics get across?'

The last third of her life was spent in a loose form of semi-retirement in her beloved Capri. Monty Banks died from a heart attack on the Orient Express in 1950, and two years later she married Boris Alperovici, an unassuming radio engineer from Bessarabia, who had long been domiciled on the island. She lived happily with him to the end of her days: perhaps she had spotted that his surname was an anagram of 'I love Capri.' Frequent trips would bring her back home or across to America for concerts and television shows. In 1968 she was even paid a king's ransom to play two weeks at the Batley Variety Club, where observing that scampi and chips was on the menu she quipped, 'I was born over a fish and chip shop, and now I'm singing in one.' The whole world now accepted that the exotic island in the Mediterranean was her home. It never stood in the way of her direct appeal at grass-roots level. Indeed, the idea of Capri kept her mystique alive in a way that a villa in Lytham St Annes could not. She remained down-to-earth to the end. The humble lass from Lancashire who had never been ashamed to admit that as a girl she used to clean the neighbours' outdoor privies for a few extra pennies later confirmed to a journalist that she had once scrubbed out the star dressing room at the London Palladium. 'Yes, I did. I didn't want to leave it messy for whoever was coming after.' When in 1978 a bouquet of red roses landed at her feet at the end of her last performance in Rochdale, to commemorate a theatre named after her, she joked, 'I'll be able to sell these on the market on Monday!'

After the 1964 Royal Variety Performance

Unpretentious and generous until the end of her life – she claimed that one of the reasons for doing the Batley date was that she still had 'a few relations who can do with a little financial help' – she maintained the orphanage at Peacehaven that she had founded for the children of disadvantaged theatricals in 1933 until the late 1960s. She had been rendered unable to have children at the time of her hospitalisation with cervical cancer in 1939, when prayers were offered for her in churches of every denomination. The Queen sent her own greeting – 'Please, tell Gracie to get well soon' – and it is estimated that more than

250,000 get-well messages were addressed to her. That statistic alone underlines the love and esteem in which she was held, far more important than all the honours that came her way. She had been appointed CBE in 1938, although unaccountably had to wait until nine months before her death from a heart attack in September 1979 before she acquired the DBE that had long been rightly hers. She greeted the news with the comment, 'Yes, I'll accept, but if they're going to call me Dame, I hope they don't call Boris Buttons!' No one, however, would have seen through the illogicality of the honours system more clearly than her and she almost certainly derived greater joy from the freedom of the Borough of Rochdale, not to mention the ship christened after her in 1936 – a paddle steamer on the Southampton to Isle of Wight run that went down valiantly at Dunkirk – and the hybrid buttercup-yellow tea rose named for her in 1938.

As one imagines the scrapbook of her career, it is hard not to discern in her the first flowerings of the more suspect celebrity culture that engulfs the media of today, nurtured in the shallows of television reality shows and the hollowness of non-achievement. If so, it is down to the democracy of her success, the willingness to make herself appear to belong to everyone. But anyone back then sitting in the Palladium or the Holborn Empire who ever responded to the humanity in her voice, the vital spark in her humour, could be forgiven for thinking they had been let into the presence of the angels, however garish and lowly the setting. More importantly she clung to what journalist Kenneth Allsop described as 'the secret of eternal maturity'. That is the quality most sadly lacking today and why those who care must cling to her memory.

To meet and work with this fine lady towards the end of her life was a special privilege, if only to have confirmed at first hand that her no-nonsense Lancastrian approach to life was as genuine as her undiminished star quality on stage. It was remarkable to greet a homely old lady in an unassuming coat and hat who would have been near to invisible in the bus queue or supermarket, and then to watch the near-alchemical transition to the person whose hold on an audience never wavered, as if one's grandmother had been transformed into Marlene Dietrich and the Queen Mother combined. It all fitted with what Arthur Askey once said of her: 'She was humble and had no false ideas. We once both met Maurice Chevalier in France at the beginning of the war. She was like a twittering schoolgirl at the thought of meeting him, though to me she was as big a star as he was.' But she was not without a certain pride in her achievements and recalled the occasion when she was entertaining the troops in the Borneo jungle at the time of the Japanese surrender. Asked to sing the Lord's Prayer, she noticed cigarettes glowing in the darkness enveloping the soldiers in front of her. Instinctively she asked everyone to strike a match and was overwhelmed by the response as thousands of flames transformed the harsh makeshift arena into a cross between a cathedral and fairy land. They all sang together. In the process she initiated what has since become a tradition at pop and rock concerts. Today, to hear her recording of 'Sally' has a Proustian effect, transporting me back to the gramophone in my grandparents' front parlour with an emotional power that no other popular music can achieve.

Dame Gracie in her beloved Capri

Max Wall: In the Flesh – Not a Cartoon

I don't think I'm handsome, but what's my opinion against the mirror?

What man… what man has my looks, my physique, my intelligence… what man? (*Long accusatory pause*) I wish I knew, because I'd like 'em back!

I'm now going to do the walking up and down bit for you. *Marvellous*. I sing at the same time. It's nothing to me. I've been trained, you see.

Max Wall's background was not as abstruse as the frequent opening lines of his act might suggest.

Hello, everyone. Wall is the name – Max Wall. You've heard of the Great Wall of China? He was my grandfather. He was a brick… huh… huh. He was the first man to tell me that over in China when a baby is born, they don't allow the mother into the room. It's very interesting, isn't it?

However hard it is to believe that there was nothing extraterrestrial in the make-up of this captivating clown with the Mekon dome head, probing melancholy eyes and grinning Houyhnhnm teeth, he could trace his physical if not stylistic origins back to an idiosyncratic line of Scottish character comedians that embraced Neil Kenyon, Will Fyffe, Harry Gordon, Dave Willis and, one has it on authority, the funniest of them all, Tommy Lorne (1890 – 1935), the Scot with the cadaverous face and Keatonian resistance to the smile, perhaps in ironic foresight of his own premature death. Max Wall himself was born in Brixton on 12 March 1908, the son of breezy north-of-the-Border comic Jack Lorimer (1883 – 1920), into a family active theatrically as far back as the earliest days of the music hall. However, it was from his stepfather that he obtained his own stage name, the first half of Wallace, to complement the first half of his proper name, Maxwell.

He made his first stage appearance when fourteen years old as Idle Jack in a touring production of *Mother Goose* in Devon and Cornwall – a role he would repeat in the more prestigious surroundings of the London Hippodrome during the Christmas of 1936. It took him only three years, however, to graduate from the far south-west to his first West End appearance as an eccentric or speciality dancer in *The London Revue* at the Lyceum. As a boy he had seen Little Tich perform and the influence was obvious. Nor is it a surprise to learn that he worked in Paris during these early years with another great clown, Grock, who would leave an indelible mark upon his later comedy routine in the form of a deranged pianist. Max's brilliance on his toes led to a featured role in Cochran's 1927 revue *One Damn Thing After Another*, alongside Sonnie Hale, Jessie Matthews and Douglas Byng, a part in the first Royal Variety Performance to be held at the Palladium in 1930 (he appeared a second time in 1950 at the same theatre), and in 1932 a transatlantic spell lasting eighteen months in the tenth and final edition of *Earl Carroll's Vanities*. While on Broadway he was given the opportunity, so far denied him by producers on home shores, to inject comedy into his standard routine. On his return strenuous efforts were made to persuade managements to accept him now as a comedian, but it would take an arduous three-year tour in the Larry Adler road show *Tune Inn* rather than the transatlantic grapevine to secure for Max the recognition he craved as a jester. The Adler show gained him a footing in the verbal medium of radio, which provided him with his first widespread public acceptance, most notably in October 1944 with Robb Wilton in *Hoop-la!*, a fairground-oriented variety show, and then subsequently *Our Shed* and *Petticoat Lane*, in the second of which he featured alongside Elsie and Doris Waters. Over the years his bill matter reflected the shift in his ambitions, beginning with 'The Boy with the Obedient Feet' and progressing to 'Laughing Legs' then simply 'Irresponsible'.

Left: Jack Lorimer: 'The Hielan' Laddie'
Above: Grock: clown 'sans pareil'

For anyone who regarded Wall as a purely visual performer, his success over the airwaves would have come as a surprise. His voice proved as hilariously unpredictable at the microphone as his dancing had been on stage, the arch stilted tones savouring experimentally each syllable of a word that happened to take his fancy, pulling vowels mercilessly out of shape – 'phil-o-sophical', spiralling off into adenoidal ecstasy – 'Ooh, auntie, do let's have tea – with lashings of toast – oooooooozing with butter,' or lapsing unashamedly into a bubblegum American drawl or the slapdash street-urchin uncouthness with which he would recount his domestic misadventures with his dim brother in *Our Shed*: ''Ere, 'ere, I don' arf do a bi' o' cookin' in there. 'Ere, last night I baked ever such a lovely cake – that's what I baked – yes and I 'ad my dim brover 'elpin' me and I said to 'im – "'Ere, 'Enery, stick this 'ere knife in that there cake and if the knife comes out clean, stick all the other knives in." It don' arf make you larf!' The last six words soon achieved the status of a catchphrase, his own personal jack-in-the-box mechanism, as did his phoney upper-crust pronouncement 'Ack-tually!'

Whatever level his delivery found, it never obscured the fact that Wall wallowed in the sheer weirdness of his eccentricity, a quality that in his heyday during the late 40s and early 50s could only be appreciated fully from a seat in the stalls rather than from a disembodied radio voice, The act for which he deserves a perpetual niche among the Grocks and the Tiches is that of the concert pianist 'Professor Wallofski', he of the manic stare, panoramic black wig and ungainly black boots two sizes too big for comfort, but perfect for the walk in which the toe of one was perpetually crushed by the heel of the other. His look has evoked comparison with a Phiz cartoon, a 'cavorting black spider' and Conrad Veidt's hypnotically controlled monster in *The Cabinet of Dr Caligari*. First featured in what turned out to be his penultimate appearance in West End intimate revue, in *Make It a Date* at the Duchess Theatre in 1946, the costume was completed when during an engagement at the Empire, Leicester Square his agent suggested he exchange trousers for tights to make fun of the male dancers on the bill – somewhat unfairly because it was in this act that one saw most clearly how Wall used techniques gained from his own training as a dancer in the service of comedy. When he announced, 'Tonight, ladies and gentlemen, I've had one or two requests from thousands of people. It appears they require pianoforte music of the more classical nature and, believe me, I'm the lad to let 'em 'ave it!' the comedy resided less in making the most of the sparse musical know-how at his disposal as he set about playing Rachmaninov's 'Praaaay-Iude' – 'This I will now play with the aid of an AA map and a spirit level' – than in the physical nightmare he deliberately subjected himself to. A guru among grotesques, he would trip across the stage, his body set in a sitting position, buttocks protuberant, spindly legs knocked out at an angle like ninepins. 'I'm in a position I've never seen advertised… You can't say I didn't give you every opportunity!' Once finally settled at the piano he became racked with anguish at the discovery that he now had one arm longer, one shoulder higher than the other. No sooner had he painfully twisted himself back into shape, than, as if to play, he would dash his knuckles against the unraised keyboard lid. At the end he telescoped himself down to dwarf size and waddled offstage to the strains of 'Whistle while you work', somehow leaving his audience confident that his Snow White would be the first Snow Witch.

There was a curiously enigmatic edge to the whole act, ambiguous in the way Wall at once wooed and alienated the audience. The cosy whimsy of the sequence where finding one key out of tune, he reached into the piano to produce a miniature baby grand – 'Just goes to show you what can happen overnight! Matron!' – and the nursery vulgarity of his discovery of a 'little potty' in the commodious piano stool chafed against the demented reproving leer that greeted the laughter with its sudden, but fleeting seriousness. Here was the predominant joke, Wall making comic currency out of the sheer desperation that so often accompanies his profession, the most difficult job in show business, the loneliest in the world. While other comedians might capitalise upon their lack of height, of moderation, of courage, Wall in an adroit display of one-upmanship made play of his simple failing in becoming a comedian in the first place. When a weak gag did win applause, it would be welcomed with the cry, 'Success! Success!' If only the public realised the effort involved. After tripping over some invisible obstacle, he would explain, 'A little hole sticking up!' and then after a pause add as an aside, 'How desperate can a comedian be?' No comic ever thought aloud so candidly. When a joke did fail, he would madly exclaim, 'Success is built on failures – that's why I'm a success!' That would get the laugh, but other comedians would have skipped along to the next gag in the chain and hoped the audience would never notice the dud one. But if Max was giving everything away, one never questioned his continuing ability to do the job in hand. An inhabitant of one's wildest dream, his 'Professor' was the one whose finger had the most direct access to the cataclysmic button, insanely happy in his privileged position, yet ignorant in the insanity of his suicidal doom.

Even without this brilliant characterisation, Wall would warrant mention in these pages if only for the humour of his eccentric dancing, always his favoured way of closing his act – a potpourri of sharpshooting tap technique, loose-limbed acrobatics and witty walks that don't look as difficult but which in practice can only evolve from the other two. Max would announce his set piece with an insistence that made no claims on subtlety and ensured that all eyes were turned: 'Ladies and gentlemen, I shall be walking up and down for you, giving you the benefit of my smile, sticking my bottom out for you, and you will find it very attractive. Then there's a drum roll and off we go. Up and down, backwards and forwards, on and

Richard Hearne: 'Mr Pastry'

Dickie Henderson

on and on. Sometimes I think it could go on for ever.' The patter itself set the rhythm admirably. As early as 1927, after seeing Wall at the London Pavilion, critic James Agate correctly predicted that he would become one of the leading exponents of eccentric dance. Watching Wall one realised what Agate meant on another occasion when, talking of the French actor Sacha Guitry, he said, 'All great comedians live with the intensity of puppets.' One also recalls Richard Hearne (1909 – 1970) in his Mr Pastry old man characterisation following in the dance steps of Tom D. Newell as he essayed a set of lancers with an invisible partner, gathering the incongruous momentum of a whirling dervish in the sedate ballroom setting featured originally in Hearne's Gaiety revue *Running Riot.* More recently there was the sophisticated dance-doodling of Dickie Henderson (1922 – 1985), son of Dick Henderson (1891 – 1958), a rotund Yorkshire dialect comedian with a special line in domestic anecdote and the first to feature the song 'Tiptoe through the tulips'. Like Max, the younger Henderson was responsible for several classic comedy routines which had as their lifeblood the discipline and technique acquired from early hoofing days, including his topological entanglement with the microphone wire with his aspirant vocalist a literal marionette in the hands of the offstage stagehand puppeteer, and his would-be Sinatra coping with cigarette and glass as alcohol hazily takes over and the four legs of his tottering stool become indistinguishable from his own.

Henderson Junior came to prominence during the mid-50s, the time Wall's own career began to split apart at the seams. There were marital difficulties which in the less permissive climate of the day triggered off a smear campaign in the popular press from which it appeared he might never recover. In 1957, while starring at the London Coliseum in the hit musical *The Pajama Game* as Hines, the factory efficiency expert, the accumulative strain of playing the same role eight shows a week for sixteen months forced him to leave the cast four weeks before the completion of the run, although with typical resilience he was back for the final performance. Audiences became less tolerant and bookings dwindled.

An attempt to stem the tide against oblivion was made in 1960 with a comeback in the short-lived *Once Upon a Mattress,* again a musical, this time based on the Hans Andersen fairy story *The Princess and the Pea,* a vehicle already used by a depressed Buster Keaton during a similar career trough in America. Wall would have to wait until 1966 before regaining the support of the public, even if at first that public was restricted to a theatre-going elite.

That year he secured a notable triumph at the Royal Court Theatre as Ubu Roi, the gluttonous monster who makes himself King of Poland by slaughtering the entire population in the eponymous play by Alfred Jarry, the French forerunner of the absurdist school. Wearing a Hockney-designed pumpkin, green bowler and a large navel which he nicknamed his bumple, Max reaffirmed not merely his own powers as an improvisatory clown, but also the link between music hall and the theatre of the absurd. It is because of this link that in his play *The Chairs* Eugene Ionesco can include a stage direction to the effect that an old man is to impersonate the month of February by 'scratching his head like Stan Laurel'; that Samuel Beckett's first foray into cinema, *Film,* turned out to be a Buster Keaton vehicle; and that on Broadway in the same writer's *Waiting for Godot* Bert Lahr, ex-vaudevillian and sometime cowardly lion for MGM, could bring to the role of Estragon with its trouser-dropping and hat-juggling, pratfalls and ping-pong dialogue an instinctive flair that no legitimate actor could ever achieve in the part. And if the inner philosophical meaning of that play does not at first glance tally with the earthier tradition, one need only recall Dan Leno's own words: 'Ah, what is man? Wherefore does he why? Whence did he whence? Whither is he withering?' *Ubu Roi,* moreover, could claim to be the first modern protest play, a genre recharged sixty years later in the light of contemporary life and feeling for humanity by dramatist John Osborne with works not the least of which is *The Entertainer.*

Wall's gift for comic disdain proved itself in one dramatic vehicle. That and his personal if intermittent experience of the failure and desperation felt by the lonely world-weary applause-anxious music hall comedian painted so perceptively by Osborne prompt a plea to some enterprising management to bring about what might be the most memorable fusion of the legitimate and illegitimate theatres ever staged. This chapter may spell success in smaller letters than most in this book, itself a sombre reminder of how fickle popular acclaim can be. The talent it treats, however, is none the less rare.

AFTERTHOUGHTS

In revising the above I have resisted amending the tense and the tenor of the final paragraph. Imagine my delight when in November 1974, eighteen months after first publication, my plea appeared to have been answered when, under John Osborne's direction, Max trod the boards of the Greenwich Theatre as Archie Rice and, dare one say, revealed what may have been lacking in earlier interpretations. The *Guardian* review simply stated, 'Max Wall makes Olivier look like an amateur.' The key to his success may be contained in his own observation on the part: 'Rice was *not* an unfunny man: he was funny in a third-rate manner.'

Max, defiant as Archie Rice

By now Max's comeback both as entertainer and actor was well established, not least through his appearances on *Parkinson* and further stage triumphs, including Wesker's *The Old Ones* in 1972 and *Cockie!*, a revue in celebration of impresario C. B. Cochran, the following year. Subsequently his work in Samuel Beckett's *Krapp's Last Tape*, *Waiting for Godot* and *Malone Dies* culminated not only in a close friendship with the otherwise reclusive playwright, but the distinction of becoming one of the preferred interpreters of his work. As Barry Cryer observed, in his comedy act Max had managed to make the word stool (as in piano) sound as if it had four syllables – now, as Krapp, he invested the word spool with in effect the same four syllables. In 1979 he appeared in a remake of Beckett's *Film*, which had originally starred Buster Keaton. On the small screen his versatility extended to spells as a featured performer in three major soaps, *Coronation Street*, *Crossroads* and *Emmerdale Farm*.

In 1975 his one-man show *Aspects of Max Wall* played to capacity business at London's Garrick Theatre and proved there was so much more to his comedy legacy than the funny steps and eccentricities of the mad music professor. Here were the witty little songs to his own guitar accompaniment, the abortive attempt to sing 'The birth of the blues', the manic trumpet playing ('I'm going to play "Sweet sixteen". *(Then to the band)* What are you going to play?'). The production returned to the West End several times.

Max had kept himself afloat during the lean years by working the northern club circuit, where his resilience towards audiences was toughened out of all recognition. He referred to the experience as encasing himself in armour, dismissing the idea of obscurity as 'They thought I was dead!' Now the *International Herald Tribune*, no less, proclaimed him 'quite simply, the funniest comedian in the world'. After his death, theatre writer John Lahr cut to the quick of the man when he said that Max 'brought his sadness on stage and dumped the hostility that came with it hilariously in the audience's lap'.

In fact, both on- and offstage he gave the impression of a hard-luck story on legs: 'If they sawed a woman in half, I'd get the half that eats!' The pattern had been set in childhood. Before it was shot down at Potters Bar, a German Zeppelin released an aerial torpedo and a gas bomb over London. They *both* fell on Max's family home at Brixton, killing his younger brother. Max had to be dug out of the rubble. He went on turning adversity to advantage for the rest of his life, claiming that the years he spent in the wilderness of the northern clubs enabled him to develop 'a line of talk that largely eliminated the need for jokes or anecdotes' and set the agenda for his one-man show, in which, as he later claimed, he was bemused that his comic business found favour 'within the pale of the legit theatre, which would in former days have often regarded my antics as beneath contempt'.

It was my privilege to enjoy Max's company many times in later years. He was a walking compendium of the music hall and as a child had stood in the wings watching just about every great name you could mention from that era with the exception of Dan Leno. He would mischievously pull faces during their acts until one day he received his comeuppance from Marie Lloyd, who went up to his mother and bawled, 'What's the matter with your kid? 'As he got bleedin' St Vitus's Dance or something?' On another occasion his mother (known professionally as Stella Stahl) and stepfather were performing a dance routine on one of Lloyd's last bills when she failed to position her hands correctly. After the act the following dialogue ensued.

> *Stepfather*: What the hell went wrong?
> *Mother*: What do you mean went wrong?
> *Stepfather*: Where were your bloody hands when I needed them?
> *Lloyd* (*later to mother*): Where did 'e think they were? Up your bleedin' arse?

Wall came to regard Lloyd as a 'stage auntie' or honorary godmother and sustained her spirit and air of no-nonsense defiance of needless propriety to the end of his days. On the back of his later success he loved to announce, 'I've become a cult,' always investing the last word with a suggestive relish that telegraphed the word he was gagging to say. The accompanying leer said it for him.

My favourite personal memory involves spending a long liquid lunchtime with him in the bar of the Greenwich Theatre, where he educated me in the only way to drink his beloved Guinness – 'It's all the nourishment I need' – namely by consistently timed gulps of an inch at a time so that when the contents were completely consumed the gradation of the rings down the side of the glass told their own story. What impressed me more, however, is that over a two-hour period he downed only one glass. Maybe in the tradition of old comedy pros he was anxious about who might be picking up the tab. His company, however, was always reflective, warm and considerate. I would gladly have picked up his bar bill however large at whatever time. He died on 22 May 1990 after a lunch with friends at a favourite restaurant in the Strand as the result of a fall, allegedly of a fractured skull. Declared bankrupt in 1973, he left what was, relatively speaking, a fortune of £193,004, having lived modestly in a single room throughout the glorious days of his second career. Setback, comeback, whatever, there was no way talent as strong and as resolute as his could not bounce back, the magnificent link between the old-time music hall and a younger school epitomised by Rowan Atkinson's physical and facial contortions, Monty Python's silly walks, not to mention the rhythmic posturing of performers as significant as Madonna, Michael Jackson and Suggs of Madness fame. Max would have felt absolutely at home in their company.

Jimmy Edwards: 'Wake up at the back there!'

All right, pay attention! Sit up straight! Don't fidget! That boy – you're chewing in class. Spit it out. No, *not in the hair of the boy in front of you*! Write out a thousand times, 'I am a mindless pain in the sphincter and spotty with it.' Now, let's get on… (*Glancing out of the window, he notices somebody*) **It's our dear matron! She's going to watch the cricket match sitting on her shooting stick…** (*He registers horror*) **Matron, no!** (*He mimes turning the shooting stick the correct way up*)

One of the less obvious consequences of the Second World War was the mushrooming a few years later of a generation of young star comedians who bad been given their first real performing experience by service life. Restrained for six socially static years, they were catapulted out of barracks and into showbiz by their pent-up exuberance, desire for a wider audience and the realisation, at a time when the value of life itself had been brought home most poignantly, that they were determined to do the job they most wanted to do. One of the brashest and most physically striking of this generation and among the first to make an impact was James Keith O'Neill Edwards, better known as Jimmy. He survived at or near the top of his profession for almost forty years through the sheer ruthless power of his personality. His burly frame was offset by a face as round and as ripe as an oversize beetroot, overshadowed by the most expressive moustache since Harry Tate's. However, while Tate's tash was false, Edward's beer-stained handlebars were his own, a self-styled 'sex-barometer', a final catchment area for valuable liquor before the last drops were sucked down the gruff gravelly larynx and a built-in question-cum-explanation mark ready to express curiosity or anger.

His professional show business career began in May 1946 at the disreputably innocent Windmill Theatre, then nicknamed the Comics' Dunkirk, where since 1932 showman Vivian Van Damm had been permitted by the Lord Chamberlain to present nude tableaux on condition that the girls featured in them remained absolutely still. It is a popular misconception that a host of later comedy stars made their first impact in that intimate auditorium; in reality the warm reception was reserved not unnaturally for the girls. As Denis Norden astutely remarked, this was a venue 'where young ladies were barely paraded and comedians were barely tolerated'. No one actually came to see the comics, who existed merely as padding, and the rows and rows of newspaper-hidden faces as seen by the aspiring Edwards or Hancock, Sellers or Secombe are now as legendary as the nudes themselves. Bruce Forsyth, Alfred Marks, Tommy Cooper, Harry Worth and Michael Bentine all played there, and yet ironically the small audience and its specialised nature – at least 90 per cent would have been male – meant that even if a comic was successful, he could still not reach the top until he had left. Moreover, the law of averages meant that of all the comedians featured at the Windmill – countless numbers – some *had* to succeed in time. Van Damm should not therefore be regarded as a prophet of future comic potential. There must have been many provincial variety theatres where the above notables all played at some early stage and with far greater success than at the Windmill, if only because of the more balanced family audience they found there, theatres with equal right to be styled stepping stones to fame. However, despite its limitations, the Windmill was unique as a training ground. Nowhere else could a young performer experience the cumulative value of performing six shows a day, six days a week, and in the framework of continuous performance, which entailed constant coming and going among the audience. Here a young comedian, once he stifled his sorrows, could at least learn to die with composure and a smile.

Jimmy, Joy and Dick: 'Take It From Here'

This unconventional training aside, the Windmill engagement came to mean more to Edwards than to most of his contemporaries. Not only was his frank eruptive vulgarity in comfortable accord with the spirit of *Revudeville* – the name coined for its distinctive mix of nudity and variety – but it was while resident at the theatre that he first met the urbane and witty Frank Muir, who proceeded to write scripts for him. It was then a short step from Soho to the radio show that firmly established Edwards as a national figure and set a new casual trend in broadcast comedy. *Take It From Here* ran for twelve series and 308 episodes from 1948 until 1960, a successful – it eventually drew weekly audiences of twenty million – if at first insecure amalgam of the performing talents of Edwards, Australian comedian Dick Bentley

(1907 – 1995), whose violin-playing eternally 'youthful' insult-ridden persona owed something to America's Jack Benny, and Joy Nichols (1925 – 1992), the commère of the earlier *Navy Mixture* programme, which had also occasionally featured Edwards. The latter had been targeted specifically at the navy and was aired in England at the obscure hour of Monday lunchtime. Both Joy and Jimmy were therefore relatively unestablished before *TIFH*. Muir and his friend Denis Norden were brought in as scriptwriters and exercised a crisp verbal wit that derived in no small way from an intense respect for the intelligence and literacy of their audience. Gillie Potter, the Western Brothers and Ronald Frankau had all contributed to a specialised niche for sophisticated humour on the airwaves. What marked Muir and Norden apart from this tradition was their lack of condescension towards both material and audience, a quality that later shone through their own not infrequent excursions into performing in their own dry humorous right. *TIFH* was a deliberate experiment with at first no precise format –

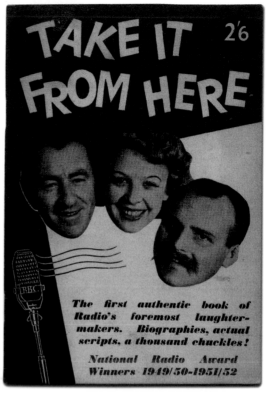

just Joy, Dick and Jimmy cool and calm in front of a microphone with no obvious indication of how they would 'take it from here'. The role of the listener was assumed to be equally carefree, the seductive tinkling of the signature tune coaxing but never coercing one into listening if one had 'half an hour that's more or less clear'. Its play-out theme, Cole Porter's 'Just one of those things', set the seal on the air of take it or leave it that made *TIFH* so refreshingly original.

In the *TIFH* world words were like lumps of modelling clay to be squeezed and moulded into what one wanted them to signify, and not what stale dull convention stipulated they should mean. The puns with which the programme became identified were completely divorced from any suggestion of the throwaway contempt for language that hallmarked the *ITMA* style. Instead one pictured the trio at the microphone revelling in their discovery of the ambiguities of English. If Samuel Johnson was not on their side, the words themselves were. The verbal dilemma could be simple or complex. One recalls the Roman soldiers numbering off from left to right: 'Eye, eye-eye, eye-eye-eye, eye-vee'! There was the surgeon and the nurse:

Doctor: Scalpel.
Nurse: Scalpel.
Doctor: Saw.
Nurse: Saw… Doctor, look, the patient is coming round.
Doctor: Circular saw.

A similar exchange took place between scientist and research assistant, the latter anxious to know what to do with some acid: 'I have an old retort for that.' A tree surgeon in a lumberjack sketch is informed, 'This hickory's a bit dickory, Doc.' There was the moment during *Swan Lake* – 'a ballet for radio' – when Jimmy as Wolfgang and Dick as Siegfried are hiding near the enchanted lake. A gentle coughing is heard.

> *Jimmy*: Did you hear that? Someone gave a sort of shy cough.
> *Dick*: Well, who'd be giving a shy cough?
> *Jimmy*: I don't know, unless it's Tchaikovsky.

The punning humour of *TIFH* was funny because it *was* audacious; the pleasure-ridden groan often its only feasible response. As if by way of easing the groan, however, there occurred throughout the programme a Perelmanesque turn of phrase that enabled, say, a fissured landscape to look 'as wrinkled as a trombone player's sleeve'. In December 1970 an article in the *Listener* by Philip French recalled the occasion *TIFH* revamped the *Radio Times* in the image of the *News of the World*. Athletics at the White City became INCIDENT IN SAND PIT – POLE HELD; Ludwig Koch's *Birdsong of the Month*, LARK IN EPPING FOREST – PROFESSOR DISCOVERED IN BUSHES; and *Have a Go*, INTIMATE QUESTIONS ASKED AT OLD PEOPLE'S HOME – STRANGER OFFERED ME MONEY, ALLEGES ATTRACTIVE PENSIONER!

Like all radio comedy shows of its era, *TIFH* developed its own catchphrases, most of which went to Edwards: 'Gently, Bentley;' 'That was a good one, was it not?' – to express satisfaction with his own jokes; 'Clumsy clot!' – the slang acknowledging his RAF days; 'A *mauve* one' – originally used to describe a sweet, but then inconsequentially to refer to anything; and most notably his ferocious reprimand 'Wake up at the back there!' – an echo from his stage act. In addition there were Bentley's 'Oh, Maaavis,' prefacing the outbursts of Dick's stiltedly naive poet, and the dry husky tones of Wallas Eaton, like Edwards a Cambridge graduate, as 'Old Wal from the Buildings', reminding Jim's insecure social climber of his supposedly humble origins: 'Come home, Jim Edwards. Learn a trade,' or, 'We're very proud of Jim back in the Buildings.' When Edwards announced real-life matrimonial plans, Eaton's 'Take the plunge, Jim Edwards' assumed headline status in virtually every popular newspaper.

In 1953 Joy Nichols, in tune perhaps with the freewheeling colonial spirit she radiated throughout the programme, returned to her native Australia, June Whitfield (born 1925) joined the team, and 'The Glums' evolved. Edwards was never more in his element than as Pa Glum, the rascally old cockney, boozy, bigoted and yet endearing, possessive yet permissive, whose efforts to destroy the romance of his 'baby boy' Ron, played by Bentley, and the insufferably loyal Eth, played by Whitfield, captured the attention of millions. The emphasis was now upon characterisation as much as fleeting jokes, the sketch developing from a slim storyline restricted to the sofa-dominated front room of the Glum household to a stronger situation played against a more extensive cockney background, the gags illuminating the situation. One recalls the day Mr Glum pawned Eth's wedding ring in order to donate the money to elderly and sick animals, not that he knew they were elderly and sick when he backed them. There was the occasion when Eth obtained a rise, enabling her and Ron to go on a continental holiday. Mr Glum will allow Ron to go only if he accompanies them as chaperone, but the budget will not extend to three. A pause and two weeks later we join the young couple anxiously awaiting the arrival home of Ron's parents from their holiday abroad. Not that one ever met Mrs Glum herself. She always seemed to be confined to some inaccessible attic or back room, her voice reduced to a muffled squeak, her appearance open to the worst the imagination could conjure from such stray remarks as

> *Jimmy*: Ron, do you remember them earrings your mum lost last summer?
> *Dick*: Yes, dad?
> *Jimmy*: Well, she's had her hair washed and guess what? There they were! In there all the time. Found two stubbed-out fag ends as well. I must give up smoking in bed.

It is, of course, unlikely that Ron did remember. His perpetually dazed verbal responses are explained by Mr Glum's own assessment of his childlike son: 'It's always the same. He starts every day from scratch. It'll be eleven o'clock before he remembers there was a yesterday. He's not so much reserved as not in use.' Eth would never have admitted as much, although her whining monotone suggests she was fully aware of the situation, in spite of her continued love for, or more accurately possessive pride in, her 'beloved'.

> *June*: Oh Ron! My heart is really beginning to pound now. Only another fortnight and then we two shall be one. Do you feel all shivery, Ron?
> *Dick*: No, Eth.
> *June*: Why not, beloved?
> *Dick*: Dad says I've been one all me life.

However much the Glums represented caricatures to be laughed at, however exaggeratedly squalid and ramshackle their immediate lives may have been, however dubious Mr Glum's own motives, the stories and characters developed to a point where they were seldom without distinct touches of pathos, an underlying quality of warmth and naturalness. When the last programme came to a close, Ron and Eth were still bickering in the Glums' front room, trapped like so many others by the limits imposed by social station and level of intelligence. The Glums at this final stage of their development were the one concession *TIFH*, at all other times a cool calculated celebration of the ridiculous, made to sentiment. In retrospect the development of the ménage was alien to Muir and Norden's prime skill as verbal pyrotechnicians. And yet the sheer gusto of Edwards and company ensured that the Glum sketches would remain more lovingly etched on the public memory than the cod investigations of a general theme by the Type agency or the stinging parodies of the movie genre currently in vogue at the local Odeon or Gaumont, other recurring features of the show over the years.

TIFH's initial success was a further indication of the way in which radio, far from killing music hall or variety, rather led to an increase in paying audiences. The sedentary listening public was determined to find out for itself what the disembodied voices that entered their homes actually looked like in the flesh. It was not long before the *TIFH* trio was appearing at such prestigious West End venues as the Victoria Palace and the Prince of Wales Theatre. Then in October 1950 the enterprising Jack Hylton presented Joy, Dick, and Jimmy in *Take It From Us* at the Adelphi Theatre. This show ran for twelve months, even though Joy and Dick left after three, thus attesting to Edwards' individual popularity. Although younger than Bentley, he was to remain the dominant member of the team and in more ways than one its father figure.

Take It From Us would be the first of three Adelphi-based revues for Edwards. Most famous was *London Laughs*, which opened in April 1952 and ran for 1,113 performances. In this he was accompanied by Vera Lynn and the emerging Tony Hancock. Sketches by Muir and Norden included 'A Seat in the Circle', in which Jimmy played a selfish discontented cinema-goer who arrives late with his brow-beaten wife. In this foretaste of 'Glum' humour they brought gradual havoc to the whole cinema through their constant wrangling, as well as despair to Hancock as a BBC commentator clinging with Reithian determination to his microphone. Then in November 1954 came *The Talk of the Town*, in which Edwards and Hancock were joined by Joan Turner. The show produced a hat-trick of memorable routines for the boisterous comic. His exuberant ego was given ample scope in 'Vote for Jim!' 'One for all, and all for Jim!' became the slogan of the moment, as he indoctrinated the audience in the principles of Jimmunism. 'Send the Relief' had Edwards as a creaking old salt in charge of a lighthouse kept going by a shilling-in-the-slot meter, and Hancock as his loyal but shattered mate, who gets all the fish and water thrown in his face and his superior's heroic sense of duty hammered deafeningly into his ears. Finally there was 'Judge for Yourself', the sketch Edwards featured in the Royal Variety Performance of 1955. The role of the lecherous judge committed to satisfying his own curiosity over the most lurid details of a breach-of-promise case was tailor-made for his ribald mock-pompous persona. At one point he had to demand of the accused, 'How do you plead?' At this the latter immediately burst into tears. 'My God,' replied Justice Jim, 'you are a miserable pleader, aren't you?' Once again the birth of a chestnut!

In the shared lighthouse and cinema sketches Edwards had a certain edge over Hancock because he was a stage comedian in the fullest variety sense, someone who could improvise on a theme, tailor each line and piece of business to the unique demands of the audience of the moment. In technique there could have been no greater contrast, Hancock being the type of performer who floundered without the safeguard of a definitive script. His subtle, quiet earnestness cut right across Edwards's bluff ebullience. And yet ironically the comic mask of each performer derived from the same source, that of the upstart, the braggart, the *miles gloriosus* of Roman comedy. Later Hancock's own persona would become more complex, and he would surpass Edwards in critical esteem, but always the laughter of the theatre audience would ring louder for the earlier star. In the early 1960s both performers made major attempts to change their image. Happily Edwards was soon back acting the buffoon in the old style, breaking box-office records in *Big Bad Mouse* with Eric Sykes at the Shaftesbury Theatre, and in overseas tours and a subsequent revival of the same 'play' at the Prince of Wales. Playwrights Philip King and Falkland Cary, sensing their work lacked a certain something, cannily allowed the pair to ad-lib around the script in the early days of the production. The result proved an improvisational tour de force in the best traditions of the Crazy Gang.

Whatever impact Edwards made as judge, political campaigner or other voice of authority in his stage revues, it is his stage schoolmaster that is most vividly remembered. Edwards broke through in *TIFH* the year before Will Hay, the original schoolmaster comedian, died. So as not to invite comparison, his act had to be ingeniously different. He achieved this by working solo, making the audience the pupils in his class, with his desk facing the footlights, the stage backdrop overlooking cloisters and playing fields. This is a school where order is kept with a gun. Halfway through his act Edwards would turn away from the window, weapon still smoking, a malicious glint in those round eyes. 'He'll never be able to make that sign with one finger!' When this latter-day Wackford Squeers was not shooting he was downing beer. 'My sweet little beauty, you go down and join your friends in Jim's tum. I'll see you sometime early in the morning!' When not imbibing, he was seething with indignation, bellowing imprecations at the audience, almost bursting out of his clothes. 'Go on, laugh. They laughed at

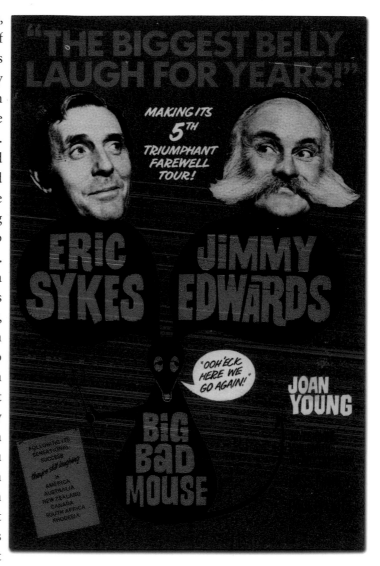

Suez, but he went right ahead and built his canal. Wake up at the back there!' Not that Professor Jim was all bluster and bombast; beneath the stern swagger was a crude naive transport-cafe blend of geniality and good cheer. Whereas Hay most noticeably polarised the two extremes of severity and lightness of heart in himself and his boys respectively, Edwards more obviously succeeded in establishing the same dialogue within his own expansive stage personality.

Onstage, the one subject of importance in the Edwards academy – the only subject – was music, more specifically that of the brass section. The word cacophony could have been coined especially to describe his sound. He did all he could to appear knowledgeable on the subject: 'Music is divided into two distinct categories – that is to say loud and soft. In soft we have piano, mezzo-piano, not-so-piano, pianissimo and, of course, pianola. In loud we have mezzo-forte, forte, fifty, fortissimo and eighty, which is, of course, double-forte.' There followed an accomplished if incoherent recital on the 'slush-pump' (trombone); cornet – 'I'll play "Eldorado" on this one' (a punning reference to an ice cream of the day); post horn – 'Stand by your buckets;' and French horn – specially cleaned out before use with Harpic and vodka: 'That gets where the brush will never get!' This particular musician was in the habit of lowering his corpulent frame where there happened to be no seat, of coaxing a pint of best bitter out of a cunningly contrived xylophone, of fighting a losing battle with a constantly disintegrating music stand and of experiencing great pain in reaching the top note on his favourite instrument, the euphonium: 'When I reached that note I couldn't have got a bus ticket between the cheeks of me arse!' It was vulgar in the ripest tradition of the authentic music hall, sheer horseplay, and as such forthright and honest. It was even more uproarious when academic cap and gown were shed for a shabby tail-suit with baggy trousers gathered in by bicycle clips and the performer assumed the tottering gait and shifty look of some absurdly downtrodden maestro of the past.

Television allowed Professor James Edwards to expand the curriculum of his academy beyond the limits of his basic repertoire. The sitcom *Whack-O!* ran for seven series between 1956 and 1960 and was revived for an eighth in 1972. Like Hay's St Michael's, Chiselbury School 'for the sons of gentlefolk' was dedicated to expanding the headmaster's bank balance first, educational advancement second. The story went that Edwards on leaving the RAF was originally set to apply for the post of school handyman. However, when his CO's references fell into his hands, he somehow finagled the top job and Mr Pettigrew, once a leader of men – played with shy charm by the actor Arthur Howard – was reduced to the secondary role of assistant master and nervous wreck old before his time, his only purpose in life the care of his golden hamster. And yet even if Edwards had no qualifications for the job and was constantly being hoodwinked by his pupils, he still managed to wriggle out of the most embarrassing situations in a way that called for a certain – albeit twisted – intelligence. When asked by the governing body why an invoice for fifty crates of pale ale should have been included in the school accounts, his mental processes took no time at all in explaining it away as a requisition for a new translation of Socrates by the famous Egyptian scholar Paleale. The wit of Muir and Norden was once more in evidence.

Born in Barnes on 23 March 1920, Edwards experienced an upbringing relatively unusual for a variety comedian. The son of a professor in mathematics at King's College, London, he did in fact spend a year teaching before going up to St John's College, Cambridge to secure an MA in history in addition to his introduction to the trombone. After a spell in the Footlights' Dance Band, he made his first impact as a musical comedian in the last *Footlights' Revue* before the war, playing the part of the shirt-sleeved old cornet player (for cornet substitute trombone) in a three-dimensional burlesque of George Belcher's famous painting, *I Dreamt I Dwelt in Marble Halls,* a work that had been exhibited with acclaim at the Royal Academy in 1936. The war saw him awarded the DFC for bravery while piloting an RAF transport plane that crashed during the Arnhem campaign. His subsequent lifestyle was no less unconventional. He enjoyed fox-hunting, shooting, farming and playing polo, and stood unsuccessfully as the Conservative candidate for North Paddington in the 1964 general election. His readiness in 1966 to rid himself of his whiskery trademark in order to play the part of the indomitable John Jorrocks Esq. in a television adaptation of R. S. Surtees's famous novels pointed clearly to a desire to foster the image of a country squire. In spite of, or because of, his middle-class origins, he had been as a child inspired by the famous Lyceum pantomime comedian George Jackley, the man with a foghorn for a voice, and George Robey's famous Falstaff at the St James's Theatre. He inherited the directness that hallmarked them both. Later Sid Field would become an idol and his own 'Professor of Music' routine a more obvious source of inspiration.

Like Falstaff, Edwards was a true Lord of Misrule. '*Jim* does the funnies!' he would thunder over the footlights with that marked air of condescension to lesser, and hence all other, men. And yet however sure of himself he may have been, however pompous, his constant readiness to plumb the depths of low comedy acted as an indispensable safety valve in maintaining audience favour. His ability to bridge the great chasm between low comedy and high pretension was, as with Falstaff, a ready recipe for laughter. The country squire *was* the village buffoon. The publicity engendered by his real-life social background heightened the comic effect of his act and played a part in explaining his popularity. The fact that everyone knew he might well go on stage having just stepped off a private plane after playing polo with 'Him' – 'Him, you clot! Him that goes about with Her!' – added an extra captivating quality to the subsequent crudities and ungentlemanly noises on the euphonium.

AFTERTHOUGHTS

The above appraisal fails to acknowledge the success of Jimmy's other radio show, *Does the Team Think?*, a comedy panel game devised by him along the lines of *Any Questions?* in which he was joined by three other comedians who tried to upstage one another in spontaneous wit. The team came to include Ted Ray as a resident member, while Arthur Askey, Tommy Trinder and Cyril Fletcher were all featured regularly. The series ran even longer than *Take It From Here*, from 1957 until 1976. Nor does Jimmy receive credit for the television series that revealed he possessed greater depths as a comedy actor than the one-dimensional persona of his boozy conniver might ever have suggested. *The Seven Faces of Jim*, reprised in a second and third series as *Six More Faces of Jim* and *More Faces of Jim*, were scripted by Frank Muir and Denis Norden, and between 1961 and 1963 saw our hero variously as an eccentric scientist, a professional wrestler, a Jane Austen patriarch and much else besides, including a first television outing for Pa Glum. The series was notable for the prominence of Ronnie Barker alongside June Whitfield at the head of the supporting cast. In later years Barker took advantage of a similar format to showcase his own versatility with the viewing public as well as to acknowledge his debt to Edwards as a mentor in general terms.

It was little known that the luxuriant handlebars of his moustache owed their origin to an attempt to disguise the plastic surgery necessary after his Dakota was shot down at Arnhem. He had ordered his crew to jump, and his gallantry saved their lives. He lost part of an ear, as well as suffering severe facial injuries. Away from the spotlight he projected an air of shy melancholy and disenchantment, which was perhaps an echo of his wartime sacrifice, perhaps of the strain imposed on him by his sexuality. That he was gay was confirmed a decade after their divorce by his ex-wife Valerie, to whom he was married between 1958 and 1969. She told the press that they had been married exactly one day when he announced he was 'a homosexual trying to reform'. When towards the end of his life journalists quizzed Edwards whether he had 'come out', he replied with typical forthrightness, 'No, they've unbolted the door and kicked me through it!' He died, not a little disillusioned, from bronchial pneumonia on 7 July 1988. As his brother Alan, who managed his Sussex farm for him for many years, admitted, 'It all got on top of him in the end.'

Frank Muir, in his autobiography *A Kentish Lad*, recalled with great relish watching Edwards on stage at the Windmill in the early days. He entered dragging an empty beer crate in one hand and a huge euphonium case in the other, sat on the beer crate to open the case and took from it a penny whistle on which he played a sprightly tune: 'He then said "Encore," pushed the mouthpiece up a nostril and played the tune again. Then he tucked the penny whistle away in his top pocket and announced, "The second encore has been banned!"' Muir also remembered his fully fledged schoolmaster act, with Jimmy striding on stage, making great play of swishing his cane and glowering at the audience as if it were a class of degenerates. His attention was then directed to a tall stand-up desk with two handbells on top. He rang one of them in conventional fashion – 'Quiet, everywhere! Fags out! Pay attention!' – then pulled at the handle of the other. It turned out to be a beer pump, which he pumped a few times, then opened the desk to produce a foaming half-pint of bitter. 'Cheers!'

In 2008 in his memoir, *Clips from a Life*, Denis Norden reminded the world of the longest pun – across five syllables – ever sustained by *TIFH*. In the sketch in question Jimmy Edwards played a rascally mill owner to whom June Whitfield's innocent young working lass is in thrall. 'May I offer you a soda scone, my dear?' The time is midnight and the girl replies, 'Nay, I never eat a soda scone so late.' 'But why not,' asks Jim. June replies, 'It makes me so disconsolate!' However, no line from the programme became more infamous than one appropriated – with permission – many years later by Talbot Rothwell for *Carry On Cleo*: 'Oh infamy! Infamy! They've all got it in for me!' As Norden remarks, 'I would judge Kenneth Williams' cry the more heart-stricken; Jimmy Edwards's declamation the more thunderous.' How a burst of that thunder would enliven today's comedy scene!

Right: one of several early film vehicles that helped Jimmy's fans put a face to the radio voice

FRANKIE HOWERD: 'AND THE BEST OF LUCK!'

Harold Macmillan? I've had no dealings with the man. I say no dealings – there was this little fracas we had about the Common Market. I thought, if you want to find something out, go to the top man. Right. So he was down at Chequers – lovely place – it goes with the job – that's why he's hanging on to it! Now, I was out on a cycle rally and we were passing by Chequers – I thought, I'll nip in. I'm sorry, I told him. I was very forthright, stupid to be anything else. I said, 'Harold, be careful.' I said, 'Harold, don't rush into this, I beg you.' I don't think he got the message. Well, it's very difficult when you're shouting through a letter box.

Frankie Howerd at the Establishment Club, 1963

In 1945 Lupino Lane, the musical comedy performer and originator of the 'Lambeth Walk' craze, compiled a small handbook entitled *How to Become a Comedian*. Prominent among the rather clinical 'suggestions to the student' were: 'Any inclination to fidget and lack "stage repose" should be immediately controlled. This can often cause great annoyance to the audience and result in a point being missed. Bad, too, is the continual use of phrases such as: "You see?", "You know!", "Of course", etc. These things are most annoying to the listener.' Frankie Howerd would triumphantly flout these cardboard conventions, his stance a-jitter, his speech a breathless string of garbled interjections and asides, and his success indelibly assured. It was as if Lane's spirit inhabited all who took delight in conspiring against this hero, whether on personal or professional grounds. Howerd, shrugging his heavy shoulders, cocked an exultant snook at the lot of them: impresario Bernard Delfont, the ominous 'Thing' of the BBC, his mercenary co-stars, the gossiping trollops he might have met in the fish queue any morning of the week. Not that Howerd was unaware of his own 'inadequacy'; rather he revelled in the aura of theatrical seediness that surrounded his every performance. Slouching on stage to the defiant strains of 'You can't have everything', he proceeded to squeeze the last drop from the most withered of old jokes. 'What do you expect at this time of night? Wit?' He was a mere menial in a profession of Gielguds and Oliviers, expecting to have to sweep the stage afterwards and knowing he was on to a good thing when he could cadge an extra twelve and six a week for pulling his own curtains. Still, he was not without pride. Appearing at the Prince of Wales Theatre in 1966, uncomfortably surrounded by faded 'Gay Montmartre' scenery and the jaded sequinned leotards of leg-flickering chorus girls, he jeered, 'I said to Mr Delfont, something bright to open with, like I had in 1952. I didn't expect him to use it all again!' Later in the same show he discovers with utter dismay that his contract has been torn up to improvise a snowstorm in a mock melodrama: 'Oh well, I shall have to go back to modelling, I suppose.' So skilful was his bluff, one never queried the presence of his 'third-rate' entertainer in a leading West End theatre. One automatically accepted it as revenge for the indignities he had suffered at the hands of the management, who were only paying him a pittance anyhow: 'For the money they're paying me, I should be dynamic!'

Howerd's whole body underlined this brilliant theatrical joke, the face in particular, haggard and lopsided, sagging like the bladder-balloon once bounced and buffeted by the Master of the Revels, of whom he was a latter-day equivalent. The patchwork eyebrows attached with makeshift indifference over the wild mournful eyes, the tousled curls, the thin pouting lips, all combined to register one moment surprise, the next cunning, one moment beaming joy, the next protestation. It was a face that in its time invoked a whole menagerie – bloodhounds and donkeys, goats and camels, even mythological hybrids – but I still favour the resort to nursery-lore taken by the *Daily Mail* theatre critic in 1950 early in Howerd's career: 'Simple Simon with mumps', a somehow precise word picture of the clown who remained 'our most original droll'. And yet the shambling pace with which his lumbering hulk approached the microphone – evoking a wild beast on the prowl rather than a clown coaxing a crowd – did nothing to belie the animal imagery. Once he had arrived centre stage, one had to wait for the crumpled figure in the sub-standard silk suit to settle down, to make himself 'comfy' – 'My trousers are sticking to me tonight. Are yours, madam? Then wriggle. There's nothing worse than sitting in agony!' – before one could see Howerd in his true colours, the scandalous gossip assuming an over-the-garden-wall intimacy with his audience, hunched forward and rubbing his hands together with the malicious satisfaction of some Dickensian ogre, his shabby toupee balanced precariously on his head. Nevertheless, in view of the willingness of the audience to enter into this conspiracy, Howerd surprisingly remained curiously isolated and vulnerable on stage, an impression emphasised by the fleeting glimpse over his shoulder into the wings to make sure, like Dan Leno and Max Miller before him, that he was *not* being overheard, followed by his insistent beckoning to the anonymous hundreds to listen all the more intently. Miller was sharp and brash enough to take care of himself, but Beerbohm's remark on Leno is surprisingly apt to Howerd: 'squirming in every limb with some deep grievance that *must* be outpoured, all hearts were his'. As long as impresarios and stagehands alike conspired against his dignity, Howerd would likewise be laughed at *and* cared about.

'Well… er – I shan't keep you long. Um – now listen – what? No – no, don't. No – listen. Before we go… er – ladies and gentlemen – I mean to say…' The words stumbling head over heels, his verbal style contained not only a sly comment on the tradition of perfect articulateness imprinted upon conventional dramatic speech in an era before Osborne and Pinter, when all was distinct and nothing pertinent left unsaid, but also a caricature of the basic failure, by contrast, of the ordinary man in the street as a talking animal. The only man to *sound* as if he was dotting his Ts and crossing his Is, he fumbled vocally amid a flurry of stunted syllables and whooping inflexions until his grievance was eventually outpoured, the scandal scattered with relish, the joke peddled with pride. One uses that last verb wisely because to Howerd jokes were essentially a marketable commodity, often a bargain. 'Listen – you're taking your time over these. There's some good stuff here. Don't waste it!' As he rambled on at uncomfortable ease with a tortuous monologue – perhaps the one about the speech he delivered on the Common Market to an audience of expectant mothers from Bromley who were all craving whipped cream and faggots, or his misadventures with a geisha girl in Tokyo, that 'inscrutable Tunbridge Wells', or even how he secured the coconut concession for the British government from the exotic island of Obbonklonx – the frequent absence of jokes per se was compensated for by the joke embodied in his own squirmish persona. Then with the furtive embarrassment but inner satisfaction of a priest eyeing *Playboy* in a barber's waiting-room, he would slip one in, certain either to be very risqué – 'Here, did you hear the one about the widow who wore black garters… in memory of all those who had passed beyond?' – or to be very bad, in which case not the joke itself but the ennui with which it was thrown away became the point. 'Isn't it whimsical? Isn't it? Please yourselves.'

'I was am – aaazed!'

Howerd's triumph was built upon several layers of ambivalence – fascinating, paradoxical and hilarious. First, the essence of his comedy, broad and brazen, was complete uninhibitedness, while he himself remained nothing if not put-upon and shy. Second, he would wheedle an audience into the palm of his hand, yet his approach would then often become increasingly truculent. He would open his act with a plea for laughter: 'Now listen, brethren, before we begin the eisteddfod, I'd like to make an appeal. No, it's not an appeal for money. You've been robbed enough as it is! No, you feel such a ninny stuck up here if no one laughs. Now, who can manage a little titter? You could? It isn't always easy to get your titters out on a wet Wednesday.' It was not long, however, before he realised that the laughter was an obstacle to his grievances being taken seriously and therefore must be checked: 'No, don't laugh. No, don't. No, don't laugh. Listen. Pull yourselves together. You'll make me a laughing stock,' 'God help us! This is gonna be a rowdy do, I can see that,' 'Look, dear, don't titter when I'm tirading – there's a good woman. I'll tell you when to titter, dear. You shouldn't be here in your condition anyway!' Third, while fully aware of his ability to impart a sexual connotation to the most innocent material, he assumed a look of outrageous indignation whenever his words *were* taken at more than their face value.

There was a gulf between Howerd's flustered stuttering – something words alone cannot convey – and the belligerent terseness of George Robey (1869 – 1954), for whom the single word 'Desist!' was sufficient to herald a similar sense of shock. But the effect was the same: the more the audience was reproved, which it was constantly, the more it laughed. Robey had styled himself 'The Prime Minister of Mirth', and for the first twenty years of the twentieth century held sway as the king of low comedy. To that style Howerd brought the more sophisticated veneer of high camp. If Robey had presented a broken-down cleric, a subtle way of planting his comedy in an exclusively masculine world, Howerd's approach was ostensibly feminine. His gossip, well within the tradition of Leno's 'Mrs Kelly', G. S. Melvin's Girl Guide and Norman Evans's wall-clinging 'Fanny Fairbottom', was at heart a woolly old woman, only without the frock. Wrongly convinced of his own immunity from the quirks and vices he detected with prying eye in other members of society, Howerd wasted no time in broadcasting them with something approaching malicious glee. The resultant sexual ambiguity only enhanced his humour. Reminiscing about the outbreak of the Second World War, he began, 'It was a prime minister that changed my life. I don't mean change *à la* April Ashley – I don't mean that type of change – but then it might come to that if things don't improve.' He did in fact aim consciously at this inverted style and so succeeded in lifting the element of bad taste, a source of all camp, to an honest entertainment level, with no snide overtones and with more than a hint of self-mockery.

The joke was most vividly displayed in his standard act with the plump lady pianist, archetype of every middle-aged accompanist with aspirations to greater things than the jumble concerts and suburban ballet galas that limp along with her services. The part was most notably taken by 'Madame' Blanchie Moore, who first met Howerd in 1941 at a wartime troop concert and would remain in his act intermittently until the mid-60s. Silent throughout, she presented a mute Margaret Dumont type, symbolising hidebound convention, deaf into the bargain, and as such the butt of the bulk of Howerd's jokes. 'I don't need a group, really, and she's cheap, that's the main thing – I tell her it's an audition!' The story went that, unwanted as a child by her 'mothers and fathers', she was left on the doorstep of London Zoo, where, brought up by the elephant keepers, she thought for years that her vocation was to give rides to children. 'Give her a bun and a prod with a stick and she's well away.' Veering between a piercing shriek to make himself heard by her and the subdued tones required to win over the audience's confidence, Howerd fluctuated between acquiescence and insult in his attitude towards this 'burden'.

> (*To the accompanist*): Yehss – we'll do the *aaaria* now.
> (*To the audience*): No – don't laugh. No – she can't hear very well – she can't hear much.
> She's a funny woman. No, she's a bit hard of hearing – a real misery – she's a real misery.

(*To the accompanist*): Ah, good evening, good evening.

(*To the audience*): No – don't laugh. Poor soul – no – it might be one of your own!

(*To the accompanist*): 'Tis chilly – *yehss* – 'tis.

(*To the audience*): Chilly? I'm sweating like a pig! Are you?

(*To the accompanist*): 'Tis *chilly – yehss.*

With Madame Blanchie Moore at the piano: 'She's a funny woman!'

Throughout she remained impervious to any attack on her stolid dignity, somehow managing to ignore Howerd's presence and, always at the wrong moment, carried away at the keys by her own conviction in her dubious musical skills. Ironically, though, the main joke was against Howerd himself, and not merely because of the creaking repertoire of hackneyed standards that he parodied with relish: 'With these hands (I could strangle her)', 'Three wives in the fountain' (i.e. a public house), and a veritable Grand Guignol version of 'Autumn leaves', not to forget his own heart-rending equivalent of the Mock Turtle's 'Beau-ootiful soo-oop', the tale of the 'Three little fishes', his hands and face assuming a carp-like form as he demonstrated the journey 'swam over the dam' by George, Perce and Cecil on their watery spree: 'Ooh – wood – dittem – dam – what – tem – day!!!' Quite simply, the reason 'Madame' was funny was the reason Howerd was funny. Both were gullible, long-suffering, ignorant of themselves as others saw them, and one feels certain that given the chance Moore would have proved as voracious a gossip as her employer. It is not too difficult to imagine them both in spirit, if not in person, attending a WVS meeting or a drill-hall whist drive on a wet Wednesday afternoon. The accompanist was another projection of the clown, viewed through the perspective of camp humour, a trait used by Howerd's idol, Sid Field, in his photographer and musician characterisations, before being exploited fully by the younger performer. At other times of Howerd's career the pianist was played by the equally effective *Mesdames* Vere Roper and Sunny Rogers.

If Howerd's general ethos was in debt to Field, his disdainful attitude towards an insensate stooge, his strained attempts at cajoling a musical key, his air of solemn, even morose defiance were all vividly reminiscent of the great Jimmy James, an equally significant influence on the impressionable young comedian born Francis Alick Howard in York on 6 March 1917. He changed his surname to Howerd after the Second World War so that down among the 'wines and spirits' on a theatrical bill it might at least stand out as a misprint. His first stage role at the age of thirteen was that of Tilly's father in Ian Hay's comedy play *Tilly of Bloomsbury,* a church-orientated production, success in which steeled him eventually to audition for RADA, where, stammering and stuttering, he was instantly rejected. A sergeant in the Royal Artillery during the war, he was turned down by *Stars in Battledress,* but still found himself unofficially entertaining the troops. And then, the war over, in spite of chronic stage fright he hit the top in a hurry. Having toured the provinces sharing bottom of the bill with Max Bygraves in a revue, *For the Fun of It,* presented by Jack Payne as a starring vehicle for vocalist Donald Peers, he got his first break as early as December 1946 on *Variety Bandbox,* radio's equivalent to the later television show *Sunday Night at the London Palladium.* He was billed in those days as 'The Borderline Case' and the *Radio Times* reported that the producer wouldn't let listeners 'into the secret of Frankie Howerd's humour because it might take some of the surprise from the first show'. The success of his nervous approach led to him quickly becoming one of the resident comedy stars of the programme, which was notable for giving him his own quota of catchphrases during the golden era of such – 'I was am – *aaazed*!' 'Ladies and gentle – men', 'Not on your nelly' – as well as a fruitful relationship with a brilliant young scriptwriter by the name of Eric Sykes. One memorable routine from those days involved Frankie's exploits as a messenger boy.

Anyway, I went along to the depot and I saw the foreman and I said, 'Look, I'll sign for these goods.' He said, 'They're labelled and ready. Get them out of here quick.' So I signed for them, you see, and I went along. They were labelled and ready all right – two elephants – two *el – eee – phants*! I was am – *aaazed*! So I got a bit of string and I tied it round their necks, you see, and I let them out into the street. Ooh, I did feel a *ninny*! I thought – no – but the way people stared. You'd have thought they'd never seen two elephants going down the Underground before.

Howerd's mood, perplexed and cautious, uncannily reflected that of a country emerging dazzled from the dark days of conflict and indecision, the distinctive verbal style that helped convey this evolving in part from the struggle for survival forced upon an essentially visual comedian in an alien medium. Now when he toured the halls it would be as top of the bill. In Autumn 1950 he was featured at the Palladium in the revue *Out of This World* with Nat Jackley and Binnie Hale, and three years later in 1953 as Idle Jack in *Dick Whittington* at the same theatre, a venue from which, apart from sporadic television and seemingly countless Royal Variety appearances, he would be bafflingly absent until returning in pantomime, in *Jack and the Beanstalk*, in 1973.

And then, as the 1950s became the 60s, his career crumpled around him in a forlorn heap. Considering his soaring rise to fame, one would not have been surprised if his reputation had nosedived after one or two years, but not so suddenly overnight after a decade or so of consistent stardom, during which the original burden of top billing on one so relatively immature had been lightened as his professional experience increased. Moreover, as he gained confidence, earnest attempts had been made to broaden his career. At Christmas 1955 he spent three months as Lord Fancourt Babberley in *Charley's Aunt* at the Globe Theatre, and two years later played Bottom in the Old Vic production of *A Midsummer Night's Dream*, proving conclusively that such parts only come to life when a genuine clown like Howerd invests them with his own personality. In October 1958 the musical *Mister Venus*, made into a vehicle for him by Ray Galton and Johnny Speight from an idea by Alan Melville, had a cripplingly short run at the Prince of Wales and the inexorable slide set in.

For three years Frankie found it hard to get work, and as his contemporaries in the comedy world – people like Bygraves and Secombe, Sykes and Terry-Thomas – soldiered triumphantly on, it looked as if Howerd was being made a scapegoat for the demise of the variety theatre. In 1961 he was out of work for nine months. Not one Blackpool manager would risk his inclusion in a summer show. Film appearances became walk-on guest spots. He did play a major provincial pantomime, *Puss in Boots* in Coventry, but with second billing to Sidney James, a brilliant comedy actor but not a bona fide panto or variety star. Matters were not helped by a nervous breakdown and the death of his mother in 1962, always a potent source of inspiration during the early years of his career. The adulation he would go on to receive from critics, producers and managements could not but be tempered with the unease left by those years of blanket disregard, when sheer silence spelt out the curt message, 'He's finished.'

The only people who didn't let him down were staunch friends like Eric Sykes, Marty Feldman, Ray Galton and Alan Simpson, and Johnny Speight, who now wrote for him for nothing. It was comforting that the cream of the country's comedy scriptwriters at the time should refuse not to believe in his great performing talent, and it only took a single guest appearance – targeting the previous week's Budget – on the BBC's late-night satirical show *That Was The Week That Was* in 1963 to bring him back into the mainstream. In time the satirists lost momentum, but their boyhood idol from the heyday of radio comedy forged ahead in spite of his own conviction 'I'm not bitter enough for that sort of comedian – I'm more the cuddlesome kind.' And yet in his satirical asides against the government and media figures of the day – 'That Robin Day, hasn't he got cruel glasses?' – Howerd, rather than cashing in on a trend, was doing little more than reaffirming the traditional function of music hall as a barometer of public opinion – a function that makes nonsense of the notion that light entertainment has no serious connection with the troubles of the world. Entertainment for the masses by its very nature reveals mass preoccupations. Indeed, when in the lead-up to *TW3* he played Peter Cook's Establishment, the controversial nightclub in Greek Street and spiritual home of *Private Eye* magazine, the joke was that a 'humble music hall comedian' like himself should have been appearing at such an 'upper-class canteen' at all. In fact it was a logical place for him to play. But if he rode back on the crest of the satire wave, he soon consolidated his regained eminence with a return to the very origins of modern comedy, in the Sondheim musical *A Funny Thing Happened on the Way to the Forum*, a musical adaptation of the plays of Plautus which unashamedly inherited that dramatist's policy of calling a spado a spado. Howerd played the slave Pseudolus scheming for his liberty in a world where adultery and defloration were the only consistent preoccupations. When he landed the part, he summed up the nature of the show to a friend: 'Ooh, it's filthy… I'm the only virgin in it!' It ran for 762 performances at the Strand Theatre from October 1963, reaffirmed Howerd as a comedy superstar, and would prove the inspiration for the triumphant television series, *Up Pompeii!*, with Howerd's slave rechristened Lurcio. The musical was followed by *Way Out in Piccadilly* – written for him by Galton and Simpson and directed by Eric Sykes – at the Prince of Wales Theatre, the venue as we have seen evoking memories for its performer of *Pardon my French,* that other tinsel and tights epic in which he featured at the same theatre in the early 50s. Howerd had come full circle back to his original giddy heights.

Like Tony Hancock, he came to epitomise all the weaknesses of man, not least a craving for affection, which he won all the more effectively in later years in view of the real sorrows and setbacks that had gone before and testified that his look of gloomy outrage and disillusion, his dry plaintive voice may have been far more realistic than the superficial equipment of the funny man. As he nudged his audience into complicity in his outrageous game, his shoulder glance a self-protective instinct, he displayed the genuine courage of the true coward ingrained in every human being. It still surprises me that his writhing frame did not duck the moment he saw the musical director raise his baton. His innate insecurity made him one of our most perfect, most natural clowns.

AFTERTHOUGHTS

After the resurgence triggered by his appearance on *TW3* Frankie never had to suffer the indignity of popular eclipse again, soon re-established as a national treasure and managing for the most part to buck the roller-coaster of fame until his death from heart failure on 19 April 1992. He had been appointed OBE in 1977 and made his last major West End appearance in a season of his one-man show at the Garrick Theatre in 1990.

In television terms, however, he never had another success to rival *Up Pompeii!* Between 1969 and 1975 the show ran for only fifteen editions, embracing two short series, one special and the pilot episode, written by Talbot Rothwell, the Carry On stalwart, with later help from Sid Colin. Howerd's ability to weave effortlessly between sitcom script and his more direct approach to the audience as he stepped out of the action to comment, say, on the improbability of the plot or the low standard of the acting, perfectly suited his confidential conversational method. It became something of an open secret in later years that his hesitant style was diligently rehearsed, every 'ooh' and 'aah', every last off-the-cuff remark, having been interpolated by him into his basic script with scrupulous care beforehand. Trademark asides like 'Oooh, no missus' and 'Titter ye not' never appeared less than spontaneous, while no comedian – with the exception of Arthur Askey – made more skilful use of the television camera to include the home audience as part of the broader hilarity taking place in the studio. However, as a professional he was not one to take liberties and had the full measure of his material. As he admitted in a *Radio Times* interview in 1984, 'When I started doing my gossipy asides to the audience on television it was completely instinctive. But it's all there in Plautus, you know.' The Roman prologue *was* tailor-made for his persona. 'Greetings, noble plebeians, crafty artisans, and arty courtesans. The bit I'm going to do now is called the prologue and... er – you see, not only is this a quick way to get into the fruity part of the plot, but also it helps me to fill you in with who is who, who does what to whom and to whom they does what to, you see, and, in addition, how, which brings me back to the fruity part...'

In 1971 *Up Pompeii!* transferred successfully to the big screen, where in a manner that foreshadowed the shift to different historical settings of Rowan Atkinson's television hit *Blackadder*, it was followed by *Up the Chastity Belt* and *Up the Front*, romps that poked fun at the crusades and trench warfare respectively. All three films were produced by Ned Sherrin, who in the same role within television had had the insight to give him that pivotal booking on *TW3* in the first place. Less effective were the attempts to rework the formula for television with *Whoops Baghdad*, *A Touch of the Casanovas* and *Then Churchill Said To Me*, in which he played the statesman's batman.

In a world of changing attitudes much of his humour, not least the routine with the deaf accompanist, would now be regarded as politically incorrect, but there was clearly a total lack of malice or prejudice in everything he did. This pinpointed the paradox of Howerd as a satirical comedian. He was better, because more acerbic, than all the young pretenders strutting their stuff under David Frost's patronage in the early 1960s; in truth he proved as inoffensive as a teddy bear, in later years taking great delight, for example, in comparing the unruliness of his eyebrows with those of the ex-chancellor Denis Healey. Today a performer would have great difficulty in replicating the pianist act without being branded disgraceful.

In spite of the heavily laden innuendo of some of his lines as the Roman slave Lurcio – 'I'm absolutely indispensable. That's why they've made me major-domo. I said domo. Let us have no misunderstandings at the commencement!' – his homosexuality, unlike his studied verbal technique, only became wider public knowledge after his death. It should not be overlooked that until 1967 active homosexuality had been illegal in England and Wales (1981 in Scotland) and potentially career-destroying. Allegedly Howerd, living in the shadow of blackmail through much of his early success, hid his sexuality from his mother throughout her life, and had he thought his audience regarded him as gay would have been devastated. It is hard not to imagine his anxiety-ridden persona as a mirror of the guilt he carried on the back of his sexuality. Perhaps he worried overmuch. Perhaps there is a tendency to underestimate the relatively sheltered life the larger public leads. Back in the 70s I remember my own mother asking me with all sincerity and seriousness whether Frankie Howerd was married. The question was not loaded – she wanted and perhaps expected the answer to be yes – and even my negative reply aroused no suspicions in her. Others ostensibly more sexually outgoing would appear to have copied his style, not least Kenneth Williams on a television foray into stand-up and Larry Grayson. Howerd made no secret of the fact that he regarded their efforts as downright plagiarism. His concern was unnecessary. While they – like Julian Clary and Alan Carr in later years – seemed to go out of their way to make fun of their campness, with

Howerd's humour there were several dimensions more. For all the floundering and fussiness, intimacy and outrage, the outward vulnerability, he remained a bully boy among funny men. At the end of his autobiography Frankie wrote, 'Audiences will forgive you practically anything, except boring them.' That he never did. For the greater part of forty-five years, give or take the occasional stutter, he dominated British comedy.

MAX BYGRAVES: 'I'VE ARRIVED, AND TO PROVE IT, I'M HERE!'

I'll tell you a story. A fellow buys a racehorse. Just before the race he goes over to the horse and puts his hand in his pocket and gives the horse a piece of sugar. The Duke of Norfolk comes running over. He says, 'What did you put in the horse's mouth?' The fellow said, 'Sugar.' He said, 'Are you sure?' He said, 'Yes, sugar. Look here. (*Max mimes reaching into pocket and swallowing cube*) Have a piece. He gives the Duke of Norfolk a piece. He says, 'That's all right, only we have to be careful.' Now the owner goes over to the jockey and has a chat with him. He says, 'Here, (*in a whisper*) I'll tell you how to win the race. The first half mile, hold him back – the last four furlongs, give him his head and let him go. If anybody passes you, don't worry. It'll be me and the Duke of Norfolk!'
(*The Duke of Norfolk was Steward of the Jockey Club between 1966 and 1968*)

Max Bygraves radiated more subtly than any of his contemporaries a mesmeric ability to please the moment he stepped on stage. To succumb to his talent was to be made joyously happy, a genuine refreshment of the spirit. And yet to explain his magic is as elusive as a snowflake in the hand. He could never claim to be the most accomplished vocalist or jester, mimic or straight actor. Rather his skill was in the creation of an atmosphere in which, as T. S. Eliot said of Marie Lloyd, full expression was given to the life of the audience, so that performer and public fused in identity. In time, because of the performer's enduring popularity, the dialogue began before he even appeared on stage. The ease and confidence occasioned by this relationship made a Bygraves appearance the stylish event it was. In their heyday Judy Garland and Maurice Chevalier, Danny Kaye and Gracie Fields all drew upon a similar modus operandi. Given their unflagging vivacity as performers, if they had not been in other respects rather ordinary vulnerable persons they would have been less than the great stars they became. They all had a combination of personality, luck and skill that could disguise a lapse in technique, make weak jokes funny and at times invest an ordinary voice with power.

Not noticed until the vintage years of radio comedy after the Second World War, Max began life in south-east London on 16 October 1922 as Walter William Bygraves, the son of a casual dock worker and ex-professional fighter who had become known as Battling Tom Smith. A cockney kid in a London dockland slum straight out of Flanagan and Allen's 'Underneath the arches', Max experienced a childhood at once stringent and rewarding. It impressed upon him the need for hard work and the sense of application indispensable for success. He showed talent as a child singer and performed solo, singing 'Jesu, joy of man's desiring' in Westminster Cathedral. Living with eight other members of his family in a two-roomed Rotherhithe flat led him at seventeen to lie about his age and volunteer for the RAF, in which for the first time he would have a bed of his own. On his first night in the service he appeared in a NAAFl concert impersonating Max Miller, his boyhood idol. From then Wally Bygraves would himself be styled Max. During the war he made six song-concert broadcasts with the RAF and then, after demobilisation and a brief return to his pre-war trade of carpenter, became a professional entertainer. He appeared like Howerd and Edwards in the radio show specifically set aside for aspiring ex-service talent, *They're Out!* and, sharing bottom of the bill with Howerd, landed a sixty-one-week run in a touring revue featuring Donald Peers, *For the Fun of It.* Then in 1950 the pace suddenly quickened. While playing Finsbury Park Empire in May, he was summoned urgently to the Palladium by a confident Val Parnell to deputise for Ted Ray, who had to fulfil a one-night charity engagement in Manchester. Max, with all his mellow, nonchalant originality, had arrived. To prove it came *Educating Archie*, the true turning point in his career.

Archie Andrews was a grinning, cheeky Pinocchio of a ventriloquist's dummy, who as the 1950s edged out the 40s became a universal figure symbolising love, friendship, comfort and mischief to a whole nation of children. He was manipulated by Peter Brough (1916 – 1999), who in forsaking perfect lip movement (or the lack of it) for clarity of diction, never – by his own admission – appeared the most technically competent of ventriloquists. What was far more important is that he was way ahead of his rivals in imparting personality to his wooden partner and in making it exceed in importance the flesh-and-blood figure working the controls. *Educating Archie*, inspired by the earlier triumph of Edgar Bergen and Charlie McCarthy with a similar format in America, ran on the BBC for eleven years from June 1950. Its long life surprised those people who argued that the ventriloquist's art had to be seen as well as heard, but this was to deny radio its true power as a means of evoking the imagination, a power to be exploited fully at a later date by *The Goon Show*. The emphasis placed upon the relationship between Brough and Archie, and the entirely original dialogue provided at first by Sid Colin and Eric Sykes and at a later stage by Marty Feldman among others, both enhanced the show. Equally important to its appeal was the uncanny ability of Brough and his producers to select supporting talent poised on the crest of a wave that would break to resounding success with the necessary national exposure. Apart from Max, who was soon promoted from the small print of the *Radio Times* to co-star billing and did three series in the role of Brough's odd-job man, others who attempted to educate Archie in the early years included Tony Hancock, Harry Secombe, Benny Hill, Hattie Jacques, Bernard Miles, Graham Stark, Bernard Bresslaw and Dick Emery; a very young Julie Andrews and Beryl Reid with her legendary 'Monica' characterisation played vastly contrasting girlfriends. The programme, or rather Eric Sykes, provided Max with a quartet of catchphrases that continued to creep into his stage act for several years: the introductory 'I've arrived and to prove it, I'm here,' the complimentary 'That's a good idea, *son*,' the mock-boastful 'Big 'ead' and the mercenary 'Dollar lolly!' Archie the dummy found in Max the entertainer the superlative sparring partner, the popularity of each far overshadowing that of Brough himself, the man who made it all possible.

'Educating Archie' from left to right: Eric Sykes, Archie, Peter Brough, Hattie Jacques, Max, Beryl Reid and Harry Secombe

While radio proved an early stepping stone to fame, the stage would remain Max's forte. In later years television provided a vivid magnification of his warmth and technique, but he never needed the additional medium and any success he achieved therein was due essentially to the studied translation of his stage technique into television terms. In a Bygraves television show you sensed that the studio audience was genuinely enjoying itself and that the guest artists, for once presented to full effect within the context of their host's personality, were in a similar position. Moreover, by limiting his appearances – to the extent that he once requested that his act be edited out of a telerecording of a Royal Variety Performance before transmission – he maintained over the airwaves that sense of occasion that surrounds any great live performance and can so easily be dissipated by the switch-over or -off vacillation of the average television viewer.

Immaculately dressed and with a wider range than the old-time music hall comedian, he remained securely in that earthy line. Most performances would contain one or two lines inherited from Max Miller, while the same influence could be seen in several of his early recordings, such as 'Chip-Chopper-Charlie', a cheeky cockney celebration of the time the guv'nor fell into the sizzling hot batter and was served up instead of the fish, and 'Once she's got you up the aisle', a plea to all bachelors not to get caught in the monotonous money-grabbing mantrap that music hall's ironical side made marriage out to be, as symbolised in the immortal song of an earlier cockney, Gus Elen's 'It's a great big shame', in which courtship is contrasted sardonically with its cat-and-dog aftermath. A great deal of the storytelling approach of Ted Ray and Vic Oliver also rubbed off on the young Bygraves. His first act would include impressions of them both, as well as of Al Jolson, the archetype of the jovial sing-along style of entertainer with which Max would come to identify. His comedy style also gained immensely from the great throwaway American drolls, performers like George Burns and Jack Benny, to whom the telling pause and the speechless stare were worth a hundred funny lines. Co-starring with Judy Garland at the Palace Theatre, New York in 1951, Max would absorb a lot about American show business at first hand, not least how to apply that lustre synonymous with the word Broadway that was essential for professional survival along the Great White Way.

The Master Entertainer

The Bygraves act was the impressive cohesion of many elements. A skilful compilation of songs, jokes and anecdotes, bravado, sentiment and razzamatazz, with no frayed edges, the end product was hallmarked by the summery individuality of its performer and his confident unhurried approach as much as by the influences of his early years. The expressive yet unobtrusive hands, the casual stroll and nomadic use of the whole stage, the face engaging and rosy and yet in repose sensitive, the eyes even a little anxious, the gently studious cockney voice capable of lapsing at will into a whole gallery of whimsical impressions, all played their part in the carefully plotted precision of the act.

Max himself once compared an audience to a group of people in danger, frightened and anxious for someone responsible to take charge, the entertainer as leader. In this situation the more competent the performer, the more relaxed they will become and the greater respect they will afford him. Bygraves' assured technique instantly converted the insecurity of a vast unwieldy audience into the excuse for a boisterous revel. He had only to shout 'Come on, everybody. Let's have a party' and everybody did. A Bygraves performance was decidedly a ball, a spree on the town, a celebration that could continue until cockcrow. Only the waving streamers, the balloons and the funny hats were missing. He could hold an audience, any audience, in the hollow of his hand with the least effort, turning to full advantage the slightest happening in the most cavernous of auditoriums. He did so without strain or vehemence, and by being completely relaxed himself cunningly lulled his audience into the same carefree attitude. And yet all the time he managed to assert at full pressure his zest and enthusiasm for the performance in hand.

While the party spirit pervaded his entire act, it set the mood for, rather than informed, the comedy element. Parties are fun rather than intrinsically funny. The comedy itself remained firmly rooted in an everyday world, implying an attitude to life tempered by genuine struggle and despair, yet always winning through on the funny side. There were the wistfully thrown-away lines about the poverty of his early years, lines that in a more affluent age it was difficult to view as anything but comic exaggeration, but which had once been so poignantly near the truth: 'We were very poor and had very little to eat. I remember once my brother and I wanted to go to a football match, so we sold the gas oven to the junk man for one and six. It was three months before my mother noticed it was missing… She went to lean on it and fell over.' There was the assumed irreverence for religion; Max, a Catholic with quasi-Jewish features and mannerisms, was equally forthcoming in poking fun at Jews and Gentiles, again by way of discreet autobiography: 'The school I went to was half-Catholic and half-Jewish. The priest in charge used to call out the bingo numbers in Latin and Hebrew so that the Protestants wouldn't win;' 'A little Jewish boy and a little Catholic boy were having a quarrel. The little Catholic boy said, "Our priest knows more than your rabbi." The little Jewish boy replied, "Well, so he should. You tell him everything!"' There was his adroitly handled mock-boastful vein, a type of comedy it would be difficult to tolerate from a performer lacking his engaging matiness: 'I don't mean to be big about this, but at thirty-five I had a house in London, a house in the country, three of the loveliest kids, an adorable wife. I had a few quid in the bank, all my tax was paid up to date and I was riding around in a Rolls-Royce. But do you think I was happy? Do you? You're bloody right I was!'

The most notable aspect of a Bygraves story was its cartoon quality, the result of his ability to mould verbally the stereotyped figures, settings, situations of a joke into something intensely visual, almost three-dimensional, so that, whether shipwrecked sailor, dizzy drunk or hackneyed trinity of Englishman, Irishman and Scotsman, they assumed form before you, not to mention a surprising freshness. Equally adept at the lazy, shaggy-dog build-up and the pungent W. C. Fieldsian one-liner, he had the knack, all a matter of presence and authority, of telegraphing to an audience that what he was saying was meant to be funny and that they should be laughing even though basically the line may have been quite the reverse.

Even when you were listening to a joke that you knew instinctively you had heard before, you were temporarily caught up in the moment of your first acquaintance with it and could laugh as before without strain. To help matters, his delivery was quietly precise and unhurried: no one would miss anything. His ethos of complete relaxation was conducive to laughter all the way. Critic Raymond Durgnat, analysing what makes jokes tick in his survey of film comedy, *The Crazy Mirror,* writes, "'I'll tell you a joke" means "Let's relax", and "I'm laughing at your joke" means "I'm jettisoning my superiority and adopting complicity", and it's this little friendship which is the source of the merriment.' This puts Max's success as a funny man in a nutshell. Even if, however, their context within the act was more important than the jokes themselves, there were still gags that spelled out 'MAX' in outsize capitals. The drunk passed in the street by two nuns, one on each side, wonders 'How on earth did she do that?' The diver, three hundred feet below the surface, is urged from above, 'Come up quick – the boat's sinking.' A favourite featured an old man walking in the Scottish mist. Suddenly he stops and taps the ground before him, then beside him, finally all around him, to find nothing. He has to stay poised on this mysterious pinnacle until morning when, the mist gone, he finds he has been standing in the middle of the road with his walking stick broken off at the handle.

Verbal cartoons like these were only part of what the public came to expect from a Bygraves performance. As long as it remained physically possible for an audience to express its solidarity with him in song, as long as it continued to join in instinctively when Max cooed his melodious way through the numbers he had made his own, he was able to present a far more extensive image as an entertainer. A happy amalgam of all that made the great traditional music hall singers so memorable – clear diction, absence of any hint of upstaging, of condescension, choice of songs that defy not to be sung – with the seeming sophistication of a later style, his singing technique was a perfect example of theatrical attack, of driving a song along with total conviction. Although it mellowed considerably after the early 50s, technically his voice could not have been described as remarkable. Where he succeeded was as an interpreter of material. The crucial issue was that a song should be acted out to the full, have every ounce of meaning and enjoyment wrung from it; the compulsive energy needed to achieve this could invest even the most superficial lyric with a far greater power than a technically good voice.

His song successes made no other pretence than to bubble over with melody and high spirits. '(The gang that sang) heart of my heart', preserved on record as a dialogue between Max and an old-time barbershop quartet, conjured up the deep personal nostalgia that can attach to any tune from the past. If this with its picture of a tuneful yet turbulent childhood gave a glimpse of Max's earlier years, 'Friends and neighbours' provided its own clue to his later extraordinary popularity, namely the ability to project a personality which, in spite of the trappings of stardom his success obviously entailed, enabled him to be at once an ordinary fellow and a star in spite of himself, friend or neighbour still to a vast public. There was 'Mister Sandman' with its musical switchback ride of a tune and Day-Glo lyrics; the hurdy-gurdy charm of ' Meet me on the corner (when the day is through)', the title song of his show at the London Hippodrome in its pre-Talk of the Town days; 'We're having a ball', another title song, this time of one of his Palladium shows, a number that on record continues to convey more spiritedly than any other the total exhilaration of a live Bygraves performance. This with its carefree rock-cum-sing-along tempo was the work of Leslie Bricusse, who would later achieve fame with his film scores for *Dr Dolittle* and *Scrooge* and whose first published song was another Bygraves vehicle, 'Out of town', written for Max's first major film, *Charley Moon*, in 1956. With a tune as relaxed as a stroll down a secluded country lane, the lyric conjures up a child's nursery picture of a spring spent away from the city grime.

> Up there the sun is a big yellow duster polishing the blue, blue sky,
> With white fluffy clouds in a cluster hanging on the breeze to dry.
> Trees everywhere, blossom in their hair, and Mother Nature wears her newest gown;
> What I'd give once more to live right out of town.

Like smudged images in crayon and pastel on the classroom wall, the lyric is charming in its naivety and a far remove from the mocking attitude of the traditional music hall towards the green open spaces as expressed in Gus Elen's 'Nature's made a big mistake' and Wilkie Bard's 'Truly rural'. And pinned alongside the drawings of 'Out of town' one can imagine similar scenes depicting 'Tulips from Amsterdam', a song that became a virtual signature tune, suggesting its own picture of blazing colour with a leisurely swing-along melody persuasively in tune with the lazily turning arms of the windmill obligatory in such a scene.

The analogy with the world of children becomes more appropriate when one considers that many of Max's early hit records were directed primarily at them, making him a sort of Pied Piper for the 1950s. The trend started in *Educating Archie*, with its enormous juvenile following. 'Why does ev'rybody call me big 'ead?' capitalised upon the success of just one catchphrase, while Brough and Archie actually joined Max on record for 'The dummy song'. This was a quaint novelty item in which 'Mr B', deciding that Archie needed a girlfriend, quickly assembled one from the legs of a table, the arms of a chair, the neck from a bottle, the hands and face from a clock; but instead of ending up with the lovely lady dummy originally intended, he gets a nagging chatterbox which is quickly dismantled with the lyric set in reverse. Max's songs for children conjured up a crazy but reassuring storybook land where pink and blue toothbrushes talk and fall in love; where lovely lasses and handsome lads live happily ever after in places with exotic names like Gilly-Gilly-Ossenfeffer-Katzenellen-Bogen-by-the-Sea; where life's biggest disappointment is to finish a lollipop and find that all you have left is the stick, as useless as a yo-yo without any string. It is interesting that Max could still include numbers like 'The toothbrush song' and 'When you come to the end of a lollipop' in his act twenty-five years after their initial impact and find an audience of middle-aged adults joining in the choruses. They were in fact never merely kids' numbers. The performer was always able to invest them with a far wider sense of fun. It comes back to the party atmosphere again. What are parties but veiled excuses for grown-ups to bring themselves down to child level, playing silly little games to forget the more pressing demands of the adult world?

'*...in Gilly-Gilly-Ossenfeffer-Katzenellen-Bogen-by-the-Sea!*'

For the record, one further number must be mentioned. What 'Underneath the arches' was to Flanagan and Allen, 'You need hands' became for Max Bygraves. The appeal of the song resided as much in its warm-blanket suggestion of security as in any notable lyrical or musical originality – as its title hints, it is basically a catalogue of gestures, from brushing away a tear to holding a loved one to expressing happiness. The number was especially significant, however, in that it built not only to a celebration in song of the almost spiritual fusion of audience and performer into one joyous abandoned whole, but also to the actual recognition by that performer of his need for their applause, of his debt to them as much as vice versa. Cunningly, it never failed to stop the show; if it had, one feels Max would have regarded this as a personal defeat. As things were, its persistent tune would linger in the minds of the audience as they made their way home, recalling an earlier song, 'We all go the same way home', sung at the turn of the century by Charles Whittle, most famous for his 'Let's all go down the Strand'. To Colin MacInnes, writing in *Sweet Saturday Night*, the latter number sums up the whole idea of friendship in music hall terms, the idea of entertainment for the people by the people and of music hall as essentially a place for letting your hair down, the several strands united in a Bygraves performance and 'You need hands' in particular.

Among the most entertaining moments in Max's act were those when jokes and songs intertwined, the singing a pretext for the comedy. One could cite his whimsical handling of a lyric like 'Hello, Dolly', his hand gestures, his overriding enthusiasm exaggerated to the point of self-caricature – the number still the show-stopper it always was but now irresistibly funny at the same time. There was no one more accomplished than Bygraves at leading an audience up a molasses-strewn path of schmaltz and then suddenly taking an outrageously astringent detour. Since few performers were able to put across an unashamedly sentimental song as convincingly as Max, there was more than a tinge of self-mockery when he employed this technique.

> I peeped in to say goodnight
> When I saw my child at prayer:
> 'Send for me some scarlet ribbons,
> Scarlet ribbons for my hair.'

And then came both antidote and laugh: 'I'm getting worried about my boy!' He never allowed his warmth to stifle his comic attack. As impressive was his ability to invest a more sophisticated ballad such as 'A very good year' or 'The folks who live on the hill' with a conscious air of burlesque, interpolating zany mock-autobiographical jokes by way of illustration between verses and yet leaving the original lyric not only intact but still oddly touching. Most memorable of all was the sheer panache of his presentation of Ralph Reader's 'Strollin''. Sauntering across the stage, top hat in hand, cane on shoulder, Max would take his audience on a tongue-in-cheek stroll around London in twilight, breaking away from the lyric to describe such sights as the Crown Jewels – 'Just shows the profit there is in wallpaper;' Madame Tussaud's – 'I used to be in there; now I'm Twiggy and Jimmy Clitheroe;' Piccadilly Circus – 'Linger for a while and be in the hub of the world; linger too long and be in the *News of the World*! No thank you, darlin'! . . . Gives me heartburn . . . Can't stand hot chestnuts;' and, of course, the London Palladium – 'where some of the greatest stars in the world have enthralled audiences – names like Judy Garland, Danny Kaye, Harry Secombe. Modesty prevents me naming others!'

One further secret of Max's appeal was the sense of nostalgia that identified so much of his act; not the 'Home town' kind which one associates so readily with Flanagan and Allen, even though this too was present, but that nostalgia consistent with a genuine love for show business, particularly the show business of his youth. In this context dancing spelled straw hat and cane and success was typified by great American entertainers like Jolson, Eddie Cantor and Sophie Tucker. Max's 'Old time movies' routine identified him in the present with their spirit. The song, a flickering succession of references to and impersonations of idols as diverse as Groucho and Garbo, Durante and Shirley Temple, stood for yesteryear, but was sung so obviously *con amore* that it became instantly acceptable many years later. This affection for the 'Jolson ethos' is what enabled him to lift out of their original context show numbers like 'Hello, Dolly', 'Mame', that optimistic rallying call from *Damn Yankees* – 'You've got to have heart', even the title number from Lionel Bart's *Fings Ain't Wot They Used To Be* with its nostalgic evocation of the 1950s, and give them his own special stamp, while sustaining, even enhancing, the qualities of showmanship, exuberance, 'heart' which they derived from their original presentation, qualities that are the lifeblood of musicals.

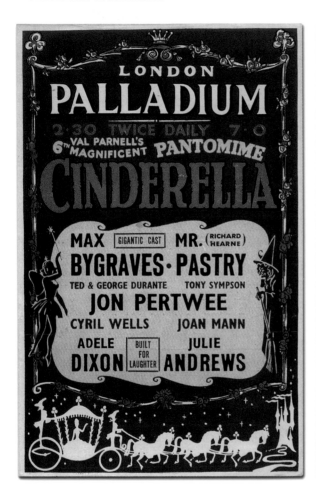

Few British entertainers of the 1950s and 60s achieved anything like Max's degree of acceptance by the masses, a success impressive in that it was entirely personal, achieved without gimmicks of any kind, unless charisma itself is classified as such. His career embraced many starring appearances at the London Palladium, including two consecutive pantomimes, *Cinderella* (as Buttons) in 1953 and *Mother Goose* (as Sammy, a Simple Simon type) the following year, and the revues *Wonderful Time* in 1952, *We're Having a Ball* in 1957, and *Swinging Down the Lane* in 1959, as well as major seasons headlining there during the last throes of variety in the late 60s and well into the 70s. The London Hippodrome played host to *Meet Me on the Corner* in 1955 and the Prince of Wales the American musical *Do-Re-Mi* in 1962 and *Round about Piccadilly* two years later. Between 1950 and 1986 he appeared in no less than fourteen Royal Variety Performances.

His long career was built on a subtly instinctive gift of being able to inspire cheerfulness and relaxation all around him, coupled with a shrewd understanding of what makes an audience tick and a warm, kindly, even if quizzical attitude to life in even its harshest aspects. A consistent box-office draw of British variety over a period of four decades, Max has had few equals with regard to sheer likeability. Appointed OBE in 1982, this most stylish of British entertainers deserves an enduring respect in a world of kaleidoscopic trends.

AFTERTHOUGHTS

The news of the death of Max Bygraves came as this revised edition was nearing completion. Having moved permanently to Australia – the scene of many successful stage triumphs – in the mid-noughties in the hope that the warmer climate would help the bronchial condition of his wife, Blossom, he survived her by fifteen months. He had recently been diagnosed with Alzheimer's disease and died at the age of 89 in his sleep during the night of 31 August 2012. It remains hard to accept that this once ever-youthful entertainer will never tread the boards again.

In the early 1970s Max adapted his singing style to a distinctive string of best-selling record albums – "Singalongamax" – which earned him something like thirty golden discs – one sold more than a million copies in less than three months – and led to a corresponding television series and two long-running stage shows at the Victoria Palace. The down side of this success was that to later generations he became identified more as a singer than as a comedian. Cynically speaking, it was to his disadvantage that this vocal peak did not coincide with a world war: his song style would have raised spirits on a par with Flanagan and Allen and George Formby.

His career wobbled uncharacteristically in the early 80s when the poor decision to host the television game show *Family Fortunes,* following the departure of its long-term resident, Bob Monkhouse, backfired on him. The decision was taken by Max himself without the input of his lifelong manager, Jock Jacobsen, who had recently died and would not be replaced. Jacobsen, whose business acumen and editorial sensitivity had helped to make Bygraves one of the wealthiest British performers of his generation, would have been the first to acknowledge that for all his skills his client lacked the spontaneity required to host such a show, ironically unlike presenters from a younger generation of comedians such as Des O'Connor and Jimmy Tarbuck, who owed not a little of their own style and technique to Max's influence. A hiccough like this, however, should not detract from his major strength: when it came to walking onstage in a seemingly effortless manner and beguiling an audience, there was no British entertainer of his generation to touch him. As Ken Dodd has said, 'He had tremendous charisma. Once he entered that stage something happened… it was like a miracle.'

Bygraves's easy-going charm and sense of fun were possibly never seen to better effect than in the Royal Variety Performance of 1960, when in tandem with an old friend, bandleader Billy Cotton, he attempted an impersonation of the puppet pigs, Pinky and Perky. Onstage Max with his gesticulating arms pinned to his body at the elbows had always given the appearance of a marionette controlled by invisible strings. Whether he was aware of the self-parody is unknown; nevertheless it doubtless enhanced what proved to be the comedy tour de force of the evening. His ability to work well with established talent had been proved at the Palace Theatre on Broadway in 1951 when he accompanied Judy Garland as one of the tramps in Irving Berlin's 'A couple of swells', originated by her on celluloid with Fred Astaire in *Easter Parade*. It was still evident on one of his television shows in the 70s when he partnered an unlikely guest, Dame Edith Evans, in the Chevalier-Gingold duet from *Gigi*, 'I remember it well'. It is a mark of their mutual stature that they each enhanced the other's performance.

Offstage he was a warm, happy-go-lucky individual whose good-naturedness came to the fore when this book was first published. A few weeks after that event in 1973 he called me – an insignificant young BBC researcher at the time – and suggested that he could help me get some publicity if I would make myself available at the Victoria Palace between his first and second houses the following Friday. Ushered into Max's dressing room on the night I saw a photographer had set up his equipment. A few minutes later Bygraves entered followed to my surprise by a dear friend of Max and my ultimate American comedy hero, Jack Benny. Max explained that I might like a photo of the three of us with the book which might trigger some publicity. Max's publicist did the rest. Over the years he never stopped thanking me for including him in the first edition. Now that he has gone, I hope that history never forgets the laid-back power of his personality on stage. Arguably he was the nearest this country has come to producing a Chevalier or a Jolson. To which I can hear him adding with the mock-boastfulness that was his trademark, "And *I* could tell jokes *as well*."

The author with Jack Benny and Max in 1973

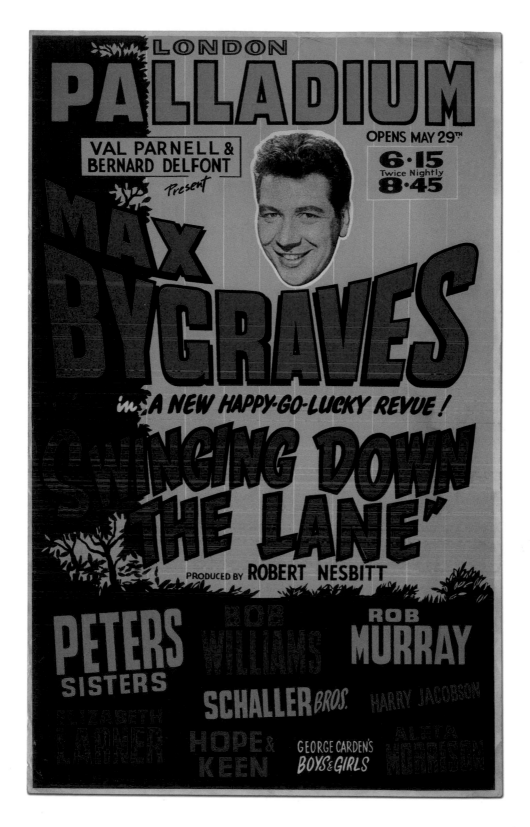

Norman Wisdom: 'Don't laugh at me cos I'm a fool'

'Mister Grimsdale!!'
(The habitual plea by the dauntless star to his persistent bête noire of an employer)

One had only to look at Norman Wisdom for him to fall down. His special preserve was the humour of physical collapse, accentuated, as so often throughout comedy history, by his size, that of the proverbial 'little man'. For all the outward swagger of experience, the anxiety to please, he was fated to act as the butt of life's indignities, never to please those placed by life in authority. The very fact, however, that he was continually knocked to the ground implies a jack-in-the-box resilience: no matter how violently he was hurled about, his eagerness and sense of bravado picked him up again. And yet, while a child will always get the better of the mechanical jack, the gaudy toy with its rouge-painted cheeks and makeshift motley will maintain its look of triumph. Conversely Wisdom, never permanently in the doldrums even if unable to dispose of the obstacles that initially tripped him up, presented the very picture of victimisation: the brooding lips, the sombre eyes with their cocker-spaniel determination, the minuscule black shoes, the shabby grey suit bursting at the seams, the askew tie, the upturned cap about to fall off in sympathy.

While the facade of the 'Gump', as Wisdom christened his character, may be at odds with that of the cheery colourful doll, it was quite consistent with his early years. Born Norman Joseph Wisden in Marylebone on 4 February 1915, the son of a chauffeur, he used to joke, 'I was born in very sorry circumstances. Both of my parents were very sorry.' His father was an alcoholic and his mother walked out of the family home when he was nine. He left school at the age of fourteen and continued to struggle and starve. During his early teens, persecution, later symbolised on stage and screen by the magnificent straight man, Jerry Desmonde, was the prerogative of a long succession of Paddington policemen, welfare authorities and employers ranging from greengrocers and headwaiters to the chief steward of a tramp steamer which the young Wisden trudged all the way from London to Cardiff to join. The Gump, firmly placed on the bottom rung of the social ladder, was in fact a simple projection of those hard early years, funny now but far from hilarious at the time. At fifteen he joined the army and his luck changed. He became a band boy with the Tenth Royal Hussars, where he would acquire the musical knowledge and instrumental ability that stood him in good stead in his stage act in the years to come. In 1930 he was posted to Lucknow, where for three years in succession he was the British army flyweight boxing champion of India. In the army gym he cultivated a comedy shadow-boxing routine in which he was knocked across the stage by his own shadow and showed the first evidence of the brilliant miming skills that would hallmark his stage and screen work. The sequence became a party piece, and people began to laugh with rather than at him. During the war he rejoined the army, and was posted to the Royal Corps of Signals. When he left the services in 1945, he was more than hungry for his first professional engagement. Billed as 'The Successful Failure', he debuted at Collins Music Hall in Islington for the week commencing 17 December 1945. At this early stage his costume consisted of a small bowler hat, striped football jersey and trousers hitched at half-mast. By April 1948 he had graduated to baggy dress-suit with long drooping tails and a humble position on a variety bill at the London Casino topped by Allan Jones of 'Donkey serenade' fame. The Gump himself would not appear until the summer of 1949, when his creator was appearing in a seaside concert party entitled *Out of the Blue* at the Spa Theatre, Scarborough. The bill featured a balding young conjuror named David Nixon, who wanted a comic stooge, a little man, to 'volunteer' from the audience to help in a trick. Wisdom, who had worked with Nixon before, quickly visited a local outfitter and purchased the prototype undersized grey-check suit, with cap to match, for thirty shillings.

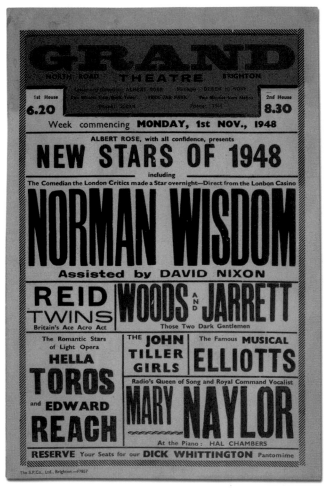

The suit was only one of several quirks that hallmarked the quintessential Wisdom, the comedian as square peg in a round hole. When he laughed, he gradually became self-intoxicated until, reduced to gulping hysteria, he lost control. This special laugh with its contagious side effects he preserved for all time on the now famous recording of 'Narcissus' with Joyce Grenfell in the early 1950s. Then there was his uncanny ability to appear to be leaning back and strutting forward at the same time. This, like his ear-to-ear grin, was an indication of triumph on his part, perhaps at his chance discovery of the increased resonance of his voice as he passed the microphone, an effect which he would go back to try again and again until the novelty and excitement palled. Perhaps the key to his whole persona, however, was in his legs, legs that defined Wisdom as an acrobat as much as a comedian. Capering on stage one moment with a jaunty, toe-to-heel swagger, the next he was slithering all over the boards, crashing helpless to the floor. One recalls the remark of Jacques Tati that film comedy is all a matter of the legs, and that Little Tich, whose 'Big Boots' dance, a compulsive combination of balancing skills and acrobatics, is happily preserved on celluloid, was the true pioneer of film comedy. Both these statements are substantiated by Wisdom, the most successful cinematically of all British post-war comedians (as distinct from comedy character actors in the mould of Peter Sellers and Terry-Thomas). Wisdom's stage act, however, was far more vigorous, more violent than Tich's ever was, a masochistic hurly-burly of collision and collapse. By the end of a performance he would have been hit in the face, punched in the stomach and, it seemed, virtually cut off from his own feet. Any chairs on stage were there either to give way beneath him or to crush him from above. The piano, when his hand was not trapped beneath the lid, became an instrument for running at, jumping over, sliding across and falling off. One felt that even his best friend would pass out of favour if a meeting between them occurred without Norman taking some kind of punishment from him. He was a one-man Mack Sennett comedy, his body a projectile in a ballistic bedlam. And yet, however much he may have appeared the true disconnected man, his act presupposed the most pliant and graceful of bodies; however much he was the original butter-legs, he possessed the poise and precision of movement of the most accomplished of ballet dancers. His routine was a frenetic spiral of continually renewed disaster, anger and isolation, pain, reconciliation and laughter, between immaculate stooge and helpless waif. One recalls the acts of Grock, Sid Field's sports novice, and Laurel and Hardy, microcosmic images of the whole human condition.

Although worked out and rehearsed to the nth degree, everything was calculated to give the impression of complete spontaneity. Shoved on as a stand-in by his straight man posing as an infuriated theatre manager, Norman as the makeshift performer is determined to grasp his one big chance with open arms. He wants to sing 'When Irish eyes are smiling' but is kept waiting by an overlong orchestral introduction. He begins, but his falsetto is too high. He tries again, but his bass is too low. The polite yet sinister straight man must now intervene. When the telephone – conveniently positioned on the piano – rings with a call for the manager, he finds himself having to sing at cross purposes with the ensuing conversation, interpreting the instructions given by the straight man to the person at the far end of the line – 'Louder, louder!' – as intended for himself. It eventually dawns that a lady friend of the manager is making the call. The face gladdens at what his fertile imagination tells him is being said, until he is quivering with uncontrollable laughter and, cutting the wire, he falls flat on the ground in his moment of exaltation.

He then gets his golden opportunity to conduct the orchestra. The conductor's back is turned and he nimbly steals the baton. The boys in the band are as amazed at his own individual conducting style, one moment over his shoulder, the next under his leg, as he is at the near-magical quality of the stick in starting and stopping the various sounds. Then the conductor waves a second baton at him – one ten feet long. This is the cue for a fencing bout between the two. Norman is triumphant, wipes off the blood and proceeds to work himself to a physical crescendo conducting the 'Poet and Peasant Overture' until he is prostrate a second time. About now the manager comes on to announce that the real star has at last arrived and that Norman must go. Not, of course, that he does. In a grovelling attempt to persuade him the straight man explains that from now on he wants Norman to regard him as a friend whom he can look up to. He puts his right hand on the clown's right shoulder and Norman seems grateful for the affection. However, when the fawning arm is withdrawn and the villain creeps stealthily into the wings, a grotesque disembodied hand remains on his shoulder. The little man, all but crowing, gabbles on as if its owner were still behind him. Then gradually the dispiriting truth dawns, not first, however, without the gory horror of amputation registering upon his mind, without the terror-stricken Norman launching himself into a nervous whirl in an attempt to come face to face with the man he imagines to be behind him.

Later the same ogre will reappear to give Norman a 'lesson in rhythm' with a gruesome Heath-Robinson-type contraption comprising 'bonker', beneath which the pupil sits, 'biffer', a converted boxing-glove operated at his side, and stool with built-in spikes. When the bonker descends on his head, Norman must beat the drum; when the biffer punches his ear, he must stop; when the spikes rise, he must 'plink the plonker' – crash the cymbal with the drumstick. Here is the answer of a more sophisticated age to the original slapstick, two pieces of wood that slapped against each other with a resounding crack when employed to hit somebody. As the savage tuition proceeds, Wisdom's body is all but reduced to a quivering blob of protoplasm to be punched and pierced, kicked and pummelled, doomed to failure from the very beginning.

While he may fail to get beyond the first line of 'When Irish eyes are smiling', one should mention that along the way despite the above catalogue of torture and knockabout Norman somehow manages to give accomplished performances on post horn, trumpet, clarinet, saxophone, xylophone, piano and drums. Whatever his shortcomings, he does possess a saving grace, a hidden talent, the equivalent of skill on tabor and pipe displayed by Shakespeare's clowns. However gullible and clumsy he may be, he does have his own specialised contribution to make to society. Even more redeeming in the Wisdom persona was his gallant resolve to succeed – even if we always knew that success was impossible for him – and his continual desire for fresh experience, traits that added depth to his pathetic little man character.

This basic characterisation carried Wisdom through a succession of West End shows in the 1950s, including the Folies Bergère revue *Paris to Piccadilly* at the Prince of Wales Theatre in 1952 and *The 1954 Palladium Show* and *Painting the Town* at the London Palladium – the theatre where he had already appeared in the first of five Royal Variety Performances in 1952 – in 1954 and 1955 respectively. Two record-breaking pantomimes triumphed at the same theatre, where – breaking tradition in newsworthy fashion as the first male principal boy in forty years – he featured as Aladdin in *The Wonderful Lamp* at Christmas 1956 and then as *Dick Whittington* four years later. He also widened his scope on stage to encompass successful stage musicals like *Where's Charley?*, the musical version of *Charley's Aunt*, in which he played the role created by Ray Bolger in America, at London's Palace Theatre in 1958, and *Walking Happy* at the Lunt-Fontanne Theatre on Broadway in 1966. Unbeknown to the public, the latter, a musical adaptation of *Hobson's Choice*, had been conceived as a vehicle for Fred Astaire and contained in its title number by lyricist Sammy Cahn, in collaboration with composer Jimmy Van Heusen, a challenging attempt to deliver what they hoped would be the definitive Astaire number. The maestro could not be tempted back onto the boards that late in his career, and Norman in an astonishing display of hoofing skill made the number and the star role his own. The legendary *New York Times* drama critic Walter Kerr, describing him as a 'zany original', praised Norman as the show's 'principal asset'.

Norman as Aladdin with producer Robert Nesbitt

Wisdom also steered his basic character through the most prolific screen career of a native music hall performer since Hay and Formby. His first film, *Trouble in Store*, made to capitalise upon his early television success, broke house records almost everywhere it was shown during its first four weeks of release in 1953. This set the trend for a chain of annual comedies, films like *One Good Turn*, *Man of the Moment*, *Up in the World*, *Just My Luck*, *The Square Peg*, *Follow a Star*, *The Bulldog Breed*, and *The Early Bird*, in which he usually played the hapless character Norman Pitkin, an extension of his stage persona. For at least a decade Wisdom's success at the box office gave the impression of keeping together the body and soul of the British film industry: he even held off the challenge of James Bond as the nation's top box office draw. The chain and the spell were broken in the late 60s by an unwise decision, probably at the bludgeoning insistence of the critics, without whose aid his films had long succeeded, to change his cosy, homely image to a more sophisticated adult one, with *What's Good for the Goose*, a so-called 'light sex comedy'. The decision to change – or adapt – his image was a brave one; the result disastrous. Moreover, for personal reasons he was unable to pursue further film opportunities in America following his success there in the vaudeville saga *The Night They Raided Minsky's* in 1968. From that point his career concentrated upon stage and television appearances.

NORMAN WISDOM in **ONE GOOD TURN** *also starring* JOAN RICE · SHIRLEY ABICAIR · THORA HIRD

Norman's early film career inevitably invited comparisons with Chaplin, both frail little men in a tough outsize world, both performers with a grounding in music hall. It was also continually blackened by intellectuals as derivative. The point is that Wisdom's enthusiasm, his ability to bounce back from the most precarious of scrapes, placed him more obviously in the line of the almost superhuman Harold Lloyd and Lloyd's immediate successor Joe E. Brown, than of Chaplin, Buster Keaton and Harry Langdon. Moreover, if derivative, his films were never self-consciously so, unlike pretentious comedy epics like *It's a Mad, Mad, Mad, Mad World* and *The Great Race*, where the comedy was hampered by the misguided assumption that to be successful the slapstick, the chases, even the number of comedians participating had to be on a far larger scale than in earlier days. More importantly, one must not lose sight of the fact that even the comedians of the silent screen had a reserve of traditional comedy material inherited from music hall and vaudeville which was regarded as common property. Chaplin himself had no scruples about using this material. Hal Roach, who nurtured the talents of both Lloyd and Laurel and Hardy, remarked how once Chaplin had exhausted the material gathered over the years as a member of Fred Karno's company, so the quality of his pictures and his own reputation, began to deteriorate. I have already mentioned Chaplin's debt to Max Linder, while Donald McCaffrey, in his book *Four Great Comedians*, though himself far from sympathetic to Wisdom, shows that while Harry Langdon is often accused of blatantly imitating Chaplin, the reverse imputation is much more justifiable. The use of the blind heroine by Chaplin in *City Lights* in 1931 had been anticipated by Langdon's feature *The Strong Man* in 1926; the climactic thrill sequences at dangerous heights in *The Gold Rush* (1925) and *The Circus* (1928) had already been developed by Langdon in *Safety Last* (1923) and earlier one- and two-reelers. The dance of the bread rolls, which Chaplin brought to perfection in *The Gold Rush*, had already been featured seven years earlier by Fatty Arbuckle in *The Cook*.

Like Chaplin, Wisdom realised at an early stage in his career that his lack of inches was conducive to pathos, which, if correctly applied, could only intensify his appeal. The public began to see Norman not only as the tumble-down clown with the footloose walk, but also as the perpetual victim of unrequited love, the wistful waif anxious to take the girl he loves, but by whom he is spurned or at most only liked, on an extravagant night out, knowing only too well that his pockets are threadbare and empty. As if to consolidate this aspect of his appeal, the little man in the battered suit would close his act alone on stage in almost complete darkness, singing in precise plaintive tones his self-written signature song, 'Don't laugh at me 'cos I'm a fool', a melodic plea for his lucky star to come out of hiding to smile on him and deliver someone who will really love him.

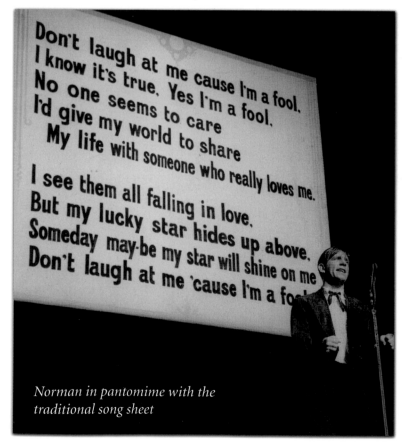

Norman in pantomime with the traditional song sheet

He was ever hopeful, always dreaming of the rosy horizon. The dangers of this kind of approach are obvious. With Wisdom the sentimentality became accepted by his public as an integral part of the act, so it was not seriously inimical to the comic effect. Colin MacInnes's strictures on the Chaplin little man figure are, however, applicable here: 'It does not engage my sympathies, chiefly because I am so aware that this figure is so insistently inviting them.' This may be a valid criticism of Wisdom, but the fact remains that for every individual who found the self-pity maudlin, his success would indicate that there were many more prepared to see him merely as a reflection, even if an exaggerated one, of themselves, the demeaned personification of the average man, overwhelmed, cut down to size by a formidable world. Wisdom's status as slapstick comedian in that world enabled him to act out child-fashion the impulses an adult would suppress. If he didn't emerge triumphant, he at least tried – the most redeeming aspect of his characterisation and the one that more than any other enabled his public to believe in their hero as they did in themselves. He did, however, have the additional compensation that as they placed their faith in this hero, they were also laughing and admiring his sheer physical dexterity at the same time.

AFTERTHOUGHTS

Shortly after the above was published it was drawn to my attention that I may have misrepresented Norman on the matter of sentimentality, having omitted to mention the device that cut the pathos in the finale of his stage act. After his signature closing with 'Don't laugh at me 'cos I'm a fool' he would walk to the wings with his head down, then shoot a sudden glance straight at the audience, break into hysterics and say, 'You ought to see your faces!' So he gave himself the last laugh, or at least the last laugh short of the Rank Organisation, possibly the true guilty party when it came to compromising his genuine comedic ability with pathos.

Many aspects of his stage act were preserved for ever on the recording of the 1961 live transmission of *Sunday Night at the London Palladium*, in which he appeared as the sole guest alongside host Bruce Forsyth. Their efforts were the culmination of Wisdom's insistence on twelve full rehearsal days. The result showed most notably in the slapstick wallpapering routine, which – with a nod to Naughton and Gold – was performed with exquisite timing and in virtual silence, with Bruce as the surly foreman and Norman as his put-upon workmate. Nothing proves as easy as it seems: setting up the two planks on the trestles without Norman getting trapped between them, unrolling the wallpaper determined to stay coiled, applying the paste to paper not person. Norman, holding the wallpaper out in front of him, at last takes the first pasted strip and climbs the stepladder to stick it to the wall; inadvertently he treads on the paper step by step, decorates the ladder instead and is bewildered to find he is left with only the merest corner to complete his task. Forsyth, watching with mounting frustration, shows how it should be done by walking backwards up the stepladder with the paper. All goes well until in a display of absolute choreographic brilliance Wisdom ends up with his boss on his shoulders as he goes to replenish the bucket of paste. Bruce at last brings the paper into contact with the wall, but as he goes to apply more paste to his brush, the bucket finds its way to Norman's head and the little man is deluged with gunge. It is hard to imagine that this was performed live, without any of the technical tricks and short cuts that filming would have allowed, and may well stand as the greatest exhibition of precision teamwork in the annals of physical comedy on the small screen.

Bruce's professionalism also came to the fore performing as the butt of another gambit that became a sure-fire device for Wisdom whenever he ventured onto somebody else's show, namely the challenge of completing a joke without laughing. He starts off with tentative coyness: 'I was walking down the street the other day and I saw this man lying in the road with his ear to a manhole cover… (*He stifles the first giggle*)… so I went over to him and said, "What are you doing down there?"' As he struggles to continue, he can't restrain himself from the giggles, which now swell into hysterics. The joke is never finished, Norman collapsing on the floor as he clings to the trousers of the distraught host as if gasping for his last breath. Even the distinguished American host Ed Sullivan allowed himself to be humiliated in the cause of Norman's comedy in this way. Any showman would have understood that no one knew the value of the infectious nature of laughter more astutely than Wisdom.

In the years that followed first publication of this work Norman's versatility came even more to the fore, not least as a straight actor who sadly never pursued this facet of his talent as assiduously as his admirers would have wished. His virtuosity would have come as no surprise to anyone who had seen his performance in *The Square Peg*, in which he played a double role as Pitkin and the Nazi General Schreiber. He played the latter straight, but for laughs none the less, and showed a sense of comic understatement of Alec Guinness class. His impressive participation – 'endearingly gentle and funny', according to the *New York Post* – in Richard Rodgers's musical version of Shaw's *Androcles and the Lion* opposite Noël Coward as Caesar for American television in 1967 fell into this category. Arguably the highlight of this side of his career, however, was as a dying cancer patient attempting to come to terms with his condition in *Going Gently* – directed by Stephen Frears from a screenplay by Thomas Ellice from the novel by Robert Downs – on BBC Television in 1981. Playing alongside Judi Dench and Fulton Mackay, he contributed a BAFTA-winning performance of such heart-stopping intensity that his well deserved knighthood in 2000 might well have come on the strength of that alone. When he walked away from the Queen at the investiture he performed his trademark trip. Even Her Majesty smiled and laughed. His screen character had played cat and mouse with protocol throughout his career. Why stop now?

In spite of his American stage success, his films were unable to make an impact there – the US had an edgier version of the type he played in Jerry Lewis – but nonetheless his fame spread worldwide, to regions as diverse as South America, South Africa, Australia, China, Iran and the Eastern bloc countries, most famously to the USSR and Albania, where he appears to have assumed the status of a demi-god. At some sacrifice to himself he expressed his thanks for this adulation in genuine work for children's charities in these places. After the 1986 Chernobyl tragedy he travelled throughout the area, entertaining children tirelessly, and helped to endow a hospice named in his honour. That he was able to subject himself to the physical and emotional strains involved largely came down to a fitness regimen that also enabled him to continue performing his stage act well into his eighties, including his *pièce de résistance* in which he took a running dive at a grand piano, slid over the top and came out unharmed from underneath. As he once explained to me, that was nothing to someone whose education in the school of hard knocks had involved being thrown against the ceiling by a violent father when he was a child. No wonder he was able to perform all his own stunts in his films. Give Norman a revolving door or a laundry chute, a teetering ladder or four wheels out of control and he came doubly alive.

I have long cherished a special affection for Norman Wisdom. In my life and career spent working with top entertainers he qualifies as the first star I ever met. In the autumn of 1956 I entered a competition in a children's comic weekly that involved matching the names of characters to their pantomimes, making sure that Widow Twankey did not pester Dick Whittington and that Abanazar kept out of the orbit of Humpty Dumpty. To this I had to add a line or two explaining why I wanted to win. The prize said it all – a trip to the London Palladium to see Norman Wisdom in pantomime with a behind-the-scenes visit to meet the cap-crowned king of comedy. To a bespectacled youth in short trousers the likelihood of winning was as far-fetched as Christmas in August, but one day late in November a telegram was delivered to our house with the news that would magic my mother and me to Argyll Street in London's theatreland a few days before Christmas.

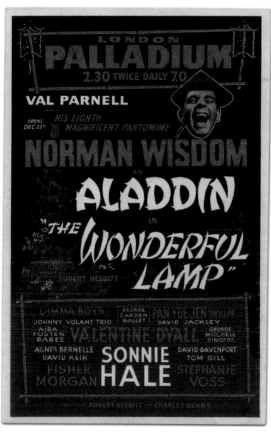

The author with Norman in 1956

The production, an ornate confection by that grand master of spectacle Robert Nesbitt, was the 1956 version of the Aladdin story rechristened *The Wonderful Lamp*, in which Norman was accompanied by musical comedy star Sonnie Hale as his mother Twankey, and Valentine Dyall, of the sonorous voice and radio fame as 'The Man in Black', as Abanazar. During the interval I was escorted into the wood-panelled splendour of the Palladium's Number 1 dressing room to meet my special comic hero. To the wide-eyed eleven-year-old from the provinces, Norman showed nothing but friendliness and warmth at a time when he was under pressure I could not have understood at that time in my life. This was the *first* night!

Little did I know then that in later years I would not only meet him again but work with him on a number of television productions. To do so was to appreciate at first hand the qualities I have tried to communicate above, not least his versatility and physical agility, his vitality and enthusiasm, as well as a painstaking perfectionism. Norman remains just about the most humble star I have known. Maybe that is why he continued to shine so bright for so long. I often wonder how great a part that early visit to see our greatest physical comedian at our most famous theatre played in steering my life and career along the course it finally took. If any performer in this book assumed for me the status of a lucky mascot, he did.

The author with Norman in 1994

When Sir Norman died at the age of ninety-five on 4 October 2010 the eulogies were unstinting, reminding us that above all else he was Chaplin's favourite clown. My guess is that Sir Charlie rated the Swiss legend Grock as highly, but together they would have made a special trio which it would be difficult to replicate among the star comedy talent of today. The frenetic Lee Evans has often been compared to Wisdom, and there can be no denying the similarity in their body language on stage, but Norman belonged to a more innocent age when the belly laugh was king. Can it be a coincidence that when he semi-retired to live on the Isle of Man in 1980, although continuing to pay British taxes, he resided in a house with the name Ballalough, even if that does translate directly from the Manx dialect as Farm of the Lake?

Norman prepares for 'Walking Happy' on Broadway

Tony Hancock: The Lad Himself!

Tonight you are getting the lot. You'll be getting Terpsichore – dancing, sword-swallowing – painful but lucrative, impressions, Shakespeare. I shall be going through the card – because you are looking at Mr Show Business himself… I've got my finger on the pulse of the nation, don't you worry.

Nothing summed up Hancock's air of sagging melancholy more aptly than his own appearance. And yet however much the hunched shoulders and penguin feet, the crumpled suit and deflated stance spoke for themselves, he still found time to pass his own morose judgement. 'I look like a bloody St Bernard up the mountain without a barrel' was a line that frequently crept into his act. What his body lacked, however, in definition, he made up for in the quicksilver precision of his features, capable as they were of conveying every single nuance of the human character with effortless ease, summarising in the twirl of a lip or the quivering of a cheek the tightrope nature of the whole human condition poised precariously between pathos and hilarity. It was this quality that made him so right for the medium of television, which comedy-wise he dominated in the late 1950s as Handley had radio fifteen years earlier. It is ironic that he made his first radio broadcast – as a guest on *Variety Bandbox* – on 9 January 1949, the day Handley died.

If *ITMA* had shown the way in the development of the narrative single-theme comedy show, *Hancock's Half Hour*, itself on radio before graduating to television in 1956, broke new ground with its emphasis on genuinely solid character-building. To say that either show introduced what amounted to situation comedy to this country is misleading, as a form of the genre had already proved its appeal on the British variety stage in the sketches of Harry Tate or Robb Wilton, which lasted up to fifteen, even twenty minutes at any one time. Where *Hancock's Half Hour* proved significant to British audiences is that a single theme was allowed to run consistently and credibly over the air for twice that time, with a minimum of characters and no superfluous musical interludes. From this developed shows like *Till Death Us Do Part*, *Steptoe and Son* and *Dad's Army*, and yet in spite of such an impressive legacy, Hancock's triumph over the new medium was a pyrrhic victory. Situation comedy appeared to become obligatory for many comedians who would have made far more successful television material if they had persisted with more conventional comedy styles, styles not themselves old-fashioned if approached – vide Morecambe and Wise – from a contemporary angle. Moreover, so much television comedy itself came to rely upon the performances of actors proper rather than those of pure comedians. Hancock's talent subsequently made things easy for the medium that had given that talent its most impressive platform, but it also set back several years the cause, television-wise, of the genuine funny man like Hancock himself.

Surprisingly, what now impresses one most about the half-hours is not their plots, debatably a *sine qua non* of the form. These were often cyclical, the end predictably mirroring the opening situation, so that when Hancock and Sid James decide to return home by charabanc to avoid the noisome company they encounter on the outward journey by train, it is inevitable that those same passengers should make a similar decision and end up sharing the back seat of the coach with our heroes. Their stay in hospital as a result of the economies taken after a holiday abroad occasions the same pile-up of stale bread, sour milk, dated newspapers that prompted the economy drive in the first place. When he is eventually freed from a night's imprisonment in a lift stuck between floors, of those released it is Hancock who must return to the lift in search of a lost season ticket and end the programme as desperately incarcerated as before. The point is that neither Hancock nor scriptwriters Ray Galton and Alan Simpson needed plots as such. Their forte was the non-plot; their skill lay in extracting comedy from the minutiae of existence. Hancock was never seen to greater effect than when he was simply doodling – verbally, facially, manually – to relieve the tension of life's boredom. It was probably the classic radio episode featuring the infamous residents of 23 Railway Cuttings plodding their listless way through a barren suburban Sunday afternoon that first proved that Hancock was funniest when nothing was happening. As the afternoon drew on, the bored comedian began to imagine pictures on the wallpaper: 'There's an old man with a pipe. Screw your eyes up. Stare hard. Concentrate on that bit by the serving hatch.' The deadpan realism of Hancock's desperate buoyancy and the cool indifference of his mates were only heightened by the revolutionary long pauses when even silence became hilarious. Hancock at his funniest personified the mood of aimless tedium that reduces grown men to drawing matchstick men on steamy train windows and greeting the first sight of cows out of London as an eighth wonder of the world.

My happiest memories of this comedian relate to his solo television performance alone in his bedsitting room, the ultimate proof of his theory that great comedy could arise from 'frustration, misery, boredom, worry and insomnia'. Here was Hancock nonchalantly trying to blow smoke rings and then burning his lip; lying there lifting his feet alternately heel to toe until the strain on his stomach muscles was too great – 'Getting old!'; rummaging through a medicine cabinet for ointment to soothe his lip only to find rows of pre-NHS medicine, the white sediment as revolting as the brown liquid it has displaced, a nose dropper with nothing to put in it, and 'Oh! Me nightlight – I've been looking for that!'; pondering his teeth in the mirror: 'Is that loose or is it my fingers going in or out? I wonder which one's the bicuspid. Wanted to know that for years. Bicuspid. It's a funny word that, isn't it? Bicuspid. Bicuspid. Bicuspid. "Bicuspid, he's a handsome fellow, Sir Charles." Ha ha ha! "Have at you, sir. Have at you!" Bicuspid. Yes, that's probably from the Latin. Bi meaning two, one on each side. Cus, meaning to swear. Pid, meaning – pid. Greek probably, pid. Yes, Greek for teeth. So bicuspid – two swearing teeth!'; veering through lack of concentration between Bertrand Russell and Lady, Don't Fall Backwards, the dictionary proving as indispensable for either: 'Well, why don't they say so, if that's what they mean?'; bemoaning that the one chocolate left in the box is the marzipan; shaving: 'Ah, you can't beat the cold steel and the badger. All that electrical rubbish – little wheels spinning around all over the place – for callow youths and peach-fluff – not for a man's beard. Razor blades for men!'; and then applying aftershave: 'Why I put that stuff on I do not know. Fancy paying good money for stuff that hurts you!'; announcing that 'to waste one second of one's life is a betrayal of one's self' and instantly tuning in to a television western in preference to the intellectual stimulation of Professor Bronowski.

Amid this brilliant testimonial to Hancock's comic philosophy what slight semblance of a plot does exist – the tenuous thread of telephone invitation to party from anonymous girl, preening in preparation for the event, reversal of invitation when her original partner does arrive – seems unnecessary, if not entirely irrelevant. It was not essential to be told so blatantly that Hancock was the 'middle' – if not physically the little – man, so anxious to be 'in', trying to keep pace with an increasingly formidable world, yet fated to remain on the outside for ever. As such he represented something in all of us, his comedy a mirror of the fears and foibles, the bewilderment and frustration of the new working-cum-middle class of the 'You've never had it so good' era. Partly defiant and aggressive, partly overwhelmed, his own rebellion against a hostile environment epitomised by advertising and the mass media, local rivalries and snide officialdom, struck a common chord because it was so petty and therefore believable – our own pathetic thoughts articulated; because his crusade was always so pompously, and therefore honestly, self-centred; because the hack philosophy with which he retaliated was so peppered with inaccuracies.

Tony at the start of his career

In Hancock the comedy of recognition reached its peak. He had a bloodhound's scent for the clichés of our existence, however slight and trivial they may have been. He could raise laughter with the mere mention of an 'individual fruit flan' or the plastic soldier he was anxious to find in the cereal packet, while only hours before members of that same audience had been purchasing such items with thoughts of laughter far from their minds. But the following breakfast time, the next visit to the supermarket, the remark would again ring true with the viewer and produce a second, even greater laughter response. When Hancock applies as a blood donor: 'I've come in answer to your advert on the wall next to the Eagle Laundry in Pelham Road. There's a Red Cross lady with a moustache and beard – pencilled in, of course – next to "Chamberlain must go", just above the cricket stumps;' or later assesses his contribution to charity: 'It's all in my diary. Congo Relief – two and six. Self Denial Week – one and eight. Lifeboat Day – sixpence. Arab Refugees – one and two. Yes, it's all down here. My conscience is cleared. And when I'm finally called by the Great Architect and they say "What did you do?" I shall just bring my book out and I shall say, "Here you are, mate! Add that lot up!"' he invests the event with a depth of detail common to all his best work, detail in itself often mundane, but which because so close, true, identifiable, assumes a brilliant comic piquancy on those lugubrious lips. The same comedy of recognition was even apparent in his invented middle names Aloysius St. John and mythical address 23 Railway Cuttings, East Cheam, both destined to become shorthand references for the shabbiest genteelism, giving themselves away the very first time they were heard.

The popularity of his characterisation was especially due to the scope it gave the audience for self-identification. 'The lad himself' was not, in fact, particularly likeable or sympathetic, but the embodiment of all those failings we detest in ourselves. Hancock was short of none of them. He bubbled over with his own self-importance, was stubborn and petulant, volatile and ignorant. Nowhere were all his faults better emphasised than in the famous blood donor sketch. By this time Hancock had discarded the astrakhan collar, overlong black overcoat and Homburg hat, sartorial symbols of the grandeur of the actor's profession that he so accurately guyed. But if his extra-long periods of resting had now dispelled any hopes of ever being elevated by the honours system to the ranks of 'Sir Laurence Olibrier, Sir Ralph Richardson, Sir John Gingold, and that mob', he was as convinced as ever of his own special place in the order of things. When told that his blood group is 'AB negative – rhesus positive – one of the rarest groups there is', he replies, 'Rare eh? Of course I'm not surprised. I've always felt instinctively that I was somehow distinctive from the rest of the herd, you know. Something apart. I never fitted into society. That explains it. One of nature's aristocrats.' Racist as well as class-conscious – 'one hundred per cent Anglo-Saxon with perhaps just a dash of Viking, but nothing else has crept in' – he is indignant at the thought that his blood should be given to anyone beneath the rank of baronet. Asked whether he has given blood before, he contrives the true braggart's licence to reminisce about his wartime experiences.

> Given, no. Spilt, yes. Yes, there's a good few drops lying about on the battlefields of Europe. Are you familiar with the Ardennes? I well remember von Rundstedt's last push. Tiger Harrison and myself, being in a forward position, were cut off behind the enemy line. 'Captain Harrison,' I said. 'Yes, sir,' he said. 'Jerry's overlooked us,' I said. 'Where shall we head for?' 'Berlin,' he said. 'Right,' I said, 'and the last one in the Reichstag's a cissy!'

Hattie Jacques as his formidable secretary, Miss Pugh, had more feasibly summed up his wartime experiences in an earlier radio show: 'He joined the Pioneer Corps in 1939, deserted after three days and hid in a cave on the Yorkshire Moors for six years.' Not that Hancock needed others to give him away. For all his Napoleonic ambition, social ideals and cultural aspirations, he always fell short of total accomplishment. Lines like 'I'll be a missionary, I think. Help the underprivileged people of the world. Hear it pays quite well too' and '"This is a far, far better thing I do now than I have ever done" – Rembrandt' bring him clearly to mind. Or Hancock lighting a cigarette, announcing in a deep voice, 'Dreadnoughts – for men. Get the girl of your choice with a Dreadnought,' then in his normal accent, 'Two and seven for twenty,' yet spluttering before he can get the last words out. His turgid, cliché-ridden, but often ornate speech would suddenly give way to the uncouth if more honest slang of 'hooter', 'bird', 'bonkers', 'Stone me!' It all happened in a way inevitable with someone who wanted the whole world and yet had no means of achieving it except on the cheap.

SYDNEY HOWARD

Ray Galton and Alan Simpson described the persona for which they were so largely responsible as that of a 'shrewd, cunning, high-powered mug'. And yet for all his cunning, his extreme suspicion of life around him, he was never free from self-deception, a trait of which one was constantly reminded during his palmier days by the presence of Sid James, ever ready to involve 'the lad' in some shady scheme and invariably succeeding, whatever Hancock's initial doubts. What Hancock did possess in his favour was an intense vulnerability, which, in the tradition of his idol W. C. Fields, he never allowed at any time to lapse into pathos. More determinedly than any British comedian of his time he sounded the death knell to the theory that pathos was an indispensable part of the clown's equipment. There were many comedians who inspired Hancock in his early years, not least Sid Field, Jimmy James and Sydney Howard (1883–1946), a musical comedy star of rotund build, rotund speech and his own moments of comic mournfulness. However, it is with W. C. Fields that the parallel appears most marked, at times even haunting. It was not merely that both flaunted a persona that represented a composite of all human weakness. The arrogant rejection of all sentiment whatever disasters and frustrations fell across his path, the weary, exasperated tones that could turn the most mundane line into the humorous quote of the year, the pathetic decline behind the scenes in which alcohol became at once soul-saver and life-destroyer, are all foreshadowed in the Fields story with alarming accuracy.

Although a hatred for children as abrasive as that espoused by Fields was never allowed to develop in Hancock, the seeds of what could have grown to equally monstrous proportions were clearly visible in his first success, namely as the supercilious tutor of Archie Andrews in the *Educating Archie* radio show, that stepping-stone to fame for many great comedians. But whereas Secombe, Bygraves and Hill projected satisfaction and friendship in their association with the wooden schoolboy, Hancock's conviction that the job was beneath him, his indignant catchphrase 'Flippin' kids!', the frequency with which the precocious dummy gained the upper hand over his wheedling superior, immediately cast him in the Fields mould. Hancock could not fail to have been aware of the parallels with his hero. While Hancock's place in the Brough and Archie circus had given him his first big break, Fields had been grateful to their earlier American counterparts, ventriloquist Edgar Bergen and principal dummy Charlie McCarthy, for an equally vital second chance. When the career of the great Hollywood character sank into a trough of ill health, despair and alcoholism in the latter part of the 1930s, it was the Bergen radio show that gave him a new lease of professional life, the series developing a feud between Fields and McCarthy that would extend into film work with *You Can't Cheat an Honest Man* in 1939. The Hancock – Archie relationship never crossed over into the cinema, but it is significant that in that soul-searching solo performance alone in his Earls Court bedsit Hancock, or at least Galton and Simpson on his behalf, found time to refer back to those early years. Clenching his teeth before a mirror he ponders his own ventriloquial ability: "'Hello, Brough.' 'Hello, Archie.' 'You're going gack in the gox.' 'I'm not going gack in the gox.'" Swivelling his head back and forth, Hancock might have had Brough's arm up his back as he speeded through the alphabet in time-honoured fashion. Only the glass of water is missing. It is a touching moment in a moving show, but, in the way Fields would have wished, never pathetic in the sense of evoking pathos.

In an earlier radio half-hour Hancock had enjoyed an even greater opportunity to display his remarkable gift for carrying on conversations with imaginary people. The recent recipient of threatening letters, he has barricaded himself into his home. Footsteps sound up the path. They stop. Hancock will bluff whoever it is.

All right, men. Aim the machine gun on the door. You fifteen men get ready to pounce on him. Have you got the hand grenades ready, Sergeant?
Yes, sir.
Corporal?
Sir.
Tear gas ready?
Yes, sir.
He's walking into a trap. He doesn't know it. Machine-gun crew, you all ready?
Yes, sir.
Ah, sir.
Yes, sir.
Ah.
Yes.
Ah.
Right men, he can't get away. If he's any sense, he'll go back to Durham while he's still got the chance. Have the battalion of paratroopers arrived yet, Sergeant?
They're hidden in the garden.
Stand by and the minute he comes in let him have it with all guns. (*Someone knocks at the door and Hancock gives up the pretence of make-believe*) I give in – don't come near me – don't touch me!

The speed of delivery and the constant vocal fluctuations were wholly convincing. But to those who knew of Fields' real-life trait of conducting loud conversations with imaginary bodyguards in bed at night to warn off the kidnappers he continually feared, the episode would have carried even greater conviction.

Above: with Peter Brough and Archie

At the beginning of the 50s *Educating Archie* represented the major breakthrough for the young Birmingham-born comedian whose career so far had embraced an amateur period decked out in check jacket, jaunty hat and co-respondent shoes as 'The Confidential Comic' in homage to idol Max Miller in concert party in Bournemouth, where the family moved when he was three and his father ran a theatrical hotel; a spell with Ralph Reader's RAF *Gang Show*, where he met up with Robert Moreton, later to become famous as the original tutor in *Educating Archie* with his mixed-up *Bumper Fun Book* approach to joke-telling and ironically as the victim of suicide in 1957 as his own career disintegrated; and in 1948 the almost de rigueur Windmill apprenticeship amid a niggardly run of small-time dates. The record-breaking touring version of *Educating Archie* enabled Hancock at last to play top theatres. To confirm that his career was in the ascendant came in quick succession the stage shows *London Laughs* and *Talk of the Town*, with Jimmy Edwards at the Adelphi in 1952 and 1954, not that Hancock, with his paranoia about long runs, was able to remain with either show for its duration. Also in 1954 the BBC launched the radio version of *Hancock's Half Hour*, the logical progression of an association with producer Dennis Main Wilson, who had already helped to steer Hancock through a principal comedianship in popular shows like *Calling All Forces* and *Star Bill*. The unprecedented successful translation to television of a radio series followed in 1956.

Although he became a master of situation comedy, and despite his abhorrence of long runs in the same theatre, Hancock never abandoned the stage act with which he served his apprentice years in variety. As his career waned he clung to this routine as his last hope, even though his television success meant that to many he never seemed as natural a performer on stage as he did in the studio. The act always ended with his classic, compressed, one-man version of the sportsmen featured so energetically behind the opening titles of the Gaumont British News, in later years a torturous metaphor for a far-from-athletic entertainer flinging himself into his own physical Armageddon. Less original were the impersonations of a whole gallery of Hollywood veterans, themselves either dead or passing out of fashion when Hancock entered show business, not least Edward Everett Horton, of the fussy manner and disapproving gaze, and George Arliss, Hollywood's monocled Disraeli prototype, introduced with mock indifference by Hancock later in his career as 'And now here's one for the teenagers.' Arliss had died in 1946, yet remained in Hancock's act until the end. But the mainstay of this repertoire was Charles Laughton, whether bellowing 'Mistah Christian' to an imaginary Clark Gable on the quarterdeck of *The Bounty,* or as a one-eye-whirling Hunchback of Notre Dame: 'I'm so UGLY, I'm so UGLY – shocking weather for humps!' As Quasimodo, Hancock would launch into a recitation of 'The Bells' ending with the cry 'Sanctuary! Sanctuary!' Then suddenly ceasing his clumsy histrionics-gone-mad, he would announce 'Sanctuary much!' and lurch off stage. Hancock's talent for eye-rolling also triggered the entry into this select company of Robert Newton in his scene-stealing role as Long John Silver. Hancock would hobble about one-legged on an imaginary crutch with the microphone for occasional support, his head tilted to one side to accommodate an imaginary parrot on his shoulder: 'How these storks keep this up all day, I'll never know.'

As 'Mr Rhythm' in a routine devised for him by Galton and Simpson he featured a parody of the Johnnie Ray type of American crooner who dominated the British variety scene as the 1940s became the 50s. The pale blue zoot suit, string tie and thick crepe soles originally worn for this characterisation later made way for a tight-fitting Italian suit and shoes, but the merciless way in which he guyed the squirming, saccharine style of the earlier period remained relevant. In a hybrid accent to which neither Birmingham nor America would wish to lay claim he would go into his introduction: 'Now, I'd like to sing you a little toon, a toon which we recorded over there and would like to bring over here from over there to over here, our latest record which didn't sell so many back in the States – because they didn't drill a hole in the middle of it!' This provided the cue for the band to launch into a fast-tempo version of 'Knees up Mother Brown'. At intervals he would break out of the American persona with a remark like 'How they do an hour and a half at the Palladium in shoes like these, I'll never know... I've got toes like globe artichokes.' Always, with Hancock, dignity ended at the ankles. Nor was the act without its physical challenges, as he jumped in the air and brought his feet together scissors-fashion. 'Oh, it's ridiculous. A man of my build and calibre, leaping about like a porpoise, spending half me life three feet off the ground. I think I'll get myself a violin and a few jokes.' In Hancock-speak, of course, calibre was always pronounced with the stress on the middle syllable. Also penned by Galton and Simpson was the sketch in which he played a budgerigar in a cage, complaining about its treatment by its owner. 'Stuck here all day with nothing to eat. Haven't had a decent piece of millet since last Thursday! Although cumbersome to stage with the birdcage needing to be constructed to human size, it was effective enough for Hancock to feature in his second and last appearance in a Royal Variety Performance in November 1958; the first had been in 1952.

Tony and Sid at 23 Railway Cuttings, East Cheam

Towards the end of his career few members of his audience were in a position to measure the accuracy of his impressions. But theatre critics who found his act jaded and out of date because of this would appear to have been out of step with the essential Hancock character as built up by radio and television. Because he never appeared on a theatre stage in a set depicting 23 Railway Cuttings and only very seldom wearing the Homburg hat and astrakhan coat, many seemed unable to accept his stage performance within the context of his television characterisation. And yet if one did this, everything fell into place. As J. B. Priestley commented, 'He was not a routine comedian doing an act, but another kind of comedian despairing of an act.' It would have been a flaw in his popular persona to have updated the ancient repertoire of impersonations, let alone to have insisted on accuracy in them; to have continued singing 'There's no business like show business' when convinced that he 'can't go on with this load of rubbish'; to have achieved an Astaire-like proficiency in his attempted dance routine; to have treated his audience with the charm and bonhomie exercised by his flourishing contemporaries. This was 'the lad himself', frustrated pretender and buffoon, on view in all his incompetence and pigheadedness. By the end of his life, however, he had jettisoned all those features that had given flesh and blood to this characterisation. Admittedly he had proved that he could convince without the stalwarts of his radio show: Bill Kerr, the inarticulate colonial cousin from the Australian outback; Hattie Jacques as his curt and mountainous secretary; Kenneth Williams, East Cheam's multi-faceted figure of authority

From top to bottom:
Sidney James, Tony,
Bill Kerr and
Kenneth Williams

with the braying nasal tones that gave 'Good evening' and 'Stop messing about' a snideness they would not convey in normal conversation. He even acquitted himself, although less comfortably, without his major sidekick, Sidney James, whose brilliantly crass aggressive cynicism added its own distinction to both the radio and television shows until the end of Hancock's penultimate television series for the BBC in May 1960. But, although the exact circumstances of their separation are open to varying interpretation, it was his rejection of Ray Galton and Alan Simpson in 1963, ostensibly in a dispute over film scripts, that led most conclusively to what has been interpreted as professional suicide. In their association Ray and Alan had provided him with over 160 scripts of the highest quality for both broadcasting media, as well as the screenplay of his first major feature film, *The Rebel*.

With Hancock's real-life character as their raw material they provided the exquisite detail of dialogue, comic business and characterisation that produced the most expansively idiosyncratic of British comic heroes. Fellow scriptwriter Denis Norden put their achievement in a nutshell when he declared they had written not a succession of scripts but a novel, so fully rounded was the character they defined and refined over seven momentous years. Perhaps feeling that his reputation leaned too heavily on their talent, Hancock had become obsessed with thoughts of international star status, a status at odds with the parochial domesticity of East Cheam or Earls Court; with the constant desire to regard each new venture as a development in style; with the gnawing conviction that he must do it all alone. J. B. Priestley likened him to a man in a leaky lifeboat throwing away one pair of oars after another. But as ambition bred independence, so it became all the more evident that he still needed scriptwriters and acting support, not to mention agent and producer. Sadly he came to lose the loyalty – if not the professional admiration, even affection – of those who had already revealed their own pre-eminence in the restricted field of working with him. Hancock was acting out a tragedy in the precise Shakespearean sense of the word, his rejection of his original success leading by way of initial isolation, double divorce, alcoholism, covered-up breakdowns, excessive pill-taking to his self-destruction, first professionally, then physically, an end made to appear even more brutal, more degrading by the trail of petty scandal it left behind and by the fact that it took place unnoticed in some inconspicuous Sydney basement-flat, far away on the other side of the globe while attempting a comeback on Australian television, which on the evidence of what was recorded would have been beyond hope. His death on 24 June 1968, caused by an overdose of amylo-barbitone washed down by an excessive quantity of vodka, came only three days after the granting of a decree nisi to his second wife. Possibly the discovery that he would not be welcomed back by his first wife, whose love was still of the greatest importance to him, triggered the fatal decision. A note left for his producer to be conveyed to his mother argued, 'This is quite rational… things seemed to go wrong too many times.'

In 1960 at the height of his career, in a line of subjects that embraced figures of the intelligentsia as notable as Bertrand Russell, Edith Sitwell and Carl Jung, Hancock was interviewed by John Freeman on the television programme *Face to Face*. Among the surgically incisive questions posed by the later British ambassador to the United States – which revealed obliquely that for Hancock comedy represented a one-man face-to-face experience, the distorted mirror in which were revealed our true selves and certainly not least those human characteristics one despised, even feared – were the seemingly innocuous 'Are you happy?' and 'Would you want to change your life?' Hancock replied, 'The only happiness I could achieve is to perfect the talent I have, however small it may be… If the time came when I found that I had come to the end of what I could develop out of my own ability, I wouldn't want to do it any more.' Caught in the snare of his own perfectionism whereby each subsequent project had to be impossibly bigger, funnier, better; jealous of other people's success; unable to help himself when isolated, he had presumably in a moment of despair reached the point where he could see nothing ahead but further decline. Certainly his early death enhanced his fame, guaranteed that he would be remembered for the great achievements of his relatively short career. Had he lived, it is doubtful whether he would have regained his previous sense of timing, essential memory power, brilliant facial control, all of which eroded during his latter years. Alcohol had reduced devoted professionalism to slipshod indifference. It is painful to think that he might have faded into the type of oblivion he himself had pondered in the final television script Galton and Simpson wrote for him.

What have you achieved? What *have* you achieved? You lost your chance, me old son. You contributed absolutely nothing to this life. A waste of time you being here at all. No plaque for you in Westminster Abbey. The best you can expect is a few daffodils in a jam jar, a rough-hewn stone bearing the legend 'He came and he went' and in between – nothing! Nobody will even notice you're not here. After about a year afterwards somebody might say down the pub, 'Where's old Hancock? I haven't seen him around lately.' 'Oh, he's dead, you know.' 'Oh, is he?' A right *raison d'être* that is! Nobody will ever know I existed. Nothing to leave behind me. Nothing to pass on. Nobody to mourn me. That's the bitterest blow of all.

It sounded funny at the time.

Hancock had betrayed the love of a public. Having gained admission to the ranks of comic heroes, he lacked a full understanding of the main qualification needed to stay in that company. It has little to do with art or ambition; it simply demands a readiness to be seen over and over again in the same situations wearing the same mask, a fixed quality with which Hancock could never be content. Part of the symbolism of the theatrical term star is that the heavenly kind do on the face of it remain unchanging. Having gained the love of the British public, he craved that of the world. But in trying to achieve it, the original goodwill gradually slipped through his fingers, his persona now drab and conventional, the world of his later television series – for ITV and Australia – synthetic and largely alien to his talent. Perhaps sensing that in real life he was beginning to attract the pathos he refused to let into his act, he took what he saw as the only way out. It was an exit most poignantly described by Spike Milligan, another clown who once found himself on the brink of self-destruction but had the courage and humility to fight back: 'One by one he shut the door on all the people he knew; then he shut the door on himself.' This was the one episode he played out that did embody a meaning applicable far beyond the limits of downtrodden suburbia. He had locked himself out, and neither Sid James nor Galton and Simpson were at his side with a spare key in their illegal possession.

AFTERTHOUGHTS

It was never my intention to underplay Hancock's effectiveness as a stage performer in the prime of his life and career, a thought that occurred to me when I revisited this chapter while writing my biography of the comedian in 2008. Dennis Main Wilson summed up the impact Hancock made on him in the early days at the Adelphi: 'He had this incredible presence on stage – you could stand at the back of the stalls looking down on thousands of people and literally see rows of shoulders rocking with laughter.

I've never seen anything like it.' Not that I needed telling. If Norman Wisdom was the first great funny man I ever met, Hancock was the first I ever saw live, on my inaugural visit to a variety show when the *Educating Archie* tour came to the Southampton Gaumont Theatre in November 1951. I was less than two months short of my seventh birthday, but I can still recall the acts on the bill in vivid detail, not least the solo turn delivered by Archie's tutor of the day.

Tony the visual comedian...

... and as 'Mr Rhythm'

As a *visual* comedian he excelled – a quality that makes his success in radio all the more remarkable – and my memory of the occasion is dominated by two physical routines, one of which, as we have seen, survived in his act until the close, by which time he was happy to acknowledge its antiquity as 'a piece of material I wrote just after the First World War. Ladies and gentlemen, I give you the Gaumont British News.' His all-round sporting prowess at school would have stood him in good stead for what must remain one of the most strenuous routines ever attempted in the name of comedy, although it was never easy to equate Hancock with the high energy level required to bring off this and much else in his act. Beginning with his take on the bulbous town crier bellowing 'Oyez' as he swung his bell up and down in the centre of the cinema picture, he then flung himself into an impressionistic one-man montage of the kaleidoscopic images of the sporting world that appeared in the four corners of the screen around him. Rowing, throwing, boxing, bowling, riding, driving, kicking, leaping, Hancock hurled himself around the stage in a physical maelstrom of activity, finishing with four well orchestrated dives to the floor press-up fashion. He claimed it kept him in the pink of condition. Apart from wondering how he never came to harm himself, I have tried many times to get inside the psyche essential for pulling off so demanding a piece of business night after night, the comedic equivalent, I imagine, of facing the diving board or the penalty shoot-out. In the early days he did wear padding to protect himself, but when this proved ineffective he engaged a trained acrobat to teach him how to fall without hurting. As the years progressed, the routine did become shorter, the dives to the ground fewer, but it must never lose its place in the top rank of Hancock moments.

My recall of the other routine is far sketchier – he never clung to it as possessively as he did the newsreel act – but it too conjures up an image of Hancock as a source of nearly inhuman energy. Fortunately we still have the lyric of the song he sang to accompany his actions. It was called 'The mechanical man' and featured Hancock's far from satisfactory experiences as a factory hand.

> I clocked in in the morning, feeling more dead than alive,
> And the foreman said, 'Now, Spurgeon, you must help the export drive.
> You'll operate this here machine from six o'clock till five.
> Get cracking – no slacking – or I'll know the reason why.'
> So I started – bing – bang – bong – bing…
> This went on to ten o'clock when we had a break for tea.
> Bing – bang – bong – bing…
> On again till four o'clock and then we had a change and went
> Bang – bong – bing – bang…

Maintaining a hangdog seriousness throughout, each time he returns to the workplace he is assigned to a different, more demanding machine; each time the jerky movements that accompany the spoken sound effects become even more frantic, spreading from hand to arm to leg to the point where his whole body is in spasmodic overdrive. Eventually he can take no more.

> They took me away on the Thursday
> Shaking in all of my joints,
> But I'm sure once again,
> Except when on a train
> It goes rattling over the joints and I go… (*Sound effects and actions*)
> So if when you're travelling you happen to see
> …(*More sound effects and actions*)… it'll be me.

As he put words to the pictures for a radio audience in May 1952, commentator Brian Johnston made the observation that the result of all his stiff and jerky movements was to make Hancock resemble 'a wound-up clockwork toy'.

Sadly no recording of Hancock's 'Mechanical man' appears to exist in any medium. To appreciate his gift for mime one has to turn to those special moments in the television shows when Galton and Simpson acknowledged that he possessed visual skills that transcended even his basic body language and talent for facial expression. The classic sequence takes place in a library where the enforced silence dictates that Hancock has to mime the entire plot, playing all the characters of a detective novel for the benefit of Sid James. This tour de force conjures up the passion between buxom girl and broad-shouldered guy, the sudden intrusion of her husband, the ensuing struggle, the firing of the bullet that kills the lover, the death scene, the sadistic pleasure of the killer, the pleading of the girl, a further struggle, another death scene as the girl is killed by accident, the remorse of the husband, his attempt to revive her, the interception of the police, the submission to handcuffs, the judge in session, the donning of the black cap and the final macabre touch as Hancock grabs the back of his collar to signify the hanging. At this moment he is spotted by the librarian, played by Hugh Lloyd, and his own embarrassment brings the curtain down on the scenario. The sudden mercurial changes he effects between each stage of the narrative are dazzling to observe. In variety's heyday an expanded version of just one such routine would have kept an old-fashioned trouper on the boards for years.

I last saw Hancock live on the occasion of his London Palladium season in *Swing Along* in 1963, when as a gesture to impresario Billy Marsh he stepped into the shoes of the sick Arthur Haynes for eight weeks. The newsreel sequence was still to the fore, even if his 'Mechanical man' had been assigned to a scrap-metal yard of comedy fragments. Among the impressions of Hollywood's yesteryear and the attempt to define himself as Britain's answer to Sammy Davis Junior was his Shakespearean masterstroke, which as late as 1967 he described as one of his two favourite routines, the other being the newsreel pastiche. 'I shall kick off with Richard III and go straight through the book,' Hancock would rant, 'all four thousand pages... Richard III... who, as you know, was a hunchback... fortunately for me!' Here Hancock would buckle his leg and shift his bulk out of kilter to suggest – not for the first time in his act – a hump on his shoulder. With hardly a moment to spare for 'the winter of his discontent made glorious summer', he would head straight for Henry V. With a hop, skip and a jump to the microphone, nothing could stop him. 'In peace there's nothing so becomes a man as modest stillness and humility. Stillness or humility or not to be? *That*... is the question. Whether 'tis nobler in the mind to suffer the slings (*He mimes a sling*) and arrows (*And fires an invisible arrow*) of outraaaageous (*With outrageous stress on the middle syllable*) fortune or to take arms (*He spreads his arms*) against a sea (*He dances a hornpipe*) of troubles (*He breaks into giggles*)... It's a game, innit?' The 'outrageous' line was one of the very few times he hit a note of campness in his performance – it lasted no longer than the middle syllable itself.

The sequence proved one of the highlights of his season as compère on *The Blackpool Show* for ITV in 1966, arguably his last credible exposure on the medium, but by then his private life had become a tabloid disaster area and it was difficult to cut through the debris to fully appreciate the magic that he could still convey. Nothing however should be allowed to stand in the way of the success of *Hancock's Half Hour*. When it switched to television, Friday night became Hancock night, still possibly the most garlanded show of its kind, gathering audiences the size of which the BBC will never attain again.

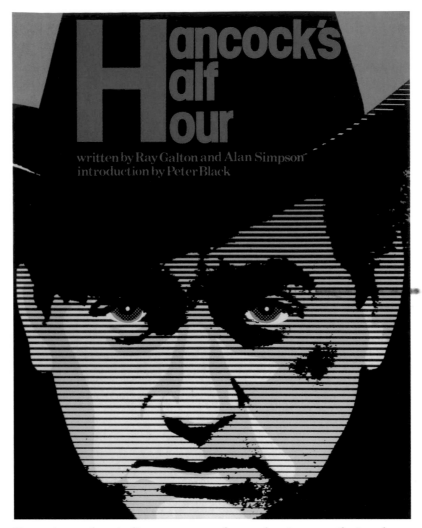

Deserving a place in literature: one of several script compilations by Galton and Simpson

We should remind ourselves that the tragedy that befell Tony Hancock clouded the last few years of a twenty-one-year career, during the larger part of which he enjoyed immense fame as a household name as an entertainer in the country of his birth. His influence – with an assist from Galton and Simpson – was prodigious. At the risk of repetition, without Hancock there would have been no Steptoe, no Alf Garnett, no Alan Partridge, no David Brent. But his greatest achievement was summed up by scriptwriter Denis Norden when he said, 'For a comedian to leave behind that kind of echo of remembered laughter – it is hard to think of his life as a complete tragedy.' Few comedians have affected the lives of their public in the way Hancock did. Even today, more than forty years after his death, it is impossible for people who were there at the time to realise they have forgotten to cancel the newspapers, to endure the agonies of the common cold, to be bored senseless on a Sunday afternoon, to get stuck in a lift, to give blood without enjoying again the bonus of the laughter he created.

Tony: How much do you want then?

Doctor: Well a pint, of course.

Tony: A pint? Have you gone raving mad? You must be joking.

Doctor: A pint is a perfectly normal quantity to take.

Tony: You don't seriously expect me to believe that. I mean, I came in here in all good faith to help me country. I don't mind giving a reasonable amount, but a pint – that's very nearly an armful. I'm sorry. I'm not walking around with an empty arm for anybody!

It is a paradox that one to whom life became unbearable should continue to make life bearable for others. As such he more than qualifies as a hero.

Tony as his friends remember him

Harry Secombe: The Golden-Voiced Goon

Anyone who, for twenty-five years, has built a career on such tenuous foundations as a high-pitched giggle, a raspberry and a sprinkling of top Cs needs all the friends he can get!

My voice is not so much bel canto as can belto!

In the 1960s the variety veteran Tessie O'Shea was fêted on Broadway as 'London's own' singer of music hall songs. The irony was that she had been born in Cardiff and achieved her greatest success on the variety stage at Blackpool. One could as easily have made the same mistake about that Humpty Dumpty of a clown Harry Secombe. He was born, the son of a commercial traveller, in Swansea on 8 September 1921, and yet while exploiting his Welshness assumed a distinctly English image, almost that of a John Bull of comedy, his big, broad, instantly likeable personality as consistent with the heyday of the Victorian music hall as with his native valleys. His famous tenor voice came to project 'Rose of England' as loyally as 'We'll keep a welcome'. In return the English appear to have adopted a Welshman as their mascot, the personification of that romanticised idea of a national heritage – Dickensian style.

Secombe represented another comic talent nurtured in service life and released in the explosion of clowns that was an aftermath of the Second World War. His first civilian sketch has become almost legendary: the shaving routine with its frenzied lathered impressions of the absent-minded shaver, the nervous shaver, and so on. He recalled in later years how he devised the sequence in Italy for army concert party.

> I was desperate to think of something to do; you had to do something new each week or you got booted back into action again and I didn't fancy that. It was cold out there!… I did a small boy shaving with his father's razor and then a man shaving in a bucket of ice-cold water at four o'clock in the morning with a blunt blade, and a man who got embarrassed when people watched him shaving. I finished up by drinking the shaving water, which wasn't very good for my heartburn!

The act accompanied him into civilian life and was still scoring laughs for Harry near the end of his days. Notorious, however, was one engagement at Bolton circa 1947 when the embryonic star was confronted by the theatre manager. 'You're not shaving in my bloody time – here's your money!' Irrepressible as ever Harry sent a telegram to Michael Bentine. It read, 'Audience with me all the way. Managed to shake them off at the station!'

Equally important to his act was the routine in which he performed a duet between Hollywood favourites Nelson Eddy and Jeannette MacDonald singing 'Sweethearts', switching between the tenor of one and the falsetto of the other accordingly: 'SWEETHEART… Sweetheart.' When they had to sing together he

The infamous shaving act

segued to a high-pitched yodel. Along the way an altercation broke out between the star-crossed lovers, the line 'When we were lovers in June' prompting the diva to suggest it might have been May. The sequence ended with someone getting a finger in the eye and the almost inevitable trademark raspberry. Occasionally Secombe would include a Stanley Holloway monologue or an impression of Stainless Stephen with his spoken punctuation or of Sandy Powell asking 'Can you hear me, mother!' At the end of 1946 he passed the almost foregone conclusion of a Windmill audition. It is alleged that impresario Vivian Van Damm forbade the raspberry, which Harry skilfully used to pre-empt the audience's displeasure at a joke; within a few days Van Damm had reversed his prohibition, acknowledging that it did add a certain gusto to the Secombe performance. However, Harry's most decisive steps to fame were provided a few years later by three separate radio series: *Welsh Rarebit*, broadcast from the BBC's Cardiff studios, a showcase for Welsh talent such as Ossie Morris, Gladys Morgan and Stan Stennett, *Educating Archie*, in which he replaced Hancock as the tutor, and the show listlessly misread on air in the BBC schedules by some staid Reithian figure as 'The Go On Show'! Even more ominously he then went on to misconstrue the corrected 'Goon' as 'Coon'. From 1952 to 1954 the latter two shows ran simultaneously in Harry's schedule. While *Educating Archie* meant contending for laughs with a ventriloquist's dummy, *The Goon Show* began by presenting the far more exacting challenge provided by three equally erratic comic talents.

Ex-trad trumpeter Spike Milligan (1918 – 2002) first met Secombe in North Africa during military service in 1943 – a howitzer fired inexpertly by Spike in Harry's direction effected the introduction – and has been likened to a combination of Gandhi and Groucho Marx. The analogy provides a clue both to the freewheeling comic inventiveness of his double-edged career as performer and writer (all the Goon scripts were Spike's work, often in collaboration with Larry Stephens, and later with occasional support from Eric Sykes, who stepped in to help his friend when the pressure got too much) and to his genuine, tormented concern for mankind. Born in India, he would become the most humane and influential humorist of his generation, brilliant at extending the anarchic surrealism of his creative fantasy into the non-theatric arena of both his public and private life. Peter Sellers (1925 – 1980), introduced to Spike by Harry in 1949, was the brilliant ex-drummer variety impressionist ('Speaking for the Stars') who had had the nerve to recommend himself to producer Roy Speer for his first radio broadcast in the telephone-disguised voices of Richard Murdoch and Kenneth Horne. Later the nerve would give way to subtlety as he proved himself the cinema's most versatile character comedian.

Harry, Michael, Peter and Spike raise the opticians' toast

Also present at that meeting was Michael Bentine (1922 – 1996), the odd man out among these odd men out. Born in Watford, the son of a Peruvian scientist, educated at Eton with an accent to match, he already by the time of the first *Goon Show* in May 1951 had an appearance in the 1949 Royal Variety Performance to his credit. Bearded, mop-haired and billed in those days as 'The Happy Imbecile', he presented an act with a broken chair back that took on a myriad of unexpected uses as machine gun, axe, flag, key, pneumatic drill, handcuffs, cow's udders, plough, comb and harp as he rattled through an excited panegyric to the dying days of empire. In a similar routine a sink plunger enabled him to impersonate Long John Silver, the Statue of Liberty, a trolleybus and Paul Robeson. All this was entirely in contrast to a brief earlier spell as a Shakespearean actor. In 1952 Bentine broke away from the Goons after only two series to launch his Moomin-type characters, the Bumblies, on television, and would later – with *It's a Square World* in 1961 – come as close as anyone at that point to the successful translation of Goon humour into the visual medium, although all along he saw a fundamental difference between his own 'logical nonsense' and their 'nonsensical logic'.

Bentine with a chair back...

...and a sink plunger

It was auspicious that the ideas of four such diverse personalities should have been allowed to coalesce when they did. *The Goon Show* represented one of the most influential breakthroughs in British humour, even if few were aware of it at the time. The performers were too engrossed in their sheer enjoyment of the project, while BBC executives were more anxious to file the show away under its original title *Crazy People*, which, while at least more acceptable than their original suggestion *Junior Crazy Gang* (sic), would, one senses, have been conducive to inevitable obscurity. If one person should be accorded the honour of foresight in this direction, it is Jimmy Grafton, whose London pub in Strutton Ground first provided an amenable forum for their unconventional comedy ideas and who had financed and co-written with Spike the first pilot recording of a Goon-type show under the title *Sellers's Castle* – thanks to his inclusion in *Ray's a Laugh*, Sellers being by a margin the best known of the four at the time. Appointed by the quartet their official spokesman, KOGVOS (Keeper of Goons and Voice of Sanity), Grafton remained a guiding light in Secombe's career until his death in 1986.

The show was eventually named after a rubbery dim-witted abominable-snowman-type creature invented by the American cartoonist Elzie Segar for his *Popeye* cartoon series – along with Lear, Carroll, Leacock, Beachcomber, Rabelais, the Marx Brothers and W. C. Fields, one of many admitted influences on the young Milligan's extravagant comic vision. Simply because it was a radio show, free of sets, locations, all physical limitations, *The Goon Show* had much in common with the ethos of the conventional film cartoon of the 1930s and 40s, of the gaudy, exaggerative world of the comic strip, an atmosphere in which violence and pain become anaesthetised and in which characters may become utterly ruthless without becoming fascist, simply because the violence is not for real. *The Goon Show* was a violent show, achieving its effect through an explosive barrage of barrier-breaking sound effects rather than lurid technicolour and the graphic style of 'BAM', 'POW', 'ZAP', and by the compliant imagination of the listener rather than the surrealist scope of the draughtsman's pen. Certainly the show was a total embodiment of George Orwell's assertion, 'Whatever is funny is subversive,' subversive in this case not only of authority and the Establishment, dull routine and menial conformism, but of the whole machinery required to transmit a programme at all: 'This is the BBC. Hold it up to the light – not a brain in sight!' Not only did it seem they were making the show up as they went along, for their own obvious enjoyment as much as that of the listeners, but that with each step towards total anarchy the programme format itself, such as it was, would disintegrate. It is a disappointment that however close they came, this never happened, or, more accurately, was never allowed to do so.

Spike, Peter and Harry light up with leeks

The conservative British public was at first unable to keep up with the show's persistent near-nihilistic drive, but eventually its barbed anti-Establishment stance caught on, proving especially popular (over ten series between 28 May 1951 and 28 January 1960) among students and the young, a generation that included among its members the then malleable stalwarts of *Beyond the Fringe*, *I'm Sorry I'll Read That Again* and *Monty Python's Flying Circus*. The show provided an essential link between these later university-orientated performers and the variety theatre in which all four Goons had been reared but which only Secombe went on to dominate to any extent. Employing more than a sprinkling of service jargon, the show also consciously reflected the absurdity of national service at a time when defence was couched increasingly in nuclear terms. Painting coal black and polishing boot studs were pure Goonish activities, for all their pointless military reality. Binding the whole unwieldy structure together was a spontaneous sense of derision, innate in all four participants and not artificially applied by scriptwriters, an attitude derived from collective years of playing theatrical dumps in grimy provincial towns and now with a tinge of malicious pleasure used to uncover the absurd latent in all aspects of reality: 'Open the door and let's get the room in.'

A rare stage appearance by the trio

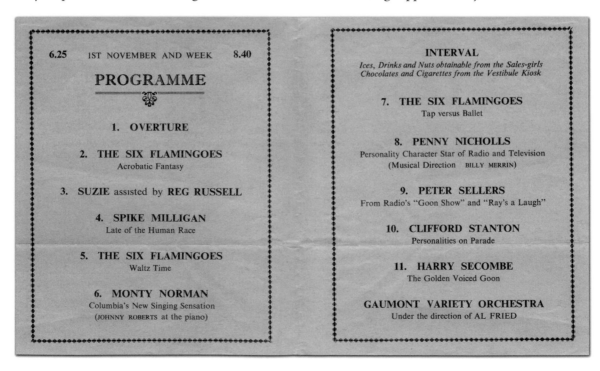

6.25 1ST NOVEMBER AND WEEK 8.40	INTERVAL
PROGRAMME	*Ices, Drinks and Nuts obtainable from the Sales-girls Chocolates and Cigarettes from the Vestibule Kiosk*
1. OVERTURE	**7. THE SIX FLAMINGOES**
	Tap versus Ballet
2. THE SIX FLAMINGOES	**8. PENNY NICHOLLS**
Acrobatic Fantasy	Personality Character Star of Radio and Television
3. SUZIE assisted by **REG RUSSELL**	(Musical Direction BILLY MERRIN)
4. SPIKE MILLIGAN	**9. PETER SELLERS**
Late of the Human Race	From Radio's "Goon Show" and "Ray's a Laugh"
5. THE SIX FLAMINGOES	**10. CLIFFORD STANTON**
Waltz Time	Personalities on Parade
6. MONTY NORMAN	**11. HARRY SECOMBE**
Columbia's New Singing Sensation	The Golden Voiced Goon
(JOHNNY ROBERTS at the piano)	**GAUMONT VARIETY ORCHESTRA**
	Under the direction of AL FRIED

The Goon world of flamboyant misrule was a world most readily conjured up by its inhabitants, a bizarre mixture of upper-crust snobs and subhuman simpletons. Sellers provided the voices of the suave patronising Hercules Grytpype-Thynne; the oppressive Major Dennis Bloodnok, decorated for emptying dustbins in battle and of the same Anglo-Indian line as Colonel Blimp; the vocally myopic Bluebottle, given to mouthing his own stage directions; the niggardly Henry Crun and much, much more. Milligan brought to life the Machiavellian Count Moriarty; twittering Minnie Banister; the lugubriously demented Eccles and the will-of-the-wispish Little Jim ('He's fall-en in the wa-ter!'). The central character of Neddie Seagoon was played by Secombe. Their combined voices, through an impression of startling originality, inveigled their way into the subconsciousness of the whole country, and yet, as the journalist and broadcaster Richard Mayne explained in a 1970 *Listener* article, not a few of them had extraneous roots. Eccles was reminiscent of Edgar Bergen's second-string dummy, the country-yokel Mortimer Snerd; Bluebottle recalled the incoherent Horace of Harry Hemsley's 'radio family'; Grytpype-Thynne suggested a cut-price George Sanders. Minnie Banister possessed a tenuous link with Arthur Lucan's Old Mother Riley; Bloodnok with Jack Train's Colonel Chinstrap; Moriarty with the villain of many a radio serial. Even Henry Crun evoked echoes of the inventor-cum-magician of the Children's Hour favourite *Toytown*. Presumably the cohesion of so many varying accents made them sound fresh or, to quote Mayne, like 'a squealing wriggle of eels' as they writhed from one burst of nonsense to the next.

The programme also gave occasional clues to the appearance of its characters. One recalls the classic description of Bluebottle as a 'trilby with legs' and exotic lines like 'Take your tongue off my boots.' It was, however, predominantly the schizoid vocal distortions of Sellers and Milligan alongside Seagoon with his screeching tenor and 'rough Welsh' that marked them out as grotesque. Physically they were as grotesque as one could imagine them to be. The more the imagination ran riot, not only did they become more hysterically funny, but they carried to the limit the whole idea of anarchy-by-proxy, of hunchback-as-jester, their very deformity allowing them special outrageous and destructive privileges on our behalf. But however close *The Goon Show* came to being a radio freak show, there was never any doubt that the grotesques were living, feeling creatures, capable of pain, joy and often clearly defined relationships between each other, innocent in so far as being impervious to the surrealism of the situation in which they were set. More importantly, however, they represented the masks of entertainers, and as such contradicted the quote from Mencken summoned by cinema authority Allen Eyles in his appraisal of the Marx Brothers: 'The liberation of the human mind has never been furthered by dunderheads; it has been furthered by gay fellows who heaved dead cats into sanctuaries and then went roistering down the highways of the world, proving to all men that doubt, after all, was safe.' Eccles and company were not only 'gay fellows' but also archetypal 'dunderheads', and, as the latter, furthered considerably if unconsciously that 'liberation of the human mind' Mencken deemed impossible for their kind. Moreover, when one conjures up an image of Goons 'heaving dead cats into sanctuaries', there seems no group more apt for the task.

If they had been required to undertake this bizarre task, there is no doubt that like all their lunatic adventures it would have been shrouded in the type of comic secrecy associated with Gunpowder Plot caricature. Of the many erratic exploits conducted in such an atmosphere one recalls the ascent of Mount Everest from the inside; the transportation, complete with inmates, of Dartmoor prison to the south of France, a cardboard replica being left in its place; the sabotage of a haddock-stretching factory behind the Iron Curtain; the aftermath of the Last Tram of London ceremony, driver and vehicle, still waiting for their official send-off, discovered in the Kingsway tunnel two and a half years later (needless to say Eccles is a passenger); smuggling dynamite into the boots of the Hungarian football team. Theirs was a world where unearthed skulls and shirt-tails explode and trains get diverted from the Elephant and Castle to the middle of the Sahara. All this was acted out against a battleground of offbeat sound effects and reactions typified by the volcanic eruptions of Major Bloodnok's curry, the often repeated chant of 'Rhubarb!' and the occasion when Seagoon knocked at the door of the Teahouse of the Auguste Goon '6,000 times' (about 125 on recording) before being told he wanted the house next door. 'It's always next door in China!' There was the occasion a bewildered Henry Crun, disturbed by footsteps pounding down some thirty flights of stairs, casually reflected, 'Funny – we live in a bungalow!' Seagoon decides to join the navy to win back his self-respect and the listener is treated to at least thirty seconds of a rousing orchestral treatment of 'Rule Britannia' followed by Neddie's rejoinder 'No. I'll join the army; it's too damn noisy in the navy!' On another occasion one heard a speechless forty-five-second montage of resounding footsteps, clanking chains, slamming doors while Neddie went and performed a special request for Grytpype-Thynne; eventually he returns exhausted. 'What was it you asked for?' And if sounds were mostly irrelevant to what plot existed, both were irrelevant to the third memorable factor of a Goon script, those fashionable exchanges, smacking of Marx Brothers dialogue and delivered with a similar breathless contempt.

How many sexes are there?

Two.

It's not enough, I say. Go out and order some more.

Ten miles he swam; the last three were agony.

They were overland.

Here's my visiting card, sir.

But it's blank.

I know – business is bad.

Secombe's characterisation of Neddie Seagoon remains his most memorable achievement in comedic terms. It not only gave him scope for the comic spontaneity and abandonment of discipline that pervaded all his comedy performances, but showed how radio could extend the limits of the conventional stand-up comedian to a dimension impossible on stage. Seagoon was a futile flag-waving British idiot with a garbled Welsh accent punctuated at irregular intervals by cackling giggle or exultant shriek. He represented at once catalyst, chorus figure and scapegoat in his relations with the inspired defectives voiced by Milligan and Sellers. Bumbling his way through a script with natural good humour, he always seemed to inspire the other two. His emotions kept just in check, he was the Goon with whom the audience identified. He represented the Odysseus on the madcap expedition who, however moonstruck himself, encountered its ordeals as the audience would have done. As scapegoat, he also underlined the theme of persecution which ran throughout the show, the embodiment of all institutions and individuals ever hated. But however much he was clubbed, burnt, whipped, even blown up, Neddie was indestructible, perhaps too indestructible. Towards the end of its delirious decade *The Goon Show*, rickety pillar of the anti-Establishment, had itself become established. For the Goons themselves this was close to professional suicide. At the same time it added greatly to the future staying power of the performers behind the masks. Ironically, while playing his glorious part in radio's ritual destruction of humanity, civilisation and empire, Secombe himself became revealed as the warm humane person he was, an image that would eventually overpower the surrealism and irreverence, the anti-John Bull ethos in which the earlier character moved. Not that the real Secombe was entirely absent in Neddie Seagoon. Of all four original Goons he and Milligan had known each other longest, and, as Harry explained, Neddie was simply how Spike saw him.

Whether in *The Goon Show* or on stage there was one quality that no one could fail to see in Secombe, the bubbling ebullience symbolised by that gasping gurgling quack of a giggle, the waddle of a walk, the grimacing fish-cum-frog footman-type face, not to forget the cautious cartwheels. There was the engaging tendency to laugh maniacally at his own jokes, a trait inherited from personal idol and inspiration, American clown Red Skelton, and excusable in both, implying not that the performer conceitedly regarded himself as funny, but simply that he was happy making others laugh. While Wisdom and Cooper used the ploy to point up their own feigned comic inadequacy, with Secombe his own laughter, however hysterical, was an innocent reaction. Certainly Charles Lamb's remark about the man who laughs at his own jokes is relevant here: to expect him not to laugh is to expect him 'to give a treat without partaking of it; to sit esurient at his own table and commend the flavour of his venison upon the absurd strength of his never touching it himself'.

Secombe was certainly never one to be imagined among the gastronomic abstainers. During the 1950s and 60s, titles of Palladium starring vehicles like *Large as Life* (1958) and *Let Yourself Go* (1961) provided a clue to his special personal chemistry. Improvisation, simply *being*, was Secombe's strongest point. In Victorian drag as a balloon-shaped bathing belle or a bursting, bouncing 'Florrie Forde', in drooping khaki shorts or ragged kilt, coy as a roly-poly ballerina, blustering and twitching as a yeoman of the guard stuck in a barrel about to explode in a Guy Fawkes sequence, he became irresistibly funny. In these situations he would have fared even better had he been left more to his own devices and confined less frequently to the straitjacket of a script. The only restriction that should be clamped upon the work of a pure clown is the one implied by the obvious need to raise a laugh.

Secombe was, though, more than a clown. As a pop-opera singer with an exciting four-octave tenor voice, he was one of the few bel canto tenors in Britain during his heyday, his vocal talent quite as responsible as his clowning for his mass appeal and making the latter acceptable to an even larger audience. However, it was difficult for him to sustain the impression of taking his singing seriously. Mockingly self-described as 'can belto', he was always ready to interpolate a raspberry between numbers; make frightening gurgling noises with a glass of water – threatening his accompanist with the resultant spray; and, scratching an imaginary corset with malicious glee, introduce an aria 'by Mr Fred Puccini, who unfortunately couldn't be with us tonight – he's in bed with a broken leg'. Then there was his invitation to community singing: 'If you join in, we'll have some 'armonising – that's the stuff they put on wedding cakes!' Audiences clamoured to hear him one minute reciting nonsense limericks in a voice crackling like overdone Welsh rarebit and lapsing into Italian opera the next. 'Italian's easy to sing. If you forget the words you just make them up and no one will know!'

Secombe's voice had a far wider range than that of the typical music hall or variety star and led him inevitably into the world of stage and film musicals, the most notable being the first, *Pickwick*, at the Saville Theatre in 1963. The show, in spite of its own rigid straitjacket, ran in London for over two years before touring in America, and consolidated his image as a singing mascot for the British tourist industry. Courtesy of Leslie Bricusse and Cyril Ornadel it also provided him with the memorable song 'If I ruled the world', which soon became his signature tune. From December 1967 his fourteen-month tenure of the star dressing room at the Theatre Royal, Drury Lane during the run of the musical *The Four Musketeers*, in which he played D'Artagnan, constituted a further artistic triumph. Then in 1968 as Mr Bumble he set his stamp on Carol Reed's Oscar-winning film version of the Lionel Bart musical *Oliver!* That all said, possibly no part fitted him more snugly than the title role in *Humpty Dumpty* in the London Palladium pantomime at Christmas 1959. Between 1951 and 1993 he was also featured in eleven Royal Variety Performances.

It was a mark of his genuinely endearing nature that he never allowed 'If I ruled the world' to sound irksome or pretentious. A compulsive clown, who never appeared to possess a sombre side, he skilfully evolved a persona in which courtesy and caricature, sympathy and satire, innocence and zany abandon all managed to achieve a subtle if complex balance. To all of which his immediate response would probably have been: 'Rhubarb!'

AFTERTHOUGHTS

It seems bizarre that to most people under the age of thirty Harry Secombe will most probably be remembered not as a comedian, but as the presenter of the Sunday evening religious television programme *Highway*, which he introduced for a decade from 1983. That those who cherished his many comedy appearances on stage and screen were not thrown by what might have appeared somewhat blasphemous casting says much for the ease and skill with which Secombe was able to tread the line between the ebullient joky exterior and his calmer inner self. Possessed of deep emotional intelligence and dependent upon the solid rock of a genuinely secure marriage to his devoted Myra, whom he wed in 1948, he avoided all the pitfalls – financial, artistic, emotional – that appeared to make the demons that drove Milligan and Sellers a consistent tabloid presence.

It is difficult to think there was ever a time when Secombe was without his feet on the ground. Not that he was ever confident about his own talent or insensitive to the demands of his profession. In later life he reminisced to author Roger Wilmut about the challenge he faced as a young second-spot comic, 'You had to get the audience's attention… whereas a comic is paid to get the laughs, the audience is not beholden to give up its laughter… you went out to face the enemy in some cases. They came to see the top of the bill and you had to be sat through. Someone said to me at Oldham, "Nearly had me laughing when you were on, you know." That was a compliment!' It is not widely known that Harry was an accomplished writer, and, apart from occasional journalism – not least for *Punch* – and volumes of autobiography, his novel *Twice Brightly* is so evocative of the tail end of the variety era one can almost smell the rancid digs, the tired desperation of the pros committed to living in them, trapped like hamsters in a cage on a treadmill circuit that for most held little reward or promise.

Although my original chapter attempted to make clear that only Secombe fully succeeded in variety, it omitted to mention that in the early days of *The Goon Show* various attempts were made by managements to feature the zany trio as a theatrical attraction. Spike and Harry had already worked together in this way. As members of the Central Pool of Artists in Italy after the hostilities ended, the war-weary pair had toured the country in a variety show entitled *Over the Page*. Back in England, Milligan was less than successful at his Windmill audition, at which his opening line, 'Sorry, I came fully dressed!' was greeted with an emphatic thumbs down. Milligan had greater success – on guitar – as part of a jazz trio with

Spike Milligan at the Metropolitan Theatre Edgeware Road. (about 1953), taken when he was singing "Laura".

Items from Spike's scrapbook

Bill Hall and Johnny Mulgrew, who mixed comedy with music on violin and double bass respectively. However, after a short time Milligan left and the group broke up.

Meanwhile Sellers, like Tony Hancock a graduate of Ralph Reader's RAF *Gang Show*, had surer claim to having an act, a slowly evolving routine of impressions that included George Formby complete with uke, Peter Lorre, Robb Wilton, radio action hero Dick Barton and the *ITMA* cast. This was enhanced by occasional flights of fancy that took advantage of his vast repertoire of accents, like the Red Indian journalist filing his observations of London back home to *The Pawnee Graphic*. When Peter arrived at the Palladium low down on a Gracie Fields bill in 1949, he announced his impersonation of Queen Victoria 'when she were a lad'. Emerging from behind a screen decked out in wig, large ginger beard, unlaced corset and heavy army boots with a stuffed crocodile under his arm, he solemnly announced to the audience, 'I'd like to be the first to admit that I do not know what Queen Victoria looked like when she were a lad.'

SPIKE MILLIGAN

wishes it known that when he played the Metropolitan last week there was a queue a mile long — outside the Palladium!!

All Coms.: c/o B.B.C., London

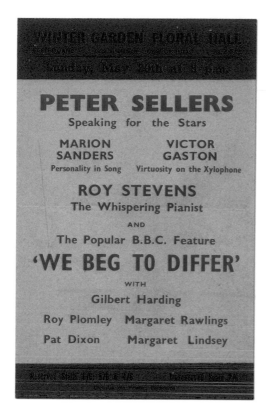

Radio's man of many voices

Unlike Secombe, both Milligan and Sellers nursed a paranoiac resentment of the venues and the audiences that sustained the business. Sellers put it succinctly when he said 'to stand on stage and be the centre of such hostility is a frightening experience'. But aside from their relative disdain for the crowd, there appears to have been within both Spike and Peter a sense that something was willing them not to succeed as traditional stage comedians. The heart of the matter may be contained in Spike's declaration in an *Observer* interview in 1995: 'Myself and Sellers always thought of ourselves as comic Bolsheviks. We wanted to destroy all that went before in order to create something totally new. We were very serious about that.' In the early days theatre audiences proved more resistant than radio ones.

The most important stage engagement that brought the trio together was a long season at Coventry in 1955. Copyright reasons prevented them performing as a group in their famous characters, but they did come together on the bill in a comedy acrobatic sketch as 'Les Trois Charleys', resplendent in red cloaks, white tights, leopard-skin trunks and gold headbands. Otherwise they were more or less restricted to their solo spots. One night Peter Sellers cast aside his repertoire of stunning doppelgängers and took a gramophone on stage. Totally serious, he announced, 'Now I'm going to play a record for you.' When the first track was over he applauded and to his surprise the audience applauded too. The record was an LP of Christmas tunes. The band sat back and relaxed and when it got to 'Jingle Bells' the audience even sang along. Sellers did nothing but invite an encore. His contempt for the audience had achieved its fullest expression.

Milligan's tolerance threshold was even lower. During the same season he objected to the catcalls his trumpet playing received and advanced to the footlights with the rebuke 'You hate me, don't you?' When the audience acknowledged the fact in unison, Spike jumped up and down on his instrument, retreated to his dressing room, locked himself in and tried to hang himself with a makeshift noose. By now Peter and Harry, needing Spike back onstage, had managed to force their way in and disentangle their friend. In later life Milligan played down the incident as a joke: 'What, hang myself for Coventry?' Whether tragedy averted or comedy at its most needlessly macabre, the incident underlined the fact that Spike, who took pleasure in billing himself variously as 'The Performing Man', 'The Fully Clothed Nude' and 'Late of the Human Race', was nothing if not unpredictable. One evening he went on stage at the Metropolitan Music Hall, Edgware Road with a loaded gun. The weapon misfired, fortunately avoiding the audience but causing blood to spurt profusely from his foot. Every week the variety profession subscribed to a trade magazine called the *Performer*. One well-regarded act who advertised frequently in its pages was the magician Kardoma, whose billing matter was 'Fills the stage with flags'. News of the Spike incident got around like wildfire, but he had the last laugh. When the next edition appeared, he had taken his own ad to read 'Spike Milligan – fills the stage with blood!' It was unfortunate that in those early years he could never structure such brilliance into an acceptable format for the stage.

Meanwhile Secombe could usually be relied upon to save the show. If his comedy died, he could always fall back upon his repertoire of operatic standards. Spike and Peter were gracious enough in later years to acknowledge how often his talent and temperament saved the day for them both in those experimental times. Not that Secombe's contribution was not recognised financially. The respected agent Joe Collins recalled in his autobiography that in the early 1950s he paid Harry and Peter £350 and £175 per week respectively when they were on the same bill for him at Southend-on-Sea. Similarly it is unlikely that Milligan would have commanded as much as Sellers. Onstage Harry was always the biggest draw. Offstage he was equanimity personified, a quality that to managements softened the blow of the even larger fees he came to command.

Eventually both of his colleagues would make amends for any shortcomings they displayed in those declining years of the halls. Sellers, unquestionably at his best in the cinematic medium, delivered one of his most affecting performances as a failed old-time variety comic in the film *The Optimists of Nine Elms*. Spike would put together a stand-up act that showed many another bill-topper how it could be done. Milligan always projected hesitancy about why he was under the spotlight at all, but as he conducted an orchestra of clockwork teeth, demonstrated paper-tearing to music and created a dazzling sound impression of a multi-instrumental version of 'The flight of the bumble bee' he at last succeeded in not disappointing in the live medium any of the admirers of his surrealist excesses in radio. 'I wanted to play one of Chopin's études; then I said, "Why should I? He never plays any of mine!"' His position as the most influential comic talent of the second part of the last century was recognised with an honorary (vide his Irish citizenship) knighthood in 2000. In the words of Eddie Izzard, Milligan was the godfather of modern comedy to whom virtually every comic carrying the label 'alternative' owes a debt. Without Spike they simply would not have known what was possible.

Secombe's stature within his profession together with his ever-present generosity – not least his charitable work for the Army Benevolent Fund – was acknowledged by a knighthood as early as 1981, upon which he took great delight in dubbing himself Sir Cumference. For much of his life he had been overweight and in 1983 he was ordered by doctors to address the issue drastically. He did so, reducing himself from nineteen to fourteen stone. Two strokes and diabetes further complicated his latter years. He succumbed to cancer on 11 April 2001. Capable of making every day seem like Christmas to anyone who was in his company, wherever, whenever, he will be remembered both as a natural clown and as a walking cornucopia of bonhomie and grace.

BENNY HILL: BRITAIN'S BRIGHTEST BOY

(*Benny recalls his first lesson on the facts of life from his father*)
He said, 'Now remember Uncle Joe and that picnic a while ago – how he went off into the woods with Auntie Pat? And how I chased old Riley's daughter and what happened when I caught her?'
I said, 'Yeah.'
He said, 'Well, birds and bees does that.'

As a live performer on stage Benny Hill may have been the least effective of all the subjects of this volume. Nevertheless, in finding his true métier on the floor of a television studio he communicated the honest vulgarity and seedy grandeur ingrained in music hall and variety humour to a wider audience than anyone else in history and became, albeit by default, the most successful comedian of his peer group, certainly the highest paid and internationally the best known. He made up for what he lacked in confidence in a theatre with a shrewd understanding of the hopes and dreams of the common man as they related to wealth and status, appetite and sex. He voiced for the masses all the things they thought in secret, but were too craven to say out loud. In the words of the drama critic Ivor Brown, 'like Dickens, Benny Hill has the key of the street'.

He knew he wanted to become a comedian from the moment his grandfather, a one-time circus performer, began to take him at the age of twelve to the touring revues that came to the local variety theatres in Southampton, where he was born Alfred Hawthorne Hill on 21 January 1924. Benny secretly identified with the special adulation accorded the star comedian and the squeals of delight he triggered in the ladies in the audience: 'I thought, hey, he must get more money than anybody else, because he's got top billing; he's surrounded by beautiful girls; everybody loves him. That's for me!' The shows, with titles like, *Ooh, You Saucy Girls*, *Ooh La La* and *Ici Paris*, were not straight variety bills, but corresponded to a milder version of the American burlesque tradition with their emphasis on gags and gals in a sketch/dance/scena format minus the stripping, a pattern Hill would unashamedly bring to television screens many years later, some would argue in an even raunchier guise. The touring revue standby of the short-skirted sexy coquette given any excuse to bend over to reveal the promise of stocking tops, bare thighs and the frilliest of knickers became as identifiable a motif of Hill's oeuvre as the failed magic tricks of Tommy Cooper and the mock buffeting between Morecambe and Wise.

In those early amateur days the precocious young pretender acquired the almost obligatory loud suit in homage to his hero, Max Miller. During another phase he donned a more sober overcoat, flat hat and scarf to bemoan the weather in the lugubrious style of professional variety depressives like Sam Mayo (1881 – 1938), always billed 'The Immobile One', as he stood stoically on stage singing his mournful songs.

'Eeeh, what a night!' Benny would sigh as he dipped his hand into his pocket and grabbed a handful of white confetti to create a snowstorm to illustrate the line. More consistent with Hill's later work was the comic vicar with a back-to-front collar courtesy of his mother's needlework skills. 'Will all those bringing eggs for the harvest festival please lay them in the vestry after the service… and will the ladies who want to be in the Young Mothers' League kindly come and see me in the vestry.' The jokes were pilfered from the variety acts he saw. In addition, impressions of radio favourites, one-man accounts of films he had seen and mock commentaries on events as they occurred were other by-products of an enthusiasm that augured well for his future. Creative sessions at his mother's dressing table eventually led his father to buy him an actor's make-up box. There was certainly no trace then of the theatrical shrinking violet to come.

Upon leaving school at fifteen he busied himself with semi-professional shows on the side while pursuing more conventional jobs. His most notable period of employment was as a milkman. In later years it provided the inspiration for the most successful of his many comic songs. Topping the hit parade for five weeks in 1971 – it sold more than 600,000 copies – 'Ernie, the fastest milkman in the west' chronicled the adventures of Benny's amorous doppelgänger as, bottles rattling, he drove his horse and cart at full gallop, fantasising that the Southampton suburbs were Dodge City and he was Errol Flynn.

> Now Ernie loved a widow, a lady known as Sue.
> She lived all alone in Linley Lane at number twenty-two.
> They said she was too good for him; she was haughty, proud and chic,
> But Ernie got his cocoa there three times every week.

In the summer of 1941 he took himself to London and found employment working backstage and helping with small parts in a touring revue called *Follow the Fun*, in which the principal comedian, the now forgotten Hal Bryan, paid him the compliment Benny claimed was the nicest thing anyone ever said to him, after he stepped into the breach to rescue the old stager at the start of his crosstalk routine when his official straight man went missing. Afterwards a relieved Bryan slipped a ten-shilling note into his hand and said, 'Well done, son. You're going to be a trouper.' He meant in the theatrical sense, but Hill was soon to become a trooper of another kind. His apprenticeship in touring revue was cut short by war service when in December 1942 his call-up papers caught up with him in Cardiff. Life in the army eventually became more tolerable when after the end of hostilities he was transferred from the Royal Electrical and Mechanical Engineers (REME) to the *Stars in Battledress* unit.

Benny would not be demobbed until the summer of 1947. What he often referred to as a road-to-Damascus moment had occurred a couple of years earlier when he visited the Windmill Theatre and saw a young comedian called Peter Waring (c.1919 – 49). Within a few years this tragic performer had taken his own life, but on that small stage, debonair in tails and smoking a cork-tipped cigarette, he displayed a flair for throwaway humour that sneaked up on you. 'A bachelor is a man who's got no children…

to speak of.' Delicate and highly strung, he managed to succeed without the robust attack of the standard variety comic. 'Not many in tonight – there's enough room at the back to play rugby. My god, they *are* playing rugby.' Hill described him as 'the biggest influence on my life', sensing in Waring's approach the answer to a niggling doubt, whether he had the ability to connect with audiences much beyond the first few rows in larger venues.

By all accounts Waring's intimate insouciance would have been a natural for long-term television success. The gap he left and the influence he had on the younger man may well have paved the way for Benny. However, research into the material Hill was using during these early years suggests he was continuing to explore all the comedy options. A favourite ploy was included in his first radio broadcast in September 1947: 'On a serious note, ladies and gentlemen, I shall now give you Abraham Lincoln's Gettysburg address… it's No 345a, Main Street, Gettysburg.' By November he had managed to gain a showcase booking for two nights in the *Spotlight Revue* at the tiny Twentieth Century Theatre in Notting Hill Gate. Here he introduced to a London audience his character Toto, no relation to the great Italian clown of the same name. Jamming a bowler hat down on his head in such a way that his ears stood out from under the rim, he launched into an approximation of an eager German eccentric: 'Guten haben, meinen Damen and Herren – und to the British gentle and ladies' men, who have come here all the way from London, from Edgwarestrasse, Chelwasser, Guilders Groin and Marble Art, we wish you a good body every evening. And, oh boy, have we got a show for you tonight! Have we got a show for you tonight? (*Turns to wings*) *Have* we got a show for them tonight?' Benny had spent time in Germany with the army, much of it in charge of prisoners of war, with many of whom he became friendly. The experience paid dividends when the character resurfaced on his television shows in later years.

Another sequence that stood Hill in good stead around this time was a routine entitled 'Ribbing the Hips', in which 'Hips' referred to the Hippodromes of variety tradition. It was a fairly broad send-up of the variety genre, but the ambience of intimate revue – whether in the *Spotlight* show or at the exclusive Boltons Theatre in Chelsea, where he made an impact during the Christmas of 1948 – enabled him to label it 'satire'. Performers evoked by Benny in this fast reprise of a fading genre were the opening two-girl chorus, the 'Dreadful Dancing Sisters', beset by 'foot and mouth disease' as they hollered and stomped their way through 'Hello, hello, how do you do you do?'; the awful inebriated concert party baritone; the third-rate impressionist with the overworked Peter Lorre – Sydney Greenstreet combination;

and an over-the-top pastiche of everybody's worst nightmare of a front-cloth comic, best characterised by the red tie he was wearing: 'Whenever a gag falls with a sickening thud, he looks down and says, "Cor-bli, I thought my tongue was hanging out!"' It reads rather thin, but already he was investing the words with the lascivious repertoire of smirks, smiles and assorted facial tics that would come to hallmark his style.

By the summer of 1948 the best work he could find was as straight man in a Margate summer show to another comic, Reg Varney, not that Varney himself at that stage had achieved anything like the fame that would come to him later with television successes such as *The Rag Trade* and *On the Buses*. At the audition another comic destined to become famous internationally had been in contention for the job, but Hill's calypso satirising the Attlee government won out over Peter Sellers' George Formby impression.

> We have two Bev'ns in our Cabinet.
> Aneurin's the one with the gift of the gab in it.
> The other Bev'n is the taciturnist;
> He knows the importance of being Ernest!

Benny had by now changed his own name from Alfie Hill, partly in tribute to his American comedy idol Jack Benny and partly, as he admitted, to make himself sound Jewish. He had already registered how much of the business was controlled by Jewish managers and agents. His duties were to partner Varney in sketches and to deliver a solo spot of his own. The partnership endured on and off over three summer seasons and assorted variety dates until one night at the Sunderland Empire in April 1951 Benny started to receive the slow handclap during his solo act. Not prepared to stay in the combination as Varney's feed alone, Benny left the show after another partner had been rehearsed.

His confidence as a stage performer had already been shaken considerably when during a matinee performance at the Boltons he caught sight of an agent who some months before had threatened to destroy Hill's career over a contractual matter in which Benny had been totally in the right. He went to pieces, gasping for breath on stage, his legs quivering, his mouth dry. Things were only compounded by the Sunderland disaster, where the audience took exception to his quick-change routine based on the balcony scene from Romeo and Juliet in which amid all the comic business, much of it suggestive, he insisted on keeping to the Bard's words.

Most performers are beset by stage fright in varying degrees. The adrenaline triggered by the fear of failure powers their talent, while the agony of the process provides the psychic justification both for the sense of liberation that performing gives and the exhilaration of success that might otherwise seem unearned. The extreme example was Tony Hancock, but he never doubted that he became fully alive once he *was* in the spotlight, and never – throughout all his personal problems – gave up on the challenge of entertaining a live crowd. It just did not seem to work that way with Benny. Stardom only brought matters to a head, showing up his unsuitability for large venues as part of the problem. He headlined in two top West End revues, *Paris by Night* at the Prince of Wales Theatre in 1955 and *Fine Fettle* at the Palace Theatre in 1959. The excuse made for his lack of success in the former was that his humour failed to engage the foreign tourists who comprised the greater part of the audience as the run progressed; it didn't help that Tommy Cooper who was billed second to Hill stole the show every evening with no trouble at all. *Fine Fettle*, subtitled 'a musical romp in cloth cap and tails', was an attempt to devise a show that would work in a smaller venue better suited to intimate revue. It disintegrated when it was staged in the large auditorium of the Palace. After *Fine Fettle* he decided to concentrate on television work, where he seemed more than happy to engage with small studio audiences at a personal level and where the unlimited resources of a wardrobe department could more or less guarantee that he would never have to face the camera as himself. The closing moments of his shows, in which he would appear out of character and pepper his adieux with self-conscious sentiment, always seemed the most uncomfortable parts of the production.

Hill's immediate reaction to the Sunderland debacle was to concentrate on writing. He retreated to his parents' home in Southampton and before long had secured an interview with Ronnie Waldman, head of light entertainment at BBC Television. Waldman responded well to the scripts Benny submitted and then surprised him further by suggesting that Benny should appear in them. Hill had written them with no specific performer in mind and certainly not himself. He debuted as the star of his own show in the one-off *Hi There* as early as August 1951. Before long he was acting as compère of *Showcase*, a programme devised to give opportunities to new talent, and by 1955 was starring in *The Benny Hill Show*. For almost two decades he enjoyed a position as one of the BBC's more prestigious stars, without question the first British comedian to be made famous entirely by television. His lack of presence on a stage was transformed on the small screen into an intimate cheeky charm that insinuated itself into people's living rooms as naturally as butter melting on toast. Askey had broken new ground in allowing his personality to play with the new medium, but Hill went further in opening a treasure chest of new comedy devices and technical innovations. He wasted no time in drawing upon his impersonating skills and became the first performer to satirise the medium employing him, expanding his range away from the film and variety regulars of the standard impersonator's repertoire and targeting the new breed of personalities, pundits and commentators upon which television still thrives.

What many remember as his first genuine tour de force was a take-off of the panel game *What's My Line*, in which – in homage to the quick-change performers who had fascinated him on the halls – he played on live television all four members of the panel while his first television straight man, the elegant Jeremy Hawk, sitting in for the host Eamonn Andrews, gave Hill cover with his cutaway interjections. Benny expertly caught the measure of the show's four contrasting panellists: the exuberant Canadian blonde comedienne Barbara Kelly, the elegant faux-aristocratic brunette Lady Isobel Barnett, the kindly comedy conjuror, bald David Nixon, and the permanently riled bespectacled Gilbert Harding, as gruff as the military moustache that bristled as a warning to anyone who might cross his path. This triumph would later be surpassed by Hill's treatment of *Juke Box Jury*, where pre-filming enabled the director to cut instantly between him as one character and another, but also for the first time used split-screen technique to show all four versions of the performer on the television screen at the same time. To the audience at home this was a miracle, while to Benny the technical challenge – he was the first British performer to cut film, previously a preserve of drama, into a television variety show – accorded him greater satisfaction than he could ever gain on the stage of the largest theatres in the land. He was unquestionably the first comedian to harness the scope of the new medium and free comedy from the confines of the variety stage. His *Juke Box Jury* triumph resulted in the BBC switchboard being jammed with a record number of congratulatory calls, ten times more than the previous record. It also triggered an internal memo from Cecil McGivern, deputy director of television to Ronnie Waldman. He wrote of the show, 'This, I thought, was in places brilliant. (At the same time, I am always worried that Hill will say or do something unacceptable!)' The spirit of his idol Max Miller and all the principal comics he had ever seen by his grandfather's side lived on.

Individual triumphs in these shows included his portrayals of the bland Barry Bucknell, the DIY wizard; the wildlife experts Armand and Michaela Denis and their underwater counterparts Hans and Lotte Hass; the flamboyant hairdresser Mr 'Teasy-Weasy' Raymond, a camp Beau Brummell for the modern age who could cause housewives to faint with a flourish of his scissors: 'We're combing the 'air over this ear. This 'ere ear. Then over that ear, over 'ere;' the fussy bearded chef Philip Harben, who with floured hands and characteristic earnestness explained to the viewer how to make Gorgonzola cheese: 'First shred the gorgon into a basin. Make sure it goes in first. If you put the zola in first, you will get zolagorgon. And there is no such cheese.' On more traditional ground, his versions of Hollywood legends as diverse as W. C. Fields, Oliver Hardy, Richard Burton and Marlon Brando were especially memorable, and if his Elizabeth Taylor only amounted to a token pastiche, his Mae West was more than up to

Benny as 'Rich Burt' in 'Who's Afraid of Virgin Wool?'

the standard of the males. Most of his impressions required considerable support from the make-up and wardrobe departments, but this cannot disguise the fact that he had an uncanny ability for getting inside the skin of a character. Single-handedly he pioneered the approach taken in years to come by talents as diverse as Alan Melville, Stanley Baxter, Mike Yarwood, Rory Bremner and a whole string of lesser dead ringers. From the beginning he wrote all the material for his television shows, both words and music, sometimes in collaboration with Dave Freeman during the first few years of his career.

Occasionally a routine would work so well that it would graduate to the stage on those occasions when Benny could be persuaded back onto the boards. With Jeremy Hawk in tow, the *What's My Line* sketch had a short life in variety. Audiences could now see his lightning costume and make-up changes for themselves; this possibly made things funnier. Equally popular was the fashion parade in which Benny played a male mannequin wearing different kinds of clothes, with Hawk providing the commentary as Hill sauntered mincingly along the catwalk: 'The short-length trousers with matching jacket are in an entirely new material. Have you guessed? Yes, pinhead!' The display even extended to beachwear, with Benny anxious to cover his nipples with inadequate braces as the beach ball he was holding took on a life of its own. 'This year the Riviera super-dark glasses protect the traveller from midday glare,' intoned Hawk, as Benny, who apparently couldn't see a thing, crashed into the scenery. Equally visual was the square-dancing sketch. Without mugging in any way, Benny and a group of dancers set about a perfectly acceptable dance in the traditional manner. However, no matter which way he turned or to whom he advanced, Benny always ended up with the least attractive of the women involved.

From the first success of *The Benny Hill Show*, the star refused to yield to the gaping maw of overexposure on television and with a weight-watcher's diligence limited himself to a mere handful of shows a year. Audiences will not remember now that during his long tenure at the BBC he kept its executives on their toes by occasional forays with his one-hour format to the new commercial television and specifically

Lew Grade's ATV. However, he was never away from the BBC for long, which made his decision to sign a long-term contract with Thames Television in 1969 even more surprising, although the promise by the new company to make his shows in colour played its part. He stayed there for twenty years. At first viewers would have seen little change in the format, the showcase for a versatility that saw banal jokes and comic songs jostling with pastiches of avant-garde drama and art-house films, dazzling displays of wordplay and inspired mime sequences.

There was still room from time to time for the clever pastiche material that characterised his BBC days, as when he portrayed Katie Boyle – 'our own Katie Boiler' – as hostess in a version of the *Eurovision Song Contest*, in which he played all the performers competing from various countries. Best, because funniest, of all was his portrayal of another cookery expert, Fanny Cradock, who insisted on working in haute couture gowns way beyond the means of the typical housewife, whom she addressed in a deep rasping voice that would have made Gilbert Harding quail. She suffered no fools as her husband Johnnie, played mischievously for Benny by Bob Todd, lurked amiably in the background, resplendent in tuxedo and with glass akimbo, only just this side of plastered as he stole the cooking sherry or whatever else was to hand – 'Don't do that, Johnnie' – when he thought his other half was distracted.

> This is the time of year when Johnnie likes to get his hands on a nice plump bird, making a change from the old boiler he gets the rest of the year… I'm just going to give it to Johnnie, and he's going to stuff it, into the oven and we are going to – don't do that, Johnnie – and into it you pour some red wine and this is a very, very good red wine, and this is called Nuits-Saint-Georges (*Pronounced newts*), which means you can get as pissed as a – Johnnie do be careful!

The Cradock combination was a self-pastiche (in Hill-speak read piss-take) in the first place. Benny succeeded in guying the original against all the odds. However, at Thames straightforward impersonation began to take more and more of a back seat to his growing repertory of generic characters.

We have to thank his wicked flair for mimicry for an impressive pageant of sly eccentrics, among whom the most prominent was the lisping salute-prone skew-eyed Fred Scuttle in his trademark wire-rim spectacles, dim but ever the opportunist, whether master-minding pirate radio station, pickle factory, art gallery or holiday-camp empire. Here he is as a supermarket security guard explaining the special treatment reserved for shoplifters to Henry McGee, who was by far and away Benny's crispest straight man during the Thames years:

> *Scuttle*: When one of our lads gives her a tap on the shoulder, she is shocked back into the straight and narrow path, sir, never to deter and go off again. You see, cured, cured, completely cured.
> *McGee*: And she's never picked up by the fuzz?
> *Scuttle*: No, sir… just tapped on the shoulder by one of us. We don't involve the police, you see.

There was the camp Mervyn Cruddy, who spoke through tight lips in a disconcertingly high pitch and whose smiling eyes hinted that he was fully aware of the double meaning behind his innocent remarks; Benny's not-so-innocent bumpkin droll, looking for all the world like a grown-up Cabbage Patch Kid, whose outlook reduced all behaviour to the level of farmyard and stable; the wily Mr Chow Mein making chop suey of the liquid embarrassments presented by the English language whereby 'blessed with two nippers' becomes in all innocence 'breast with two nipples'; Primrose Hill, an early excursion into drag, a 1950s caricature of Diana Dors-style glamour, forever making references to her 'dumplings'; Herbert Fudge, the saucy madrigal singer beneath shaggy black wig, whose look alone is enough to suggest the main preoccupation of our most celebrated diarist when he was not writing his diary:

> A fair young maid has took a room down at the local inn,
> Her bedside light is oh so bright and the curtain's oh so thin.
> At nine o'clock she enters her room, at ten o'clock she sleeps,
> Lord Clarendon, he just walks on, but naughty Samuel Pepys.

Each surface disguise was underpinned by the same twinkling full-moon face, aflame with wickedness and simpering with naivety at the same time. His mastery of the television medium confirmed this as his finest asset, his artful grin irradiating the whole world of his shows, that of squashed hats and baggy shorts, speeded-up Keystone-style chases and McGill misunderstanding. Their success showed that the television public still had a penchant for the rortier traditions of the variety stage, even though Benny had now firmly left the proscenium arch behind him.

And then a short while into his tenure at Thames a sea change occurred. Possibly pining for the chorus line that adorned the revues he saw with his grandfather, maybe influenced by what other more permissive shows purveyed, he let loose the scantily clad bikini-bursting beauties known as Hill's Angels. There had been dancers on his shows before, but they were always incidental and no more threatening in their sexuality than the standard row of high-kicking starlets that were an opening fixture of the variety tradition. They now began to appear in sketches and to get involved with Benny onscreen. His humour, once tolerated at the level of schoolboy naughtiness, now began to appear coarser and became unacceptable to many, as if a favourite broadsheet had become a tabloid overnight. In Benny's defence, it should be stressed that in making these changes he was reflecting an increased permissiveness in the media generally. With apposite timing, his first show for Thames had been transmitted on 19 November 1969, a mere two days after the first publication of Rupert Murdoch's *Sun*: within a year the first topless girl had made her appearance on page three. This did not stop feminist groups directing their rage at Hill personally, although more rational commentators like the writers John Mortimer and Anthony Burgess went out of their way to underline Benny's place in a rich literary tradition that embraced Aristophanes and Chaucer. As Burgess said, 'Orwell would have loved him; Orwell would have understood; Orwell might well have written the definitive essay.'

The earlier appraisal of Max Miller in this volume shows how close Orwell did come to understanding, in his assessment of the seaside postcard artist Donald McGill. It seems unfair that Benny took this flak while, among his contemporaries, British institutions like the Carry On team, Frankie Howerd and the Two Ronnies could on occasion tread a similar route and go unscathed. The pretty girl had long been a natural comedy foil; it is just surprising that Benny had not made capital of the device at an earlier stage. As he pointed out, in his sketches it was the men who lost their dignity, not the girls. He did not chase them, they chased him. 'My would-be lovers never succeed. A man who succeeds is not funny… if my sketches reveal anything it is that, for the male, sex is a snare and a delusion. What's so corrupting about that?' If a sexual predator lurked within Benny's males, their sheer inadequacy removed any suggestion of lust by their very ridiculousness.

Bringing Donald McGill to life

Matters were not helped when in 1987 in an interview in *Q* magazine Ben Elton came out against Benny in a burst of flawed self-righteousness that was tantamount to an accusation of incitement to rape: 'You have Benny Hill in the late 80s chasing half-naked women around a park when we know in Britain women can't even walk safe in a park any more. That for me is worrying.' That a fellow comedian should criticise him so openly upset Hill far more than the detail of the comment. As feminist groups and high-minded editorials compounded the injury, Benny – at the end of one of his actual shows – took refuge in one of the forms of humour he knew best – wordplay.

Me, sexist?… I had to look it up in my *Boy's Own Dictionary*. Nowadays I'm almost afraid to say dictionary, because 'dic' is masculine, you see. It should be Bettytionary. I looked up 'sexist' and it wasn't there. So I looked up 'feminist'. It said, 'See sexist.' Because you hear a lot about feminists don't you, eh? You never hear of masculinists. Perhaps there's no such word. Perhaps the masculine equivalent of a feminist is a male chauvinist pig. It's a bit unfair. You never hear about female chauvinist sows, do you?

When it came to sex, frustration and failure were the name of the game as far as Hill was concerned, maybe providing an insight into his own private life, which remains a discussion for a volume other than this one. It is reasonable to assume that as a fascination, if not a full-blown obsession, sex had loomed larger earlier in Benny's life than in that of other comedians. In Southampton his father had owned a shop selling surgical appliances and contraceptives. 'Hilly's dad sells French letters,' was a playground taunt that he had to get used to as a child. The stigma of having to enter his father's emporium never left him. Once inside, observing the sheepish parade of customers, he learnt about adult sexual embarrassment far earlier than most. In later years all of this was channelled into his comedy. But to his professional detriment a sleazy quality *had* intruded into another aspect of the show, namely the dance routines, and here no tradition of comedy could provide an excuse. Indeed the overall production of the programmes had become lazy, indiscriminate and shoddy. Benny had also become guilty of being greedy with a principle: a much-needed independent script editor would have leavened the emphasis on innuendo and in the process achieved with it even greater effect. Hill was probably too close to it all, while those around him were so dazzled by the show's global impact that any sort of criticism must have seemed irrelevant.

When he did take notice of one critic, it was too late. That commentator was no less than Hal Roach, the veteran comedy producer responsible for the success of Harold Lloyd, 'Our Gang' and Laurel and Hardy. During a lecture in London in 1986 the nonagenarian noted that Hill's potential was limitless, if he would only clean up his act, adding that he could be 'one of the greatest – only for one thing. His comedy is all below the belt. That's no use for comedy. It won't do for children, and in the end it's children who have made all the great comedians – Chaplin, Laurel and Hardy, all of them.' Hill responded, cutting dancers out of sketches, raising necklines, even misguidedly introducing kids – Hill's Little Angels – into the shows. These steps did little to change the prevailing view. His popularity meant that his older shows were repeated and recycled many times over, and any reversal of the sea change hardly registered. But other considerations were coming into play at Thames. The budget for the show was escalating out of control at the same time as viewing figures were on the decline, possibly as a result of the adverse publicity. These factors led to the much-publicised non-renewal of his contract in 1989. In truth the issue of political correctness per se never came into it.

However hurtful this dismissal proved to Benny – it cast a considerable cloud over his last few years – there was a crumb of artistic satisfaction to be gained from the incredible success the shows had by now achieved in the USA. That they had done so was something of a fluke. When in the late 1970s American distributor Don Taffner was looking for material on the Thames shelves to package for

American exploitation, the sheer bulk of the Hill catalogue, rather than any other quality, won out over that of any other comedian. The show was edited into faster-paced half-hour versions that would win for Hill the international recognition that eventually entailed being seen in over one hundred countries. This was in spite of his reluctance to be shown in America in the first place; his basic contract carried an exclusion clause in this respect. His long-term agent Richard Stone held out for a deal whereby Thames and Benny would share all profits equally. To his surprise, the broadcaster conceded and Benny, who had a complete disregard for money beyond his basic needs, became one of Britain's richest entertainers. After his death probate established his wealth at £7,548,192.

His success confounded the accepted view that Americans had difficulty accepting grass-roots British humour. In the edited versions the emphasis was placed firmly on his sexual humour and mime skills. Taffner claimed that one sketch alone helped his sales pitch more than any other, the wishing-well sequence, in which both these facets of the star's humour fused beyond even Don's wildest dreams. A humdrum Benny enters with a jaded housewife on his arm. He throws a coin into the well and she disappears. His smile lights up the sky. He throws in another coin and a bikini-clad lovely appears on his arm. The smile gives way to a smirk. She throws in a coin and an Adonis figure in swimming trunks materialises. Benny's face registers gloom. The hunk lobs in a coin, the girl disappears and he makes a grab for our hero. In homophobic horror Benny drops in the last coin and the guy changes into the housewife. Benny registers resignation and they walk off together. Nobody saw it as an omen at the time, but this sketch was the first item in Benny's debut show for Thames back in 1969.

His international success inevitably resulted in offers to appear in live performances all over the world. He refused them all, including what seems to have been virtually an open cheque from Las Vegas. To appease Thames he *did* appear in an Eric Morecambe tribute show at the London Palladium in 1984 and a promotional gala for the company at New York's Lincoln Center three years later. He kept his material basic, mainly confining himself to a written text for the latter and a lectern for a schoolmaster skit in the former, devices perfect to prevent his hands from trembling and to save the day word-wise should he dry up. He just managed to conceal his dread on both occasions.

A shy and simple man who kept himself to himself and had few possessions, he died a lonely death from a heart attack in a functional flat at Teddington within walking distance of the studio where he only really came alive. It was probably two days before his body was discovered on 20 April 1992. As one might have expected given his spectacular popularity and the controversy much of his achievement engendered, the eulogies veered from hypocrisy to hyperbole. He *may* have been the most successful British funny man since Chaplin, but that he was anywhere near as significant or would prove as enduring was wishful nonsense. Chaplin, for all that his comedy was rooted in class, had been classless as well as international in his appeal. He was also the first comedian not only to make audiences laugh out loud but to give them cause for thought at the same time. This need not be a *sine qua non* of hilarity, but if comparisons are to be made between the two men, it should be stressed that Hill was never on that side of the fence where one might find Charlie hobnobbing with Keaton, Hancock, Jacques Tati, Woody Allen and a few more.

Paradoxically, possibly his finest moments of later years were when he set aside the Donald McGill approach and gave free rein to his love of silent visual comedy, as observed by him on frequent visits to European cabarets and harking back to the speciality act tradition he observed in the touring revues he saw as a child. His orange-haired red-nosed clown character may have been his finest creation and could have provided another less resourceful performer with a whole career. In one sequence the clown begins by performing a striptease down to his skin. Then, using the principle known to magicians and puppeteers as black art, he peels away the skin to reveal his skeleton and in turn with anatomical precision disconnects and discards his left arm, pelvis, legs, ribcage and skull. All that remains in the black void is an eerie disembodied right hand that slithers offscreen. It is a chilling motif with which to end this appraisal, though somewhat apt that he should be remembered for a routine in which after the removal of his facial features, he became totally anonymous – as one senses on balance he would like to have been in life itself.

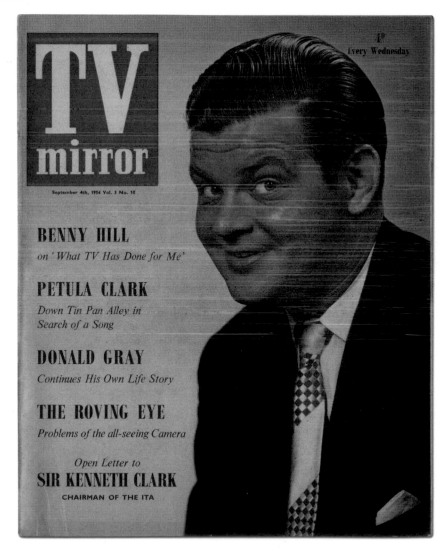

MORECAMBE AND WISE: TWO OF A KIND

Ernie: Do you have to wear those glasses?
Eric: Yes, because when people talk about us – which they don't very often –
I'm known as 'the one with the glasses'.
Ernie: Well, what am I known as?
Eric: You're known as 'the other one'!

One moment a candlestick in silhouette, the next two identical profiles in stern confrontation; one moment a frail wisp of a girl, the next a repellent hag with a jutting chin. Eric Morecambe and Ernie Wise enjoyed a curious affinity with those intriguing puzzle pictures that alternate between two entirely different visual interpretations, lending light relief to the heaviest of the psychological textbooks in which they appear. Aware in a television age of the short life-expectancy imposed by constant exposure on the traditional double act, they evolved to a point where the jester's cap and bells became interchangeable between them, where neither was cut and dried as comic or straight man.

One might have assumed that Eric, uneasy and hysterical in fancy dress, was the clown, as with the stunned look of a quizzical owl he asked,

Eric: Why am I dressed like this?
Ernie: We are going to do *The Three Musketeers*.
Eric: But there are only two of us?
Ernie: It doesn't matter. I'll play one and you can play the other two.

The last exchange betrayed the shift in focus, the intelligence of the supposed fool, the idiocy and illogicality now invested in the self-importance of the straight man. But if the comic balance was now tipped towards Ernie's shortcomings, then, as if to emphasise the flexibility of the whole arrangement, came the less than logical reply:

Eric: Can I really? That's very good of you, Ern.

Eric for all his foolery was in fact as cunning and intelligent as any straight man ever was, only the willpower to resist, the power of concentration was lacking. When this became desperate, Wise would enquire,

Ernie: What's the matter with you?
Eric: I'm an idiot – what's your excuse?

But later Eric would himself wish to qualify that.

Eric: I'm not a complete fool.
Ernie: Why, what part's missing?

The smugness with which he delivered that last line, the zany logic of his ideas, revealed Ernie, for all his solemnity, as fully capable of making up for Morecambe's self-avowed deficiency.

There were even times when Ernie stood exposed as a complete fool himself, as when Eric was buying a dress for his wife and only Ernie could supply the necessary details of style and size. In the end Morecambe, increasingly suspicious that there might be more to this than met the eye, gave in and rattled off a completely different set of measurements to the shop assistant.

Ernie: What do you want to buy a dress like that for?
Eric: Well, it's the only combination of measurements I know.
Ernie: But it won't fit your wife.
Eric: No, but it will fit yours! Ho-ho-ho-hey!

That final exultant shriek was Morecambe's own concession to vanity, its high-pitched tones piercing enough to prick those pretensions of Wise as actor, playwright, singer that Eric undermined throughout their act. 'Look at him – he believes it all, you know,' he would confide disrespectfully to the audience. The height of Wise's presumption occurred in a television show when he answered successfully an advertisement in the *Stage* for the job of Bob Hope's head writer. The tall, gangling Eric kept his feet firmly on the ground as he attempted to dispel Ernie's misconception of the Hollywood of the 1970s as an autograph hunter's playground, exposing Donald Duck as a cartoon and Shirley Temple as 'Lee Marvin's mother', but Ernie persisted in the conviction of his own talent, until, that is, the misspelt club comic Bob *Pope* arrived to introduce himself.

At other times Wise would revert to the well defined hauteur of the bullying straight man, Morecambe to his temporary membership of that maladjusted breed so sensitive they turn a guilty scarlet when someone else makes a faux pas. In one of their well honed stage routines, Ernie took Eric through the steps of his Swiss dance, explaining carefully that when he pretends to slap Eric's face, Eric must simultaneously clap his hands together and vice versa: 'It's all pretence!' Wise's own sound effects are coordinated with hair's-breadth precision, but Eric, although he picks up the rhythm with uncanny speed, ends up at the real mercy of Ernie's buffeting and in the end slapping himself, in spite of taking time off halfway through to go into a frantic private practice of all the judo cuts he knows. The whole routine with its theme of retaliation successful and thwarted was a brilliantly economical demonstration of the code of conduct basic to the traditional double act. A similar sequence featured Wise teaching Morecambe to play the bongos to accompany his impression of Sammy Davis Junior. The instrument represented uncharted territory as far as Eric was concerned. Determined not to be taken in, he nurses them tentatively in his arms. 'You don't blow them! You thump them with your digits,' explains Ernie brusquely. The puritanical streak in the clown causes Eric to step back, fearful that Ernie may just have thrown decency to the wind. 'You play them with both hands. Put them between your legs.' Eric can't believe this. 'Get on?' he queries, with the dazed curiosity of the Wonderland caterpillar, as he carries out the instructions, inevitably getting the drums the wrong way round. 'The *other* way round,' shouts Ernie, and Eric turns around. He ends up standing as near as straight, straddling the twin orbs, legs akimbo, allowing Ernie to quip, 'You look like a Ford Zodiac. Now follow me.' Not recognising the musical terminology, Eric takes Ernie at his word, leaving the drums suspended eighteen inches above the ground against the backcloth.

In Tyrolean guise

In the comic literalism of this last routine, as well as in much of the casually violent interplay between them, one can see the undoubted influence of Sid Field and Jerry Desmonde in their golfing and billiards sketches – not surprising when one recalls that Eric and Ernie appeared individually as juveniles in Field's first West End revue, *Strike a New Note*. Other early influences were America's Bud Abbott and Lou Costello, who achieved a cinematic fame out of all proportion to their slick but average wisecracking talent. Nevertheless, because they happened to be in vogue at the time, they were responsible for much of the material of all aspiring double acts in the late 1940s. The flavour of the meagre breadwinning material of the younger pair is captured in the exchange that featured in Eric and Ernie's first booking as a double, when Eric sauntered across the stage carrying a fishing rod with an apple attached to the line.

Ernie: What are you doing?
Eric: I'm fishing.
Ernie: But you can't catch fish with an apple; you catch fish with a worm.
Eric: That's all right. The worm's inside the apple.

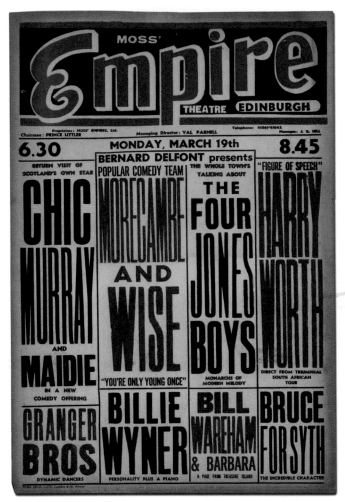

However, as the quality of their performances rose, they soon showed that they had links with Laurel and Hardy, the greatest double act the cinema ever produced. There were obvious individual parallels, Stan and Eric sharing a Lancastrian warmth and simplicity, Ollie and Ernie a fastidious but never objectionable concern for their own self-importance. At the same time all four represented a degree of idiocy to which Abbott as the smart-aleck straight man of the brasher duo would never have been party. Perhaps most significant was the ability of both pairs to reconcile a simple homely style with the most surreal flights of fantasy. One recalls the moment when in the rush of the show Eric and Ernie come on wearing each other's trousers. Their subsequent adroit exchange of pants without seeming to take them off was a concept not far removed from Stan and Ollie's agile retreat in the film *You're Darn Tootin'*, yoked together in one oversized pair of trousers. There are many more.

Morecambe, real name John Eric Bartholomew and the son of a corporation worker, was born in the town of his adopted name on 14 May 1926, the year after Wise, real name Wiseman, was born in Leeds on 27 November. At an early stage in their partnership they decided against calling themselves 'Morecambe and Leeds' as sounding 'too much like a railway return'. It is, however, in Ernie's railwayman father that we find the first hint of a show business influence. Out of working hours he was an amateur entertainer among the working men's clubs of Yorkshire. At the age of seven, his stage-struck son joined him illegally on stage to form an act that became known as Carson and Kid. At one point he sat on his father's knee while the parent sang 'Little pal, if daddy goes away'. Meanwhile the more reluctant Eric, goaded by a mother with more ambition for her son than he nursed himself, had discovered his own way of leaving not one eye unmoistened with a gormless 'I'm not all there' characterisation in the tradition of veteran comic Jack Pleasants (1874 – 1923), most famous for his song 'I'm shy, Mary Ellen, I'm shy'. In those days Eric's glasses had to vie with kiss curl, beret, a giant Shirley Temple-style lollipop and the huge safety pin that fastened the jacket of his cut-down dress suit, the last item a basic uniform common to Ernie as well.

Both boys found their way into *Youth Takes a Bow*, a juvenile version of Bryan Michie's *Discoveries*, variety's answer to all the radio and television talent shows that would follow. Sensing her son's lack of enthusiasm, Sadie Bartholomew suggested he team up in a double act with Wise. The decision to do so was taken on a train journey from Birmingham to Coventry during the 1940 Blitz, although it was not until nine months later on 28 August 1941 that the act made its debut on stage at the Liverpool Empire. It was well received, but only after the war – by which time Wise had served a stint in the Merchant Navy and Morecambe down the mines as a Bevin boy – did they have any real chance of becoming established. That came with the same freakish good fortune already seen at work reuniting Flanagan and Allen. Prior to this, however, Eric would team up for a short while with Gus Morris, brother of Dave Morris, later to achieve fame as the straw-hatted heavily bespectacled guv'nor of the *Club Night* radio and television programme. Then around 1947 Eric

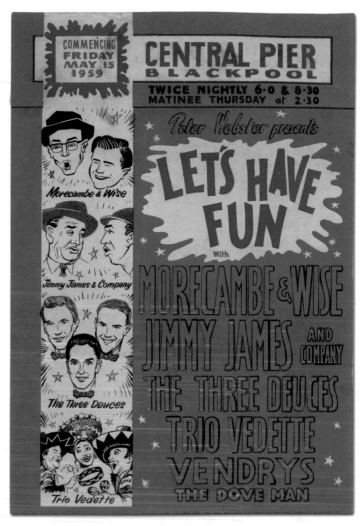

applied for a job as feed (his role with Morris) to a comic in *Lord George Sanger's Circus and Variety* which was appearing at Godalming. The comic was Wise, and the partnership took off, taking in tatty nude shows with titles like *Fig Leaves and Apple Sauce* and *Come In For a Bit*, sporadic radio work in shows like *Workers' Playtime* and *Variety Fanfare*, then their own radio series *You're Only Young Once* for BBC North, and the plunge into television with the six-part series *Running Wild* for Ronnie Waldman in April 1954.

For performers whose greatest success would come on the small screen, it is hard to imagine they could ever have warranted the scathing remarks the critics produced on the occasion of that first series: 'So feeble, it's a wonder the show can totter as far as our sets;' 'Alma Cogan stands out like a sunflower in a rubbish heap;' and most cruel of all: 'The definition of a TV set – the box they buried Morecambe and Wise in.' The backlash from their initial television failure no doubt explains why for the next seven years, in spite of an indelible presence in the top provincial pantomimes and Blackpool summer seasons and gradually spreading fame, they never became bona fide top of the bill names, but staunch support to the acts or egos of the big American singing stars who invaded British variety in the 1950s. Certainly they had a lot to live down. One radio script soon after the television debacle called for someone to ask, 'Are you Morecambe?'

> *Eric*: Have you a television set?
> *Man*: No.
> *Eric*: Well then, yes, I'm Eric Morecambe.

Eric and Ernie in their Abbott and Costello days

Perhaps they realised they weren't quite ready, but it is difficult to believe they could have seen themselves ever becoming the fashionable entertainment commodity they became in the 60s. They were given a reprieve by the BBC during the summer of 1957 with the short series *Double Six*, a revue format in which they appeared with the gormless Ted Lune. However, it was a television appearance on *Sunday Night at the London Palladium* in the spring of 1960 that led by way of return bookings to their own series for Lew Grade's ATV. This ran for sixty-seven episodes in six runs between 1961 and 1968. The format, essentially a sketch show with elements of both stand-up and sitcom, remained more or less consistent until the end of their career.

Their subsequent triumph within the medium is all the more impressive considering the theatrical orientation of their act. However, if the television studio was lacking in red-plush cosiness, they went out of their way to use as many other theatrical trappings as possible, performing for the studio audience on a raised platform as distinct from the studio floor, making their announcements in front of a set of tabs (once, that is, Eric had fought his way through the gap in the middle), taking their call at the end, all the time acting out what may have been no more than personal superstition in the wider cause of atmosphere and individuality. But their luckiest mascot for television was their least separable, their own physical appearance. One thinks less of the contrast in stance and size than of facial detail: Eric's inquisitive features kept from disintegration by the heavy scaffolding of his significant horn-rims, or his mouth agape in fearful agitation, accusing and aghast without a word escaping; the beaming complacency of Ernie's smile. And if Wise's face was less readily identifiable, Eric at least provided his partner with virtual compensation, namely the mythical – 'You can see the join!' – toupee, butt of a thousand gags, not least the one cracked by Eric at Madame Tussauds at a preview of their waxen effigies. After a careful inspection of first Ernie and then his double came the satisfied judgement 'He's got a better one than you!' But with Ernie's height – or lack of it – it is perhaps not surprising that the very top of his head should have become the centre of attention.

Eric: Ern, *you* are the pocket Hercules!
Ernie: I suppose you're right.

Their television work gained for them – Eric especially – a formidable reputation as ad-libbers, certainly for imparting a distinct sparkle to whatever material they tackled, however old. Morecambe once described himself as a haphazard man, someone for whom the stress of adhering to a set script was greater than the stress of

393

ad-libbing itself with its need for split-second reactions. Television's greatest asset is its fallibility, something Morecambe and Wise realised to their advantage at an early stage. The irony was that while the audience came to love Morecambe and Wise for their unpredictability, the results of that spontaneity soon became old favourites themselves. Into this category come all the catchphrases, even catch-actions, used by Eric on 'little Ern' like the repeated reference to his 'short, fat, hairy legs'; 'There's no answer to that!'; 'Just watch it, that's all' as Eric grabbed Ernie by the lapels; the two-handed slap on the cheeks and shoulder-hug in a passing moment of endearment; 'Get out of that,' as he put a hand under Ernie's chin, a remnant from their early judo routine, in which Eric as the self-styled expert tries to demonstrate the art to Ernie, but can't understand when he's the only one to get hurt. Most famous was 'What d'you think of it so far?' to which the response, 'Rubbish!' – often ventriloquised by Morecambe through whatever prop presented itself at the time – became something of an audience rallying call.

'There are these two old men sitting...'

Summoned instinctively in moments of panic when something has to be said or done while the mind is groping for the next stage of the routine proper, lines like these have passed into a memory bank of comic gambits, a lucky dip which always guaranteed them a laugh. Here were old favourites like the joke with the mystery ending never to be divulged on television: 'There are these two old men sitting in deckchairs in the Sahara and one says to the other...; using the lens of the television camera as a mirror, Eric adjusting his tie, baring his teeth in a ventriloquial grin until hypnotised by his own stare, with Ernie, at first puzzled, speedily following suit; Eric's sure-fire impersonation of Jimmy Durante – 'Sittin' at my pi-har-no the udder day' – with paper cup for schnozzle. Their use of incidental props in this context was unerring, Eric trying to attract the audience's attention as Ernie sings by bouncing an invisible ball which he catches – complete with sound effect made by concealed middle finger – in a paper bag, until Ernie himself and members of the audience are taking turns at throwing the missile; Eric flattening the same bag behind his spectacles to give his impersonation of 'The Invisible Man'; demonstrating that the handkerchief in his top pocket is really the tail of his shirt, only needing a slight pull for his opposite leg to shoot up, at which Ernie is adamant: 'You ought to be ashamed of yourself. The band, yes; but you, never!'

In similar vein they genuflected to the folklore of variety, as when the bulky presence of Janet Webb, who appeared nowhere else in their act, barged into the limelight to monopolise their final applause and then thank the audience 'for watching my little show here tonight. Good night and I love you all.' Everyone in the business knew this was meant – good-naturedly – to guy Beryl Formby, who gratuitously shared the spotlight with husband George whenever she could inveigle her way onstage. Or it might have been the presence of Arthur Tolcher, the veteran harmonica player, anxious to finish his number at opportune moments throughout the show in a last desperate fling to keep the dying corpse of third-rate variety alive, only to be told by Eric, 'Not now, Arthur.' The list appears never-ending, each device a trademark for the mechanics of the relationship they built up over the years, as well as the password for an assumed intimacy between audience and performers.

As the above hints, one of their strongest cards was demolishing the conventions of their own profession, show business, a task made more credible by the willingness of actors of the stature of Michael Redgrave, John Mills, Eric Porter, Edward Woodward, Peter Cushing and Flora Robson to help them enact Ernie's plays 'what I wrote' on their television show. The honour invested in the indignity of Morecambe failing to recognise them or get their name right became a significant one. The plays also allowed Eric with his spring-heeled enthusiasm a fancy-dress field day as he portrayed Toulouse-Lautrec with boots on his knees, a crutch-bearing Long John Silver dancing in his uncertainty of which leg to cock up, or Octavius Caesar with hussar's hat and an eagle-topped standard reading Luton FC on the reverse side of SPQR, while all the time Ernie was fussing around, apologising to the guest stars using the very clichés he had given them to say. But in spite of the joyful marriage between their talents and those of their 'legitimate' guests (a triumph as much for the impresario skills of their key BBC producer, John Ammonds) they remained at their most hilarious when guying their own scene, the world of the performer as individualist. It may have been Eric as Erico Morecambeovicz attempting to play Grieg's Piano Concerto in the testing company of virtuoso André Previn, or 'Andrew Preview' as Eric introduced him.

Ernie: But you're playing all the wrong notes.
Eric: Oh no. I'm playing the right notes, but not necessarily in the right order.
Ernie: Oh!

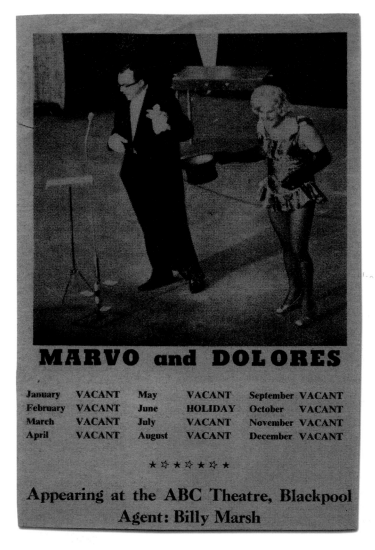

MARVO and DOLORES

January	VACANT	May	VACANT	September	VACANT
February	VACANT	June	HOLIDAY	October	VACANT
March	VACANT	July	VACANT	November	VACANT
April	VACANT	August	VACANT	December	VACANT

★ ☆ ★ ☆ ★ ☆ ★

Appearing at the ABC Theatre, Blackpool
Agent: Billy Marsh

For the record, the original premise of this routine, alongside the device of Wise as self-esteemed author, belonged to Sid Green and Dick Hills, who first wrote it to feature piano star Peter Nero in the ATV days.

More usually, however, the inspiration would refer back to their earliest days in variety. So were born 'Marvo and Dolores', the archetype of every third-rate magician and his quasi-glamorous assistant ever to tread the boards. Ernie played the upholstered tutu-flaunting blonde in attendance on Eric, who released a steady stream of telltale feathers from his bedraggled tails rather like the whiffs of a smoke signal the cavalry weren't supposed to see, as he stumped around the stage, interrupted only by the alarming bird-like noises coming from somewhere on his person. They chose to feature this routine at the London Palladium in the third of their four appearances in the Royal Variety Performance in November 1966, the others being in 1961, 1964 and 1968. 'The boys', as they were affectionately referred to in the business by their agent, Billy Marsh, also brilliantly extended their burlesque into reality, taking out trade advertisements for the magic act announcing they were 'Vacant' for January, February, March, April and so on throughout the year, with the exception of June, which was reserved for 'Holiday'. At no point were their own names mentioned in the ad. In a similar vein theatre programmes printed the act as just another speciality act on the Eric and Ernie show, giving no clue at all to audiences that this would turn out to be the comedy bonus of all time.

There was their top hat and tails routine, harking back fondly not merely to their mutual love of the old Hollywood, but also to Ernie's training as a song and dance man – or boy – under the aegis of impresario Jack Hylton in the days before he met Eric; at the time he had been dubbed Britain's answer to Mickey Rooney. In the most memorable of their many variations on this basic theme they were joined by Glenda Jackson on a staircase of MGM proportions. There was no difference in the panache they displayed each time they threw their canes out of vision and then caught them nonchalantly on the rebound, except that at each stage Eric's cane grew in size until he was nursing a pole as tall as himself. On another occasion they featured an adagio routine with a phantom girl partner, swinging her around by the ankles, spinning her into the air and, adamantly refusing not to believe in their total concept, disclaiming any responsibility as she plummeted to the bare boards, a fate similar to that suffered by Jackson as the climax to the earlier routine when she toppled over the prop staircase.

Topping it all was Morecambe's love–hate relationship with ventriloquism, a theme pursued along standard Sandy Powell lines in their stage act, but expanded to surrealist dimensions on one precious occasion for television. This time the dummy was three times Morecambe's height, enough to cause him to sway backwards and forwards under the strain. 'Solid oak! You know that clearing in Epping Forest? This is him. Here, hold it a minute,' he says to Wise, who buckles at the mere thought. Ernie is more anxious to know how it works. 'You mean how do I reach his thing?' asks Morecambe. At Wise's suggestion a stepladder is brought in which Eric climbs to work the lips. Of course, he is then too far away for the dummy to be heard through his clenched teeth. He comes down for a conference with Ernie, but before he gets there the dummy has fallen crashing to the floor, pinning a struggling Wise beneath it. There was seldom a performance when their basic act did not include their private homage to the doyen of variety vents, Arthur

Arthur Worsley and Charlie Brown:
'He thinks I'm real – don't you, son?'

Worsley (1920 – 2001), whose dummy, Charlie Brown, did (almost) all of the talking and was continually berating its owner, 'Look at me, son, when I'm talking to you!' Ernie or a guest had only to look away from Eric to cue the line.

Their greatest strength as they drove these routines along to their wildest limits was that they never lost sight of the fact that they were guying themselves at the same time. The following exchange frequently found its way into their performance:

Ernie: You're turning the whole thing to ridicule.
Eric: What d'ya mean?
Ernie: Well, you're making us look like a cheap music hall act.
Eric: Well, we *are* a cheap music hall act.

Their imaginary day-to-day existence behind the scenes informed much of their television comedy, especially in the sequences that depicted them relaxing in the cosy banality of the flat they shared. This was more a time/space vacuum than a home, and yet for all its anonymity as meaningful to their relationship as the more specific address of 23 Railway Cuttings was to Hancock. Here they would discuss the old touring days, the lost Empires, the theatrical landladies that went with them. This was the situation of their comedy, the double act playing itself, so that what would in other circumstances have been regarded as theatrical in-jokes became not merely acceptable to the wider public, but essential as the background detail the decor of the flat visibly lacked. In this way Eric would settle down with Ernie's copy of the *Stage*.

> *Eric*: 'Herbert and Sylvia Makepeace – still at it on the grand piano.' Does your mother know you read stuff like this?
> *Ernie*: There's nothing wrong with that.
> *Eric*: 'Bernard Delfont still looking for girls.'
> *Ernie*: For the summer.
> *Eric*: Doesn't he do it in the winter, then? 'Elsie and her Disappearing Canary'. 'ATV becomes 53rd American State'.

In this same flat in later years a routine that always gave Wise the dolly bird and Morecambe the sour-faced best friend was realigned to the point where the prospect of a date with Princess Anne or a glimpse of Ada Bailey's knickers on the line next door were equally meaningful. But one could never be sure that either would get the girl, and if Eric seemed more sex-mad than his partner it was probably because his short-sightedness added an additional sense of adventure to his sexual escapades. Moreover, each would take turns in adopting a display of puritanism to drive home their recurrent use of innuendo. It may have been Ernie during their ventriloquist sketch:

> *Ernie*: Have you ever done it while drinking a glass of water?
> *Eric*: No, but I had a glass of water instead of it once.
> *Ernie*: That's not what we're talking about!

It may have been Eric: 'Maracas? Please, no words like that in front of the ladies.' Puritanism has most opportunities in a one-track mind.

The flat itself stood for the larger-than-life pantomime horse's skin that being a double act for over thirty years must entail. Their popularity was best testified to, not by box office returns, not by television ratings – huge as both were – but by the avalanche of public affection and concern that greeted the screeching halt in their activity caused by Eric's near-fatal heart attack at the end of 1968, the result of much worry and considerable overwork. When they returned, it was to restrict their appearance to British television and the occasional one-night stand, a routine they continued to follow under the shadow all double acts must dread, namely the loss of the other half. But there were other obstacles to overcome around that critical time. A few months before the tragedy, disappointed by their earlier failure to live up to Lew Grade's expectations of them as potential international stars as well as anxious to record their shows in colour, they had failed to reach anything but a monochrome agreement with ATV and recorded a series – this time flesh-tinted – for the BBC. Few performers switch channels successfully, but reunited with producer John Ammonds, who years before had helped to launch them in radio in Manchester, they soon achieved a form equal to their best for the commercial company, where their producer Colin Clews had instilled into their work a freshness and novelty that never faltered. It did not help Eric's recovery that in the uncertainty of the moment the brilliantly inventive Green and Hills, their writers since 1961, signed an exclusive writing contract with ATV. Memories of Hancock's experience in changing writers at the height of his success could not have helped Eric's convalescence. The services of Eddie Braben, who had already served a spell as Ken Dodd's principal writer, were imaginatively secured on their behalf by Bill Cotton, the BBC's head of variety. Braben proved to be far more than, in Eric's words, 'a gift from heaven', bringing in character developments and stylistic innovations that in retrospect would have been eventually necessary for professional survival given the rate of exposure they had committed themselves to on television.

Established as the BBC's top stars, when they now appeared in the provinces they achieved a reception not far removed in spirit from that reserved by the people of Cobh, near Cork in Ireland, for Laurel and Hardy in 1953. John McCabe quotes Stan's account of their arrival in his biography, *Mr Laurel and Mr Hardy*: 'There were hundreds of boats blowing whistles, and mobs and mobs of people screaming on the docks. We just couldn't understand what it was all about. And then something happened that I can never forget. All the church bells in Cobh started to ring out our theme song, and Babe looked at me, and we cried.' In short, love was in the air. The real key to their popularity was the loyalty and camaraderie that appeared to bind the two, each obviously regarding the other as a genuinely funny man, a camaraderie never impaired in the audience's view by Ernie's show of pomposity or Eric's barbed defiance. It is hard to believe that any double act can last such a long career without at some time one or the other believing he was demeaning himself for the glory of the other. There would inevitably have been tensions in their partnership, but for the most part, for all Eric's protestations to the contrary, Morecambeandwise – well, you really couldn't see the join.

AFTERTHOUGHTS

Their later years were plagued by Morecambe's health problems and an unwise career move. At the beginning of 1978 they made front-page news when they switched allegiance back to ITV under the banner of Thames Television. It took time before Braben could make the transition with them. In 1979 Eric underwent open-heart surgery. He recovered sufficiently to be able to rehearse and record at a slower pace, but they never regained the stature they had enjoyed at the BBC, where their audiences were unparalleled in ratings history and their signature tune, 'Bring me sunshine', lit up the heart of any executive needing to justify the licence fee as value for money. Their 1977 Christmas show is said to have attracted 28,835,000 viewers. The casting of the guest stars at Thames maintained its high standard – Alec Guinness, Judi Dench and ex-prime minister Harold Wilson all played along – and there were comic moments to rival the best of their previous work. Their pastiche of the Disney film version of *The Jungle Book* revealed Morecambe at his physically funniest as, upholstered to high heaven in fur as Baloo the bear, he wobbled uncontrollably to 'I wanna be like you' while Ernie had a field day as a hyperactive orange-coloured King Louis. However, after so long at the BBC, the ambience of the commercial station seemed out of kilter, although in retrospect perhaps their greatest work took place at ATV first time around, before the arrival of the sometimes distracting guest stars, whose presence tended to tilt the product towards the formulaic. Their later shows at Thames played down the guests, but by then the energy had been lost.

The 'Jungle Book' sketch

Eric died from a further heart attack on 28 May 1984, having collapsed onstage at the end of an evening being interviewed at the Roses Theatre, Tewkesbury by his friend Welsh comedian Stan Stennett. Only six weeks earlier Tommy Cooper had died in not dissimilar circumstances and many close to Morecambe have speculated that his demise may have been accelerated by the shock of the departure of his old friend. Ernie had been strangely absent onstage that night. He now struggled bravely to pursue a solo career in showbiz – mercifully, rumoured attempts to pair him with Bernie Winters came to naught – but as he veered between panel games, the odd pantomime and a run in a West End musical based on Dickens' *The Mystery of Edwin Drood*, he must have been the first to appreciate that something was missing that could never be recreated. He himself died in the wake of triple heart bypass surgery on 21 March 1999. Since then television reruns have kept the pair in the public eye, especially at Christmas, although there is a danger that they have now overstayed their welcome as part of the medium's seasonal charivari, used by the BBC to disguise the low quality of much of its contemporary output. That said, as a double act they succeeded in their day in appealing to all classes and could best be summed up as the Marks and Spencer of British comedy. Their quality constitutes the what-might-have been if Sid Field had flourished within the television age.

Guinness with Genius

The relative lack of success Ernie subsequently enjoyed without Eric invites the question of how well the latter would have fared had their departures been reversed. It is impossible to imagine so reactive a performer working as a single act. It is equally hard to envisage Morecambe with any other partner: the onstage telepathy developed over thirty years would not have been there with anyone else. Moreover, Eric possessed an undeniably cynical streak in his humour, the edge of which was softened by the geniality exuded by Wise. For all Morecambe's brilliance, there is no guarantee that the public would have taken him to their hearts had he not been so cosseted, allowed to shine under the unselfish long-suffering gaze of so professional a partner. To be in their company offstage was always to sense a chip on the Morecambe shoulder beneath the well developed protective shield of put-downs and comic bravado, maybe a legacy from the earliest years, when his mother had set the agenda for his future career and cannily tied him to the apron strings of the young song-and-dance man. He admitted in *Eric and Ernie*, their joint 1973 autobiography, that he had found performing as a juvenile a chore and that it was his mother who 'pushed me into show business and kept me there until I was safely in Ernie's hands: he's been doing the pushing ever since'. If this was the case, it says much for Eric's loyalty through the years, just as it also speaks volumes for his insistence on a private life that seemed to shut the door on the act the moment he arrived home, although he was more than happy to be publicised in a solo capacity, promoting his other interests like Luton Town Football Club, birdwatching and fishing. To make up for his partner's alleged lack of interest in business matters, Ernie assumed an air of managerial responsibility for the act: not for nothing had Jack Hylton been his mentor. In public and private Wise might be said to have kept the act on the straight and narrow, at times showing reserves of tact and discretion when the public might not have expected it. It was churlish that in 1998, when Eric was included in the special Royal Mail stamp issue to honour comedians, Ernie, who had a year to live, was not by his partner's side, an omission justified by the explanation that no living person is allowed to be featured in the space alongside the Queen. But exceptions have been made when it suits the interests of the postal authorities. Morecambe and Wise had both been appointed OBE in 1976: no one then would have envisaged honouring one without the other.

Nothing however should be allowed to cast doubt on Morecambe's comedic qualities, not least his speed with a barbed line in the best spontaneous tradition of Groucho himself, doubtless the positive by-product by way of defence mechanism exercised to cope with any grudge borne, however subconsciously. No one proved more vulnerable to this approach than the entertainer Des O'Connor, who for years figured as an invisible straight man in their act. When Eric had his first heart attack, Des asked his theatre audience to pray for his speedy recovery. When Morecambe was told this, he replied, 'Tell him that those six or seven people made all the difference.' When Des got to appear on their show in person, he asked if he could sing. Eric replied, 'Sing on our show? You can't even sing on your own show!'

Until Eric's health got in the way, the boys closed each show with their distinctive take on a Groucho Marx dance, skipping towards the horizon, away from the camera, shifting their hands alternately between the backs of their heads and their backs. For the audience of the day it approximated to a modern equivalent of Chaplin's trademark waddle into the distance, a poignant indication that nothing will last for ever. Subliminally it marked the fading of the variety era. For almost twenty years the pair conveyed on the small screen variety's combined ethos of glamour, fun and communication across the footlights. As traditional variety on television went into decline at the expense of situation comedy and game shows, their show never constituted less than the blue riband of the old formula.

Incidentally, the publication of their autobiography marked an amusing moment in my own life. Imagine my surprise when the day after the launch, to which I had been invited, *The Times* reported on the event with a photograph of Eric and Ernie standing side by side. Lurking between them is a strange, anonymous face. You've guessed! Eventually I managed to get my copy signed by the pair. Ernie wrote, 'To Mr Show Business,' to which Eric added, 'Yes, but what do you do for a living?' To them both I owe my pictorial presence in the broadsheet press of the day, but sadly, Eric, it made no difference. I'm still looking for a proper job. To which he'd probably reply, 'There's no answer to that!'

TOMMY COOPER: ALMOST A MAGICIAN!

I can't help laughing. I know what's coming next!

I found these in the attic the other day. So I took them to an expert and he said, 'What you've got there – you've got a Stradivarius and a Rembrandt. Unfortunately… Stradivarius was a terrible painter and Rembrandt made rotten violins!'

It has been said before and it will be said many times again, 'You just had to look at him and you laughed.' It wasn't as simple as that, of course. Tommy was as much subject to the occupational hazards of insecurity and self-doubt as any comedian and as a highly conscientious professional would retreat into a private world to which the public was not admitted. At those times he could be vehemently serious, but essentially the message is loud and clear. More than anyone featured in this volume, Tommy Cooper was born funny: he not only had funny bones, he had funny genes. Once described with loving accuracy as 'picking his way through the debris of fumbled conjuring tricks like a gigantic stork pecking for sustenance in a morass', he was arguably the most physically funny man in the world, the key, one feels, to Thomas Mann's idea, in *The Confessions of Felix Krull*, of clowns as 'basically alien beings… side-splitting, world-renouncing monks of unreason, cavorting hybrids, part human and part insane art'. His lumbering bulk contained a compendium of hilarity from the massive twitching hands – 'See that one there, look. Well this one's just the same!' – to the outsize splayed feet, from the anxious lumpen features to the shrugging shoulders capable of registering success and disappointment with equal flair. But not all was weighed down by gravity. There were times on stage when he resembled a football star with his ability to change direction with amazing cunning, the feints and swerves of his body adding a balletic quality to the performance. Cooper was as capable of doing double takes with his legs and his feet as with those deep-set soulful eyes. Revelling in a brilliantly deceptive air of under-rehearsed confusion, he mined a rich vein of burlesque humour with gusto. The momentary look of intense bewilderment when his conjuring tricks misfired, followed by the maniacal cackle that was at once his wand and safety valve, launching hopes and greeting failure alike, guyed the self-importance of every second-rate jongleur who could pull anything out of a hat but his own self-esteem.

Over the years Cooper developed as assured a sense of personal branding as Charlie Chaplin, George Robey and Max Miller before him. Take away the fez and smooth down the tufts of jet-black hair trained to sprout like a pair of upturned inverted commas from beneath its brim and you might as well put Santa Claus in a kilt. This led to him becoming the most impersonated entertainer in recent British show business and helps to keep him in the forefront of our shared comic consciousness almost thirty years after his death at a time when most of his comic peers have begun to recede into oblivion. The fez was exotic enough as an item of headgear to have been worn by a whole parade of relatively insignificant

FUNNY WAY TO BE A HERO

magicians before him, but none wore it with such authority, such abandon as Cooper. Tommy told the story a million times of the night soon after the end of hostilities when he mislaid the pith helmet he was wearing in his act as a struggling forces entertainer in Cairo and happened to reach out to grab the fez from the head of a passing waiter as a replacement. It paid instant dividends, adding even further height to his already impressive six feet three inches. Once he was launched on his professional career back home, it soon became a beacon of fun and frivolity as he strode to the footlights, inseparable in the public consciousness from the rolling gait and the catchphrase that also labelled him.

He always claimed that 'Jus' like that!' came about by accident. In later years he was only too happy to embroider upon it with those expressive hands pointing down in counterpoint at waist level: 'Not like that! Like that!' followed by some incomprehensible incantation of dubious foreign extraction that might have been spelled 'Zhhzhhzhhzhh' but probably wasn't. In retrospect it was the perfect verbal trademark for a comedy exponent of a demonstrative art like magic. The catchphrase and the hat were obviously made for each other, as Tommy found with his wife Gwen when he returned on holiday to Egypt at the peak of his fame.

> We were in Cairo and we came across a guy selling fezzes in the market. I went up to try one on and the guy turned to me and said, 'Jus' like that!' I said, 'How do you know that? That's my catchphrase!' He said, 'What's a catchphrase? I know nothing about any catchphrase. But I do know that every time an English person comes up here and tries on one of these fezzes, they turn to their friends and say 'Jus' like that!' And you're the first one not to say it!' Marvellous, isn't it!

Thomas Frederick Cooper was born in Caerphilly on 19 March 1921. He was three years old when his family relocated to Exeter, where one Christmas he received the life-defining gift of a box of conjuring tricks from his Aunt Lucy, who lived nearby. In 1933 his parents moved again, to the outskirts of Southampton, just outside Fawley, where he left school at fourteen to take up an apprenticeship at the British Power Boat Company in Hythe, the principal employer in the area. Here his talent for burlesque and relish for laughter were discovered by accident when one Christmas he was cajoled into giving a performance in the works canteen. When the time came, his body turned to jelly and his throat to sandpaper. Everything let him down, not least his big trick where the milk was supposed to stay suspended in the bottle when it was upended. As he remembered it, 'The stage was swimming with milk. I dropped my wand. I did everything wrong. But the audience loved it. The more I panicked and made a mess of everything, the more they laughed. I came off and cried, but five minutes later I could still hear the sound of the laughter in my ears and was thinking maybe there's a living to be made here.' By the outbreak of war he had already enlisted in the Horse Guards, where he spent seven years before becoming a professional funny man. 'Trooper Cooper – huh – huh!' he used to joke. His height made him a natural for the Blues. More importantly the experience he gained doing shows in the NAAFI and later for Combined Services Entertainment proved invaluable.

The fez that launched a thousand quips

In November 1947, a few months after his demob, he came to the attention of Miff Ferrie, a jazz musician and band leader anxious to get into management. Their partnership lasted until the end of Cooper's life, as tempestuous as many marriages but tempered by a mutual respect that Tommy found difficult to acknowledge in public. Within weeks Miff's influence had secured him a spot on a gala Christmas Eve television variety show hosted by musical comedy star Leslie Henson, in spite of Tommy making a lacklustre impression at the BBC audition he had attended a short while before Miff made his acquaintance. Before long Cooper was a fixture on the London cabaret circuit and by July 1950 was filling in as a replacement for Michael Bentine as the top comedy attraction in the Folies Bergère revue at the London Hippodrome. His success secured him a permanent place in the second edition of the show. When *Encore des Folies* opened on 6 March 1951 the critic from the *Daily Telegraph* considered the ensemble lacked inspiration and rehearsal, but conceded that 'the best individual turn was provided by Tommy Cooper… I have never before seen anybody do as little as Mr Cooper and yet be so terribly

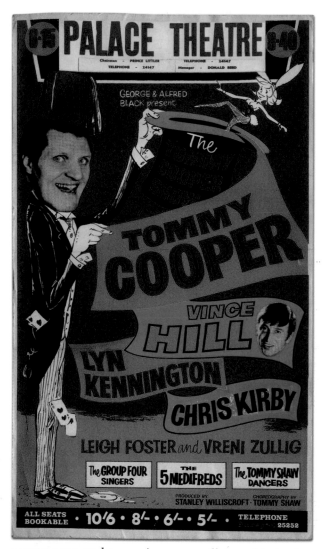

funny.' Future long-running West End appearances would include working alongside Benny Hill in *Paris by Night* at the Prince of Wales Theatre in 1955 and co-starring with Shirley Bassey in *Blue Magic* at the same venue in 1959. He made a modest, but show-stopping Palladium debut in a bill topped by the forgotten American comedy team Peter Lind Hayes and Mary Healy in July 1952 and returned several times over the years: for the Coronation variety season in 1953; for the pantomime *Robinson Crusoe*, in which he played the sidekick, Abu, to Arthur Askey's dame at Christmas 1957; and alongside Frankie Vaughan and Cilla Black in *Startime* during the summer of 1964. He at last achieved undisputed top-of-the-bill status at the theatre in the summer revue *To See Such Fun* in 1971. However, if one event turned the tide of recognition during the early years of Cooper's career, it was probably the BBC's live *Television Christmas Party* of 1952. Being essentially a visual performer, Cooper did not have the benefit of radio to advance his cause in the manner of so many of his ex-service colleagues at this time. By the end of 1952, however, television had expanded beyond leaps and bounds from the privileged plaything of dubious picture quality that it represented in 1947. Nor did it hurt that newspapers and magazines were all tuned into the event. Cooper stole the show from established stars and newcomers alike as he got up to his usual tricks and magicked a block of wood – from ear to ear – through the head of the host, McDonald Hobley. Cooper always looked back on this one appearance as the turning point in his perception by the public.

It surprises many to learn that there had been a long string of burlesque magic men on the halls before Cooper made the role his own. These included Carlton, Frank Van Hoven, Artemus, The Great Claude, Walton and Lester, billed as 'The World's Worst Wizards', and Arthur Dowler – 'The Wizard of Cod'. Some were more slapstick than others, some more anxious to weave their comedy around a residual display of manipulative skill. A little of most of them rubbed off one way or another on Cooper, but none of them approached the task with the inner reserves of charisma, the heaven-sent comedic gifts that Cooper was endowed with at birth. At a more serious level, the star magicians of the day were all slick and sophisticated, neat and necromantic in the nicest of ways, and the contrast could not have worked better in Tommy's favour. In contrast to the swallow-tailed elegance of a Jasper Maskelyne appeared someone with the hands of a labourer and the legs of an ostrich who looked nothing like the regular model. As such he had the edge over all others who had styled themselves comedy magicians.

Dominating his stage were two large tables, the tops of which represented some surreal car boot sale that had spiralled out of control. Here were props for playing with, like the spoon in the jar with the invisible thread attached: 'Spoon, jar! Jar, spoon!'; props for throwing aside: 'Here we have a skipping rope – so we'll skip that!'; props for dropping for the sole purpose of picking them up: 'See that. I'm not afraid of work!'; props for questioning: 'I don't know what that's for!'; props for talking to like the wooden duck trained to find the chosen card: 'You may have seen a duck do that before,' he would screech, 'but, to be fair, blindfolded?'; props to debunk mystery, as when he produced a supposed dove from his crumpled handkerchief and then rolled up the pitiful rubber object to place in his pocket; props to suggest his versatility, like a tap on a string that he would pick up and jiggle: 'Look, a tap dance!'; props to show his dexterity, as when he threw an egg into the air only for it to shatter the plate that was supposed to catch it intact; props that hint at some vestige of domestic routine, like the flower in the pot that wilts the moment he turns away from watering it, not once, not twice, but ad infinitum; props with no apparent reason at all, like the portable white gate through which he would stroll as he went from one routine to another; and occasionally props for genuinely succeeding with, providing moments when the magic came right and his look of triumph was a wonder to behold. His enthusiasm was contagious. Driving the routine was an anarchy that was nothing if not liberating, ahead of its time in reflecting the message of modern stress therapists to rid ourselves of the clutter of our lives – the Christmas presents never used, the gadgets that never worked.

Totemic were the bottle and the glass which were supposed to change places beneath their cardboard covers. 'The bottle has now changed places with the glass,' he would announce without lifting the tubes, then continue, 'The most difficult part of the trick is to make them go back again.' He'd eventually segue into a series of simultaneous reveals – 'Glass, bottle! Bottle, glass!… Bottle, glass! Glass, bottle!' – before disastrously letting the audience see two glasses at one time, then two bottles, then in quick succession leaving all four objects in view and flinging the tubes aside. Sometimes in an unexpected conclusion the table would end up swamped by more than thirty or so bottles. The speed of the finish was incredible, while words on a page can give no impression of the overpowering presence and nervous energy that drove the whole routine along. The skill with which he ruined his act was dazzling. Magic provided him with the perfect metaphor with which to comment upon the human condition. He was every one of us who has ever fumbled his or her way through a conjuring trick in a social situation. And when a trick came off, his success became our success. He was clever enough to ensure that from time to time triumph sneaked up on him regardless, however much he adopted that blissful head-in-the-clouds attitude of not seeming to know what was going on. In truth, he left nothing to chance. A stagehand once commented on his habit of treble-checking every prop before a show: 'Tommy's no fool. He knows where every single bit of gear is. It's like a space-launch countdown.'

The precision of his technique gave the lie to his apparent clumsiness, and in his preparation he was as painstaking as the greatest practitioners of serious stage conjuring ever were. There is no better example than his cabinet routine. At Tommy's beckoning two stagehands would wheel on a wardrobe-size piece of apparatus with red curtain in lieu of door. It comes on faster than expected. At the split second it reaches centre stage, Cooper, clearing the decks for its arrival, just so happens to be standing in its path. The collision leaves him dazed and disoriented until, pulling himself together for the miracle ahead, he draws our attention to the pitch-black interior. As he turns the prop first to the right and then to the left, no one in the audience can have a single doubt about its innocence: 'Empty! Empty! Empty!' Reaching over the threshold he raps his clenched fist against the inside walls to prove the point further. Genuine hurt steals over his features as he hits too hard, but the show must go on. With all the bravura of one of the great masters of the past he steps inside, draws the curtain across and almost instantly whips it back again. There has been no time at all for anything to have occurred, but his expression

'Egg, bag – bag, egg!'

suggests that this makeshift Tardis has revealed the ghost of Rasputin. Back on terra firma he pulls the curtain across once more and proceeds to make a series of fussy mystical passes towards it, each pointedly from a different direction and loudly accompanied by a tymp roll. Then with studied intent he jerks the curtain back sharply. There is no one there. Nothing has happened. Nothing will happen. For a nanosecond expectancy hangs in the air before Cooper succumbs to disdain and dismissal. For one incredible moment the audience ceases to exist. He shrugs almost subliminally to the stagehands to take the cabinet back whence it came, slapping the side nearest to him as he does so: 'Right!' The bathos of his delivery tells us all we need to know. In that one word is wrapped up more than the secret admission of his own failure, but the guilt and frustration of every one of us who sets out high-handedly to achieve a personal goal we know we can never attain. The underplaying of the end says a thousand words. The basic emotions of pain, fear and guilt are enacted with his whole body at a level with which the audience for all its laughter truly empathises. More importantly the immediacy of the sequence never left him. However many times he played the routine, he never left you in any doubt that what you were seeing performed was taking place for the very first time. No wonder that today thespians as distinguished as Anthony Hopkins, Michael Gambon and Simon Callow regard him as highly as they do.

As his confidence grew, so Cooper – alert to the straitjacketing effect magic might have on him – widened his comic horizons into skits and routines that had not a magic wand in sight. His comic idols included Jack Benny, Bob Hope, Laurel and Hardy and Arthur Askey, whose outward display of energy on stage he emulated, but no one more so than Max Miller. Tommy would go to watch Max time after time and admitted to learning wide swathes of his patter off by heart, even though ostensibly their styles were far apart. Innuendo was never part of Cooper's comic arsenal. After Max's death he began to use much of his material – with his blessing I am sure. A few years before Miller died he had befriended the younger comic and later entrusted him with his trademark white trilby. Tommy's verbal dexterity failed to match that of the master, but in his inability to match the flow and rhythm of Max's timing he created a rough poetry of his own and somehow the material stayed funny. Tommy would in time build up a lexicon of jokes culled from all four corners of the joke book universe, but destined to become indelibly his own. None of them were funnier than those bequeathed by the Cheeky Chappie. 'I was talking to this girl the other day and I said to her, "Are you familiar with Shakespeare?" She said, "As a matter of fact I am. I had dinner with him last night." I said, "What are you talking about? He's been dead for years." She said, "I thought he was quiet!"' Then there were the wife jokes. It possibly helped in the devoted eyes of Cooper's wife, Gwen – Dove as he called her – that Miller had delivered them first: 'I've got the best wife in England. The other one's in Africa!' and 'The other day I came home and the wife was crying her eyes out. I said, "What's wrong?" She said, "I feel homesick." I said, "This is your home." She said, "I know. I'm sick of it."' Miller – and Cooper by default – had millions of them. 'My wife came in the other day and she said, "What's different about me?" And I said, "I don't know. What is different about you? Have you had your hair done?" She said, "No." I said, "Have you got a new dress on?" She said, "No." "Have you got a new pair of shoes?" She said, "No." I said, "Well, I don't know. What is different about you?" She said "I'm wearing a gas mask!"' Tommy was still making audiences cry at the latter almost forty years after the gas masks had been stored away.

In time Cooper's act appeared to become a repository for jokes in most categories. People associated doctor jokes with him as readily as they did bungled hocus pocus: 'So I said to the doctor, "How do I stand?" He said, "That's what puzzles me!" I said, "Doctor, I feel like a pair of curtains." He said, "Then pull yourself together." "Doctor, doctor," I said, "There's something wrong with my foot. What should I do?" He said, "Limp."' There were the dog jokes: 'My dog's a one-man dog – he only bites me. He took a big lump out of my knee the other day and a friend of mine said, "Did you put anything on it?" I said, "No. He liked it as it was."' There were the waiter jokes: 'I said to the waiter, "This chicken I've got here's cold." He said, "It should be. It's been dead two weeks." I said, "Not only that, it's got one leg shorter than the other." He said, "What do you want to do? Eat it or dance with it?" I said "Forget the chicken. Give me a lobster." So he brought me a lobster. I looked at it. I said, "Just a minute. It's only got one claw." He said, "It's been in a fight." I said, "Well, give me the winner."'

He rejoiced in one-liners, shaggy dog stories, schoolboy howlers and visual puns like when he ignited the explosive in the baking tin and announced 'Just a flash in the pan!' To Cooper jokes were like tricks, to be performed, then discarded with the reckless abandon with which he would cast aside the playing cards, dice and silk scarves of the magician's trade. It is no coincidence that jokes also derive their energy from twists in logic or language or both, in the way that conjuring takes liberties with the accepted realities of the world. Cooper's philosophy of humour was basic but sound. He never concerned himself with the possible antiquity of much of his material: 'It doesn't matter how old the gag is. It doesn't matter how many times the audience has heard it before. If it's funny, it's funny.' When asked once to explain his humour, he replied simply that the two funniest things were a surprise and a funny picture. His entire repertoire is a cartoon gallery of the unexpected.

The other night I slept like a log; I woke up in the fireplace.

Last night I dreamt I ate a ten-pound marshmallow. When I woke up the pillow was gone.

Sometimes I drink my whisky neat. Other times I take my tie off and leave my shirt hanging out.

Someone actually complimented me on my driving the other day. They put a note on my windscreen that said, 'Parking fine.' So that was nice.

My feet are killing me – every night when I'm lying in bed they get me right round the throat like that.

A definitive Cooper gag had qualities of conciseness and an outrageous courting of the obvious that might seem to contradict the surprise theory. But you seldom saw it coming, even when you had heard it before.

His funniest routine came completely from left field, a fancy-dress romp through a Pandora's box of assorted hats upon which he made a series of frenzied smash-and-grab raids to impersonate a seemingly never-ending stream of characters in a stirring mock-dramatic ballad in the tradition of 'The Shooting of Dan McGrew' by the Edwardian balladeer Robert William Service. An earlier sequence entitled 'A Few Impressions' had pointed the way. Here he shuttled back and forth between the theatre tabs in a series of daft impressions – each signified by the hat he was wearing – of 'famous people of the past, the present, and the future'. In quick succession came Uncle Sam, John Bull, Napoleon, English sailor, American sailor, 'two sailors at once', Napoleon again, 'We should not have lost the war!' (*Nazi helmet*), 'Why?' (*British Tommy*), the King of Norway, 'the other way' (*Turns hat through ninety degrees*), Nelson (*With a hand over his right eye*), half-nelson (*Same as before, but down on bended knee*) and so on. Sometimes he would become hopelessly entangled with the curtains, sometimes completely out of sync with the invisible assistant backstage readying each hat for him.

The cardboard box provided audiences with a new focus and enabled Cooper to garner even bigger laughs as the time approached when curtains would no longer be a *sine qua non* of performance. The effortless ability to switch with lightning speed from one hat to another, signifying a whole procession of characters that included tramp, sailor, banker, cowboy, soldier, little old lady, fireman, pilot, policeman and a few more along the way – while attempting to keep some sort of order in the box – would alone have qualified many a lesser performer for a place in variety's hall of fame. The words of the doggerel that began

> 'Twas New Year's Eve in Joe's bar, a happy mob was there.
> The bar and tables were crowded, lots of noise filled the air.
> In the midst of all this gaiety the door banged open wide.
> A torn and tattered tramp walked in. 'Happy New Year, folks,' he cried.

were largely inconsequential – and sometime incomprehensible – but provided a springboard for his gift for comic looks like no other routine in his repertoire. Two thirds of the way through – '"Them's shooting words," a cowboy said. "Are you aimin' to be shot?"' – he would forget the words and have to go right back to the beginning whence he proceeded to mumble his way back on to the right lines, going through the motions with the hats all over again, all the while insinuating to the audience that it will soon be business as usual, as if nothing has happened. The laughter was now twice as loud. Inevitably at one stage he can't find the hat he needs: 'I've got to get a bigger box!' It's then time for the fireman to have his say. Tommy brings the helmet up so sharply, he appears to hit himself with considerable force on the forehead. Registering pain as only he can, he appeals to the wings, 'Now that's dangerous, that is. You should have padded that a bit. I could have cut my head open on that.' The poem concludes as the bar-room brawl gets out of hand and the law has to intervene.

> In the midst of all this fighting you could hear the knuckles crunch,
> When all of a sudden they heard a policeman's whistle…

It doesn't come.

> They heard a policeman's whistle…

No luck this time either.

> They heard a policeman's whistle…

At last the sound effect is heard from the wings. Tommy looks with disdain at the disgraced stagehand and utters the line that sums up amateur theatrics everywhere. 'Isn't it marvellous, eh? That's all he has to do. And he's wearing make-up as well!'

> Then a policeman came in and pinched the whole damn bunch!

Cooper never quite conquered the medium of television at a critical level in the manner of Hancock, Howerd or Morecambe and Wise, but his various series and specials, principally for Thames and ITV, were always guaranteed ratings winners. Tucked away in them are classic sketches that in another medium would have serviced a performer like Sid Field for a lifetime. In one he played a ventriloquist entertaining an audience on board a cruise liner as the ship is buffeted from side to side by a raging storm. Anyone who saw it will be laughing still, as well as impressed by the special effects that enabled the whole set to teeter backwards and forwards on a rocking mechanism as Tommy staggered this way and that on the tiny cabaret stage. The chair, the table, the performer and his dummy slither to and fro as Cooper attempts to prove that he is as fine a technician as the best of them. Much of the business where the head of the dummy becomes detached from the body and then disappears was anticipated by the comedy ventriloquial act of Sandy Powell. Cooper battles on against all the odds, coaxing the little fellow to sing for us – 'Gye, gye glues!' – and engaging in a frantic wrestling match as he attempts to restore the doll to its suitcase. This becomes a losing battle and as he concedes an encore to the doll water begins to pour through the first of four portholes in the wall at the back of the stage. No sooner has he closed this than water gushes through the second, then the third, then in pairs and so on, until in defiance of his efforts to stem the flow, it is cascading through all four together. All the while the stage is heaving to and fro, the magician and dummy drenched to desperation levels as they continue to slither in whichever direction gravity dictates. At the conclusion Tommy is literally poured into the wings. Had it been a sequence in a movie, the routine would be talked of today with the same reverence with which cineastes discuss the scene in the stateroom where the Marx Brothers manage to compress more people in a confined space than is humanly possible. At one point a stray lifebelt rolls across the tiny stage like a wistful comment on this very fact.

The sketches in which Cooper appeared to work the best were those that showed him fighting against the conjuring tricks played by fate, not least the caprices of inanimate objects. Appropriately another unforgettable sequence from his television career makes verbal acknowledgment of this, although fitting less obviously within the mould itself: the sight of Tommy in doublet, hose and flaxen wig confirmed our gravest suspicions that the boards at Stratford East and not Stratford-upon-Avon were his rightful habitat.

To be or not to be, that is the question.
Whether 'tis nobler in the mind to suffer
The slings and arrows of outrageous fortune...

Breaking off he immediately shifts into stand-up mode: 'I had a bit of bad luck yesterday. I was pinched for parking. I said to the officer, "But I'm in a cul-de-sac." He said, "I don't care what kind of car it is. You can't park here."'

Or to take arms against a sea of troubles...

'I usually travel by sea…' And so the verse of the original is brought up against the dire reality of the comic's lot, a double-edged comment on the two performing traditions. Other aspects of variety are brought into the mix, with Yorick's skull the pretext for further bad ventriloquism, this time in open parody of the already mentioned Arthur Worsley, who allowed his dummy Charlie Brown to do virtually all the talking as he stood there bemused and – a technical tour de force – tight-lipped, the almost unsmiling butt of a thousand jests, daring the audience to catch the merest lip movement. Tommy keeps his teeth clenched in defiance as with a nod to Worsley's catchphrase he attempts to coax words from the grotesque papier mâché head: 'Look at me, son. Look at me. Here's a joke. Here's one for you now.' But the jokes are incidental. Before long the real laugh becomes the impossibility of knowing who is supposed to be speaking to whom at any one time. The routine culminates with a song and soft-shoe in homage to Ophelia, a reworking of an old Max Miller number.

In the loose tradition of both 'Hats' and 'Hamlet' with their play on confused identity was the one-man play in which Tommy donned a half-and-half costume portraying a Nazi officer in one profile and a British brigadier in the other. As the two soldiers wrestle with the uncertainties of monocle and clip-on half-moustache and the constant turning from one profile to the other, the two parts become hilariously out of sync until it slowly dawns upon the brigadier that he is speaking the part of the Nazi. Thanks to the script of Johnnie Mortimer and Brian Cooke, they are discussing escaped prisoners.

Kommandant: When zey are caught, zey vill be shot.

Brigadier: Oh no, they won't.

Kommandant: Oh yes, zey vill.

Brigadier: Oh no, they won't

Kommandant: Oh yes, zey vill.

Brigadier: And ven zey are caught everyone vill be shot because…

(*Cooper thinks quickly and turns again*)

Kommandant: Vy are you imitating me?

The real joke, of course, was that he could become neither, remaining unmistakably Tommy Cooper whatever the costume, the accent or the facial appendage. And yet at another level, in order to make this very point, he was resorting to comic acting of considerable expertise.

The late 1960s and early 70s saw Cooper at his peak, his skills refined by the constant benefit of repeated performance, his health still on top of the skills themselves. As variety theatres and traditional summer seasons became scarcer or less remunerative, Miff Ferrie shrewdly moved his client into the burgeoning network of cabaret clubs opening throughout the country. No comic played these more successfully than Cooper, enabling him during the 70s and early 80s to become the highest-paid live British comedy attraction of his day. At the height of his client's career Ferrie was able to boast to one newspaper, 'If I told you how much Tommy gets, the other comedians would turn communist overnight!' A favourite of royalty, he almost inevitably stole the show whenever he appeared in the Royal Variety Performance, as he did in 1953, 1964, 1967, 1971 and 1977, or on similar gala occasions. In 1964 the whole country responded to his prize joke: 'I've brought the wife. I said, "How much is a ticket?" They said, "A hundred pounds." I said, "How much is a programme?" They said, "Six pounds." I said, "Give us a programme. She can sit on that."' In 1977 with half an eye on the Royal Box he took a sword from his table, carefully placed it on the ground and knelt expectantly in the direction of Her Majesty. After a hushed silence he stood, replaced the weapon and shrugged: 'Well, you never know, do you?'

Triumphs of this kind, however, were tempered by a rapid deterioration in his health caused by excessive smoking and drinking. As we have seen, the uncertainty that an audience may or may not find you funny on any one night, in any one town is an occupational hazard for the stand-up comedian. No one summed it up better than Ted Ray when he explained what it meant to sign a contract as a comedian: 'What you are doing, in effect, is saying to a future employer, that sometime next year, at a given date, time and place, *you will be funny*. It doesn't matter what happens between now and then. You can be ill, broke, lose everything you have ever held dear. On that night you *have* to make them laugh, because you have signed a contract that says so.' Tommy knew in his bones that no one ever forgave mediocrity in a comedian and faced up to the challenge of his own particular situation. He once confided to his friend Eric Sykes, 'People say I've only got to walk out onstage and they laugh. If only they knew what it takes to walk out onstage in the first place. One of these days I'll just walk out and do nothing. Then they'll know the difference.' In his early days Cooper had been close to being teetotal. When he did begin to drink in larger quantities, it was because he was successful and could now afford to do so. Sadly what began as a well earned luxury with which to wind down after a show became the crutch that helped him through the challenge Ted Ray had articulated so well. His pace slowed down, and the look that had once been a darting glance of comic acknowledgement as a trick misfired now took on a more searching, more contemplative aspect. Audiences still laughed, but the mood had changed from springtime to autumn. At the end of the 1970s, although far too late for his long-term health, he did attempt to arrest the decline and, knighthood or not, could still steal the show working at a slower pace, but he was in fact living on borrowed time.

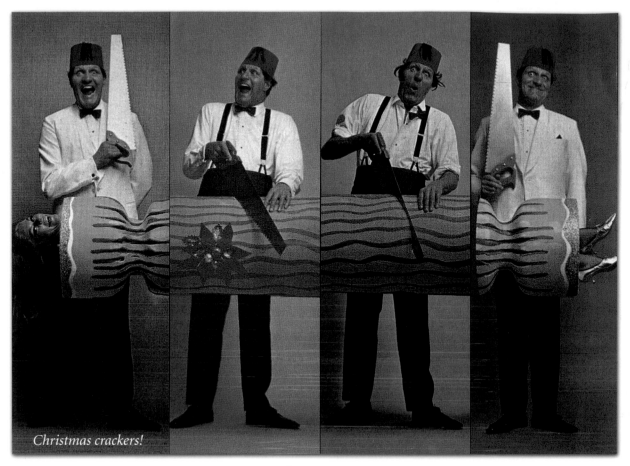

Christmas crackers!

He died the most visible of deaths as a result of coronary complications on live television during the transmission of the variety show *Live from Her Majesty's* on 15 April 1984. Curiously he was truly on form that night. Wearing a giant tube of Tunes cough sweets attached to his fez, he delivered the portentous opening line, 'Do you believe in reincarnation? Sometimes I think I'm Beethoven come back. I do really, because I've had tunes through my head all day.' From that moment the laughs flowed until he appeared to crumple to the floor under the weight of the voluminous scarlet cloak from which he was intending to produce – quite obviously through a gap in the curtains – a ludicrous assortment of objects that included a plank, a ladder, a beer crate and a leg for displaying nylon stockings in a shop window. At first the audience and technical crew assumed the collapse was all part of the act. Then gradually the truth dawned and a country went into mourning. The consensus was that this was the way he would have wanted to have died, but sadly his public had no say in the matter.

Some of the happiest moments of my life were spent in his company. He had a way of creating instant carnival when the mood was right, which was much of the time. To walk down a street with him was to expect everyone else to trail behind wearing their party hats and bashing their improvised musical instruments in a heady crocodile of exhilaration and fun. Magic was his life's blood: the simple tricks that spilled out of his pockets and enabled him offstage to display a more than competent skill essentially out of kilter with the dysfunctional facade that predominated in his act provided both relaxation and a favoured means of communication at the same time. But he always knew where the line had to be drawn between his own amusement and the stringent commercial demands of the repertoire that kept him at the top, even if the layperson would have been hard-pressed to read greater seriousness into an exploding top hat or a re-zippable banana than a relatively complex show of sleight of hand. In many ways he was the amateur and the professional combined. To those close enough to him it was not difficult to see the dividing line, as in one of his absurd half-and-half costumes. Paradoxically, however, the appeal he represented to the mass public was predicated on the blurring of the two, the supposedly shambolic and the obviously accomplished coming together as perhaps in no other performer.

Today he endures as part of the fabric of British folklore, a larger-than-life legend on a par with John Bull, Winston Churchill and Mr Punch, his jokes, mannerisms and catchphrases living on in the manner of nursery rhymes and playground chants, a vibrant part of the heritage of a nation at play. More offstage anecdotes and funny stories contribute to his memory than that of virtually any other performer in recent show business history. There cannot be a person who has not heard of the time he asked the queen if she liked football and if not could he have her cup final tickets. Des O'Connor tells the tale of how in their shared variety days he answered a knock on his dressing-room door to discover Cooper standing there stark naked with mug in hand asking for a cup of sugar. Once he arrived late for a cabaret date to be greeted by the distraught organiser, 'You were on half an hour ago!' Without batting an eyelid he replied, 'Was I? How did I do?' He was incorrigible and he was irresistible. Today his ongoing popularity flies the flag for innocence in an increasingly cynical age. It is hard not to imagine that as long as there is scope for magic in the human spirit and for laughter in our hearts, there will always be a place for Tommy Cooper.

No single anecdote can sum up all his qualities, but here, with acknowledgment to theatre executive Richard M. Mills, is possibly my favourite. On one occasion when Tommy was appearing at the Prince of Wales Theatre, he noticed that one of the speciality acts in the show invariably made straight for the stage door after his performance, made a telephone call that never appeared to get answered, and only then returned to his dressing room. One day Cooper's curiosity got the better of him and he asked the performer what was going on. The act replied that he had to leave his dog at home. The dog tended to get lonely and the sound of the telephone cheered him up. Tommy said nothing, but one night as soon as the act stepped on stage he popped into his dressing room, pinched his keys, skedaddled round to his flat – he lived only a short walk away – let himself in and waited for the phone call. When the phone rang Tommy lifted the receiver and went, "Woof, woof!" Who could be angry with a man like that?

'Thank you very much!'

LES DAWSON: A CARD FOR THE CLUBS

I won't say my act is bad, but the night variety died, they held my script for questioning!

For a stand-up comedian Les Dawson had a way of standing there like none other. He sort of settled behind the footlights like a sack of potatoes, lumpen and immobile, but solid and reliable nevertheless. Any movement displayed by this rotund Rumpelstiltskin of a clown seemed reserved for his face. His sad runcible features, in despair at the sheer thought of living, at times resembled a latex mask scrunched and contorted from behind by an unseen hand. The expressions were never as subtle as those of Hancock, who was capable of conveying thought by the twitch of an eyelid, the twirl of a lip, but were therefore better able to communicate to the back rows of the cavernous auditoriums whose pantomimes and summer shows he came to adorn. Anyone who ever saw Dawson's hilarious telling of the tale that involved the blowing out of a candle and – to achieve this – the incessant switching between the right side of his mouth, the left side and the upward movement of a lower lip that appeared capable of swallowing his nose, will testify to the athleticism of his facial muscles.

He originated, of course, in the northern club circuit of the 1960s and can be regarded today as the one indisputably outstanding funny man to have been nurtured by it, his memory interwoven securely into the fabric of British humour even more tightly than many of the great northern comics who inspired him. Unlike other successful graduates from the clubs, he was able to reveal a coherent comic attitude shaped by it, as distinct from a relatively superficial talent polished within it. To understand that attitude one has to appreciate the disheartening sleaziness of much of that world, a living hell where according to Dawson himself 'a comic was more like a human sacrifice. It was a matter of pride on the part of the audience to turn a normal human being into a quivering wreck in as short a time as possible.' As he was fond of reminding interviewers, 'If they liked you, they didn't clap, they let you live!' It is difficult to know which was worse, to die at the mercy of priggish insults and tossed pennies or to be given the sort of cold shoulder Dawson once experienced when the whole audience walked out halfway through his act. As he started to remonstrate he was shouted down by the chairman: 'Nowt to do with you. The pies have come.' As for the residual glamour of the milieu, that was summed up by the announcement of one concert secretary: 'Tickets for t' annual do – to Garstang – are available from the Polynesian Bar which is next t' urinals.'

Dawson fared no more successfully in this kind of environment than the rest, until one night at a fishermen's club in Hull, fortified by the Dutch courage he had imbibed to face what he later described as 'an alcoholic El Alamein', he followed the path of all great entertainers – witness Sinatra's menace, Garland's frailty, Jolson's egotism – and turned his weakness into his strength. That evening, amid an atmosphere reeking of Icelandic cod and beer squirted at him from bottles shaken by a persistent audience, he saw the light of disenchantment. As he recalled the moment, 'I got absolutely bevvied. And when the curtain opened on this makeshift podium I'm slumped over the piano because I couldn't get up and I couldn't remember the act so I improvised.' He forgot the piano and began to insult the crowd: 'It's a great pleasure for me to be here in this superbly decorated kipper factory.' (The club had in fact just been redecorated at a cost of £20,000.) He also channelled the discomfort of his earlier life for comic effect: 'I don't have to do this for a living. I just do it for luxuries – like bread and shoes.' A link was forged as he explained the 'celestial conspiracy' that had dragged him down to their level. But now the audience was laughing and Les found himself playing midwife to his characterisation of the slightly pompous individual with the deadpan face who is a failure, knows it, but can rise above it. He had found his voice. In time the persona would expand, all subjects subjected to his glum cynicism and self-pity, but especially, in the great tradition of north-country humour, those that revealed a shared identity between the comedian and his audience, one rooted in adversity.

Dawson need never have been scared of dealing in clichés. He possessed a brilliantly fertile mind, if not for disguising them, at least for decking them out in new clothes. When he described his mother-in-law as having a face 'like a sack full of spanners' or referred to his wife as 'so ugly that *I* had an affair with the milkman' the picture was deft, powerful, complete, not to mention funny. As adept as he was at the one-line gag, his style, hallmarked by its highfalutin vocabulary – a legacy from his idol W. C. Fields – rich incidental detail and sheer love of the English language, contrasted superbly with depths of despair to be turned into comic gold. 'When the going gets rough and the vicissitudes of life turn your dreams into a positive maelstrom of despair, be not of faint heart. Two years ago I went through such a period of desolation. I invested a lot of money in a company that made ladies' bonnets and the government cancelled Easter!' He had no illusions about the business he was in and loved to recount the moment he was approached by a member of his audience. 'He said, "Would you mind a word of constructive criticism?" I said, "Not at all." He said, "Well, I think you're crap!"' Here was a maestro who never rose above his station. As he was fond of proclaiming, 'My act is to the cultural heritage of this country what Julie Andrews is to *Deep Throat*.'

may have been at his best when he embarked on one of those rambling monologues with the kind of line that kept in step with logic yet totally pulled the rug out from under the audience's expectations. he was spiritually back in that Hull club, twisting the clichés of show business itself, describing the entures of a juggler who had seen better days, urged on 'from the gin-sodden lips of a pockmarked scar in the arms of a frump in a Huddersfield bordello' to make a pilgrimage to the Himalayas, where he monks of a remote monastery would make available 'the tincture of life' that would restore his lost sense of vocation. When the juggler gets there, however, he finds that only artists and intellectuals are allowed across the sacred threshold. He begs to be allowed to stay, convinced that eventually his true destiny will be revealed. Admitted as a menial, he spends the next twenty years sweeping floors and washing dishes, until the great night of the festival when the initiates display their talents and the oracle speaks. Can his moment have come? He sneaks into the temple, secretly takes out his juggling clubs and puts himself through his old routine. In seeming response the candles flicker, the wind howls, the bronze figure of the oracle creaks tentatively. The juggler, transfixed, strains his ears in anticipation of the message for which he has waited all that time. 'Don't call us,' booms the oracle. 'We'll call you!'

Les was born on 2 February 1931 in a two-up two-down terraced slum in Collyhurst, a suburb of Manchester: 'You can tell how poor we were – till the age of fifteen I thought knives and forks were jewellery.' In later years his facility with words enabled him to paint a more serious but still vivid picture of this environment: 'That tiny abode rubbed alongside countless others of a similar ilk – soot-bearded and gazing eyeless onto cobbled streets. Large women with arms akimbo gossiping on the doorsteps; flat-capped men, unemployed for the most part, grouped in ill-clad knots near shuttered inns. When open, pubs were the nub of one's social life, dark cheerful places where yellow piano keyboards jingled out the tunes of the day.' The description provided a template for his comedy at all levels. With his nod to the camaraderie of the social clubs and his deadpan observation of the foibles of both sexes, his act in many ways came to represent a one-man *Coronation Street*. His was a rough upbringing: he claimed to owe his ability to extend that lower lip upwards to a Mancunian youth who smashed his jaw during a scrap in the early 40s. At school he had nursed aspirations to write, but upon leaving found himself employed unpromisingly in the drapery department of the local Co-op store.

National service then intervened. Upon demob he headed to Paris in the footsteps of Hemingway to pursue his literary ambitions, but ended up playing piano in the bar of a brothel instead. He was so naive that it was several weeks before he grasped what was going on upstairs. His stint at the keyboard had a far greater influence on his destined career than he could have imagined at the time. Once he acquired star status as a comedian the piano became useful to break up the comedy in the extended act now required of him in an interlude that owed as much to the Danish-American musical comedian Victor Borge as to Mrs Mills, the buxom singalong pianist of television's *The Billy Cotton Band Show*. Interestingly the piano by now was necessarily a concert grand: a pub upright would never have struck the right contrast between the lugubrious misfit and the classical instrument with its cultural credentia. For many the favourite moment in his act came when he asked the audience to sing along to accompaniment of a medley of old standards. Once they were on song he would suddenly disconc them by switching to a new key, a different tempo, urging them, 'Come on, sing up. You all know t one!' Often you weren't sure if your ear had gone or his fingers had slipped. Soon the laughter drown the discord. Pandemonium had never been so musical. Had Mrs Mills been born a generation or so lat she would have been physically well equipped to become a member of the Roly Polys, the dance team o well endowed middle-aged dears who performed their sub-Tiller routine to fill further gaps in Les's television and summer shows. The idea came to Les after watching an anorexic group strutting their stuff in a summer show in Brighton. 'Let's hear it for *les femmes*,' he would announce before dashing off to do a quick change into sequins and leotard to add himself to the line for a resounding finish.

After the Paris sojourn he began to juggle club dates as a musical act – the traditional combination of a song, a smile and a piano – with spells of more humdrum employment, most notably as a vacuum cleaner salesman. If his own road-to-Damascus moment eventually occurred in a Hull working men's club, the big breakthrough came in 1967 when he won Hughie Green's television talent show *Opportunity Knocks*, back in the days when that kind of format was exempt from the chilling shiver of 'reality TV' that obtrudes today. Even then it was unusual for a comic to take the honours; usually they were bestowed on vocal and musical acts. It is to Les's credit that today he remains the most credible winner. While the reputations of the others who won have mostly faded away in the manner of the musical formats on vinyl and magnetic tape that gave them passing commercial value, his triumph was so complete it can be seen as larger than the show itself. Television would soon shoehorn him into a variety of sketch and variety formats of his own with pedestrian titles like *Sez Les*, *Dawson and Friends*, *The Dawson Watch* and *The Les Dawson Show*.

Inevitable comparisons were drawn between Dawson and Hancock, another comedian to whom melancholy acted as a catalyst. In 1975 Galton and Simpson, Hancock's best writers, found themselves writing a short-lived series for Dawson with the title *Dawson's Weekly*. There were of course essential differences between the two clowns. While Hancock's character could always muster a vestige of hope from somewhere in the recesses of his mind, Les knew nothing but gloom; while Hancock was a loser who refused to admit it, Les was a loser who knew from the outset that his luck would never change. There was, however, an even more basic distinction. While Hancock, after a long apprenticeship in variety, found his greatest fame as an interpretative artist enacting someone else's words, Dawson was funniest delivering wonderfully idiosyncratic material of his own creation. In television situation comedy he was a pale presence beside the Dawson who stood centre stage with the air of a discontented sumo wrestler glaring resignedly over the footlights.

Aside from his stand-up routines the highlights of his television shows were often provided by two characterisations that firmly underlined his debt to the northern variety tradition. The sex-crazed Cosmo Smallpiece with his absurdly thick pebble lenses and pursed-lipped cry of frustration 'Where's the crumpet?' was in direct line of descent from the edgy old satyrs played by rapscallion-in-chief Frank Randle. In partnership with actor Roy Barraclough as Cissie, Les as Ada played similar homage to Norman Evans's immortal northern housewife Fanny Fairbottom, right down to the sunken toothless features and the brazen adjustment of her waywardly bloused breasts with which he punctuated the routine. In Cissie and Ada's universe the most trenchant or embarrassing remarks are unsaid, a legacy of the tradition known in Lancashire as mimo-ing, the skill of lip-reading acquired by female mill workers to communicate with each other over the rattle of the looms and useful away from the din to convey the unmentionable as it relates to the law of slander, major surgery and gynaecological procedures. Cissie nursed delusions of being slightly above Ada in the social scale and always managed the right expression of disgust tempered by an eagerness to hear when her friend wanted to convey news of a colleague's bodily circumstances. One famous line went – as far as the mimo-ing allows it to be transcribed – 'She's having women's troubles – you know – a hysterical rectomy!' The use of two socially sidestepped old dears also nodded back to the success of Elsie and Doris Waters as Gert and Daisy. The subtle mix of single and double act redefined both originals and kept homage this side of plagiarism.

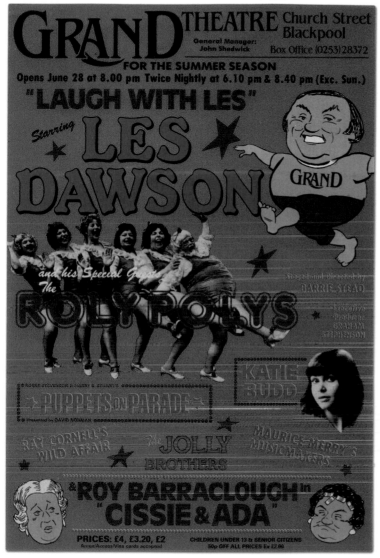

With or without Cissie and Ada, the northern matriarch was never far from the Dawson act. In retrospect it seems remarkable that as late as the 1980s, with so-called alternative comedy gathering momentum, one man could continue to use the mother-in-law joke in so shameless a fashion escape the opprobrium from feminist groups that might have been expected at that time. 'I'm not saying she's ugly, but every time she puts make-up on, the lipstick backs into the tube.' He'd than pause before telling us, 'For all that, she does possess some things men admire – like muscles and a duelling scar.' He built this poor soul up – or down – into a figure of unspeakable grotesqueness. 'I'm not saying the mother-in-law's fat, but she hung her bloomers out to dry and a camel made love to them.' In real life his mother-in-law came to regard his taunts as something of a privilege. 'She said, "You sicken me, but I'll have the last laugh, because one day I'll dance on your grave." I said, "I hope to God you do – I'm going to be buried at sea!"' In more serious moments Les would defend himself: 'Women don't understand the power they have. That's why I can't understand this feminist thing… Since the dawn of time the mother-in-law was the central pivot of the whole hierarchy of the family structure.' He was referring to the almost routine necessity of young couples having to share that traditional two-up, two-down with the wife's parents, something within his own family experience. He also well understood that amid such poverty the structure of life itself would have caved in without the dominance of the strong female adept at keeping hardship and want on the right side of hunger and squalor.

Maybe we all need a battle-axe in our lives to keep us in line, one who looks capable of eating us. Les certainly got the chance of a lifetime in 1991 when, in a move that could have led to a second career as a straight actor, he was coaxed by BBC Television into playing the part of Nona in the black farce of the same name. The play, written by the Argentine dramatist Roberto Cossa in the wake of the Falklands war, represents a parable of capitalist greed in which a hundred-year-old grandmother with a compulsive eating disorder eats everybody else in her family to death, as amid the collapse of the Argentine economy they contrive to fund her appetite and endure the effects of her dementia at the same time. In a twist for the feminists, the title role – imagine a more sinister version of the granny from the family created by cartoonist Giles – is usually played by a man to make the character less likable. Dawson rose to the occasion amid a prestigious cast that included Jane Horrocks, Jim Broadbent, Timothy Spall and Liz Smith, all on the threshold of ongoing dramatic success that would be denied Les in the short time he had left in this world.

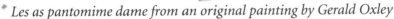

Les as pantomime dame from an original painting by Gerald Oxley

The courage to break new ground shown with *Nona* first manifested itself in 1975 when Dawson starred in a series of three half-hour television plays by Alan Plater about a recluse living halfway up a Yorkshire hillside. Each episode focused upon what happened to him when he set foot outside his home to contend with the wider world. Plater perfectly caught the strain of melancholy which so regularly came to the surface in Dawson's act. Indeed, after Dawson's death, he claimed that the original *mise en scène* had come from Les himself. The trilogy was called *The Loner,* and no title could have resonated more tellingly with his earlier fans. Although played without a studio audience, it served to remind the world that no stand-up comedian of his day projected a greater loneliness than Les. As he himself admitted, 'If any comic's basically honest, he's a lonely person. It's the loneliest job in the world. It really is. In the final analysis, when all the back-slapping is done, it's you and you alone against them. It's as simple as that.' Few came to know Les better than Plater, whose literary success Les aspired to emulate. Over the years he had several

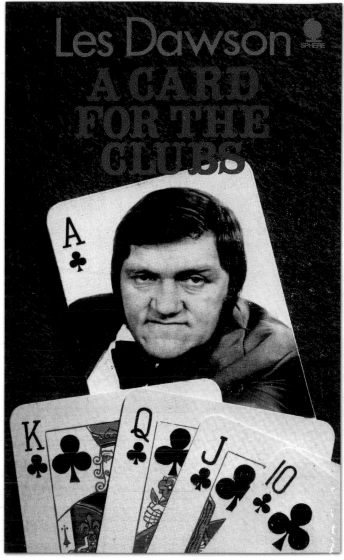

novels published – some more serious than others, often pastiches of favourite authors – with titles like *A Card for the Clubs*, *Well Fared My Lovely* and *A Time Before Genesis*. In today's changed comedy scene all comedians are expected to have a novel within them. If we exclude the great Spike Milligan – *Puckoon* was published in 1963 – Les can be seen as something of a pioneer. He would have given anything to have secured for himself the literary reputation that is now rightly Milligan's. Dawson once begged of his second wife, Tracy, 'Always remind them I was a writer too.' More than anything he would have been proud of the thoughtful eulogy that Plater gave after his death: 'I think he realised that you could not expect the world to make sense – he would be a fool to try – but being a fool he had to keep on trying.' While Dawson may not have articulated hope, the laughter he raised was its own light at the end of a tunnel of doom and self-deprecation. As he used to say in his act, 'Failure doesn't bother me – I was a failure during the boom.'

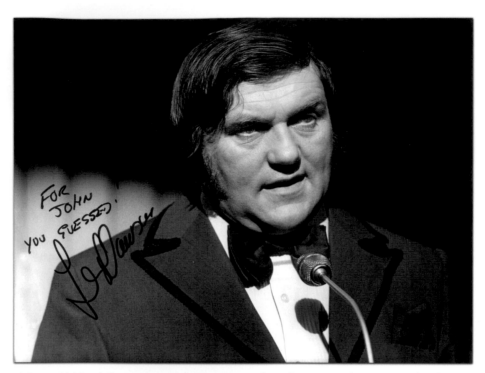

He died on 10 June 1993 while undergoing treatment for a heart condition, not the first member of his profession to fall victim to too great a fondness for alcohol and cigarettes. He never reached the starry heights of London's West End – his theatrical triumphs were confined to provincial panto and summer shows – and the climax of his television career was considered by many to be *Blankety Blank*, an uninspired game show underpinned by little rhyme or reason and previously hosted by Terry Wogan, in which Dawson bravely adopted the piss-taking approach that Wogan himself used so profitably over the years on another hackneyed warhorse – the *Eurovision Song Contest*. No one was safe. Les would turn to a hapless celebrity contestant and in his trademark mutter-speak growl, 'I've got your picture on my mantelpiece. It keeps the children away from the fire.' The show lasted from 1984 to 1989 and began to lose its appeal when the powers that be insisted on awarding prizes worth winning. Les had taken delight in the fact that many punters would discard their useless trinkets and trophies in the foyer of Television Centre on their way home.

No one more effectively pinpointed the alchemy of Les's comic/melancholic way with words than the journalist Nancy Banks-Smith, when in an appraisal of Dawson's roots she quoted Chaplin, no less. Charlie, who had also known dire poverty as a child, added this caption to one of the illustrations in his autobiography: '[This is] where we lived, next to the slaughter-house and the pickle factory after mother came out of the asylum.' The caption was not meant to raise a smile, but try imagining it voiced by Les Dawson at his most resigned and basic. It cries out for laughter, but more importantly it also reminds us that like Chaplin in another medium, Les knew intuitively that the most direct way to an audience's heart was through the truth.

Les with Mo Moreland, the leader of the Roly Polys

The Two Ronnies: 'And it's good night from him!'

Corbett: Yes, sir?

Barker: Four candles?

Corbett: Four candles? Yes, sir. There you are.

Barker: No – fork handles.

Corbett: Four candles. That's four candles.

Barker: No, fork handles – handles for forks.

Corbett: Oh, fork handles. (*He retrieves a garden fork from the back of the shop*) Anything else?

In the early days of radio broadcasting a parade of entertainers ostensibly more refined and less flamboyant than their music hall counterparts paraded before the microphones at Savoy Hill and subsequently Broadcasting House. Sometimes in pairs, they often sang witty songs at the piano, traded inoffensive banter, had a nifty way with a monologue, and frequently had roots in concert party. Names like Flotsam and Jetsam, Norman Long, Nan Kenway and Douglas Young, Jeanne de Casalis and Leonard Henry come to mind. The most important thing about them is that under the watchful patronage of Lord Reith they exuded respectability, almost as if the nation's entertainment had been brought within the civil service. Half a century later, through the new medium of television, another pairing dominated the airwaves. Even allowing for the diminutive size of one of them, they too could have been reputable civil servants, bank managers, country solicitors or City executives. Indeed, the smaller and slightly younger one could have been articled to the larger. Fortunately for them Lord Reith was no longer an obstacle to the transmission of humour that once might have made a maiden blush and they flourished to an extent that won for them the hearts of the nation. They were the Two Ronnies.

They were never a conventional double act in the manner of Flanagan and Allen or Morecambe and Wise. Both owned up to the difficulty they had in performing off the other, unless they were playing well defined character parts within a sketch. Even within two-handers, the parts were virtually interchangeable: sometimes Corbett would play the more eccentric character, Barker the straight man, at other times vice versa. Their shows always began and ended with them taking turns to tell their individual jokes and relishing each other's performance but never intruding upon it. Mutual respect and the fact that, once brought together, they continued to team up voluntarily and not through force of circumstance enhanced their relationship and underpinned a genuine and lasting friendship between the two. But the idea of them standing side by side at a microphone in the semi-scripted cut and thrust of the old-fashioned double act was inconceivable to them. In the words of Corbett, there was none of the traditional blather between them. He never joked about Barker's weight, nor did his partner ridicule Corbett's lack of inches. It was left to the individual to mine the personal vein of humour for himself.

Barker: I'm on a seafood diet. I see food and then I eat it.

Corbett: I did nine holes of golf today, played four and fell down five.

They first met in the early 1960s when Ronnie B. was a jobbing character actor passing through the Buckstone, a West End drinking club for the profession, where a resting Corbett was employed as a barman. Barker's passion for wordplay meant he never forgot the crates the little man had to stand on behind the bar. There were two of them, one marked AGNES and the other CHAMP. Only later did it connect that they were sawn-down parts of the same box and that the letters in their correct order spelled CHAMPAGNES. A few years later in 1966 they found themselves cast together as resident members of *The Frost Report*, the satirical BBC sketch show starring David Frost. Also in the cast was an emerging John Cleese. Most people's memory of that series is crystallised in the sketch 'An Understanding of Class', penned by Marty Feldman and John Law. Arranged in descending order of size to correspond to the hypotenuse of a right-angled triangle, the trio submitted their opinions on their respective positions in society.

Cleese (*Wearing bowler hat and carrying umbrella*): I look down on him (*Barker*),
because I am upper class.
Barker (*Wearing trilby*): I look up to him because he is upper class, but I look down
on him (*Corbett*), because he is lower class. I am middle class.
Corbett (*Wearing cloth cap and muffler*): I know my place.

Seldom in television comedy have words and the visual image come together as neatly as a comment on their own time with the etched precision of a Punch cartoon.

Barker: We all know our place, but what do we get out of it?
Cleese: I get a feeling of superiority over them.
Barker: I get a feeling of inferiority from him, but a feeling of superiority over him.
Corbett: I get a pain in the back of my neck.

There might have been a modest difference in inches between Ronnie B. and Ronnie C., but they bonded from the beginning, feeling themselves excluded from the varsity-oriented camaraderie of the rest of the cast: their formal educations had stopped at grammar school. Spurred on by Corbett's background in nightclubs and revue, they attempted successfully to bring a vaudeville edge to much of the satirical writing. After two series the show was reinvented for commercial television as *Frost on Sunday*, but as the pace of Frost's career accelerated, this was soon considered to have run its course by ITV. Bill Cotton spotted the combined potential of the pair as they were filling in during a technical hitch at an awards ceremony in 1970. It was not until after he had signed them both for the BBC that he discovered they would soon have been out of contract with ITV and out on a limb as a result. Thanks to Cotton, they never looked back.

Ronnie Barker was born in Bedford on 25 September 1929, the son of a Shell Mex oil employee, and worked briefly as an apprentice architect and a bank clerk before gravitating to the theatre. While he was young the family relocated to Oxford, where during the Christmas of 1947 he made an early appearance on stage, running up from the auditorium to help present the Ugly Sisters with burlesque bouquets fashioned from onions, carrots, cabbages and bottles of stout. The more charismatic of the two siblings was played by no less than the young Tony Hancock. Within a year Ronnie was playing in pantomime himself, at Aylesbury, as one of the comic policemen, Punch and Trunch, in *Red Riding Hood*. He was now firmly locked into the repertory structure that stipulated a new part in a new play week in, week out for the foreseeable future. This provided a learning experience that would take him to theatres all over the provinces. Repertory also gave him the ability to deliver a punchline with unerring ease and formed the basis of the remarkable repertoire of voices and characters that served him well during the triumphant years of *The Two Ronnies* and more. His epiphany occurred at the beginning of 1949, the moment he got his first real laugh on stage, playing the part of Charles the chauffeur in Peter Blackmore's play *Miranda*, the story of a mermaid surreptitiously introduced into London society as an invalid in a wheelchair. David Tomlinson had played Charles in the film version the previous year. Ronnie later admitted, 'I get goose pimples even now thinking of it. This is what I want to do, I thought. I want to make people laugh. Never mind *Hamlet*. Forget *Richard II*. Give me *Charley's Aunt*. My mission in life was now crystal-clear.'

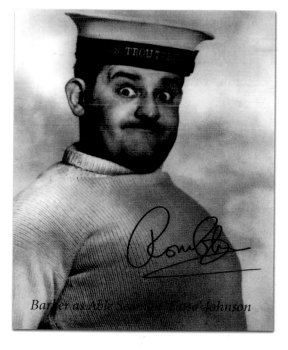

Barker as Able Seaman 'Fatso' Johnson

By 1955 he had come under the wing of legendary theatre director Peter Hall, who cast him as Joe Silva in Eugene O'Neill's *Mourning Becomes Electra* at the Arts Theatre Club, by which time Ronnie had appeared in something like 350 different plays. However, he did not truly register on the national comedy radar until he assumed the role of the disgruntled Able Seaman 'Fatso' Johnson in *The Navy Lark*, a situation comedy for radio by Laurie Wyman set aboard HMS *Troutbridge*, which ran for thirteen series between 1959 and 1977 and was always introduced as 'a surely fictitious account of events in a naval detachment only loosely connected with the Senior Service.' Although Ronnie did not receive star billing, the exchanges between him and Chief Petty Officer Jon Pertwee provided the funniest parts of the programme, as the latter laid into him with one size-related insult after another: 'you barrel of lard', 'you great balloon-faced bumpkin', 'my little rotund podge'. This was far closer to the traditional double act than he ever came with Ronnie Corbett.

> *Pertwee*: If you're gonna do a thing, do it right and proper. That's what I say.
> *Johnson*: I know you do. I've been done right and proper ever since I knew you!

Equally significant, in 1962, was Barker's supporting role in *The Seven Faces of Jim*, a versatility-testing showcase on BBC television for moustachioed Jimmy Edwards, a better actor than he was given credit for and much of whose comic bluster would rub off on Ronnie's later Lord Rustless persona in his early sitcom *Hark at Barker*, a character also influenced by the more abstruse Fred Emney. *Seven Faces* was followed by *Six More Faces of Jim* and *More Faces of Jim*, all authored by Frank Muir and Denis Norden. Tucked away in the second series was an episode entitled 'The Face of Fatherhood', in which Jimmy reprised his role of Pa Glum from radio's *Take It From Here*, June Whitfield (another regular)

Barker as Lord Rustless

her role of Eth, and Ronnie translated Dick Bentley's character of Ron Glum to television for the first time. In later years the same device – a series of disconnected half-hours each featuring individual characters – was appropriated by Ronnie himself, both in *The Ronnie Barker Playhouse* (his first full starring role in a series) in 1968 and *Six Dates with Barker* in 1971, both for ITV, and then as *Seven of One* for the BBC the following year.

Ronnie Corbett's early theatrical career was less formalised than that of his friend. Born in Edinburgh on 4 December 1930, the son of a master baker, the little man avowedly received an early boost to his confidence from a spell in the Boy Scouts. Before long he was a pilot officer in the RAF, an indication in those formative years of the determination and personality he would later bring to the business of being a comedian. His national service acted as a bridge between the amateur theatricals that attracted him in a church youth club and the decision to move to London to pursue an acting career. Casting directors immediately targeted him as someone whose height allowed him to play younger than his years, a school cap fast becoming an obligatory item of wardrobe. More important was the social scene in which he found himself through his friendship with Edward Hardwicke, son of Hollywood luminary Sir Cedric. Before long he was a guest at the table of Sir Cedric's ex-wife, Helena 'Pixie' Pickard, enjoying the conversation of the likes of J. B. Priestley, Ralph Richardson and cabaret star Hildegarde. Noël Coward was somewhere around – his cabaret season at the Café de Paris left an abiding impression – and Evelyn Laye gave the young hopeful singing lessons.

This grounding in style contributed to Ronnie's insistence on keeping his dignity as a comedian. He was not cut out to be the put-upon member of a knockabout act, which makes footage that survives of him as the resident fall guy in the children's television show *Crackerjack* during the late 1950s more embarrassing to watch than it should be. Meanwhile a string of small parts in films, appearances in summer seasons and a spell as the lowliest member of the cast in Harry Secombe's Palladium show *Let Yourself Go* all contributed to his experience as a performer whose role models were Jack Benny, Bob Hope, even Max Wall, masters of self-deprecating humour all. But he found his forte in the revues at two West End nightclubs that helped to characterise the Swinging Sixties, first at Winston's and then at Danny La Rue's. Now Noël Coward was watching *him*. The contemporary scene had a certain *je ne sais quoi* that appealed to his sense of purpose, while the comic elegance of the transvestite star meshed well with Corbett's own, not least in a pastiche of Margot Fonteyn and Rudolf Nureyev. It was at Winston's that Ronnie was first seen by David Frost.

The Two Ronnies was first transmitted on BBC Television on 10 April 1971, and clocked up ninety-eight episodes over twelve series and assorted specials up until December 1987, during which time it never ceased to be a critical success or a ratings winner. The title emerged when it became known that on the Frost show they had often been bracketed together by the rest of the team: 'Oh, the two Ronnies can do that sketch' had become a kind of default response. The chemistry between the two owed a great deal to their divergent professional backgrounds. Essentially Barker was an actor, Corbett a product of light entertainment, if not variety as such. It was not the first time that the two disciplines had coalesced so spectacularly. The most successful double act of all time, Stan Laurel and Oliver Hardy, brought a similar exchange of experience to each other, while in later years – although never perceived as a twosome in the same way – Tony Hancock and Sidney James had helped each other considerably in understanding the other's métier. Arguably Barker's innate shyness was his hardest challenge. As he took pains to stress throughout his career, he had great difficulty in projecting himself or a variation of himself. That is why the shows commenced with them sitting at a desk as a pair of all-purpose newsreaders or announcers, in other words playing a part.

Corbett: In a packed programme tonight, I'll be telling you about the woman who has just sold her Victorian brass bedstead, as she is no longer on squeaking terms with her husband.

Barker: We had hoped to be bringing you the star attraction of Lord George Davidson's circus – Alfredo, the human bomb. But we've just heard that he's gone off on holiday.

Corbett: But first the news. By the terms of Lady Oenome Smith-Maggs' will, published today, her fortune will be divided between her cat and her dog. The will is to be contested by her parrot.

Barker: The Irish Guinness shortage was solved today. From tomorrow, customers will be served with lager and sunglasses.

Once that opening had been established everything else seemed to fall into place, their mixed palette of skills providing a greater range of options than most comedy shows of the kind and disguising the fact that the programme unashamedly used the most formulaic of all formats. This embraced regular and well defined solo spots, two-hander sketches, the recurring filmed serial often featuring the pair as two seedy private eyes, Piggy Malone (Barker) and Charley Farley (Corbett), and the rousing and spectacular musical pastiche – with the couple featured as the likes of charwomen, road sweepers, brass bandsmen and folk singers, dancing, marching, strumming and always singing together – with which the show all but concluded, prior to the signing-off back at the news desk that became their trademark.

Corbett: So it's good night from me.
Barker: And it's good night from him.
Together: Good night!

Barker came into his own playing a whole gallery of ever-so-slightly pompous authority figures and public service spokesmen, in which his love of wordplay was never far from the surface. He wrote most of his own material, and many of their joint sketches and parodies as well, seeking no credit for so doing by hiding behind a range of pseudonyms, of which, once the cat was out of the bag, Gerald Wiley became the best known. The favourite of many was his address to those who couldn't help getting their words in a twist.

Good evening. I am the president for the Loyal Society for the Relief of Sufferers from Pismonunciation; for people who cannot say their worms correctly. Or who use the wrong worms entirely, so that other people cannot underhand a bird they are spraying. It's just that you open your mouse, and the worms come turbling out in wuk a say that you dick knock what you're thugging a bing, and it's very distressing.

Equally effective was the president of the Getting your Wrongs in the Word Order Society, who had been 'asked to come a night too long to aim the society's explains and picture you firmly in the put'. It was no secret to his colleagues that the precision of delivery required to deliver these self-imposed verbal hurdles was what set him apart as an actor and therefore allowed him to find his own comic voice.

Barker's general fascination with the twists and turns of which language was capable had their origins in many of the comedians who had entranced him on radio and gramophone records as a child. These included Milton Hayes (1884 – 1940), who billed himself as 'The Laugh-Smith with a Philosophy' and developed the quirk of reading across the columns of a newspaper with hilarious results, as well as Stainless Stephen (1892 – 1971), purveyor of spoken pronunciation to the nation, as in this top and tail to a wartime broadcast: 'This is Stainless aimless brainless Stephen semi-colon broadcasting semi-conscious at the microphone semi-frantic… and so countrymen semi-colon all shoulders to the wheel semi-quaver we'll carry on till we get the Axis semi-circle and Hitler asks us for a full stop!' Leonard Henry (1890 – 1973) had a way of getting sidetracked into lists at the microphone. 'On the evening of 30 (*sic*) February, a large party might have been observed at closing time coming out of Potter's Bar… This contained Doctor Doges Bodie, RATS, Colonel Sulphuric, H_2SO_4, the Rev. Tinklepippin of St Cricks-in-the-Necks, fourteen beaters, two sweepers, a dozen natives, some brown bread and butter, six gross of assorted corkscrews, and one white woman.' Taken at a vocal gallop, that could be Barker speaking. When it was, it all appeared so effortless.

Milton Hayes *Stainless Stephen* *Leonard Henry*

In contrast, when it came to the other Ronnie's solo routines, the impression was of anything other than exactness. Drawing attention to his size and vulnerability by sitting on the edge of a chair that might have contained a giant, Corbett would lean forward to win us all over: 'I wonder if it's true that Mickey Mouse wears a Ronnie Corbett watch.' As discursive as a runaway train and looking a cross between Val Doonican and Pinocchio in his V-neck golf sweater, he then proceeded brilliantly to take vacillation to levels a metronome might not have considered. It all came down to acting again, helped not a little by the sort of top-drawer accent that makes colloquialisms sound posh. You don't expect someone with such assured tones to be making things up as he goes along. All he set out to do each week was to tell a simple joke. The fun came from his obvious enjoyment at being sidetracked by this tangent here, that diversion there, before homing in on the tag line, the very weakness of which perversely became even funnier the longer he kept it from you. The more oblique the introduction in the first place the better.

'I actually found this joke in an old *Reader's Digest* in between an article called "Having Fun with a Hernia" and a story about a woman who brought up a family of four with one hand… while waiting for Directory Enquiries.' Along the way Ronnie would introduce stray lines like 'We were so poor that on a cold night my father used to suck a peppermint and we all sat around his tongue.' The producer was often an excuse for a distraction: 'Before we go any further, I must blow a kiss to our producer – the man who makes Boy George look like Charles Bronson!' As comedy routines, Corbett's ramblings were greater than the sum of their parts and exhilarating in a reassuringly comic-nostalgic way. Much credit for the effectiveness of the 'Ronnie in the Chair' device must go to the writer Spike Mullins, a retired builder who helped to originate the idea and put most of the early words onto Ronnie's lips, and then to David Renwick, who scripted the routines in later years.

Corbett's influences are less discernible than Barker's. There has to be a hint of Askey there, and not simply because of size: Ronnie is an inch or so the shorter of the two. Although he lacks Arthur's absolute spontaneity and *joie de vivre*, he manifests a great deal of the sheer pride in his own work as well as the absolute professionalism of his big-hearted predecessor. The self-deprecation picked up from watching the likes of Hope and Benny early in his career obviously made its contribution. More importantly, Corbett was reared on a great generation of Scots comedians like Harry Gordon, Jack Anthony, Jack Radcliffe and Dave Willis, who would have meant little to Barker until he became a serious student of humour in his adult years. From Willis, a bedraggled little Woodbine of a man with a Chaplinesque moustache, Corbett would certainly have absorbed the unintentional pathos that has made him an exceptional Buttons in pantomime and – proud man that he is – unashamed to use his size as an important weapon in his comic armoury in any medium. In Anthony, before the latter cultivated more clownish make-up, he would have discerned the debonair flair of a lighter comedian, aspects of the style that characterised their fellow countryman Jack Buchanan – Corbett has always given the impression of being able to twinkle on his toes. His most important decision before moving south was to attend drama classes in an attempt to eradicate all trace of his Scottish accent. In his own words, 'It was how now to brown cow and goodbye to the broon coo'. His independence was such that he would never be shoehorned into a pattern that would make him somebody else's man.

Jack Anthony

Harry Gordon

DAVE WILLIS

Many of the sketches in which they featured together have passed into comedy folklore as memorably as Hancock sequences and Cooper routines. From Barker's pen came the encounter in one of those hardware shops that sell everything, in which he begins by asking Corbett, who is behind the counter, for 'Four candles.' When they are handed over, it transpires he was asking for 'fork handles – handles for forks'. The ambiguity born of the terseness of Barker's requests continues to confuse the issue on plugs, hoes, pumps, washers.

Barker: Got any plugs?
Corbett: What sort of plugs?
Barker: Bathroom – rubber ones.
(*Corbett gets box of bath plugs and holds up two different sizes*)
Corbett: What size?
Barker: Thirteen amp.

Corbett's frustration builds through the piece and does much to convey the underlying believability of the absurd transactions. The perfection is in both the playing and the composition, although interestingly such was the dynamic of their partnership it would have lost none of its effectiveness had their roles been switched.

More contrived but equally memorable was the parody of the quiz show *Mastermind* in which Corbett's contestant has chosen as his specialist subject, 'answering the question before last'. This was the work of David Renwick again, one of the pool of quality writers that serviced the show when Barker's inspiration flagged or energy waned. The arrangement whereby the programme was not held hostage to the talents of any one writer or team helped to ensure a high standard throughout its long run. Also prominent within this group were Barry Cryer, Ian Davidson, David Nobbs, Peter Vincent and Dick Vosburgh. In the sketch Barker as the question master has just asked, 'What sort of person lived in Bedlam?' He continues:

Barker: What is a jockstrap?
Corbett: A nutcase.
Barker: Correct. For what purpose would a decorator use methylene chlorides?
Corbett: A form of athletic support.
Barker: Correct. What did Henri de Toulouse-Lautrec do?
Corbett: Paint strippers.
Barker: Correct. Who is Dean Martin?
Corbett: Is he a kind of artist?
Barker: Yes. What sort of artist?
Corbett: Er… pass
Barker: Yes, that's near enough.

Superb as the performances and much of the material were, there was nothing truly ground-breaking about the show. Even the casting of two bespectacled comedy performers with contrasting styles had been attempted, albeit unsuccessfully, with Arthur Askey and Alan Melville in *Raise Your Glasses* by the BBC way back in 1962. The show that most vividly foreshadowed *The Two Ronnies* was without doubt *The Benny Hill Show*. If one sets aside the dual casting of the later programme, virtually all the key ingredients had been featured by Hill on BBC Television in the 50s, including informed parodies, musical pastiches, sketches motivated by puns and double entendres, wordplay spun from misplaced letters and other devices, all tied together by the identifying ambience of a revue made to work for the small screen. The parallels between Hill and Barker are telling, including their intrinsic shyness and reluctance to face the public as themselves, their creative satisfaction in writing and compiling their best material, the willingness – some would say need – to exert an influence over all technical aspects of their productions (Corbett never felt that necessity), and most significantly their fascination with the bawdier byways of human nature in the cause of comedy.

It is difficult not to see a double standard operating at the time the shows were running concurrently on opposing channels. In later years the production of *The Two Ronnies* was a far more polished, more assured affair than that of *The Benny Hill Show*, but while Hill was being slated for the supposed filth and sexism in his material, the Ronnies seemed to emerge relatively unscathed. And yet throughout the run of their show Barker's material, like Hill's, revealed a continuing obsession with the seaside-postcard approach to life. He could not even refrain from ending the magnificent 'Four Candles' sketch with an obvious reference to the knockers (*not* door knockers) of the big-bosomed shop assistant. To discover that during his career he amassed a large private archive of saucy material from the Victorian era – some of it republished in picture books carrying his byline – substantiates what his BBC boss Bill Cotton once told me: 'He has the filthiest mind of anyone I know.' To think that everyone thought that no one had a filthier mind than Benny! Incidentally Bill meant it as a compliment, hearty and jocular, but the fact remains that Benny would never have been able to get away with a sketch on breastfeeding or the serial about the world being run by women in sexy uniforms. It helped that the public image of Barker was 'respectable married man with three children', whereas Hill was quite content to be perceived as a bachelor with a roving eye. It is ironic, though, that many who devoured *The Two Ronnies* never deigned to watch the show on the rival channel, as if a cultural divide existed between the two, the onstage respectability of the duo chafing against the cheeky lasciviousness of Hill's persona. Part of it may have been linked to the class divide symbolised by the BBC and ITV at the time. In consolation, Hill did have the satisfaction of succeeding in the international marketplace, an achievement denied the other two.

The success of *The Two Ronnies* was underlined in May 1978 when the show was translated to the stage for a virtually sell-out three-month season at the London Palladium. Barker might have initially baulked at the idea, again anxious at being exposed as himself onstage, but took strength from Corbett's advice that he confront the theatre audience as an expanded almost caricature version of his normal self, 'the avuncular, prosperous sort of fellow in specs'. If he lacked the stage presence of a Dodd or a Cooper, the smaller Ronnie had by now matured into a sure-footed stand-up comedian of stature, and thus the weight of the production shifted more onto his shoulders. For once there was nothing technical like editing, dubbing and filming for Barker to worry about. To Corbett it all came as second nature: he had triumphantly topped the Palladium bill as Buttons in *Cinderella* in 1971, volunteering for the solo role when the less-assured Barker played the fly in the ointment and vetoed the idea of the two of them appearing as the Ugly Sisters in the same pantomime.

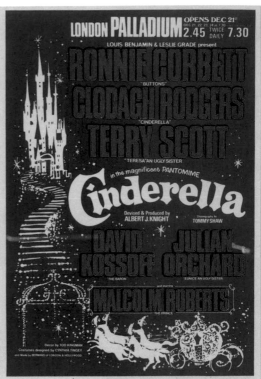

The 'Four Candles' sketch proved no less effective framed within the Palladium's proscenium arch, while their musical escapades as morris dancers and the shaggy country singers Big Jim Jehosophat and Fatbelly Jones arguably benefited from the theatrical setting. Ronnie B. delivered a sermon in cockney rhyming slang – as the Vicar of St Cain and Abel Church, Hampstead Heath – and Ronnie C. performed stand-up at the top of his game. There was much else besides, both from the two stars – solo and in tandem – and from exhilarating speciality acts in the best variety tradition. The success of the venture led to an eight-week season in Sydney followed by five weeks in Melbourne in 1979. Bristol, Coventry and Southampton were British cities treated to extended seasons along the way. Then in February 1983 they reopened with an entirely new production at the Palladium for a further three months. This time around the evening was launched by the *Mastermind* sketch and crowned by 'A Load of Balmoral', featuring Barker as Victoria and Corbett as her faithful gillie John Brown. It was said of the sketch that it would never have got past the Lord Chamberlain in his heyday. Audiences were also reintroduced to old favourites from their television repertoire, including the two near-monosyllabic men in a pub and Barker's solo turns as a Chelsea Pensioner pining for the girls he left behind and as a cinema commissionaire whose speech is littered with the star names of yesteryear. The latter two routines complemented Corbett's signature solo spot.

These live theatre seasons set a special stamp on the success of *The Two Ronnies* and would unquestionably have qualified them for inclusion in this book, had the variety style and ambience of their programmes not already staked their own claim. Barker used to joke that he must be the only performer to commence his career in variety at the top of the bill in the top theatre in the land. Of course, their individual triumphs away from the variety arena were noteworthy, principally in situation comedy, where Barker the actor, notably as the cunning old lag Norman Stanley Fletcher in *Porridge* and the stuttering tight-fisted grocer Arkwright in *Open All Hours*, had the edge over Corbett the comedian, although the little fellow registered effectively as Timothy Lumsden, the middle-aged son not quite able to release himself from the apron stings of a forceful mother, in *Sorry!* But Barker himself was not infallible. *The Magnificent Evans*, a situation comedy in which he played a florid Welsh photographer, is best forgotten, while *Clarence*, the saga of a short-sighted removal man, struggled to make an impact.

This last vehicle – the only one scripted by Barker himself (under the pseudonym of Bob Ferris) – aired for six episodes at the beginning of 1988. Halfway through transmission of the series, on 17 January, he announced his retirement, a decision prompted not only by health considerations but also by his fear of sliding standards. The message on his answer machine left no one in doubt: 'I am retiring from public and professional life so I am unable to undertake any more commitments. To those people with whom I have worked, I would like to express my gratitude and good wishes. So it's a big thank you from me and it's goodbye from him. Goodbye.' He more or less kept to his word, aside from occasional appearances in documentaries and at gala evenings, often showcasing the work of the Two Ronnies. Cameo roles as Churchill's butler in the television drama *The Gathering Storm* in 2002 and alongside Maggie Smith in *My House in Umbria* the following year were too tempting to refuse and confirmed that television's earlier gain had been the British cinema's loss. The decision came as a shock to most people, although he had told Corbett in advance. In the understanding words of Michael Grade, his boss at the BBC at the time, it was time 'to stop and smell the roses'. Corbett was equally sympathetic and at least had massive reserves as a solo performer to draw upon. For almost a quarter of a century he has kept himself at the forefront of British show business with characteristic flair and dignity, although none of the projects entrusted to him by broadcasters since his friend's demise has received anything near the acclaim of *The Two Ronnies*.

Barker died of heart failure on 3 October 2005. At the time the other Ronnie claimed that there had never been a cross word between them. Unlike many conventional partnerships – comic or otherwise – they had never had cause to resent their dependence on the other. But while they never became an exclusive team, it is difficult not to see *The Two Ronnies* as their major professional triumph. The diversity of the characters that the variety format enabled Barker to play showed off his skill as an actor more dazzlingly than any number of sitcoms and drama series, while few solo stand-up comedians have fitted more comfortably, more amiably into a television format than the little man through whom the word class is spelt like the letters through a stick of his native Edinburgh rock.

Their long list of credits, individually and together, stands as its own monument to their success, but maybe their greatest achievement resides in what they came to represent rather than, for all their combined talent, what they actually did. This was predominantly a world where gentlemen's clubs, old-fashioned shops, pipe bands and allotments conveyed an air of dependability, personified by the professionalism of the comics themselves, as week in week out they continued to tease and amuse us in their jaunty regatta blazers and complementary horn-rim specs. Something approaching the empire comes to mind – reassuring if not entirely flawless. It was their secret that beneath a cloak of respectability they were never smug and sanctimonious. Who said that comedy had to be respectable anyhow? As Orwell indicated, the risqué joke is not itself an attack on morality, even if it represents 'a sort of mental rebellion, a momentary wish that things were otherwise'. Buried beneath his piles of bawdy Victoriana, no one understood this better than an actor with an antiquarian's instinct called Ronnie Barker. As for Ronnie Corbett, he knew his place.

Shortly before his death, Barker told me, 'I have one ambition – to own a tree that grows mistletoe on it.' It was a surprising and humble claim from a man who throughout his career appears to have got his priorities right. He also explained what he regarded as the quintessential duty of a star, namely to ensure that at all times you are better dressed and appear healthier than everyone in your audience. 'They expect it of you.' Today expectations have changed, but the standards implicit in his words are still kept up meticulously after his death by the other Ronnie. In his autobiography Corbett recalls his delight on a visit to his favourite patisserie in Marylebone High Street: '…then there is that wonderful final flourish when they tie up the box with ribbon, then scrape the scissors along the ribbon so it curls up. I feel like shouting "Bravo!" Or perhaps even "Encore!"' There was scarcely a show they performed together that didn't live up to their criteria, that didn't have the big bow of quality around it, that didn't have their audience clamouring for more.

KEN DODD: 'HOW TICKLED I AM!'

By Jove, what a wonderful day for ramming a cucumber through the vicar's letterbox and shouting, 'Look out – the Martians are coming!'

I'd love to be chancellor of the exchequer – that way I'll be united with my money!

Christmas is coming;
The goose is getting fat;
Who'd have thought the gander
Would have done a thing like that?

To see Ken Dodd at the frenzied peak of his act when he dominated the live comedy scene in the 1960s was not necessarily to realise that he was the newest in the tradition of genuinely great stage comedians. The protruding triangular teeth, the popping scatterbrain eyes, the hair as distraught as a dandelion puffball, the fingers sticking out at all angles in their own expression of erratic surprise, all combined to present an image of an age less immediate, less sophisticated. Doddy burlesquing 'On the road to Mandalay', a Union Jack erect on an outsize tropical helmet, his body weighed down by an 'any old iron' assortment of pots and pans, the shapely leg of a shop-window dummy strapped to his waist, recalled the bizarre military outfit of none other than Victorian clown Grimaldi, in which coal scuttles became boots, a poker his sword, a lady's muff his hat. The appearance of the younger comedian cried out for the pictorial homage the robust and detailed graphic style of *Film Fun* would have paid him in its heyday, when the antics of Laurel and Hardy, George Formby, Frank Randle, and Old Mother Riley filled its compact pages, and one was led to believe that a mountain of sausage and mash could be happily served on a silver platter, a meal fit for a comedy king.

On a more serious level, the writer J. B. Priestley said that all great clowns have a transient look which makes them appear not men of this world, but people from another planet, puzzled by the mundane problems of the earth. However much Dodd's own humour is tinged with the everyday, one is aware from the moment he capers on stage, his tickling stick in the form of feather duster poised for the fray, that 'Ken Dodd' spells 'misfit'. Today he no longer has to roll the expressive eyes so excitedly, twist his shock of hair into a three-cornered jester's cap so assertively, to prove the point. To trace, though, his 'misfit' to another planet goes too far. His whole ethos embodies the mystique of the circus and fairground, travelling homes for the most colourful, most admirable of society's dropouts. The symbols are obvious. If the tickling stick resembles an everlasting candyfloss, the audience represents the figures in the rifle range waiting to be shot down by the barrage of his quick-fire gags. The crazy props that have appeared in his act down the years – the exploding guitar and the giant snake-like accordion which take on lives of their own as he struggles to play them, the life-size cow that plummets to the stage when he shoots at the moon, the colossal footballs hand-kicked around the auditorium – all evoke the tang of the sawdust ring as much as the whiff of red plush and greasepaint. His colourful jester outfits, complete with fluorescent beehive hats, vie with the traditional Gypsy caravan and the 'Galloping Horses' carousel in their garish appeal. His sheer electric vitality reminds one of the placarded emphasis placed by fairground sideshows on their attractions, whether 'voodoo woman' or 'television chimps', being ALIVE, LIVING, ANIMATED, REAL. To experience a performance by Ken Dodd is as reviving for a jaded, spiritually dead public as any visit to fair or amusement park. He often jokes in his act, 'What a wonderful atmosphere here tonight – just like a clinic!' 'Just like a carnival' would be more accurate.

His success is the happy culmination of a career that began in his native Liverpool with the gift of a Punch and Judy show on his eighth birthday. Two years later he graduated to ventriloquism, having answered an advertisement in a children's comic that read, 'Fool your teachers, amaze your friends – send sixpence in stamps and become a ventriloquist.' Soon after this his father bought him a dummy and even today a ventriloquial cameo in which he performs with a doll based on Dicky Mint, one of his Diddymen puppet characters, features in his stage shows.

Dodd: Would you like a big bottle of brown beer – watch my lips – a **b**ig **b**ottle of **b**rown **b**eer and some **b**rown **b**read and **b**utter – or a shandy?
Mint: A shandy.
Dodd: Good!

If his early theatrical activities bore little resemblance to straightforward comedy, fate was already determining the course his talent would take. In his youth a head-over-handlebars cycling accident while he was trying to ride with his eyes shut was responsible for the protruding teeth, one day to become a heavily insured comic trademark. These played their part in his first serious venture as a comedian, as 'Professor Yaffle Chuckabutty, Operatic Tenor and Sausage Knotter'. The act was built around burlesques of ballads that audiences had refused to take seriously when attempted straight by the ex-choirboy. Wearing the dishevelled tail suit that became a talisman throughout his career, he made his full-time professional debut at the Nottingham Empire on 20 September 1954. Within a year the ex-boy-ventriloquist was topping his first bill at the Royal Court Theatre, Warrington. Billed as 'Ken Dodd, the Unpredictable', he would before long be undisputed cock of the north, four consecutive Blackpool seasons between 1955 and 1958 providing a unique comic apprenticeship. It is interesting to recall the names of other performers featured in those early shows at Blackpool's Central Pier. In 1955, with star trumpeter Kenny Baker topping the bill, both Morecambe and Wise, at that time second-string radio comedians, and Jimmy Clitheroe (1916 – 1973), the perpetual 'boy' comic even then upsetting the magician's act by stirring the goldfish in their bowl, were also featured. The following summer saw veteran Jimmy James as top, and then in decreasing order of status Dodd, Clitheroe again, Dennis Spicer – the brilliant young ventriloquist tragically killed in a motor accident a few days after his triumph at the Royal Variety Performance of 1964 – and Roy Castle. Morecambe and Wise would return to the Central Pier in 1957, while Dodd held sway at the Hippodrome. Then in 1958 he was back at the Central Pier, top of the bill at the theatre that had given him his biggest opportunity. Over the following years an impressive

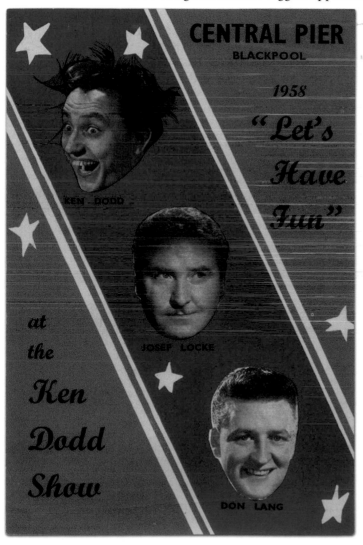

career embraced six record-breaking seasons at Blackpool's Opera House, the country's largest theatre, and the shows *Doddy's Here* and *Doddy's Here Again* at the London Palladium in 1965 and 1967, to which he returned for extended autumn variety seasons in 1974 and 1980. There were show-stopping Royal Variety Performances to coincide with the first two Palladium shows, as well as further appearances in 1972, 1986, 1999 and 2006. He made the first of countless television appearances – principally in his own series and specials – on Barney Colehan's production *The Good Old Days* on BBC Television on 11 March 1955, a music hall format that could have been invented for him, although television conveys little of the power of his performance as he works a live audience towards hysteria with his high-energy humour. Less predictable was his highly praised season as Malvolio in *Twelfth Night* at the Liverpool Playhouse in the autumn of 1971. On an equally rare excursion into film, he portrayed Yorick the Jester in Kenneth Branagh's version of *Hamlet* in 1996.

Backstage at the London Palladium on opening night

While Dodd was resident at the Palladium, playwright John Osborne took the entire company of the Royal Court Theatre several times to see this 'real comic artist at work'. Even in those days, his act, which could never be tamed to run for less than an hour, even though it might be split into two or three spots within a show, ran the whole gamut of comic invention. In this way it reaffirmed its links, and indeed those of the variety bill in general, with the fairground and the carefree premise that allows audiences to accept those aspects of the entertainment they like and reject without embarrassment those they do not. There would be the occasional political gibe, which in the late 60s often belied the much-publicised pictures of Dodd entertaining the chief resident of Number 10 in his dressing room: 'It's very sporting of you to come here tonight when you could be watching Harold Wilson on the telly. He says he wants to get us out of this mess as soon as possible because he's got another mess lined up which he wants to get us into.' 'Joey-Joeys', the traditional mainstay of the circus clown – finding the coat hanger left in his jacket, discovering an actual miniature ladder in his sock, then pulling half a sock up to his knee – would vie for laughter with more physical visual humour, as when he twisted his hair into all kinds of erratic shapes: 'Pal does this, missus. P-A-L – Puts 'Airs on Lads. P-L-J – Puts Lumps on Judies'; or launched into a series of impressions of people walking along wearing 'Little-X bras', 'Y-Fronts' or 'Jockey shorts': 'As it happens I'm wearing me yodelling trousers!' Running through the whole act was a fizzily incoherent chain of tongue-twisting nonsense language with its own vocabulary in words like tattiphilarious and plumsciousness, diddilation and goolified, and with phrases like 'nikky nokky noo' reminiscent of T. E. Dunville's 'bunk-a-doodle-I-do' and 'pop-pop-popperty-pop' at the turn of the century. In contrast there was the wry wordplay especially associated with Liverpool which just stops short of becoming a pun: 'My dad loves Handel's "Largo" – he won't drink anything else;' 'It's these plays on the telly – *Armpit Theatre*'; 'This morning I woke up in bed with misgivings.' Nor did he disown the puerile *Comic Cuts* tone of lines like 'Tonight we've the great Russian striptease artist, Eva Vestoff, and there's that well known contortionist, Willy Snappit!' The naivety, however, was always tempered with a vivid surrealism. One recalls the episode of the marmalade divers rowing out into the vat with a basket of orange peel singing 'Heaven preserve us'. A brisk sequence of one-line gags would suddenly make way for a wholly irrelevant limerick, innocently defiant of the clouds of political incorrectness on the horizon.

> There was a young man from Sydenham,
> Who lost his pants with a quid in 'em.
> He saw them again in Petticoat Lane…
> They were walking about with a Yid in 'em.

And almost as a bonus there were the brilliant burlesques of songs like 'The floral dance' and 'Granada'. In the latter the gags assumed a mock-romantic nature: 'He kissed her neck, a lump came in his throat – it was her earring,' and Dodd himself took on an orchestral quality, the chattering of his teeth suggesting castanets, the twang of his braces double-bass strings, and his body evoking the sounds one would expect from a swallowed harmonica. His main props for this number were a floppy sombrero with ping-pong balls suspended from the brim and a battered guitar used to bat at least one of these maddening obstacles to vision into the audience: 'I'm sorry, missus, but you shouldn't have had your mouth open!'

Hand in hand with this vast comic range was – and remains – an obsession with the physical aspect of man that never attempts to shun vulgarity, is never free from innuendo. Stark nudity is a favourite theme, not confined to the steaming fish and chip shop Dodd mistakes for a Turkish bath. 'I took all my clothes off – a lady looked at me and said, "I'll have four pennorth,"' nor to the nature-cure clinic where again he disrobes: 'The medical superintendent looked at me. "Ho ho," he said, "you'll have to diet." I said "What colour?"' but extending vicariously to the auditorium itself: 'Come on – let's take all our clothes off and parade past the Town Hall. We'll show 'em!' Legs would appear to hold a special comic fascination, whether those of a man on the beach in khaki shorts 'like two sticks of celery sticking out of a carrier bag' or again, in direct encouragement to the audience, 'When you go to bed, take a torch, shine the green light on them, nudge the wife and say, "We'll have to keep off the lettuce, Alice."' Even more fascinating are the reminders of Billy Bennett and Dan Leno where the physical veers off in the direction of the absurd as in the case of the Gypsy girl who had two long hairs stretching all the way down from her chin into her blouse: 'I couldn't resist it. So I cut 'em. Her stockings fell down!' or in Dodd's plans for modifying the human anatomy. An extra mouth on the top of the head would enable one to pop a sandwich under one's hat and eat breakfast on the way to work; or one could have another eye at the tip of a finger, at the thought of which the mind, wherever it may be by this time, boggles. This obsession with the odd and incongruous aspects of life extends to his confusion of people with objects: 'My grandad used to stand with his back to the fire; we had to have him swept.' The same confusion informs his own aims and decisions: 'What a beautiful day for putting on a kilt, standing upside down in the middle of the road, and saying, "How's that for a table lamp?"' It all bears out his generalised definition of comedy as a topsy-turvy viewpoint, seeing things from new angles, new perspectives. His ability to project verbal into visual, together with a seemingly inexhaustible sense of comic invention – far more spontaneous than the fantasy of Leno and of Bennett, both of whom were hampered to an extent by the comparative rigidity of the song and metrical form that their presentations most often demanded – have enabled Dodd to exist convincingly in the imagination of his public, and not least because however inspired the surrealism, it is firmly rooted in the basic, niggardly, undignified, yet easily recognisable world of sliced bread and Shredded Wheat, knees, pimples and toenail clippings.

A mere catalogue of specific lines and gambits, only mildly funny when presented out of context, can give no indication of the stunning overall effect that his act continues to have upon an audience. His trump card is the breathtaking tempo at which the material is delivered. 'Seven laughs a minute and you're motoring' is a much-quoted precept, each laugh encroaching upon its predecessor, so that by the end of his act the audience is so distracted with laughter it may well be laughing before the punchline is out, incapable even of grasping exactly what he is saying. There are even times when he gives the impression he is himself startled by his chain of thought, puzzled at what possible connection there could be between the idea of groping around naked for the cauliflower in a steaming vat of piccalilli and the fact that – a favourite line from the period in question – when we join the Common Market we will all have to sleep on the other side of the bed. His mind is constantly operating on several wavelengths at once, and in this respect he is as handicapped as any of Beckett's vaudeville-inspired characters.

No other performer has proved more conclusively that laughter is contagious, as it ricochets on its zigzag journey through an audience with the casually devastating effect of a stray spark in a box of fireworks. His method is such that the chuckles raised in the first few minutes accelerate by the end into one tumultuous roar of laughter. He pulls out all the stops to make certain of this, to convert the last sceptic, flinging himself into a final frenzy that substantiates his earlier declaration: 'It's exactly fifteen years ago today that I went out of my mind!' Unfinished limerick tumbles over unfinished limerick. His body is whirled into an uneasy spastic spectacular. 'They're coming to take me away, ha ha!' In a tantrum with the musical director he resorts for revenge to the resounding beat of the great Drum of Knotty Ash'. 'This drum was my grandad's. I expect he can hear me now. He's up on the roof pinching lead.' 'It's ideal for a lullaby,' he confides before bashing the instrument to high heaven and booming out at the top of his voice: 'GO TO SLEEP, MY BABY!' By the time he has nudged the whole auditorium into standing for what they think is the National Anthem – after the first few misleading bars it turns out to be 'Down at the Old Bull and Bush' – all barriers are down between performer and audience.

In this final relationship with his public Dodd's essential spirit becomes most obvious. He is the modern equivalent of the Puck or Robin Goodfellow of medieval times, not only in the way he jumps and skips about the stage, but in that he is at once both mischievous and innocent. His misdeeds never become more serious than jests or pranks, whether putting sunglasses on a hen destined to spend three weeks trying to hatch out a black pudding or suggesting to the audience they should all march down to the Chinese embassy and squirt rice pudding through the letter box. A knave, but not disciplined enough to be a villain, he is – like Puck – totally unpredictable. There is a redeeming childlike zest about both of them, reducing all of life to one big game. 'If my mother knew I was doing this, she'd be ashamed – she thinks I'm in prison!' The same playful innocence is maintained in the image he presents of the adulterous door-to-door salesman, purveyor of lechery to the masses. It is no coincidence that before he became a full-time pro he had his own travelling hardware store, the source of the 'Hello, missus' that punctuates his act. Salesman and showman combined, he vaunts his sexuality before the ladies in the audience in a game pure and simple: 'Have we any hen parties in tonight? We have? Cock-a-doodle-doo!'; 'By jove, I feel fit – as fit as a boarding house tomcat!' If Puck spent his time scaring 'the maidens in the villagery', there was Dodd in Blackpool during the summer of 1968 explaining how Engelbert Humperdinck at a rival theatre had promised to kiss a girl from the audience on stage at every performance and how he, Doddy, had an even better idea, but the management wouldn't play ball! However, just as he involves his audience in his puckish pranks, he still allows sexual participation by proxy: 'Come on, you daft lot, let's have an orgy!' Earlier, when he substitutes his tickling stick for a giant version – 'The size of it!' – the phallic connotation is obvious. As he points it in the direction of the giggling rosy-cheeked housewives in the front two rows, he explains, 'This is me knockers-up pole. If I can get this through your bedroom window, I'll send you to work with a twinkle in your eye!' His mastery of sexual innuendo is such that, as with Marie Lloyd and Max Miller before him, everything he does say is irreproachable. If the audience wishes to add its own interpretation, it can, may, and of course does. But whether Dodd is acting as prankster or lecher, no offence can be taken, because none is meant. His ambience is too celebratory for that and he is totally upfront about the importance of sex to his act: 'Sex is funny. We have a saying in Liverpool, "If the good Lord had anything better, he kept it for himself!"'

Among his generation Dodd proved himself to be the funniest of the live stage comedians, simply because no other performer aroused a greater volume of sustained laughter, caused an audience literally to ache until it could laugh no more for the pain in its sides. In the face of such tangible proof, theories as explanations are superfluous. When it comes to communication with an audience, he has had few equals, from the instantaneous contact of his opening line: 'First of all, I'd like to say how tickled I am;' through the byplay of those personal exchanges that make every single performance a unique experience: 'Did you all get your free sausage on the way in? – No? – Then you'll get it on the way out!' or, 'Are you all enjoying yourselves? You are? Then what are you doing?' to the final ultimatum: 'Do you give in?' By this time the audience is physically exhausted, but no more anxious that he should stop than he is to leave. Now no Ken Dodd show ends on time. In this respect his passion for performance is, as Leno's grew to be, insatiable. We have seen other points of similarity between the two comedians, but it is possible that Dodd is funnier now than the averred master ever was. In *Fifty Years of Vaudeville* by Ernest Short, published in 1946, we are told that 'the essence of the Lenoesque humour was the speed with which absurdity was piled upon absurdity, leaving time for nothing save laughter'. So far we are on common ground, but then Short adds, 'When Dan was on the stage the laughter was not noisy.' When Dodd is on the stage the laughter is raucous. The journalist Alan Brien likened the relationship between stand-up comic and audience to that between matador and bull, the former desperately determined to exhaust the latter before it can exhaust him. The analogy is most applicable if Dodd is pictured in the ring, because he appears the least exhaustible of clowns. There is an energy, a sense of urgency about his every performance that spells this out, and not merely in his own leaping wildly semaphoric physical presence, not merely in the zing of his delivery, but in the way he imparts a new life force to the old people he talks about so frequently. 'My grandad goes to the Darby and Joan club. I don't know what he does there, but he's got three notches on his walking stick. He used to be a model for jelly babies, but one day he went too far!'

Unfortunately in a Dodd performance there is the ever-present fear that one day the ultimate orgasm will be achieved, the audience go so far in the direction of exhaustion that it succumbs to hysterics, sulks, even chaos. The Danny Kaye legend lost much of its potency during his third Palladium season in the early 1950s. Convinced that the audience, which he held in the palm of his hand, would become even more compliant, he sat on the edge of the stage and asked them to follow his actions, clapping their hands, touching their elbows in unison. It seemed a fair enough request to make, but he had miscalculated. The essential give and take had given way. It is like placing the last fateful coin on that perilous pillar of pennies on the pub counter. The great entertainer will persist in adding to the column until the last possible moment, but ensure that it is left standing sensationally – however precariously. The danger is in trying too hard. Dodd has skirted this pitfall through his ability to switch the mood at a crucial moment and in a warm unpretentious mezzo-tenor silence the laughter with the melancholy of songs such as 'Love is like a violin', 'Pianissimo', 'Let me cry on your shoulder' and 'Broken-hearted'. All tell a tale of unrequited love, not least his biggest hit 'Tears', which in 1965 at the height of Beatlemania sold one and three quarter million copies, more than any other British-made single to that point, and stayed in the charts for forty-two weeks, five of them at the top.

> Tears have been my only consolation,
> But tears can't mend a broken heart, I must confess.
> Let's forgive and forget,
> Turn our tears of regret
> Once more to tears of happiness.

His most relevant song, however, is the infectious calypso-rhythmed 'Happiness'. When the curtain goes down the laughter must subside, but the exhilaration and joy of his performance as a whole remains embedded in us all. It is a case of 'Happiness' first and foremost, and has nothing really to do with making people laugh, which is only the first hurdle. His presence has come to represent the spirit of joy incarnate and never more so than in the grotesque company of the Diddymen, the Lilliputian inhabitants, by way of popular Liverpudlian mythology and Dodd's own surrealistic imagination, of Knotty Ash, an actual village now swamped by suburbia a few miles outside Liverpool, where he was born Kenneth Arthur Dodd, the son of a coal merchant on 8 November 1927 and where he still lives in his family home. Played by energetic young dancers the Diddymen have long formed an integral part of his stage act; as television puppet stars in the 1960s and 70s they won for a predominantly adult comedian a devoted juvenile audience.

With the distilled essence of an earlier generation of Merseyside comedy greats trickling (tickling?) through his veins – Askey, Handley, Bennett, Wilton, Ray – Dodd remains the one great Liverpool comedian who has never thought for a moment of cutting himself off from his roots. With his statue in pride of place at Lime Street Station and a special licence to tease – 'We've always been environment-conscious you know in Liverpool. In Liverpool we've had unleaded churches for years!' – he maintains an objective view of life as lived by the people he has to entertain, namely the masses. It is a view not a little responsible for his prominence. His unique air of impish tenderness also plays its part. The most crucial factor in his success, however, was alluded to in Dodd's own appraisal of George Robey in a television tribute to mark the centenary of that performer's birth. In style and appearance Robey and Dodd are as different as curled cane and feather duster, but I have no qualms about substituting the name of the younger comedian between his own inverted commas: 'A lot of comedians perform *at* an audience. They use the audience as a sounding board for their jokes. But Ken Dodd performs *with* an audience. He is a one-man situation.'

AFTERTHOUGHTS

It is hard to believe that almost sixty years since he turned professional Dodd is still touring with his act today and that substantially the same formula that convinced John Osborne at the Palladium back in the 1960s still works, even if the name of the prime minister has to change every few years or so. As the public allowed Tommy Cooper to become older and hence slower and yet found him hilarious still, so it has found no difficulty in allowing a man who is now more than twenty years senior to Cooper at the time of his death to preserve an ageless sense of mischief. As he approaches his mid-eighties, Dodd's energy remains indefatigable, not only in the spotlight but behind the scenes, where his dedicated approach to his craft ensures that every book published on humour is read, every effort made in the exploration for new material to keep his act crisp and topical. While he almost certainly has the largest working repertoire of any comic of his kind, it is not unusual to enter his dressing room during the intermission of a show and discover him on the phone to one of a dedicated group of personal writers scattered throughout the country, scribbling lines in biro onto his wrist in an attempt to be as topical in the second half as the news allows him to be, possibly with reference to headlines he has not yet even read.

There was a time in the late 80s when it looked as if what was on course to become one of the most enduring careers in British entertainment might be derailed when charges of tax evasion were brought against him. For months it seemed he dominated the headlines. It was seriously on the cards that if convicted he would serve a prison sentence and there was also the risk of being stripped of the OBE he had been awarded in 1982. At this point I have to declare an interest in having been called as a character witness in the trial by Dodd's QC, the legendary George Carman. I had known Ken since he helped cultivate my interest in comedy while I was an undergraduate, when he performed a three-week season at the New Theatre, Oxford. His genius and inspiration had an intrinsic part to play in the genesis of this book. Once established in my own career as a television producer, I had the privilege of working with him on frequent occasions, not least in his own series. I knew above all else that behind the veneer of

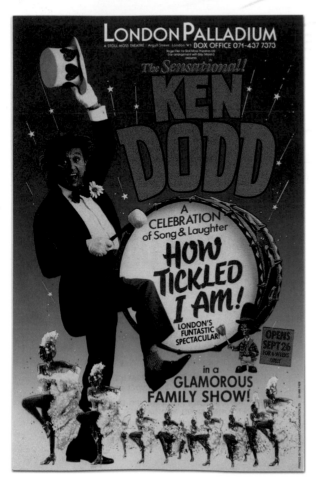

eccentricity he might have chosen to cultivate at times – the trial revealed that he once kept in excess of three hundred thousand pounds in cash stashed away in suitcases in his attic – he was an extremely caring man of many secret good deeds and certainly not a criminal. Roy Hudd and Eric Sykes, who once gallantly referred to him as 'a Chippendale in a room full of G Plan furniture', also testified on his behalf. On 21 July 1989 Dodd was cleared of all charges.

He immediately ploughed himself back into his exhilarating but exhaustive regimen of one-night stands, vowing where possible to return to his native Knotty Ash at the end of each evening, however late that may be. The following year he confirmed his status with another triumphant Palladium season, *How Tickled I Am!* In the latter half of his career he has assumed a personal mission to keep theatres open as a home for popular entertainment and play every single one of them in the process. NO ONE GIVES KEN DODD A GRANT, DO THEY? ran the famous headline. His is one of the truly great success stories of British entertainment within my lifetime.

At the front line of comedy

It was typical of the man and his humour that rather than attempt to tuck the indignity and embarrassment of the tax ordeal out of sight, he turned the episode and his attitude to his finances as portrayed by it to his comic advantage, in a manner not too far removed from the way in which the great American droll Jack Benny traded on a fictitious meanness. Soon lines like the following were at home in Dodd's act: 'I told the Inland Revenue I didn't owe them a penny because I lived near the seaside! You know where their headquarters are? Andover! I filled in my forms in pencil – it's not my fault they might have smudged. And what's their latest trick? Self-assessment! They pinched that one from me!'

In the same way his enthusiasm to stay on stage past the time when the last bus has left and the stage doorman has shut up shop has become an additional leitmotif. In recent years – well into his fifth hour on stage – he has been known to quip, 'Don't worry – you'll all be safe. You'll be going home in the daylight. Those in the cheap seats get coffee and you in the stalls get full English breakfast.' His determination to give value for money on stage is without question, even though he has his own philosophical take on the passing of the hours, minutes and seconds. 'Time is an illusion' is a constant mantra which those who work with him have to get used to!

Rereading what I wrote about Dodd many years ago I realise that I underplayed then an important aspect of his talent, one that reveals an even wider grounding and versatility than the highlights of his act already reported. Quite simply, no one can surpass Dodd's way with an anecdote or story joke, like the tale of the three-legged chicken immortalised on *Parkinson* in 1981.

This man had his brand new Jaguar – a beautiful car. He was driving up the M1 – just keeping it at 69 mph, like Jaguar drivers do – and he happened to look in his mirror and he sees a chicken running alongside him. A chicken – a three-legged chicken! So he put his foot down and he gets through to about 90 and he says, 'That'll fix him – cock-a-doodle-doo!' Now the chicken's still there. Suddenly the chicken puts his right wing out and overtakes him and he's doing about 150 mph up the M1. He's in the Jag – the chicken ahead. He says, 'I'll catch him! Come here, you little beggar, come here.' Suddenly the chicken puts his left wing out and is off up a slip road. So he chases him up the slip road, down all these little country lanes and suddenly the chicken puts his right wing out again and shoots into a farmyard. So into the farmyard. He pulls up – no sign of the chicken, just an old farmer crossing the farmyard – as farmers do! I don't know why they walk like this – there must be a reason! So he says, 'Where is he?' He says, 'What?' He says, 'Where's the chicken?' He says, 'Oh, you chased him, have you?' He says, 'Yes. I chased a three-legged chicken in here.' 'Oh yes,' the farmer says. 'Ooh aahh, ooh aah. I breed 'em.' He says, 'You breed three-legged chickens?' 'Yes,' he says, 'I breed three-legged chickens' He says, 'Why?' 'Well,' the farmer says, 'I like a leg.' He says, 'And the wife, she likes a leg and the son, he likes a leg.' He says, 'What do they taste like?' He says, 'I don't know. I've never caught one!'

The point was never in the joke per se. Dodd didn't just tell it, he became it. In a display of perpetual motion to rival moments of his stage act, his body became a veritable cyclone of activity, veering from the chicken punching against the air for speed to the pop-eyed amazement of the driver; from the bird signalling weirdly with its wings to the driver's every change of direction at the steering wheel; from their zigzagging along the country lanes to the legs-akimbo tread of the farmer through the mud. No detail was lost. It is impossible to add up the number of laughter cues Dodd achieves in the telling of the tale. All merge into a glorious whole revealing an actor and mime of considerable skill.

No comedian has pursued his craft with greater evangelical zeal, religiously numbering the venues he continues to play around the country with the dedication of the devotee counting off the beads on his rosary. No performer of his kind is more vitally at home on a stage, while none has revealed greater loyalty and commitment to his public off it. I once walked with him the relatively short distance from his dressing room to a hospitality suite at the BBC Television Centre. It took sixty minutes as one person after another seemed to step out of the shadows to chat and offer thanks to a man who has always been happy to give the public his time in return. He has openly admitted, 'You can only be as good as the audience will let you be,' and has always resented being labelled a stand-up comedian, feeling that his unique relationship with the audience qualifies more as a double act. If Max Miller – one of his heroes – goes down in the annals as the king of stand-ups, Dodd somehow demands his own special category. As he rides the merry-go-round of his imagination, no performer has pulled together so many strands of talent and timelessness, music and mayhem, energy and hilarity, sheer hokum and humanity. He does represent the end of an era. It is difficult to imagine that he will ever be surpassed.

At the top of his game

Billy Russell: 'On Behalf of the Working Classes'

...To See Such Fun!

It will always depend, as it has in the past, right to the beginnings of ballad and song, on the sympathy between artist and audience... on 'timing'.
[Sir John Betjeman on the British music hall, 1965]

However comprehensive one strives to make a book within its carefully defined limits, as the last chapter approaches the scary thought persists that full justice has not been done to certain talents and key individuals. Figuratively speaking, the vignettes that follow represent an attempt to plug the last remaining holes in the bucket of the pantomime clown. Should water continue to spurt out, the author only hopes that he himself gets the backlash of the slapstick and not the comic heroes considered by others worthy of inclusion whom he may have omitted. Happily, the paperback publication of this volume in 1976 enabled me to continue to make up what might have been interpreted as the deficit of the first edition and those additions, with a few others, are included here.

Prominent in the front line is Billy Russell (1893 – 1971). He had a wheezy high-pitched line in domestic patter, which he delivered especially 'On Behalf of the Working Classes'. His 'Old Bill in Civvies' character was based on the clodhopping walrus-moustached pipe-chewing veteran of the Flanders mud created during the First World War by cartoonist Captain Bruce Bairnsfather. Possibly Bairnsfather's most famous cartoon depicted Bill and a colleague under fire in a shell hole somewhere in no-man's-land. The caption read, 'Well, if you knows of a better 'ole, go to it!' Thanks to Russell, a generation later 'Old Bill', now a navvy, was able to carry on joking in adversity from a civilian standpoint. Blackout misadventures, 'RIP' patrols, the 'Ministry of Inflammation', and newspaper headlines like BABY GORILLA BORN AT THE LONDON ZOO... HITLER BLAMES WINSTON CHURCHILL were all grist to his earthy mill. In later years Russell achieved distinction as a character actor, but the warmth of his variety self never failed to shine through the most cantankerous of the roles he played.

Not too far removed from the spirit of the great Jimmy James was his close friend the pawky Middlesbrough-born Dave Morris (1896 – 1960), whose imaginary heraldic shield – a device that would have appealed to his pretensions to worldliness – would have had to include his torpedo cigar, squat straw boater and those pebble lenses through which he hazily surveyed his world, a Mr Magoo of the British working classes. With a well defined retinue of stooges, most notably Joe Gladwin as the gormless Cedric, he wove a web of verbal fantasy that in his heyday, the 1940s into the 50s, was somewhat ahead of its time. One routine depicted him as the greatest lion tamer on earth, who happened to be in a cage 'with fifteen forest-bred lions when the chair broke. Picture these thirty forest-bred lions clawing their way out of the cage. So there I was being pursued by these fifty forest-bred lions when I realised I'd run into a cul-de-sac with a ten-foot wall. And there were these 150 forest-bred lions behind me. Just imagine a cul-de-sac with this hundred-foot wall and 350 forest-bred lions after me.' Timid, yet sceptical,the stooge could no longer contain his curiosity. 'What happened?' 'What happened?' replied Morris. 'I just

Dave Morris

turned me hat back to front, gave a false name and walked away.' Badly gassed during the First World War, he battled with ill health and poor eyesight for the rest of his life. When asked by a reporter how he managed to contend with his disabilities, he replied, 'Well, for a start, this cigar is primed with pot. Then, after a shot of Benzedrine and a glass of Coke, I hobble on with the aid of my stick. I do it because *the show must go on*. And I go on because I need the money!'

In the same robust northern tradition was the raucous yet brilliant combination of cousins Jimmy Jewel (1909 – 1995) and Ben Warriss (1909 – 1993). Performing together from 1934, they were the most successful traditional double act in the period between Flanagan and Allen and Morecambe and Wise. To someone reared on the cut and thrust of their radio sketches in the hit series *Up the Pole*, which ran between 1947 and 1952, it is easy to overlook the fact that in their heyday on stage they gave an outrageous three-dimensional reality to the sort of fantasy world that might have seemed impossible outside the broadcasting studio. In one famous Blackpool sketch Jimmy entered a shop to buy a pen that he hoped would write underwater. Ben, the officious salesman, would not let his customer leave until satisfaction had been proved. Forcibly stripped down to lurid striped underpants, Jimmy was submerged in a ten-foot-deep tank of water, his usual pop-eyed stare assuming a goldfish vulnerability, while the severe look of his complacent straight man took on a gloating catfish menace. Each time Jimmy bobbed up to the surface wielding the giant phallic writing implement, Ben would push him under once more. It was all miles away from the close-harmony singing of Irving Berlin's 'You're just in love', with which they would appealingly bring their act to a close, the 'I wonder why' self-questioning of the lyric informed at a level the lyricist could never have intended by Jimmy's daft comic persona. In another sketch planks of timber cascaded threateningly from the flies as they sang a novelty number of the day that went,

Jimmy Jewel and Ben Warriss

'Timber! Timber! Can't you hear us calling for timber?' No one expected the avalanche at the end. In the latter period of his life, Jewel, long since separated from Warriss, became a stage and television actor of considerable stature.

Gillie Potter

There were also the early solo radio humorists with a grounding in variety, most prominent among whom was Gillie Potter (1887 – 1975), chronicler of events in the mythical village of Hogsnorton and of the Marshmallow family in particular. His standard attire consisted of rimless glasses, Harrovian boater and ample blue blazer with an exclamatory arrow on its breast pocket. He assumed a schoolmasterly air of superiority – 'Good evening, England. This is Gillie Potter speaking to you in basic English' – coupled with a gift for the commonplace by way of anticlimax. In real life he did in fact have an impressive scholastic record, as archaeologist, heraldic expert, and practising writer and lecturer, traits that showed through in his work and were doubtless one reason why his approach was often accused of being too subtle for some of the rougher halls. He lived during his retirement in Bournemouth, from where the odd letter found its way to the correspondence columns of *The Times* to remind us that the squire of Hogsnorton was still alive and well and speaking to us in basic English.

At a later date no solo radio performer colonised the airwaves more effectively than Salford-born Al Read (1909 – 1987), whose individual talents marked him out as the pioneer of the observational humour now beloved of a generation of newer comedians to whom the joke has become anathema. However, rather than simply draw attention to our faults and frailties, the inconsistencies and banalities of daily existence, Read single-handedly (he portrayed all the voices, including the dog) peopled his radio half-hours with a cast of recognisable types which included the inquisitive schoolboy, the fellow with the uncontrollable dog, the harassed car park attendant, the know-it-all in the doctor's surgery or on the Old Trafford terraces, the henpecked husband with the harridan of a wife who always seemed to be shouting from the kitchen: 'Are you going to mow that lawn – or are we putting some sheep on it?'

Al Read

In the 50s British working-class mores knew no more accurate observer than Al Read, who had trod an unconventional path into show business. An executive with his family's meat pie firm, he was spotted in a Manchester bar describing to some of his business associates his first encounter with the obstreperous decorator summoned to provide an estimate for doing up the back bedroom for his mother-in-law's impending stay. As the laughter subsided, BBC radio producer Bowker Andrews introduced himself and was in no time launching Al into broadcasting work. This led to a distinguished career which embraced the catchphrase-titled revues *You'll Be Lucky* and *Such Is Life* at London's Adelphi Theatre, numerous Blackpool seasons and a radio series that ran intermittently between 1951 and 1968. 'Right, monkey!' was another Read catchphrase that swept the country.

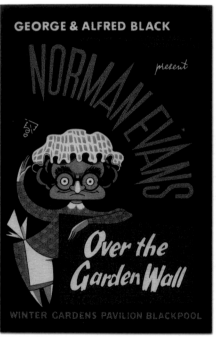

In similar proletarian vein was Norman Evans (1901 – 1962), a protégé of Gracie Fields, like her a native of Rochdale and best known for his characterisation of Fanny Fairbottom in his sketch 'Over the Garden Wall'. Here you could take the humour on a purely physical level – Fanny getting her balloon-sized breasts trapped between bricks and chin as she struggles to maintain her balance on the other side of the wall ('That's the third time on the same brick!') and wielding her gums with the toothless flexibility of Popeye the Sailor – or on a more subtle enemy-in-the-camp level as exploited later by Danny La Rue, a fellow letting in this case not the birds but all those busty northern matriarchs, once the lifeblood of *Coronation Street*, know he has caught on to them. He had a special line in confidential chatter as he gossiped away to his invisible next-door neighbour, whether targeting pungent moggy ('Whew! It does whiff – I could smell it in t' custard last Sunday!') or randy coal man ('Don't tell me it takes thirty-five minutes to deliver two bags of nuts!'). It would, however, be unfair to characterise Evans as simply a dame, although it was this facet of his work that brought him greatest prominence, including star billing in pantomime at the

London Palladium and the Coliseum. In male attire he also featured a hilarious mime routine portraying persistent dentist – 'This isn't going to hurt' – and obstinate patient in the throes of an extraction using a screen, in much the same way that Marcel Marceau would later enact David and Goliath, and an endearing sequence with a glove puppet teddy bear that crept sheepishly out of his jacket. forerunner of Sooty and featured several times in his television shows during the twilit 1950s.

Arthur Haynes

At the time of Evans's death at the beginning of the 1960s, another older-style comedian, Arthur Haynes (1914 – 1966), a graduate of Cheerful Charlie Chester's *Stand Easy* radio show, was also achieving prominence through his portrayal of the obstreperous tramp character created for him by Johnny Speight – alongside *Hancock's Half Hour*, one of the first television comedy ideas to make any real comment about social class. The basic formula was a reversal of the traditional double act with Haynes's gleefully insolent underdog demolishing the Establishment figure played with upper-crust authority by Nicholas Parsons. Brandishing his sole credentials, a sagging string of First World War medals, Haynes would tell Parsons, 'There I was up to me neck in muck and bullets fighting for me country, mate.' The atmosphere of almost Pinteresque menace that hovered behind the laughter that the tramp provoked is underlined by the real-life situation that gave birth to the characterisation. A tramp thumbed a lift in Speight's car and, revelling in its comfort, settled down to deliver the first authentic Haynes dialogue: 'I prefer Bentleys. A little Anglia offered me a ride, but I wouldn't take it. I mean you meet a better class of person in a car like this. Toffs, like.' A glowing stage performer with a fatherly presence, Arthur featured at the close of his act a hilarious burlesque of a much-wounded soldier parading the rousing 'Goodbye' number from *White Horse Inn*. He topped the Palladium bill in 1963 with the revue *Swing Along*. Sadly ill health absented him from much of the run and he died from a heart attack at the premature age of fifty-two three years later.

Few comics were of more eccentric bent than the boyishly rotund Fred Emney (1900 – 1980), a famous son who followed in his famous father's footsteps as a prominent fixture in musical comedy and revue. However, it was television that brought him national fame and a presence in variety in his later years. As trademarks, his top hat, Churchillian cigar and monocle, all conveying an air of aristocratic disdain, were overshadowed by his gargantuan girth. He was a veritable barrage balloon of a man, who when someone once commented that he had possibly lost a little weight replied, 'Yes, I've given up mint sauce!' He was also an accomplished player and composer of light piano music, and his gruff throwaway verbal style provided the perfect accompaniment to his deftness at the keys: for all his size his touch was as light as the hippos dancing in *Fantasia*, not so unlikely an analogy given his late-life success on the small screen as straight man to puppet favourites Pinky and Perky. His piano routine had a wonderful piece of business when he tried to settle his vast bulk on the piano stool with a cushion, eventually throwing it aside in disgust with the line 'Never could stand heights!' One television sketch depicted him as a variety agent. An act came into his office to audition, a human pyramid of three performers on two bikes, the woman juggling as she balanced precariously on the shoulders of her male partners. As they rode round the room, Fred's expression gave no hint of surprise or interest. Eventually they left and after a

Fred Emney

brilliantly timed pause he declared, 'I wonder what *they* do!' Arguably his greatest stage success came in 1950 in the musical comedy *Blue for a Boy* at Her Majesty's Theatre. The incongruous image of his vast mass swathed in blue baby rompers hugging a teddy bear was enough to coax anyone into the theatre irrespective of the flimsy plot he fought desperately to save.

To the pantheon of great stage drunks already celebrated one must attach the name of Freddie Frinton (1909 – 1968), whose tipsy routine, while derivative of that of Jimmy James, was in the eyes of many second only to it. His characterisation was seen to best advantage in a sketch entitled 'Dinner for One' originally performed by Bobby Howes and Binnie Hale in West End revue in the 1920s although considerably embellished by Freddie after he first performed it in 1945. In this Frinton, playing butler to a dowager (played by May Warden) celebrating her ninetieth birthday, has to serve dinner – and drinks – to an assorted gathering of long-dead grandees seated around the table in her imagination. The sequence revolves around their oft-repeated exchange as the procedure for each course is addressed.

> *Frinton*: The same procedure as last year, Miss Sophie?
> *Warden*: The same procedure as *every* year, James.

In an effort to follow her wishes he pours each drink in turn, gives a short and suitable toast and then, circling the table again, quaffs it himself. Staggering between table and sideboard, he gets tighter and tighter with each course, each time making more studied play of circumnavigating the ravenous gaping head of a tiger-skin rug as he returns for his orders. Then it is time for the old lady to retire to her bed. Frinton accompanies her up the stairs.

Freddie Frinton with May Ward

> *Frinton*: The same procedure as last year, Miss Sophie?
> *Warden*: The same procedure as *every* year, James.

Frinton's discombobulated frog face says it all. In a bizarre quirk of fate a recording of the sketch made by Frinton for German television in 1963 has become a New Year's Eve tradition in that country, where it has been repeated annually from the early 70s. Subsequently the tradition has also flourished throughout Scandinavia.

The slapstick skill and physical adeptness required by the sketch – not least the moment when Frinton finally did trip on the tiger rug sending his tray of drink and glasses towards the ceiling – would have come as second nature to the plump and minuscule Charlie Drake (1925 – 2006), famed for the seemingly beguiling innocence of his catchphrase 'Hello, my darlings!' As a clown Drake was a cherub with a touch of the hoodlum about him, as well as one of the first comedians to be reared in British television, the medium where he registered his greatest success, having begun as one half of the children's slapstick duo Mick and Montmorency. Jack Edwardes played the straight man, Mick. This background, however, should not detract from the memory of a breathtaking routine, featured in many variety appearances, in which, playing a carnival salesman swathed in balloons of all colours, he hurls himself at the least pretence into a whirlwind of disaster, incorporating a sensual dance with a buxom blonde, the balloons popping in turn to highlight the frenzy, until like Old Mother Riley's final china plate, one last persistent balloon is left.

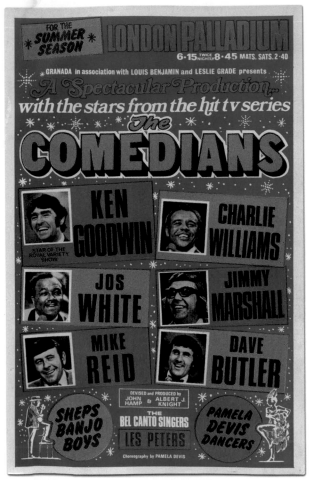

And so the glorious parade passed by. For a while the buzz in comedy became centred upon the emergence of the northern working men's club scene as a late music hall substitute and the distinctive brand of joke purveyors that served as both staple diet and cannon fodder for the audiences they attracted. The trend was distinctive enough for Granada Television, maybe taking a hint from Dawson's *Sez Les* success on Yorkshire Television, to package some of the best of these 'funny men in suits' in a series imaginatively called *The Comedians*! Under the skilled editorial eye of producer Johnnie Hamp, the idea caught on to the extent that in 1972 a selection of the bunch played a Palladium season in a stage show built around the format, although sadly the pace achieved on the small screen by editing and cross-cutting between the jokers was noticeably missing. Of those performers, only two succeeded in outlasting the original impact of the show to enjoy an enduring comedy career and any real status, namely Frank Carson (1926 – 2012), whose hearty Irish horseplay enabled him to get away with the most unkempt of shaggy-dog stories as he assured his audience, 'It's the way I tell 'em;' and the controversial Bernard Manning (1930 – 2007), squat as a Toby jug, whose salty rough-diamond authority was not diminished by his experience of clubland at another level, namely as the proprietor of Manchester's Embassy Club. In addition, the bludgeoning fast-talking cockney Mike Reid (1940 – 2007), to whom a hand mike was superfluous and whose rabble-rouser facade failed to do justice to a subtler range beneath, proved himself a creditable actor within the environs of the soap opera *EastEnders* in the character of Frank Butcher. Jim Bowen (b.1937)

Frank Carson

Bernard Manning

also acquired a deserved reputation as a television host and demonstrated an intelligence in his attitude to comedy that won him many admirers among younger audiences, possibly to the surprise not least of himself. Colin Crompton, Ken Goodwin, George Roper, Roy Walker and Charlie Williams were others who achieved considerable, if passing, fame through the format.

Jimmy Tarbuck

Aside from Les Dawson, arguably the most successful of the new breed to emerge from the northern theatre clubs – and well established long before the Granada format – was Jimmy Tarbuck (b.1939), the 'Lad from Liverpool', who in a single live Palladium television show broke through during the early 1960s to satisfy understandable public demand for a comedian in the Beatle image and, exploiting his own brand of cock-sparrow brashness, went on to consolidate his popularity as the perennial host of any number of television formats that would once have fallen upon the shoulders of Tommy Trinder. From the same school came Freddie Davies (b.1937), an original eccentric with an esoteric line in budgerigar stories, who became known more affectionately, especially amongst his many young fans, as Mr Parrot Face, although parrots with his jug-handle ears and popeyed stare are rare, and those with the volcanic splutter reserved for his ornithological jokes even rarer. Tarbuck and Davies were just about the first to span the chasm between beer-stained club platform and Palladium stage, helping to undermine the cliché that with the closing of so many theatres training places for the apprentice funny man had become harder to find.

Alas it was not to be. The club-as-music-hall boom proved a passing fancy. The exorbitant sums paid to stars, some worthier of the name and the cash than others, upset the economics of it all, while the humour on offer, regardless of accusations of political incorrectness made against much of it, quickly became lazy and stereotyped, revealing itself bereft of imagination and invention, allowing the university-orientated purveyors of so-called alternative comedy to grasp their opportunity. Of course it is never quite as simple as that, but comedy was given a wake-up call, and, with the wind of *Beyond the Fringe* and television's *Monty Python, Not the Nine o'Clock News* and *The Young Ones* behind it, a new generation adapting to new working conditions imposed by specialised comedy clubs and large arenas took the reins.

Roy Hudd

As the variety era breathed its last a promising live comedian arrived on the scene in Roy Hudd (b.1933), whose early progress appeared to be hindered by his enthusiasm for and allegiance to idols from Leno through Bennett and Miller to Dodd himself, resulting in an impressive series of memory-lane stage and television impersonations when he might have been searching more profitably for an individual comic persona that he could indelibly call his own. Hudd has since developed into a character actor of standing, as well as proving me wrong by evolving into the public face of and spokesman for the old traditions. His amiable persona both on and off stage is a happy reminder of a time when successful comics were friends of the family to be rooted for and when material – albeit sometimes risqué – had an innocence harder to find today.

Ken Dodd has expressed his disdain for the foul language and studied cruelty that often pass for comedy now. To quote the master, 'My job is to send people away from the theatre feeling better than when they came in. We all know there's plenty of misery in the world, but that doesn't mean it's a miserable place.' The greatest fear, as the briefest glimpse at the television schedules and subsequent ratings reveals, is that comedy has come close to losing touch with mainstream public taste and will pass into the hands of a middle-class elite. An obsession with the cult experience has to be guarded against. But life has to evolve. I am just truly grateful that I was there when Hancock grumbled, Wisdom stumbled and Cooper fumbled, while Morecambe and Wise requested the sunshine that Ken Dodd radiated with such zany bonhomie.

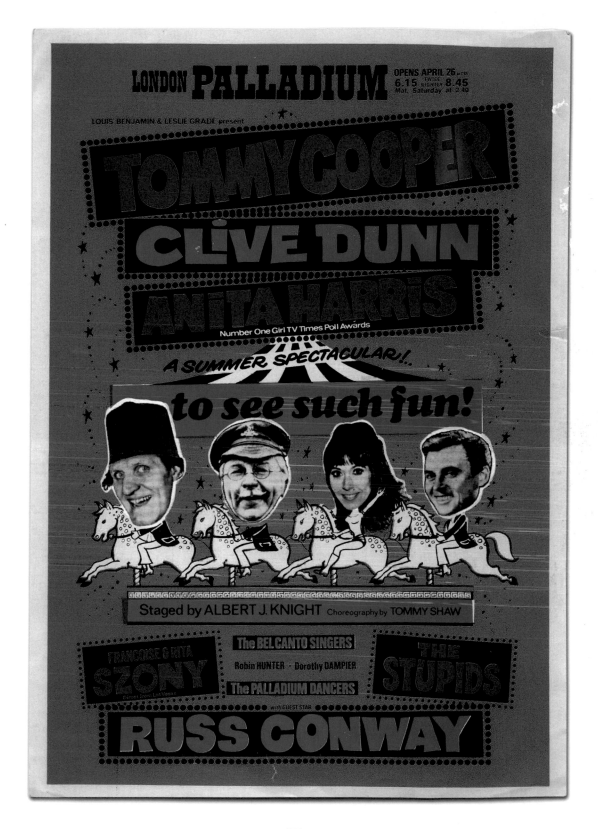

'Bring Me Sunshine': Des O'Connor, Ernie Wise and
Sir Michael Parkinson backstage at the London Palladium
on the occasion of the Eric Morecambe gala tribute

Afterword by Sir Michael Parkinson

About the only fact missing from this book of loving care is the date of my first appearance in a m hall. It is worth recording not because it has any importance to the grand pattern of the halls, but it has real significance in my own development. The time was during World War Two. The place: the Theatre Royal, Barnsley. The occasion: my parents' wedding anniversary. To celebrate this event and my baptism in the music hall the old man brilliantined his hair and mother bought a new coat. Moreover, father saved up enough money to take a box. That box at Barnsley was unique in that it is the only one I have ever encountered which contained deckchairs instead of conventional seats. Perched on the edge of my deckchair I was soon drunk on the smell of Barnsley bitter and Woodbines, hypnotised by the lights and the beefy chorus girls in their darned tights.

Top of the bill was a brace of comedians, famous in their time but not famous enough to warrant mention in this book. There was a tall thin one and a short fat one as there always has been and, please God, always will be. The tall thin one had his eye on my mother and became so saucy that he angered my old man. The comedian's career would have been considerably foreshortened if my father's plan to chin him had materialised. As it was, his deckchair collapsed at the point where father was about to launch himself out of the box and across the footlights. It got the biggest laugh of the evening. The significance of this event, beyond the pantomime in the box, was that from that moment on I was hooked on music hall. I grew to love, everlastingly, the men who made me laugh. Being a Yorkshireman I became addicted to those comedians whose humour grew out of the grimness of northern industrialised society. Case-hardened comics epitomised by the greatest of them all, the incomparable Jimmy James, whose heritage has been so brilliantly grasped by our finest modern comedians, Morecambe and Wise.

All this is merely a preamble illustrating how much I have enjoyed this book. It is more than a good read; it is a loving analysis of a unique sense of humour. John Fisher is both my friend and my colleague. As someone who works alongside him I take for granted all the dedicated and intelligent care he reveals in the book. But I am still amazed that one so young can be so perceptive and wise. I think I have read an important book and I know for a fact that the comedians we both adore have been paid due homage.

Michael Parkinson

1973

Author's footnote:

The team alluded to by Sir Michael is (Will) Collinson and (Bobby) Breen, an act which before the upheaval of personnel triggered by the Second World War had consisted of Collinson and (Alfie) Dean. To the best of my knowledge both combinations enjoyed the same billing matter: 'Lilies that fester smell far worse than weeds,' which may just qualify as the *reductio ad absurdum* of all such sobriquets.

Above left: Ted Kavanagh

Above right: Ray Galton and Alan Simpson with agent and producer Beryl Vertue

Left: Frank Muir and Denis Norden

Below left: the author with Eric Sykes

Below right: much treasured support from Eric Morecambe and Ernie Wise

To John.

Mr Showbusiness

ERIC & ERNIE

Eric Wise

'But what do you do for a living'

Eric

ACKNOWLEDGEMENTS

From the first edition:

Thanks must be extended in many directions for the completion of this volume. Research was facilitated by the staff of the original Enthoven Collection at the Victoria and Albert Museum, and in particular Tony Latham; the Bodleian Library, Oxford; the BBC Gramophone Library and Dennis Dexter who both made available rare recordings of the earlier performers; the National Film Archive which likewise made available rare film; the Information and Stills Departments of the British Film Institute; Ellis Ashton, John Lungley and Don Ross of the British Music Hall Society; the Publicity Department of Thames Television Ltd and the Press Office of Moss Empires Ltd.

I also recognise the kindness, attention and inspiration received from the following individuals, together with the permission to quote from copyright material as apparent in the text: Chesney Allen, Arthur Askey, Hylda Baker, George Bartram, Eddie Braben, Peter Brough, Max Bygraves, James Casey, Sir Bill Cotton, Ken Dodd, Richard Drewett, Clifford Elson, Miff Ferrie, Mrs Sid Field, Mrs Bud Flanagan, Ray Galton, John Gibson, Jimmy Grafton, James Hartley. Dickie Henderson, Nigel Hollis, Patricia Houlihan, Frankie Howerd, Jock Jacobsen, Tony James, Roger Johnson, P. J. Kavanagh, Max Kester, John Kennedy Melling, Mrs Max Miller, Sir Spike Milligan, Eric Morecambe, Frank Muir, Denis Norden, Sir Michael Parkinson, Stan Parkinson, Phyllis Pleydell, Mrs Frank Randle, Ted Ray, Mike Regan, Winifred Relph, Max Russell, Rex Russell, Sir Harry Secombe, Alan Simpson, Albert Stevenson, Richard Stone, Jacques Tati, Beryl Vertue, Peter Vincent, Max Wall, Elsie and Doris Waters, Sir Norman Wisdom, Ernie Wise, Ken Wrench, April Young, and Sonny Zahl.

Original copyright holders are noted as follows: "Scarlet ribbons", © Copyright 1949, Belwin-Mills Music Ltd; "Chinese laundry blues", reproduced by permission of B. Feldman & Co. Ltd, 64 Dean Street, London WIV 6AU; "Run rabbit run", reproduced by kind permission of Noel Gay Music Co. Ltd; extracts from *The Prime Minister of Mirth* (1956) by A. E. Wilson, reproduced by kind permission of The Hamlyn Publishing Group Ltd; "Out of town", copyright 1955 Ed. Kassner Music Co. Ltd, by Robin Beaumont and Leslie Bricusse and reproduced by kind permission of Ed. Kassner Music Co. Ltd; extracts from Max Kester's radio scripts reproduced by kind permission of Max Kester Ltd; "Free" (Kennedy and Carr), "On the outside looking in" (Carr), " Mary from the dairy" (Miller, Kern and Walsh), © 1936, 1939, 1950 by the Peter Maurice Music Co. Ltd; "Under the bed" (Castling), reproduced by kind permission of the Mechanical-Copyright Protection Society Ltd; "Tears" (Ubre and Capano), by permission of Keith Prowse Music Publishing Co. Ltd; "Hindoo man" (Formby, Gifford, Cliffe), "The Lancashire toreador" (Formby, Gifford, Cliffe), "Riding in the T.T. races" (Gifford, Cliffe), "The best of schemes" (Gifford, Cliffe), "With my little stick of Blackpool rock" (Formby, Gifford, Cliffe), "In a little Wigan garden" (Gifford, Cliffe), "When I'm cleaning windows" (Formby. Gifford, Cliffe), "Mr. Wu's a window cleaner now" (Formby, Gifford, Cliffe), "There's nothing proud about me" (Gifford, Cliffe), © 1963 Lawrence Wright Music Company Ltd and reprinted by kind permission.

For the new edition:

In the forty years since publication during a lifetime spent in the world of entertainment many more people have informed and encouraged my love of comedy. It would be impossible to credit every single individual, but I would like to make special mention of the following, linked again with thanks for permission to quote from copyright material where appropriate: Roy Addison, Val Andrews, Brad Ashton, Tom Atkinson, Richard Anthony Baker, Ronnie Barker, Larry Barnes, Laurie Bellew, Michael Bentine, Sir John Betjeman, Michael Billington, Sir Peter Blake, Mike Brown, Colin Burnett-Dick, Simon Callow, George Carl, Seamus Cassidy, Jonathan Cecil, Malcolm Chapman, Barney Colehan, Alistair Cooke, Gwen Cooper, Tommy Cooper, Vicky Cooper, Ronnie Corbett, Barry Cryer, John Howard Davies, Russell Davies, Dabber Davis, Les Dawson, Tracy Dawson, David Drummond, John M. East, Jimmy Edwards, David Elstein, Dick Emery, Pierre Etaix, Di Evans, Norma Farnes, Colin Fay, Marty Feldman and John Law, Dick Fiddy, Dame Gracie Fields, Jerome Flynn, Bryan Forbes, Dave Forrester, Sir Bruce Forsyth, Colin Fox, Nancy George, Denis Gifford, Brian Glanville, Lord Michael Grade, Barry Grantham, Sir Peter Hall, Jeff Hammonds, Annie Hancock, Roger Hancock, Tim Hancock, Anne Hart, David Hemingway, Benny Hill, Dick Hills, Roy Hudd, Peter Hudson, Barry Humphries, Valerie James, Brian Johnston, Philip Jones, Tudor Jones, Jan Kennedy, John Lahr, Anita Land, Tessa Le Bars, Mark Lewisohn, Laurie Mansfield, Clive Mantle, Marcel Marceau, Billy Marsh, Jay Marshall, Sandy Marshall, Keith Mason, Paul Merton, Dave and Elizabeth Miles, Geoff Miles, John Miles, Cyril Bertram Mills, Richard M. Mills, James Moir, Bob Monkhouse, Gary Morecambe, Joan Morecambe, Mo Moreland, Johnnie Mortimer and Brian Cooke, John Muir, Spike Mullins, Norman Murray, Des O'Connor, Philip Oakes, Gerald Oxley, Patrick Page, Dan Peat, Arthur Pedlar, Michael Pointon, Slava Polunin, Peter Prichard, David Renwick, Charles Reynolds, David Robinson, Lynda Ronan, Phyllis Rounce, Patrick Ryecart, Neil Shand, Madeline Smith, Johnny Speight, David Suchet, Eric Sykes, Barry Took, Lyn Took, Tommy Trinder, Jack Tripp, Kenneth Tynan, Beryl Vertue, John Watt, Colin Webb, Len Whitcher, June Whitfield, Kenneth Williams, Audrey Worsley, Michael Worsley, Gerald Wiley, Dennis Main Wilson, Doreen Wise, Andrea Wonfor, Duncan Wood, Chris Woodward, Laurie Wyman and Cy Young.

For the new edition I acknowledge fair usage of material from the following sources: "The bee song" by Kenneth Blain, published by Keith Prowse Music Publishing; "The seagull song" by Arthur Askey © 1940; "Hello to the sun" by Noel Gay and Frank Eyton published by Cinephonic Music Co Ltd/Richard Armitage Ltd; "Sally" by Will E. Haines, Harry Leon and Leo Towers published by Keith Prowse Music Publishing Co. Ltd; "Take me to your heart" by Gracie Fields; "I took my harp to a party" by Noel Gay and Desmond Carter published by Chappell Music Co Ltd/Richard Armitage Ltd; "In my little bottom drawer" by Will E. Haines and Jimmy Harper, "I never cried so much in all my life" by Will E. Haines, Jimmy Harper and Harry Castling, "The wickedness of men" by Will E. Haines and Jimmy Harper, "She fought like a tiger for 'er 'onour" by Will E. Haines and Jimmy Harper, "Walter, Walter, lead me to the altar" by Noel Forrester, Will E. Haines and Jimmy Harper, "The biggest aspidistra in the world" by Tommy Connor, Will E. Haines and Jimmy Harper, all published by Campbell Connelly and Co. Ltd;

476

"The Rochdale hounds" by Harry Gifford/Fred E. Cliffe published by Francis, Day and Hunter Ltd; "Sing as we go" by Harry Parr-Davies published by Francis, Day and Hunter; "Ernie" by Benny Hill © 1970; "Don't laugh at me ('cause I'm a fool)" by Norman Wisdom and June Tremayne published by David Toff Music Publishing.

Photographs included in the original edition are credited as follows: Chesney Allen (page 11, 60, 80); Anglo-EMI (138); ALS Management Ltd (303); ATV Network Limited (446, 465); Blackpool Tower Company (217, 464 left); BBC Pictorial Publicity (156, 288, 361); British Music Hall Society (131); Butcher's Film Services (215); James Casey (234, 237); Collingham Press Representatives Ltd (470); Clifford Elson Publicity (386); London Weekend Television (218); Moss Empires (37 top left, 45, 107, 228, 250 bottom, 258); The Rank Organisation (2, 46, 55, 71, 174, 200, 202, 204, 207 right, 324); Ted Ray (193); Winifred Relph (25 left); Don Ross (257 right); Max Russell (460); Saxon Films (286); Thames Television (404, 191); and Warner Brothers (112 top right).

All other images are from the author's collection with the exception of those kindly provided by Richard Anthony Baker (187), David Drummond (82), and Gerald Oxley (426). The image of Gracie Fields on page 260 derives from the personal photograph album of Max Miller now in the author's possession. The photography of Max Wall by Stephen Moreton-Prichard featured on pages 276, 280 & 283 appears by kind permission of Celia Moreton-Prichard. Special additional credit is acknowledged as follows: Aquarius Library (430); General Theatre Corporation Ltd (74); Graham Sunderland (336, 474 bottom left); Harold Fielding Ltd (442 left); Jack Hylton Ltd (86 left, 86 right, 351 right); Mancunian Film Corporation Ltd (221); Norma Farnes (368); Ray Burmiston (438); Roger Hancock (345, 349, 355, opposite 496); Thames Television (298, 301, 314, 336, 373, 379, 382, 389, 394, 400, 401, 415, 457, 472, 474 bottom left); Ralph J Wald (337).

While every effort has been made to trace the owners of and ensure accuracy with regard to copyright material produced in this volume, the publishers would like to apologise for any omissions and will be pleased to incorporate missing acknowledgements in any future editions provided that notification is made to them in writing. Parts of the chapters on Tony Hancock and Tommy Cooper have been modified from material and observations that first appeared in my biographies of the two performers.

Finally I wish to acknowledge the help, support and encouragement I have received this second time around from my managing editor, Nicola Taplin, her colleague Katherine Murphy and copy editor, Hugh Davis. I am grateful to designer Andy Spence for excelling himself in making the book reflect the ambience of its subject. Especially I thank Trevor Dolby of Preface at Random House and my representative, Charles Armitage, for their enthusiasm and faith in a project that goes back so many years. Ultimately, those who know us both well will need no telling that without the love and tolerance of my wife, Sue, this book – then as now – would never have emerged into the spotlight.

John Fisher

Arthur Askey's Annual

FEATURING
BIG-HEARTED ARTHUR,
'STINKER' MURDOCH,
NAUSEA & MRS. BAGWASH,
ERNIE BAGWASH,
LEWIS THE GOAT,
AND OTHER OLD FRIENDS

Fred Bennett

BIBLIOGRAPHY

All publications London unless specified otherwise:

Agate, James: *The Ego Series (Ego 4 – 9)*, Harrap, 1940 – 48

Agate, James: *Immmoment Toys*, Jonathan Cape, 1945

Allen, Steve: *The Funny Men*, Simon and Schuster, New York, 1956

Anon.: *The Tommy Trinder Story*, W. H. McKechnie, Melbourne, 1952

Babington, Bruce (edited by): *British Stars and Stardom*, Manchester University Press, 2001

Baker, Richard Anthony: *British Music Hall: An Illustrated History*, Sutton Publishing, Stroud, 2005

Baker, Richard Anthony: *Old Time Variety: An Illustrated History*, Remember When, Barnsley, 2011

Barker, Ronnie: *All I Ever Wrote*, Essential Books, 1999

Barker, Ronnie: *Dancing in the Moonlight*, Hodder and Stoughton, 1993

Barker, Ronnie: *It's Hello – From Him!*, New English Library, 1988

Beerbohm, Max: *Around Theatres*, Rupert Hart-Davies, 1953

Beerbohm, Max: *Mainly on the Air*, Heinemann, 1946

Bentine, Michael: *The Long Banana Skin*, Wolfe, 1975

Bentine, Michael: *The Reluctant Jester*, Bantam Press, 1992

Bentley, Eric: *The Life of the Drama*, Methuen, 1965

Bergson, Henri: *Laughter*, in Sypher, Wylie: *Comedy*, Doubleday Anchor, New York, 1956

Bevan, Ian: *Top of the Bill*, Frederick Muller, 1952

Billington, Michael: *How Tickled I Am*, Elm Tree Books, 1977

Billington, Michael: *The Modern Actor*, Hamish Hamilton, 1973

Boothroyd, Basil: *A Shoulder to Laugh On*, Robson Books, 1987

Braben, Eddie: *The Best of Morecambe and Wise*, Woburn Press, 1974

Braden, Bernard: *The Kindness of Strangers*, Hodder and Stoughton, 1990

Brandreth, Gyles: *The Funniest Man on Earth: The Story of Dan Leno*, Hamish Hamilton, 1977

Brough, Peter: *Educating Archie*, Stanley Paul, 1955

Bullar, Guy R. & Evans, Len (compiled by): *Who's Who in Variety*, The Performer, 1950

Burgess, Muriel, with Keen, Tommy: *Gracie Fields*, W. H. Allen, 1980

Busby, Roy: *British Music Hall: An Illustrated History*, Paul Elek, 1976

Bygraves, Max: *I Wanna Tell You a Funny Story*, Robson Books, 1992

Bygraves, Max: *I Wanna Tell You a Story*, W. H. Allen, 1976

Bygraves, Max: *Stars In My Eyes*, Robson Books, 2002

Byng, Douglas: *As You Were*, Duckworth, 1970

Castle, Roy: *Now and Then*, Robson Books, 1994

Cheshire, D.F.: *Music Hall in Britain*, David and Charles, Newton Abbot, 1974

Collins, Joe: *A Touch of Collins*, Columbus Books, 1986

Corbett, Ronnie: *My Autobiography: High Hopes*, Ebury Press, 2000

Cotes, Peter: *George Robey*, Cassell, 1972

Craig, Mike: *Look Back with Laughter (1 – 4)*, author publication, Manchester, 1996 – 2000

Crowther, Bruce & Pinfold, Mike: *Bring Me Laughter*, Columbus Books, 1987

Dacre, Richard: *Trouble in Store*, T.C. Farries, 1991

Dawson, Les: *A Card for the Clubs*, Sphere, 1974

Dawson, Les: *No Tears for the Clown*, Robson Books, 1992

Disher, M. Willson: *Clowns and Pantomimes*, Constable, 1925

Disher, M. Willson: *Winkles and Champagne*, Batsford, 1938

Dodd, Ken: *The Big Doddy Book*, Panther/Souvenir Press, 1966

Donovan, Paul: *The Radio Companion*, HarperCollins, 1991

Double, Oliver: *Stand-up*, Methuen, 1997

Durgnat, Raymond: *The Crazy Mirror*, Faber and Faber, 1969

East, John M.: *Max Miller: The Cheeky Chappie*, W. H. Allen, 1977

Edwards, Jimmy: *Take It From Me*, Werner Laurie, 1953

Eliot, T. S.: *The Sacred Wood*, Methuen, 1920

Eliot, T. S.: *The Use of Poetry and the Use of Criticism*, Faber & Faber, 1933

Empson, William: *Some Versions of Pastoral*, Chatto and Windus, 1935

The Era, 1920 onwards

Esslin, Martin: *The Theatre of the Absurd*, Eyre and Spottiswoode, 1962

Everson, William K.: *The Art of W. C. Fields*, Bobbs Merrill, New York, 1967

Fairlie, Gerard: *The Fred Emney Story*, Hutchinson, 1960

Farnes, Norma: *Memories of Milligan*, Fourth Estate, 2010

Farnes, Norma: *Spike: An Intimate Memoir*, Fourth Estate, 2003

Fawkes, Richard: *Fighting for a Laugh*, Macdonald and Jane's, 1978

Feiblemen, James: *In Praise of Comedy*, Macmillan, New York, 1939

Fergusson, Louis: *Old Time Music Hall Comedians*, author publication, Leicester, 1949

Fields, Gracie: *Sing As We Go*, Frederick Muller, 1960

Fisher, John: *Call Them Irreplaceable*, Elm Tree Books, 1976

Fisher, John: *George Formby: The Ukulele Man*, Woburn Press, 1975

Fisher, John: *Tommy Cooper: Always Leave Them Laughing*, HarperCollins, 2006

Fisher, John: *Tony Hancock: The Definitive Biography*, HarperCollins, 2008

Fisher, John (not the present author): *What a Performance*, Seeley, Service and Co, 1975

Flanagan, Bud: *My Crazy Life*, Frederick Muller, 1961

Fletcher, Cyril: *Nice One, Cyril*, Barrie and Jenkins, 1978

Foster, Andy & Furst, Steve: *Radio Comedy 1938 – 1968*, Virgin, 1996

Gallagher, J.P.: *Fred Karno: Master of Mirth and Tears*, Robert Hale, 1971

Galton, Ray & Simpson, Alan: *The Best of Hancock*, Robson Books, 1986

Galton, Ray & Simpson, Alan: *The Best of Steptoe and Son*, Robson Books, 1988

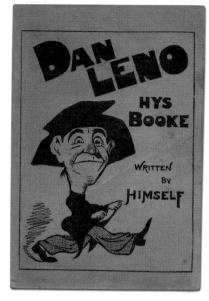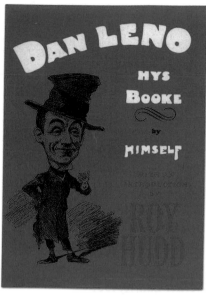

Galton, Ray & Simpson, Alan: *Hancock*, André Deutsch, 1961

Galton, Ray & Simpson, Alan: *Hancock's Half Hour*, Woburn Press, 1974

Galton, Ray & Simpson, Alan: *Hancock's Half Hour*, BBC Books, 1987

Gammond, Peter: *Your Own, Your Very Own*, Ian Allan, 1971

Gifford, Denis: *British Cinema*, Zwemmer, 1968

Gifford, Denis: *Entertainers in British Films*, Flicks Books, Trowbridge, 1998

Gifford, Denis: *The Golden Age of Radio*, Batsford, 1985

Glanville, Brian: *The Comic*, Secker and Warburg, 1974

Grantham, Barry: *Playing Commedia*, Nick Hern Books, 2000

Grantham, Barry: *Commedia Plays*, Nick Hern Books, 2006

Green, Benny (edited by): *The Last Empires*, Pavilion, 1986

Guinness, Alec: *Blessings in Disguise*, Hamish Hamilton, 1996

Hancock, Freddie & Nathan, David: *Hancock*, William Kimber, 1969

Hill, Leonard: *Saucy Boy*, Grafton, 1990

Holloway, Stanley: *Wiv a Little Bit of Luck*, Leslie Frewin, 1967

Hoggart, Richard: *The Uses of Literacy*, Chatto and Windus, 1957

Howerd, Frankie: *On the Way I Lost It*, W. H. Allen, 1976

Hudd, Roy, with Hindin, Philip: *Roy Hudd's Cavalcade of Variety Acts*, Robson Books, 1997

Hudd, Roy: *Roy Hudd's Book of Music Hall, Variety and Showbiz Anecdotes*, Robson Books, 1993

Humphries, Barry: *More Please*, Viking, 1992

Humphries, Barry: *My Life as Me*, Michael Joseph, 2002

Jewel, Jimmy: *Three Times Lucky*, Enigma Books, 1982

Johnston, Brian: *It's a Funny Game*, W. H. Allen, 1978

  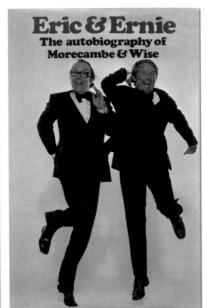

Kavanagh, Ted: *The* ITMA *Years*, Woburn Press, 1974

Kavanagh, Ted: *Tommy Handley*, Hodder and Stoughton, 1949

Kilgarriff, Michael: *Grace, Beauty and Banjos*, Oberon Books, 1998

Kilgarriff, Michael: *Sing Us One of the Old Songs*, Oxford University Press, 1998

Kilgarriff, Michael: *It Gives Me Further Pleasure*, Samuel French, 1996

Lahr, John: *Dame Edna and the Rise of Western Civilisation*, Bloomsbury, 1991

Lane, Lupino: *How to Become a Comedian*, Frederick Muller, London, 1945

Le Roy, George: *Music Hall Stars of the Nineties*, British Technical and General Press, 1952

Le White, Jack and Ford, Peter: *Rings and Curtains*, Quartet Books, 1992

Lee, Stewart: *How I Escaped My Certain Fate*, Faber and Faber, 2010

Leno, Dan: *Dan Leno, Hys Booke*, Greening and Co, 1899

Leno, Dan: *Dan Leno, Hys Booke (2nd edition)*, edited by John Duncan, Hugh Evelyn, 1968

Lewis, Roger: *The Life and Death of Peter Sellers*, Century, 1994

Lewisohn, Mark: *Funny, Peculiar: The True Story of Benny Hill*, Sidgwick and Jackson, 2002

Lewisohn, Mark: *Radio Times Guide to TV Comedy*, BBC, 1998

Little Tich: *Little Tich: A Book of Travels (and Wanderings)*, Greening and Co, 1911

MacInnes, Colin: *Sweet Saturday Night*, MacGibbon and Kee, 1967

McCabe, John: *Mr Laurel and Mr Hardy*, Grosset and Dunlap, New York, 1966

McCaffrey, Donald W.: *Four Great Comedians*, Zwemmer, 1968

McClean Jr, Albert F.: *American Vaudeville as Ritual*, University of Kentucky Press, Kentucky, 1965

McGough, Roger: *Watchwords*, Jonathan Cape, 1969

Macqueen-Pope, Walter: *The Melodies Linger On*, W. H. Allen, 1950

Mander, Raymond & Mitchenson, Joe: *British Music Hall: A Story in Pictures*, Studio Vista, 1965

Mander, Raymond & Mitchenson, Joe: *Musical Comedy: A Story in Pictures*, Peter Davies, 1969

Mander, Raymond & Mitchenson, Joe: *Pantomime: A Story in Pictures*, Peter Davies, 1973

Mander, Raymond & Mitchenson, Joe: *Revue: A Story in Pictures*, Peter Davies, 1971

Marshall, Martin (compiled by): *The Book of Comic and Dramatic Monologues*, EMI/Elm Tree, 1981

Martin, Steve: *Born Standing Up*, Scribner, New York, 2007

Mellor, Geoff J.: *Northern Music Hall*, Frank Graham, Newcastle upon Tyne, 1970

Mellor, Geoff J.: *They Made Us Laugh*, George Kelsall, Littleborough, 1982

Milligan, Spike: *Peacework*, Michael Joseph, 1991

Monkhouse, Bob: *Crying with Laughter*, Century, 1993

Montgomery, John: *Comedy Films 1894 – 1954*, George Allen and Unwin, 1954

Morecambe, Eric & Wise, Ernie, with Holman, Dennis: *Eric and Ernie*, W. H. Allen, 1973

Moules, Joan: *Our Gracie*, Robert Hale, 1983

Muir, Frank (compiled by): *The Book of Comedy Sketches*, EMI/Elm Tree, 1981

Muir, Frank: *A Kentish Lad*, Bantam Press, 1997

Muir, Frank & Norden, Denis: *The Glums*, Robson Books, 1979

Nathan, David: *The Laughtermakers*, Peter Owen, 1971

Norden, Denis: *Clips from a Life*, Fourth Estate, 2008

Nuttall, Jeff: *King Twist*, Routledge and Kegan Paul, 1978

O'Gorman, Brian: *Laughter in the Roar*, author publication, Westbury, 1998

Oakes, Philip: *Tony Hancock*, Woburn/Futura, 1975

Orwell, George: *Critical Essays*, Secker and Warburg, 1946

Osborne, John: *A Better Class of Person*, Faber and Faber, 1981

Osborne, John: *Almost a Gentleman*, Faber and Faber, 1991

Osborne, John: *The Entertainer*, Faber and Faber, 1957

Powell, Sandy & Stanley, Harry: *Can You Hear Me, Mother?* Jupiter Books, 1975

J. B. Priestley: *Particular Pleasures*, Heinemann, 1975

Radin, Paul: *The Trickster*, Philosophical Library, New York, 1956

Ray, Ted: *Raising the Laughs*, Werner Laurie, 1952

Read, Al: *It's All in the Book*, W. H. Allen, 1985

Rinaldi, Graham: *Will Hay*, Tomahawk Press, Sheffield, 2009

Robinson, David: *Chaplin: His Life and Art*, Collins, 1985

Rogers, Dave & Higgs, Mike: *Fun Films*, author publication, Bilston, 2004

Rose, Clarkson: *Red Plush and Greasepaint*, Museum Press, 1964

Rust, Brian: *British Music Hall on Record*, General Gramophone Publications: Harrow, 1979

Rust, Brian: *London Musical Shows on Record*, General Gramophone Publications: Harrow, 1977

Scott, Harold: *The Early Doors*, Nicholson and Watson, 1946

Seaton, Ray & Martin, Roy: *Good Morning, Boys*, Barrie and Jenkins, 1978

Secombe, Harry: *Arias and Raspberries*, Robson Books, 1989

Secombe, Harry: *Goon for Lunch*, M. & J. Hobbs/Michael Joseph, 1975

Secombe, Harry: *Strawberries and Cream*, Robson Books, 1996

Secombe, Harry: *Twice Brightly*, Robson Books, 1974

Short, Ernest: *Fifty Years of Vaudeville*, Eyre and Spottiswood, 1946

The Stage, 1935 onwards

Staveacre, Tony: *Slapstick*, Angus and Robertson, 1987

Stone, Richard: *You Should Have Been in Last Night*, Book Guild, Lewes, 2000

Sutton, David: *A Chorus of Raspberries*, University of Exeter Press, 2000

Sykes, Eric: *If I Don't Write It, Nobody Else Will*, Fourth Estate, 2005

Tarbuck, Jimmy: *Tarbuck on Showbiz*, Willow Books, 1985

Tich, Mary & Findlater, Richard: *Little Tich*, Elm Tree Books, 1979

Took, Barry: *Comedy Greats*, Equation, Wellingborough, 1989

Took, Barry: *Laughter in the Air*, Robson Books, 1976

Took, Barry (compiled by): *The Max Miller Blue Book*, Robson Books, 1975

Took, Barry: *Star Turns*, Weidenfeld and Nicolson, 1992

Tynan, Kenneth: *Curtains*, Longmans, 1961

Tynan, Kenneth: *He that Plays the King*, Longmans, 1950

Tynan, Kenneth: *Persona Grata*, Allan Wingate, 1953

Tynan, Kenneth: *Profiles*, Nick Hern Books, 1989

Tynan, Kenneth: *Tynan Right and Left*, Longmans, 1967

Tynan, Kenneth: *The Sound of Two Hands Clapping*, Jonathan Cape, 1975

Wall, Max: *The Fool on the Hill*, Quartet Books, 1975

Warner, Jack: *Jack of All Trades*, W. H. Allen, 1975

Watt, John: *Radio Variety*, Dent, 1939

Williams, Philip & David: *Wired to the Moon*, History on Your Doorstep, Ashton-under-Lyne, 2006

Wilmut, Roger & Grafton, Jimmy: *The Goon Show Companion*, Robson Books, 1976

Wilmut, Roger: *Kindly Leave the Stage*, Methuen, 1985

Wilson, A. E.: *Pantomime Pageant*, Stanley Paul, 1946

Wilson, A. E.: *The Prime Minister of Mirth*, Odhams, 1956

Wilson, A. E.: *The Story of Pantomime*, Home and Van Thal, 1949

Wisdom, Norman, with Hall, William: *Don't Laugh at Me*, Century, 1992

Wisdom, Norman, with Bale, Bernard: *'Cos I'm a Fool*, Breedon Books, Derby, 1996

Wood, J. Hickory: *Dan Leno*, Methuen, 1905

Worsley, Francis: *ITMA 1939 – 1948*, Vox Mundi, 1948

INDEX

Page numbers in italics indicate images